Continuing *the* Struggle *for* Justice

Continuing *the* Struggle *for* Justice

100 Years of the National Council on Crime and Delinquency

Editors

Barry Krisberg

Susan Marchionna

Christopher Baird

National Council on Crime and Delinquency (NCCD)

SAGE Publications

Los Angeles • London • New Delhi • Singapore

For information:

Sage Publications, Inc.
2455 Teller Road
Thousand Oaks, California 91320
E-mail: order@sagepub.com

Sage Publications Ltd.
1 Oliver's Yard
55 City Road
London EC1Y 1SP
United Kingdom

Sage Publications India Pvt Ltd
B 1/I 1 Mohan Cooperative Industrial Area
Mathura Road, New Delhi 110 044
India

Sage Publications Asia-Pacific Pte Ltd
33 Pekin Street #02-01
Far East Square
Singapore 048763

Printed in the United States of America

Library of Congress Cataloging-in-Publication Data

Continuing the struggle for justice : 100 years of the National Council on Crime
and Delinquency / edited by Barry Krisberg, Susan Marchionna, Christopher Baird.
    p. cm.
Includes bibliographical references and index.
ISBN 978-1-4129-5190-6 (cloth)
ISBN 978-1-4129-5191-3 (pbk.)
  1. National Council on Crime and Delinquency—History. 2. Criminal justice,
Administration of—United States. I. Krisberg, Barry. II. Marchionna, Susan. III. Baird, Christopher.

HV9950.C655 2007
364.97306—dc22

                                     2006033701

Printed on acid-free paper.

07 08 09 10 11   10 9 8 7 6 5 4 3 2 1

Acquiring Editor:	Jerry Westby
Editorial Assistant:	Kim Suarez
Production Editor:	Sarah Quesenberry
Copy Editor:	QuADS
Typesetter:	C&M Digitals (P) Ltd.
Proofreader:	Dorothy Hoffman
Indexer:	Nara Wood
Cover Designer:	Michelle Kenny
Marketing Manager:	Jennifer Reed

CONTENTS

Continuing the Struggle for Justice: The Legacy

A Brief History of an American Institution

The National Council on Crime and Delinquency (NCCD) was founded on June 17, 1907, by 14 probation officers who met at Plymouth Church in Minneapolis, Minnesota. They were attending the annual meeting of the National Conference of Charities and Correction. This first meeting was an exploration of whether it was time to organize a professional association to advance the emerging field of probation. The leading force behind this meeting was Timothy D. Hurley, a Chicago lawyer and key participant in the movement to create the first juvenile court in America. He later served as Chicago's first probation officer.

In 1907, Theodore Roosevelt was President of the United States (there were only 46 states at the time), and the nation was still confronting unresolved issues from the Civil War. Legally sanctioned racial segregation was the norm. Lynching of African Americans and other racial minorities was epidemic. The United States was accumulating colonies in the Pacific, the Caribbean, and Central America. Women were permitted to vote in only four sparsely populated western states and not yet in federal elections. The Congress had passed a number of laws denying citizenship rights to immigrants from Asia. The average worker earned $13 for a 60-hour work week.

The criminal justice system was still in its infancy. For example, the juvenile court had just been created in 1899; many states and the federal government did not yet recognize probation as a legitimate penal sanction, and in most states children continued to be confined in adult correctional facilities. There were no established standards for those who worked as probation officers and few, if any, published materials about the practice of community supervision of law breakers. It was decided that the newly established National Probation Association (NPA) would seek to "offer a broader medium for the exchange of ideas, methods, reports, and questions" and to arrange for future meetings of probation officers from across the country. Initially, only probation officers were allowed to be members of the NPA, Timothy Hurley was elected as its first president, and the annual dues were 25 cents. The NPA remained an informal and voluntary association until 1921. The life of the organization consisted primarily of annual meetings of the membership. During the early years, the membership of the NPA became actively involved in the growth of the juvenile court movement and the emergence of child guidance clinics that helped assess the treatment needs of delinquent youth. Julia Lathrop, the newly appointed head of the U.S. Children's Bureau, enlisted the aid of the NPA to conduct a national survey of the progress of the juvenile court in its first decade. The NPA also helped promote the use of psychiatric expertise in the criminal justice system. The members drafted and advocated for the first federal probation law in the U.S. Congress.

There was a growing sense that the NPA should seek funding and create a paid staff. Through the energetic work of Charles L. Chute, who headed the New York State Probation Commission, the NPA was able to garner major contributions from the Milbank Memorial Fund, the Commonwealth Fund, and many other private philanthropies. With its paid staff and as the only national organization, the NPA was called upon to conduct surveys of juvenile courts and corrections systems in many jurisdictions. These surveys permitted the NPA to make recommendations for urgent reforms of the American justice system. Often these reports stressed the inhumanity of housing children in adult jails and led the NPA to organize local communities to open juvenile detention facilities for wayward youths.

Over the next 100 years, the NPA expanded and became the National Council on Crime and Delinquency. In 1947, the NPA merged with the American Parole Association to become the National Probation and Parole Association (NPPA). In 1952, the NPPA began publishing a number of professional journals, including a newsletter designed for citizens, *Crime and Delinquency*. Leadership of the Board of Directors included such notable figures as former Attorney General George W. Wickersham, U.S. Supreme Court Justice Charles Evan Hughes, and Harvard Law School Dean Roscoe Pound.

Also during the early 1950s, the NPPA began organizing regional offices in a number of locations. With financial support from the Mary Reynolds Babcock Foundation and the Ford Foundation, the NPPA explored the creation of citizen councils to support its growing policy agenda. In 1960, the NPPA was renamed the National Council on Crime and Delinquency (NCCD), reflecting its growth and broad public policy interests. The first citizen council was in Westchester County, New York, and by the early 1970s there were 38 state offices or regional affiliates of the NCCD. That same year, Don M. Gottfredson organized the NCCD Research Center, which became a world renowned center of empirical studies of the justice system. In 1953, the prestigious Council of Judges was formed by the NPPA to advise the organization on sentencing issues. A prominent Federal District Judge was the first chair of this Council; later in the 1990s the group was chaired by U.S. Supreme Court Justice William Brennan.

When President Lyndon Baines Johnson created a Presidential Crime Commission in 1965, he called on the NCCD to conduct a national survey of the corrections system. During this same period, the NCCD recruited America's top corporate leaders to advocate for and endorse the bold reform proposals of the Johnson Crime Commission. One of the most significant outcomes of that Commission was growth of the federal role in funding criminal justice research and demonstration projects under the Law Enforcement Assistance Administration. The NCCD was one of the principal recipients of federal grants over the next decade.

During the early 1970s, the NCCD was an integral part of a national coalition to pass the Juvenile Justice and Delinquency Prevention Act of 1974. The NCCD emerged as one of the leading national research centers on juvenile justice and delinquency prevention programs. The focus on sustaining the large number of state-affiliated councils was supplanted with a greater participation in federal reform efforts, especially under President Jimmy Carter.

Like most long-lived social institutions, the NCCD has had its periods of challenge. During the Reagan Administration the NCCD almost went out of existence due to a reduction in federal funding that resulted in severe financial problems. It was rescued by the support of many progressive professionals in the criminal justice system who wanted the Council to survive, and by generous contributions from the Edna McConnell Clark Foundation, the Guardsmark Foundation, and a number of private individuals. Board leadership in the 1980s came from one of the nation's most revered corrections experts, Allen Breed, who had just retired as Director of the National Institute of Corrections.

During the 1990s, the NCCD enjoyed the support and confidence of Attorney General Janet Reno. The Council rebuilt its base of substantial federal funding, including a 40-community effort to help the Office of Juvenile Justice and Delinquency Prevention implement its Comprehensive Strategy for Serious, Chronic, and Violent Juvenile Offenders. In 1993, the NCCD created the Children's Research Center (CRC) and expanded its work into reform of the child welfare system. The CRC has helped over 15 states provide better care of maltreated young people. The CRC is also conducting research on innovative educational approaches for disadvantaged youth.

Today the NCCD works with many states, and receives funding from national and state foundations such as the Jessie Ball duPont Fund, the Annie E. Casey Foundation, the Cowles Charitable Trust, the JEHT Foundation, the San Francisco Foundation, the Gerbode Foundation, the Rick and Regina Roney Foundation, The California Endowment, and the California Wellness Foundation.

Bedsides reform of child welfare systems, the NCCD research and policy agenda focuses on crucial issues such as race and justice, mental health services in the juvenile justice system, women and girls in the justice system, and prisoner reentry. Together with the University of California, Berkeley, the NCCD has just launched a multi-year research project on immigration, culture, and youth violence prevention. This work builds on NCCD's previous work on youth violence prevention in Asian American and Pacific Islander communities and reaches out to youth and families in Latino communities. Both these projects were funded by the U.S. Centers for Disease Control and Prevention and represent NCCD's continued emphasis on violence prevention utilizing a public health model.

Throughout its 100 years of service to America, the NCCD has been involved in many policy debates and professional engagements. Remarkable has been the consistency of themes and values expressed in that history. This volume offers a selection of some of the best writing by individuals who were members of the NCCD Board of Directors or its staff. We have organized these contributions around the themes that have always mattered to the NCCD. Those themes will guide its course into the next century. First and foremost, the NCCD fought and continues to struggle to maintain a separate justice system for children. Children are not little adults, and our legal system must take into account their unique needs for protection and guidance. The old NPA advocated for the expansion of probation as a scientific alternative to incarceration. The NCCD has continued this tradition of opposing the growth of policies favoring mass imprisonment, offering instead research evidence on safe alternative penalties.

Early in its history, the NCCD examined the impact of child abuse and violence against women as a major factor in crime rates. The NPA was an early proponent of Domestic Relations Courts that would confidentially and dispassionately seek to reduce the harm in families experiencing severe conflicts. In contemporary scientific terminology, we refer to the ideas of Cathy Spatz Widom and her perspective on "breaking the cycle of violence." Put simply, the research demonstrates that children who witness violence or who are victims of violence in their homes are at greater risk to become violent offenders themselves. As noted earlier, the NCCD launched its Children's Research Center to work on these issues. The NCCD's Executive Vice President S. Christopher Baird played a key leadership role in this area and reminded the NCCD that if it did not work to prevent child maltreatment, "we would spend the rest of our careers counting the number of prison beds that would be needed."

A major theme of the NCCD is the inextricable link between the pursuit of social justice and a criminal justice system suited for a democracy. The NCCD continues to emphasize the social forces such as racial divisions, gender inequalities, and class prejudices that plague our nation. Over the years, the NCCD has pointed out needed reforms of policing, sentencing practices, and correctional policies that could alleviate some of the wounds of social injustice. When our cities were in flames during the urban riots, civil rights protests, and antiwar movements of the last century, the NCCD consistently urged measured responses based on the expansion of opportunities and rights for all Americans, rejecting harsh state suppression of protests and disorder. Finally, the NCCD has long opposed the use of capital punishment because it has been applied in an arbitrary and capricious manner, and the death penalty has historically been applied disproportionately to racial minorities. The NCCD has long advocated that state-sanctioned murder has no deterrent effect, and it is antithetical to the core values of our civilization.

ACKNOWLEDGMENTS

The compilation of this book would not have been possible without the help of many people. Primary thanks go to Jerry Westby at Sage Publications. His belief in the project made it possible to pursue.

Also, thanks go to Phyllis Schultze of Rutgers University, whose patient tending of the NCCD library has ensured the preservation of unique and valuable materials.

Thanks also to Tanya Montes for doggedly pursuing the permissions necessary to reprint the articles in this volume originally appearing in a variety of publications, which we would also like to acknowledge as follows:

Charles L. Chute, "Rational Crime Treatment," originally appeared in *The American Review of Reviews*, May 1923, pages 521–526.

Will C. Turnbladh, "A Critique of the Model Penal Code Sentencing Proposals," originally appeared in *Law and Contemporary Problems*, Volume 23, Number 3, June 1, 1958, pages 544–566.

Joan Potter, "Milton Rector: 43 Years of Reform," originally appeared in *Corrections*, June, 1981, pages 19–27.

Orlando Martinez, "Creating Effective Juvenile Justice Systems" is reprinted with permission from the author.

Allen Breed, "The State of Corrections: A Triumph of Pluralistic Ignorance," originally appeared in *Criminal Law Bulletin*, Volume 23, Number 3, 1987, pages 262–274. Special thanks also to the Edna McConnell Clark Foundation.

Norval Morris, "Impediments to Penal Reform," originally appeared in the *University of Chicago Law Review*, Volume 33, Number 4, 1966, pages 627–656.

Raelene Freitag and Madeleine Wordes-Noya, "Improved Decision Making in Child Maltreatment Cases," originally appeared in the *Journal of the Center for Families, Children & the Courts*, Volume 3, 2001, pages 75–85.

Rose Matsui Ochi, "Racial Discrimination in Criminal Sentencing," originally appeared in *The Judges' Journal* of the American Bar Association, Volume 24, Issue 1, 1985, pages 7–11, 53–54.

Patrick V. Murphy, "Organizing for Community Policing," originally appeared as a chapter in *Issues in Policing, New Perspectives*, published by Autumn House Publishing, 1992, pages 113–128.

Hubert G. Locke, "The Color of Law and the Issue of Color: Race and the Abuse of Power," originally appeared as a chapter in *Police Violence: Understanding and Controlling Police Abuse of Force*, published by Yale University Press, 1996, pages 129–149.

Anthony C. Thompson, "Navigating the Hidden Obstacles to Ex-Offender Reentry," originally appeared in the *Boston College Law Review*, Volume XLV, Number 2, 2004, pages 255–306.

Kim Taylor-Thompson, "Taking It to the Streets," originally appeared in the *New York University Review of Law and Social Change*, Volume 29, Number 1, 2004, pages 153–201.

Marvin E. Wolfgang, "We Do Not Deserve to Kill," originally appeared in the *Thomas M. Cooley Law Review*, Volume 13, 1996, pages 977–990.

PART I

THE VIEWS FROM NCCD'S FIVE PRESIDENTS

Since 1921, five individuals have led the staff of the National Council on Crime and Delinquency (NCCD). The following essays give a sampling of their perspectives on the continuing struggle for justice. While they each differ in their family backgrounds, political ideologies, educational training, and professional experiences, these essays show the amazing continuity in the themes and issues they have embraced.

Charles L. Chute was the first paid executive director of the National Probation Association (NPA). Trained in social work, he worked for many years in the field of child labor and was later appointed the head of the New York State Probation Commission. Heading the NPA from 1921 to 1948, Chute helped draft, and lobbied for the passage of, the first federal probation law and was very influential in the evolution of the juvenile court in its early years. He was a prolific writer who authored many essays during his tenure at the NPA. His essay in this volume, "Rational Crime Treatment," reflects his visionary perspective, calling for the abolition of contemporary prisons as early as 1923. He was a firm believer that science and research would perfect the penal system. He forcefully advocated for special courts to deal with domestic violence and to respond to child abuse. His views were solidly based in the belief that every individual could be redeemed.

The next leader of the National Probation and Parole Association (NPPA) was Will C. Turnbladh, who served as its executive director from 1948 to 1959. He went on to be named the first commissioner of the consolidated Minnesota Department of Corrections, which was known as one of the most progressive adult and juvenile corrections departments in the nation. We have included here his excellent "Critique of the Model Penal Code Sentencing Proposals." The Model Penal Code was drafted by the American Law Institute (ALI) and was intended to shape legislation on sentencing in many states. Turnbladh argues that the Model Penal Code undervalues the role of probation, parole, and other alternatives to incarceration that together make up a comprehensive penal system. He complains that some of the sentence lengths suggested by the ALI are too long, going beyond prudent confinement needed for public protection. Anticipating concerns that would be expressed by the NCCD in its opposition of Three Strikes laws of the 1990s, Turnbladh criticizes enhanced penalties and life sentences for "habitual offenders" as costly and susceptible to unjust application.

For most criminal justice professionals, the NCCD is synonymous with Milton Rector. A graduate of the University of Nevada in social work, Rector was a probation officer and later ran the Western Regional Office of the NPPA. He was the executive director from 1959 to

1

1982. During his long tenure, the organization became the NCCD and expanded its policy focus beyond the concerns of probation and parole. Milton G. Rector was one of America's most respected penologists for over two decades. He was skillful at "talking truth to power," contradicting the views of national politicians. A self-styled conservative Republican, Milton G. Rector was able to enlist the support of top corporate leaders in what today appears a very liberal policy agenda. Rector led NCCD to oppose the death penalty, he called for a moratorium on all new prison and jail construction until all alternatives had been explored (echoing the views of Charles L. Chute), and he pressed for the decriminalization of minor drug crimes as well as prostitution, gambling, abortion, curfew violations, and truancy. Rector advocated for the abolition of the Federal Bureau of Prisons, pointing out that many federal prisoners were nonviolent and that the violent few could be better managed in state corrections systems.

In an era during which debates over criminal justice were becoming increasingly bitter and partisan, Rector was a courtly and gentle person who never publicly vilified his opponents. He managed to remain a respected adviser to Democratic and Republican Administrations alike, although he often opposed the view of professional associations of judges and corrections officials.

Later in this volume, we have reprinted his classic essay, "The Extravagance of Incarceration," but in this section we have included an in-depth interview with Rector, conducted by Joan Potter. The interview provides unique insights into the intellectual and moral foundation of Rector's views. He inspired a generation of young NCCD staff with his humanity and vision. Particularly memorable was Milton Rector's warning that "in our zeal to punish offenders, we must be careful not to punish ourselves."

Between 1981 and 1983, the NCCD was led by Harvard Law School graduate, Diana R. Gordon.

She argued forcefully against the increasingly tough crime policies of the Reagan Administration. We have reprinted her trenchant critique of federal crime policy that was offered by Reagan's attorney general William French Smith. This essay was an important rallying cry for those who sought to oppose the rightward drift of sentencing and penal policies. Gordon briefly led the NCCD during a period in which crime policy debates were harsh and personalized. Attorney General Edwin Meese viewed the NCCD as part of the "criminal lobby" that was led by the American Civil Liberties Union. During this period, the substantial support of the NCCD by corporations evaporated as they perceived criminal justice as "too controversial." A group of former NCCD board members decided to use the National Crime Prevention Council, organized by NCCD staff, as a vehicle for a more politically neutral national crime organization.

Diana R. Gordon now teaches political science and criminology at the City University of New York. She has authored a number of impressive books documenting the failures of the War Against Drugs and the movement to recriminalize homelessness, the mentally ill, and other nonviolent offenders.

Barry Krisberg is the current president of the NCCD. A criminologist trained at the University of Pennsylvania, he was a student of America's most renowned crime researchers, Thorsten Sellin and Marvin E. Wolfgang. Heading up the organization from 1983 to the present, Krisberg first joined the NCCD as a researcher in the mid-1970s, after teaching at the School of Criminology at the University of California. He increased the role of research in the formulation of NCCD's policy positions and emphasized issues of juvenile justice and delinquency prevention. Most important, Krisberg has led the NCCD to play a national role on issues of racial justice. The essay in this volume reflects his views on how racial dynamics and the opportunism of politicians led to disastrous juvenile justice policies in California.

1

RATIONAL CRIME TREATMENT

CHARLES L. CHUTE

The amazing progress of science in revealing the physical universe is making the world an increasingly reasonable place. During the great gathering of scientists at Cambridge, Mass., in December last, thrilling discoveries and unheard of advances in knowledge were reported at nearly every session. Man was shown controlling the physical forces of nature in proportion as he more fully understands them. But the general note of optimism was somewhat broken by speakers who deplored the lack of scientific knowledge of man himself and the forces of society. Said Professor Mead of the University of Chicago: "What we are called upon to do in our conduct is to pursue the same method in dealing with social questions that we pursue in dealing with scientific ones."

We realize clearly enough today that there are other worlds to conquer. Much have we to learn about our own minds; we must understand better, if we are to control, the springs of human conduct; a great deal remains to be done to bring organization into our chaotic social life. Ghosts, witches, devils—the dark brood of ignorance and fear that haunted men's minds for ages—are passing; but we have still much to unlearn as well as to learn and in no field more than in that of treatment of man's antisocial behavior, broadly known as crime.

THE SCIENTIFIC APPROACH

But the insatiable mind of man, ever seeking and finding new truth, is today as never before entering upon the greatest study of mankind. We are just beginning to build up a science of human behavior which alone will make it possible for us to understand the so-called criminal. In the advances of psychology, in the new sciences of psychiatry and psychoanalysis, in the recent studies of human behavior and in the increasing knowledge of the child mind, rather than in the older pseudo-sciences of criminology and penology, lies the hope for a solution of our vast crime problem of today.

As yet few grasp the significance of the scientific approach to this problem. The great mass of people are still hopelessly irrational and unscientific in their consideration of it—more so, perhaps, than in almost any other field of human experience. Why is this so? Because it is a field in which emotions have long ruled—primitive emotions; fear, hatred, revenge. Then too, it is a field largely monopolized by that most conservative of all professions, the law. Treatment of crime has been largely hampered by rigid criminal codes, based upon outworn principles of equal responsibility, "punishment to fit the crime," and the essentially unjust and discredited principle of the need for severe

3

punishment to deter others. Through inertia, conservatism and the accumulated fears and prejudices of generations, the law has changed but little, although increased knowledge and social advances have made fundamental changes imperative.

FAULTS OF THE PRESENT SYSTEM

Eventually, if we are to solve the crime problem, as it has by no means yet been solved, we shall of necessity have to scrap much of our wholly unscientific criminal law; we shall abolish or greatly modify our present system of courts and do away with the kind of prison existing today.

"This," it may be said, "is a sweeping statement, based on mere hypothesis." But consider these facts: In the first place, is it not clear to every one who studies the problem that our present agencies for dealing with crime have largely failed? They do not even result in an understanding of the offender; they certainly do not cure, or what is even more to be desired, *prevent* crime.

The criminal law, as everybody knows, attempts to mete out punishments for each crime regardless of the many individual variations in motives and degrees of responsibility and the greatly varying needs of the offender. It sets up a rigid, impractical scheme, based on classical ideas of crime deterrence. Already it is being modified and will some day be replaced by a system more just and more scientific.

It is but natural that conservative lawyers with eyes on the past, ever seeking precedents, should explain, as some of them have attempted to do, the unquestioned failure of our treatment of crime as due to departure from the orthodox principles and methods of the past. The modern innovations: indeterminate sentence, probation, parole, psychiatric examinations, which are in reality attempts to apply some of the conclusions of science through the developing study of the individual and society, are blamed as causing or increasing the crime problem. The fallacy of such a view is apparent to the open-minded student.

FUTILITY OF SEVERE PENALTIES

If any fact is well established in the world today, it is this: Severe penalties do not deter from crime and therefore do not protect society. We have always had severe penalties and crime has increased. No country has ever carried the theory of deterrence by intimidation further than supposedly Christian England. History records that there were 72,000 executions for crime in England during the twenty-year reign of Henry VIII in the sixteenth century. Blackstone, writing his "Commentaries" in 1765, describes 160 kinds of crime punishable by death. The records of those days tell of mere children who were hung, transported, or who died in prison for no worse crime than stealing, perhaps only to appease their hunger. All kinds of inhuman punishments were imposed for trivial offenses.

But history also shows that during these periods of greatest severity crime flourished and increased. The more hung, the more there were to hang. Brutality bred brutality. A striking illustration of the failure of punishment to deter is contained in the following melancholy incident which has come down to us on good authority: It was a capital offense in the eighteenth century in England to pick a pocket, yet at the great public hangings, when scores were executed, pickpockets were caught plying their trade in the very shadow of the gallows.

To this day English law and our own, which came from England, reflect the spirit and ideas of those times, though a more humane age has required some modification. It is only in comparatively recent times that fixed prison sentences have been substituted for the death penalty and capital punishment relegated in most of our States, though by no means in all, to first-degree murder. Long prison terms are still commonly imposed, mainly to deter others. Such, for instance, was the case of the boy K-, sixteen years old, sentenced recently in Queens County, New York, to *not less than* thirty years in Sing Sing prison for committing burglary and highway robbery.

HAS CRIME ACTUALLY INCREASED?

During all these centuries, crime has held its own and even increased. No statistical evidence has been presented, however, showing in recent years a serious increase of crime in this country. In fact, before the war, a marked decrease in prison population had begun. In the last few years, statistics compiled by the police departments of a number of our larger cities, like New York, show some decrease in the total number of crimes committed and arrests made. However, the reportorial phrase "crime wave" has been somewhat justified by a sporadic increase in the major crimes of violence, and in the atrocious efficiency of the perpetrators. Stealing is now done wholesale, and there has been of late unusual disregard for human life, due to the reckless use of firearms.

The apparent increase in spectacular crime today is due to several things. First, aftereffects of the war: unemployment, unsettled conditions, general lawlessness, familiarity with weapons. This result has followed every great war. Other factors in the situation today are: The availability of the high-powered automobile; the unrestrained publicity given to successful crime through the moving pictures and especially the newspapers. But more important than any of these is the growing inadequacy and incongruity of the old system of law and treatment to meet modern conditions. There is increasing disrespect for a system so unscientific and ineffective. We must find a new way. That way leads to a thorough overhauling of our machinery of law, courts and prison, to enable us to determine in every case the causes, both individual and social, back of the offense and then establish a system which will remove and correct these causes.

THE CRIMINAL COURTS—ATTITUDE OF THE LEGAL PROFESSION

The greatest blame must be attached to our criminal court system. It is hardly necessary to cite authorities to prove that it has worked badly, especially in the higher criminal courts. Eminent lawyers, like Secretary Hughes and Chief Justice Taft, have borne eloquent testimony to this fact as has recently the Committee on Law Enforcement of the American Bar Association. Unfortunately, that Committee, composed of eminent and conservative lawyers, themselves a part of the system, fails to suggest any adequate remedy. Minor improvements in the criminal courts to speed up the rusty wheels of justice and to make punishment more severe and "sure" will never accomplish the results desired. The attitude of the Committee was legal and not scientific. Must we look to other professions for the remedies which will reform our laws and court system, the necessity of which is well recognized by the lawyers?

The criminal courts, however, are now being modified, slowly but surely. In time they will be revolutionized. Courts should be, and in some places have today become, clinics for studying the causes of crime and for fitting treatment to the individual criminal. The old system and practice dies hard in so conservative a profession as the judiciary and the public is not yet fully awake to the need.

PROBATION AS A SCIENTIFIC METHOD

One remedy for a rigid and unscientific court system has been found and is making headway. This is the extension of the power to place offenders on probation. The development of this system has done more to modify criminal law and court procedure than any previous reform in a generation. As a method for individualizing justice and bringing social treatment to bear in suitable cases, probation is generally endorsed; but in no State is its administration adequate.

Probation laws now in effect in every State of the Union, and to some extent in nearly every civilized country, give the court not only the power to suspend the sentence imposed by law but, most important, to prescribe instead of imprisonment a social treatment. Although released in society the probationer is under the watchful eye and personal, helpful influence of the probation officer. The probation officer is, or should be, a trained social case worker, skilled in following a large number of cases, not losing sight of any, but influencing and guiding each one. The probation officer is also the social investigator of the court, bringing to the judge a complete knowledge of the previous history, social condition, individual character of the accused, and probable causes of crime upon which evidence many courts are now largely basing their sentences.

Probation is essentially scientific, based on a study of the facts in each case, using just so far as public safety permits, the powerful forces of persistent kindness, self-help, encouragement and rewards for achievement, all the while maintaining strict disciplinary conditions of the court, often very strict ones, for the protection of society.

INSTANCES FROM LIFE

With probation every possible incentive is given to the delinquent to succeed. No publicity is given to his offense or the fact that he is under supervision. His attitude, almost without a single exception, is one of gratitude to the court for the chance given him to go "straight." I have often heard probationers express this feeling with touching sincerity and earnestness. More important, their acts show it. Usually they respond to all suggestions and directions of the probation officer as to employment, associates, use of leisure time, family life and other matters varying with the case.

John R was a young man of fair education and many good character traits. He was from a good family and had a devoted wife. He held a position with an express company, commanding very good wages. Bad company and drink got the better of him. He fell to the depths, lost his position and even went so far that his wife could not live with him or help him. While intoxicated he slept in the open, in gutters and under stables; he became filthy and vermin ridden. It was while in this condition that he became a felon. While he was with boon companions, somewhat under the influence of liquor as usual, a horse and carriage were stolen from a farmer, driven off and abandoned. He was arraigned for grand larceny, pleaded guilty and, it being his first time in court, was placed on probation.

An admirable probation officer was assigned to the case. The officer became a brother to the man. He found his task by no means easy. The man showed a real desire to get back to respectability, but his character was weakened by long indulgence. Conditions had to be very strict: No drink, a job, no association with former companions, reporting to the probation officer every week and giving a full account of himself.

Regular reporting, while an essential part of the probation system, is far less important than the constructive work of the probation officer. The officer visited the man frequently, got him work, kept him at it and finally brought about a reconciliation with his wife. At first the man "fell" more than once, but gradually grew stronger, took courage, gave up his bad habits entirely, got back his original position, was reconciled to his family, and after a period of a year and a half on probation, toward the close of which the supervision was somewhat relaxed, received his "honorable discharge" as a completely successful case. Best of all he has "made good" ever since his discharge and has kept in touch with his friend and former probation officer. This is a true story

and, far from being exceptional, is typical of a large percentage of probation cases.

As the probation treatment is a "testing out" process many inevitably fail, but not nearly as many as do so after the heartbreaking, desocializing experience of a prison sentence. During 1921, according to the carefully compiled statistics of the New York State Probation Commission (an official State department supervising probation work in all courts of the State), 78.2 per cent of the 19,452 persons of all ages and both sexes, who finished probation terms within the year, were discharged as successful; that is, they lived up to the conditions of probation and committed no further offenses. Approximately 80 per cent of successes have been reported by Massachusetts authorities for several years. Individual afterstudies made in New York State of all the probationers successfully discharged from probation in certain courts during a given period have shown over 70 per cent (72.1 per cent in one study of 200 consecutive cases) completely restored to good citizenship with no more offending. Many of them had made truly remarkable progress, industrially, socially and morally.

In advocating the extension of probation to all courts (for it is used extensively today in only a few States) great emphasis must be placed on the selection of offenders and the securing of enough skilled probation officers to supervise them thoroughly. One office should not supervise more than fifty cases—better less. Few cities have made adequate provision for this work, although it is an undoubted economy to do so. Most of the failures of the system are due either to selecting probationers without full investigation or the overcrowding of the officer so that he cannot get results.

It should be remembered by critics of the system that with the skillful probation officer, not overworked, the community is well protected. The probationer *must* be industrious, *must* keep good habits and out of further crime. Otherwise he is practically sure to be found out with speed by the officer, brought back to court, and given much more drastic treatment than he would have received if sentenced in the first place.

THE COURT CLINIC

In recent years another agency has developed in some of the courts, especially those dealing with children. This is the court clinic. Its establishment followed and in part resulted from the introduction of the probation system. In the growing number of courts which have clinics (and all need them) their work is always closely associated with the work of the probation staff—the clinic making the physical and mental diagnoses, the probation staff making the social investigations and frequently carrying out the recommendations of the clinic for social treatment.

In the best-equipped courts a majority of cases are examined in the clinic; its report, made to the judge before final dispositions, often revealing serious mental and physical defects as the principal causes of the individual's misconduct. Both a psychiatrist, i.e., a physician skilled in treating mental diseases, and a psychologist, are essential to the complete court clinic.

The work of these clinics has been of untold value when well conducted. They enable the court to understand the offender and to recognize many feeble-minded, insane, epileptic or defective delinquents who otherwise would escape notice. From 10 per cent to 50 per cent of the individuals brought before the average court have been found to be more or less mentally defective, or diseased, requiring in many cases to be sent to the special institutions for these classes, which are being developed in all States. The advice of the clinic is also of the greatest value to the probation officers, enabling them to understand and so better aid those placed under their care. It safeguards the use of probation and helps in selecting delinquents who can safely be given a chance.

JUVENILE AND DOMESTIC RELATIONS COURTS

Besides the probation system and the court clinic, which adapt themselves to all courts dealing with delinquency, the movement for special socially organized courts is also a hopeful factor in the situation.

First comes the Juvenile Court, which has been established, legally at least, in all but two of our States. In most of our large cities today there are successful Juvenile Courts. Men of the highest type of devotion to the public interest, outstanding men, with a keen understanding of the needs of delinquent and neglected childhood, are serving in these courts. The fundamental

principles of the Juvenile Court—individual study and understanding of each child, protection of the unfortunate one from publicity and contamination, social treatment through probation—have been and are leading the way for the application of the same principles to all courts.

As yet, however, in no State have all delinquent children the benefit of juvenile court procedure. In many States children are still tried like adult criminals and mingle with them in police stations, courts and jails; their first contact with the State is anything but parental. Detention in jails, those breeding places of crime, is common in nine-tenths of the States of this country, especially in rural districts, but also in cities. The separate court for children, with its special detention home, avoids this early introduction of the child into associations which cannot but harden him, developing instead of correcting every evil tendency.

The newer Domestic Relations of Family Courts, dealing with the problems of broken homes and domestic quarrels, especially cases of desertion and non-support and including divorce jurisdiction in some States, use practically the same social procedure as the Juvenile Court. Even more than the Juvenile Court, their work involves the adjustments of families. There must be the same protection from publicity and disgrace and continued supervision of the home through probation, rather than the former method of breaking up the home and scattering its members. These courts, well conducted, not only prevent untold misery to wives and children, but prevent crime.

HOSPITALS AND REFORMATORIES AS SUBSTITUTES FOR PRISONS

What, finally, shall we say of the place of prisons? The problem of prison reform cannot be considered apart from the whole system of crime treatment. As long as the courts continue to send to prisons the heterogeneous group that now go, without study of the individual and his needs, fixing determinate or partly determinate sentences which make rational treatment impossible, the prisons will continue to be the hopeless travesties upon just and scientific treatment of crime which they now are.

The failure of the prison as now conducted is an age-old problem to be met, not by prison reform (that has always proved ephemeral) but by abolishing the prisons of today and in their place establishing the following:

1. A well-supervised probation system in each community for the treatment of every offender who is not a confirmed repeater or so abnormal as to be a menace to society. A majority of the so-called criminals in our courts are young, early offenders, often more sinned against than sinning, accidental offenders, victims of environment or associates; they are largely reclaimable if taken in hand at the time of the first offense and then thoroughly treated.

2. Special hospitals where all feeble-minded, insane, epileptic and physically sick offenders shall be sent. Here their defects, the principal causes of the antisocial behavior, may be treated and if possible cured. This will take a large number of so-called criminals. Studies have shown in many prisons and reformatories that nearly 50 per cent of the inmates belong to one of the above classes. They should not go to prisons but to institutions where they will not be stigmatized of punished, but cured if possible or, if incurable, kept as long as they are a menace to themselves or society, often for life. They should be kept busy with wholesome work and recreation and helped to lead as normal a life as possible.

3. Reformatory institutions where the residue, a small one and gradually decreasing as more thorough work is done with the first offenders, may be given closer supervision than the probation plan can hope to give. To these institutions will go the confirmed criminals to be confined until "cured." They should be kept busy, taught trades, made to live as normal and healthy lives as possible, though safely confined. All good influences should be brought to bear upon them, through keepers and guards selected for their ability to understand and reform men. When released they should be placed under strict parole.

SOCIETY'S RESPONSIBILITY

This scientific plan of crime treatment, whose aim is to lift up and save rather than to crush down and destroy, should prove not only more successful and more safe, but also more just. How prone are we to forget that the debt is not all on one side! Every delinquent child, every criminal adult, no matter how deliberate may seem his offending, is to some extent at least the victim of bad social conditions for which society and all of us as members thereof are surely to blame. Small wonder that the boy growing up in the city or the country slum, surrounded by wretchedness and immorality from his very birth, with suitable education often denied, soon learns from parents, perhaps, or associates, the ways of evil. Well may we ask ourselves the question—we who would inflict retaliative social vengeance: What have we done to prevent this natural result? These victims, for such they often are—victims of others and of social neglect—deserve help, deserve what may be perhaps their first real chance to live normal lives. The court experience with its awakening, especially when kindness is shown, often affords very favorable soil in which new determination to succeed may grow.

We are so far today from the rational program of crime treatment outlined that it will take time to attain it, but progress should be more rapid than at any previous time in history because of the growing scientific spirit and approach to the problem.

Why do not we adopt such a program at once? Because of inertia and conservatism; the many selfish interests involved in the present system; the incompetency of many public officials, hampered by politics and the distrust in which they are held by the public; ignorance of the scientific gains in this field; persistence of the instinctive emotions of fear and hatred of the criminal and the primitive demand for vengeance. Last, and perhaps most of all, comes our "penny-wise" economy—the objections of the taxpayer to the outlay necessary to establish through probation systems, special courts, and the diversified institutions required. This last and greatest objection will be overcome, however, as will the others, by greater public knowledge, as unquestionably the expenditure will prove an investment in manhood and womanhood bringing large social returns. "The greatest enterprise in the world," says Emerson, "for splendor, for extent, is the upbuilding of a man."

2

A CRITIQUE OF THE MODEL PENAL CODE SENTENCING PROPOSALS

WILL C. TURNBLADH

The effort of the American Law Institute in the drafting of a Model Penal Code is one that deserves the attention not only of the bench and the bar, but of those in the field of criminal correction, and, sooner or later, the leading organizations of the lay community. It is the kind of effort that is made only at rare intervals, and it may well have an impact that will last for generations. All of these factors render critical examination urgent, to ensure that the final product will reflect the best thinking available and conform with the goals of progress.

With this realization, the National Probation and Parole Association (NPPA) has, since the initiation of the Code project, endeavored to elicit the opinion of those in the correctional field on its various proposals, particularly those dealing with sentencing and correction. It has, through meetings and the submission of briefs, presented the distillate of this canvas to the Code Reporters, as well as to the ALI Council. Much of the material in this paper, indeed, is drawn from briefs, submitted or in preparation.

It is not difficult for people dealing with correctional administration or reform to concur on certain general principles. All could agree, for example, that punishment is necessary, but that it should serve a constructive purpose. Opinions, however, may well diverge when specific means of achieving this end are considered. It is to these matters, accordingly, that attention and energy must primarily be devoted, so that through counsel and discussion, differences may be resolved, if possible, and an accord reached that will advance correctional work and the welfare of the country.

The opinions expressed in this paper are those of the writer, but they are not his alone. They reflect, as well, the views of the Advisory Council of Judges of the NPPA, a group of leading trial and appellate court jurists drawn from all sections of the country, the Advisory Council on Parole of the NPPA, and various advisers from the field of correction who have studied the Code proposals.

Source: From Turnbladh, W. C., "A Critique of the Model Penal Code Sentencing Proposals," in *Law and Contemporary Problems, 23*(3), Summer 1958. Published by Duke University School of Law. Reprinted with permission.

TABLE 2.1

Grade of Felony	Maximum Term—Ordinary	Maximum Term—Extended
first degree	life imprisonment	life imprisonment
second degree	ten years	ten to twenty years
third degree	five years	five to ten years

I. IMPRISONMENT

A. Maximum Terms

The Code would prescribe maximum terms for felonies, to be automatically imposed, as follows.[1]

There is considerable evidence that the scale of prison terms employed in this country is too high. The number of prisoners is steadily growing not only absolutely, but also relatively to the general population.[2] This has resulted in the overcrowding of prisons and a more urgent need for additional facilities; and the pressure certainly will not abate unless means are found to change existing sentencing practices. A pattern of maximum terms lower rather than higher than those now prevailing must be sought.

Experience indicates that prisoners can safely be released earlier than is generally the case, particularly if they are professionally supervised and helped while on parole. Experience further shows that many offenders now in prisons could safely have been granted probation if effective probation service had been available in the court which committed them. The scale of punishments under the proposed Code, however, conjures up a picture of the average offender as an extremely dangerous individual; it would deter judges from the use of probation, when the social need is to the contrary. What is required, instead, is a scale of punishments that will encourage the use of community correctional treatment and make parole a flexible tool, enabling earlier release at the discretion of the parole board. This would conform with the lessons experience has taught, and to this end, the Code should point.

A statement by Professor Henry Weihofen in his book, *The Urge to Punish*, seems appropriate to quote and consider.[3]

> It is not only criminals who are motivated by irrational and emotional impulses. The same is true also of lawyers and judges, butchers and bakers. And it is especially true on such a subject as punishment of criminals. This is a matter on which we are all inclined to have deep feelings. When a reprehensible crime is committed, strong emotional reactions take place in all of us. Some people will be impelled to go out at once and work off their tensions in a lynching orgy. Even the calmest, most law-abiding of us is likely to be deeply stirred. All our ingrained concepts of morality and "justice" come into play, all our ancient tribal fears of anything that threatens the security of the group. It is one of the marks of a civilized culture that it has devised legal procedures that minimize the impact of emotional reactions and strive for calm and rational disposition. But lawyers, judges and jurors are still human, and objective, rational inquiry is made difficult by the very irrationality of the human mind itself. . . . It is time we Americans realized that we have probably the most ferocious penal policy in the whole civilized world.

Parole boards have a considerable interest in the maximum terms prescribed. It is not sufficient to suggest that if a parole board considers a maximum term to be excessive, it can discharge the individual from parole, thus terminating the commitment altogether. There are several things that this overlooks. Most importantly, it is not the province of the parole board to exert absolute authority over the matter of the duration of a commitment, and it is not helpful to give it such authority. The judge should be equipped with a presentence investigation, just as the parole board should be equipped with a parole study, and like the parole board, he must exercise his discretion to implement the requirements of individualized treatment. If he fails to do so with respect to the maximum term, the parole board is deprived of the guidance of his judgment. Moreover, when faced with a very high maximum term, whether legislatively or judicially-fixed, the parole board, being a responsible body, accords it a measure of respect. Indeed, experience shows that the length of time during which the parole board keeps an offender institutionalized and supervised is directly related to the maximum term that has been imposed.

To avert excessively long imprisonment, therefore, two things are necessary: First, the judge must have a discretion to fix a maximum term less than that prescribed under the statute. Second, the scale of punishments must be reduced substantially below its present levels.

B. Extended Terms

The extended terms proposed under the Code purport to serve a purpose somewhat similar to that of the habitual-offender, repeated-offender, or recidivist statutes found in most jurisdictions. Their rationale is that among convicted offenders, there are those who constitute an especial danger to the community, or those who are particularly difficult to deal with in any ordinary therapeutic or custodial way; and this technique is supposed to furnish a suitable mechanism for sentencing such offenders.

If the statutes exacting heavier penalties for recidivists actually operated in this manner, they would be unobjectionable. Experience, however, shows that they do not. It is notorious that the offenders who have been committed to extended terms under these statutes have not been the most dangerous, but more typically are the underlings of the rackets, the "small fry." Almost all professional observers have concluded that these recidivist statutes have been inconsistently applied and are of little value. One commentator, for example, has said:[4]

> It can hardly be said that the popularity of this practice was, or is, due to the theoretical possibilities of deterrence and reformation inherent in such penalties. Whatever the belief was formerly, present knowledge does not support it. Rather, revenge, and protection gained by eliminating the culprit from society, seem to be the reasons for its continued use. . . . It may be justly said that in the United States the recidivist laws have never been successful.

And another has written:[5]

> Evidence of the failure of the habitual offender laws has come from numerous sources during the writer's inquiries into the problem. It adds up to a conclusion that nowhere do these statutes effectively control organized criminal enterprise. They simply do not touch the problem.

Why is this so? For these reasons: The recidivist statutes play havoc with the orderly procedure of accusation, since the potential unjust penalties are avoided by the prosecutor in negotiations for pleas of guilty or in other ways. They similarly adversely affect trial procedures, involving the judge in negotiations regarding plea and sentences.[6] Moreover, they prejudicially affect sound jury procedures, resulting in a variety of rules for proving the prior offenses, with a confusion of effects and purposes in giving such evidence to juries or withholding it. The mandatory aspects of some of these statutes also deprive the courts of considerable discretion, essential to a sound penology, with respect to not only the limits of commitments, but also the use of probation. And, finally, they limit parole authorities in their discretion, because of the increase in minimum terms they prescribe. The result is a chronic "prison problem" in America, with a variety of destructive effects on the people imprisoned, on their families, and on correctional services.

The present Code approval wisely leaves the matter of the extended term within the discretion of the judge,[7] a feature that is found in a number of the existing statutes as well. To be useful rather than destructive, however, such a statute should further do or attempt to do two other things: First, it should provide a definition and the legal criteria of "dangerous offender" which actually accords with the security needs of the community. Second, it should provide for the most efficient means of detecting such a "dangerous offender," subjecting only him to the extended term, while excluding others, for whom the extended term would be excessive.

It is felt that the present Code definition and apparatus do not provide effective instruments for these purposes. Here, again, however, it should be noted, issue is taken not with the objective, but rather with the means through which its attainment is proposed. The NPPA is currently formulating an alternative "dangerous offender" code provision which, it is believed, will be an improvement over the instant proposal and which, it is hoped, the ALI will study and draw upon. Like the Code proposal, it is based on the realization that the community will be ready to accept a more moderate sentencing structure for the ordinary offender if it is confident that the dangerous offender will not be free to prey on society.

TABLE 2.2

Grade of Felony	Maximum Term—Ordinary	Maximum Term—Extended
first degree	not less than one nor more than ten years	not less than ten nor more than twenty years
second degree	not less than one nor more than three years	not less than one nor more than five years
third degree	not less than one nor more than two years	not less than one nor more than three years

C. Minimum Terms

The Code would prescribe minimum terms for felonies, as follows:[8]

One of the truly destructive elements in present-day sentencing practice is the imposition of minimum terms, especially those which, at the discretion of the sentencing judge, may (in some states) be inordinately high. It must be recognized that a high minimum term limits parole flexibility and handicaps the entire correctional process. Parole boards need the power to release the offender when his adjustment seems to them to warrant it. If the parole board does not have this power, then the commitment is obviously one of sheer punishment, depriving not only the individual, but the parole board—and, hence, the community—of the opportunity of applying what may be the most appropriate form of rehabilitation.

D. Misdemeanants

The Code prescribes sentences for misdemeanors and petty misdemeanors, too—a definite term of not more than one year, with parole seemingly impossible.[9] Again, the pattern of ordinary and extended and minimum terms is used, and its only apparent justification is one of symmetry with the proposals for felony commitments, since it is hardly related to correctional treatment. There is little to recommend a form of commitment which abolishes the possibility of parole even for minor offenders serving terms up to one year. Nor is it sound to conclude that parole cannot be used for such offenders, simply because it is little used at present. On the contrary, it is necessary for leaders in the judiciary and in the correctional field to make every effort to develop proper parole procedures in this area. Experiments in local parole are, in fact, being carried forward in a number of places, and workable systems are being devised. Most judges

of lower criminal courts, moreover, vigorously endorse such systems.

II. PROBATION

The Code originally articulated what amounted to a presumption in favor of imprisonment and proposed a series of criteria which had to be met before probation could be granted.[10] It was the opinion of the Advisory Council of Judges of the NPPA, however, that the proposed criteria would deter rather than encourage the appropriate use of probation. Accordingly, in order to gauge the prevalent sentiment not only in the immediate matter, but also as to the use of criteria in general—for they are widely employed elsewhere in the Code—a questionnaire survey was conducted among a number of judges of criminal courts located in different parts of the country, none of whom were members of the Advisory Council.

Most of the judges who opposed the incorporations of criteria in the Code felt that they would either decrease a court's latitude in the use of probation, or not affect it at all. But these judges criticized the criteria for other effects they would have as well. A number stressed the fact that the judge ought not to be circumscribed in the exercise of his discretion by any such detailed provisions. Some observed that the criteria might encourage unnecessary litigation, in that they would tend to encourage defense counsel to attempt, in any given case, to place their clients within one of the categories in an effort to establish their right to probation. Several also pointed out that offenders would assume that they were entitled to probation as a matter of right if they could qualify under the criteria set forth, and the statute might, thus, encourage a rash of habeas corpus proceedings where probation had been denied.

The view was expressed by a number of judges, too, that even if the criteria are proper for consideration by the judge, they should not be incorporated in the Code, since this might encourage their routine, mechanical use. Moreover, it was remarked that the criteria proposed do not embrace all of the cases in which probation might be appropriate. Furthermore, some of the specific criteria were questioned. One judge declared "they do not stress the court's expectation of future reform strongly enough. They stress the past, not the future. They are negative, not positive."

In any event, Professor Wechsler, the Chief Code Reporter, and the ALI Council are redrafting the relevant provisions, taking these views into account, and the latest material appears to incline in a direction consistent with a more progressive use of probation.

III. Procedure on Sentence

A. Mandatory Presentence Reports

The Code contains a laudable proposal requiring a presentence investigation in all serious cases and in all cases affecting youth.[11] This is a forward-looking step, and it merits widespread adoption. Only with a presentence investigation available can a judge confidently sentence on the basis of knowledge, rather than hunch.

B. Confidentiality of Presentence Reports

The Code provides that before imposing sentence, the court shall advise the defendant or his counsel of the factual contents and the conclusions of any presentence or psychiatric investigation and afford to the defendant an opportunity to controvert them.[12] As is pointed out in the commentary, however, this provision is a controversial one. The NPPA's Standard Probation and Parole Act deals with this matter as follows:[13]

> The presentence report, the preparole report, and the supervision history, obtained in the discharge of official duty by any member or employee of the board, shall be privileged and shall not be disclosed directly or indirectly to anyone other than the board, the judge, or others entitled under this act to receive such information, except that the board or court may in its discretion permit the inspection of the report or parts there of by the defendant or prisoner

or his attorney, or other person having a proper interest therein, whenever the best interest or welfare of a particular defendant or prisoner makes such action desirable or helpful.

The information-gathering function of the probation and parole service is supported by this provision, which enables the staff to assure persons providing information that it will not be routinely disclosed. This policy also supports the relationship of the probation or parole officer to persons under investigation or supervision by avoiding disclosures which might be damaging to the individual or cause recrimination. A policy of routine or mandatory disclosure would have to be interpreted to informants and might inhibit the free disclosure of information that might otherwise be forthcoming. On the other hand, since it is desirable in certain situations to disclose a report or parts of it to the defendant or prisoner or his attorney, the Standard Probation and Parole Act authorizes the court, in its discretion, to make such disclosure or permit inspection.

IV. Parole

A. Separate Parole Term

Underlying the Code provisions regarding the length of terms is a proposed division of terms—or a multiplication of terms—so that an offender faces two terms—one, a term of commitment, and the other, a wholly new concept, an additional term of parole.[14] That is, at the time of parole release, the term of imprisonment would come to an end and a parole term of a specified duration would commence. The minimum parole term would be at least one year or one-half of the period of time that the offender actually served in the institution, whichever were longer; the maximum parole term would be ten years or twice the period of time actually served in the institution, whichever were shorter.

At the present time, in all states, a term of commitment embraces both the term of institutionalization and the term on parole. In other words, at present, a commitment of ten years may represent five years in the institution and five years on parole. But under the Code proposal, a ten-year term of which the offender served five years would actually be a term of five years plus a possible maximum term of ten years on parole, or a total of fifteen years. In fact, it would be possible for the so-called ten-year term to become a term of ten years (perhaps less one day) in an institution plus a term of ten years on parole, or a total of twenty years for a term which was actually designated as only ten years.

Apart from lengthening the combined period of sentence, the proposed separate parole term is perhaps intended to afford a parole board a longer period of supervision than is possible at present. The extension of parole terms, however, is neither necessary nor useful, for if parole is to succeed at all, it will in most cases be in two or three years.

B. Mandatory Parole

The Code proposes that all offenders shall be released on parole, and it seeks to accomplish this, as described above, by providing that when an offender is released from an institution, whether before or upon the expiration of his term of imprisonment, a new separate term, the parole term, comes into being. The resultant universalization of parole is a sound goal, of course, but whatever possible gain might be achieved by this plan would largely be offset by the increase in the total term. It must be remembered that even under existing laws, where parole is a matter of discretion, not of right, there are jurisdictions in which sixty, seventy, eighty, and even over ninety per cent of releases are attained through parole. Moreover, under the Code proposal, not only the poor risks, but also the good ones might have their terms considerably extended, since both the minimum and maximum parole terms would be based on the amount of time served in the institution, and a parole board which might otherwise be inclined to release an individual at an early date—for example, perhaps after one year—might feel it necessary to postpone the granting of parole in order to increase the period of supervision beyond the automatic two years prescribed under the Code. Thus, a parole board could not grant an early release with a long parole period, even if this were indicated in a particular case.

The Code proposal would, moreover, foster a mechanical approach to administration. All too often, parole boards, like prisoners, become more concerned with arithmetic than with attitudes, more solicitous about calculating the term than preparing for release at the most beneficial time.

C. Representation by Counsel at Parole Hearings

The Code grants to a prisoner the right to consult with his own legal counsel in preparing for a hearing before the parole board. The provision was later amended to give the prisoner the right to be represented by counsel at the hearing.[15] The Standard Probation and Parole Act, however, provides that "the Board shall not be required to hear oral statements or arguments by attorneys or other persons not connected with the correctional system,"[16] and this position is endorsed by most of the correctional and parole administrators in the country. The following comment which appears in the Standard Probation and Parole Act, explains its provision:

> Improper activities of paid attorneys have done much to bring parole into dispute in many states. Some attorneys solicit business from prisoners, representing that they have influence to get paroles for a fee. The representation is unfortunately, well founded in some states. Even attorneys who are members of the legislature present cases before some parole boards in spite of the fact that in doing so they may be exerting improper influence by reason of their power to oppose appropriations and policies of the state officers who compose the parole board.

In general, it is undesirable to have attorneys or relatives and friends of the prisoners present when the parole board is interviewing him and discussing his potentialities for parole. But in order to hear the arguments and pleas of these persons, some parole boards hold special meetings at which they may appear, but at which decisions are not necessarily made. These meetings make it easier for board members to discourage such persons from attempting to interview them individually, a most undesirable practice.

D. Criteria

The Code declares that when the parole board deliberates, it shall order the release of a prisoner unless any one of four specified criteria exists.[17] Boards of parole use many criteria and guides in arriving at their decisions, but the variety of situations and kinds of offenders are such that no simple guides, as are here proposed, are likely to be adequate or even substantially agreed upon. Furthermore, these criteria might be interpreted as creating a right to parole, inviting countless writs by prisoners whose paroles had been denied.

V. TREATING THE YOUTHFUL OFFENDER

Several years ago, when Tentative Draft Number Three of the Code was first published, the field of correction, and especially of youth treatment, was alarmed at the proposals which, in effect, totally repudiated the ALI's Model Youth Correction Authority Act. This Act, promulgated in 1940, had served as an effective tool for the organization of approximately ten equivalent authorities among the states and in the federal system. It was one of the most important incentives to a surge in philosophy, legislation, administration organization, and expansion of services relating to youth treatment. At the request of the NPPA, the ALI, in April 1956, called a meeting of youth authority leaders from many parts of the country, who affirmed to the Code Reporters and the ALI Council their belief in the youth-authority idea. But when Tentative Draft Number Seven of the Code was presented to the ALI membership in May 1957, it was found to be essentially a statutory version of the proposals originally set forth in Tentative Draft Number Three.[18]

A. Terminology

The key term used in the Code proposal for a special part of court as well as for correctional services for youth is "young adult" or "young adult offender." It would appear, however, that the preferable term is "youth" or "youthful offender." Among the existing courts for offenders, those which deal with children are universally denominated juvenile courts; the others, dealing with adults, simply criminal courts. It is evident that the instant group of offenders is between the two—above juvenile-court age, but still minors (although there may be some control after an individual becomes twenty-one). Where intermediate courts or procedures have been established—for example, in New York and in the many jurisdictions with youth authorities—the term used is youth. This terminology accords with the realities of personality development, since the offenders are still in their adolescent period.

B. Youth Court Organization

The Code proposes supplemental provisions establishing a special part of court for "young adult offenders."[19] Based on general principles of judicial organization, which appear applicable here, however, it would seem best that a separate part not be established by statute. Certain very important procedural and substantive matters must be provided for with respect to the court procedure and disposition in youth cases, but none of these depends on the organization of a separate part.

The establishment of separate parts, divisions, or courts for special purposes is a tendency which has had adverse effects on the efficiency and quality of not only the special courts, but the whole court structure. Experience has shown that specialized courts or parts in general do not acquire the same status or receive the same budgetary support as do the courts of general jurisdiction. The pyramiding of courts also confuses administration as well as litigants. Moreover, where special courts exist, they necessarily compete for limited services, and the burgeoning vested interests become a barrier to effective administration and any reform. Consolidation, the obvious need sooner or later, thus becomes an extraordinarily difficult problem. Then, too, the variety of methods of selection of judges that prevails where special courts exist increases the difficulty of attracting the best men to the bench. Special judges, in addition, tend to be out of the mainstream of the regular judiciary.

Nor are specialized courts or parts necessary to achieve the objectives contemplated for the special part for youth; they can be achieved within a general court system. If the problem is one of additional judges, this can be solved. If the problem is one of obtaining judges with a specialization in one phase of the law or another, this, too, can be remedied through special assignment within the general court system. Establishing the special functions within the general court system, moreover, has an additional advantage, in that neither constitutional nor legislative changes are needed to meet new situations. Changes can be made within the judiciary itself and its organization.

Accordingly, the NPPA has proposed that the ALI consider the plan of prescribing certain powers and procedures in the courts of general criminal jurisdiction; authorizing these courts to determine when and where a special assignment, which could be designated as a part or division, should be set up; and empowering it to do so. This would enable the establishment of a special part, where indicated, without the need for a statutory change. Actually, only in the larger cities is there a sufficient volume of such work to warrant the establishment of such a division or part.

C. Procedure and Jurisdiction

The Code proposal of a special part of court for young adult offenders does not offer any special procedures for dealing with youth. It refers to approval of places for the detention of persons awaiting proceedings, to probation and other services, and to assignment of counsel. These are not new tools, however, and do not add greatly to existing procedures and techniques. There are sources in existing law, however, offering precedents for special procedures which have, in fact, proved quite effective and appropriate for youthful offenders. The New York youthful offender procedure, for example, which has been in existence since 1943,[20] provides for a screening of offenders in the criminal court to determine which ones are suitable for treatment as a special noncriminal category, designated as "youthful offender." About thirty-eight per cent of eligible youth have been dealt with in this way in that state. In addition to the noncriminal disposition, this procedure features an early investigation upon which the court, with consent of the youth, determines whether youthful offender procedure shall be applied; the sealing of the indictment and the protection of records; and the usual dispositions—probation, fine, commitment—except that the defendant is not deemed to have been convicted of crime, and where there is a commitment, its duration is limited.

The Code proposes that in sentencing a young adult offender to the special term provided or in imposing any sentence other than one of imprisonment, the court may order that so long as he is not convicted of another felony, the judgment shall not constitute a conviction for the purposes of any disqualification or disability imposed by law upon conviction of a crime. It further proposes that when any young adult offender is unconditionally discharged from probation or parole before the expiration of the maximum term, the court may enter an order vacating the judgment of conviction.[21]

Although such provisions would seem to be quite progressive, they are, in fact, quite limited as compared with some existing provisions in a number of jurisdictions, and they fall short of the optimal provisions that could be proposed for youthful offenders. For one thing, they do not actually provide a noncriminal disposition; rather, they only avoid certain disqualifications which are the consequence of a conviction. All too often, however, we encounter the tragic experience of youthful offenders, many of whom are convicted of crimes which are the results of youthful impulse and not representative of a criminal pattern, youth who are headed for successful careers or respectable lives, whose future opportunities for professional work or satisfactory employment are grievously impaired, to their own detriment and to that community, by the existence of the criminal conviction which inexorably follows them. This effect can be mitigated and the community, at the same time, can be amply protected by the provision that the disposition shall be deemed noncriminal, so that the youth may accurately say that he has not been convicted of a crime. Expunging the record later on comes too late.

Judge Sylvia Jaffin Singer, of the New York City Domestic Relations Court, for ten years assigned to the youth parts of the New York County courts wherein the youthful offender law was operative, writes as follows:[22]

> The volume of cases I handled during those years ranged from 1200 to 1800 annually. The hope of noncriminal adjudication was in my experience a great incentive to rehabilitation in many instances. Many young people who were adjudged youthful offenders and not criminals were encouraged to try to keep their records clean. Many who adjusted themselves in the community came back to thank us for the consideration they had received and reported that their progress had been made possible by the absence of a criminal record.

> To expunge the record after a youngster has borne it and been identified in the community as a criminal, provides little help to him. The proposed code bids him fly but weights his wings so he cannot get off the ground. It would prevent some of the near miracles the judges in New York County have known. I cite merely one, a youngster originally charged with armed robbery ultimately adjudged a youthful offender who is now a physician after a distinguished record in college and medical school. None of this would have been possible had he been stigmatized with a criminal record at the age of sixteen when he perpetrated his criminal act.

Under the New York plan, it should be emphasized, the determination of whether a youth shall be tried as a youthful offender is made at the outset of the proceeding. This is a desirable feature, as it puts the stamp on the proceeding at once, thereby facilitating all subsequent steps. It would be anomalous to attach a noncriminal disposition to a completely criminal proceeding. This determination also governs the applicability of a special commitment, limited to three years, which is prescribed for those who are retained for trial as youthful offenders. A recent statutory modification, enacted in 1956 but not yet in effect, would add that where the underlying act is a felony, a five-year indefinite term may be imposed.[23] These terms seem practical.

D. Organization of a Youth Authority

As has been noted above, Tentative Draft Number Seven of the Code does what Tentative Draft Number Three proposed—it rejects the youth authority plan. It declares than an offender sixteen years of age or over but less than twenty-two years of age shall be committed to the custody of the Division of Young Adult Correction of the Department of Correction. One may agree with the present Code position that the power to sentence—that is, the power to select among probation, suspended sentence, fine, or commitment— should remain with the judge. When commitment is determined upon by the judge, however, it should be to a "youth authority," an autonomous administrative unit, either independent or a separate division in a state department, responsible for the whole youth correction program, including institutions, diagnostic facilities, and both state-wide leadership and assistance to communities in crime and delinquency prevention. This authority should be authorized to receive commitments of youth beyond juvenile court age only, or to receive commitments of both minors outside of juvenile court age and juvenile court commitments; and a model act for youth treatment should authorize either of these forms. Although similar advances in the correctional treatment of adults are desirable, the specialization of the youth authority is vital. It should, therefore, not be necessary to increase the age level in order to embrace a wider group of individuals in a modern youth correctional program.

The Code also sets up a Young Adult Division of the Board of Parole.[24] Although such a plan has some realistic meaning for a board like the United States Board of Parole, with eight members, whose youth correction division has three members, for most boards this is not feasible. There are very few boards with more than three full-time members. A youth division of the board would, therefore, consist of the same members as the adult parole board. It should, however, rather be a separate board of three members or more, depending on the volume of work, and it should be empowered to grant a parole at any time, as is true of all the existing youth authorities.

VI. Conclusion

A high proportion of sentences today are too long—twenty-five per cent are commitments of ten years or over.[25] Such terms are inconsistent with present correctional knowledge and experience. They mislead the public as to the dangerousness of most offenders. Under the Code proposals, they would be lengthened, through the proposed maximum terms, minimum terms, parole terms, and other provisions.

Montesquieu wrote: "As freedom advances, the severity of the penal law decreases."[26] Public protection does not require and is not best served by a punitive penal code. Rather, one providing the framework for the fuller development and more effective application of correctional treatment is a better guarantee of public protection and, in the boarder sense, of our freedom.

Notes

1. Model Penal Code §§ 6.06, 6.07 (Tent. Draft No. 2, 1954).

2. *Compare* N.Y. Prison Ass'n, Third Report 358 (1847), and U.S. Census Office, Statistical View of the United States, A Compendium of the Seventh Census table CLXXIX (1850), *with* U.S. Bureau of Prisons, Dep't of Justice, National Prisoner Statistics, Prisoners in State and Federal Institutions, 1956, table I (1957). See also Rubin, *Long Prison Terms and the Form of Sentence*, 2 N.P.P.A.J. 377 (1956).

3. Henry Weihofen, The Urge to Punish 130, 148 (1956).

4. Brown, *The Treatment of the Recidivist in the United States*, 23 Can. B. Rev. 640, 664 (1945).

5. Tappan, *Habitual Offender Laws and Sentencing Practices in Relation to Organized Crime*, in Organized Crime and Law Enforcement 113 (1952).

6. These aspects of sentencing are treated more extensively elsewhere in this symposium. See Ohlin and Remington, *Sentencing Structure: Its Effect Upon Systems for the Administration of Justice, supra* p. 495.

7. Model Penal Code §§ 6.06, 6.07 and comment thereto (Tent. Draft No. 2, 1954).

8. *Ibid.*

9. *Id.* §§ 6.08, 6.09.

10. *Id.* § 7.01.

11. *Id.* § 7.07(I).

12. *Id.* § 7.07(5).

13. NPPA, Standard Probation and Parole Act § 5 (1995).

14. Model Penal Code § 6.09A (Tent. Draft. No. 5, 1956).

15. *Id.* § 305.II(2).

16. NPPA, *op. cit. supra* note 13, § 22.

17. Model Penal Code § 305.13 (Tent. Draft. No. 5, 1956).

18. *Id.* §§ 4.10, 402–3, 6.05 (Tent. Draft No. 7, 1957); *cf. id.* at 2–4 (Tent. Draft No. 3 1955).

19. *Id.* app. A (Tent. Draft No. 7, 1957).

20. N.Y. Crim. Code § 913.

21. Model Penal Code § 6.05 (Tent. Draft No. 7, 1957).

22. Letter from Judge Singer to author.

23. N.Y. Unconsol. Laws § 4356 (McKinney 1957).

24. Model Penal Code § 402.3 (I) (Tent. Draft No. 7, 1957).

25. U.S. Bureau of Prisons, Dep't of Justice, National Prisoner Statistics, Prisoners Released from State and Federal Institutions, 1951, table 6 (1955).

26. Quoted in Charles L. Chute and Marjorie Bell, Crime, Courts, and Probation 8 (1956).

3

MILTON RECTOR

43 Years of Reform

JOAN POTTER

For most of this century, the most constant and persistent organization advocating criminal-justice reform in the United States has been the National Council on Crime and Delinquency. Founded in 1907, the NCCD started out as the National Probation Association to lobby for alternatives to incarceration for juvenile and youthful offenders, who at the turn of the century were housed in the same bastille-like institutions as adults. The NCCD had great influence in the "movement" 60 years ago to create special juvenile courts. In 1960 it took its present name.

For the last several decades NCCD, which is supported by private donations and foundation grants, has been an advocate of corrections reform for both adults and juveniles. Its administrators favor a radical reduction in the number of offenders incarcerated; they even foresee the eventual abandonment of the prison as a penal sanction in favor of community alternatives.

Despite its radical positions on many corrections issues, the NCCD remains the most "respectable" of the nation's prison reform groups. This is partly because its administrators have been careful over the years to involve criminal justice practitioners, especially judges, in the formulation of NCCD's position papers and

research projects. But it is also because of the respect that its long-time executive director, Milton Rector, is accorded among correction officials. Corrections reform will therefore lose one of its most eloquent and effective spokesmen when Rector retires in January.

Though NCCD employs 65 people at its Hackensack, N.J., offices, many say that Milton Rector is the NCCD. Since he took the office of NCCD executive director in 1959, Rector has fought tirelessly, sometimes against insuperable odds, in an effort to persuade criminal justice officials and legislators to reduce their reliance on imprisonment. Rector has argued his way through endless conferences, seminars, workshops and legislative hearings. He and his staff are constantly churning out position papers and critiques of the latest get-tough-on-crime proposals from politicians. Part of Rector's appeal is that he is an eminently reasonable man, willing to state his positions on criminal justice issues with a minimum of rancor. He is also a gentleman; he never makes personal attacks on those whose policies he opposes. Though Rector's advocacy of humane alternatives to imprisonment grows out of a general sympathy for the poor and downtrodden, his correctional politics are not part of a general leftist ideology. In fact,

Source: From Potter, J., "Milton Rector: 43 years of reform" in *Corrections*, June, 1981. Reprinted with permission.

the tall, gray-haired 63-year-old Rector says he has always been a "conservative Republican." Given the annual rise since 1969 in the nation's prison population, and given a spate of legislation in recent years mandating that more and more offenders go to prison for longer and longer terms, it is a wonder to his friends and acquaintances that Rector is able to continue his work so cheerfully and with such energy. He attributes the fact that he has not "burned out" to strong religious convictions.

Rector based his decision to retire partly on his own experience as a young man at NCCD. NCCD was incorporated in 1918 by its first executive director, Charles Chute, he pointed out. "Having respected Mr. Chute, my first boss," he says, "but having seen him stay until he was 70, I know you have to get out of the way for young people."

Rector will take a year-long sabbatical starting in January to update a history of the NCCD begun by Chute. He will formally retire in January 1983, after his 65th birthday.

Rector lives with his wife of 41 years, Harriet, in River Edge, N.J., where he is active in the Grace Lutheran Church. They also have a home in Cape Cod, Mass., where they like to sail. They have three children. Their son is an engineer; one daughter is a nurse, and the other, Rector says, is "a happily married mother of two." Since he travels so extensively for the NCCD, his wife, Rector says, "has lived for 35 years with me gone half the time. She has raised the children and practiced what I preach."

After his retirement, Rector plans to write in the field of theology. He is interested in examining the conflict between the church's teachings of reparation and restitution and the current criminal justice system, which he says is based on "punishment and revenge." He also looks forward to traveling with his wife. "Maybe a university or two will let me come to town and lecture during a semester and she can come with me and we can rent an apartment. I want her to meet friends I have all over the United States who are just pictures and names to her now."

Rector spent several hours recently talking to Contributing Editor Joan Potter about his 43 years as a corrections reformer. Following are excerpts from that interview.

Potter: I understand you had your first contact with the criminal justice system when you were a boy in Nevada.

Rector: After the loss of my mother [when I was a small child] I was taken by an aunt and uncle who lived in San Francisco. . . . When I was about 12, my uncle had some financial reverses—it was during the Depression—so I went back to the ranch [in Nevada to live with my father]. I used to ride out repairing fences and would sometimes be gone overnight. One day I took my dad's best horse and kept going. I finally got over to the Mono Lake area which was over the pass near Tehachapi [Calif.]. I guess by then the word had gotten out and I wasn't too hard to find. I was picked up and put into jail. It was a severe shock. I stayed there two nights and then my father came to get me. He thought it would be good for me, would teach me a lesson. After that, I was allowed to live with my aunt and uncle, who had moved to Long Beach [Calif.].

What was your life like in Long Beach?

We weren't living in the best part of town. I was a heller, and I started getting into street gang activity. Then in high school, I was very fortunate to get involved with a group of kids who went to a small Baptist church. My baptism in that church and my friendship with those kids was really kind of a turning point. I didn't realize that impact on my thinking and in my life until trying to sort out with NCCD why some of the ideas and programs we see taking root in communities lose their staying power. For a number of years, I've been saying to our board of directors and program staff that if good programs at a neighborhood level were going to last, we had to somehow strengthen the forces for positive social control. I want to bring in a council of top religious leaders, those who were the real philosophers, to look at the impact of religion on the life and behavior of people. So now we have at NCCD the National Council of Religious Leaders.

What role should the churches actually play?

Well, I think the church has to get into the debate—on federal and state criminal codes, on juvenile justice codes. Church leadership in the United States invented the prison as a place for long-term service of sentence, for penitence. Fortunately, the Quakers have now rescinded their early discovery.

[Churches] can't just be there to receive people on their holy days. They have to be concerned about their neighborhood. It's like Karl Menninger's book, Whatever Became of Sin? Karl's saying that the things the churches used to be concerned about—the behavior of people—that as they become crimes the churches are no longer concerned. It's in another arena. Sure, we'll have committees visiting our local jails and visiting our prisons, but we've been content to leave the people in these hellholes and not be too concerned if we can save their souls.

I recently met with the Conference of Bishops at the New York State Catholic Conference. I was there as a lay person, to bring this message: that your people are the people in the neighborhoods who are being robbed or raped or are fearful that they're going to be, and all you're doing is saying, "Well, we need more police and more prisons and more courts." I can tell you with authority that police, courts and corrections cannot stop violence in the United States.

I started out working with Mexican-American gangs in Los Angeles over 40 years ago. I go back now and there are more young people on the same streets; there is more youth unemployment than there was in the depression days of the 1930s. And Los Angeles is now wondering, Why do we have so much gang warfare? All they have done is build additional detention cells for those kids, add more police—no more jobs, no better schools, no better housing. They're willing to accept the gang violence as a part of the culture of the Mexican-Americans.

How long did you work with Mexican-American gangs?

For about a year and a half. When I was at the University of Southern California, I answered an ad placed by the Los Angeles sheriff for young people to work with gangs in the East Los Angeles area. I was a trainee deputy. To make a little extra money, I took a night job in the juvenile hall. One night, a young man came up to me and said, "Aren't you the guy who arrested me?" He had been in a stolen car with a couple of other kids, and [when we arrested him] the deputy I was assigned to and I both had torn our uniforms and it was raining and we were angry. Later, I had to figure out why I had a different perception of this young man as I talked to him. I think I saw myself in him. He was no longer being chased, and I was no

longer the chaser. I think that had something to do with my switching to the probation department. I was uncomfortable making arrests.

What was your job with probation?

I joined the probation department as a trainee and worked for about a year and a half as a counselor in some forestry camps. Then I came into the central office and eventually became a full-fledged probation officer. Before I left to go into the Navy in 1944, I was directing a camp institution for delinquent youngsters. While I was in the service, the man who was the head of the juvenile division of the Los Angeles County Probation Department became the director of the western office of the National Council on Crime and Delinquency. . . .

I joined the organization when I came out of the Navy. I was sent to the state of Washington to do a study of the juvenile court system there and to help develop a state citizens committee to lobby for legislation. In 1948, I got a permanent spot in the San Francisco office. I traveled to all western states as a consultant on juvenile courts and probation and parole. I came east in 1952 and became chief executive officer in 1959.

The NCCD played a role in the creation of separate courts for the prosecution of juveniles, and also in the establishment of juvenile detention centers separate from adult jails. I understand that you and other NCCD officials now regret some of those developments.

I am now encouraging a policy position that raises for public debate the abolition of the juvenile court. The way we're looking at it is this: In what other area of human services do we publicly tolerate a system for the adult members of the family that is so bad, so antiquated, so violent, that we can't have the children in that system? One of the prime defenses against using the criminal justice system for juveniles is that it is so inhuman, that they keep offenders so long, brutalize them, and destroy any ability to develop self-esteem . . .

I have terrible guilt feelings of having had a part in the planning and design of practically every large juvenile detention home in the United States through an early campaign to get kids out of jail. . . . It was a staff member who left NCCD and said, "Milt, if we had gotten out in front in how to keep kids out of detention and in better defining who needs detention at all, we wouldn't have the number of kids locked up that we have today."

I would think it would be easier for people to respond to juveniles.

I always thought that, but I've always been dismayed at how lay citizens really want to avoid the real issues in juvenile justice. . . . A lot of them feel that kids need a good, sharp lesson, and a lot of judges satisfy that feeling. I went up to Butte, Montana, for a meeting, and a child welfare worker took me down to the jail to show me the number of kids there. I said, "Why? It's a weekend." He said the parents call the sheriff [and tell him] to keep them in over the weekend.

By the way, let me correct for the record that the NCCD is not announcing that it's going to support the abolition of the juvenile court. That's in staff debate and preparation. We are pulling in people from the outside to stretch our minds, and then a position paper with the data will go to a program and policy committee of the board of directors. . . . [We are discussing the abolition of juvenile courts] because the juvenile justice system is stretching and stretching. Alternative programs are bringing in kids that used to be let alone and it's getting big and fat and rich. We we're saying it's inconsistent to work for one thing in juvenile justice and another for the adults. Maybe we ought to look at justice for human beings. And the whole system has got to be changed. When it is and it's decent, we won't have one standard of indecency for adults and another for kids.

Over the years, how has the public responded to the need to make changes in the criminal justice system?

I think the great movement came during the 1960s. The 1970s was a very traumatic kind of experience.

From what we read in the newspapers, the law-and-order mentality in this country is stronger than ever. Are things as bad as they seem?

I hope I'm not being falsely optimistic. Last week I participated in the National Conference of State Legislators in Connecticut. They're considering mandatory sentencing laws. I told them that, because of what has happened in Western Europe and Scandinavia— countries that in my 43 years in the field we have generally followed by ten to 15 years—I know that prisons are on their way out, that civilization is better than it was before, that where we can no longer use whipping posts and disembowelment and so on, the public will soon begin to see incarceration in that same light. I said that community forces and resources, with leadership and funding, are going to be the principal correctional resources in the future.

How did the legislators respond?

Some, I guess, thought I was whistling Dixie, because it's not what they hear. . . . In Connecticut and elsewhere I say to the legislatures. "Don't get out and promise the public that the death penalty is going to stop crime and violence, that mandatory sentencing is going to stop the use of handguns. You're going to be found out. You're going to be shown up as a public fraud. Because now, as one of the major contributions of the LEAA, we have the data. It's not going to be long before the public builds a few more of these $100,000-a-cell institutions and then asks, "Why did you lead us down this street?"

But it often seems to work the other way. Legislators appear to be led by their constituents.

Well, they're fearful. Their constituents are fearful. The people at the church Sunday [a New York City church where Rector spoke] wanted Mayor [Edward] Koch's promise of the death penalty. When asked why, it was because it would reduce violence, it would be a deterrent. They were shocked at all the data that's available that shows it won't be a deterrent.

Would you advocate determinate sentencing if the sentences seemed fair and reasonable and equally applied?

If we can get sentences down to where the maximum time served does the least damage—a year, maybe two years as the maximum—and, like the Scandinavian nations, stop trying to fight crime and violence by incarceration, then, simultaneously, we'll have most offenders in for less than a year.

But what about violent offenders?

Then we'll begin to put our money in other kinds of resources to deal with violence. Most of the violence that's occurring in the United States today is between family members, acquaintances, neighbors. We're beginning to remedy this with the involvement of community mental health, family services. . . . But for the minority of crime, the high fear, stranger-to-stranger crime, we addressed this on the commission on criminal justice standards and goals [in 1973]. It said that those who commit street crime, stranger-to-stranger crime, are mostly poor people, undereducated people. Kids with an education and a job with hope don't commit street crimes. Well, then, that has to say that there's another resolution to that kind of violence. And it's less costly. For the $26,000 a year it costs to lock up a person on Riker's Island [the New York City jail] you can build a decent place to live and have some subsidized employment.

In your experience, has there been a time when the public outcry against crime has been equal to the current one?

Not quite equal. In the 1960s, we had the debates between presidential candidates Johnson and Goldwater. That was the first time crime was ever raised as a key political issue. But what is happening now is more severe because most governors and most mayors have picked it up as a campaign issue.

I recently heard the New York State corrections commissioner, who once talked about expanding community corrections, say that everyone in prison in New York belongs there and that we need more prisons.

I think he's being politically loyal. The man he replaced is a man I've known for many years, Dick Hongisto. When Dick was appointed commissioner of corrections, I knew what he stood for and I saw real hope for no more prisons in New York. I invited him to our board of directors meeting. Dick called me personally and said, "Milt, I have to stay under wraps. I promised that until my appointment is confirmed I will take no controversial positions, and anything that deviates from the plan to build more prisons is controversial."

I've had young staff at NCCD who accused me of being too conservative, too slow, who then went out to become

directors of planning commissions for states, or directors of prisons. Then they call me and say, "Well, out here you have to be pragmatic." I've said to them, "All right, I understand, if your governor has promised that his solution is to build prisons, to get the death penalty, and if you're going to keep the job you have to be loyal to the governor. But let us help you. Make sure we get invited to testify at your key hearings. Make sure your data are correct."

So, when people who have these government jobs feel they have to be careful not to lose them, you can come in as an independent organization and present facts?

Yes, and we owe it to the professionals in the system not to attack them personally. When [former U.S. Attorney General] John Mitchell and President Nixon announced that they were going to rebuild the federal prison system and asked Norman Carlson to develop a master plan, it was going to be a model all the states could follow. I went down to meet with Mr. Mitchell and Norman Carlson. I said, "Norm, I want you to understand, it's not personal, but if community corrections comes to the United States, there will be no place for a federal system that transports residents hundreds and thousands of miles from their homes." Well, Carlson has come to see it as a personal fight when I testify against his budget.

I understand that you had another run-in with John Mitchell in the late sixties.

We had a member on our board, a very powerful industrial leader, who brought us into a series of meetings with John Mitchell and the Nixon administration. We were to discuss becoming the principal volunteer organization in the United States. But the theme was wrong. The theme was law and order. The theme was not system change; the theme was increase the system, make arrest easier by diminishing the rights of the accused. But the NCCD refused to fight crime with pamphlets and promises that a stronger criminal justice system would reduce crime. That would have been a fraud.

We could have raised a lot of money. We had the promise of millions and dollars. I went through a series of meetings. This board member was so powerful and brought such leadership together that I was meeting with the president of the American Bar Association, National Legal Aid and Defenders, the International Association of Chiefs of Police. . . . We were all summoned. We were all going to work as a coalition and NCCD was going to be the principal funding body. When we refused to become a law and order organization, well, we almost went bankrupt [because Mitchell and members of the NCCD board who supported Mitchell's plan urged the corporations and foundations that supported NCCD to cut off funding]. . . .

Finally, at one meeting, John Mitchell left the room with a string of profanities. My board member, who shall go unnamed, had created a new organization called Citizens for Justice with Order, and it became the thrust of Mr. Mitchell and others to have the NCCD merge with them and they would become the umbrella organization. When Mr. Mitchell left the room he said, "You'll have to tell me why NCCD won't be a part of this." And I said, "I will, I'll tell you in writing." I wrote a 13-page memorandum and sent copies to National Legal Aid, American Bar Association and other groups that I thought were being conned. I told them we were being asked to join a fraudulent money-raising organization to increase fear. To the credit of our board of directors, we not only survived, but that organization [the Mitchell-backed one], in a face-saving move, was merged into NCCD. My chairman of the board at that time, Carl M. Loeb Jr., a conservative Republican, stuck with us through it all and gets credit for NCCD being what it is today.

You support a moratorium on all prison construction. How do you feel about the prisoners who are jammed into overcrowded state prisons right now?

That's one of the most difficult parts of our policy position. The NCCD supports the moratorium, but if you read our policy position it says that nondangerous offenders should not be incarcerated. It says there should be a halt to construction until all possible community alternatives are funded and developed, recognizing that until knowledge increases beyond where it is, we are going to need places to incarcerate offenders who are persistently violent. John Conrad [now of the

American Justice Institute] and I wrote a series of letters to each other about this. He said to me, "You're taking the NCCD down the wrong street. You haven't been in Walla Walla, you haven't been in Leavenworth." I said, "John, there's hardly a prison in the United States I haven't been in." For a while, even when I'd go abroad on U.N. meetings, I went out to see prisons like I was collecting them. I suddenly realized they're all the same, and there isn't a good one.

Conrad said I was immoral because I didn't want to build any more prisons while people were crammed in there. And I was glad he chose [to talk about Washington State]. Because I used to visit the women's prison, which was part of the men's prison in Walla Walla, Washington, for NCCD and I had never seen more than 50 or 60 women in the prison. It was a hellhole. I saw the state of Washington improve it by building [a new institution] for 185 at Purdy [in 1970]. It's one of the most beautiful campuses. That's the best we can do, and it's been overcrowded ever since they built it. Women who used to make it in the community are now going to Purdy. I don't feel I have to apologize to anyone for saying we cannot design an inmate cage no matter how decent or how plush.

You mentioned NCCD's struggles during the Nixon administration. How did you get along with Carter?

Well, President Carter used to be on our state citizens council in Georgia. That was where I first met him as a farmer and a businessman. . . . He called me personally during his campaign—I couldn't believe that he was running for president—and wanted some help. . . . I prepared some briefing papers, on decriminalizing victimless crime, reducing lengths of sentences, a stronger federal role in helping states and cities, and phasing out the federal Bureau of Prisons.

Did he use any of your ideas?

No, I can't say we got any real support from the Carter administration except in juvenile justice.

How do you feel about Reagan?

I worked with President Reagan when he was governor. His director of corrections [Raymond] Procunier, and Allen Breed, who headed the youth authority, asked if we could help persuade

Gov. Reagan to not issue his executive order due the following week to eliminate furloughs from the California prison system. Ed Davis, who as L.A. police chief and president of the California Peace Officers Association, was using a murder and an attempted murder by men on furlough to pressure the governor. I got three of our board members who were very conservative Republicans to go with me to talk to Gov. Reagan. After a two-hour meeting, he tore up the executive order. He'd had no idea that people of this substance saw furloughs as essential to a good correctional system. So I'm hoping that NCCD won't have trouble getting our position heard, in getting a Republican administration that will work for criminal justice change.

I've heard you say that you are a conservative Republican.

Yes, I always have been. As a Republican and a fiscal conservative I feel that any administration of a city or a national government that spends more than it takes in is repulsive. I point out the economic issues, the expense of incarceration. It's phony to say that Republicans can't stand for a good justice system. It's not a conservative or a liberal issue; it's either rational or irrational.

People who have observed your spirit and optimism want to know how you have had the energy to keep going in a field that is often so disheartening.

A belief. This is why, I guess, in my current study and reminiscence, I find when I get backed into corners—as I was last Sunday on the death penalty—I can only answer, "It's because I believe that man is better, or will be better." I began to see that NCCD wasn't a job; it was a mission. There is too little identification with a sense of mission today among criminal justice leadership and too much following public opinion rather than leading it. I've had a strong sense that what is happening now is not right, but I'm going to change it. And one of the great things about being in the field a long time is perspective, and that gives you hope.

4

DOING VIOLENCE TO THE CRIME PROBLEM

A Response to the Attorney General's Task Force

DIANA R. GORDON

I. INTRODUCTION

Street crime has reemerged as a major public issue in America within the past year. 1980 was described by *Newsweek* as "the year that mainstream America rediscovered violent crime," and that discovery took many forms. Hundreds of thousands of Californians now have tear gas permits, and polls indicate that growing numbers of citizens now own guns for protection. Within a few weeks of each other in the spring of 1981, the three major national news magazines ran prominent stories on violent street crime, and in many cities local radio and TV stations now begin their daily news programs with the latest muggings and murders. Political figures are giving voice to public fears by running for office on law-and-order platforms.

Public concern, media attention, and the recent political debate over crime have all created a situation which calls for dispassionate and thorough analyses of the problem and the appropriate responses to it. Expectations that such an analysis was forthcoming were raised when, on April 10, 1981, Attorney General William French Smith created his Task Force on Violent Crime. Its members[1] were to develop, as the Attorney General put it, "a more effective federal role in combating crime."

The work of the Task Force took four months. Testimony was heard from nearly 80 witnesses in seven cities, many criminal justice experts submitted written testimony, and the Task Force staff conducted literature searches and interviews. Phase I recommendations, presented in June, dealt with measures which could be undertaken immediately and administratively. The Phase II report issued on August 17, proposed changes which would necessitate new legislation and new or reallocated funding.

The Task Force Final Report contains 64 recommendations covering a very broad range of criminal justice issues. Generally intended to raise the costs of crime as perceived by potential offenders, the proposals, if enacted, would provide mandatory prison terms and expanded prison capacity, institute procedural changes to increase convictions, and extend federal jurisdiction over some kinds of criminal investigations and prosecution.

This response to the Attorney General's Task Force Report is not comprehensive. The Report contains a number of recommendations on which the National Council on Crime and Delinquency does not presume to be expert. This paper addresses a group of proposals on which the organization has taken positions in the past and which are likely to damage the cause of effective and fair criminal justice. In general, these changes would not reduce violent crime and could be implemented only at great social and economic cost.

II. RESPONSE TO SELECTED RECOMMENDATIONS OF THE TASK FORCE REPORT

The Final Task Force Report contains some welcome endorsements of such measures as continued research on crime and its causes, more extensive training for local corrections and law enforcement personnel, exploration of gun control measures, and victim assistance. But the Report, as a whole, does not guide the new Administration toward constructive federal involvement in the control of violent crime. This response to the Attorney General's Task Force will be limited to commentary on selected recommendations: preventive detention (Recommendation 38); the exclusionary rule (Recommendation 40); the sentencing provisions of the Federal Criminal Code (Recommendation 41); federal funds for state and local prison construction (Recommendation 54); and the extension of federal jurisdiction over juveniles (Recommendations 58–61).

Preventive Detention

Section a of Recommendation 38 calls for amending the Bail Reform Act of 1966 to allow the denial of bail to those found "by clear and convincing evidence" to be dangerous to others. Section b would withhold bail from one who had committed a "serious crime" while previously released pending trial. These proposals may well be found unconstitutional. They will surely be impractical to implement and ineffective in reducing violent crime.

Denial of bail and the detention that results constitute punishment of one who has not yet been found guilty. To rule that such punishment is justified requires turning away from nearly a century of judicial interpretation of the due process clause of the Fourteenth Amendment.[2] Certain Supreme Court decisions on which current practice is based cite as well the Eighth Amendment prohibition of excessive bail to support the principle that detention is justified only to ensure appearance for a trial.[3]

Predictions of human behavior for the purpose of determining dangerousness have been demonstrated to be notoriously unreliable. Prediction of dangerousness is difficult partly because, as a matter of statistical frequency, violent or dangerous events are relatively rare. Even where a defendant has been known to engage in violent behavior in the past, the risk of overpredicting dangerousness is very great indeed.[4] Estimates of the number of defendants who must be detained in order to prevent the violent behavior of one person vary widely. Some scholars think the number is as low as four, but many think it is as high as ten.[5] One researcher expresses the conclusion of many when he says, " . . . available research has demonstrated that predicting a defendant's propensity to commit (dangerous) crimes while on pretrial release is at present nearly impossible."[6]

It is unclear from the Task Force recommendation what would constitute dangerousness justifying pretrial detention. While some might consider any propensity toward felonious behavior sufficient evidence, others would include only behavior that caused permanent physical harm to a victim. The inherent subjectivity of standards of dangerousness illustrates well the concern of Supreme Court Justice Robert H. Jackson when he said many years ago that preventive detention is "fraught with danger of excesses and injustice."[7]

The Report's provision for denying bail to one who has proved his or her untrustworthiness by committing a serious crime while previously on pretrial release is no more precise. Similar problems of defining what is a "serious" offense pertain. In addition, that provision would have very little effect on violent crime, simply because such a small proportion of defendants are arrested for violent crimes while on bail. The most recent major study of pretrial release in the United States found that, while about 16 percent of pretrial releases were rearrested before their trial dates, only 2 percent were people who had been initially charged with a violent crime and were picked up during their pretrial period for either a property or a violent crime.[8] Furthermore, fewer than half of all rearrests occurred during the first four weeks on release. The Task Force notes that the federal system brings defendants to trial promptly, and relatively few charged with federal offenses have demonstrated a propensity to engage in violence. These facts suggest that the serious crime prevented by detaining defendants would be minimal. If detaining those charged with a narrow range of violent crime does not significantly reduce the incidence of violent crime, disillusionment may open the door to application of the policy to those charged with only minor offenses. Preventive detention could quickly become a legal and fiscal nightmare. The problem of pretrial crime could be much more effectively addressed with further efforts to ensure speedy trial.

This proposal, along with several others, is far more relevant to the states than to the Federal government—since most violent crime is prosecuted at the state level—and seems to have been promoted less for its impact on the Federal system than for the message it might send to the states. But preventive detention could potentially have a greater negative effect locally, as the Task Force acknowledges. The pretrial detention period is often much longer at the state level, and is likely to cause a defendant to lose his job and force his family onto the welfare roles. Imprisoned defendants have less opportunity to work on their cases with their lawyers, and research suggests that defendants in custody are more likely to be found guilty and tend to receive longer sentences than those who have been released before trial, regardless of the seriousness of the charge.[9]

The Exclusionary Rule

Another important Task Force proposal would allow evidence acquired in violation of the Fourth Amendment prohibitions against unreasonable search and seizure to be admitted at trial if it "has been obtained by an officer acting in the reasonable, good faith belief that it was in conformity" with constitutional standards for search and seizure. The recommendation further provides that evidence obtained pursuant to a warrant should be *prima facie* evidence of good faith on the part of the officer obtaining it. The NCCD has not taken a formal

position explicitly in support of current interpretations of the exclusionary rule, but has generally supported the Supreme Court rulings on criminal procedure with regard to the protections of the Bill of Rights. The Task Force recommendation would eviscerate the exclusionary rule without significantly increasing the number of convictions for violent crime.

One of the justifications for the change proposed is that the original, legitimate purpose of the rule—to deter illegal police activity and promote respect for the Fourth Amendment—has been abused by the courts in allowing its application where there has been merely trivial investigative error. But the evidence does not support this allegation. The exclusionary rule is infrequently invoked and has been found by one Federal General Accounting Office study to have a "minimal" impact on federal prosecutions.[10] The study found that in only 1.3 percent of court cases was evidence excluded as the result of an illegal search. (It can be inferred that the exclusionary rule is seldom invoked because it keeps police searches within legal bounds. If enforcement of the Fourth Amendment protections were weakened, more evidence might be collected illegally.) The GAO study is confirmed by others, one of which concludes that the exclusionary rule has "little impact on the overall flow of criminal cases after arrest."[11] Where it is invoked, the circumstances generally indicate very substantial violations of the Fourth Amendment.[12]

Objections by law enforcement officers to the exclusionary rule are generally based not on the rule itself but on the limitations to the police power inherent in the Fourth Amendment. The Task Force appears to share these reservations. It would allow "unintended or trivial" violations of the Fourth Amendment in the interest of getting at the truth as proved by the evidence. But that approach begs the issue. Loosening the enforcement mechanism for illegal searches is not merely a means of strengthening legitimate cases against serious criminal offenders; it is an acknowledgement that we are willing to extend the police power at the cost of the right of the people guaranteed in the Fourth Amendment "to be secure in their persons, houses, papers, and effects. . . ." This erosion in federal law would become a model for the states, in which the majority of police agencies are small departments, which experience large turnover and whose members receive far less training than is given to federal officials. Proscribed conduct does not become less offensive because entered into a spirit of "good faith"; one's home or person is no less violated because the violator mistakenly thought he was acting under color of law.

It has been suggested by some that a better means of enforcing the Fourth Amendment protections than the application of the exclusionary rule is to punish police officers who conduct illegal searches. This practice is followed in England. But English training and discipline for police differs greatly from ours. Furthermore, the exclusionary rule protects a judge from implicitly becoming a party to violations of the law by allowing illegally seized evidence to taint the proceedings they oversee. To weaken or abandon it in favor of disciplining police would diminish the rule's protection of judicial integrity.

One of the difficulties inherent in making hard choices about how the Bill of Rights applied is that the application of its protections is most evident where the conduct of someone under suspicion is concerned. Because debate over the desirable extent of Constitutional standards generally arises only when the government is eager to get a conviction, we tend to think these standards are beneficial only to criminals. Their fundamental significance lies in the protection they provide all of us, most of which is never noted because if falls into the intangible category of harm prevented. It is particularly important to reaffirm the significance of that larger benefit, however, when we feel threatened by crime. For it is then that our passions prompt us to regard scrupulous adherence to the Bill of Rights as the observation of mere "technicalities."

Federal Criminal Code

The Task Force Report proposes the enactment of the sentencing provisions of the proposed Criminal Code Reform Act of 1981 (S. 1630). These provisions would abolish the United States Parole Commission and establish a Sentencing Commission to develop guidelines for sentences for all federal offenses.

The Task Force commentary states correctly that there is widespread agreement on the need for reform of the federal criminal laws. It also properly endorses the idea that structuring the discretion of those who impose criminal dispositions (whether judges or Parole Commission members) can add certainty and reduce disparity

in the sentencing process. But, like its predecessor bills S. 1, S. 1743, and S. 1722, S. 1630 is fundamentally flawed in not addressing the excessive use of imprisonment for less serious offenses and not providing for a range of non-incarcerative sanctions. This was one of the sources of opposition that prevented all three bills from being enacted.

The American Bar Association was one of many organizations that criticized the sentencing provisions of the proposed federal Criminal Code. The NCCD and others concurred with the ABA recommendations delineating seven sentencing alternatives which judges should be required to consider in every case in which a sentence is imposed: Fine, restitution, suspended sentence, discharge, reparation, community service order, and probation.[13] Finally, if incarceration were the sentence of choice, first consideration should be intermittent incarceration, then non-secure incarceration, and finally imprisonment. To include a broader and more progressive perspective on sentencing alternatives, especially restitution sentences requiring offenders to repair the harm done to victims or community, would be consistent with the Task Force's expressed concern for victims of crime.

The Task Force commentary labels the proposed code "a truth in sentencing" package because the imposition of determinate sentences with "modest good time credits" would make it possible to inform both the public and the offender of the real sentence to be served. In terms of the Task Force's focus on violent offenders, this designation of the proposal as "truth in sentencing" is ironic. A major consequence of the provisions—a large number of nonviolent offenders being swept into the federal prisons for longer terms than under present law—is unstated.

With the exception of Russia and South Africa, where there are many political prisoners, the United States imprisons a larger proportion of its people than does any other industrialized country. On a per capita basis, this country locks up more than twice as many people as does Canada, three times as many as great Britain, and four times as many as West Germany.[14] A federal sentencing policy which overlooks the use of alternatives to imprisonment can only worsen this situation. Increasing the imprisonment rate is particularly inappropriate at the federal level, where only 11 percent of prisoners during the 1970s were convicted of crimes classified as violent.

The Task Force Report speaks to a cost-conscious administration and public. During the 1970s, expenditures for government programs at all government levels, excluding defense, rose 37 percentage points more than disposable income.[15] The Reagan Administration is trying to address this problem by cutting government spending in many areas. Taxpayers should not be asked to support greater government expenditure for correctional policies which will not reduce violent crime. The report of the U.S. Senate Appropriations Committee on federal sentencing policy and practice put the issue of alternatives to prison in this context when it said:

> Because cost makes imprisonment a scarce resource, it is essential that imprisonment only be used where necessary to assure the protection of society or the administration of just punishment. In those cases in which imprisonment is not necessary, the range of alternatives currently available in S. 1722 is clearly unsatisfactory.[16]

Funds for Prison Construction

There are several proposals in the Task Force Report that would provide extra resources for corrections. Recommendations 3 and 56 would allow the use of surplus federal property, including abandoned Army bases, for local incarceration; Recommendation 41 would add to the federal inmate population by supporting sentencing provisions of S. 1630; and Recommendation 36 would allow federal assistance for "enhanced jail capacity to handle the increased burdens of recent years, including overcrowding." But the principal recommendation in this area calls for $2 billion to be made available to states for the construction of prisons and jails. Governor Thompson calls this proposal the "linchpin" for all the other recommendations and, at the August 17 press conference releasing the Report, underscored its importance by saying that the "bottom line" of the Task Force's findings is that "we have to lock up more violent offenders and we have to keep them locked up." This proposal will not do that. Furthermore, even if it could do so, violent crime would not be significantly reduced. Finally, the cost of this proposal far exceeds $2 billion and renders it an impermissible drain on the taxpayer.

The $2 billion proposed (which would actually be $2.7 billion worth of cells, assuming the 25 percent local matching contribution called for

in the recommendation) would pay for only 38,000 one-person maximum security cells, at an average cost of $70,000 per cell, which the Report itself cites and many experts now use in calculating building costs. These 38,000 cells would house less than 12 percent of the present state and federal inmate population of 329,122 and less than two-thirds of the 60,000 increase in that population in this country over the past three years. The added cells would leave 68,000 places still needed to close the gap between the 1978 rated capacity (at a standard of 60 square feet of floor space per inmate) of our state and federal prisons and the number of prisoners.[17] In short, that number of cells might reduce the current overcrowding somewhat, but it would not accommodate new offenders brought into the system. Furthermore, overcrowding would continue to be a serious problem during the time required to build prisons, usually four years.

The provision of new cells might not even relieve overcrowding, under any one of several situations.

The Task Force commentary notes that more than half the states have one or more prisons where conditions have been held unconstitutional, and for this reason "replacement or renovation" of existing cells is deemed an appropriate use for the federal dollars which would be spent. As the Task Force itself states, "The provision of assistance in building or renovating correctional facilities need not necessarily mean that the total capacity of institutions be increased. . . ." Surely, many states will regard the new federal money as a chance to get out from under court orders by upgrading what they have, rather than using it to increase cell capacity.

The cells built might not reduce overcrowding if the current trend in criminal justice policies continues. Many people—including those who drafted the Task Force commentary—mistakenly believe that it is the rising crime rate which increases incarceration. In fact, there appears to be no relationship between crime rates and incarceration rates. A 1976 study by the American Foundation's Institute of Corrections found that while some states with high reported crime rates had high incarceration rates, others had low rates of incarceration; the group of states with low reported crime rates also contained some with high and others with low incarceration rates.[18] In many states the incarceration rate in the 1970s went up far faster than the reported crime rates.

Between 1972 and 1979, the reported violent crime rate in New York State went up 23 percent and the incarceration rate 87 percent; in Ohio the reported violent crime rate went up 53 percent and the incarceration rate 62 percent; in Illinois, the reported violent crime rate actually decreased by 5 percent, but the incarceration rate rose by 97 percent.[19]

Various policies are pushing the incarceration rate up. In California, where mandatory sentences for serious crime has gone into effect, time served has increased and the imprisonment rate is rising.[20] Between 1975 and 1980, states which had moved toward determinacy experienced substantial increases in state prison populations: Florida had a population rise of 68 percent; Illinois a rise of 73 percent; and Arizona a rise of 59 percent.[21] Even the states which continue to use indeterminate sentencing, with the judge setting a minimum and maximum penalty, and the parole board exercising its discretion with respect to the point at which the offender will be actually released, judges have been more willing to give prison terms. If this trend continues, prison populations will continue to rise without encouragement of the federal government and without any systematic effort to see that these increases represent a higher detection and conviction rate for violent offenders. Overcrowding is likely to be just as serious after construction of the 38,000 cells made possible by the Task Force recommendations.

A serious effort to provide more space for handling violent offenders should include in the strategy support for alternatives to incarceration for *non*-violent offenders. The implementation of a rational process for sentencing lesser offenders to restitution and probation, for example, can be an important tool for managing convicted populations so that proper priority is given to violent offenders. The severe overcrowding that characterizes many state systems will prevent them from concentrating attention on predatory criminals as long as the only policy solution taken seriously is the impossibly costly one of increasing bed space. Far more feasible is the development of classification procedures which separate property offenders from personal offenders and find less restrictive solutions than confinement for the former. Experiments with alternative sanctions for lesser offenses have shown that recidivism is no greater following the imposition of such sanctions than it

would be if offenders were sent to prison. Public expense is reduced, but not at the cost of public protection.[22]

Even if the federal subsidy proposed by the Task Force were spent on new cells to increase state prison capacity and all the cells were filled with violent offenders, the proposal would barely touch the violent crime problem. Victimization studies conceived and supported by the Federal Bureau of Justice Statistics and conducted by Census Bureau survey teams have found that only about 30 percent of serious crimes are reported to the police; of reported crimes, only about 20 percent lead to an arrest.[23] Only six percent of court cases involving serious crimes, therefore, even enter the criminal justice system. Many other cases dropped for lack of evidence or dismissed for other reasons would not be affected by increasingly tough stances taken by prosecutors and judges.

The recent experience of California and New York suggest the lack of causality between increased imprisonment and reduction in reported crime. In California, the average daily prison population is up 7,000 since 1978. Because of tougher sentencing policies, those convicted of felonies stand an 83 percent chance of going to jail or prison.[24] Yet reported crime has risen very significantly there. Similarly, New York has, for several years, been implementing "get-tough" policies enacted by the legislature—longer and mandatory terms for drug offenders, repeat felons, and violent youth. The proportion of felony defendants sentenced to at least a year more than doubled in the 1970s; the state's new career criminal program has been meting out longer sentence to serious repeat offenders; and the state's prison population has almost doubled.[25] Yet the New York Police Department reports a 1980 increase in robberies of 21.7 percent.[26]

The belief of the Task Force that more incarceration will reduce violent crime seems to be based on two of the classic rationales for punishment—deterrence and incapacitation. For the violent street crimes that the Task Force is most eager to control, neither of these rationales is likely to be valid.

The deterrence rationale is often supported with a kind of economic calculation. As James Q. Wilson, a Harvard professor and member of the Task Force, puts it, "If the expected cost of crime goes up without a corresponding increase in the expected benefits, then the would-be criminal . . . engages in less crime. . . ."[27] To a certain extent, we would agree with this formulation. But the likelihood of a prison sentence—and of apprehension—is only one element in the potential criminal's calculation of the risk of the act he is contemplating. While it is impossible to tell how each person will weigh the costs and benefits of crime, we can assume a wide variety of calculations. Each individual, for example, will place a different value on the time he might have to spend behind bars, according to how he perceives his opportunities and pastimes in non-prison society.

Perhaps the threat of incarceration is particularly meaningless for the street criminal the Task Force is most eager to deter. Low income repeat offenders often describe the city streets from which they come as a kind of prison. This attitude is not likely to be measurable by economists as they assess the decision making of potential offenders.

The Task Force has declared its intention to keep violent inmates locked up, but some of the policies the Task Force supports would probably prove counterproductive. As Professor Wilson points out, "The more severe the penalty, the more unlikely that it will be imposed."[28] The truth of this observation is apparent in looking at the strict drug law that went into effect in New York in 1973. While incarceration became more likely for those convicted (up from 33 percent to 55 percent), there was a corresponding decline in the percentage of felony drug cases that resulted in indictment (down from 39 percent to 25 percent) and conviction (down from 86 percent to 80 percent); researchers attribute that decline to the unwillingness of prosecutors and judges to give free rein to such a harsh law.[29]

Incapacitation—that is, the imprisonment rationale that holds that at least the community is protected from crime while the criminals are locked up—is theoretically valid only if those imprisoned would, in fact, have continued to commit crimes if left at large. The problem here is like the problem with preventive detention: behavior cannot be predicted. If we assume that some convicted offenders will commit further crimes in the community, but we do not know which ones will do so, incapacitating the future criminals will require locking *all* the others up, too. While we cannot say what level of imprisonment would be necessary nationally to accomplish that amount of incapacitation, estimates exist for some states. One study has estimated

that a 57 percent increase in New York State imprisonment would be required to reduce violent street crimes by only 10 percent.[30] Another study holds that sending all Ohio felony offenders to prison for five years would reduce violent crime in that state by only four percent.[31]

The costs of significantly reducing violent crime through incapacitation would exceed the expenditure for prisons recommended by the Task Force by many billions of dollars. The social costs would also be enormous. America would become a garrison state, with huge numbers of *nonviolent* people imprisoned along with the violent. Vastly increased police surveillance over the innocent as well as the guilty would be needed to arrest a significantly higher proportion of offenders.

The real costs of the prison construction assistance the federal government would provide are difficult to assess, but the states' financial burden would surely be massive. $667 million in matching funds would have to be raised by localities already facing extreme fiscal pressures. The debt service they would have to pay would inflate local operating budgets for many years to come. Taxpayers might end up paying several billion dollars for the local contribution alone, depending on the maturity date and the interest rates on the bonds that would be floated. To qualify for the assistance, states would have to show that they could afford the maintenance costs for the cells to be constructed. That cost could run close to $1 billion a year if the cells cost $25,000 a year to maintain and were all additions to present capacity. The Task Force commentary itself points out that "some states have found (prison construction) so costly that they cannot complete their efforts or have vacant facilities because they cannot afford staffing and operation." And yet the Task Force is prepared to ask the states to incur staggering additional costs.

The prison assistance program will generate other federal costs of exactly the kind the Task Force says it wishes to avoid. While the commentary says the money is to be provided with as few strings attached as possible, the recommendation does include conditions with which applying states must conform and some indication of a process to be followed in obtaining funds. This suggests a compounding of the federal bureaucracy, a phenomenon much inveighed against in other areas. During the time when inflation has doubled consumer prices, annual expenditures—federal, state, and local—for police, courts, and corrections have increased by 600 percent, from under $5 billion in 1967 to nearly $30 billion in 1980.[32] In many states, criminal justice is the fastest growing item in the budget. The Task Force recommendation for prison expenditures, if enacted, would necessarily make criminal justice even more of a growth industry.

There are many dangers in implementing a prison construction policy which will be both costly and ineffective. For one thing, public confidence will be dealt another blow, and disillusionment and anger are likely to be keen. The Task Force hoped to strengthen the public's view of the efficacy of the criminal justice system; this proposal will work against, not for, that aim. In addition, reliance on this ephemeral "solution" distracts both the public and the decision-makers from understanding and dealing with other serious issues related to the violent crime problem: for urban black youth an unemployment rate of 50 percent, neighborhood and family disintegration, the shrinking economic base of many American cities.

Criminal justice professionals often understand the futility of such proposals as the Task Force prison-building recommendation better than anyone else. While corrections officials understandably welcome the opportunity to ease their population management problems, they do not expect that new cells will mean significantly less crime. The New York State Parole Board Chairman, Edward R. Hammock, for example, has grave doubts that changes in sentencing have an impact on crime; Amos Reed, President of the American Correctional Association and head of corrections for the state of Washington, recently told an audience of officials at the annual ACA Congress that prison construction would have "little effect on the rate of crime."[33]

Youth Proposals

Recommendations with regard to youth crime are aimed at establishing the means for the federal government to reduce both individual and gang violence. Recommendation 58 provides for greater federal access to information on juveniles; Recommendation 59 would create original jurisdiction for the federal offenses; Recommendation 60 would use organized crime resources to investigate and prosecute gang activities; and Recommendation 61 would lump funding for programs for juveniles in with other criminal justice program initiatives at the federal level. These recommendations would extend federal authority over juveniles without including adequate protection for young people or for the local programs addressed to their problems. Furthermore, the proposal would be expensive and would do very little to reduce youth violence.

The commentary for Recommendation 61 dealing with funding mechanisms for juvenile justice programs says, "We believe the federal government can play an important and cost-beneficial role as a program catalyst to state and local jurisdictions in their attempts to alleviate (violent juvenile crime)." This endorsement of the usual view that juvenile justice matters are best dealt with as close to home as possible is contradicted by the thrust of all the recommendations with regard to young offenders. The Task Force is prepared to bring in the U.S. Attorney to prosecute any violation of federal law by a minor. It would disregard state information-sharing policies with regard to juveniles so that the FBI could have fingerprints and criminal histories of an undefined class of youthful offenders. It would conflict with gang programs—prosecution and crime prevention efforts—under way now in many cities. In short, the Justice Department would take on the role of juvenile officer and prosecutor.

In no area of social policy is it more firmly established than in work with problem youngsters that local efforts are the key to a solution. Erosions of family and neighborhood bonds are widely blamed for much youth violence, and most programs—law enforcement and social welfare programs alike—stress the importance of local solutions which relate the juvenile offender to the institutions of his community. Currently, the Federal Office of Juvenile Justice and Delinquency Prevention (OJJDP) is mounting a program initiative for dealing with violent juvenile offenders. While federal funds and national evaluations are provided, and technical assistance is available, local agencies will run the programs. It is assumed that they will have a better sense than do federal officials for the programs. The federal role ought not to extend beyond the provision of training and technical assistance, research and program development, and funding for special needs.

Recommendation 61 would, however, reduce the role that *does* seem appropriate for the federal government. In many respects, adolescence is a crucial period for the growth of social attitudes. OJJDP has provided the tools for local and state governments to use in giving special attention to social development. To abolish that agency and disperse youth programs, as is suggested by the Task Force, is tantamount to abandoning a coordinated effort to give special attention to youth problems.

Much attention has been given in recent years to the effects of overinstitutionalizing young people who violate the law. It has repeatedly been found that, even in the best of reformatories, the environment stimulates, rather than corrects, antisocial behavior.[34] Two midwestern studies have found that juvenile crime appears to accelerate among young offenders who have been repeatedly incarcerated.[35] The recommendations provided in the Task Force Report would increase the incarceration of young people, with the consequence of alienating them still further from the world to which they will eventually return. Prosecuting youth more harshly may thus prove counterproductive, stimulating violence rather than reducing it.

The reduction of juvenile violence as the result of Task Force recommendations seems very unlikely for other reasons. Transferring the juvenile mail tamperer to a federal prosecutor, for example, will not have a bearing on violent juvenile crime. Similarly, the substitution of federal for local police and prosecution efforts with regard to gangs has very little to recommend it by the standards of efficient law enforcement. Federal investigations of gang warfare would lack the advantages of neighborhood intelligence that characterizes local police work. It also seems unlikely that original jurisdiction over all federal crime will bring in many violent young people for non-gang related offenses. Young offenders do not usually commit the offenses, violent or otherwise, that fall under federal jurisdiction.

III. THE PERSPECTIVES
OF THE TASK FORCE

This paper contends that many of the major Task Force recommendations will not be effective at reducing violent crime. In addition, the Task Force approach seems likely to perpetuate misconceptions about the problem of violent crime and the ability of the criminal justice system, acting alone, to stem it. This section considers the general perspectives and scope of the Task Force and its report.

The Final Report accepts without question certain attitudes prevalent among politicians and the media. In particular, it takes as given that the country is experiencing an unprecedented crime wave and that the best way to address that problem is to strengthen the apparatus of criminal justice—through enacting tougher laws, increasing the police power, and building new prisons to permit incarceration of more offenders for longer periods of time. There is a wide body of literature which casts serious doubt on these basic perspectives. Why, then, did the Task Force adopt its approach so uncritically?

Within the last several years, the public and the media have become more vocal about street crime and grown increasingly skeptical of the ability of the criminal justice system to control it. The Task Force also undoubtedly felt the press of recent events—the attempted assassination of the President; the murders of Atlanta children; and a series of brutal killings in California. Task Force members appear to have sought some means of reassuring the public—addressing the crisis of public confidence rather than the crisis of crime in the streets.

But such reassurances can backfire. Groups like the Task Force have tremendous impact, not only on federal policy, but also on the directions state systems will take in the future. It is imperative, therefore, that their recommendations reflect their knowledge, as expressed in the Preface to the Report, that there are no easy answers, that the criminal justice system alone cannot provide all the remedies, and that there may be realistic (although perhaps unpopular) alternatives to the "get-tough" polices that must be seriously considered. It is important that commissions and task forces examine closely some of the myths and realities concerning violent crime.

Take the question of whether the country now has what Chief Justice Warren Burger has called "a vast increase in crime." While everyone should recognize that violent crime is an extremely serious matter in America, there is major confusion about its dimensions and trends.

The federal government collects two very different kinds of data on crime; the Uniform Crime Reports compiled by the FBI and based on local police department reports, and the National Crime Surveys prepared by the Bureau of Justice Statistics and based on interviews of households around the country to determine the extent to which they have been victimized. The former data base shows substantial increases during the 1970s for serious violent crimes (murder, rape, robbery, and aggravated assault), while the victimization surveys indicate that personal crime rates have remained relatively stable since 1973 when the studies were begun. Although there are methodological problems with both sets of data, criminologists warn that the UCR data are particularly susceptible to manipulation. Because UCR data are based on *reported* crime only, and reporting technology has greatly improved in recent years, some of what is perceived as a crime wave may in fact be a crime *reporting* wave. Policy prescriptions should be based on an assessment of *all* the data, not only on the most dramatic statistics.

Another problem with the Task Force approach rests in its failure to consider the sources of criminal violence. It wrote to the Attorney General two months after it began its work, "We have not addressed the many social and economic factors that . . . may tend to increase or decrease crime rates." Such a choice reduces the Task Force mandate to the promotion of mere containment measures. For, as Tom Wicker put it in *The New York Times* on August 21,

> If every person who has already committed a violet crime could be identified and convicted today, sent to prison tomorrow, and kept there for life, and *nothing else was done,* a new group of violence-prone persons soon would rise from the same economic, social, legal, psychological and class conditions that produced their predecessors.

While the focus of the Task Force was too narrow in some respects, it was too broad in others. Its definition of violet crime explicitly included residential burglaries, which, while they can be accompanied by violence and are often terrifying to their victims, are not, without aggravating circumstances, generally considered violent offenses. Many of the targets of some recommended changes in the justice system—particularly young people who would be newly subjected to federal prosecution and to law enforcement surveillance in school—would not be people who commit the violent crimes we all fear.

The Task Force stressed that "the control of crime and the administration of justice are primarily the concern of state and local governments, and of private citizens." But implementation of many of the specific recommendations would extend federal jurisdiction over many areas of law enforcement traditionally reserved to states and localities. State standards for the sharing of criminal history information for example, would be threatened by the proposed Interstate Identification Index; local policies with regard to the prosecution and treatment of juveniles would be overridden; even local boards of education would come under pressure from the Attorney General's proposed public education campaign against drugs and violence in the schools. This is a puzzling direction from responsible conservatives who vigorously defend state interest in other areas. The Final Report conveys no message as to why increased federal activity is appropriate in criminal justice and not in other areas of domestic policy.

The Task Force also gave inadequate attention to the expenditures—at all government levels—necessary to carry out its recommendations. The only major item in the Report which has a clear price tag attached is the prison construction plan, but many others would be very expensive indeed. Professor Kenneth Laudon of John Jay College of Criminal Justice in New York City estimates that the criminal history system proposals, for example, would cost the federal government $350 million. Other proposals would add to the work load of federal units such as the FBI, the Drug Enforcement Agency, the Navy and Defense Department, the U.S. Attorney's Offices, and the Immigration and Naturalization Service. No assessment of that factor is made, although there are acknowledgments that provisions must be made at some indefinite time in the future. Many of the agencies whose costs would increase are those cut back in the 1982 budget.

There are a number of reasons for the limitations of the Report. The Task Force was given a deadline of only four months, which must have made it difficult for members and staff to review relevant studies and take into consideration all the factors that bear on such complex problems. The Task Force also sought the opinions of a narrow range of professionals; the membership of the Task Force was heavily weighted toward law enforcement and prosecution, and it is perhaps not surprising that the group, faced with limited time for hearings, sought testimony primarily from those with the same perspectives.

Few corrections officials or judges testified. Few invitations to appear went to those who defend the accused, to those who run programs that divert defendants from criminal justice processing, or to those who advocate the use of criminal justice as the system of last resort. Few scholars were asked to present their views.

The perspective and scope of such a report are as important as the recommendations that define its outcome. The Final Report is likely to influence not only the Attorney General and the President but also the media, local policymakers, and the public. Its perspective will suggest policy directions for the country as a whole. All concerned groups should therefore respond to the Task Force Final Report, launching a dialogue which the Task Force has itself welcomed. This dialogue should pay particular attention to the underlying perspectives of the Task Force and popular misconceptions about violent crime.

The Attorney General and the President will be well served if the work of the Task Force can lead to greater involvement in policy formation by a wide range of criminal justice professionals and citizen groups experienced in research and analysis of justice issues. No one has all the answers to the problem of violent street crime. Expectations of perfect solutions would be unreasonable. But groups like the National Forum on Criminal Justice—representing 29 organizations of criminal justice practitioners, advocates, and researchers—can contribute a varied and careful assessment of the crime problem to help the Reagan Administration address violet crime effectively while preserving cherished American values. Federal officials should go beyond the Task Force Report to expand the public debate and determine the shape of final policy.

IV. CONCLUSION

In the preface to its Report, the Task Force says that the violet crime in American society "reflects a breakdown of the social order, not the legal order." That statement is surely correct. Yet the recommendations made by the Task Force are not aimed at restoring social order; instead, the enforcement measures advocated may, at best, plug up a few leaks in the legal order. Many of the proposals, indeed, are likely to disrupt social harmony further by curtailing fundamental liberties of the innocent or by using resources badly needed for social benefits to expand official social controls.

It has been popular for many years to use military metaphor when talking about reducing crime. President Johnson talked about the "war on crime." Chief Justice Warren Burger's speech to the American Bar Association in February spoke of crime control as "national defense," and likened its importance to the Pentagon budget. The Task Force, too, analogizes the effort that must be made to investment in war. Its commentary on the recommendation of a new LEAA-type program states: "(Some) people believe that American citizens who see billions of dollars sent to fighting enemies in other lands have every right to see substantial federal sums for fighting crime—an internal enemy."

If the general perspective of the Task Force prevails, crime will be the only domestic policy area deemed important enough for new federal aid—essentially a war effort. Like some international war efforts, the Task Force program gives little evidence of concern for the preservation of peace.

It did not have to be this way. The Task Force could have analogized its role to the peaceful side of international relations. It could have supplied aid as well as defensive weapons. It would have provided technical assistance in addition to building up the militia.

Specifically, the Task Force could have invested in reducing prison overcrowding in more effective and less expensive ways than a $2 billion grant-in-aid program. It could have provided management experts to show how, through classification procedures and other techniques, states and cities could put nonviolent offenders into alternative programs and give the violent ones adequate space and supervision.

Still more important, the Task Force could have acknowledged the importance of all the other forces besides criminal justice that can be enlisted in community crime prevention. It might have recommended the kind of community development that would provide young people with alternatives to crime. It could have provided the opportunity for volunteer community organizations around the country to make crime prevention an integral part of their agendas.

This kind of program may not appeal to political leaders concerned that the federal government has already involved itself too much in the education, employment and welfare problems of the states. But the Task Force did not apply such principles of federalism when it recommended aid for prisons or expanded federal jurisdiction over juveniles. And the effort need not involve a massive federal bureaucracy or overregulation of local efforts. The federal government can and should play an enabling role, leaving local groups largely free to determine their constituencies' most pressing needs.

Many of those who must preside over the most extreme form of control—the prison officials—know best the dangers of concentrating the "war on crime" on the capture and conviction of the enemy. They know that they cannot—and should not be expected to—deal effectively with the problems that brought their charges to them. Many complain bitterly that corrections are blamed for the failures of the schools, the parents, and the courts. Some go a step further and say, with Amos Reed, "We believe the greatest priority for attacking crime should be directed toward children and families and schools."

To fight the war on the narrow battlefield defined by the Attorney General's Task Force is to risk tragic failure. The war on crime, as the Task Force conceives it, is likely to become an expensive offensive waged against combatants whose identity is obscure and whose techniques are not well understood. Perhaps the greatest danger lies in the divisiveness that may result from escalating the offensive. If, as a society, we make increasing use of the criminal justice system to address what the task Force calls the "breakdown of the social order," we run the risk of separating groups of Americans—rich and poor, urban and rural, black and white—from one another. Restoring the social order—and thereby addressing meaningfully, the problem of violent crime—will require unity and participation. These are not values promoted by the narrow range of legal system changes recommended by the Task Force.

NOTES

1. The Preface for the Final Report lists the names, titles, and experience of the Task Force members as follows: It was co-chaired by former Attorney General Griffin B. Bell and Governor James R. Thompson of Illinois. Griffin B. Bell was a judge of the U.S. Court of Appeals for the Fifth Circuit from

October, 1961, to March, 1976, and was Attorney General from January, 1977, to August, 1979. Governor Thompson was U.S. Attorney in Chicago from November, 1971, until June, 1975. The Task Force also includes: James Q. Wilson, professor of government at Harvard University and author of numerous books and articles on criminal justice; David L. Armstrong, Commonwealth Attorney of Louisville and President of the National District Attorneys Association; Frank G. Carrington, Executive Director of the Crime Victims Legal Advocacy Institute, Virginia Beach, Virginia; Robert L. Edwards, Director of the Division of Local Law Enforcement Assistance of the Florida Department of Law Enforcement; William L. Hart, Police Chief of Detroit; and Wilbur F. Littlefield, the Public Defender for Los Angeles County.

2. See, for example, *Wong Wing* v. *United States,* 163 U.S. 228 (1896), and, more recently, *Ingraham* v. *Wright,* 430 U.S. 651 (1977).

3. See *Stack* v. *Boyle,* 342 U.S. 1 (1951).

4. Teri I. Martin, "The Prediction of Dangerousness in Mental Health and Criminal Justice," *Pretrial Services Annual Journal* (Washington, D.C.: Pretrial Services Resource Center, 1981), pp. 9–14.

5. For a range of conclusions and discussions of prediction problems, see Andrew von Hirsch, *Doing Justice: The Choice of Punishments* (New York: Hill and Wang, 1976), Ch. 3; John Monahan, "The Prediction and Control of Violent Behavior." Testimony before the U.S. House of Representatives Subcommittee on Domestic and International Scientific Planning, Analysis and Cooperation, Committee on Science and Technology, January 10, 1978; and John S. Goldkamp, *Two Classes of Accused: A Study of Bail and Detention in American Justice* (Cambridge, Mass.: Ballinger, 1979).

6. Goldkamp, *supra,* p. 100.

7. *Williamson* v. *United States,* 184 F.2d 280, 282–283 (1950).

8. See *Pretrial Release: An Evaluation of Defendant Outcomes and Program Impact: Summary and Analysis Volume,* unpublished draft (Washington, D.C.: Lazar Institute, 1981).

9. See, for example, William M. Landes, "Legality and Reality: Some Evidence on Criminal Procedure," *Journal of Legal Studies,* Vol. 3, 1974, p. 287; and Hans Zeisel, "Bail Revisited," *American Bar Foundation Research Journal,* Vol. 4, 1979, p. 769.

10. U.S. General Accounting Office, "Impact of Exclusionary Rule on Federal Criminal Prosecution," GDD 79–45, April 19, 1979.

11. Institute for Law and Research, 1979, "A Cross-City Comparison of Felony Case Processing." See also Institute for Law and Research, 1979, "What Happens After Arrest."

12. Personal interview with Ira Glasser, Director, American Civil Liberties Union, August 31, 1981.

13. Testimony of William Greenhalgh, Chairperson of the ABA Criminal Justice Section

Legislative Committee, before the Senate Judiciary Committee, September 28, 1981.

14. Eugene Doleschal and Ann Newton, "International Rates of Imprisonment," unpublished document, National Council on Crime and Delinquency, 1979.

15. Computations based on *Economic Report of the President, 1980* (Washington, D.C.: Government Printing Office, 1980), Tables B-72, B-69, and B-22.

16. Senate Appropriations Committee Report 94–964, at pp. 21–22.

17. Bureau of Justice Statistics, "Prisoners in 1980" (Washington, D.C.: U.S. Government Printing Office, 1981); Joan Mullen et al., *American Prisons and Jails,* Vol. 1, "Summary Findings and Policy Implications of a National Survey" (Washington, D.C.: U.S. Government Printing Office, 1980), p. 65.

18. William G. Nagel "On Behalf of a Moratorium on Prison Construction," *Crime and Delinquency,* April 1977.

19. Computations based on FBI *Uniform Crime Reports* and LEAA, *Prisoners in State and Federal Institutions,* both for the years 1972–1979.

20. Albert J. Lipson and Mark A. Peterson, "California Justice under Determinate Sentencing: A Review and Agenda for Research" (Santa Monica, California, RAND Corporation: June, 1980).

21. Computations based on LEAA, *Prisoners in State and Federal Institutions.*

22. Bartell, Ted; Winfree, L. Thomas. "Recidivist Impacts of Differential Sentencing Practices for Burglary Offenders." *Criminology* (Beverly Hills, Calif.), 15(3):387–396, 1977. Andrew Peter Hopkins, *Return to crime: a quasi-experimental study of the effects of imprisonment and its alternatives.* Ann Arbor, Mich: University Microfilms, 1974. 150 p. (Dissertation.)

23. Bureau of Justice Statistics, *Criminal Victimization in the United States, 1978* (Washington, D.C.: U.S. Government Printing Office, 1980).

24. Barry Krisberg, "The Task Force on Violent Crime: Implications for California," *Los Angeles Times,* August 31, 1981.

25. Diana R. Gordon, "Toward Realistic Reform: A Commentary on Proposals for Change in New York City's Criminal Justice System" (Hackensack, N.J.: National Council on Crime and Delinquency, 1981), pp. 3–5.

26. *Uniform Crime Report,* 1980 Preliminary Annual Release, Table 5.

27. James Q. Wilson, *Thinking About Crime* (New York: Vintage Books, 1977), p. 197.

28. *Ibid.,* p. 201

29. Joint Committee on the New York Drug Law Evaluation, *The Nation's Toughest Drug Law: Evaluating the New York Experience* (New York: Association of the Bar of the City of New York and Drug Abuse Council, 1977).

30. Jacqueline Cohen, "The Incapacitative Effort of Imprisonment: A Critical Review of the Literature," in Blumstein et al., eds., *Deterrence and Incapacitation: Estimating the Effects of Criminal Sanctions on Crime Rates* (Washington, D.C.: National Academy of Sciences, 1978), p. 226.

31. Van Dine, Dinitz, & Conrad, "The Incapacitation of the Dangerous Offender: A Statistical Experiment." *Journal of Research in Crime and Delinquency* (January, 1977).

32. Speech by Milton Rector, President of National Council on Crime and Delinquency (to New School Associates), March, 1981.

33. Mr. Hancock told a N.Y. State Senate committee on criminal justice that "the sentencing system has no impact on crime at all," according to *The New York Times,* October 25, 1980. Mr. Reed's comment was quoted by *The New York Times* editor Tom Wicker in his column of August 21, 1981.

34. Bartollas, Miller, & Dinitz, *Juvenile Victimization: The Institutional Paradox* (New York: Sage Publications, 1976).

35. Statement of Charles A. Lauer, Acting Administrator, Office of Juvenile Justice and Delinquency Prevention, before the Senate Subcommittee on Juvenile Justice of the Judiciary Committee, July 1981.

5

HATE THE PLAYER AND HATE THE GAME[1]

The Politics of the War Against the Young

BARRY KRISBERG

THE GAME

Without question, our young people have paid a heavy price in the so-called War Against Crime. The most vulnerable political targets of the demagogues on crime policy were adolescents (Krisberg, 2005). The next most vulnerable political targets were women who were incarcerated in unprecedented numbers due to mandatory drug laws. The young children of these incarcerated moms were the civilian collateral damage of the Drug War, receiving less than benign attention by state criminal justice and welfare officials (Krisberg & Temin, 2000). To the extent that obscene levels of spending on the War on Crime have led to reduced funding for education, health care, after school programs, and job training, low income youngsters have paid an indirect and egregious tax to finance the attack on them by cynical politicians.

The War Against the Young has taken many forms. The most significant assaults on children in California were new legislative and voter initiatives (Proposition 21) that were designed to try children as young as 14 years old in criminal

courts. Other states created even lower age limits for youths to be tried as adults. For example, Michigan prosecuted children who were as young as 9 years old. Related to this trend of "cracking down" on juvenile crime, many localities adopted aggressive anti-gang campaigns, including automated police intelligence files that contained the names of tens of thousands of adolescents who were merely suspected of having some gang affiliation. Not even minimal standards of "probable cause" were required to place names in these files, and there were no clear methods through which a young person could remove his or her name from the gang intelligence systems. These law enforcement files were not covered by the usual confidentiality protections that normally apply to juvenile court proceedings. Further, vague evidence that a young person was "gang affiliated" could be used in criminal sentencing to greatly enhance penalties. A recently released documentary entitled *JUVIES* presents the tragic story of twelve young people aged 14–16 who were all sentenced to very long prison sentences. In several of the cases, the impact of gang enhancements produced enormous increases in the sentences. For example, the film profiles a 16-year-old Vietnamese boy with no prior arrests who is now serving a prison term of 35 years to life. He was driving a car when one of the passengers fired a gun. No one was hit by the bullet, and there were no injuries. Still, the young driver was convicted of attempted murder with gang enhancements that will keep him in prison for many decades. There was very little hard evidence that the young man was involved with any gangs.

The hysteria over juvenile gangs, partially fueled by the media, led to a virtual cottage industry of "gang experts" who allegedly could decipher graffiti for gang messages. With little objective evidence, some members of the law enforcement community created fantastic mythologies about how Los Angeles street gangs were spreading their ominous colors of red and blue across the country, and even around the world. Long before the September 11th bombings of the World Trade Center and the Pentagon, the Patriot Act, and the Department of Homeland Security, the United States was gearing up for a life or death struggle against juvenile gangs. Ironically, juvenile crime was dropping during most of this period, and the violent presence of youth gangs was more prevalent on television or the cinema than in urban neighborhoods.

During this period, police agencies launched high profile "made-for-television" crackdowns on gangs. The Los Angeles Police Department organized massive weekend offensives (known as "Operation Hammer") in South Central Los Angeles that resulted in thousands of arrests. So many young people were taken into custody that the LAPD set up a temporary booking operation at the University of Southern California football stadium. These mass arrests were usually for minor crimes; the arrests resulted in few convictions and virtually no referrals to the California Youth Authority (Krisberg, 2005).

Fear of violent juvenile gang members persuaded California juvenile justice officials to send many more youths convicted of crimes to its juvenile prison system without even the pretense of considering alternatives to incarceration. In 1997, that system was almost at 200 percent of its housing capacity. It was at this time that the Youth Authority's traditional emphasis on treatment and education was eroded, with increased use of custodial staff who dressed and comported themselves more like prison guards than

counselors. Youth Authority employees were being organized by the California Correctional Peace Officers Association (CCPOA), which also represents the prison guards. This movement away from the rehabilitative model was illustrated by the practice of having some Youth Authority residents receive their educational programs in cages. These were steel mesh devices that were the size of a telephone booth. The teacher would pass the student his or her textbooks or lessons through a small slot in the cage. The Youth Authority also instituted the use of attack dogs in some of its facilities to prevent escapes and quell riots. Juvenile correctional facilities continued to utilize the attack dogs long after the Department of Corrections decided to abandon this practice. Funding for rehabilitation, mental health, and medical care in state juvenile facilities was severely cut back. In the mid-1990s, the Director of the Youth Authority adopted the rhetoric of the prison guards union and claimed that his facilities were among the "toughest beats in the state."

At the local level, correctional boot camps and the ideology of "tough love" dominated community conversations about youth crime. Schools jumped into the War Against the Young by creating mandatory suspension and expulsion policies such as "Zero Tolerance" programs that claimed to be making schools safer. Many urban schools required that youths pass through metal detectors to enter school buildings. Some public school districts debated requiring students to wear uniforms to classes so as to discourage "gang clothing." Students were pressured to submit to mandatory drug testing if they wished to participate in extra-curricular programs and sports teams. More police than ever before were assigned to work on high school and junior high school campuses; other school districts hired their own private security officers. Unannounced searches of student desks and lockers became much more common. Students who allegedly were wearing gang colors were summarily kicked out of school.

There are only partial data on how many young people fell victim to pernicious Zero Tolerance policies. The California Department of Education website reported that there were almost 25,000 students recommended for expulsion in fiscal year 2002–03. Of those students, approximately 83 percent were actually expelled (California Department of Education, 2004).

In recent years the numbers of California pupils expelled from school has increased steadily. While there were some limited legal challenges to these new rules, the general picture was of informal and arbitrary enforcement practices that were not guided by due process or equal protection of law. By all accounts, students of color were the most likely targets by these Zero Tolerance policies. Data from the Oakland Unified School District for 2003–2004 showed that white students accounted for just 6 percent of the 4,297 students who were suspended that year. African American students made up 71 percent of those suspended. The very limited data on the reasons for school suspensions and expulsions suggest that most of these severe actions were not taken against students who brought weapons to school or engaged in violence. For example, in the Berkeley Unified School District the overwhelming majority of suspensions and expulsions were for "defying authority," i.e., talking back or arguing with teachers and other school staff (Berkeley Unified School District, 2002).

Another crucial aspect of the War Against the Young was the movement to re-criminalize juvenile status offenses. These are offenses such as truancy, curfew violations, running away, and "incorrigibility" that are only law violations if committed by minors. In the 1970s there was a national reform movement to divert these youths from secure detention centers, keep them out of the formal juvenile court system, and expand the use of community-based organizations to deal with these family issues. California enacted legislation in 1978 (AB 3121) to remove status offenders from locked facilities and the formal justice system. Young women historically had been the primary targets of the status offense laws. Whereas young men were about as likely as girls to be arrested for juvenile status offenses, it was young women who were incarcerated for these behaviors. The perverse and prejudicial logic behind these policies was that girls needed to be protected from themselves, especially their nascent sexuality. The new law limiting the application of juvenile status offense laws significantly reduced the number of girls in state and county juvenile correctional institutions.

There was a rediscovery of the alleged value of strict enforcement of laws against truancy, the need to reestablish curfews for juveniles, and increased incarceration for runaways. Many communities passed new local ordinances to restrict the behavior of young people. Courts and probation agencies used the pretext of violations of probation or violations of court orders to charge youths with offenses that could result in their incarceration. Thus, youths who were brought into Court were ordered to attend school regularly, to be at home before a specific time, or to cooperate with their guardians. Young people who allegedly failed to meet these rules could be sentenced for more serious charges. In a practice known as "boot strapping," youths who got into aggressive arguments with their parents or guardians could be charged with domestic violence. Children who were placed in foster care or group homes could be labeled as delinquents if they left these placements without official permission. Law enforcement and school officials asserted that threatening young people and their parents with criminal prosecutions would reduce truancy rates. All of these severe restrictions on young people were loudly justified as measures required for increased child protection.

The campaign to arrest and incarcerate young people for status offenses was sold to the public based on heightened fears about child abductions and sexual exploitation of young children. In California and across the nation, there were well-financed media campaigns focusing on missing and exploited children. The federal government pumped millions of dollars into publicity about missing children through the National Center on Missing and Exploited Children. Despite these millions of taxpayer funds, there is no documented case in which the Center actually found a missing child.

Parents were frightened to death about the potential kidnapping of their children by strangers. Faces of children showed up on milk cartons. Other commercial enterprises sold identification and fingerprinting equipment to petrified parents. Schools and nonprofit groups started training programs to teach young children to avoid abduction. Despite these scare campaigns, the evidence grew that most of the missing and exploited children had either been taken by their non-custodial parents, usually in the context of bitter divorce proceedings, or they were teenagers that had run away from home. Some research suggested that many of these runaways were actually escaping from abusive living situations. The Federal Bureau of Investigation estimated that there were fewer than 200 abductions by strangers a year in the entire nation. Of course there were a very small number of child kidnappings and murders such as the Adam Walsh and Polly Klaas tragedies that galvanized worldwide media attention and further fueled the hysteria about missing children. Motorists were often greeted with highway signs and broadcast "Amber Alerts" telling us about the most current missing child. Many of these alerts proved inaccurate and created false impressions about the frequency of child abductions.

Young people are virtual sitting ducks for politicians and other public officials who want to push "get tough" crime policies. The immediate costs to cynical elected officials of fighting the War Against the Young appear to be minimal. Adolescents cannot or do not vote. Young people do not sit on the boards of directors of corporations, foundations, universities, religious organizations, or large nonprofit organizations. Few unions regard young people as their constituents, rather adolescents are often viewed as economic threats to older unionized workers. Youths were not invited to be active participants in the political discussions and decision-making forums that led to the War Against the Young. In the mainstream political process, youth are often used as "window dressing" and as a means to create campaign photo opportunities.

A school-based curriculum on civic engagement of the young is sorely lacking. Education in the politics of social justice is almost nonexistent in most public educational settings. Young people do not belong to well-heeled political lobby groups such as the American Association of Retired People, the National Rifle Association, or the Chamber of Commerce. The conventional media rarely seeks out a youth perspective on critical public policy questions. The viewpoints of adolescents are generally not measured by influential public polling organizations. The organizations that seek to be advocates for young people are chronically underfunded, understaffed, and largely ignored by the political establishment.

Adolescents in this society are a lucrative market for a broad range of commodities including tobacco, alcoholic beverages, fast food and snacks, trendy clothing, grooming aids, expensive electronic toys, music, and movies, to name a few products. Genuine aspects of youth culture are often co-opted by the media which sells these images to young and old alike. For instance, the mass media embraced a powerful portrayal of violent, sexually promiscuous, drugged, urban minority youths that is retailed to suburban and rural youngsters so that they can spend their disposable income to cultivate the "Gangsta" look at the carefully protected and sanitized suburban shopping malls. These harsh racist stereotypes promoted by the media are, in turn, used by adults to justify the need to increase social controls on the young.

The great American criminologist Marvin Wolfgang observed that fear of the young by adults is as old as human history. He wrote about a Sumerian tablet that revealed deep-seated fear that young people were the "barbarians at the gates" that would bring down the social order. Whether it was the sexually explicit young people of the Jazz Age of the 1920s, the Rock and Roll rebels of the 1950s, the culturally subversive Hippies of the 1960s, or the Hip Hop Generation of the 1990s, adolescents have almost always signaled that the social norms could be changed, sometimes in ways frightening for adults. These concerns may be on the rise as the baby boom generation is aging and facing retirement, and senior citizens become the largest voting block in the nation. These fears intensify as young people of diverse racial and ethnic backgrounds make legitimate claims to be seen and heard. The perception that the young are wildly out of control and need tighter regulation is a longstanding and powerful cultural theme easily exploited by politicians, some religious leaders, and the media.

THE PLAYERS

While we can comprehend The Game in sociological terms and focus on the structural forces that led to bad social policies for the young, it is equally important to expose the perfidy of those power hungry politicians, government bureaucrats, and academic mountebanks that have fueled the War Against the Young. I would like to present a brief review of three dramatic California instances in which powerful and influential adults betrayed our young people. Besides talking about the main villains in the piece, I will discuss the smaller roles that others played in these examples of bad public policy.

AB 136 and the Rise and Fall of Chuck Quackenbush

For more than a half century, California law mandated that persons under age 16 were to be tried in juvenile courts regardless of the gravity of their crimes. While there were very limited examples of persons between the ages of 16 and 18 being tried as adults, the vast majority of minors were handled in the juvenile justice system and served their sentences in the California Youth Authority, the mission of which was to pursue the goals of treatment and rehabilitation, not punishment. Before 1994, the maximum sentence that could be given to a youthful murderer under the age of 16 was to be confined in the Youth Authority until age 25. Other states began amending their laws to permit serious juvenile offenders to be tried as adults and placed in prisons. For example, New York State revised its sentencing laws in 1978 to allow young offenders above the age of 14 to be handled in the adult criminal justice system. Throughout the country in the 1980s, states debated and passed new laws that sent more youths to the adult system. California was virtually alone among the large urbanized states to resist this urge to stiffen penalties for very young juvenile murderers.

All this changed as a politically ambitious Republican Legislator Chuck Quackenbush launched a media-focused set of hearings to support his bill, AB 136. The proposed legislation dropped the age at which children could be tried for murder in criminal courts, and could face a potential sentence in prison of Life Without the Possibility of Parole. Quackenbush used a time-tested method to push his agenda—organize events at which the surviving relatives of murder victims talked about the tragic loss of their family members and publicly shared their unremitting sorrow.

The media, especially the local television evening news, has come to adore these stories. Cynical news directors often say, "if it bleeds it leads," and the focus on the suffering of ordinary citizens is compelling television. Not only is the viewer drawn to the drama of the tragic testimony, but there is an emotional "rush" to viewers as they realize that the story is about someone else and not them. This is not unlike the emotional charge that is offered by horror movies or suspenseful television dramas—we get a chance to vicariously experience the pain or fear of others without paying the price. Some years ago, Danish sociologist Svend Ranulf (1938) pointed out that this sort of very emotional news coverage is often used by totalitarian regimes to build support for repressive government actions.

Most important, this sort of journalism generally does not address questions about why these terrible events occur, nor what the citizenry might do to make their families safer. Violence is portrayed as the random and irrational acts of strangers, despite the fact that most violence occurs among people who are well acquainted with each other.

Quakenbush used AB 136 to strengthen his image as a crime fighting conservative. He broadened his political rhetoric about AB 136 to encompass other conservative social concerns such as the alleged decline in personal responsibility and the claimed corrosive nature of the welfare system. As he noted, "Once you bring government into the family, you really are zapping the energy of society. People think, 'Why should I bust my tail to raise a family? Government will take care of all of that for us'" (Hubner & Wolfson, 1996: 259). Chuck Quackenbush's argument for AB 136 also suggested, without providing any evidence, that the juvenile justice system was incapable of handling the "new breed" of young murderers. Pushing all the fear buttons, Quackenbush warned that "The Little Monsters we have today who murder in cold blood are very dangerous individuals. They have to be punished and walled off from society for a very long period of time, if not forever" (Hubner & Wolfson, 1996: 260). He asked if voters were willing to bet their lives or those of their family members on the ability to rehabilitate young killers. He went on to explain "The way you turn things around is to make crime hurt. If you hurt a person in this society, then society has to hurt you back. It's very primitive, but people understand it" (Hubner & Wolfson, 1996: 261).

These arguments certainly resonated with a strain of American social values that suggest that "an eye for an eye" or social revenge is an appropriate and effective response to crime. Further, there were several academic "players" such as James Q. Wilson, Charles Murray, and John DiIulio who were providing seemingly valid intellectual cover for these political arguments. These professor-crime warriors told us that America was about to be overrun by a generation of "super predators" who were psychologically damaged and possessed lower than average intelligence and would only respond to blunt social reactions to their criminal behavior (Wilson & Hernnstein, 1985; Murray & Cox, 1979; DiIulio, 1995). Employing language designed to scare white, middle-class voters, John DiIulio wrote about a coming "Crime Bomb" carried by the new generation of "fatherless, Godless, and jobless" juvenile super predators that would be flooding America's streets (DiIulio, 1995).

The highly questionable science produced by these conservative academics was trumpeted by right wing "think tanks" and given enormous coverage in the press. They were invited to present their flawed research to legislators, to the United States Congress, and to other gatherings of elected officials.

More moderate members of the California legislature could not resist the pressures from the fear-mongering right wing, the strong, publicity-savvy, victim's advocacy groups, and the hysterical media. AB 136 was quickly passed and signed into law in 1994. This was the same year that Californians were discussing the "Three Strikes and You're Out" ballot proposition for habitual and violent adult offenders. Trepidation about violent crime was on the political and media front burners, with the rhetoric flame turned up high.

AB 136 affected a relatively small number of young defendants, but the break with past juvenile justice traditions emphasizing the possibility of rehabilitation for very young criminals signaled the start of a stampede among elected officials to demonstrate who could be tougher on juvenile criminals. A few years later, this trend resulted in another politically motivated campaign to pass Proposition 21, which amended juvenile law to move the State toward becoming the harshest juvenile sentencing system in the nation.

And what of the payoffs for the major player behind AB 136, Chuck Quackenbush? The formerly obscure Santa Clara County lawmaker used the publicity gained via his support of AB 136 to spearhead a statewide campaign to become elected as California's Insurance Commissioner. Virtually all of Quackenbush's well-funded television advertisements centered on his role to toughen laws against juvenile criminals. This might be an appropriate electoral theme if one was running for Governor or Attorney General, but crime control was not part of the job description of the Insurance Commissioner. Despite this logical disconnect, Quackenbush became California's elected Insurance Commissioner. Politic pundits declared that the former Notre

Dame University graduate was a rising political star who might be destined for even higher statewide or even national elective office.

Then something happened to derail the Quackenbush political bandwagon. A very high profile series in the *Los Angeles Times* written by top investigative journalist Virginia Ellis (2000) presented an alarming set of facts. It turned out that Commissioner Quackenbush had made several secret deals with major insurance companies that allowed them to escape fines for mishandling up to thousands of claims resulting from the terrible Northridge earthquake. Quackenbush ignored the advice of his own legal staff that might have produced hundreds of millions in fines for the offending insurance companies. Further, the investigation revealed that Quackenbush and his aides had "strong-armed" some of these same corporations to donate more than $12 million to nonprofit foundations that he created. Ms. Ellis uncovered confidential documents showing that Quackenbush used his powers as Insurance Commissioner to create a "political slush fund directed by highly paid consultants, to further his quest for higher public office." Pressures to have Quackenbush resign his office grew rapidly, but even in his last days in office, the erstwhile crime fighter approved contracts that obliged taxpayers to pay more than $1 million for his legal fees and those of his top staff for the investigations of wrongdoing.

Commissioner Quackenbush received no jail time for these alleged felonies. He resigned his office and was able to move to Hawai'i to avoid further legal entanglements. It does not appear that he was made to "hurt" for the damage that he inflicted while in public office. Tragically, while Quackenbush is now a long forgotten "trivia question" in California politics, the harm to young people created by AB 136 continues.

Governor Pete Wilson and Proposition 21

Many liberal legislators argued that the passage of AB 136 would calm the panic over juvenile violence, and would really only harm a very small number of youths. In 1994, 234 young people between the ages of 14 and 16 were arrested for homicide in the state of California (California Department of Justice, Criminal Justice Statistics Center, 1994). Opponents countered that AB 136 would just whet the appetite of ambitious politicians for more "raw meat" juvenile justice law reform. Unfortunately, Californians did not have to wait very long to see who was correct about these future predictions. After the enactment of AB 136, virtually every legislative session contained additional bills that made it easier to try juveniles as adults by expanding the list of crimes that could result in adult prosecution. Other bills moved the burden of proof from prosecutors to defendants to show that young people should *not* be transferred to criminal courts. Yet even these further "crackdown" measures did not satisfy the players.

Recall that juvenile violent crime rates in California were sharply decreasing after 1993, but the media continued its focus on juvenile gangs and violent crimes by young people. In March of 2000, the voters were asked to approve a ballot measure entitled "The Gang Violence and Juvenile Crime Prevention Act" or as it became known more popularly, Proposition 21. This voter initiative rewrote over 50 pages of law covering the California juvenile justice system. It made it even easier to try young people in criminal courts for a long list of crimes. Under Proposition 21, the decision to try youths as adults could be made at the discretion of prosecutors, without any judicial review or hearing. Proposition 21 mandated secure confinement and stronger penalties for a wide range of juvenile offenders, including offenses such as vandalism of property costing over $50. The ballot measure expanded the definition of gang crimes to cover almost all offenses committed by three or more youths, and permitted large increases in penalties for alleged gang-related crimes. Proposition 21 made clear that juvenile offenses would count under the existing draconian adult Three Strikes Law. Taken together, the provisions of Proposition 21 were viewed by both its critics and defenders alike as the toughest juvenile law in America.

Many of the provisions of Proposition 21 had been advocated for years by the California District Attorneys Association, but these ideas had gained little headway in the Legislature. Enter the major player, then-Governor Pete Wilson, who embraced Proposition 21 as a main component of his political agenda. It was broadly speculated in the political watering holes of Sacramento that former Governor Wilson wanted to make a run for the U.S. Presidency. The three big issues to establish the

conservative bona fides for Wilson were his proposal to require labor unions to get annual permission from each member to use their dues for political purposes, an anti-teachers union program for school reform, and tough new laws against juvenile crime. It was alleged by some that Wilson's staff had purposely delayed placing Proposition 21 on the ballot until the March 2000 California Primary Election to aid his national political ambitions (Shrag, 2000). Wilson's spokespersons have denied this charge saying that they lacked the adequate funding to qualify the measure earlier.

Governor Wilson had perfected the art of using racially charged wedge issues and ballot measures to solidify his conservative white voter base. Interestingly, some political observers felt that Pete Wilson was too moderate to capture the support of the very conservative California Republican party, let alone the very right wing national party apparatus. He had won two elections as Governor and was elected twice to the United States Senate pushing for tighter restrictions of undocumented workers (Propositions 187 and 227), denying them driver's licenses as well as basic health, welfare, and educational benefits that were available to other California residents. He fought to pass another voter initiative that made state Affirmative Action programs virtually illegal (Proposition 209). Wilson led the statewide campaign to pass Proposition 184, the Three Strikes Law.

Raising large amounts of funds from his corporate supporters, Wilson solicited and received major contributions for the Yes on Proposition 21 campaign from Pacific Gas and Electric, ARCO, Unocal 76 and the head of Hilton Hotels, who each paid $50,000. A spokesperson for Chevron admitted that his company gave $25,000 to the Proposition 21 campaign at the request of then-Governor Wilson. None of these businesses had any obvious corporate interest in supporting tougher juvenile sentencing laws, but they could scarcely turn down the request of the powerful Governor who was aiming for the White House (Ching, 2000). At least one advocate who opposed Proposition 21, Kimi Lee of the ACLU, stated that "The corporations had no idea what they were supporting" (Ching, 2000). Later, after Wilson's Presidential prospects faded, many of the corporations that gave large donations to pass Proposition 21 withdrew their support of the measure. For example, when confronted by youthful protesters, PG&E publicly retracted its corporate endorsement of Proposition 21.

Wilson claimed that Proposition 21 was not connected to his political goals. He professed to just trying to be helpful to the California District Attorneys and Sheriffs who wanted the proposed "get tough" provisions of Proposition 21. It is worth noting that Mitch Zach, who was Pete Wilson's top political director, was the primary strategist of the Proposition 21 campaign.

As Wilson's efforts to become the Republican Party nominee for President faded, so did his highly visible presence as the chief advocate for overhauling the juvenile justice system. After Wilson's exit from the campaign, the prosecutors and sheriffs soldiered on to pass Proposition 21. They were assisted in their efforts by Governor Gray Davis who embraced Proposition 21 and sometimes confided to audiences that he thought that the Singapore juvenile justice system had got it right; presumably this meant that Governor Davis favored public caning as an acceptable juvenile correctional program. Davis had received over $2 million in campaign contributions from the prison guards union (CCPOA) during his run for Governor in 1998. Proposition 21 and other new laws that further swelled the inmate population and the budget of the Department of Corrections were good business investments for the CCPOA.[2]

Attorney General Bill Lockyer also played a significant role in the passage of Proposition 21. Critics of the measure claimed that the very short and simple language that would appear on the ballot summary obscured the radical nature of law changes that would follow passage of the proposition. Unless one took the time to carefully review the full text of Proposition 21, most voters thought that they were being asked to endorse a measure to prevent juvenile violence and to fight dangerous street gangs. The ballot summary language emphasized the provisions about violent youth felons, but did not explain that Proposition 21 permitted police to wiretap groups of more than three juveniles whom they suspected of committing any crimes. Nor did the ballot summary language point to the elimination of much of the confidentiality of juvenile court hearings, or the stiff new penalties for juveniles committing property damage valued as low as $50. Appeals to Attorney General Lockyer to use the ballot summary to describe the wide ranging nature of the changes in California law

fell on deaf ears. Polls suggested that the more voters knew about the specifics of Proposition 21, the less support that it received. Other statewide leaders either offered mild support for the Proposition, or remained mute. The principal opponents of the measure included juvenile court judges, youth advocates, civil rights groups, many labor unions, the state PTA, and the League of Women Voters. However, the groups that opposed Proposition 21 were unable to raise any significant funds to counteract the statewide campaign that was launched by the proponents and bankrolled by the corporate friends of Governors Pete Wilson and Gray Davis.

Proposition 21 was passed by a large majority of California voters. Within months of its passage, a fascinating case in San Diego County derailed the implementation of the ballot measure. As a lark, a group of eight middle-class white students decided to chase down and beat some Latino migrant workers. The San Diego District Attorney decided to charge each of these youngsters as adults under the new law citing: (1) the violent nature of the crime; (2) the fact that the offense was committed by a group of teenagers that could be defined as a gang under Proposition 21; and (3) the circumstances of the offense that suggested a hate crime. Immediately, the financially capable parents of the boys filed a series of appeals attempting to void Proposition 21. Signifying the racially tinged nature of opinion on Proposition 21, Tim McClain, the editor of the business magazine *Metropolitan*, reflected on the views of his readers: "These kids, these teenagers, as heinous as the crime that they're being accused of, are not your prototypical person that you would see prosecuted under this . . . They're not from low-income families. They're not gangbangers. You know they're not minorities. They're white, upper middle-class kids going to one of the best schools in San Diego" (Edwards, National Public Radio, 2000). Ultimately, the California Supreme Court found that the sentencing provisions of Proposition 21 were constitutional. Although no definitive data are yet available, it appears that Proposition 21 slowly is being implemented across the state.

The Fight Over the Alameda "Super Jail" for Youth

Expanding local capacity to incarcerate more young people was another aspect of the

California War Against the Young. Beginning in the late 1990s, the state Legislature voted to reallocate federal funding that was meant to support the construction of new prisons to renovate and expand local juvenile correctional facilities. Legislative staffers thought that this move would force the Department of Corrections to give greater consideration to alternatives to prison for adults. Further, there was a general consensus that local juvenile detention facilities were in a state of disrepair; many of the buildings were over 50 years old and were plainly inadequate for their current mission. The Chief Probation Officers Association had tried to get a bond measure before the voters to help remedy these conditions. However, California voters had consistently rejected bonds for the improving or expanding juvenile correctional facilities, or even for building new adult jails and state prisons. To meet the financial needs to expand the adult incarceration capacity, state and local officials did an end-run around the voters, relying instead on private financing to support prison and jail expansion. This method of public financing entailed higher interest rates to be paid to private investors—adding as much as an additional one-third to costs of prison and jail construction. Under President Bill Clinton, the federal government began making grants to the states to partially defray the building of new lockups. The California share of these funds exceeded $275 million per year. In the early years of this federal program, almost all of the grants went to adult facilities. Although most of the monies could be used for renovations and improvements, the federal program mandated that there be some, if only token, expansion in the number of custody beds.

The legislature assigned to the Board of Corrections (BOC) the job of working with counties who wished to improve existing juvenile facilities or to build new ones. The BOC created a protocol for counties to submit plans for improving and expanding their juvenile detention facilities. Counties received small planning grants and could apply to the BOC for a share of the federal monies. This led to a virtual boom in detention bed construction across the state. Grants were given to 40 of the 58 counties, and collectively these projects expanded the detention bed capacity by 3,150 new beds, or a 50 percent expansion in juvenile beds. Besides the expanded capacity, the BOC grants partially paid for replacing

another 1,300 detention beds. This all happened during the late 1990s while juvenile arrests continued to decline. Moreover, California had traditionally possessed one of the very highest rates of juvenile detention in the nation. Thus, the Golden State, which used secure juvenile lockups more than any other large state, was creating the ability to greatly increase its ability to incarcerate more young people.

The case of Alameda County and its proposed expansion of detention provides a fascinating case study of how an irrational public policy can be promoted. The county operated an aging 299-bed detention center that was located in the northern part of Alameda County—close to the neighborhoods in which most detained youths lived. The facility was in urgent need of repair, and probably replacement. There were few youth advocacy groups in the community that opposed spending funds to improve the conditions of confinement in the old juvenile hall. The county hired a Georgia-based planning firm that specialized in helping build new adult prisons to conduct a study of the needed renovations. Amazingly, the Georgia group proposed that the county build a new 540-bed juvenile hall to be located near the existing jail in the City of Dublin, far from the neighborhoods in which most detained youths lived. There were few accessible methods of public transportation that would permit the families of these incarcerated young people to visit their children. It was asserted that the existing detention center could not be retrofitted, because it sat on top of a major earthquake fault line.

The data provided to support the vast expansion of the juvenile hall were suspect, at best. The Georgia-based planners apparently misinterpreted Alameda County juvenile justice data, showing supposed increases in juvenile arrests and detention bookings, even though the Probation Department's own statistics showed a significant decline in these juvenile crime trends. The plan justifying more detention beds assumed a 50 percent growth in the county's youth population. However, these data relied on projections of population growth in the suburban and rural parts of the county. In fact, the growing numbers of new county residents who were moving into high-priced "gated residential communities" were unlikely to be candidates for the new expanded juvenile detention center. Rising real estate values were leading to more "gentrification" of traditional urban communities, driving the poorest families to seek housing in other Bay Area counties. The plan also used data on the highest recorded monthly detention hall populations, exaggerating the real level of crowding. Finally, the Georgia group assumed that the Alameda juvenile justice system was functioning in an optimal manner, making maximum use of alternatives to secure confinement. None of these assumptions were true, but these premises allowed the plan to conclude that Alameda County must increase its detention bed capacity by 81 percent.

The county assembled a facility-planning group and applied to the BOC for funding. They secured grants of almost $30 million to pay for needed renovations, and approximately another $3 million to subsidize bed expansion. It should be noted that these BOC funds would cover only a small proportion of the costs of the new 540-bed juvenile hall. Further, it was unclear how the financially strapped county would find the funding to add all of the additional staffing that would be required to operate the new facility.

At this point, the players who were mostly county bureaucrats and some elected officials were operating with little public scrutiny of their ambitious game plan. Enter a small band of dedicated youth organizers calling itself Books Not Bars (BNB). This group questioned the need for the expanded detention capacity that would result in many more young people, especially minority youths, being locked up. In addition, Books Not Bars questioned the perverse investments in more juvenile jail beds just as local budgets for youth programs, public school funding, welfare supports, and health care were being slashed. The proposed Dublin detention complex became known as "the super jail for kids." Books Not Bars held a number of public forums and rallies that raised serious questions about the value of the county's plans. Theses idealistic and politically involved young people worked closely with a number of local and nationally respected juvenile justice research and policy groups such as the Center for Juvenile and Criminal Justice, the Commonweal Institute, the Youth Law Center, the National Juvenile Law Center, the Justice Policy Institute, and the National Council on Crime and Delinquency to support the case that the super jail was ill conceived and that more alternatives to detention should be created.

The mobilizing efforts of BNB received intense media attention as they pled their case before the County Board of Supervisors. They traveled to a statewide meeting of the BOC to protest the grants to Alameda County. The BOC decided to avoid the adverse publicity and voted to ask the county to revise and resubmit its application for funding. This was the first time that the BOC actually turned down, if only temporarily, a local proposal to build more detention beds.

Next, the game turned ugly as the supporters of the super jail felt the need to discredit all those who questioned their plans. In a whispering campaign, BNB was labeled as a subversive organization with ties to radical political entities. More establishment adult critics of the plan were accused of withholding their views from county planners, even though the actual planning process involved only the input of the Georgia firm and local officials. Juvenile justice officials announced to the media that the existing building was unsafe and prone to severe earthquake damage. How could the local officials disregard the potential harm to the incarcerated children? When confronted with the question of why the Juvenile Court and the Probation Department leaders were willing to wait several years for the building of a new facility to "save these endangered children," and why there were no emergency steps to move the children to safer housing, these inquiries were met with silence.

Referencing Proposition 21, the backers of the super jail told the community that this new law required the building of a much larger detention capacity. Yet only about 12 percent or about 40 of detained youth were there pending trial as adults. It was claimed that the detained population contained a high percentage of very violent youths, however, at least 25 percent of the juvenile hall residents were being held while awaiting placement in community group homes. Another group of young inmates were locked up for violating court orders or the rules of probation, not for new crimes. When pressed to bring in national experts to look at the existing youths in confinement and propose viable alternative programs, county officials decided to defer this analysis to a more global and more costly study of the entire juvenile justice system. This study was scheduled to be completed after the ground was broken for the expanded juvenile hall. The Request for Proposals (RFP) for this study explicitly instructed the bidders not to focus on criticisms of the juvenile court, nor to revisit the need for a new and expanded juvenile hall.

The proponents of the super jail were eventually undone, because residents of the Dublin community opposed the situating of the super jail in "their backyard." These suburban activists joined in common cause with BNB to raise many additional questions about the need for such a large facility and the logic of placing it many miles from where the detained youths and their families resided. The Dublin activists found that the county officials claimed to have performed a thorough analysis of alternative locations for the super jail, but no such study could be located. The super jail planners had to retreat and restart the process. Next the Sheriff proposed that the county take over an abandoned jail located in downtown Oakland that had been closed because the Sheriff lacked the funds to operate it. Now the county juvenile justice leaders were fighting amongst themselves as BNB was steadily but surely converting more members of the community, especially those in faith-based groups, to the view that the super jail was a big mistake. Several of the largest religious congregations in Alameda County went on record as opposing the super jail.

At their best, the Alameda proponents of the super jail could only marshal a 3-to-2 vote of the Board of Supervisors to go forward with the Dublin juvenile facility. The two opposition votes came from Supervisors Keith Carson and Nate Miley, who represented the predominantly impoverished, minority communities of the county. The strongest support for the super jail came from Supervisor Scott Haggerty in whose district the new detention complex would be built, thereby creating an important revenue source for the local construction businesses. Supervisor Gail Steele also represented many of the more prosperous suburbs. She also was viewed as the champion of the probation officers union that stood to benefit financially as more officers were hired to run the bigger facility. The last Supervisor, Alice Lai-Bitker, represented a predominately white and politically conservative suburban community. She was heavily lobbied by youth advocates to oppose the super jail, and actually switched her vote to oppose the project. The politically powerful Sheriff announced that he would actively support a challenger to Lai-Bitker in the next election. Supervisor Lai-Bitker reversed herself again and rejoined the backers of the super jail. Despite this announcement, the Sheriff still vigorously supported an alternative candidate to Lai-Bitker in the upcoming election.

Although few county employees were willing to be quoted for attribution, it was clear that county administrators were demanding loyalty to their agenda. One top county public health official was told that he would lose his job if he publicly questioned the need for the super jail. He declared that his job with the county did not mean the loss of his right to freely express his views about what was best for the public health of young people.

The opposition from Dublin residents, combined with the continued crusade by BNB, caused the players to retreat. With successive votes of the Board of Supervisors, the size of the facility began to shrink, although no new planning data were presented to justify these alterations. Next, the county planners reconsidered the safety of rebuilding the new facility on the existing site; apparently the problematic earthquake fault was less serious than it had seemed. In the end, the Board of Supervisors voted unanimously to rebuild on the existing site and to add the minimum number of beds required to qualify for the federal funds. The super jail was dead and the tens of millions of taxpayer dollars that were invested in the planning and design of the Dublin facility resulted in a compromise that would have been acceptable to the youth advocates at the very beginning of the struggle. There were significant personnel changes in the top leadership of the Probation Department and the Juvenile Court, and this meant that some of the most forceful advocates of the super jail were no longer in the game.

THE REMIX

In the vernacular of contemporary music, a Remix is a blending of components to reach a new creative level. One version of the Remix involves sampling from classic popular music of the past 50 years that is combined with complex rhythmic additions and the innovative use of the spoken word. This form of the Remix seems very applicable to finding the strategies to "beat down" the players and their game on behalf of young people. Expressed in more formal social science jargon, we might think of the Remix as a pathway to social reconstruction.

The brief case studies presented in this paper suggest some ways to resist the War Against the Young. Some of the best of these approaches use very conventional methods of research and the presentation of solid evidence to stand up to the players. Public demonstrations and community mobilization proved to be crucial tools against the players and the game. Many of these direct community action strategies were very successful during the Civil Rights Movement and the mobilization to end the Vietnam War. These successful social justice campaigns taught us the value of forging broad community coalitions that bring diverse groups to the table. These organizing efforts rest on a profound respect for all people, including the need to listen and respond to their immediate concerns.

The Remix used litigation strategies, voter mobilization, and publicity to expose injustices and to educate the public. While there was ongoing dialog with the players ("keep your friends close, and your enemies closer"), the progressive groups never lost sight of the lesson that real social change needed to happen at the grassroots level.

The current generation of social reformers consists of a variety of very dedicated youth organizers who are savvy about using the mass media and come armed with research data to back up their arguments. Contemporary advocacy groups exhibit an impressive ability to sustain a diversity of ethnicity, gender, and age in their organizations. I remember that, after an early meeting with representatives of BNB, I confided with a colleague about how polite and respectful these young people were with us "old heads" from the 1960s. We were a lot angrier, I concluded. My very wise colleague educated me that "They are just a whole lot smarter than we were in the 1960s," and had gotten everything they needed without resorting to confrontational tactics. The new generation of social justice advocates shows a very sophisticated grasp of how to balance confrontation and accommodation. Most important, the new generation of reformers is focused on getting results.

In this Remix of old and new, justice reformers can make a real difference in the lives of young people. First and foremost, strategies of social reconstruction demand that the players not be let off the hook. The cynical leaders in the War Against the Young must be publicly held to account for their actions. Second, we should not assume that most citizens know the abuses being practiced in their name. Helping the media to expose abusive and corrupt government practices is an important part of social reconstruction.

Equally important is the ability to put forth real-world examples of what a better social policy should resemble. People must be inspired by positive and practical solutions to seemingly intractable problems. The players want us to believe that "nothing works."

Recently in California, the justice reformers have turned the tables on the players by using the tool of voter initiatives to usher in progressive policies. For too long these ballot measures brought us reactionary social policies such as Three Strikes and Proposition 21. Just a few years ago, advocates of progressive reform of state drug policies successfully passed Proposition 36, which allowed minor drug offenders to be diverted to treatment programs in lieu of jail. This measure was almost universally opposed by criminal justice system officials. Most establishment politicians avoided taking a public position on the measure. The proponents employed sophisticated polling and focus group techniques to craft their message. They learned that most Californians reported that someone in their immediate family was suffering from an addiction problem, and that they felt that jailing their family members was an expensive and counterproductive approach. Proposition 36 passed by a wide margin.

Another progressive reform measure, Proposition 66, is designed to amend the pernicious Three Strikes Law and is supported by 65 percent of Californians as measured in a recent public opinion poll. The Yes on 66 Campaign is utilizing similar and sophisticated electoral strategies to those employed for passage of Proposition 36. Progressive reformers have also learned that recruiting financial supporters, especially via the Internet, can enable a serious statewide campaign to build momentum. Another voter initiative, Proposition 63, places a modest tax on millionaires to help fund badly needed programs to prevent and treat mental illness. Neither of these bold reforms could have successfully survived the onslaught of special interests if the game had played out only in the Legislature and Governor's Office.

The Remix has rediscovered the enormous power of giving young people back their voice. Jerome Miller, a champion of the old school justice reformers, built public support for closing the terrible youth prisons in Massachusetts in the early 1970s by using this approach. As Commissioner of the Department of Youth

Services, Miller set up public forums around the Bay State that featured youthful inmates who told their stories of maltreatment to civic and religious groups, and to the media. Their message was compelling and persuasive. Current reformers are also very attentive to the value of empowering young people. Groups such as The Beat Within work with incarcerated young people, encouraging them to write down their experiences, and then communicate these powerful insights to the public. Books Not Bars has organized families of incarcerated young people to share their hopes and dreams that their children's lives can be redeemed. Organizations such as Youth Radio teach disadvantaged youths to use the tools of the electronic media to tell their stories.

The players in the War Against the Young can be very ruthless and the game can be very "cold," but the Remix for social justice is showing us that the rules of the game can be changed and the players can be defeated. We have learned that the cynical exploitation of our frustrations, anxieties, and psychic distance from the young is too harmful to our communities for any of us to sit on the sidelines.

NOTES

1. The title of this paper takes poetic license with the Hip Hop phrase, "Don't hate the player, hate the game." This saying is often used to excuse the behavior of people involved in exploitive and dishonest actions as part of the "survival of the fittest." The phrase suggests a sense of pride in the abilities of some streetwise individuals to employ their wit and resiliency to overcome harsh social conditions that are often out of their control. By altering this phrase, I mean to say that the powerful and influential officials who push for destructive legal and social policies need to be held publicly accountable for their personal choices. These establishment players do have the ability to change the circumstances in which they operate.

2. Despite its role as a stratagem to further the political ambitions of Wilson and Davis, Proposition 21 rendered little help to either politician. As noted earlier, Wilson's quest for the White House stalled. Indeed, it is argued that his anti-immigrant ballot measures so alienated Latino voters that the California Republican Party lost tremendous voter support. Some have observed that national Republican leaders such as George W. Bush tried to distance themselves from Wilson's perceived anti-minority image, and instead were working to win back Latino voters to the

GOP. Governor Gray Davis's political fortunes were not helped by Proposition 21. In 2003, California voters decided to make him the first California Governor in state history to be recalled from his office. The close association of Davis and CCPOA was used by his opponents, especially the current Governor Arnold Schwarzenegger, as evidence of how Davis was beholden to the powerful interest groups such as the prison guards union.

REFERENCES

Berkeley Unified School District (2002). [Berkeley Unified School District Suspension Report, Spring 2001–2002] Unpublished raw data.

California Department of Education (2004). Retrieved October 13, 2004 from http://data1cde.ca.gov/dataquest/searchname

California Department of Justice, Criminal Justice Statistics Center (1994). [Juvenile arrests reported, age by specific offense] Unpublished raw data.

Ching, C. (2000, February 14). Lock up: Cracking down on California's youth. Why are big corporations backing the state's prison-industrial proposition? Retrieved October 13, 2004 from http://www.metroactive.com/papers/sonoma/02.17.00/proposition-0007.html

DiIulio, J. (1995). Arresting ideas: Tougher law enforcement is driving down urban crime. *Policy Review, (72),* 12–16.

Edwards, B. (Author). (2000, September 12). *Morning Edition* [Radio broadcast]. National Public Radio, Inc.

Ellis, V. (2000). The fall of Commissioner Chuck Quackenbush. *Los Angeles Times.* [Series of articles from March 26 through November 30.]

Hubner, J., & Wolfson, J. (1996). *Somebody else's children: The courts, the kids, and the struggle to save America's troubled families.* New York: Crown.

Krisberg, B. (2005). *Juvenile justice: Redeeming our children.* Thousand Oaks, CA: Sage.

Krisberg, B., & Temin, C. (2000). *NCCD focus: The plight of children whose parents are incarcerated.* Oakland, CA: National Council on Crime and Delinquency.

Murray, C. A., & Cox, L. (1979). *Beyond probation: Juvenile corrections and the chronic delinquent.* Beverly Hills, CA: Sage.

Ranulf, S. (1938). *Moral indignation and middle class psychology.* Copenhagen: Levin & Munksgaard.

Shrag, P. (2000, February 2). Prop. 21 tale of Wilson, ghost of politics past. *The Fresno Bee.*

Wilson, J. Q., & Herrnstein, R. J. (1985). *Crime and human nature.* New York: Simon and Schuster.

PART II

THE NEED FOR A SEPARATE SYSTEM OF JUSTICE FOR CHILDREN

The American juvenile court was created in 1899 in Chicago, Illinois, and Denver, Colorado. The new "children's court" built on more informal practices in several cities in which wayward youth were placed with volunteer probation officers in lieu of being sentenced to adult or juvenile corrections facilities. It was to become the model for handling delinquent youth throughout the world.

The National Council on Crime and Delinquency (NCCD) was intimately involved with the expansion and growth of the juvenile court. The NCCD developed standards for the qualifications and training of juvenile court judges and court staff. Through its surveys, the NCCD spread the movement to remove children from adult facilities and to create specialized youth programs. As noted earlier, various federal agencies called on the NCCD to help push the juvenile court movement forward. Not surprisingly, a significant amount of writing by NCCD board members and staff was devoted to defining the standards of juvenile justice.

In this chapter, we have included a selection of some of those essays and reports. The first essay by NCCD Board Chair and Harvard Law School Dean Roscoe Pound was written on the 50th anniversary of the children's court. In "The Juvenile Court in the Service of the State," Pound, who was America's foremost legal philosopher, comments on the progress made to date and the

road still to travel. He notes that the growth of criminology, psychology, and social work has greatly added to the sophistication of the methods employed by the juvenile court. He observes that the signal insight of the juvenile court is that the court must not "merely adjust or readjust the individual, but deal with the conditions which make for maladjustment for so many of his kind" (Pound, 1949, p. 23). This unique vision of preventive justice will, according to Professor Pound, be the lasting contribution of the juvenile court. He also notes that America is evolving into a "Service State" in which government is playing a larger role in the lives of ordinary people. The juvenile court is admonished not to try to overreach its expertise and to work collaboratively with other community institutions and agencies.

The next selection by Sherwood Norman expands on this theme of durable community partnerships on behalf of delinquent youth. Norman wrote and lobbied on behalf of the NCCD vision that communities needed to establish strong multi-agency networks to best serve youth. His publication on the Youth Service Bureau influenced policy makers and practitioners on the state and national levels. The NCCD was one of the very first groups that advocated for handling youth outside the court system when possible, especially those youngsters who were runaways, school truants, curfew violators, or beyond parental control. This NCCD view often created strains with some juvenile court judges, but Sherwood Norman's vision of the Youth Service Bureau stimulated a national movement to create options to divert youth from the formal justice system. Most recently, these ideas were reflected in efforts by many communities to create Community Assessment Centers that would provide services to youth in lieu of arrests and detention.

Orlando L. Martinez has been a board member of the NCCD for over a decade. He is a respected juvenile corrections leader who has accomplished major and progressive changes in Colorado, Puerto Rico, and Georgia. With his former research director in Colorado, Dr. Claus D. Tjaden, Orlando L. Martinez spells out the lessons learned by a practitioner on how to reform juvenile justice systems. His perspective illustrates the valuable interplay of the practical experience of system insiders with the NCCD's research and policy proposals.

This chapter also contains a summary of the investigation of the California Youth Authority conducted by Dr. Barry Krisberg. At the request of the California attorney general and the lawyers for incarcerated youth, Dr. Krisberg led a panel of experts that looked at virtually all aspects of the Youth Authority. What they found was shocking—a virtual collapse of the entire system. Dr. Krisberg documented incredible levels of institutional violence, excessive use of force, inappropriate use of solitary confinement, and "cages" unfit for zoo animals that were used for many youth as their classrooms. Especially appalling is that the California Youth Authority was once regarded as the best system for rehabilitating youthful offenders. It was the very essence of a separate justice system for troubled young people, but it has become a very bad prison system. This study became the basis of a consent decree to dramatically reform the system, and Dr. Krisberg was appointed by the court to help monitor those reforms.

6

THE JUVENILE COURT IN THE SERVICE STATE

Roscoe Pound

THE PATH OF PROGRESS

In fifty years there has been enormous advance in scientific preparation for social work and in the training of those who have to do with the treatment not merely of children but of adolescent and adult offenders. Only as one compares the books of today with those with which I began as a teacher of law in 1899 can he see how much more prepared those who are coming after us will be than were those who have gone before. Take the one matter of psychology. In the last two decades research in connection with juvenile delinquency has put us immeasurably in advance of where we were in the formative years of the juvenile court.

As it was in the beginning we saw only the individual child. We sought to do for the individual child what normal households had done in the everyday conduct of the family. Later we came to see that the delinquent child with whom the juvenile courts had to do was a product of conditions which had operated to bring about delinquency long before he came before the court and that we had a preventive no less or even more than a correctional task. We had not merely to adjust or readjust the individual but to deal with conditions which were making for

maladjustment of so many of his kind. In other words, the juvenile court was not enough. It had to be put in a setting of institutions doing more than salvage of individual children. But after this was perceived the difficulty was that we had hardly yet perfected the court for the purposes for which we had set it up. Too few of our courts, in the country as a whole, have even now the facilities and equipment for what we have demanded of them. In the last few years, however, more and more we are seeking to organize comprehensive prevention, not for the locality merely but for the state, and to bring all agencies and programs of prevention into effective relation. Here is a great administrative problem; one which deals not only with juvenile delinquency but with the whole area of social control in its relation to delinquency, and indeed, with the whole program of the welfare or service state. Many states in the present decade have been moving in this direction. But expense in the multiplication of demands upon public revenues, lack of experience of administration on such a scale, and a certain American instinct for non-cooperation have been in the way. Yet here is one of the most hopeful activities of the service state. If we are bringing up a generation equal to developing this movement as ours did the movement for the juvenile court, we shall have done much for a social control for urban industrial America even as the formative era from the American Revolution to the Civil War did for rural pioneer agricultural America.

Much in this new direction is experimental. Much will require education of the public. Much will require a great deal of research beyond what has been done even if along lines that have been definitely indicated. But the juvenile court in its inception was experimental. It required education of the legal profession and of the public. It has required and has brought about a great deal of productive research. We have only to compare the knowledge we have achieved through two generations of research with what we called criminology when I began to teach criminal law, in order to be assured that we are in the path of progress.

So much for the coming pathway. As to the going pathway, the way before us, for the most part in many states and to no little extent in all, we shall for a time be going forward from the first level of development, the correctional level, thinking only of the individual child after he has been brought to the attention of the court. Correction, to use the legal term, of the individual child is a highly important function. But this function can only be performed effectively as doing it is integrated in the whole process of social control in a modern society and works in harmony and cooperation with other agencies toward the same ends. Moreover, in the exercise of the immediate function itself there is a like and difficult task of integration. Our progress in the going pathway will depend much upon our appreciation of these tasks of integration.

Integration does not mean making a whole by merging each part in one of them which swallows up the rest. It means instead a weighing and balancing whereby each part is preserved while joining it in the whole so that each is given effect with the least impairment of any.

BALANCE

Radbruch, whom I regard as the outstanding writer on philosophy of law today, tells us that in the law we have to do with three ideas which are in irreducible contradiction in the sense that no one of them can be carried out to its full logical development consistently with a full logical development of the others or either of the others. These ideas are: (1) justice, the ideal relation among men, (2) morals, the ideal individual character, and (3) security both of the individual and of the social order. Let me illustrate. Criminal procedure is embarrassed by an internal conflict between quest of effective prosecution to maintain the general security and quest of protecting the individual against coerced confessions and unreasonable searches and seizures. When we think only in terms of the general security we may be tolerant of third-degree methods, may make no objection to the searching of person and house and seizure of papers which are employed so effectively in criminal investigation in France, and may not be offended by wire tapping. On the other hand, when we think only in terms of the ideal relation among men we repudiate the third degree and limit search and seizure by strict limitations in bills of rights rigidly enforced. When we think only in terms of morals we are likely to agree with Lord Coleridge that while barristers and judges are gentlemen the question of requiring a priest to testify to what is disclosed to him in the confessional can never arise, and to concur in the pronouncement of Mr. Justice Holmes as to wire tapping. Yet the exigencies of the general security have led a majority of the courts to deny privilege to disclosures in the confessional as a matter of common law, while half of the states have established the privilege by statute. So difficult is it to hold the three ideas in mind at one time and put and keep them in balance. In legal history there has been a continual movement back and forth between stress on the general security at the expense of the other two ideas, and stress on the ideal relation among men at the expense of the general security.

I have been speaking here in terms of the criminal law, and you will tell me that the juvenile court is not a criminal court but is administering an equity jurisdiction. I grant this freely and grant that this feature of the juvenile court is fundamental and is to be preserved sedulously. But both criminal court and juvenile court are parts of a regime of social control through a politically organized society. They should work in cooperation not so as to negate each other.

It is said that the fear of the Lord is the beginning of wisdom. Over and again the Bible tells us of the God-fearing man and commands us to fear God. But that does not mean the fear the slave has of the overseer or that the subject has of a tyrannical despot. It means the fear born of an overawing respect and such a fear of the law of the land is a powerful agency of social control. Our agencies of individualization, responding to the social interest in the individual life, should be kept in balance with this requirement of the social interest in the general security. This is something we must weigh carefully in extending by analogy the ideas and methods of the juvenile court to older offenders. Overemphasis on either side must be avoided. A balance conduces to the general security, as overemphasis on the general security may threaten it and in experience has resulted in impairing it by the reaction to the other extreme which it induces. So also overemphasis on the social interest in the individual life impairs the security of that interest by the reaction it induces.

All legal history shows the difficulty of maintaining this balance in showing a constant fluctuation between reliance on rule and justice administered in accordance with established norms on patterns of conduct and of decision, on the one hand, and reliance on discretion and unfettered judgment of judge or magistrate in molding his decision to the case in hand and the parties individually, on the other hand. The nineteenth century, following an era of personal government and of judicial discretion in the rise of the court of chancery, turned to rule and pushed discretion into a corner. The present century by a like reaction turns back again to discretion; and individualized justice according to the personal ideas of judge or administrative official for the time being is called socialized justice, as if social interests are only to be secured by wide judicial or administrative discretion. Because the nineteenth century overemphasized history, the fashion of thought of the moment tends to ignore history. Also the necessarily minute specialization of today divorces the history of law from study of the new agencies of social control. There are, however, signs that we must relearn much of what the law has had to learn in the past.

Indeed, the problem of balance is universal. To begin with, the individual needs the law to keep the two sides of his own nature in balance no less than to make adjustments of the desires and demands and activities of his neighbors to his own, and of his own to theirs. The word instinct has been so overworked and made to cover so many things that one hesitates to use it.

But using it to mean certain fundamental tendencies of human behavior, appearing in childhood and manifest throughout life, there are two groups of classes of these tendencies, one which may be called the aggressive or self-assertive instinct, the other which may be called the social instinct. In other words, man's nature is not a harmonious one except as he learns to bring about a working balance through training and the exigencies of life in society. The aggressive or self-assertive instinct leads him to think of his own demands and desires for himself alone and to seek to satisfy them at the expense of others and to overcome all resistance to them. Bringing up and education seek to bring about control of the tendencies involved in this instinct. But it is deep-seated and experience shows that it requires a backing of force. The exercise of that force, however, is something which in itself requires control, since the aggressive instinct of those who wield it may govern its application. Thus we get a problem of balance of force and of control of force which is at the root of an internal contradiction in criminal law and criminal procedure from which we have thus far found no escape and is in the background of most of the difficulties of government and of the legal order. This, however, is external to the man himself. Aggressive self-assertion even to the point of violence is potential in almost every one. It is excited in different men in different ways and different degrees, often spasmodically and contrary to the normal intention and mode of conduct and even in ways for which he finds it difficult to account. The significant point is that it runs counter to the social instinct of the individual and he usually repudiates it. But its potential existence and frequent manifestations require a reserve of force somewhere to keep it in control. The task of social control, and hence of the highly specialized form of social control which we call law, is to hold down this individual tendency to aggressive self-assertion to satisfy individual desires. That this is so we have abundant evidence whenever the reserve of force is withdrawn or suspended, as for example, in revolution or a police strike, or in some sudden great catastrophe—conflagration or flood or pestilence—when the coercive agencies of politically organized society are in abeyance and violence seems to break out spontaneously. I remember that a generation ago at the time of the police strike in Boston, respectable people who would not normally think of such things were seen to take goods from show windows on main streets and walk off with them.

PREVENTIVE JUSTICE

Delinquency is a product of imbalance of the two sides of the individual nature so that the instinct of aggressive self-assertion gets the upper hand. Preventive justice is directed to developing, maintaining and strengthening this balance. Modern methods of penal treatment are directed to restoring it. But in developing, maintaining and restoring this balance we must have an eye to the general security as well as to the individual life. Hence deterrent measures operating through punishment and fear of punishment cannot be left wholly out of account. Lack of inner balance and self-control which lead to delinquency is a problem not merely of juvenile delinquency but of all delinquency. Also it is a problem not merely of criminal law but of all law; and not of law merely but of all the agencies of social control.

Today we seek a way out from the difficulties of the criminal law and criminal procedure by developing preventive justice and preventive measures of social control. Equity had developed preventive remedies and in making the juvenile court to the model of equity those who set it up built wisely. The progress in preventive justice, not in the form of forcible interference in advance of delinquency, by police and agencies of detection and investigation, discovering planned offenses and thwarting their execution, but by treatment of the causes of imbalance and endeavoring to create or restore balance, has gone far in the present century.

When I came to the bar in 1890 there were no traffic rules for ordinary vehicles and no special traffic policemen as we know them now. Beyond a custom of turning to the right, everything was left to the judgment and the good sense of pedestrian and of driver. When one walked upon the street, on coming to a crossing he exercised his own judgment as to when and where and how he should cross. When a driver came to a crossing he also exercised his free judgment. Each made up his own mind for himself at the crisis of action. If injury resulted, the judgment he had formed for himself was scrutinized after the event by a tribunal which then told him

whether or not he had lived up to the legal standard. Today, on the other hand, lines down the middle of the road tell where to drive, lines upon the pavement tell where to cross the street, and other lines tell where to park cars. Also signals and signaling traffic officers tell when to cross the street and when to stop and await one's turn. This change is typical of what has happened in every sphere of activity. On every hand we now seek to handle concrete situations concretely at the time and when they arise instead of referring to abstract generalizations and handling them out of their setting of time and place. We seek to prevent rather than to repair after the event. We give, so far as we may, individualized treatment to the case in hand instead of generalized treatment to an abstract situation.

Nowadays also we conceive of the legal order, of the regime of adjusting relations and ordering conduct by systematic application of the force of a politically organized society, as only one part of social control. A significant characteristic of thought in the present generation is the breakdown of the water-tight-compartment theory of the social sciences. We no longer hold each self-sufficient. We no longer believe that we may give each a sufficient critique in terms of itself. We recognize that in the past century, while each was largely formative, each like Baron Munchausen, sought to pull itself out of a bog by its own long whiskers. Carrying out this unification of the social sciences there is special need of the fullest team play between law and social work. In order to bring about this team play, in order to make use of all that has been done and is being done for preventive justice by courts, by administrative agencies, and through social work, we need the same creative spirit and inventive activity which Americans and American lawyers displayed so abundantly in the formative era of our institutions. The needed team play has been growing up, largely in connection with the juvenile court. There is much more to do in many places in order to make it what it should be. But when I compare what I could say about preventive justice in my address on that subject before the National Conference of Social Work in 1923 with what I could say today were I to rewrite it, I can see that we have on the whole gone forward steadily and far.

Preventive justice as we knew it twenty-five years ago, the preventive justice administered by a court, while it makes an advance in our dealing with delinquency, is by no means the solvent of all our problems which we took it to be. We have to go deeper and find out how to deal effectively with things which cannot be reached by courts of any sort. In the first place, preventive justice such as courts can administer, even with the administrative machinery which we have learned to give them, does not always or wholly prevent. The studies of Professor and Mrs. Glueck have made us aware of this. Tribunals must still deal with a great mass of cases in which the preventive methods we have been able to set up have not achieved their ends. We must still deal with a great mass of cases where there are serious crimes before such preventive methods as we have are indicated. We must still deal with many cases which are not amenable to preventive methods; which at best only admit of what we have called correction, and probably only of deterrent correction if that can be made to deter. The adventurous type of boy who used to run off to sea, the adventurous youth who used to go abroad to fight in revolutions or foreign wars, is limited by the conditions of life today to conducting holdups and is not easily deterred by the best of machinery of police, criminal investigation, and penal treatment. We cannot wholly dispense with conviction and penal correction as deterrents if only as a means of holding down this type.

Secondly, our experience of preventive justice on the criminal side is recent and limited and we have still much to learn in order to give what we have devised a maximum of effectiveness. While it is yet in a large measure formative, we need to be careful not to impair the general security by zealous experimenting at the expense of demonstrated experience of penal legislation and administration. We need to bear in mind that preventive justice and penal and correctional measures after the event are parts of one system of social control. Neither is to claim our exclusive attention at the expense of the other. Neither should be a wholly separate self-sufficient system.

Proof may be seen in the phenomenon of which I have already spoken in another connection, namely, in what happens in oft repeated experience when the ordinary machinery of forcibly maintained order by governmental authority is for a time in abeyance in some emergency. In time of earthquake, fire, flood, or even riot it becomes necessary to call out the military when the instinct of aggressive self-assertion which is latent at least in each of us breaks over the limits established by bringing up, social custom, and the inner order of the groups and association which make up society; when even steady-going citizens are seen to need the restraint of the strong arm of the law backed by government. Let me repeat: In preventive justice we have to do with an agency of social control and so should view it in its place in social control as a whole, that is, in its relation to all other agencies and to how they all may be made to work without friction or waste toward the end or ends of social control.

COOPERATION OF SOCIAL CONTROL AGENCIES

Because of the difficulties just set forth a writer of an able paper on the legal character of juvenile delinquency has urged that the juvenile court should not attempt more than its original function and that in trying to be an agency of preventive justice as well as one of treatment of the individual before the court, the court is likely to fall down between two tasks. There is no doubt much to be said for this point. It is never wise to impair the doing well of whatever an institution has been set up to do and has learned to do well, by trying at the same time to do also something else which it has not been set up to do and has yet to learn how to do or even whether it can do it. I am looking at social control as an integrated whole and at the view of that whole as giving the end and spirit and guiding method to each of its agencies. The juvenile court should not impair its usefulness by seeking to do what it cannot well do. But it can make the most of its usefulness by the fullest realization of the task of prevention which confronts all institutions and agencies having to do with delinquency and the fullest exercise of its powers in cooperation with and by utilizing the help of those other institutions and agencies.

An eight-year-old child friend of mine, when I said to her that it was dangerous to climb up on the hand rail of an ocean liner from which she was apt to be thrown and injured if the boat pitched, told me sorrowfully that there were many so many things she couldn't do that she couldn't remember them all. There were things her father and mother would not let her do, and things her aunt would not let her do, and things her big sister would not let her do. And then, too, she said, I have to remember that there are things that God won't let me do. In the crowded world of today, in which individuals and groups and peoples are brought into so many and so close contacts with each other, in which so many reasonable desires and demands conflict or overlap, in which the opportunities for misunderstanding and misjudging each other are so numerous, we are all much in the position of the small girl. There are so many things we can't do if the world is to move smoothly. But because there has to be so much regulation of what we do or seek to do and because the measures of regulating and forbidding are so often not easy for the individual to recognize in a complex social order, it is the more needful that the agencies of social control be made to operate in effective and harmonious cooperation. If each is made or allowed to operate by itself without regard to what is done by the others or even some of the others, not only is the end of social control impaired but the working of those so operating is itself impaired if not thwarted.

Hence when I address bar associations I preach the need of understanding and cooperating with social workers, and when I address social workers I preach the need of understanding and cooperating with lawyers and courts. However, as I look back forty years to the time when I first became interested in the relation of social work to the law, it is gratifying to see how much progress has been made on both sides toward understanding and working with each other. Yet there is still much to be done, though more in some parts of the country than in others, to make the machinery of justice according to law and the machinery of individualized justice operate as one, without friction and without waste. In the social sciences we are all, whatever our special field, engaged in some part of a job of social engineering: a job of maintaining, furthering, and transmitting civilization—the development of human powers to their highest possibilities—with a minimum of friction and waste.

HISTORICAL DEVELOPMENT

In the nineteenth century, in reaction from the idea that law and morals were to be made identical which governed in the science of law in the seventeenth and eighteenth centuries, and consequent uncertainty of the law in action, in reaction also from the extreme of personal discretion which had obtained in the formative stage of English equity and the arbitrary conduct of common-law judges appointed for political purposes under the Stuarts, there was a quest for certainty at any cost and a rejection of judicial discretion, a seeking to make the administration of justice a matter of mechanical logical application of rigid rules attaching definite detailed consequences to definite detailed states of fact and making legal procedure overtechnical and rigidly mechanical. The results of this reaction made the law of the third quarter of the nineteenth century quite out of line with the needs of that time and created popular dissatisfaction with the administration of justice lasting well into the present century. We were for a time slow in ridding the law of the burden it accumulated in the course of that reaction. But the substantive law has taken it off and procedure has been modernized in the federal courts and is more and more becoming modernized in the states. While the process of emancipating law and legal procedure from the mechanical methods of the last century was going on slowly, administrative agencies, set up in continually increasing number to meet the exigencies of the rising service state, brought back for a time the unchecked personal discretion and arbitrary methods which had characterized the administrative tribunals of the Tudors and Stuarts. Personal justice rather than justice according to law became the fashion. Many who remember what legal procedure was two generations ago, or having read what it was then, have not learned of the overhauling that has been going on, and would prefer an out and out administrative agency instead of a court. It is significant in this connection that in continental Europe, where the Roman administrative tradition prevails, courts rather than administrative agencies have been set up for juvenile delinquency except in the Scandinavian countries. But in Sweden recently there has been a demand to substitute judicial for administrative tribunals as to all decisions involving deprivation of liberty. The example of totalitarian states has taught distrust of administrative agencies with power over individual liberty. The founders of the juvenile court did a lasting service by basing it upon the individualized justice of the court of chancery (the court of equity) in England. For two reasons I have preferred to say "individualized" rather than "socialized" justice. First, the justice administered in the juvenile court has the characteristic of the chancellor's justice in that it individualizes remedial treatment, dealing with each case as in great measure unique and yet does this on a basis of principle derived from experience or, one might say, experience developed by reason. Secondly, the law has always been directed to social ends. Today we are directing its application toward those ends by individualization whereas in the last century we sought to do so mechanically.

Thus the juvenile court has been and is a court with the tradition of the Anglo-American teaching of the supremacy of the law and respect for the liberty of the concrete human being and yet the flexible procedure which an individualized justice demands.

CONSERVATION OF JUDICIAL POWER

There are those who advocate a truly separate and independent local juvenile court with its own judges and its own probation department. But the specialization which is sought in this way may be achieved sufficiently by a well-organized branch of a general court, presided over by a specialist judge with its own probation officers, part however of the staff of the whole court, without the serious disadvantages which multiplication of independent separate courts, each with an independent administrative staff, brings in its train. A notion of dignity of specialized functions of administering justice has often led to establishment of separate independent courts. Perhaps the extreme example is a court for St. Louis created by statute in 1855. It had jurisdiction of everything in which real estate agents might be interested, and of nothing else. In eras of boom in town lots the real estate agent is a person of much consequence and the dignity of his calling required that he have a court of his own. Such tribunals are seldom long lived. On the basis of experience with separate independent courts of more or less concurrent jurisdiction, of which there has been much in England and in the United States, I deprecate separate juvenile courts and separate domestic relations courts instead of juvenile courts and domestic relations courts as branches in the ordinary courts of general jurisdiction with specialist judges and specialist staff. A modern organization of the judicial system calls for specialist judges rather than specialized courts. Specialist judges, exercising their powers in the way their special knowledge and special experience has taught them, with specialized equipment and specialist staff, may still be part of a court of general jurisdiction with more than one branch. Conservation of judicial power is a requisite of efficiency under the circumstances of the time. There are so many demands pressing upon our state governments for expenditure of money in the service state of today that so costly a mechanism as the system of courts cannot justify needless and expensive duplications and archaic business methods. The principle of a unified court cannot be insisted upon too strongly. Specialist judges in a unified court can devote themselves to their special function in a special branch. But if work in that branch falls off they may be utilized elsewhere where there is need of them, and if their work accumulates or they become ill or disabled, other judges of the court may be assigned to help out. This does away with problems of concurrent jurisdiction, clashes of jurisdiction, and technicality and expense of appeals. There ought to be as few appeals as possible from a juvenile court. They should be as few as possible both in the number of decisions appealed from and as to the questions reviewed. But we cannot allow one-judge tribunals without review. Habeas corpus as the only remedy is inadequate, and appeal with a new trial in a superior court and prospect of review of that trial in an appellate court is not merely expensive and time consuming, it is destructive of the purposes of a children's court and impairs the effectiveness of a domestic relations court. A hearing before a bench of three judges in the court of which the juvenile court is a branch can be as individualized as the exigencies of the juvenile delinquency jurisdiction demand, and if only a question of law is involved, can be as formal as a proper determination of a question of law demands. Where everything is done in one court questions of interim custody and the like will cause no delay and give rise to no conflicts.

BROAD VIEWPOINT NECESSARY

Fichte pointed out that in modern society each man is trained or has trained himself specially for some profession or vocation or walk of life, and as he has perfected himself for the purpose of that profession or vocation or walk of life, has tended to narrow his outlook upon the world and to look upon his fellowmen as it were through the spectacles of his calling. Looking at other callings through those spectacles he has tended to become suspicious, prejudiced, and intolerant of them. Hence Fichte urged an all-round training instead of the one-sided vocational development which he saw in the educational system of his time. The purpose, he said, must be an all-round development of men as men, not merely as fellows in a calling. It is indeed hard to be a specialist and at the same time the all-round man whom Fichte called for. On the other hand, the all-round man whose all-roundness is due to equally superficial development on every point is not what is called for. Rather our need is for specialists of sufficient knowledge of many other fields bearing on social control to make them aware of the problems in those other fields and of the necessity of adjusting their ideas to those problems as well as to their own.

Let me give an example of how a one-sided view from the standpoint of one specialty only may result in rules which have bad effects in other parts of the administration of justice. Wigmore has called attention to this in his monumental treatise on evidence. A feeling of the dignity of some of the old professions and the urge of newer callings to claim the dignity of professions and assert that dignity, has led in many states to legislative provisions for professional privilege as to testifying which are sometimes seriously embarrassing to ascertainment of the truth. You are familiar with provisions as to juvenile courts keeping no records. Here the question is not one of dignity but of protection of the delinquent child. But when later questions as to probation and parole arise as to an adult delinquent, it may not be the child that is protected but instead an adult criminal whose nature and record need to be known for the purposes of adequate individualized penal treatment.

One result of the narrow specialization in research which is inevitable in relatively formative social sciences in the complex social order and service state of today is the persistent fallacy of the single cause for particular ills or for the ills of society in general. Very likely the cause

which the specialist sees and investigates is truly a cause of ill. But it is usually not the only cause even of the ill investigated. Zeal to reach this cause which he sees in the light of his specialty leads to ignoring of other causes and to advocating measures which do not consist with those designed to meet other causes equally valid. What I would emphasize is the need that the different callings, which should cooperate in making individualized preventive justice effective, come completely to understand each other. When they fully understand each other will be time enough to criticize; and when they understand each other they are not likely to wish to criticize. As necessary co-workers in the task of social engineering I have described, these callings need to know and appreciate each other's accumulated experience, each other's problems born of their experience, and each other's methods devised to meet those problems.

RISE OF THE SERVICE STATE

Along with the demand for preventive justice, the rise of the service state known to the English-speaking world only in the present century, has greatly complicated the task of social control. From the relatively simple subject known to law and government in the past, it has become a many-sided one with effects upon every feature of what had seemed fundamental in the analytical and historical jurisprudence of the nineteenth century. A state which instead of maintaining the general security began to render to the people service of every sort, so that a French jurist writing at the time of the First World War could say that a railroad company, a banking company, an insurance company, an endowed school, and the state were equally public service companies, makes the law look very different from the way it looked when I was a law student. Also the great expansion of administration and setting up of bureaus with staffs of lawyers and physicians and experts of all kinds is having a marked effect upon the professions. When Blackstone wrote he could classify public law as a part of the private law of persons. Now a teacher of administrative law in England can tell us that public law is swallowing up private law. As we could think a generation ago, when the service state in America had comparatively little development, the juvenile court represented a service to children as wards of the state which had succeeded to the position of the English king as *parens patriae*. As the sphere of activity of the service state increased we could think of it as a necessary part of the oldest service which the state had been rendering, namely, that of adjudging the disputes, adjusting the conflicts of interests, and ordering the conduct of its citizens, without which the social group would dissolve. But that service instead of standing out as paramount, is now taking its place along with satisfying the material wants and meeting a multitude of other demands incident to life in an urban industrial society. In consequence, there is a growing tendency to rely on official rather than on individual private initiative and to commit all things to bureaus of politically organized society. Today the service state has become jealous of public service being performed by anyone else. What the effect of this may be upon social work I leave it to you to answer. All this is so out of line with the traditional mode of thought of the Anglo-American that it is difficult to guess what it may portend.

But of one thing I am sure. We shall not be changed radically over night. As Isaiah puts it, he that believeth shall not make haste.

HALF A CENTURY OF PROGRESS

If we are inclined to be impatient we may take heart from the progress made in half a century. I have been at the bar now for fifty-nine years— substantially two generations, counting thirty years as a generation. The well-educated lawyers who came to the bar in 1890 had had a college training primarily in Latin, Greek, and mathematics, with some modern languages, Mill's political economy, and some elementary science. In law school they were trained in the analytical and historical methods which had been worked out in the nineteenth century and have gradually given way

in the last forty years to social philosophy with sociological or realist methods. The lawyers of 1890 came mostly from apprentice training in law offices or from law schools conducted on the apprentice type. It is only since 1900 that the bulk of the profession has come from university law schools training college graduates.

How far all the callings which need to contribute to effective treatment of delinquency in its many phases can agree upon the ends of social control is a question not easy to answer. If we distinguish immediate ends from ultimate ends, the former will be seen in the light of the latter as we see them. No subject has been longer and more heatedly debated and is now more in dispute than the ultimate end or ends. The philosophers, whose special province is here, have been in disagreement since the Greek philosophers first raised it as a philosophical question, and philosophers, clergymen, economists, political scientists and jurists are disputing the matter both with each other and among themselves. But there is no need for social workers and lawyers to conduct a sit-down strike until the philosophers have, if they ever succeed in doing so, settled the exact goal. We have sufficiently practical problems for which we may devise practical methods by experience and prove them by practical use.

It took seventy-five years to make a common law for nineteenth-century America out of the English seventeenth-century and eighteenth-century land law and procedure in a time of political and social change after the American and the French revolutions. This has been regarded as a record of achievement in the history of law. When we consider the progress which has been made in developing a law for twentieth-century America out of what had been achieved in our formative era, the development in comparison will not seem slow. Progress at the same rate for another twenty-five years may well establish another record.

7

THE YOUTH SERVICE BUREAU

A Key to Delinquency Prevention

SHERWOOD NORMAN

The Juvenile Court is in the process of change. Recent Supreme Court decisions—*Kent, Gault,* and *Winship*—have explicitly stated that minors are entitled to the same constitutional protection as adults. Yet over half the cases referred to juvenile and family courts concern truancy, incorrigibility, waywardness, and other behavior that would not bring an adult to trial. Such behavior—as well as petty theft and other minor offenses—is often an indication that the youngster and his family need social services, not court processing. Furthermore, if community situations have contributed to his behavior, these should be changed.

It is imperative that states and communities take greater responsibility for providing effective out-of-court services for youth when their troubling behavior first comes to public attention. Some youngsters need no intervention beyond police warning or friendly counseling. Others need to be helped—without being stigmatized by involvement in the justice system—if they are to solve the problems that led to their misbehavior. They are not getting this kind of help, for a number of reasons.

For one thing, there are serious gaps in the availability of services. Established social agencies tend to reject children with behavior problems. Moreover, those young people most in need of help generally avoid seeking it unless they are encouraged to do so by someone in whom they and their peers have confidence.

In its report, *The Challenge of Crime in a Free Society,* the President's Commission on Law Enforcement and Administration of Justice suggested a promising approach to delinquency prevention—Youth Service Bureaus. These agencies would divert from the justice system (1) children who have not committed criminal acts but whose problems at home, in school, or in the community may lead them to do so if they do not receive help, and (2) minor offenders whose behavior is rooted in similar problems.

The Commission's report stated:

Communities should establish neighborhood youth-serving agencies—Youth Service Bureaus—located if possible in comprehensive neighborhood community centers and receiving juveniles (delinquent and nondelinquent) referred by the police, the juvenile court, parents, schools, and other sources. These agencies would act as central coordinators of all community services for young people and would also provide services lacking in the community or neighborhood, especially ones designed for less seriously delinquent juveniles.[1]

Because no nation-wide guidelines to the establishment of Youth Service Bureaus existed in December 1968, the National Council on

Crime and Delinquency sought and received a grant from the Pinkerton Foundation to publish such a guide. There were no precedents from which to develop the guidelines. We had to start from scratch. The process was complicated and time-consuming. In brief:

1. NCCD's Library and Information Center undertook a literature search relating to Youth Service Bureaus.

2. Letters were sent to the directors of state agencies for children in all fifty states— departments of welfare, youth authorities, state committees, and commissions for children and youth—announcing the study and seeking information about all Youth Service Bureaus known to them.

3. We selected a panel of fifty consultants to review drafts of the manuscript and suggest changes and additions.

4. We corresponded with all existing Youth Service Bureaus known to us to obtain information about their programs.

5. We visited ten Youth Service Bureaus throughout the country and, on the basis of an extensive questionnaire, interviewed their staffs. We also interviewed law enforcement, probation, and social agency personnel in each community we visited.

6. Meetings were held on Youth Service Bureaus at the 1969 National Institute on Crime and Delinquency and at the 1970 NICD, and at the 1969 National Conference of Social Work and at the 1970 NCSW. In addition, workshops were held in Chicago with the National Conference of Public Youth Agencies and in Washington with staff from nine federal agencies. We attended U.S. Department of Health, Education, and Welfare workshops on problems of state planning at Fordham University and New York University.

In 1969 the project staff found fewer than a dozen agencies directly or indirectly involved in delinquency prevention which (1) were strictly noncoercive, (2) were planned on a jurisdiction-wide basis, (3) were neighborhood-based, (4) received referrals from law-enforcing agencies, schools, and other sources, and (5) coordinated appropriate resources on behalf of the child and

followed through to see that he received the appropriate service. Only a few bureaus attempted to develop new resources, and only one focused its efforts on working cooperatively with other agencies to modify existing systems which contributed to the problems of young people.

Of course there were many prevention programs that met some of the above requirements but could not be considered Youth Service Bureaus in keeping with the total YSB concept formulated by the Crime Commission or the National Council on Crime and Delinquency.

In 1958, long before establishment of the President's Crime Commission, Youth Service Bureaus were established in Chicago and in Pontiac, Mich., to divert children of juvenile court age from the justice system. The Cooperating Services Centers in Chicago were set up under the Chicago Youth Commission as a centrally administered program with units in high-delinquency areas. They are now part of the city's Department of Human Resources. Unfortunately there was no objective evaluation of this $700,000-a-year operation as a delinquency prevention measure. Furthermore the offices of the CSC were housed with those of probation and parole personnel. Thus the noncoercive image of this program was confused.

The Oakland County (Michigan) Youth Assistance Program, a noncoercive, citizen-oriented program, is jointly sponsored by the juvenile court, local municipalities, and their public school districts. The agency includes citizen volunteers organized into a variety of committees. Like most of the early Youth Service Bureaus, it has not been objectively evaluated; however, it may not be mere coincidence that the county it serves (population of 800,000) has an extremely low state training-school commitment rate and a detention population that rarely exceeds forty children.

In Arlington, Mass., the stabbing of a young boy by a group of teenagers so aroused the town that a youth council of citizens and professionals was formed. This became the parent organization of a Youth Resources Department, sponsored and financed by the Town Meeting and in operation since 1964.

In Winston-Salem, N.C., a chief probation officer was fired for daring to use an ex-offender as a probation aide. Four other graduate trained probation officers resigned with him, and in a matter of weeks they secured funds from public and private sources to establish a YSB under the sponsorship of Wake Forest University. The bureau's focus was on developing resources and modifying systems which contributed to delinquent behavior rather than on the acceptance of direct referrals, although it is the agency's intention to include this function in the course of time.

In California the first Youth Service Bureaus were initiated in each of four counties by the county Delinquency Prevention Commission, which competed with twenty-four other local commissions for state funds by submitting a plan to the State Delinquency Prevention Commission. The $25,000 provided by the state for a coordinator and secretary for each program selected was supplemented by local contributions of agency personnel, equipment, office space, etc. These were the first Youth Service Bureaus to be initiated and funded by a state.

Because communities differ widely in population density, ethnic composition, and youth mores, appropriate means of reaching youth in one neighborhood or one part of the country may be quite inappropriate in another. Likewise, agency organization, citizen action, and government involvement will differ from city to city and from state to state, affecting the financial and administrative feasibility of any particular type of program.

Although experience and observation may offer clues to good preventive programs, research has yet to be developed to the point where certain types of organization, techniques, and programs can be positively identified as more effective than others. Therefore, maximum experimentation in the operation of Youth Service Bureaus and demonstration projects is to be encouraged, provided that evaluation by a reliable, well-qualified research organization is built into the operation from its inception.

The purpose of this book is to furnish basic principles and guidelines (not blueprints) for establishing and operating Youth Service Bureaus. They should be creatively adapted to local needs.

Purpose

The tremendous magnitude and complexity of any realistic solution to the problem of juvenile delinquency are seldom grasped by the layman or the professional. The layman tends to generalize about the problem in current clichés or scapegoat theories, and the professional, engrossed in the day-to-day demands of his job, often fails to see the problem in perspective or, seeing it, is seldom in a position to take broad-scale action.

Seldom do either professionals or laymen experience the justice system from the point of view of a child, and they probably know much less about practical delinquency prevention than the youngster who has gone through the entire process of arrest, detention, court adjudication, probation, and institutionalization.

Any effort to reduce delinquency and youth crime must concern itself with three general matters:

1. *The mores of our society and the specific culture or environment to which children are exposed.* These include the tensions of the times, the ways in which our stated ideals and beliefs— religious, educational, judicial, social, etc.—fail to jibe with established attitudes and practices, and their impact on the growing child.

2. *Voluntary services provided to alter the behavior of children when it conflicts with that which can be tolerated by their parents, school, and community.* These are the health, educational, and social services designed to correct disturbing behavior short of court referral. If these fail, the child may sooner or later be referred to the justice system.

3. *Authoritative measures applied to adjudicated delinquents by police, detention, the court, probation and institutions.* The failure of authoritative measures to correct problems underlying unlawful behavior produces a backlash of delinquency and crime which affects children susceptible to the delinquent subculture in the community.

The purpose of the Youth Service Bureau[2] is to divert children and youth from the juvenile justice system. It functions primarily in the second concern mentioned above; i.e., it makes services available to parents and children on the verge of trouble and in need of help. However, through its citizen-action arms, it reaches into the other two areas, thus providing a key to the three basic approaches to delinquency.

The Youth Service Bureau concept provides a foothold for public action. Its structure offers citizens, professionals, and youth an opportunity to join forces in solving problems underlying troublesome behavior *before* youngsters are labeled delinquent. This calls for an entirely different approach from that of authoritative intervention.

WHAT IS A YOUTH SERVICE BUREAU?

The Youth Service Bureau is a noncoercive, independent public[3] agency established to divert children and youth from the justice system by (1) mobilizing community resources to solve youth problems, (2) strengthening existing youth resources and developing new ones, and (3) promoting positive programs to remedy delinquency-breeding conditions.

The YSB should preferably be organized on a town-, city-, or county-wide basis with neighborhood-based branches in high-delinquency areas. It should be independent of other agencies and systems.

The YSB should make its services available to children seven to eighteen years old (a) who have been referred to the justice system but for whom the authoritative intervention of the court is not needed or (b) who have problems that might eventually bring them within the jurisdiction of the court. Although this is the primary target group, neither older nor younger children need be excluded.

The Youth Service Bureau is *not* a part of the justice system, although it may accept referrals from it. Its immediate goal is to keep children from becoming involved with the justice system. Its long-range goal is to reduce home, school, and community pressures to which children react with antisocial behavior.

WHY IS A YSB NEEDED?

In the early days of the juvenile court, few social agencies were available to handle the large number of problems relating to children. Consequently, in addition to offenses committed by children which would be defined as crimes if committed by adults, the juvenile court's jurisdiction covered a wide range of noncriminal behavior—e.g., truancy and "stubbornness"—for which a child could be adjudicated delinquent. This is still true of most juvenile court laws, which make no distinction between criminal and noncriminal offenses. Even in states that *do* make the distinction (New York, Ohio, and Oregon), children who have committed noncriminal offenses, although spared the "delinquent" label, are often treated no differently from the delinquent group. They may be detained in secure custody with older, more sophisticated youth or committed to institutions for delinquents, where they soon acquire a delinquent self-image.

Many of the children who come before the already overburdened courts require social services more than they require court processing. Some probation departments do attempt to render social services by counseling children informally or referring them to a social agency—if an appropriate agency is available—but it is not the function of a probation officer to follow up cases of children who have not been adjudicated, to coordinate services on their behalf, to keep an inventory of gaps in needed services, and to promote the establishment of such services.

While some youngsters may be deterred from further delinquency by the mere display of court authority, usually they are not the ones most in need of help. Furthermore, those most in need are usually the least motivated to seek that help even when they are referred to an appropriate resource. If we hope to steer young people away from the juvenile justice system, some means of doing so must be found outside the system by one of their peers or by an advocate of youth who can help them obtain, without coercion, the help they need *before their behavior reaches the point where judicial intervention becomes necessary.* Such an advocate must be someone in whom they have confidence.

For generations, individuals and agencies have been involved in delinquency prevention efforts. Some programs, such as family counseling or mental health services, attempt to resolve specific difficulties. Other programs offer educational and recreational activities to occupy mind, body, and spirit. However, traditional character-building organizations, whether religious, educational, or recreational, are oriented to adult standards and are regarded by many of today's youth as representative of the adult establishment's attempt to do things "for" them and thus to destroy their independence. In most communities the appeal of such services is primarily to middle-class youngsters and to low-income families who are the least likely to become involved in delinquent activities.

Many juvenile offenders, especially those from minority groups living in poverty pockets, are trapped in situations from which they cannot escape without help. The existing procedures for providing assistance are haphazard, since schools, social agencies, and police differ widely in philosophy, understanding of behavior, and approach. There is no single agency that (1) provides assistance to parents and troubled youngsters by coordinating community services on their behalf and mobilizing concerned citizens to correct delinquency-breeding conditions, (2) identifies and statistically records gaps in urgently needed youth services in order to promote their establishment and obtain the necessary local, state, and federal funds, and (3) coordinates the effort of community residents—professionals, private citizens, and youth—to change those attitudes and practices of established institutions that contribute, directly or indirectly, to delinquent behavior.

Many boys and girls referred to the police for truancy, incorrigibility, or minor infractions of the law are on the threshold of serious delinquency and crime. As things stand now, they (1) are warned and released or given "station adjustments" by police officers, (2) are referred to other agencies—sometimes inappropriately and without follow-up, (3) are placed in jail, a detention home, or a juvenile hall, often under appalling conditions, or (4) are referred to court without receiving community-based corrective services. Many youngsters who are picked up repeatedly are told, in effect, "Come back when you are more delinquent; we can do nothing for you now." When they do come back, they are either rejected or punished. As hundreds of juvenile court surveys have demonstrated, many of those who are declared delinquent by the court and most who are detained and sent to institutions should have received a variety of helping services in their own homes and in their own neighborhoods without having been branded delinquent.

For the *court*, the YSB provides a relief from many "nuisance cases" and a source of follow-up services for nonadjudicated children.

For *probation officers*, the YSB provides a reduction in time-consuming "informal adjustment" cases, which are more effectively worked with outside an authoritative framework.

For *police officers*, the YSB provides an alternative to detention and court referral when, in the officer's judgment, release with warning is insufficient but filing a petition is not imperative.

For the *public schools*, the YSB provides a link with the social work community so that truancy and other school behavior difficulties may be handled through cooperative problem-solving with other agencies.

For *citizen volunteers*, the YSB provides a chance to turn from frustration over juvenile deliquency to constructive efforts on behalf of youth and youth-serving agencies.

For *private social agencies*, the YSB provides an extension of youth services through citizen action.

For the *Welfare Department*, the YSB provides an advocate for troubled youth and support for protective services available to young children.

For *youth*, the YSB provides the listening ear of someone who can cut establishment "red tape" in an effort to solve their problems.

For the *community* as a whole, the YSB provides an opportunity to accept responsibility for assisting its troubled and troubling youth by coordinating services on their behalf rather than relying on court authority.

WHAT DOES IT DO?

The three interrelated functions of a Youth Service Bureau are as follows:

1. *Service Brokerage.* The Youth Service Bureau bridges the gap between available services and youth in need of them by referral and follow-up. It acts as an advocate of the child to see that he gets the service he needs, and it strives to avoid any suggestion of stigma so that those in need of assistance will not be reluctant to seek it. However, it does not intervene in the lives of children and their families if its services are not wanted. By receiving voluntary referrals and making referrals to other agencies, with the consent of the child or his parents, the YSB can free court intake departments and probation officers to deal with more serious offenders. It can prevent minor behavior problems from reaching serious proportions and can keep within the community the responsibility for—and the solution to—behavior problems. Furthermore, it avoids associating the minor

offender with sophisticated delinquent youth. All this is possible, however, only if law-enforcing agencies, parents, the general public, and youth itself have confidence in the quality of service delivered.

2. *Resource Development.* It is of little value merely to divert a youngster from the justice system unless the resources he requires to stay clear of it are identified and supplied. Therefore the Youth Service Bureau works with citizens in developing new resources where they are lacking. It also contracts for urgently needed services that would otherwise be unavailable. When such services cannot be purchased, the bureau encourages existing agencies to expand their programs or

develop specialized services for disadvantaged youth. The bureau works to strengthen these agencies rather than attempting itself to fill the gaps; it obtains data on gaps in youth services but passes the information on to whatever authority has responsibility for establishing priorities.

3. *Systems Modification.* There is little sense in helping a young person adjust to home, school, and community difficulties without also intervening to change the conditions that create them. Therefore the Youth Service Bureau seeks to modify, in established institutions, those attitudes and practices that discriminate against troublesome children and youth and thereby contribute to their antisocial behavior. It constructively

FIGURE 7.1   Service Brokerage and Resource Development

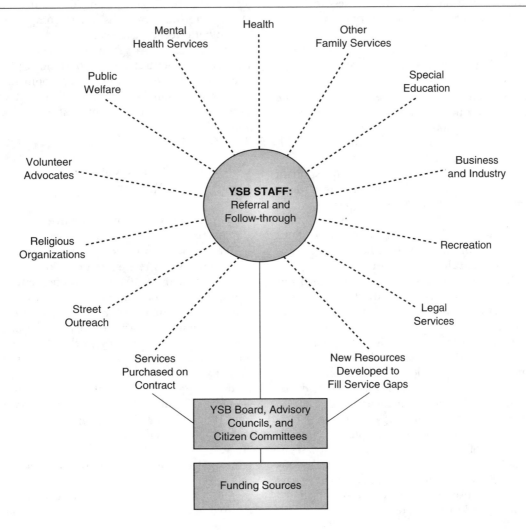

challenges public school and agency procedures that affect youth adversely, and it guides citizens and groups in fact finding and fact dissemination. It is the bureau's job to educate, to consult, to demonstrate, and to resort when necessary to political pressure to see that resources and institutions are responsive to needs.

There is no prototype for a Youth Service Bureau. Each community must determine which particular type of organization and emphasis can best divert its children from the juvenile justice system and reduce the possibility of future court involvement.

There is no reason why a bureau may not begin with one type of operation and shift its emphasis as the need to do so becomes evident. In any case, the eventual goal is to perform all three closely interrelated functions. An agency that focused exclusively on only one of them would be too limited in effectiveness to fit the NCCD definition of a Youth Service Bureau.

WHY ANOTHER AGENCY?

No one can doubt that preventive measures are needed to control delinquency and youth crime or that prevention is a community responsibility. But opinion differs on how this responsibility should be allocated.

One controversy concerns the question of jurisdiction. Many judges support the *parens patriae* concept, holding that the jurisdiction of the juvenile court should encompass all youngsters who are charged with minor infractions of the law or whose parents have lodged complaints of unruliness or incorrigibility.

If a juvenile who has committed a noncriminal or minor offense is adjudicated delinquent, he is placed in the same category as one who has committed a serious offense. Both the label of delinquent *and* the label of PINS (person in need of supervision) tend to destroy self-esteem and to cut the child off from constructive, nondelinquent peer relationships.[4] To avoid saddling a child with a delinquency record and to conserve the time and energy of probation officers for more serious cases, it would be better to settle out of court as many noncriminal cases as possible. Moreover, many Youth Service Bureaus have been successful in working with youngsters whose offenses would have been considered criminal had they been referred to court.

Wide gaps in youth services in most communities are partly the result of the inability of traditional agencies to reach alienated youth and partly the result of insufficient public knowledge about the special needs of acting-out youth. Some services exist somewhere in the community but not in the neighborhoods where they are most needed; some are not available anywhere in the community. Other services exist but are available only theoretically because of long waiting lists. There is no assurance that a child referred to a social agency by the court will actually get the help he needs.

The Youth Service Bureau is not itself a service agency so much as an agency for organizing the delivery of services to children and their families. Its uniqueness lies in its relationship to youth and to agencies serving youth. Although it may conduct demonstration projects and perform an information, counseling, and referral function, it is not in competition with other direct-service agencies.

In fact, one long-range aim of the YSB should be to achieve such a change in court intake practices and such coordination and development of youth resources in the community that whatever direct services it may have temporarily provided will no longer be needed.

OBJECTIONS TO THE CRIME COMMISSION'S REPORT

Many people have been confused by conflicting statements about the Youth Service Bureau in the Crime Commission's Report.[5] Most of the Commission's references to the bureau are consistent with NCCD's recommendations. However, it is not entirely clear whether the Commission would have the YSB (a) fill all the gaps in community services to youth through direct service or (b) simply work with citizens and planning agencies to see that the most urgently needed resources are created. The report stated that the Youth Service Bureau should be established to "provide and coordinate programs for young people."[6] Were this to be done, it would indeed become a bureaucracy, a monster direct-service agency whose basic purpose of diversion would be all but eclipsed.

Another issue is coercion. Once a child is referred to the Youth Service Bureau, he should not be subject to court action unless he subsequently commits an offense that warrants court referral by a law-enforcing agency or is referred to court (but *not* by the Youth Service Bureau) for judicial determination in a neglect petition. We would take issue with the Crime Commission, which appears to straddle the issue of whether the YSB should or should not be coercive. "It is essential," the Commission stated, "that acceptance of the Youth Services Bureau's services be voluntary; otherwise the dangers and disadvantages of coercive power would merely be transferred from the juvenile court to it. Nonetheless," it went on to say, "it may be necessary to vest the Youth Services Bureau with authority to refer to the court . . . those with whom it cannot deal effectively."[7]

We also find ourselves in disagreement with the Commission's statement that, "in accordance with its basically voluntary character, the Youth Services Bureau should be required to comply with the parent's request that a case be referred to juvenile court."[8] NCCD believes that the Youth Service Bureau should be an advocate of the child, even if the child's wishes differ from those of his parents. To do otherwise, or to refer to court upon the child's failure to cooperate, would be a clear indication to him that the YSB was not a voluntary agency but rather part of the justice system and therefore coercive. How long, then, would youngsters respect the relationship of confidence and trust fostered by the bureau as the cornerstone of all its activities and operations?

CONCLUSION

The successful operation of a Youth Service Bureau depends upon (a) the concern of the power structure and its willingness to invest sufficient funds on behalf of the troubled youth of the community; (b) the readiness of the social work community to join with the YSB in a cooperative effort to arrive at solutions to the problems of youth; (c) the availability of citizen leadership and of the volunteer services of both adults and youth, with youth taking an active role in decision making; (d) the willingness of the court and the police to cooperate with the bureau's objectives, particularly the diversion of

children from the juvenile justice system; and (e) the personality, creativity, and skill of the director and his staff in working with citizens, professionals, and youth in solving individual and community problems affecting youth.

How effective the Youth Service Bureau can be in the inner city is not yet known. Delinquency and youth crime have become a fact of life in the urban ghetto. Until the citizens of large metropolitan areas compel their governments to correct the social and economic conditions that produce overcrowded housing, massive unemployment, racial discrimination, and similar evils, the ghettos will continue to be cesspools of crime.

The Youth Service Bureau, then, is no panacea for delinquency. However, it does challenge citizens and government to break through the inflexibility of officialdom and open up new lines of communication by means of YSB boards, block associations, and other local groups. Even if at first only a few youngsters are diverted from the justice system by the YSB, it will be a worthwhile beginning.

NOTES

1. Presidents' Commission on Law Enforcement and Administration of Justice, *The Challenge of Crime in a Free Society* (Washington, DC: U.S. Government Printing Office, 1967), p. 83.

2. The name "Youth Service Bureau" was used by the President's Crime Commission and, because of its widespread adoption, has been retained in this book. The YSB is found in practice under several other names: Youth Resources Bureau, Youth Assistance Program, Listening Post, Focus on Youth, etc.

3. Under certain circumstances, pending acceptance of responsibility by government, a YSB may be operated by a private agency.

4. For a description of the effects of labeling, see Charles Mangel, "How to Make a Criminal Out of a Child," *Look*, June 29, 1974, pp. 49–53; Lisa Aversa Richette, *The Throwaway Children* (Philadelphia: Lippincott, 1969).

5. President's Commission on Law Enforcement and Administration of Justice, *The Challenge of Crime in a Free Society* (Washington, DC: U.S. Government Printing Office, 1967).

6. *Id.*, p. 69.

7. *Id.*, p. 83.

8. *Ibid.*

8

SAFETY AND WELFARE REVIEW OF THE CALIFORNIA YOUTH AUTHORITY

BARRY KRISBERG

BACKGROUND

This review was completed at the request of the California Attorney General (AG) and the Youth Authority (YA). Issues to be examined were cited in federal and state court lawsuits filed by the Prison Law Office (PLO). My charge was to answer a set of specific questions, and to make recommendations for improvements as needed.

To complete this study, I reviewed current and draft YA policies in each of these areas, as well as the entire manual for the Institutions and Camps Branch. Also examined were the content of YA training materials in the relevant areas. I reviewed statistical data provided by a broad range of YA staff. The effort to identify and assemble these data was greatly facilitated by staff members in the YA Central Office. Data were also provided by institutional staff at many YA institutions. Few of these data were readily available and required special data collection and analysis. In no instance was I denied access to any reports or documents, nor was I prevented from talking on a confidential basis with any staff or wards.

Besides file reviews and analysis of statistical data, I conducted intensive visits to the following YA institutions: the N.A. Chaderjian Youth Correctional Facility, the Heman G. Stark Youth Correctional Facility, the Fred C. Nelles

Youth Correctional Facility, the Preston Youth Correctional Facility, the El Paso de Robles Youth Correctional Facility, and the Ventura Youth Correctional Facility. These onsite visits were generally three days in duration. Over the course of the visit, I toured each institution and inspected all the restrictive housing units, as well as a cross section of regular living units.

Interviews with institutional staff usually involved individual one-hour sessions with the Superintendent, the Parole Agent III (PA III), the Chief of Security, the Ward's Rights Coordinator, the Risk Manager, the Chaplains, and other staff. I also attended regular scheduled meetings of the Use of Force Review Committees, Institutional Classification Committees, Special Management Program (SMP) Reviews, and the Suicide Prevention Committees. In the course of my facility tours, I had unlimited opportunities to talk with line staff, both Youth Correctional Counselors (YCCs) and Youth Correctional Officers (YCOs).

Most important, I was able to conduct completely private and confidential interviews with nearly 100 wards at the facilities that I visited. Wards were chosen at random across all living units, and represented different "phases" or behavioral ratings in each living unit. Wards, including those in SMP and Temporary Detention (TD) units, were brought to an interview room for these conversations. Usually ward interviews lasted 30–45 minutes. I told them that I was talking to them in connection with pending lawsuits filed by the PLO, and that my role was as a neutral fact-finder. I was neither an employee of the YA nor the PLO. They were free to participate in the interviews if they wished (only a few, very select wards declined to be interviewed). I took notes but assured the wards that they would not be directly quoted. I was looking for general patterns and not specific allegations. My intention was to keep their responses confidential, but I promised to report their concerns to the facility superintendents or Central Office staff if they wanted me to address specific issues. Many of the wards sought my help in getting answers to questions that they had on a wide range of issues. I made it clear that I would report circumstances in which I believed that they or other wards were in danger.

These ward interviews were conversational in style, covering their views on the specific topics of my review, but I also asked about how they were doing in school, what were their plans for the future, how their families were doing, as well as any concerns that they might have about visiting, mail, and telephone privileges. I always asked about their medical care. The interview also probed whether they felt safe in their current living unit. I would always end the interview with open-ended questions about "the hardest thing for you personally about being in the YA," and any "good or positive things that were happening because they were in YA." The wards were very open and candid in their comments. They usually thanked me profusely just for listening to them. Several of the wards showed me injuries that they claimed were the result of attacks by other wards or were the result of use of force by staff.

At the end of each site visit I conducted a one-hour debriefing with the institution's superintendent in the presence of staff from YA Central Office and, sometimes, staff from the AG's office. These meetings were intended to give some of my key observations, and to clarify areas of confusion. I wanted to have no surprises, and I wanted to let institutional staff correct any errors in my data collection or perceptions, as needed.

As to professional standards in the pertinent areas of my review, I examined YA policies, standards available from the United Nations, the Welfare and Institutions Code, the American Correctional Association, the Council of Juvenile Correctional Administrators, and the National Institute of Corrections. In some instances, I will be referring to standards that have been applied by federal courts to other youth correctional systems.

I. CLASSIFICATION

There is a growing professional consensus that effective classification systems are central to the safe and efficient operation of correctional systems. In the 1970s, the Federal Bureau of Prisons and the California Department of Corrections pioneered the use of objective classification systems to manage offender populations. Almost all prison systems and most large jail systems now employ objective criteria that are statistically associated with serious inmate misconduct to assign offenders to appropriate custody and security levels within these correctional systems. Correctional classification systems are designed to reduce threats to the public and to increase the safety of inmates and staff. Objective classification approaches can also be used to plan for new facilities. We have learned that large proportions of inmates can be housed in lower levels of custody without endangering inmate, staff, or public safety, resulting in substantial cost savings in operations and construction.

Formal systems of classification are less common in juvenile corrections. Most states have only one long-term juvenile correctional facility. Further, juvenile corrections systems have been more focused on assessing treatment needs rather than on custody and security concerns.

The Youth Authority invests a substantial amount of staff time and resources collecting detailed information about its wards, but these data are not organized into an effective system to guide either security or custody needs. Typically wards are given a very thorough assessment at one of the YA Reception Centers as they enter or reenter YA. Reception Center staff utilize data provided by the committing county, but also conduct an extensive series of medical, psychological, educational, and social case histories. The YA Reception Center also conducts detailed interviews with the wards to determine the nature and extent of their gang participation. The reports are very comprehensive, and potentially of great value in determining institutional placements and treatment planning. It is unclear, however, whether this excellent diagnostic and assessment effort is readily and routinely utilized by those YA staff who supervise the wards on a daily basis. It does not appear that the YA has developed a coherent strategy that integrates security and treatment concerns. Fear of violence, and especially of gang behavior, dominates the thinking of many staff in living units. Staff seem confused as to how to maintain the safety of staff and wards while still meeting the rehabilitative mission of YA. Without a clear and consistent correctional philosophy, and lacking a structured classification process, most decisions about wards are made on an ad hoc basis—with less than ideal results.

The YA does employ one security classification form that screens for those youths who can be safely placed in Camps or Forestry programs. This security risk classification identifies wards that might qualify for placement in a minimum security Camp setting. The criteria on this form have not been subject to a validation study, so nobody knows if this risk assessment effectively selects those wards that will function best in a Camp setting. This screening form is filled out on virtually all new YA admissions, but it is not used to make assignments to any YA institutions other than the Camps. A YA working group led by Sterling O'Ran has explored expanding this risk screening for making advisory decisions for institutional placements. This group did not arrive at a consensus for action, and YA still does not possess an organized risk classification process.

Reception Center staff make recommendations for institutional placements. Typically there are three placement options. These recommendations are prioritized by the Clinic staff, but sometimes only one placement option is given.

I looked at a random sample of approximately 20 files that had been processed by the Population Management Unit. This review included examining the case file, the Reception Center reports, and the scores on the Camp Screening tool. I could find little rhyme or reason to the recommendations for specific institutional placements. Recommendations were not based on the severity of the commitment offense or the ward's prior criminal history. Because many of the wards had been in the YA before, and were returning on parole revocations, it was common that prior disciplinary records were referenced in this placement report. The

allegation that a youth might be a sex offender was often decisive in making a placement determination. However, there were unclear guidelines as to what constituted sex offending behavior, which could run the gamut from aggressive sexual assaults or more passive sexual contacts, to masturbation. The ward's age was generally the most important factor, followed by alleged gang affiliations, and other geographic considerations such as keeping Southern California wards in Southern facilities, and others at Preston or Stockton. The Central classification process does not recommend the specific living unit to which the ward will be assigned. This determination is made at the institutional level and is typically staffed by the PA III.

In requesting transfers to more restrictive settings, the Institutional Classification Committee (ICC) reviews large and cumbersome files for each ward. These files are not well organized and are not user friendly. There are no summary sheets that concisely list the main risk and treatment factors. Often the ICC needs to puzzle over when and where certain events, such as attempted suicides, took place. This process is informal and is often influenced by an ICC member who reports that he knows something about the ward, or by the Gang Coordinator who may have pertinent information. Also discussed is the wards' behavior while they are temporarily housed at the Reception Center intake unit of the facility. It is common that the ICC asks the wards their suggestions on where they should be housed. Placement in special mental health units requires the concurrence of facility clinical staff, who make an initial living unit assignment and transfer the ward from the intake unit to a regular living unit. There appeared to be significant variability among institutions in how the ICC process was accomplished. The growing ward files are then sent to the units as the ward is assigned to a specific Youth Correctional Counselor (YCC). The living unit staff must wade through this small mountain of paper to develop their treatment plans. The PA IIIs conduct periodic audits of the YCC treatment plans to ensure that they are being completed and followed, but there is significant variation among individual institutions in terms of how carefully the treatment plans are monitored.

Wards are reviewed by the ICC at a maximum of every 120 days or when a transfer to another living unit or facility seems warranted. This reassessment process is also handled slightly differently at each facility, and the process is conducted in an informal manner. The ICC comes up with a preliminary recommendation that is usually presented by the ward's parole agent. Typically the ward is invited to these meetings and asked to give input into placement decisions. The ICC members sign a form that shows they agree or disagree with the group's decision. No formalized instruments addressing risks or treatment needs are employed as part of this process. The ward is asked to sign a form indicating that he or she understands the decisions, and that he or she has the right to appeal that decision to the institution's superintendent.

There is also an informal and traditional arrangement that allows superintendents to request the transfer of a ward who poses a danger to others or who is in acute danger from other wards. Usually this is accomplished via telephone conferences between the superintendents of the sending and receiving facilities. The Central Office Population Management Unit is informed once these agreements have been reached. There is generally no Central Office review of these or other assignments to living units unless a formal complaint is lodged by the ward. These complaints are generally in the form of letters to the Director of the YA, who in turn will send these matters to the Central Office for review.

Another major problem for classification is that, unlike the Department of Corrections, the YA does not rate its institutions by security or custody levels. With the exception of the Camps, all the other YA institutions are treated as if they are equivalent in security and custody levels. It is generally understood that Chad and HGS handle more difficult wards and thus operate with a higher concern on security issues when compared with Ventura or DeWitt Nelson and Preston. Nelles and El Paso de Robles are viewed as more security conscious than OH Close, but these understandings are not formalized in policy or practice. Whereas some mental health units have enriched clinical resources, presently the YA does not assign differing levels of staffing to living units based on custody and security risks posed by the wards assigned to those living units.

Most of the YA facilities possess a mix of single locked rooms, open dorms, and unlocked rooms in some of the dorm units. Due to the shrinking population of the YA, most of the rooms hold single wards, but there have been times in the recent past when many of these rooms were double-bunked. Even the single rooms are not necessarily appropriate for secure confinement. For example, at Ventura and some of the other living units, the rooms have electrical outlets, and wards are permitted to have televisions, radios, or other electrical devices in their rooms. The potential for these electrical outlets to facilitate suicide attempts, fire setting, and other security problems is significant. The YA employs an elaborate assessment approach that invests significant staff time and resources in knowing many aspects about the wards. Unfortunately, there is no effective system to ensure that these data are incorporated in day-to-day custody, treatment, and training decisions. While the YA seems to do a good job at monitoring the development and delivery of individual case plans, it is not at all clear that the process is grounded in the extensive casework that begins at the Reception Centers. More important, the detailed information on wards is not systematically utilized for assignments to living units or facilities. YA has become more focused on program assignments of wards to formalized drug treatment units, Intensive Treatment Programs, and Specialized Counseling Programs. It is still unclear how many wards that ought to be placed in these special programs are currently housed in other units.

Assessment data are not coherently translated or summarized for those staff who supervise the ward in current living units. Assessment data are not passed on to YA parole staff who prepare the youth for return home, or to those field staff who must supervise the ward on release.

Because the detailed Reception Center assessments are not routinely repeated, there are concerns expressed that these data are badly outdated for those youths who remain in the YA for substantial terms. Adolescence is a time of rapid change and development in a young person's psychosocial development, thus, the value of the excellent work at the Reception Centers is of diminished utility as time goes on. In particular, parole staff find these initial assessments of limited value, and perhaps misleading.

The current assessment process is not very helpful in making custody decisions, with the exception of dramatic psychiatric problems or immediate past histories of gang-related violence. While other juvenile correctional systems have been slow to embrace a custody-focused classification system, it is very common that prisons and jail systems across the nation have adopted the sort of objective classification approach advocated by the National Institute of Corrections (NIC). There is no inherent reason why custody classification would conflict with the primary mission of the YA—to provide high-quality treatment and educational services within a safe environment. Indeed, it is impossible to imagine how an effective rehabilitative program could be provided in unsafe and often chaotic living units. Custody classification creates a "platform" on which good treatment and education can take place.

Achieving an NIC model of classification for the YA is very desirable for short-term ward management and long-term institutional planning. This is a complex process that needs to have unequivocal support from top management, especially from the Central Office. There are many materials available from NIC that could be used by YA to move toward an objective classification process.

The YA should establish a high-level management group to implement an effective custody classification system. This group needs to come up with standardized criteria for categorizing each living unit in the YA according to different levels of security and custody. Most institutions will have various custody levels within the facility. Next, YA needs to develop a research-validated security classification instrument that can classify youths into differing levels of risk in terms of escape and serious institutional misconduct, especially assaults on staff and other wards. The YA should examine the current security of the ward's current housing assignment, as compared with the presumptive placement of the youth based on the validated risk instrument. This process will reveal the mismatch between actual security and custody needs and current YA resources and options. These data can be used to plan for additional facility renovation or replacement that is more in synch with ward security needs. Further, the YA should consider developing new staffing ratios that are tied directly to the security and custody needs of the wards under supervision. Further, the YA should implement a full set of policies and procedures that cover initial security classification and reclassification.

Some YA staff have expressed concerns that a focus on security and custody classification would undermine the traditional focus on treatment and rehabilitation. This is a "red herring."

Effective treatment and training cannot occur in environments that are perceived by staff and wards as unsafe. Moreover, it is entirely feasible to implement a system of treatment needs assessment that is appropriate for youths in every security classification. Juvenile correctional systems tend to break down when security and treatment considerations are not attended to with equal weight. Staff in such systems are given conflicting messages, and wards experience arbitrary and capricious decision making.

The changes outlined above will be difficult and potentially costly to implement. In the immediate term, the YA should consider a more moderate approach that systematically collects data on ward security and treatment needs and attempts to make placement decisions that are more aligned with the observed needs. Until staffing and physical plant deficiencies can be rectified, the YA could train its living unit staff on improved offender management techniques that have been demonstrated to reduce violence among high-risk inmates. One place to look is the Prison Management Classification system that was tested by the Washington DOC and evaluated by NCCD under a grant from the National Institute of Justice. The Washington approach showed reductions in serious institutional infractions in one prison in which staff were trained in improved inmate supervision techniques compared to another prison that housed very similar inmates. YA staff generally lack sufficient training in managing different types of offenders, and there are living units that clearly could benefit from increased levels of staffing. The preliminary results from the YA pilot project, in which the number of wards assigned to a living unit was decreased, and staffing ratios were increased, suggest that YA needs to explore a more complete implementation of this approach. An effective custody classification system would be the best way to actualize this new approach on a system-wide basis.

II. PHYSICAL SAFETY OF WARDS

It is abundantly clear from a range of data that I collected as part of this review, that the YA is a very dangerous place, and that neither staff nor wards feel safe in its facilities. One might easily conclude that an intense climate of fear permeates California's state youth corrections facilities. Although the YA Director has taken important steps to rectify this situation, the organization has a very long road to travel.

Virtually all of the chiefs of security (COS) at the institutions that I visited expressed concerns that these facilities possessed serious physical design issues that created security difficulties. Most YA facilities are 40 years old or older; even the newer living units were built over a generation ago. One chief of security told me, "These places were not designed to be safe." He pointed out myriads of "blind spots" in which assaults could take place without witness. I also saw buildings in which broken windows and other readily available materials could easily be fashioned into lethal weapons. Even though there were cameras installed in many of the living units, I observed that the on-duty staff did not know how to operate this equipment—get close-up views of individual rooms or even find the remote control needed to work the cameras. In-room cameras were often vandalized by the occupants, or covered with cloth towels, clothing, paper, human waste, or dirt. This is especially problematic when trying to monitor youth at high risk for suicide.

Electrical outlets are common in many YA single rooms (although not the newer units). These can be used to start fires or to self-inflict injuries. Permitted televisions, radios, and other electrical devices can easily be used to fashion weapons, or can become part of an underground bartering system.

The COS staff also complained about "dead spots" in fences that were supposed to be monitored via cameras or by alarms. No COS felt that they possessed adequate staffing to achieve a desired level of institutional security. While very proud of the professionalism of their staff, virtually all of the COS staff asked that more training be made available to staff, especially in the area of the use of force.

Some living units, such as the "270" units, have better security than the open dorms or older lock-up units, but COS and other staff repeatedly complained that there are serious design flaws even in the newer units. Often entryways to outdoor recreation areas create "blind spots," and the general disrepair of concrete floors, steps, and fences create potentially hazardous conditions for both wards and staff.

Because most of the YA institutions are so antiquated and in a general state of disrepair due to budgetary priorities, many of the units lacked safe and effective methods of feeding wards who were confined to their rooms. Staff complained about the risks of "gassing," in which wards throw an unknown and potentially toxic substance at staff that need to enter the rooms to deliver food or other materials. In the older living units, one could see a variety of staff attempts to reduce the risks of "gassing" via the use of duct tape, temporary fixes involving wooden or metal strips attached to the doors, and other non-standardized security methods. One wonders if these "patches" create additional health and safety issues for both the wards and the staff.

Perimeter security was a major issue at every facility that I visited. Some of the facilities once had security checkpoints as one entered the grounds, but these posts were abandoned to consolidate security staff within the institutions. At other facilities the visitor drives right into a parking lot near the front entrance. Once at the facility, the visitor goes through a sally port and must provide a valid ID to the security. Never once was I asked if I had any weapons with me, nor was my briefcase or computer searched by YA staff. I never passed through a metal detector of any type, nor was I asked to comply with policy and wear a protective vest. Put simply, I was subject to greater security screenings at airports as I flew to YA facilities than at the facilities themselves. Moreover, I wonder if other visitors, including volunteers, workmen, and vendors, are examined any more closely than I was.

Security practices vary widely across the facilities that I visited and seem unconnected to actual risk. For example, ward movements are rigidly controlled by staff at some institutions, but they are much more relaxed and informal at others. Practices relating to wards' personal items alternated between permissiveness and arbitrary raids. Although correctional agencies must have flexibility, patently inconsistent and ever changing policy and practice is not desirable.

The general YA approach to safety and security appeared to me to be primarily reactive in nature. The principal control device that was used by staff was lockdowns of whole units or institutions for indeterminate periods of time, or immediate transfer of certain wards to TD units. Stepped up security measures are often geared up to respond to the most recent problems.

Recently, the YA has instituted the staff position of Risk Managers, who are supposed to compile statistical data about the time and place of security problems, and to identify any patterns. The Risk Managers provide this information to institutional management staff, however, the degree to which these Risk Managers are funded (fully budgeted or just an additional job assignment for existing staff) varies across facilities. Generally, YA administrators seem to lack early warning data about potential problems that might be brewing before actual outbreaks occur. Typically, the gang coordinators are relied on to "take the temperature" of rival groups and to anticipate potential outbreaks of violence, but the YA has only recently invested in upgraded training and better Central Office support for the gang coordinators at the individual facilities.

Data on Ward Safety and the Use of Force

YA Director Jerry Harper has been instrumental in starting efforts to collect system-wide data on ward safety and the use of force. These efforts, while laudable, are still in the pilot phase, and there is considerable variability in reporting across the YA institutions, especially on the use of force. Greater attention is needed on increasing the consistency and quality of reporting in these crucial areas. The following limited data paint an alarming picture of violence issues in the YA.

Perhaps the most conservative estimate of violence in the YA comes from data on sustained disciplinary level B infractions. Not included are violent incidents that do not come to the attention of staff, or events in which a lesser violation is charged. This latter situation might occur when eyewitness accounts are absent or the evidence is contradictory.

This very conservative measure reveals a stunning amount of violence in the YA. In the six institutions that I visited, there were over 4,000 sustained Level B infractions for ward-on-ward assaults and battery—at least 10 such assaults every day—in 2002.

Besides the ward-on-ward assaults and batteries, there were nearly 1,000 incidents of sexual harassment, as well a number of sexual assaults by wards on other wards. Also in 2002, there were 84 Level B infractions for wards who committed assaults and batteries on staff with weapons or vile substances (referred to as *gassings*). These levels of ward-on-ward or ward-on-staff assaults are unprecedented in juvenile corrections in the nation. While there are no reliable data kept on disciplinary infractions in juvenile corrections across the states, many national corrections leaders were astounded by the apparent frequency of assaults in the YA.

As noted, each of the institutions uses different categories for reporting either violent incidents or the use of force, necessitating the review of these data for individual facilities. In addition, terms such as "necessitating security dispatch" or "unnecessary or excessive use of force" are only generally defined in YA policies. But the responses to the ward violence in question include the use of a pepper ball launcher, chemical restraints, physical restraints, and mechanical restraints. At times these responses have led to serious medical emergencies.

Other Data Sources

Letters that wards and their parents have written to the Ombudspersons or the Director of the Youth Authority further support the picture of frequent violence in the YA. I reviewed all the letters received by the Director for the first six months of 2003. Of the 136 letters written from wards or their parents at all YA institutions, 23 expressed concerns over physical safety, another 18 involved transfer requests, which often involved issues of ward safety, and 16 involved complaints about staff misconduct, especially verbal abuse. Ward complaints over safety issues and excessive force also appeared in grievances filed by the wards, although the Ward Grievance System does not have very high confidence among the confined youths and consequently yields questionable information. More common were complaints about everyday denials of requested services.

My confidential interviews with almost 100 wards and with several staff were consistent with the statistical data. Few youths feel that the YA is a safe place. Those who do, manage their personal safety either by keeping a very low profile or banding together for protection. Few wards felt that staff were responsible for the unsafe conditions. Most feel that "this is a jail, and it is filled with dangerous people." Many wards felt that the staff did what they could to provide safety, but that the YCCs and YCOs were generally unable to prevent the frequent violent attacks of wards on wards. In only a few cases did wards complain that individual staff knowingly placed wards in harm from other wards.

The primary staff response to curtailing institutional violence is the use of gang intelligence information, the frequent resort to lockdowns of living units, expansive use of temporary detention, the disciplinary system, and prosecuting wards in local juvenile and criminal court systems. Although there are treatment programs that cover anger management and avoiding gang involvement, there is little evidence that these programs are having any positive impact on institutional violence. The dominant YA response to ward violence is reactive and after-the-fact.

Preventive strategies are either nonexistent or very rudimentary. For example, I sat in on a number of meetings of the institutional use of force committees. The committee typically reviews statistical data on the number of incidents in the preceding several months. The general sense of the meetings was for staff to convince each other that either "things were getting better," or that no specific actions were required. There seemed a consensus that more prosecutions and harsher sanctions could help make the institutions safer. Many staff were concerned that Central Office edicts that limited the use of the SMPs or required shorter stays in these units were not promoting safety. I never observed institutional managers planning proactive efforts to reduce the level of violence at their facilities. The focus on reactive and punitive approaches to ward violence has necessarily led to more formality in the investigative process (to meet due process and equal protection concerns), and was consuming ever larger amounts of managers' time at both the institutional and Central Office levels.

Both wards and staff suggested that the most vulnerable youths were those with mental health problems, those labeled as homosexuals or as sex offenders, or wards who were attempting to disengage from their prior gang affiliations. Open dorms were viewed as the most dangerous housing assignments, although attacks sometimes occurred in the lockup units. Group fights or individual attacks also commonly occur in classrooms, vocational areas, and recreational areas, and periodically in the chapels.

Only Chad had a living unit devoted to wards who pledged to remain not involved in gang activities. Staff at Central Office and at almost all of the institutions talked about the possible need for a protective custody (PC) classification and specialized housing arrangements. While some YA staff expressed concerns that PC units created a different set of ward management issues, I was repeatedly told by superintendents and security staff that many wards attempted to achieve some measure of personal safety by getting placed in mental health units where there was somewhat

enriched staffing and single rooms. YA staff also reported that some number of wards in the lockup units try to get into these programs as a means of self-protection. Some wards build up a legacy of conflict with other wards, and see transfer to other institutions as their only option. Ironically, institutional staff and some wards reported that Central Office policies that are designed to better regulate entrance into mental health or restricted programs limited their ability to use these existing options to provide a measure of short-term safety.

A topic that came up in many of the ward interviews was the problem of wards designating other wards as "green lighted," "black lighted," or "rainbow lighted"—signals that encourage others to violently assault this ward. Green lights and black lights refer to attacks by Latino or African American wards. A rainbow light means that all the wards are encouraged to attack. The designation creates tremendous fears and reluctance to attend school or be placed in living units with open dorms. Lighting feeds into the intense climate of fear among the wards.

Staff readily acknowledge the existence of the "lights" system. Wards are lighted for being "snitches," for engaging in verbal abuse, or other perceived offenses. For some gangs, attacking a lighted ward is a point of honor among peers.

Use of Excessive Force by YA Staff

Suspicions that YA staff were engaging in the use of excessive force were found to be well grounded in a number of audits and investigations that were conducted by the Office of Inspector General (OIG). These reports documented the dangerous and potentially fatal use of high-powered weapons that delivered chemical agents. These chemical restraints were designed by their manufacturers to be used by correctional staff to quell riots in prison yards, but YA staff were using these same powerful chemical agents during extractions of wards from their rooms and other secure areas. Since these powerful chemical agents absorbed the oxygen in the small ward rooms, there are real dangers that YA inmates can be asphyxiated. The OIG also found instances of wards that had been severely burned because they were not permitted timely access to showers after being sprayed. At one facility, wards were made to spend long periods on their knees, in some cases on sharp surfaces, with their hands bound behind them in mechanical restraints. The staff called this "Gym TD." Other wards were made to strip down to their boxer shorts and were forced to sleep on cement slabs in very cold rooms. Some staff also struck the wards during these situations. Based on the OIG report and internal reporting, the YA launched a number of internal affairs investigations resulting in several early retirements and some transfers. Three cases were referred to the local District Attorney's Office. One case was successfully prosecuted.

As with other YA correctional issues, statistical data on the use of force are scant and not consistent across the facilities. Central Office staff review only a fraction of potential incidents involving force, and the primary responsibility for investigating these issues rests with the superintendents of each facility. There are no extensive reports that are available to assess the thoroughness and quality of these local investigations. Behavioral reports that are prepared by YA staff to accompany these serious incident reports are often very brief and not very helpful in understanding what transpired. At virtually all of the institutional use of force committee meetings there are concerns expressed about the thin content in the behavioral reports and the need to train YA staff to produce more in depth and detailed accounts of these incidents.

During confidential interviews with over 100 wards, I asked various questions about whether these youths had been physically or sexually abused by the staff. I asked about staff abuse in a variety of ways, and only after I had established a rapport with the ward and he or she was talking freely to me about their experiences in YA. There were only one or two instances in which wards related stories about the alleged abuse by staff. These wards would show me injuries that they attributed to staff physical abuse such as twisting mechanical restraints too tightly or allegedly throwing a ward against a wall. In these cases I worked with the assigned YA staff to further research these claims. They were unable to come up with any reports or records indicating whether excessive force was used. The attached behavioral reports that were forwarded to me about these youths were generally not very detailed, and it was unclear from the reports whether unusual force had, in fact, been used. In one case, the staff member had been investigated by the Central Office, but no staff disciplinary actions were taken as of this date.

Most of the wards did not feel that they had been personally subjected to excessive force, nor did they report being witness to others being physically harmed by staff. The wards told me that staff used force to stop fights. While they did not relish being sprayed by chemicals as part of staff activities, the vast majority of the wards felt that the staff were not attempting to use excessive force. Their attitude was that some wards provoked staff reactions by their own behavior and that the staff use of force was appropriate.

It should be noted that virtually all of the YA wards that I interviewed had spent time in county juvenile detention centers. It is fairly common that county staff use chemical and physical restraints in these institutions, so the YA wards may have perceived their treatment by YA staff as a continuation of the expected treatment of young inmates of California juvenile justice institutions. Further, many of these young people have endured long personal histories of violence directed at them by family members, gang peers, and other law enforcement personnel. It is quite possible that these young people find it difficult to gauge the level of physical abuse against them that actually crosses the line of acceptable adult behavior. I could not unequivocally conclude that isolated incidents of staff use of excessive force did not happen. But, my ward interviews suggested that such behavior was not widespread or systemic in the YA.

However, regarding verbal abuse, there were almost unanimous complaints. Wards say that YA staff make demeaning and angry comments to the YA wards on a daily and routine basis. One of the YA Ombudspersons reported to me that she received many complaints from wards about verbal abuse of staff and that the youths, and even their families, were the subject of routine disrespect by staff. This Ombudsperson observed that verbal abuse seemed to be "inherent in the staff culture," and she wondered why staff come to believe that their behavior was therapeutic.

The wards complained about demeaning comments that are clearly meant to make them feel they were worthless and without chance for rehabilitation. Wards told me that some staff routinely yelled in close proximately to their faces, attempting to elicit a physical response that could lead to disciplinary write-ups, the use of temporary detention, or the escalation to the use of chemical restraints. Some courts have held that this verbal harassment of inmates by staff constitutes a violation of their rights. Few correctional experts would defend these practices as beneficial in terms of the treatment process. Indeed, adapting the military boot camp model in juvenile correctional programs has proven to be ineffective. There is speculation that harsh verbal behavior by staff makes facilities more dangerous for staff and wards.

Many YA institutional managers criticized the use of verbal abuse by staff. They argued that the staff should not try to "act like wards," and that there was a clear need to maintain a standard of professionalism. There was a range of opinions among YA managers as to whether they could do very much to stop the verbal abuse. There had been some inquiries and investigations about individual staff, particularly as a result of grievances filed by wards. However, staff action grievances often took a long time to complete. Union agreements and other state personnel rules made it quite difficult to enforce sanctions against offending staff members.

The reported extensive use of verbal abuse by staff, and the dubious theory that this behavior could be a positive motivational tool, is reflective of the very limited amount of training that YA staff have received on ward management issues. Staff are asked to perform a difficult job, managing many youths with severe behavioral and mental health problems. Training and ongoing coaching on the most effective strategies of managing ward behavior by supervisors with their line staff appear to be quite limited.

Secure Area Extractions

Force is used by the YA primarily to stop ward-on-ward fights and to curtail group disturbances. However, force is also exercised to extract wards from secure areas, principally their rooms, which often entails significant risk of injury to both the staff and wards. A relatively new YA policy requires that all of these extractions be videotaped. As part of this review, I requested permission to view random samples of these videotapes. The YA complied with my request, and I was able to view 36 such videos. In addition to the specific tapes, I had the benefit of reviewing all of the behavioral reports written by staff in the wake of these secure area extractions. Not inconsequential is the apparent lack

of staff training in the use of the video equipment and the objectives of the taping. The accompanying behavioral reports that were submitted by staff were equally thin on details as to the reasons force needed to be used or the alternative conflict resolution approaches that were attempted. The written reports were generally focused on the amounts and timing of the use of various methods of restraint that were employed in the secure area extractions.

It was often quite difficult to understand the necessity to escalate to the use of secure extraction. Apparent reasons were: a ward refusing to come to the door of his room and submit to being handcuffed, a ward barricaded under a mattress, a ward that had placed a towel or paper over the door window, or a ward had created a disturbance by banging on the door or making excessive noise. The video would generally show the staff giving a curt warning that chemical restraints would be used if the ward did not comply with staff requests. The balance of the video would document the sequence in which force was escalated, including the use of pepper ball launchers and physical entrance by counselors. There was little evidence in the videos or in the accompanying files that the YCCs had reviewed or were briefed by mental health or medical staff on any pertinent issues that might be useful in responding to the situation.

In every case, the ward would ultimately submit to staff instructions, although the process could take well over one hour to complete. Typically these events occurred during the Third Watch and tied up almost all of the security personnel at the institution during that time period. Once the ward was placed in mechanical restraints, they were moved to a shower and permitted to wash off the chemical agents. Other YA staff washed down the ward's room to remove chemicals from the environment. The ward was usually seen by a medical technician who washed out his eyes and examined him for any injuries. In most cases the ward was then returned back to the original room. This often appeared to me to be a great deal of investment of staff time and effort to slightly pacify the ward. None of the videos showed the counselors utilizing the advice or support of clinical staff or other non-security personnel. I was repeatedly told that once the security staff were called, the counselors were supposed to back off. Ironically, the management of a very angry and upset ward is passed over to the staff that probably know the least about that individual's psychosocial background. It was likewise unclear from the YA records, whether there was any subsequent mental health intervention for their wards by YA staff.

There is no doubt that YA staff must aggressively intervene in situations in which ward safety is a major consideration. However, it is not clear that the secure area extractions are always warranted, or if some lower level of force, including attempting a sustained conversation with the ward, might not produce a better result with less risk to staff and wards. Although there are no national data on this topic, my strong impression is that secure area extraction conducted by security staff alone is a very rare practice in juvenile corrections across the nation. Even more troubling, the secure area extractions are often perceived by staff and wards as contests of will. The YA needs to take a comprehensive look at the occurrence of secure area extractions, including the policies and procedures that govern these events. Greater use of counseling resources or assistance from medical staff or chaplains might obviate the need for many of these situations in which large amounts of force or chemical restraints are employed against wards.

Monitoring the Use of Force

Top YA management has taken several steps to build more review and accountability about the use of force. But the YA seems to take a very long time to actually institute new policies. Management staff often cites extensive consultation with CCPOA representatives as a major hurdle to finalizing new policies or revising older ones. Further, the traditional organizational style of the YA is to delegate most of the details on implementation to the facility superintendents. This practice was justified due to the different types of wards that each institution was managing, but this highly decentralized model led to widely disparate practices. In the past, there was almost no Central Office oversight or monitoring on how each facility was interpreting basic YA policies. This traditional relationship between the Central Office and the facilities is starting to change, engendering a substantial amount of complaining at the facility about unnecessary Central Office paperwork requirements and general meddling into daily operational issues. As a result of this history, the

Central Office has tried to solicit input and ideas of facility-level staff, adopting a consensus-building model as part of the development of new policies.

The YA takes these allegations of excessive force very seriously, and requires a process that is very deliberate and cumbersome and takes a substantial time to complete. Given the very frequent incidents involving the use of force, especially chemical agents, it is obvious that current investigatory resources are stretched very thin. The small number of sustained adverse staff actions does not appear to provide very much accountability, except in the most severe cases. The YA must rely on the aggressive pursuit of its policies by the institutional superintendents to reduce the use of excessive force. These superintendents, in turn, must depend on their middle managers to convey the YA mission and culture, providing continuous reinforcement to line staff to do the right thing.

The YA suffers from a serious problem of violence in its institutions. This plays out in terms of large numbers of assaults of wards on wards, as well as a significant number of ward assaults on staff. Of equal importance, the climate of violence has engendered high levels of fear among wards and staff that affect virtually all aspects of daily operations. These tensions produce an extensive use of force, especially chemical agents. Further, the YA staff are mostly relying on a reactive response to the violence, involving the use of discipline and the resort to extensive use of restrictive programs and temporary lockdowns. YA policies in these areas are relatively new and are still being field-tested at the individual institutions. Training resources for line staff are limited, especially in the areas in which interim rules are being enacted. The absence of new training academies means that most frontline staff are receiving limited training, and supervisors and other middle managers are not being trained under these efforts. Training costs come out of the institutional budgets, requiring the superintendents to juggle expenditures to find budgetary resources for training. While greater Central Office oversight on critical incidents and the use of force is a very positive step forward, the levels of resources being devoted to this oversight by the Compliance Review Unit or through Internal Affairs are not yet sufficient to fully implement the goals of the Central Office.

Staff in the Central Office and at the various institutions claimed that levels of violence had gone down as the ward population was lowered. Living units hold fewer wards, especially when compared with the chronic crowding of just a few years ago. The YA has generally responded to the declining ward population by closing housing units, or proposing to close whole facilities. These plans are clearly driven by budgetary pressures, especially from the legislature.

There is some convincing evidence that lowering the size of living units and enriching staff resources can reduce violence in the YA and promote better rehabilitative outcomes. Impressive research that was conducted by the YA Research Division from the 1960s and 1970s showed that lowering the size of living units to no more than 50 wards substantially improved correctional management and advanced treatment goals. This research has been influential for the design of juvenile correctional facilities across the nation, and was important to establishing professional standards on the appropriate size of living units. Ironically, California policy makers chose to ignore the findings of their own research and attempted to operate living units that were too big.

Saving money was the rationale for the larger units, but this justification may have fueled the problems that now plague the YA. Staff overtaxed by the number of wards that they must manage have resorted to seemingly time-saving approaches that employ greater use of restraints and force. Many staff complain that they lack enough time to even talk to the wards on each shift, and were consequently unaware of the emotional state of the wards under their supervision. The staff freely admitted that daily interaction with wards was very important to creating safer environments. The YA needs to consider implementation of cost-effective methods to reduce the size of living units and to increase the level of positive interactions among the YCCs and the wards.

One very promising step in this proposed direction was the deployment of the Enhanced Casework Pilot Program. The Pilot Project reduced the living unit to less than 60 wards. It also incorporated the YCOs into many of the daily operation assignments, so that YCCs could be free to conduct more small and large group therapy sessions, provide more hours of individual contact with wards, and to devote more time to developing and monitoring individual case plans.

The early results of the Pilot Program were quite encouraging. The wards were involved in 4 times as many hours of treatment than previously. The wards are more involved in small groups, and they are getting more hours of individual counseling. Of equal importance, there were many more time credits for good behavior being awarded to the wards in these special units, and they were receiving fewer time adds for serious disciplinary infractions. Fewer wards in the Pilot Program units are placed in lockup.

Although not all of the Pilot Program sites have fully implemented the model, due to shifting staff or ward populations that have reduced the full effect of the program, the most stable and consistent Pilot Program sites have witnessed reductions in Level B infractions and other troublesome ward behavior. These units have seen a reduction in serious incidents and in the need for the use of force.

Staff in all the Pilot sites report that ward behavior has improved and that the milieu has improved. Levels of treatment services have increased, and they report that the wards seem to absorb more of the treatment curriculum. The YCCs have more time to complete their casework responsibilities because they are freed, by the presence of the YCOs, of some of their responsibilities. The staff report that they are getting to know the wards better, their files are better organized, and YA supervisors suggest that case work preparation has improved.

The use of YCOs to perform some of the living units duties was employed by the YA administration as a cost savings strategy for the Pilot Programs, rather than increasing the number of the YCC staff. At present it appears that the Pilot Program is not substantially more expensive to implement than the conventional model.

The early results of the Pilot Program, as well as past research conducted by the YA and other jurisdictions, suggest that the Pilot Program be expanded throughout the YA. A special task force should be immediately created to develop plans for an expansion of the Pilot Program concept. This planning group would estimate the needed startup costs and training requirements, draft a detailed program manual, and resolve other operational issues such as potential union concerns. Projected savings in terms of reducing the lengths of stay in YA facilities for those assigned to the Enhanced Casework program, as well as savings due to reduced need for disciplinary and other investigatory functions, would appear to make this effort very marketable to the legislature and the Governor's budget staff. Further, the Pilot Program represents a proactive strategy that could de-escalate the violence experienced by both wards and staff. The expanded Pilot Program should be evaluated by an independent research group that is very knowledgeable about juvenile corrections.

Also important to reducing violence in the YA is to upgrade and expand the training of staff at all levels. Current curriculum on the use of force is good, but is not delivered with the frequency and intensity that is required. The current curriculum is primarily aimed at getting greater staff compliance with the newest Central Office Use of Force policies and monitoring requirements. Staff need interpersonal skills to allow them to anticipate violent situations and to prevent them, guidance in working with very emotionally troubled, and often mentally ill, wards, creativity in building solutions to institutional challenges.

I heard about many new ideas that might be implemented at different sites. While this practice is desirable, it also means that there is a tremendous amount of flux in terms of suggested approaches, few with solid research support. The YA should commit to implementing a limited number of approaches to managing disruptive wards that are based on rigorous research and testing. These strategies need to be formalized in training materials, and integrated into the daily operations of each of the institutions. Ideally, approaches to preventing violent behavior by wards should involve teams of security staff, counselors, and health and mental health clinical personnel. Other YA staff including the teachers and the chaplains can be valuable resources in heading off violent confrontations and providing support and guidance to the frontline staff. There are juvenile correctional agencies that have been very successful in enlisting the support and assistance of their youthful inmates to increase the safety of facilities. One national leader in this "Normative Model" is the North American Family Institute in Danvers, MA, which runs juvenile correctional programs in several states.

Monitoring of serious incidents must also improve. The current use of force committees are meeting regularly, but the mandate and responsibilities of these groups are ambiguous. They must set very tangible goals for the reduction of ward violence and the use of force and develop plans to meet these goals. They would become responsible for achieving sustained measurable declines in institutional violence, rather than conducting after-the-fact assessments of institutional statistics. The YA should explore ways of providing incentives to line staff, supervisors, and managers who can de-escalate the violence in their living units and facilities.

The YA needs to substantially increase its budgetary commitment to ensuring compliance with new policies on the use of force, and other key policies. The current investigatory process is too limited and takes too long to complete to be the primary tool that the Central Office employs to implement its crucial policies.

At root, the Central Office needs to infuse a "new organizational culture" that does not accept the current levels of ward violence or staff use of force. Few YA institutions have witnessed the same level of breakdown of basic rules of how wards should be lawfully treated as this facility. The abuses that were uncovered by the OIG and the YA Internal Affairs Unit were abhorrent. While current leadership at El Paso de Robles has moved firmly to change practices, it was stunning to me to hear the prior investigations referred to as "The Witch Hunt." Many current middle managers felt that it was the staff at El Paso de Robles that were victims of overzealous investigators, not the wards who had been brutally treated by some staff.

More frequent visits by Central Office staff to each of the facilities are a must. These visits should last over several days and be focused on monitoring compliance with important policies. These site visits should also provide institutional staff a chance to offer their suggestions on how best to achieve organizational goals. Regular site visits should include confidential interviews with random samples of wards (similar to the interviews that I was able to conduct). Giving wards a clear way to raise issues of concern to them with Central Office staff sends a very important message to the wards and the staff. The Compliance Review Unit staff making these visits ought to be selected for their proven track records to be completely objective and professional. Instituting a very intensive schedule of routine facility visits could be a crucial step to building and strengthening the hold of a new YA organizational culture throughout the entire system.

III. Restrictive Programs

In response to a number of concerns expressed by wards, their families, and other complaints, the Office of the Inspector General conducted a series of reviews of YA lockup programs in 2002. There were very specific reports of abuses at the O and R living units at HGS that brought urgency to this OIG investigation. This initial review, which covered lockup units at Chad, El Paso de Robles, Preston and Nelles, found "a system of disciplinary detention fraught with identified and potential constitutional rights violations; and a mental health delivery system in complete disarray" (OIG, *Statewide Review of California Youth Authority Lockup Units*, June 28, 2000). The OIG review team concluded that many of the abuses stemmed from systemic problems and inadequate department policies and procedures.

As a follow-up to the initial OIG review, a subsequent investigation covered Temporary Detention (TD) programs in November of 2002. This review found that 10–12 percent of wards were confined to their rooms for 23 hours a day, with one hour outside their rooms under close supervision. During this one hour, the wards may be in wrist and leg shackles, or they are moved to small cage-like confinement areas known euphemistically as Special Program Areas (SPAs). The wards in lockup units receive their educational services and counseling in these cages.

It was very difficult to determine from YA data the precise reasons that wards were placed in these lockup units or how long they were confined there. The OIG found that institutional staff exercised broad discretion on placement and release from these 23 and 1 programs. There was little Central Office oversight into this process, and no clear data flowing into the Central Office on these restricted programs. Wards in restricted programs complained of a lack of legally required services—not getting their one hour outside the room, religious services, allotted phone calls, or visits from their treatment teams. The YA record keeping on the mandated services to wards in lockup was insufficient to either refute or validate the claims by the wards. The OIG review also found that many of the restricted housing units were in disrepair, with walls filled with graffiti, dirt and odors, poor lighting, and inadequate temperature controls. Wards in these units were kept dressed in underwear and lacked basic hygiene items and writing materials.

These alarming findings by the OIG have led to major restructuring of YA policies and procedures about restricted housing programs. Top YA leadership has placed a major emphasis on greater Central Office control over who enters these units and how long they are confined. Data on the wards in lockup are somewhat better. Serious attempts are being made to shorten lengths of stay in restricted housing units. There are increased efforts to train institutional staff on the importance of ensuring that the wards in lockup receive the legally mandated services and care to which they are entitled. The YA Director has been very clear in his communications that restrictive programs are not intended as punishment. In Jerry Harper's view "the courts send wards to the Youth Authority *as* punishment not *for* punishment." Harper also began the process of removing all wards with mental health issues out of the lockup units, and is attempting to close down the lockup units that are in the worst physical condition. All these efforts have met with opposition from some CCPOA members who accuse the Director of coddling offenders and somehow endangering their membership.

The Current Status of YA Restricted Programs

As part of the current review, I toured the lockup units at each of the facilities that I visited. Several of the wards with whom I conducted confidential interviews were current residents of lockup units. I also asked wards from other living units if they had spent time in a lockup unit and asked them questions about that experience.

In the aftermath of the OIG reports, the YA developed a very detailed set of policies governing the operation of restricted housing programs. There is far more Central Office oversight on lockup programs than in the recent past. YA manager Mark Blaser has worked very intensively with institutional staff to develop more uniformity in admissions criteria for lockup, and to reduce lengths of stay. The YA has instituted a new policy in which all wards assigned to restricted living units must be considered for transfer within 60 days of their assignment of units. A team consisting of Central Office staff and a multi-disciplinary team from the facility reviews each ward and either approves a three-day extension of the time in lockup, or develops a plan to move the youth to another program setting. The regularly scheduled visits of Central Office staff to each facility to conduct reviews of the status of every ward in a restricted housing program has introduced an important set of "checks and balances" into this process.

The data available to YA on the restricted housing programs are still less than ideal. For example, there are weekly snapshots of this population, but no efficient way to determine how many wards go through these programs in a given year, or how many wards are multiple admissions to these programs. Further, it is not easy to calculate the actual time that wards spend in lockup if they are first sent to Temporary Detention and then placed in Special Management Programs. YA can track current cases that are in lockup on court holds, but lacks accurate data on how long these youths stay in restricted programs until their court cases are finally resolved. Still it is clear that lengths of stay in lockup have declined. At the time of the OIG investigation, the expected stay in SMPs was over nine months. This extraordinarily long time in 23-hour-a-day lockup began to drop as the YA Central Office starting monitoring these cases more closely. Today, wards are generally housed in SMPs for 60 to 90 days. After 60 days, the institution must justify holding the ward for additional time. This added time must be subsequently reviewed every 30 days by teams that include institutional parole officers, treatment team supervisors, education staff, mental health personnel, and gang coordinators. The deliberations of this group are monitored and approved by Blaser and other assigned Central Office staff. The lockups are now viewed as short-term interventions requiring the team to formulate strategies to return the ward to more suitable housing units.

YA staff are also more focused on assessing the potential for suicide and other mental health issues of wards placed in lockup units. The YA has developed increased awareness that lockup units are unacceptable places to house wards with mental health problems. Director Jerry Harper has already ordered that all wards with mental health designations should be removed from the Tamarack SMP at Preston. The review teams led by Mark Blaser have moved aggressively to facilitate the timely transfer of wards with mental health issues out of lockup and into the mental health units. At Preston, the YA has opened a special program designed to manage mentally ill wards whose behavior is violent or extremely confrontational. The YA Central Office has clearly communicated its policy that lockups are not designed for mentally ill wards.

I attended several reviews of the current status of the residents of restricted programs. These reviews were quite comprehensive and allowed many YA staff to provide their suggestions. The process seemed to work best for youths who were identified as mental health cases. In these instances the mental health staff seemed to work effectively with the Central Office and other institutional staff to plan for transitions out of lockup into mental health units. This was more of a problem for facilities that lacked sufficient onsite mental health programs.

More difficult were the cases in which the ward's assaultive behavior seemed unlikely to change. Wards who had already hit their maximum confinement time and who were set to be released posed the most serious challenges for the review committee. Another issue was the reduced number of general population living units. As the YA has witnessed a greatly reduced ward population, the response has been to close down living units and to consolidate the remaining wards in fewer housing units. Although this might make sense from a budgetary standpoint, it means that institutions must balance the problems of violence and gang conflicts in fewer places. For example, if a ward in lockup was regularly involved in fights with rivals in their previous dormitory, sending that ward back to the same living unit might simply create a replay of the original confrontations. Further, grudges and perceived insults that evolved during ward stays in lockup could easily spill over to the regular living units.

The restricted program review committee struggled with these problems on an ad hoc basis. One sensed that the group felt that there were few real options and that the original behavior that got the ward into lockup might well continue. The major criteria that seemed to govern the review decisions (except in those cases in which mental health issues were clearly involved) were the degree to which the wards followed staff instructions and did not receive additional disciplinary charges while in the restricted program. There was little discussion about whether the ward's participation in the

SMP program had accomplished a reduction in the underlying problem behavior. YA staff often told me that the really dangerous gang youths were very adept at "staying low profile" while in lockup so that they could quickly return to regular housing units to pursue their gang activities or to retaliate with other wards. It was as likely that the emotionally troubled wards or the more immature ones would continue to defy staff instructions, provoking secure area extractions, and piling up more disciplinary problems. Some staff suggested that some wards were using the lockup units as self-protection from other wards, and they would violate rules and act out to try to remain in the restricted programs, or to convince YA staff to transfer them to other units.

Despite vastly improved YA processes to regulate how youths enter restricted programs, and to expedite their return to more appropriate housing units, the restricted programs are still very problematic. First and foremost, the lengths of stay in the lockup units are still much longer than those encountered in virtually any other juvenile correctional system in the nation. For most juvenile correctional systems, restricted programs rarely last more than a week. While 60–90-day programs are better than the 270–360-day stays in the past, the duration of lockup programs in YA poses a serious problem. YA has worked to reduce stays in the detention units; however, wards facing criminal prosecutions routinely spend many months in lockup units.

It is hard to imagine that 23-hour confinement over several months has any therapeutic value. Most psychologists and mental health professionals would argue that this severe isolation is antithetical to sound treatment practices. Since the invention of solitary confinement by the Philadelphia Quakers in the 18th century, we have learned that this approach produces hostility and illness, not health. The enforced isolation of troubled wards and minimal meaningful social interactions with YA staff can only plausibly lead to their psychological deterioration. The YA has no data suggesting that the use of lockup produces more than a very short-term response to various forms of prohibited behavior by wards. The ongoing levels of violence in the YA suggest that lockup is not effective to reduce this problem.

It is worth noting that the physical conditions of many of the lockup units remain deplorable. The programs that are housed in the "270" living units are a bit cleaner, but still lack needed program or counseling space. One positive sign was the closure of an SMP unit at Nelles that was filthy, vermin-infected, and subject to flooding in the rainy season. When I visited this unit, it was filled with litter and trash on the floors. Staff and management seemed unable or unwilling to maintain even basic conditions of sanitation. In response to the closing of this unit, CCPOA objected and some of its members alleged that action was coddling the wards. Another SMP unit at Preston has been repeatedly labeled as a "dungeon" by YA Director Jerry Harper. Other units are poorly lighted and have terrible ventilation. The cells are not well designed to monitor potentially suicidal wards, and the video equipment in the rooms is in disrepair. YA staff have often made room conditions worse by blocking off doors or openings in their attempts to stop gassings. It is worth noting that gassings of staff primarily occur in the lockup units. It is difficult as one tours the lockup units to reach any other conclusion than that these conditions of confinement are designed to punish their inhabitants.

I did not find deliberate efforts on the part of staff to deny access of wards in the restricted programs to religious services, visiting, or phone contacts. However, the operation of these units makes normal forms of contact with other staff and family members quite difficult. For example, Chaplains or treatment staff are often required to communicate with wards through the doors to their cells. Time outside of the cells almost always involved full mechanical restraints or time in the cages. Wards told me that they spent most of their day in lockup units sleeping or reading. They would often sleep through most of the daytime hours and be up all night. The noise levels and chaotic environment of the lockup units led to conditions of insomnia and other forms of sleep deprivation. Some of the wards told me that they began hearing voices and experiencing symptoms of other mental health problems. Most wards reported symptoms of severe depression, including suicidal ideation. The staff felt that some wards feigned suicidal potential as a way of getting transferred out of restricted programs to the mental health programs.

A major challenge for the restricted programs is the apparent lack of a clear and coherent treatment program that would transition wards back to regular housing units. It was difficult to determine if wards in these units received any additional treatment services compared to wards in general population units. Treatment in the YA often amounts to giving the wards "canned" workbooks that cover topics such as anger management, gang avoidance, or substance abuse. Wards in 23-hour-a-day lockup often used these workbooks to pass the time, but it is unclear how much real interaction that they get from the counseling or treatment staff. Further, it is difficult to determine if there are specialized and individual treatment plans that are implemented for youths in lockup programs. As noted above, at least one SMP unit at El Paso de Robles has instituted a particular ward education and management curriculum, but other restricted units appear to lack well-defined treatment objectives. Although behavior modification approaches were once very popular in the YA, these approaches seem to be mostly operationalized in terms of the Phase System. The Phase System is differentially applied at each institution, and mostly involves the giving or taking of daily privileges based on whether the wards get sustained disciplinary charges. The Phase System does not seem to focus on promoting the positive interpersonal skills and abilities that could help wards avoid future behavioral problems. Further, many of the wards in restricted units have ongoing disciplinary investigations that may well result in time adds. This means that successful stays in lockup may still result in subsequent punishments that are above and beyond the time spent in lockup. The wards that I interviewed often complained that time in restricted programs was "dead time" during which educational advancements or completion of ordered treatment plans ordered by the parole board was very difficult. Thus, a stay in lockup frequently meant a longer stay in YA.

Thus, it appears that the same ward misconduct could result in a criminal prosecution at one facility, whereas it might be handled through the disciplinary system at another. Criminal prosecutions are more common at HGS and Chad, because the wards at these facilities are almost always over 18. Further, wards at HGS and Chad have often received many time adds while at other facilities and have already been given their maximum confinement time. Thus, staff at these two deep-end YA facilities

feel as though discipline provides no practical deterrent effect for the wards.

Wards awaiting court trials are subject to very long stays in TD units. All the problems of lengthy stays in lockup are multiplied for these wards. First, one wonders if there is any evidence that the pursuit of criminal prosecutions is, in fact, an effective behavioral management tool for the YA. Some wards who receive prison terms actually return to HGS or Chad if they have remaining time left on their YA commitments. YA superintendents and other staff have expressed concerns that wards returning from CDC institutions can create even larger problems for the youth institutions to which they return. Some believe that these wards worsen the gang problems at HGS and Chad. Wards that are sent to CDC have the option to request that they serve their remaining YA terms in CDC facilities. Second, the variability in institutional practices to pursue criminal prosecution raises issues of equal protection of law. To my knowledge, there is no Central Office review or oversight of these decisions to pursue criminal prosecutions. It is unclear why some of these wards could be screened for their further potential for violence and returned to regular housing units, or mental health units as appropriate, while awaiting the resolution of their criminal charges. Finally, there is the question of whether these wards facing prosecutions should be housed in YA lockup units as opposed to the local county jails. In some instances, the conditions of confinement in local jails would not be as restrictive as in YA units. At best, this policy should receive a top-level management review.

The Cages

Wards in restricted programs usually receive their educational, counseling, and recreational services in cages that are referred to as Secure Program Areas (SPAs). A number of outsiders have raised grave concerns about the SPAs, including the Board of Corrections, which requested that the YA conduct a thorough review of the cages. In 2002, the YA formed a task force to look at the practice of utilizing the cages. Besides YA staff, Sue Burrell of the Youth Law Center was invited to attend these meetings.

The task force found that the cages were introduced in 1998 as a method of providing legally mandated educational services to wards in restricted programs (*Secure Program Areas: Report of Committee*, May 15, 2002). Before the cages, these wards received their educational materials and communicated with teachers through a food slot in their room doors. The YA task force found that less than 10 percent of the wards in TD or SMP units that used the cages were there due to assaults on staff. Some profile data suggested that these wards were similar in their criminal histories to other YA wards and that they were somewhat younger than other YA residents. Youths who were managed in the cages were disproportionately African American, Asian, or Latino compared to the general YA male population.

Staff expressed the need to use the cages for at least some of these wards. They pointed out that the residents of the restricted programs had been removed from other general population units and did pose a danger to others. The staff liked the cages because it made them feel safer. However, other staff recognized that the use of the cages could be dehumanizing. These staff feel that the SPAs made the institutions less safe because they did not allow for resolution of the underlying conflicts that would flare up again as the wards were released. Concern was expressed by staff that the cages actually cut down on the healthy communication that should be taking place among staff and wards.

The YA task force found that no other states were using the cages. The YA basically designed their own prototypes, since these units were not being manufactured for the corrections market. Some states provide education for youths in lockup by increasing staff supervision, others do not offer education for youths in lockup units despite clear legal requirements. The Youth Law Center has suggested that the cages pose several important constitutional problems, and that providing educational services in the cages did not meet federal or state statutory requirements. For example, wards in the cages received far fewer hours of schooling or special education services than are mandated by law.

There was general agreement that not all wards that were put in cages needed this level of security. There was a sense among the YA working group that the use of the cages should be reduced. A minority of the committee called for their complete elimination. In any event, it was agreed that the YA lacked an effective screening mechanism to decide which wards should be managed in the cages and that wards should be

moved out of them after a brief period of time. Even if the cages needed to be part of a continuum of responses to the potential dangers posed by youths in the lockup units, the SPA committee recommended that more specific policies and procedures be developed about their use. It was acknowledged that the cages were symptomatic of larger issues confronting the YA such as of the prevalence of institutional violence, the control of gang behavior, the lack of effective classification, and limited training of staff in offender management strategies.

When I conducted my site visits, some of the institutions were already attempting to reduce their reliance on cages. At HGS the superintendent was encouraging staff to reduce the use of the cages after 30 days; at Preston, some wards were receiving educational services in classrooms or in teachers' offices. Institutions are attempting to allow some joint programming among wards in the lockup units.

To the visitor, the cages seem to be in stark opposition to the mission and philosophy of the YA. Without minimizing the amount of violence that plagues the YA, it is difficult to see how the cages provide more than the illusion of safety. As one of the Chaplains explained to me about the use of the cages: "The YA has a serious problem with gangs, but their solution is demonic." It also seems clear that the YA could upgrade staff and ward safety through other, less degrading methods.

Although the courts have recognized the need for juvenile corrections agencies to operate very short-term lockup programs, none of these cases has approved 23-hour-a-day lockups for as long as they are used by the YA. There is a general professional consensus that solitary confinement is not a desirable correctional strategy for either adults or juveniles, except under emergency situations. I know of no other juvenile correctional systems that operate lockup programs that are in any way similar to those of the YA. Programs for very violent juvenile offenders are often designed to provide enriched counseling and treatment resources. Youths in other states are not locked in their rooms for all but one hour per day. No other state uses cages for education and treatment purposes.

Other sections of this report have suggested a number of methods by which the YA could attempt to stem the violence in its facilities. I have indicated that I consider that this climate of fear and violence is very real and very disturbing. However, there is no credible evidence that the lockup programs, as presently operated, contribute very much to a de-escalation of these problems. Indeed, there is reason to believe that the extensive use of lockup makes the violence worse.

YA has made significant strides in better Central Office oversight of the restricted programs. There is greater accountability in terms of who is placed in these programs and when youths can be returned to other housing units. Progress has been achieved, but many of the concerns expressed by the OIG are still present.

I would urge the YA to continue to phase out the lockup programs as currently operated. Many of these decrepit living units need to be closed immediately. YA should convene a task force, including top juvenile corrections professionals from other states, to redesign programs for violent wards. It is entirely possible that YA could institute programs for their most dangerous wards that are more consistent with the best research in "what works" and with its own mission of providing treatment and education. This new program model must be rooted in the fact that all of these wards will be released to the community in a relatively short period of time, and that effective institutional programs must be integrated with preparation for returning home.

Part of this review of restricted programs should be an examination of ways to further reduce ALOS in the TD units, and to reexamine the current policies and practices relating to wards being prosecuted for alleged offenses while they are in the YA.

The cages should be eliminated as quickly as possible. They are degrading and antithetical to the mission and goals of the YA. Staff need to be convinced that other more humane approaches can be equally safe, and more effective, in stemming future assaults on wards and staff. A key area for examination is the value of much smaller living units, with greatly enriched treatment and security staffing patterns. Staff training, especially in the management of disruptive wards, must be expanded and intensified. YA staff at all levels should be enlisted in efforts to reform and replace the current lockup programs.

The YA's progress in limiting the use of the restricted programs demonstrates that further moves in this direction are possible and beneficial. YA leadership needs to continue its strong message that the courts "send youths to YA *as* punishment, not *for* punishment." If this statement is true, then current lockup programs should be ended and replaced by more suitable correctional interventions as soon as this is practical.

9

CREATING EFFECTIVE JUVENILE JUSTICE SYSTEMS

Orlando L. Martinez

Claus D. Tjaden

If youth are our future why do we keep locking them up?

Don't we understand the high cost of rotten outcomes?

In spite of major investments in both policy and funding for services to delinquent youth and their families, these questions continue to challenge policy makers and juvenile justice professionals. The challenge is to change the "how" (administration and management) and "what" (intervention) methods to improve outcomes for young offenders and their families. This review presents the position that we must take the most significant lessons learned as a guide to better outcomes. It also illustrates that we must develop a leadership mind in creating effective juvenile justice systems.

SETTING THE RIGHT DIRECTION

The first challenge is setting the *right* direction. We must bring a balanced solution to the continuing struggle on what should be the purpose of the juvenile justice system—should it be on the one hand a strict father or on the other a nurturing parent? This debate keeps juvenile justice in a permanent "white water" condition (chaos—either because of laws or because of the added complexity of what works and what doesn't work). This is a critical decision point given that the effectiveness of a juvenile justice intervention is influenced by our philosophic orientations and the assumptions made about the best way of achieving this purpose. Corrado (1992) provides a useful framework for describing philosophic orientations regarding the treatment of juvenile offenders. This framework incorporates five models of juvenile justice: (1) Child Welfare, (2) Corporist, (3) Modified Justice, (4) Justice, and (5) Crime Control. Interestingly, all of these models emphasize the

Source: Reprinted with permission from Orlando L. Martinez.

promotion of individual responsibility through the use of punitive sanctions.

Secure confinement in institutional secure facilities is a common sanction used in all states in spite of which of the five models is selected. Characterizing the conditions in these secure institutions is very difficult because they vary so much across and within jurisdictions. It is important to point out, though, that incidences of serious overcrowding and of occasional physical and emotional abuse of inmates have often been recorded in juvenile custody facilities (Feld, 1977, 1999; Greenwood & Zimring, 1985). The Office of Juvenile Justice and Delinquency Prevention analyses indicate overcrowding in 45% of institutional facilities in 1995 (Snyder, Sickmund, & Poe-Yamagata, 1996). More than 70% of juveniles in custody were in facilities exceeding their design capacity. There is also evidence that the level of security in juvenile institutions has increased and in many cases they have come to closely resemble adult correctional facilities (Snyder & Sickmund, 1995).

Confinement in an institution is generally viewed as providing protection to society. In addition to the specific and general deterrent effects of the punishment, youths do not represent a threat as long as they are incarcerated. Even those favoring a child welfare and rehabilitation orientation will usually recognize that the institutionalization of young people is necessary under circumstances where they represent an immediate threat to themselves or others. However, it has been observed that significant numbers of youths in secure custody or detention do not, in fact, represent significant threats to the community.

The evidence clearly indicates that a majority of secure custody facilities for juveniles do not offer significant programming and are designed to confine the youth for the period of the sentence (Feld, 1999; Greenwood & Zimring, 1985). We know that some types of treatment delivered in institutional settings can be effective in reducing recidivism (see Lipsey & Wilson, 1998). On the other hand, the Office of Juvenile Justice and Delinquency Prevention study of juvenile facilities (Parent, et al., 1994) indicated that, while most facilities provide some schooling for the youth (required by law to do so), treatment and rehabilitation programming is not widely available, nor are psychological or psychiatric services.

The lessons we have learned must guide our decisions in setting the right direction. Recent reviews of the effectiveness of types of treatment programs generally indicate that select intervention with delinquent youths can be effective (see Altschuler, 1998; Krisberg & Howell, 1998; Mulvey et al., 1993; Palmer, 1994). These reviewers also converge on the conclusion that, in general, judicial sanctions involving measures such as incarceration or intensive supervision are less effective than treatment programming focusing on specific individual or family needs. Also, treatments delivered outside of correctional settings and institutions are somewhat more effective than those delivered in the institution.

How should an effective treatment approach look? Unless the criminogenic needs of the youth are addressed, one should not expect the sanction to have an impact. Research indicates that intervention with delinquent youths works best when the treatment is targeted to the needs of the individual youth (Dowden & Andrews, 1999; Hoge, 2001; Lipsey & Wilson, 1998). Of course, this mandates that each youth undergoes a thorough assessment process. Structured and focused treatments are more effective than less structured treatments like counseling. Likewise, behavioral programs that teach interpersonal and social skills are more effective. Multimodal approaches that address multiple needs are more effective than programs that focus on single needs. Finally, duration and intensity are important; longer and more intensive treatment contacts produce more positive results (Lipsey, 1992).

There is finally the question of the monetary costs associated with secure custody sanctions. Figures from the United States and Canada indicate that the costs of detaining a youth in secure custody range from $100.00 to $250.00 per day. This is far more than nearly any type of community-based intervention. Within most jurisdictions, custody costs are the single largest budget item.

LEADERSHIP FOR EFFECTIVE JUVENILE JUSTICE

A second challenge in creating an effective juvenile justice system is implementing the direction selected and making it work most often in a hostile environment. Experience tells us that success is about leadership and management. We need leaders who can effectively deal with the special needs of youth, evidence-based practices, litigation, shrinking budgets and at the same time begin rethinking how human organization can get better outcomes for youth while improving public safety. We need leaders who can balance personal and professional areas of life in the middle of constant crisis and pressures. Research conducted by The Gallup Organization suggests that the major challenge for leaders over the next twenty years will be the effective deployment of human assets and not about organizational development or work place design. It's about getting one more individual to be more productive, more focused, and more fulfilled then he was yesterday (Buckingham, 1999).

It is evident that we must work smarter (not only harder), differently (not only better), and in breakthrough ways (not only incrementally). It is also evident that we have failed to improve outcomes because the methods managers have used in the attempt to transform their organizations—total quality management, zero-based budgeting, right sizing, restructuring, cultural change, and various other methods—routinely fall short because they fail to alter organizational behavior.

There is a pragmatic and a philosophic definition of leadership. The pragmatic consists of what seems to work effectively in practice. Effectiveness is the key. Leadership requires establishing a direction, aligning people—communicating, motivating and inspiring, producing change (Koestenbaum, 2001).

The most effective leaders engage employees on a personal level and communicate the values of the program. They know how to engage people not only using facts and data, but also engaging people on a personal, emotional level. Their communication and leadership embodies the standards and values of the organization. These are the kind of leaders an organization needs, beginning with the senior offices. Effective leaders have learned to:

1. Be effective. Emphasize results, both through management by objectives and by process.

2. Understand that leadership is a mindset and a pattern of behaviors: it is to have made a habit of a new way of thinking and a new way of acting.

3. Lead by teaching leadership, by empowering, by fostering autonomy, providing direction, and lending support. A teacher is an experienced and relentless learner.

4. Have faith that leadership can be learned and that it can be taught.

Leaders must understand that an effective juvenile justice system must provide protection for the community and that some offenders require secure, locked treatment settings, while others can be supervised and treated in less secure programs. Objective decision making and classification must direct placement of youth to insure public safety and address the inappropriate incarceration of youth who can be effectively treated and supervised in less secure programs.

We have learned that an effective juvenile justice system must be a balanced system that provides a continuum of security and supervision levels and that provides treatment that is not only structured but that also is targeted to the needs (criminogenic) of the individual youth.

References

Altschuler, D. M. (1998). Intermediate sanctions and community treatment for serious and violent offenders. In R. Loeber & D.P Farrington (Ed.), *Serious and violent offenders: Risk factors and successful interventions* (pp. 367–385). Thousand Oaks, CA:Sage.

Buckingham, M. (1999). First, Break All The Rules : What The World's Greatest Managers Do Differently. New York : Simon & Schuster.

Corrado, R. R. (1992) Introduction. In R. R. Corrado, N. Bala, R. Linden, & M. Le Blanc (Eds) *Juvenile Justice in Canada: A theoretical and analytical assessment* (pp. 1–20) Toroto: Bitterworth.

Dowden, C., & Andrews, D. (1999). What works in young offender treatment: A meta-analysis. *FORUM on Corrections Research, 11*(2), 21–24.

Feld, B. C. (1977) *Neutralizing inmate violence: Juvenile offenders in institutions.* Cambridge, MA: Ballinger.

Feld, B. C. (1999) *Bad kids: Race and the transformation of the juvenile court.* New York: Oxford University Press.

Greenwood, P. W. & Zimring, F. (1985). *One more chance: The pursuit of promising intervention strategies for chronic juvenile offenders.* Santa Monica, CA: RAND.

Hoge, R. (2001). *The juvenile offender: Theory, research and applications.* Norwell, MA: Kluwer Plenum.

Koestenbaum, P. (2001). *Freedom and accountability at work : Applying philosophical insight to the real world.* San Francisco: Jossey-Bass/Pfeiffer.

Krisberg, B & Howell, J. C (1998). The impact of the juvenile justice system and prospects for graduated sanctions in a comprehensive strategy. In R. Loeber & D.P Farrington (Ed.), *Serious and violent offenders: Risk factors and successful interventions* (pp. 346–366). Thousand Oaks, CA: Sage.

Lipsey, M. (1992). Juvenile delinquency treatment: A meta-analytic inquiry into the variability of effects. In T. D. Cook, H. Cooper, D. S. Cordray,H. Hartmann, L.V. Hedges, R. J. Light, et al. (Eds.), *Meta-analysis for explanation: A casebook.* New York: Russell Sage.

Lipsey, M., & Wilson, D. (1998). Effective intervention for serious juvenile offenders: A synthesis of research. In R. Loeber & D. P. Farrington (Eds.), *Serious and violent juvenile offenders: Risk factors and successful interventions* (pp. 313–345). Thousand Oaks, CA: Sage.

Mulvey, E.P., Arthur, M.W,, & Reppucci, N. D., (1993) The prevention and treatment of juvenile delinquency: A review of research. *Clinical Psychological Review,* 13, 133–167.

Palmer, T. (1994). *A profile of correctional effectiveness and new directions for research.* Albany, NY: State University of New York Press

Parent, D. G., Lieter, V., Kennedy, S., Livens, L., Wentworth, D., & Wilcox, S. (1994). *Conditions of confinement: Juvenile detention and corrections facilities.* Washington, DC: Department of Justice, Office of Juvenile Justice and Delinquency Prevention.

Snyder, H. N., & Sickmund, M. (1995). *Juvenile offenders and victims: A focus on violence.* Washington, DC: Department of Justice, Office of Juvenile Justice and Delinquency Prevention.

Snyder, H. N., Sickmund, M., & Poe-Yamagata, E. (1996). *Juvenile offenders and victims: 1996 Update on violence.* Washington, DC: Department of Justice, Office of Juvenile Justice and Delinquency Prevention.

PART III

ALTERNATIVES TO MASS INCARCERATION

Central to the NCCD is the principle that there exist safe and more cost-effective alternatives to imprisonment for nondangerous offenders. Indeed, the history of the NCCD reveals a strong legacy of research, advocacy, and training of professionals in best practices for probation, parole, and other community-based sanctions. Tragically, the NCCD view has not prevailed in the political marketplace. The number of Americans who are in prisons and jails has surpassed 2 million. The U.S. imprisonment rate is well over 700 per 100,000 citizens—the highest in the world, exceeding the incarceration rates of Russia, China, and other nondemocratic regimes.

For many decades the U.S. prison population was relatively stable, but beginning in 1979 the nation witnessed a stunning and steady growth in incarceration. This rise in the confined population was not due to rising crime rates, as prison populations grew in times of rising and falling crime rates. The primary causes of the vast rise in incarceration were the war against drugs, which swept many minor offenders into prisons and jails, and far stiffer sentencing laws. In addition, decisions to parole offenders became the subject of political campaigns. Recall in 1988 when President George Bush's campaign used the furlough of Willie Horton as a symbol that Massachusetts Governor George Dukakis was too soft on crime. The same tactic was used to attempt to defeat Bill Clinton in the

1992 presidential election. Consequently, many elected officials are reluctant to take any actions that might be used against them in the next election. The political imperative to seem to be the "toughest" on crime is powerful.

This chapter opens with Milton G. Rector's concise explanation in 1975 of the NCCD policy position that nondangerous offenders should not be imprisoned. The NCCD under Rector's leadership went further to advocate for a complete moratorium on new prison construction until a thorough study of safe alternatives was completed. This essay sets out the enormous costs and meager results to be expected from expanded incarceration. Ironically, the financial figures presented by Rector seem modest compared to current correctional costs.

Former NCCD board chair and renowned correctional professional leader, Allen Breed, reflects on the relationship of public opinion to the expansion of "get tough" sentencing policies. He finds that the public is not as enamored as the politicians with expanding incarceration. The citizenry is far more open to the concept of rehabilitation—a view reflected in the most recent opinion polls (Krisberg & Marchionna, 2006). Breed notes that politicians and the media are drawn to the pro-incarceration position, in part, due to "pluralistic ignorance." They do not want to hold views different from the majority, but they misperceive the nature of that consensus. He also notes that the politicization of the crime debate and the collapse of true professional leadership have contributed to this situation. While acknowledging that research alone has not been effective in changing the crime policy debate, Allen Breed calls for a resurgence of public information and advocacy by professional organizations like the NCCD and the American Correctional Association. He also urges private foundations and civic groups to support these efforts.

In the 1980s, a curious argument emerged at the National Institute of Justice that resonated with the policy views of the Reagan and Bush administrations. It was argued that prisons were not too costly but actually saved money due to the impact on reducing crime rates. This argument did not result from a well-designed research study but from a cobbling together of a variety of statistics from several disparate sources. It should have been dismissed out of hand. However, the backing of several conservative think tanks and the explicit support of the U.S. Department of Justice gave it credence in policy circles. Moreover, the argument was quickly picked up by the popular media and given prominent attention by "scholarly" journals such as *Readers Digest*.

NCCD's Executive Vice President S. Christopher Baird wrote the definitive critique of the "prison pays" studies. His careful look at the arguments convinced several policy makers that this line of analysis had no merit. Over time, the "prison pays" view lost its credibility in all but the most conservative policy forums. Taking on the powerful U.S. Justice Department was not an economically wise choice for a nonprofit research organization such as the NCCD, but it reflected the commitment of the council to "speak truth to power."

A key method of reducing mass incarceration is the prudent exercise of parole decision making. In the 1970s, parole release processes were coming under attack by critics of the right and left. Liberals were concerned that parole boards made arbitrary and capricious decisions that often excessively penalized racial minorities; conservatives argued that parole authorities released dangerous felons too early. The NCCD provided invaluable research to guide this debate. Don M. Gottfredson and his colleagues developed an evidence-based parole decision-making process that was first adopted by the U.S. Parole Board and later became the basis of progressive reforms of the sentencing systems in Minnesota, Pennsylvania, and Washington. The concepts presented in this essay are still at the cutting edge of policy reform in many states.

The NCCD board greatly benefited from the humanity and wisdom of University of Chicago Law Professor and Dean, Norval Morris. In his comprehensive essay titled, "The Impediments to Penal Reform," Morris sets forth his vision for the possibilities of more enlightened penal sanctions. He is also candid about the real obstacles to reform. Consistent with the long tradition at the NCCD that valued research as a guide to progressive policies, Morris offers us the view that well-done and ethically sound empirical research can improve the sentencing and correctional systems.

REFERENCE

Krisberg, B., & Marchionna, S. (2006). Attitudes of US voters toward prisoner rehabilitation and reentry policies. *NCCD Focus*. Oakland, CA: National Council on Crime and Delinquency.

10

THE EXTRAVAGANCE OF IMPRISONMENT

MILTON G. RECTOR

Adoption of a policy of nonimprisonment of the nondangerous would signal a shift from a reactive to a proactive response to crime and would result in the re-allocation of vast sums presently earmarked for institutional construction. It requires legislative action.

Short of execution, imprisonment of the nondangerous (nonviolent, nonassaultive) offender is the most violent response government can make to crime. It is a waste of lives and of public funds.

The difference between the NCCD Council of Judges' Model Sentencing Act (1972) and the NCCD Board of Directors' policy statement on sentencing (1973) is clarified: the former allows for a prison commitment of up to five years for a "nondangerous" offender; the latter abrogates imprisonment for that category. The argument that a less punitive sanction (e.g., probation) is powerless unless the more punitive one (imprisonment) is a threatened possibility is rebutted.

A policy of nonimprisonment has traditionally been applied to certain favored groups of nondangerous offenders; the policy statement

recommends that it be applied, without social or economic or racial discrimination, to all who qualify as nondangerous. Some examples are given of imaginative and ingenious sentences that demonstrate the feasibility of not committing a nondangerous person to prison.

The NCCD Board of Directors' recommendation that nondangerous offenders not be imprisoned calls for a major change in public policy. Of the broad implications and consequences of this change, the most significant is the demise of the penal institution—the cage—as a primary means of enforcing the criminal law.

A nation founded on respect for individual liberty acknowledges that a civilized way to deal with crime excludes exile, excludes mutilation, excludes the death penalty.[1] The punishments of exile, mutilation, and death have been abolished because they are excessive; imprisonment of an offender who is not violently assaultive—not dangerous—should be abolished for the same reason.

Adoption of the recommended policy rests on legislative initiative and enactment. It requires leadership and courage, qualities not conspicuously displayed by many judges and criminal justice officials, who, under present sentencing and correctional statutes, possess but fail to exercise the broad discretion that could sharply reduce the use of imprisonment. These judges, and other public officials who influence prison policy, tend to be opinion-followers, not opinion-leaders. They have endorsed proposals at all levels of government to rebuild and expand prisons and jails and have been singularly unreceptive to efforts to reduce unnecessary institutional commitments. In light of the huge cost and the glaring ineffectiveness of prisons and jails, their supine acceptance of a policy of proven waste borders on irresponsibility. They will change their ways only when legislative debate on the extravagance of imprisonment is so loud and clear that there will be no doubt about the need for change in sentencing and correctional practices.

Legislative prohibition of imprisonment of nondangerous offenders will signal a basic shift to a proactive policy, a basic shift away from the almost totally reactive policy that now determines how government responds to crime. Law enforcement, courts, and correction are part of a reactive system. Their principal contribution to a proactive effort to reduce crime is thought to be deterrence, which, according to present evidence, correlates most highly with the certainty and speed of response by each part of the criminal justice system.[2] Individually and collectively, police, courts, and correction cannot reduce crime and violence in our society. The expectation that they can and should do so unquestionably does much to reduce the proactive planning and financing of other programs and strategies that could reduce crime. A public policy change in correction that would release 80 to 90 percent of those now in prison would transfer hundreds of millions of correction's construction dollars to criminal justice operating funds for alternative programs and strategies and for other social service systems.[3]

OFFICIAL CONTRIBUTION TO VIOLENCE

Government cannot give leadership to any effort to reduce violence unless it first reduces violence in its own house by adopting a policy of nonimprisonment of the nondangerous. Short of killing the offender, imprisoning him is the most violent response a government can make to crime. Despite the great cost of imprisonment and the high ratio of staff to inmate population, government has proved itself incapable of reducing violence within its prisons or of protecting those it imprisons from severe physical and psychological damage. Its rehabilitation and vocational training programs, which are supposed to return the prisoner to his home and his community better motivated and better equipped to avoid crime, have demonstrated no capacity to protect the public or to overcome the disabling effects of incarceration, despite a well-financed governmental career service for the operation of prison systems. Government itself maintains and operates a slave-labor system in which the prisoner is exploited for the production of government-purchased goods; government itself is responsible for the exclusion of the ex-prisoner from a great number of legitimate fields of employment; government itself is responsible for the civil disabilities that set the ex-prisoner apart from the rest of the population.

If a policy of nonimprisonment of the nondangerous is not adopted, the backlash of frustration over the failure of imprisonment may produce even worse results than we have already had. The inability of imprisonment thus far to improve the prisoner by a regime of "just deserts" stimulates some prison authorities to propose more of the same—despite centuries of the expensive and well-documented failure of "just deserts" penology. Others would want to retain the current large prison population (consisting mostly of persons who are not dangerous and do not have to be confined) from which they could select persistently violent offenders for experimentation in special "behavior modification" programs and to which they could return those who choose not to "volunteer" for the treatment.[4] Before wasting more lives and public funds in new cages for the persistently violent and dangerous offender, we should direct our ingenuity and resources to the elimination of imprisonment for the nondangerous. We would then have a huge surplus of uncrowded cages to be rebuilt and refurbished for our efforts to control and change the dangerous.

MODEL SENTENCING ACT

The Model Sentencing Act, originally published in 1963 by NCCD's Council of Judges an revised in 1972, is a unique and creative document drafted by a unique and creative group of judges concerned with the need to identify the dangerous criminal who requires imprisonment. They did not pretend they had fathomed the complexities of human behavior nor did they lay a claim to scientific knowledge that could predict with accuracy the propensity of the individual for committing future crimes. They did know that judges commit far too many nondangerous offenders to jail and prison for excessively long terms and that this dispositional pattern imposes a heavy financial burden on the taxpayer. They also knew that judges are no less opinionated and prejudiced than other people and no less likely than other officials in the criminal justice system to be capricious in use of their discretion. They were aware of a prevalence of sentences which, asserting unwavering allegiance to justice, were unintelligent and irresponsible. They sensed that it was time to compose a definition of dangerousness because judges—the conscientious as well as the indifferent—had no sentencing guidelines to help them distinguish between the "ordinary" offender and the one who is dangerous and likely to repeat his violent crime.

We decided that the criteria for a determination of "dangerousness" should be defined by statute to help reduce to a minimum the disparities and inequities of sentencing. The Model Act provides for judicial discretion in fixing a maximum sentence within a statutory maximum of thirty years for dangerous offenders and five years for those who do not meet the criteria for dangerousness. It does not make prison commitment obligatory for either group, thus avoiding the injustices of mandatory sentences. It eliminates "habitual offender" sentencing, indeterminate sentences, and the death penalty.

After a decade the influence of the MSA principles was seen in the Standards for Criminal Justice of the American Bar Association and the sentencing standards recommended by the National Advisory Commission on Criminal Justice Standards and Goals. Thus far however, Oregon is the only state that has adopted the Model Sentencing Act (in slightly modified form—1971, ch. 743). Not enough time has elapsed since the new Oregon act went into effect to permit a conclusive statement on the results, but prison officials there have informed me that since 1973 the courts have reduced prison

commitments from 36 percent of total convictions to about 19 percent and that the use of suspended sentences has increased from 7 percent of total convictions to 14 percent. In the first year of operation under the act, median time served dropped from two years to sixteen months. No prosecutor or judge has criticized elimination of the mandatory life sentence for habitual offenders.

The debate has been started and the NCCD Model Sentencing Act criteria for dangerousness are under attack. This is as it should be. Public debate and a better-informed public will bring a demand for anticrime policies and strategies based on research and rational assessment rather than clichés, platitudes, and law-and-order slogans. Criteria for sentencing that cannot stand the test of assessment can be changed. In the interim both the convicted offenders and the public will be the beneficiaries of legislated criteria that reduce judicial caprice and abuse of discretion to a minimum. The Council of Judges believes that public opinion will support maximum use of criminal sanctions other than imprisonment if the criminal justice system shows itself able to select for confinement those criminals who have repeatedly hurt or endangered people physically or are participants in organized criminal activity. To make this selection with reasonable accuracy requires that criteria for sentencing be established and that research back-up be instituted to monitor the use of criteria and improve the sentencing practices of judges as deficiencies appear. Guidelines should also be devised to improve the screening and diversion practices of police and prosecutors.

No research to date has corroborated anyone's ability to predict which offenders will or will not commit further violent crimes. Attempts to make such predictions have resulted in "overpredicting" and prolonged confinement of nondangerous persons. A history of violence offers the most objective data by which dangerous people can be sentenced, but even that offers no guarantee of accuracy in predicting their future violence. The performance of prisons in trying to lessen the aggression of persons who commit violent crimes is no better than their record in trying to reduce the rapacity of property offenders. Criminal justice leaders must continue to search for humane and rehabilitative programs beyond primarily custodial care for persons who commit crimes of violence and are classified as dangerous.

The rate of imprisonment in the United States, which takes pride—in orations—in its protection of liberty and freedom, is considerably higher than the rate in any other industrial nation. In proportion to population, we imprison twice as many people as New Zealand, Canada, and Great Britain; three times more than Denmark, Sweden, and France; four times more than Italy and Japan; five times more than Spain and Norway; and nine times more than the Netherlands.[5] That extraordinary rate says it all. To ignore it is to condone the flagrant waste of money and lives and the crime-producing effects of needless imprisonment; to allow it to continue would be irresponsible support of those popular politicians and criminal justice leaders who promise that extending the number and length of prison commitments will reduce crime and who perpetuate the myth that more imprisonment means better protection of the public. That is why the NCCD Board of Directors in April 1973 adopted the policy recommending nonimprisonment of the nondangerous offender, the offender who does not meet the criteria for dangerousness set forth in the Model Sentencing Act. We and others are seeking research grants to improve these criteria, which are still too general and would imprison, up to five years, thousands of persons who are not dangerous to society.

IMPRISONMENT NOT NECESSARY

Retaining these criteria in its 1972 revision of the Model Sentencing Act, the Council of Judges dissented from the prohibition-of-imprisonment policy that the Board of Directors was then considering. The judges maintained that before the criminal justice system could abolish imprisonment of the nondangerous, it must first develop a set of punitive sanctions that would be not only less destructive than imprisonment but also at least equally effective. They maintained that without the threat of imprisonment, use of any less punitive alternative—a suspended sentence, a fine, probation, etc.—could not possibly be effective. The Board did not accept that reasoning: it contended that if the effectiveness of every sanction depends on the existence of a more punitive sanction as back-up the Council of Judges' Model Sentencing Act would not have excluded the death penalty and mandatory life sentences.

The public has been told repeatedly, by officials in whom it has confidence and by others seeking public office, that crime could be stopped if the police and the judges and the parole boards performed their functions more competently. More specifically, they say crime can be stopped by, for example, throwing out the *Miranda* rule, which "prevents police from obtaining confessions"; it can be stopped by juvenile court judges who should "stop slapping young punks on the wrist and start slapping 'em in the clink"; it can be stopped by parole boards that would not release any prisoner until he was "too old and feeble to hurt anyone"; etc. But simplistic remedies, such as the death penalty, mandatory sentences, and longer prison terms—all of them resurrected periodically out of frustration—have failed in the past and there is no reason to think they will succeed in the future. The inability of the police, courts, and correction to plan and operate as a coordinated system has intensified frustration and stimulates interagency accusations of failure. In the midst of all these empty promises, panacean proposals, and angry recriminations, criminal justice expenditures have more than tripled, from $4.5 billion in 1967 to $14.5 billion in 1974. In the past five years public expenditures for the police alone have increased from three to eight billion dollars a year, with no visible effect on the crime rate. There is a general fear that urging other societal systems to attack the problems which feed the subculture of urban violence and at the same time *not* urging tougher responses to acts of violence makes one appear permissive and soft on crime. There is a supplementary fear that the shift in policy and strategy, from reacting to crime to proacting, will result in shifting public funds from criminal justice to education, health, and other human service systems.[6] The question is one of leadership and responsibility. Should a public official fashion remedies that will "give the public what it wants" or should he construct them according to what the problem demands?

The criminals who ultimately reach the courtroom for sentencing are not at all representative of all who commit crime in our society. Most persons who commit crime are not sentenced. Most are not apprehended in the first place; of those who are, many are not officially arrested. Most victims, neighbors, and employers don't press charges. Because of the discretion allowed police and prosecutors, many arrested persons are dismissed without prosecution; others are diverted from the criminal justice process without conviction; and some, including many charged with serious offenses, are sentenced on a reduced charge not at all descriptive of the crime committed. Those committed to prison are more representative of the lower socio-economic strata of our society than of all those who commit serious crimes.

That most people who commit crimes are disposed of without being sentenced or with sentences other than imprisonment doesn't mean that the system is not working or that the goal should be to increase the number who are imprisoned. It means that we must improve the selection of those who should be imprisoned. It also means that other forces in society are working—in different ways for different people. Persons convicted of white-collar crimes are rarely sentenced to a long prison term or to a prison term of any length; for them the usual sentence is a fine and a restitution order or other conditions of probation. Why can't the same diversions from imprisonment that are now used, with general approbation, for offenders having high social status also be applied to offenders of lower social status? Research findings on the criminal behavior of children also have significance for sentencing of adults. Among them are the conclusions that the more severely punished are more likely to repeat and that those who do not go through the justice system commit fewer crimes than those who do.[7] They, too, support nonimprisonment of nondangerous offenders.

CREATIVE SENTENCING

Judges and probation officers dealing with white middle- and upper-income offenders from "good families" very often exercise considerable ingenuity in locating or creating community alternatives to imprisonment. They may not have the time to serve similarly as advocates for all the low-income nondangerous offenders from "bad families" that come before them, but with a little effort they can recruit volunteer advocates from the community. The involvement of such volunteers would enhance community support for a wide variety of alternative sentences. Communities and volunteers can devise, manage, and operate a variety of noninstitutional sanctions for all nondangerous

offenders—and can do so at a cost far lower than the amount of interest now due for amortizing the construction outlay of $50,000 per cell and the annual operating expense of $10,000 per prisoner (whose theft averages about $300).

No public outrage was expressed when a heart specialist who had stolen over $200,000 was sentenced to perform free surgery for indigent children. Nor did the heavens fall when a Phoenix physician, convicted on a drug charge, was sentenced to serve as Tombstone's town doctor as a condition of probation and when a Phoenix youth convicted of armed robbery was placed on probation for five years during which he was required to complete two years of college work. Creative use of probation can find unlimited alternatives for the unskilled as well as the skilled, for nonwhite as well as white offenders. Skilled plumbers, carpenters, and painters can give their probation time on weekends and holidays to train unskilled probationers as helpers while they repair and refurbish housing for indigent and aged people in the community. England's community service law authorizing 40- to 240-hour assignments in lieu of confinement can be adapted to our sentencing alternatives within the community for offenders who cannot afford fines or restitution on the installment plan.

Implementation of the policy of nonimprisonment of the nondangerous cannot and, of course, will not take place quickly and without debate. It undoubtedly will be preceded by a gradual retreat from the present wasteful and costly use of excessively long prison sentences to the use of short terms and nighttime, weekend, and holiday sentences to jails instead of prisons. Implementation efforts should be accompanied by increased allocation of funds for research and assessment of sentencing practices and the consequences of sentences for offenders classified experimentally to test criteria for dangerousness. Assessment should include monitoring the outcome of police and prosecutor diversion practices for comparison with the outcome of similar cases that are sentenced. Monitoring of sentences judge by judge is imperative for the gathering of data that can be used to improve judicial training for better sentencing and better use of informed discretion. Sentencing outcome should be measured by cost-effectiveness factors that relate not only to the crimes committed subsequently by sentenced offenders but also to the relative costs of the sanctions used. I am willing to predict that sentencing effectiveness will correlate highly with reduction in the length of sentences and reduction in the use of imprisonment for nondangerous persons.

Holland has one-ninth the per capita prison population of the United States. Its sentences to confinement (even for crimes of violence) are for terms of a few months; ours are for many years. Holland's underlying concept is, as ours should be, that punishment should be certain but need not be destructive. Its consistently low crime rate correlates with its change to short sentences and a heavy use of volunteers in probation sentences. The change was motivated by public officials who had been imprisoned during World War II and had first-hand experience of the destructive ineffectiveness of prisons.

We should not have to endure a similar catastrophe to understand that the kinds of sentences authorized in our statutes and administered by our judges reflect the kind of society we are and the degree of civilization we have attained. We have reached the stage when imprisonment is neither socially nor economically feasible as a punitive sanction for the great majority of sentenced persons, the hundreds of thousands who can be classed as nonviolent and nondangerous.

NOTES

1.   *Morales v. Schmidt,* 340 F. Supp. 544 (1972). See also David J. Rothman, *The Discovery of the Asylum: Social Order and Disorder in the New Republic* (Boston: Little, Brown, 1971).

2.   Eugene Doleschal, "The Deterrent Effect of Legal Punishment," *Information Review on Crime and Delinquency,* June 1969.

3.   National Advisory Commission on Criminal Justice Standards and Goals, *Corrections* (Washington, D.C.: U.S. Government Printing Office, 1973); National Council on Crime and Delinquency, Board of Trustees, "Institutional Construction—A Policy Staement," *Crime and Delinquency,* October 1972; Jessica Mitford, *Kind and Usual Punishment: The Prison Business* (New York: Knopf, 1973).

4.   Norval Morris, *The Future of Imprisonment* (Chicago: University of Chicago Press, 1974).

5.   Irvin Waller and Janet Chan, "Prison Use: A Canadian and International Comparison," *Criminal Law Quarterly,* December 1974, p. 58.

6.   Such a priority was recommended by the National Advisory Commission on Criminal Justice Standards and Goals, *A National Strategy to Reduce Crime* (Washington, D.C.: U.S. Government Printing Office, 1973).

7.   Eugene Doleschal, "Hidden Crime," *Crime and Delinquency Literature,* October 1970. See also Jay R. Williams and Martin Gold, "From Delinquent Behavior to Official Delinquency," *Social Problems,* 20(2): 209–229, 1972.

11

THE STATE OF CORRECTIONS TODAY

A Triumph of Pluralistic Ignorance

ALLEN BREED

The task of summarizing public perceptions of corrections is a formidable one. I am reminded of the story of an ancient Eastern monarch who once instructed his wise men to invent for him a phrase that would be true and appropriate for all times and in all situations. They withdrew and deliberated at length, finally returning to the king with this saying, "And this too shall pass away."

Of one thing we can be sure: Public opinion, whatever it is now, shall pass away. Whatever conclusions we reach today and tomorrow should be based on two principles. First, public opinion is constantly changing. Second, remembering Von Schiller's immutable law of events, written over two centuries ago, "In today already walks tomorrow."

But, given that, first (as the Cheshire Cat said to Alice in Wonderland, "Before we decide where we're going, we first must decide where we are"), let us ask, What is public opinion regarding corrections right now? And what influences it?

Gauging public opinion is really a very simple process. We all understand it because we are, after all, part of that public. But the Clark Foundation did not want me only to present my views of the public opinion. They also requested that I review and synthesize the key reports on crime and corrections that have been released by the federal government and other organizations, and summarize the underlying themes and ideas that surface through the media and that capture public attention.

Bear with me for a minute as I quickly relate the basic documents I reread. This will give you a flavor of the magnitude of the preparation, even though you may not be impressed with the depth of my conclusions.

With the help of the staffs at the National Criminal Justice Research Service and the National Institute of Corrections Information Center, I reviewed all the public opinion polls on crime and corrections for the past three years. I reviewed all the Bureau of Justice statistics, and

Note: It is unusual for the Bulletin to publish a speech. Allen Breed, however, is one of the quiet yet influential giants in corrections. His graceful speech easily translates into a graceful essay to be read quickly and digested slowly.

This speech-turned article was supported by the Edna McConnell Clark Foundation and, though it clearly goes beyond the narrow boundaries of law, it should be of interest to our lawyer readers.

Source: From Breed, A., "The state of corrections today: A triumph of pluralistic ignorance" in *Prisoners and the Law,* Thomson West. Reprinted with permission from the Edna McConnell Foundation.

reports of the National Institute of Justice, National Institute of Corrections, and the Office of Juvenile Justice and Delinquency Prevention for the last two years. I reviewed all news releases on corrections issued by the Department of Justice over the last four years. I reviewed, and in most cases reread, the Wickersham Report, the Katzenbach Report, the Violence Commission Report, the Eisenhower Commission Report, *Corrections Digest* for the past two years, *Criminal Violence/Criminal Justice* by Charles Silberman, *Crime in American Culture, Crime and Public Policy*, and *Thinking About Crime*, editions 1 and 2, by James Q. Wilson, *Beyond Probation* by Murray and Cox, *Weeping in the Playtime of Children* by James Wooten, *Getting Away with Murder* by Alfred Regnery, *The Watershed of Juvenile Justice Reform* by Schwartz, Krisberg, et al., and *One More Chance* by Greenwood and Zimring. I then skimmed the Rand studies on probation and prisons, Martinson's review of treatment programs, Wolfgang's longitudinal studies of delinquents in Philadelphia, the national evaluation of delinquency prevention by the National Council on Crime and Delinquency, *Delinquency Prevention: Theories and Strategies* by the Westinghouse National Issues Center, and then, just out of nostalgia, I revisited Glucks' and reread Norval Morris' books.

Now, my reeducation having been completed, and any debt I might have owed to the Clark Foundation having been repaid, I can conclude that my bibliography is a valuable compendium of usually solid and often illuminating research and opinion.

However, I must also conclude that, individually and collectively, the body of research and professional opinion has had little impact on public opinion. To some degree, several mission reports and research writings have reinforced ideological positions already enunciated by politicians or other decision makers, but one can measure little public opinion change in the directions advocated by reports in the years immediately following their release.

PUBLIC ATTITUDES OVER TIME

If the best knowledge is not molding public opinion, then what is determining public views on corrections? Historically, we Americans are basically a punitive people. Our ancestors ran away from oppressions, intolerance, and injustice and then introduced them into the colonies. The literature on corrections is replete with the cruel and unusual punishments practiced. Perhaps a bit like abused children who often grow up to be abusive parents, we appear to have brought the worst of our inhumanity to the correctional arena. And I might add that values that encouraged this inhumanity still permeate much of our citizens' attitudes toward criminal offenders. My 93-year-old aunt from eastern Colorado has always been a "liberal" in every respect, except for crime and criminals. She has never understood quite what I do for a living, but I knew that I was an embarrassment to her when she recently said, "I hope you don't do anything to make those prisons better places."

But we Americans have also always exhibited a great deal of guilt and compassion. Guilt about what we were doing to those who did not conform to the norms of the moment. Guilt particularly in terms of the principles under which this nation was founded: Liberty, Justice, Equity, Fairness, and Humaneness. And this guilt has been translated into compassion for the underdog, the underprivileged, even the offender.

Thus, over the years, punitiveness and compassion have been the conflicting and underlying forces shaping public opinion about the treatment of offenders. Throughout our history, we have gone through cycles in which we punish ever more severely, only to have our guilt and compassion persuade us to adopt more humane options. Then, either because of a real or perceived increase in crime, or a series of dramatic, often bizarre, criminal events, our fear and anger bring the return of our more punitive impulses. Looking back over time, however, it would appear that the reformist periods were more the result of charismatic reformers, individuals and groups, who were able to sway decision makers, than of any dramatic shifts in public opinion. I would assert that it is the absence of such charismatic leaders that inhibits the rebirth of the reformist spirit today.

We all recall examples of reform: the Quakers' fight against cruel and unusual punishment and their invention of the prison. The removal of children from jails through the establishment of the house of refuge in New York in 1824. John Augustus, shoemaker from Boston, who persuaded the courts in 1860 to start probation. The development of the Juvenile Court Act in Illinois in 1899. And the humanitarian Declaration of Principles adopted in 1870 by the American Correctional Association.

But, generally speaking, throughout the eighteenth and nineteenth centuries, the public wasn't concerned about corrections issues, except as crises, disturbances, or tragedies temporarily gained their attention through newspaper accounts. The public was content to let correctional leaders do what they felt best. Such leaders were seen as trusted "experts," and courts supported this view. Changes that did take place occurred when public opinion appeared to be neutral, not necessarily supportive of changes. Until recently, without strong public interest, the spokespersons for corrections were able to get principles enunciated and programs adopted. But where today are the public-minded reformers like John Augustus, Charles Loring Brace, John Howard, Rutherford Hayes, Benjamin Rush, and Jane Addams? Tragically, their often worthy pronouncements became the facade obstructing the public's view from the real inadequacies of the correctional system.

Leaders in corrections articulated the most noble objectives while presiding over squalor, fear, and degradation. We have supported the principles of fairness, justice, and humane treatment for those who are wards of the state, yet our daily practices have often been, and often are, at odds with the ideals given voice in oration. The discovery of this gap is hardly new. Shakespeare and Dickens had much to say about it. John Howard and a long succession of penal reformers have identified the shortcomings of our correctional system. But the nobility of our stated principles kept strong public sentiment about our actual practice from ever developing.

Until recently, politicians have stayed removed from corrections, gaining nothing by involving Richard McGee, then administrator of Youth and Adult Corrections, as he described innovative programs to two different governors of California, one a Republican and one a Democrat. In both cases, he said, "Give me permission to do this. Do not endorse it, because I'm here to take the heat if things go wrong." Professional and organizational leadership were the forces that influenced corrections—not political leadership.

THE EMERGENCE OF CRIME AND CORRECTIONS AS MAJOR ISSUES

Starting in the mid-1960s, a combination of factors forged today's "get tough" attitude toward offenders among the public and in the government:

- Crime rose astronomically and became more violent.
- Media coverage of crime increased dramatically.
- Civil rights issues were being addressed.
- Prison riots brought new advocates for offenders as well as hardened attitudes toward inmates.
- The courts intervened in prison matters, reversing more than a century of "hands off."
- The Warren Court's increased due process protections (for those accused of crimes) angered law enforcement, prosecutors, and the general public.
- The Vietnam War and Watergate dramatically reduced the public's trust in government.
- Researchers attacked the concept of rehabilitation, and then politicians urged reduced expectations and gave renewed emphasis to the infamous statement that "nothing works."

Crime and corrections became major political issues. In 1964, Senator Barry Goldwater campaigned for the presidency on a platform that stressed law and order, and he coined the phrase "crime in the streets." President Lyndon Johnson responded by creating the Katzenbach Commission, better known as the President's Crime Commission, to develop the blueprints of a plan to banish crime. The result was The Challenge of a Free Society and many task force reports of surprisingly high quality, which remain the most comprehensive and useful collection of information on the problems of crime prevention and treatment to be found anywhere. The Kerner Commission was appointed in response to the race riots of the 1960s. The Commission on Violence under Milton Eisenhower was an immediate response to the assassinations of Robert F. Kennedy and Martin Luther King, Jr. These and numerous other studies and reports all increased our knowledge of crime and provided creative approaches to controlling it, but appeared not to have tempered political opinion or public policy. As the American humorist Will Rogers reminded us, "Knowledge and political will do not always pull in double harness."

Let us briefly review what happened at the federal level as crime and politics moved on a collision course. During President Johnson's administration, the Law Enforcement Assistance

Administration (LEAA) was established and the Juvenile Delinquency Prevention Act was passed. These worthwhile legislative efforts were "politicized" from inception. Now, although recognizing that some good came from both LEAA and JDPA in the criminal justice area, we also must recognize that no fundamental change resulted from those federal legislative initiatives. Most of the federal funds went to block grants for the states in genuflection to local politics. President Richard Nixon came on the scene and established a "War on Crime." Money poured into criminal justice agencies, reaching the level of $900 million per year.

The federal programs raised public expectations that crime could be dramatically reduced. But crime continued to rise, and so did federal deficits. And so the "crunch" began with political attacks directed at LEAA. President Jimmy Carter cut the crime control programs drastically, wanting to reduce domestic spending. President Ronald Reagan, not needing to justify his law and order credentials recommended cutting the remainder of the LEAA programs and Attorney General Edwin Meese added the final nail with the statement: "The money has been wasted on so-called crime prevention and treatment programs, which are lining the pockets of social workers."

LEAA programs were cut—without the public supporting such action and with every conceivable criminal justice agency in opposition to those cuts. The new Administration stance was: "Don't throw money at the problem—change bad policy." A Task Force on Violent Crime was created in 1981 by Attorney General William French Smith. No expert advice was used. No one representing corrections was included. It did its work in 120 days, with seven days of hearings, and issued a ninety-six-page report with sixty-four recommendations. The Commission opted not to consider causes of crime, saying government cannot solve all problems. Although federal officials often emphasize the significance of the report, it is seldom mentioned in local deliberations about criminal justice matters.

The Federal Crime Control Act of 1984, which ended a decade or more of congressional debate, resulted in a compromise that pleased few on either side of the aisle. Its impact on corrections will be the introduction at the federal level of determinate sentencing, the abolition of parole, and the termination of all youthful offender legislation. These changes in the federal code reflect little or no public support, and run counter to almost all of the testimony given by correctional spokespersons.

More recently, the second Eisenhower Commission report, which was the Violence Commission revisited, was released. Although it received several days of media attention, there was little editorial support and few follow-up stories about the Commission's analysis of the crime problem or its potential policy implications.

THE POLITICIZATION OF CRIME AND CORRECTIONS

Politicizing the issue at the federal level became more evident in about 1979, with the use of commissions, task forces, study reports and funding of "approved" programs to modify policy positions at both the federal and state levels of criminal justice. The primacy of political and philosophical concerns has grown ever stronger since then. Never in my forty years in corrections has there been a more one-sided, ideologically based, and politicized set of views as a basis for policymaking. I don't make this statement lightly, and it is not politically motivated. I saw it developing in the Carter years, and it is expanding now in the Reagan Administration. It exists in many states that have either Republican or Democratic administrations.

An administration has a right and a responsibility to establish policy and to use its constituency and organization to develop support for that position. Historically, however, this approach has been balanced by seven factors that no longer exist:

1. Opposition leadership has always presented a counterview. Those in a minority role today will not take a position on anything in criminal justice that appears "soft" on crime.

2. There is an absence of strong spokesperson for corrections. The intellectual giants in the field of corrections such as Austin McCormick, Sanford Bates, Richard McGee, and Howard Gill do not exist today.

3. Experimentation in criminal justice historically has occurred at state levels, not within the federal government. Every progressive program in corrections has been pioneered at the

state level. Today, a wave of conservatism, an absence of professional leadership, competition for scarce resources, and the crisis of overcrowding have nearly eliminated the progressive state leadership role.

4. Historically, the federal government has supported research and development in corrections within a host of agencies—the Children's Bureau, Education, Health and Human Services, Labor, the National Institute of Mental Health, LEAA. None of these organizations currently provide grants in the corrections field. Today, little federal research and development money is available for corrections.

5. Historically, the federal government has assisted state programs even when they were not in tune with federal policy. At one time in the latter days of LEAA, an attempt was made not to fund any program that was in opposition to the LEAA position. Congress rejected the effort. However, currently the small amounts of government money assist only "approved" programs. It seems to be the intention of the Department of Justice to do away with the limited block grants to states because it cannot control such funds. Currently, the Department of Justice is opposed to parole, the expansion of probation, and pretrial services, and will not fund experimental programs or research in the crucial areas.

6. Private foundations and nongovernmental organizations formerly filled voids and spoke out on issues in corrections. Foundations such as Ford, Carnegie, and Rockefeller, to name a few, which used to take strong positions and grant large amounts of money, no longer do. Strong voices like the National Institute on Crime and Delinquency, the National Council on Crime and Delinquency, the National Association of Social Workers, the League of Women Voters, the National PTA, and the Federated Women's Club, have almost vanished from the criminal justice scene.

7. Historically, clear statements of principles, purposes and policies for corrections have been absent; and it is only recently that the American Correctional Association has even begun to develop a coherent corrections policy.

With these key elements missing or weakened substantially, the corrections establishment operates in an environment shaped by a public

that is frightened and angry and by a government that is aggressively pursuing policies based on ideology. The power of resources and the clout of political leadership are being used in ways that have never occurred before, resulting in the following:

- The only national information available to decision makers is what the Bureau of Justice Statistics (BJS) releases. BJS also interprets those data, issues news releases based on those data, and shapes those data's impact on public opinion.
- The federal government is the only game in town for information to the press, and it skillfully handles the media, effectively marketing its reports. It stresses ideological messages while toning down "inconvenient" facts.
- Funding is just not available for programs that are not "approved." One of the most interesting research proposals I've seen on parole supervision recently came out of Illinois. It was turned down because the results might indicate that parole was successful.
- Private criminal justice agencies, dependent upon fees for service from governmental agencies, feel they cannot take strong positions in conflict with current policies. And the reduction in government funding has not been supplanted by private financial support. Many nonprofit criminal justice reform groups face constant fiscal peril.

THE PUBLIC ATTITUDE TODAY

With this background, what are the key ideas, themes, and messages relating to corrections that are currently alive in the public's mind? The public, reflected in polls and surveys, is frightened, confused, and angry, and it wants greater protection from criminal activity. Beyond that, one cannot legitimately generalize about public opinion.

When I reviewed the public opinion polls for the past three years, I was amazed because the findings were not what I assumed they would be, and they were not what the media had informed me they were. Let me briefly summarize these three years of polls.

The only trend in the public views that appears to be truly consistent is on the death penalty. Support for the death penalty has moved in the last ten years from 35 percent to well over 70 percent. This probably represents our basic punitive responses to the most serious of crimes. But ten years ago almost every correctional spokesperson in the country spoke out strongly in opposition to the death penalty. No corrections leader does today. Could that have affected public opinion on this very crucial issue?

I had come to believe that the public basically believes that prisons act as the best deterrent to crime, that the public supports punishment as the primary objective of prisons, that it rejects the concept of rehabilitation, and, further, that it doesn't like the decisions of judges. However, here are some findings from the pollsters that contradict my "conventional wisdom":

- Less than 50 percent of the American people feel that prisons discourage crime.
- The question "What are prisons for?" elicited these responses:
  –Punishment: 14 percent
  –Protect society: 26 percent
  –Rehabilitation: 60 percent
- In both the United States and Canada, 50 percent of the people saw courts as too "easy" on crime, but 60 percent favored more judicial discretion.
- 83 percent favored prisoners making products or performing services, and 95 percent favored prisoners having a skill or trade before release.

Does this sound as though the American people are opposed to the idea of rehabilitation?

The most recent public opinion study I came across was in Illinois, where the question was asked, "Should we build more prisons or look for alternative sentencing?" One-third of the respondents were in favor of more prisons. Two-thirds were in favor of alternatives! One must conclude that current spokespersons on public opinion in corrections are either ignorant of the facts or have elected to distort them.

THE LESSONS LEARNED

What *are* the lessons we have learned?

First, we must recognize that today's correctional leaders are qualified survivors. They are *not* activists, and they have not been spokespersons for progressive corrections. They are persons attractive to whatever party is in power. Even so,

their tenure is short, stability virtually unknown, and long-term major policy changes are rare events. Sadly, this absence of correctional leadership will not change in the immediate future.

There needs, therefore, to be strong state and national leadership from independent, non-governmental organizations committed to the upgrading of corrections and who can provide long-term policy development and support.

Second, much of the public has been persuaded to believe that crime control can be achieved by swift and more punitive penalties, while ignoring the lack of economic opportunities, racism, discordant homes, secularized churches, intimidated and ineffective schools, and an ethos of individual self-expression. A balanced view of the causes of crime and its control must be provided and supported.

Third, the pendulum of public policy on corrections will not swing from "conservative" to "liberal," whatever those terms may mean. It will change, but the change will be something different from what used to be.

Fourth, we need to reduce "pluralistic ignorance," the term central to the current correctional dilemma. It is the systematic inaccuracy in the assessment of group opinion by members of the group. Pluralistic ignorance is caused by two unfounded and conflicting assumptions: First, that one's beliefs are uniformly shared. Second, that one's attitudes and expectations are unshared by opinion. Teenagers are most guilty of it. But recently I met with a group of juvenile court judges where one articulated eloquently the importance of shifting responsibility for probation to the executive branch of government. No one spoke up. Later, in a more informal setting, two judges agreed with this view, but stated that they had been unwilling to endorse it because they felt no one else agreed with them. There is often a great difference between what one thinks and what one thinks others think. Much public opinion in corrections is based on this harmful "pluralistic ignorance."

Fifth, public opinion can be influenced by leadership—political and professional—and by the media. But there has to be a message, a plan, a policy that is clearly articulated and readily understood. And even if a message, plan, or policy is clearly articulated, one cannot depend on the political process to develop it and to carry out its implementation. One has only to review the history of *The Challenge of Crime in a Free*

Society to realize that. Implementation is dependent on a coalition of strong professional groups, civic organizations and independent groups who can work within the political process without being controlled by it.

Sixth, commission reports, research findings, and academic publications add to our body of knowledge, and are often used by political forces when the contents support ideological positions. Such reports seldom appear to have any lasting impact on public policies.

Seventh, when looking for future trends, one should not view the federal government as the "bellwether" jurisdiction. Changes in corrections have always emanated from the progressive states, not from the shores of the Potomac. One might

better watch carefully what is happening in Massachusetts, Colorado, Utah, Washington, and Texas in the juvenile field, or Florida, Georgia, and Minnesota in adult corrections to get some early leads. And, although the general public will always be basically punitive, because of an inherent guilt and compassion, it will also be open to reasonable and responsible programs for offenders. Our efforts to change must recognize both forces.

Lastly, it is vital that we recognize that long-range planning does not deal with future decisions but with the future of present decisions. I hope that our discussion can focus on the importance of what we recommend today, as those decisions can dramatically affect our tomorrows.

12

THE "PRISON PAYS" STUDIES

Research or Ideology?

CHRISTOPHER BAIRD

In recent years, a number of articles and reports have been published documenting the rise in U.S. crime rates and advocating increased use of incarceration to reverse the trend. These reports, if widely accepted by legislatures, could have a major impact on probation and parole services. In fact, data from these studies have already been used to abolish parole in at least one state, and it's clear that the battle is just beginning. Pending legislation in a number of jurisdictions calls for limiting the use of probation, parole, and intermediate sanction programs. In one Midwestern state, a pending bill even *prohibits* counties from implementing intensive supervision programs for juveniles. Leading the charge is a group of economists and policy analysts who have concluded that incarceration, while costly, is less expensive than the crime it prevents. Edwin Zedlewski pioneered this movement in *Making Confinement Decisions* (1987). He concluded that incarceration was remarkably cost effective, because each year of prison time saved taxpayers $430,000 in criminal justice expenditures.

When serious flaws in Zedlewski's methodology were identified (Zimring and Hawkins,

1988), John DiIulio stepped into the fray, presenting himself as the voice of reason between highly disparate points of view. DiIulio conducted a study of Wisconsin prisoners and concluded that, although Zedlewski had indeed overstated the case for incarceration, prison was, nevertheless, cost effective (DiIulio, 1990). Other studies followed, advancing an "economic theory of crime" (Reynolds, 1991), which in turn led to several well-placed articles challenging conventional wisdom regarding relationships between crime, poverty, race, and incarceration (Methvin, 1992; DiIulio and Logan, 1992). According to the "economic theory of crime," crimes are committed because, after implicitly weighing the benefits and risks (cost), criminals conclude that the benefit exceeds the cost. Reynolds concludes that, at least in Texas, the cost of crime to criminals has decreased markedly in recent years. According to Reynolds, this decrease is directly responsible for the rise in Texas crime rates. Methvin extends this argument to the national level, adding Michigan and California as case examples.

Following Zedlewski's *Making Confinement Decisions*, each new study has used findings of

Note: An earlier version of this article was published as an NCCD *FOCUS* Report.

preceding reports, often without mentioning that the conclusions have been strongly challenged by respected research organizations as well as some of the nation's foremost corrections officials (Johnson, 1992; Riveland, 1992). As a result, the "prison pays" position continues to be quoted in the media and forms the basis for correctional policies advocated by no less a public figure than William Barr, a former Attorney General of the United States in the Bush Administration. Indeed, both the crime bill and the "contract with America" put most of the burden of crime control on increased use of prisons. To be eligible for federal funds, states will have to dramatically increase the proportion of sentences that are actually served behind bars.

Although criticisms of these studies have been rather cavalierly dismissed by their authors, reviews have often been incisive. In a critique of *Making Confinement Decisions*, Zimring and Hawkins concluded that Zedlewski's computations contained "compound catastrophic error." NCCD's review of DiIulio's work found "nonsensical comparisons" used to support the position that prison pays. Other reviews have been equally critical, noting that some studies use carefully selected time comparisons that support the views of the authors or rely on single factor models to explain changes in crime rates, grossly oversimplifying the complexities involved in analyzing the relationship between crime and punishment.

If it is true that these studies are fundamentally flawed, two primary questions emerge:

- How could serious researchers have made such egregious errors?
- Why have these studies continued to influence those in public policy positions?

Perhaps the answers to both questions lie more in political ideology than in research. The extent to which ideology has replaced science is critical to the American debate. Incarceration is expensive. If it is effective in protecting the public and avoiding other crime-related costs, it may well be worth the price. But if measures of effectiveness are based on data analyses shaped more by politics than scientific inquiry, the United States could continue down an expensive path that fails to improve the safety of its citizens. Such policies may represent "opportunities lost," funding an ever growing punishment industry rather than programs that could effectively reduce crime and violence in our cities.

Before addressing the issues of crime and punishment in the United States, it is necessary to provide a detailed analysis of a few of the flaws of the more recent studies. Although Zedlewski's work has been thoroughly reviewed by others, *Making Confinement Decisions* is the foundation of the "prison pays" movement. Therefore, the review begins with a short critique of Zedlewski's study before focusing on the work of DiIulio, Reynolds, Methvin, and the American Legislative Council.

MAKING CONFINEMENT DECISIONS

Following its release, Zedlewski's study was virtually bombarded with criticism from the research community. Even John DiIulio, who also has claimed that increased incarceration will reduce crime, called Zedlewski's findings "incredible" (1989). The most thorough review (Zimring and Hawkins, 1988) was harshly critical of nearly every aspect of the study. Their critique pointed out the enormity of the errors made in estimating both the number of crimes prevented by incarceration and the cost of each crime committed. Every incarceration, Zedlewski concluded, prevented 187 crimes a year and ultimately saved society $430,000 in costs associated with these crimes.

Basing their analysis on the same figures Zedlewski used to derive the benefits of incarceration, Zimring and Hawkins demonstrated that if he were correct, the increase in the number of persons incarcerated between 1977 and 1984 alone should have totally eliminated crime in the United States. Furthermore, all this would theoretically have been accomplished for a mere six billion dollars. Obviously something was seriously amiss in Zedlewski's analysis. Despite huge increases in the incarcerated population in most states, crime rates remained high and costs rose dramatically throughout the 1980s.

The benefits of incarceration presented by Zedlewski were so extreme and errors in methodology so obvious, that Zimring and Hawkins admonished the funding body (NIJ) for releasing the study "substantially unexamined." Others, including the National Council on Crime and Delinquency, produced their own critiques of the study, reiterating the issues identified by Zimring and Hawkins. Despite the onslaught of criticism from the research community, Zedlewski's conclusions continue to surface in the political forum.

Does Prison Pay?

Like the figures used in Zedlewski's analysis, estimates of both crime and costs in DiIulio's *Does Prison Pay?* have been questioned. However, there is a more fundamental error that requires attention. DiIulio's crime estimates were produced through a survey of Wisconsin prison inmates—felons who had been arrested, prosecuted, convicted, and incarcerated. Then, in determining the incapacitation benefits of prison, DiIulio compares incarceration with only one alternative—"letting (criminals) freely roam the streets in search of victims" (1990, p. 53).

Quite obviously, the conclusions of any cost-benefit analysis are wholly dependent on the alternatives compared. The travel industry, for example, could easily demonstrate that air travel between New York and San Francisco is cost effective when it is compared to walking the 3,000 miles. But walking 3,000 miles is not a viable alternative to air travel and such a comparison would be viewed as preposterous.

Likewise, letting the offenders surveyed in DiIulio's study roam the streets in search of victims is not a viable alternative, certainly not one that would ever be considered by the Wisconsin legislature. A serious cost-benefit study would compare prison costs and outcomes to those of true alternatives: house arrest, electronic surveillance, intensive supervision, or even shorter periods of incarceration followed by such community-based offender control strategies. Indeed, when NCCD compared house arrest in Florida with incarceration, we found house arrest to be quite cost effective.

Although DiIulio corrected one of Zedlewski's most serious errors in calculating the cost/benefit ratio of incarceration (and used the median number of offenses reported rather than the mean), he essentially follows the Zedlewski formula comparing the cost of prison to the cost of doing nothing. In his concluding chapter, he does mention the potential cost-effectiveness of alternatives to incarceration, but makes no attempt to include them in his cost/benefit calculations.

When DiIulio's cost comparisons were dubbed nonsensical by NCCD, he complained that his results had been "caricatured" (DiIulio and Piehl, 1991). Far from it. The approaches being compared in any cost/benefit study are of *fundamental importance.* DiIulio himself stated that his analysis "does *not* mean that it is more cost effective to imprison offenders than to intensively supervise these same offenders in the community" (1990, p. 55). Since no one has suggested that we let offenders roam freely in search of victims, we are left to wonder what, if anything, this study does mean. It certainly does not, in any sense, mean that prison pays.

Crime in Texas

Morgan Reynolds, in a publication of the National Center for Policy Analysis, advances a very simple premise. As "expected punishment" for serious crime dropped in Texas, it *resulted* in an increase in the rate of serious crimes committed. Furthermore, using a calculation of "expected punishment" that includes the probabilities of arrest, conviction, and imprisonment, he derives alarmingly low estimates of actual prison time served per serious offense committed.

While the study can be criticized at several levels, there are two issues that are of primary importance. First, while Reynolds discusses other potential causes for increases in crime in Texas, none of these are factored into his model. With all of the social and economic change occurring in recent U.S. history, to attempt to explain crime rates with a single factor model represents a serious departure from reality. Even more importantly, a scan of Texas crime and incarceration data presented in appendices to Reynolds' report leaves one wondering how he can conclude that punishment for serious crime has declined in Texas. Prison admissions relative to crimes reported have *increased* since 1960 in every category presented except robbery and theft/larceny. Furthermore, for the most serious offenses, murder and rape, the increases have been dramatic. For example, in 1960, Texas reported 821 murders and only 216 prison admissions for murder. By 1988, 2,022 murders were reported and 1,888 persons were imprisoned on murder charges. The prison admission/ murder ratio increased from 26 per 100 murders in 1960 to 93 per 100 murders in 1988. Lagging prison admissions to allow a year for arrest and prosecution produces very similar results and limiting the analysis to the 1980s (as the National Center for Policy Analysis did in its press release) shows substantial increases in admission to crime ratios for *all* categories presented in Reynolds' report.

It appears that the probability of imprisonment for serious offenses has *increased* in Texas over the last decade, yet crime increased substantially. Rather than supporting Reynolds' crime/punishment premise, the data seem to refute it. Another factor in Reynolds' "expected punishment" calculation, the median time served may have declined for some offenses in Texas, but this is true in other states faced with federal court orders to reduce crowding, usually caused, in part, by an over-reliance on incarceration. But the certainty of punishment, if not the length of time served has increased for major crimes. And indeed, there is no evidence that length of time served, is a deterrent to crime. In states where length of stay increased significantly over the last decade, crime rates have also increased as well. The bottom line is that this issue deserves a thorough analysis of all the factors involved in the complexities of crime and punishment. To recommend broad policy changes based on this "research" represents a serious disservice to the state of Texas and the nation.

DOUBLING THE PRISON POPULATION WILL BREAK AMERICA'S CRIME WAVE

Perhaps no one has been a more vocal proponent of increasing the use of incarceration to combat crime as Eugene Methvin. Certainly, no one has been more misleading in his use of statistics. Methvin relies heavily on the work of Reynolds and others to establish his arguments, then selects specific states as case studies to support his contention that as punishment declines, crime increases. What is most intriguing about Methvin's case examples is that two of the three states selected, Michigan and California, are precisely those used by researchers to demonstrate that rising rates of incarceration have not reduced crime.

Methvin's article is itself a case study in how data can be carefully manipulated to lead to the desired conclusion. Comparing Methvin's analysis to an unedited version of each state's crime and incarceration trends is illuminating. Michigan, Methvin notes, "tried it both ways" first holding prison populations relatively constant then rapidly increasing the use of imprisonment. According to Methvin, when Michigan prison populations dropped from 15,157 in 1981 to 14,604 in 1984 (a drop in the incarceration rate of one person per 100,000), violent crime soared 25%. Then from 1986 to 1991, Michigan doubled its prison population and "wonder of wonders" Michigan's crime rate dropped (1992, p. 34). Taken out of context, these data seem compelling. Now for the rest of the story . . .

• First, the crime rate in Michigan started its decline three years before the state began its dramatic increase in the use of incarceration. From 1981 through 1984, while the state's incarceration rate remained unchanged, total crime decreased 4.4%, an average of 1.5% per year. Then, while incarceration rates rose from 161/100,000 population in 1984 to 366/100,000 in 1990, the crime rate decreased 8.6%, an average of 1.4% per year. Hence, the decline in the Michigan crime rate began well before its prison construction binge. It may well have continued without a doubling of the incarceration rate.

• Second, violent crime did increase in Michigan during the 1981–84 period, but at a slower rate than Methvin reports (18% rather than 25%). But, after more than doubling the incarceration rate, the rate of violent crime in 1990 was still 4% above the 1984 rate and 25% higher than the rate at the beginning of the decade.

To support the conclusion that increased use of imprisonment resulted in fewer crimes of violence clearly requires very selective data comparisons, and Methvin is selective, not only in his choice of years to compare, but in his choice of crimes as well. He initially claims that robbery and burglary rates are the best measures of the effectiveness of imprisonment, but quickly abandons robbery in favor of other crimes when analyzing trends in California.

In California, Methvin never precisely identifies a base year but states that in the 1990s, murder, rape, and burglary rates fell a "whopping 24 to 37% from their 1980–82 peaks." However, as Table 12.1 illustrates, despite huge increases in the state's rate of incarceration, the total crime rate remained relatively stable from 1983

TABLE 12.1   California Crime Rates, 1975 to 1992

Year	Crime Rate	Violent Crime Rate	Incarceration Rate
1975	7204.6	655.4	81
1976	7234.0	669.3	85
1977	7008.7	706.0	80
1978	7116.2	742.9	88
1979	7468.8	811.1	93
1980	7833.1	893.6	98
1981	7590.5	863.0	114
1982	7285.5	814.7	135
1983	6677.4	772.6	150
1984	6468.3	763.4	162
1985	6518.0	765.3	181
1986	6762.8	920.5	212
1987	6506.4	918.0	231
1988	6635.5	929.8	257
1989	6763.4	977.7	283
1990	6603.6	1045.2	311
1991	6772.6	1089.9	320
1992	6679.0	1119.7	332

through 1992 while the rate of violent crime soared. Methvin is correct in noting that California did witness a substantial decrease in crime in the 1980s (13% versus a national decline of 3.5%), but virtually all of this decrease occurred by the end of 1983 when the state's incarceration rate was 150/100,000. Since that point, California has more than doubled its rate of incarceration with no corresponding decline in crime rates. In fact, the 1992 and 1983 crime rates are nearly identical, while violent crime in 1992 was 45% above the 1983 rate.

REPORT CARD ON CRIME AND PUNISHMENT

In 1994, The American Legislative Exchange (ALEC) released a *Report Card on Crime and Punishment* concluding there is an "indisputable relationship between crime rates and incarceration rates" and that "punishment is a proven deterrent of crime." The *Report Card* contains a myriad of crime statistics on all states, but presents no analysis at all to support its claims. In fact, the data presented can be used to effectively argue that there is *no* relationship between crime rates and incarceration rates. For example, South Dakota incarcerates at three times the rate of North Dakota, but still has a violent crime rate 2.5 times that of its neighbor. South Carolina's incarceration rate is 60% higher than North Carolina's, yet its total crime rates are nearly

identical, and South Carolina has a 38% higher rate of violent crime reported. The examples go on and on. As this article illustrates, a sophisticated, objective analysis of ALEC's figures would leave the organization hard pressed to defend the above statements. Like data used in the Reynolds and Methvin reports, the ALEC statistics can be used to effectively dispute all conclusions drawn.

SCIENCE OR IDEOLOGY?

The problems with the above studies do not always represent variances in research methods that can be defended as honest differences in approach. Instead, these reports are based on an overly simplistic analysis of complex issues, misleading comparisons of alternatives, or selective use of data to prove a point. As such, they are not the products of science, but of ideology. No serious study of crime would analyze its relationship to punishment without incorporating other important measures of social change. No serious study of the relative effectiveness of incarceration would fail to compare incarceration to important alternative sanctions.

CAUSES OF CRIME

Americans have become increasingly alarmed about crime, drug abuse, and violence, particularly in the inner cities. Crime statistics certainly justify the high level of concern. The number of crimes reported to police has indeed mushroomed over the last four decades, from 1.8 million in 1950 to over 14 million in 1990. Other societal changes have been equally dramatic; the United States has undergone tremendous social and economic change since 1950. Today, our country and the lifestyles of most of its citizens bear little resemblance to the 1950 model.

The fact that overall crime rates were actually declining through much of the 1980s provided little comfort to those coping with guns in schools, drug dealers in their community, and drive-by shootings. The threat of gangs and drugs moving into the suburbs and smaller communities has kept middle America on edge as well.

Why is our society plagued by so much crime? What are its causes? Why has crime increased so markedly since World War II? The reasons for the rise in crime rates are undoubtedly as complex as the forces molding our society.

Demographers and criminologists have always linked crime to population trends, particularly to males under age 30, given that this group is responsible for a disproportionate number of crimes. The downturn in crimes in the 1980s, for example, was long forecast as a reflection of the aging of the post-World War II baby boomers. Population is obviously an important variable, but other factors have undoubtedly played a role as well. What follows is a summary of probable contributors.

The Increasing Urbanization of America

In 1960, about 30% of the U.S. population lived in rural settings. By 1990, the rural dwellers represented less than 25% of the total population. In total, 62 million more Americans lived in U.S. cities in 1990 than in 1960. Historically, crime rates are much higher in urban environments, often three to four times those reported in small towns, smaller cities, and in rural areas. Hence, our movement toward an urban society could help explain the rise in U.S. crime rates.

Improvements in Crime Reporting

Criminologists recognize that a portion of the increase in crime rates does not represent changes in behavior, but changes in the technology of crime reporting. In the late 1960s and early 1970s, the Law Enforcement Assistance Administration (LEAA) funneled millions of dollars to local law enforcement agencies to upgrade crime reporting and tracking capabilities. Following this investment, the number of reported crimes did increase substantially. The question is how much of this increase was due simply to better reporting and how much was due to actual increases in offenses committed.

Other factors have also influenced crime reporting, including increased public awareness of such issues as child abuse, sexual assault, and drunk driving. Offenses committed within family units and many perpetrated against women and children were less likely to be reported in past decades. Although continued progress is needed, tolerance of destructive behavior has changed due to public education efforts and the work of special issue groups such as Mothers Against Drunk Driving. While it is difficult to gauge the extent to which these increases reflect changes in the number of crimes committed or the number of crimes reported, it seems clear that reporting has improved significantly and that these improvements explain some portion of the increase in the rate of reported crime.

Changes in the Workplace

The economy of the United States has undergone fundamental change over the last 20 years. In 1969, 20 million people were employed in manufacturing. By 1989, the number of manufacturing employees had shrunk by 600,000, although the total U.S. population had increased from 203 million to 245 million people. As a result, employment prospects for youth without solid educational backgrounds have declined markedly. In the 1960s, high school graduates could look forward to good jobs in industry, jobs that paid well enough to sustain a reasonable standard of living. Today, a high school education is not a ticket to a decent paying job. Without additional education, many youth face a life of poverty.

Family Disruption

Much of the blame for society's ills has been placed on the demise of "family values." While the "values" issue is open to debate, it is obvious that the structure of the American family has changed significantly since the 1950s. In the last 20 years alone, the number of single parent households has increased 137%. Today, nearly

8 million homes have only a single caregiver present. In 1970, there were just over 3 million such homes. Whether this is a cause or a symptom of society's problems may never be decided to everyone's satisfaction. Regardless of one's point of view, the absence of a caregiver adds significantly to the stress of parenting and reduces the family's ability to nurture, provide for, and supervise children. The weight of this problem has fallen principally on women, and the economic challenges facing single women raising families is well documented. The expense of adequate child care and needed medical insurance forces many into a subsistence level existence, relying on public assistance to survive.

Putting Punishment in Context

While the above issues in no way represent an exhaustive list of possible contributors to the rise in crime in the United States, they are certainly among those factors that need to be considered in any analysis of crime rates. To focus on the relationship between crime and punishment without their consideration is inexcusable, particularly when such analyses are used to establish criminal justice policy for the nation.

The following discussion is simply an attempt to put the crime and punishment relationship into a larger context. While it is obviously not an in-depth analysis required to comprehensively examine factors that influence crime rates, it does illustrate how little impact changes in correctional policy have in controlling crime.

Two simple analyses are presented. The first enters measures of the above demographic and economic issues as well as a measure of punishment into a series of multivariate analyses to estimate the relative influence of each factor on changes in crime rates. The period 1960 through 1990 is used, representing three decades of change. Variables were entered after various lagging and smoothing techniques were used to maximize the bivariate relationship between each factor and the change in crime rates. The second analysis is simply a comparison between two states (Wisconsin and Minnesota) with similar demographic profiles and very different incarceration policies.

Relationships between demographics and economic factors and the crime rate are not easily quantified. Attempts to do so are plagued

by errors in measurement, changes in data definitions over time, and simply by the complexities involved in establishing causation in social science research. On the surface, some relationships between crime and demographics seem extraordinarily strong. The correlation for the time period 1960 through 1990 between crime rates and one population subgroup, males, age 15–29, is nearly perfect (.98). However, a significant portion of the relationship is simply serial correlation—that is, since both indices generally move in the same direction over time, the beginning and ending points of the data sets account for much of the correlation attained. When annual *changes* in crime rates and population estimates are compared, the correlation between the two measures declines markedly (to .44). In attempting to determine the *causes* of changes in crime rates, it is necessary to analyze changes in data that occur within specified time periods.[1]

Generally stated, the analyses tested the following hypothesis:

Changes in the U.S. crime rate are a function of:

a. Annual changes in the population of males 15–29;
b. Annual changes in the urban population;
c. Annual changes in the number of single parent families;[2]
d. Annual changes in the unemployment rate; and
e. Annual changes in the ratio of prison admissions to the number of serious crimes committed.

The last variable constitutes the measure of punishment used. Relating prison admissions to crime rather than population has long been advocated by "prison pays" proponents.

None of the statistical analyses undertaken were particularly successful in explaining changes in U.S. crime rates. Males 15–29 accounted for most of the variance explained in total crime rates, while changes in urban population was the factor that best explained the variance in violent crime followed by changes in unemployment and single parent families. *In every instance, the punishment measure proved to be insignificant in explaining variances in crime.*

Comparisons of crime and incarceration rates in Wisconsin and Minnesota are equally telling. The two states were chosen because of their geographic, historical, and demographic similarities, and very different punishment

TABLE 12.2   Wisconsin/Minnesota Comparisons (Rates Per 100,000 Population)

	Wisconsin			Minnesota		
Year	Total Crime Rate	Violent Crime Rate	Incarceration Rate	Total Crime Rate	Violent Crime Rate	Incarceration Rate
1979	4388.0	166.1	73	4392.8	221.0	51
1980	4798.6	182.6	85	4799.5	227.8	49
1981	4766.8	187.9	93	4736.7	228.5	49
1982	4439.1	190.5	96	4454.6	219.3	50
1983	4255.7	190.9	102	4034.2	190.9	52
1984	4172.3	196.5	105	3841.5	211.5	52
1985	4016.7	206.9	113	4134.2	256.4	56
1986	4096.8	257.9	119	4362.2	284.6	58
1987	4169.4	249.9	126	4615.8	285.4	60
1988	3972.0	214.4	130	4314.7	290.1	64
1989	4164.8	222.6	138	4383.2	288.3	71
1990	4395.1	264.7	149	4538.8	306.1	72

TABLE 12.3   Violent Crime Comparisons

	Population	Violent Crime Rate*	Homicides	Gun-Related Robberies	Aggravated Assaults	Gun-Related Assaults
Milwaukee	601,000	710	112	1,153	1,281	875
Minneapolis-St. Paul	610,000	1,282	61	768	3,738	874

*Per 100,000 population

policies. Minnesota introduced sentencing guidelines in 1980 with the clearly articulated goal of controlling prison growth. As a result, the state's incarceration rate has increased slowly from 51 per 100,000 in 1979 (the year before guidelines) to 84 in 1992. Remarkably, the 1992 rate in Minnesota is about one-fourth the national rate.

Wisconsin, on the other hand, while still incarcerating far below the national average, saw its rate more than double from 1979 to 1991, nearly matching the U.S. rate of growth. If the punishment-crime relationship promoted by Barr, Zedlewski, Reynolds, and others is valid, crime rates in the two states should have taken very different courses. As Table 12.2 demonstrates, this is clearly not the case. In 1979, the year before the Minnesota guidelines were initiated, total crime rates in the two states were virtually identical. In the 12 years that follow, Minnesota reported significantly lower rates twice and nearly identical rates four times. In

1991, despite an incarceration rate twice that of Minnesota, Wisconsin's crime rate was only 0.7% below Minnesota's.

Minnesota has historically reported a higher rate of violence than Wisconsin, but that is misleading because it appears to be the result of differences in either police practices or crime reporting. A comparison of each state's major metropolitan areas indicates that residents of Milwaukee are more exposed to gun-related violence than citizens of Minneapolis-St. Paul (Table 12.3). In fact, in 1991, the number of murders committed in Milwaukee was nearly double the number reported in Minneapolis-St. Paul. In total, the higher overall rate of violence in Minnesota is due largely to a huge difference in reported assaults, very likely reflecting differences in how police handle and report domestic violence, minor street altercations, and other types of assaultive behavior.

The Minnesota experience should be particularly instructive. No other state with a large metropolitan population has managed to keep prison costs so low. Yet, Minnesota's rate of crime has also remained low. The fact that neighboring states have not followed Minnesota's example is testimony to the persuasiveness of the "get tough" rhetoric.

CONCLUSIONS

Advocates of increased incarceration have, at best, presented an incomplete picture to the American public. Their simplistic approach to complex issues and, at times, careful manipulation of data have led to a conclusion that more thorough study would not support. The huge and expensive increase in the use of imprisonment over the last decade has *not* led to decreases in crime. The evidence that the imprisonment binge has not produced the desired results is absolutely overwhelming. Attempts to manufacture a different scenario have been based on limited and slanted analyses.

It is time to abandon the "prison pays" myth and move on to affordable intermediate sanctions and crime prevention strategies that better protect the public while offering more hope for long-term reductions in crime. In a recent article on the value of prevention, William Raspberry cited poet John Malins, whose sentiments are as applicable today as when they were written:

Better guide well the young than reclaim them when old,

For the voice of true wisdom is calling,

"To rescue the fallen is good, but 'tis best

To prevent other people from falling."

Better close up the source of temptation and crime

Than deliver from dungeon or galley;

Better put a strong fence 'round the top of the cliff

Than an ambulance down in the valley.

NOTES

1. Annual differences in rates may not be the best measure of change. Annual crime rates tend to go up and down, sometimes inexplicably. In-depth research would attempt to identify crime cycles, perhaps "smoothing" these fluctuations by using 24 or 36 month changes, or moving averages.

2. The number of single parent families is available only since 1970.

REFERENCES

American Legislative Exchange Council, "Report Card on Crime and Punishment." Washington, D.C. (1994).

Bluestone, Barry and Bennett Harrison, "The Grim Truth About the Job Miracle." *New York Times* (February 1, 1987).

Branham, Lynn S., "The Use of Incarceration in the United States: A Look at the Present and the Future." American Bar Association, Criminal Justice Section (April, 1992).

Currie, Elliott, "What Kind of Future? Violence and Public Safety in the Year 2000." NCCD, San Francisco, California (1987).

DiIulio, John J. Jr., "Crime and Punishment in Wisconsin: A Survey of Prisoners." Milwaukee, Wisconsin: Wisconsin Policy Research Institute (December, 1990).

DiIulio, John J. Jr. and Charles H. Logan, "Ten Myths About Crime and Prisons." Wisconsin Interest, Milwaukee, Wisconsin (Winter/Spring, 1992).

DiIulio, John J. Jr. and Anne Morrison Piehl, "Does Prison Pay?" *The Brookings Review* (Fall, 1991).

Johnson, Perry M., "Methvin's Incarceration Argument Doesn't Hold Up Under Scrutiny." *Corrections Today* (April, 1992).

Kleiman, Mark et al., "Imprisonment-to-Offense Ratios." Washington, D.C.: Bureau of Justice Statistics Report (November, 1988): p. 21; we are using his figures without adjustment for under-reporting by the UCR, since that adjustment is only possible from 1973 on.

Methvin, Eugene H., "Doubling the Prison Population Will Break America's Crime Wave." *Corrections Today* (February, 1992).

Raspberry, William, "Better a Fence at the Edge of the Cliff." *Washington Post* (September 2, 1994): p. A23.

Reynolds, Morgan, "Crime in Texas." NCPA Policy Report No. 102, Dallas: National Center for Policy Analysis (February, 1991).

Riveland, Chase, Comments published in a Seattle Times Editorial, and presented at a Washington, D.C. Press Conference (1992).

U.S. Department of Justice, Office of Policy Development, "The Case for More Incarceration." Washington, D.C. (1992).

Zedlewski, Edwin W., "Making Confinement Decisions." Washington, D.C.: National Institute of Justice Research in Brief (1987).

Zimring, Franklin E. and Gordon Hawkins, "The New Mathematics of Imprisonment." *Crime & Delinquency*, Vol. 34, No. 4, 425–436 (1988).

13

MAKING PAROLING
POLICY EXPLICIT

DON M. GOTTFREDSON

PETER B. HOFFMAN

MAURICE H. SIGLER

LESLIE T. WILKINS

The opening section of this article discusses the need for more explicit definition of elements governing parole selection and the problem of determining the weight that should be given to each. The study then demonstrates a method by which analysis of parole board decisions may make present paroling policy more explicit. Decision guidelines developed from this method provide an aid in actual case decision-making. By structuring discretion without removing it, these guidelines permit it to be exercised fairly and rationally. A United States Board of Parole pilot project which includes guideline usage and a procedure for regular evaluation and modification of guidelines is then described.

Are Parole Boards using the right determinants for parole selection? The best answer they can offer at this time, without assurance, is: "Possibly." Ostensibly, at least, they consider the prisoner's offense, prior record, educational and employment history, military record, drug or alcohol problems, institutional discipline, and other matters. But they have not articulated the weight that should be given to each. Should a good military record, for example, outweigh a poor alcohol history, or vice versa? They might argue that every case is unique, but, if this is totally true, they cannot hope ever to establish generally applicable criteria.

UNIQUENESS AND EQUITY

By "equity" or "fairness" we mean that *similar* persons are dealt with in *similar* ways in *similar*

Authors' Note: The points of view and opinions expressed are those of the authors and do not necessarily represent the official position and policies of the above agencies.

Source: From Gottfredson, D. M., et al., "Making paroling policy explicit" in *Crime & Delinquency,* January 1975, pp. 34–44. Copyright © Sage Publications, Inc. Reprinted with permission.

situations. Fairness thus implies the idea of similarity and of comparisons. Obviously, if every person or every case were unique, there would be no grounds for comparison and, hence, no way to provide for fairness. Will an individual, then, see his treatment as fair if he sees himself as similar, in all significant ways, to another person who received exactly similar treatment? Not quite, since, if only one other person were required for comparison, it would not be unreasonable to maintain that *both* were treated unfairly. However, as the sample of similar persons increases, similar treatment among that sample becomes more likely to be regarded as fair. The idea of fairness thus becomes closely related to statistical concepts of similarity and sample size.

A complaint that a parole board is "unfair" implies that similar persons convicted of similar crimes are receiving dissimilar treatment. The factors taken into consideration in the reference sample of persons and characteristics may vary in some degree from one critic to another. Some critics will look with particular care at race (unfairness related to racial characteristics is defined as "racism" because "race" is not seen as a reasonable or morally acceptable justification of differences in treatment); others will look with particular care at the type of offense; some will look at both types of offenses and race. However, the scale and scope of comparison upon which critics may rely are not likely to be wider than the scale and scope of factors the board might consider. If the board uses a parole selection model built upon common elements of comparison (fairness criteria), it can respond precisely to criticisms. If it sustains a balance with respect to crime seriousness, probability of reconviction, and behavior in the institutional setting and ignores race, it is not likely to be accused of racial bias.

If the board has before it, in each case in which a decision is made, a chart indicating the balance among the most important factors that arise in any discussion of "fairness," it can, if it wishes to do so, still depart from the calculated figure, but, in so doing, it would be making a value judgment of further factors not included in the model. If the decision makes these further factors explicit, a sound case for it will have been established. Though the general policy of the board would not be defended by such a model, clearly the decisions *within* the model would be "fair." If attention were diverted from individual cases to questions of general principles of parole, the understanding and control of the system would, we suggest, be greatly increased. Attention could then be more thoroughly devoted to humanitarian considerations because the routine comparative work (even though highly complex) could be delegated to "models" of "fairness."

REASONS FOR DENIAL: IMPORTANCE OF WEIGHTS

To ascertain whether a parole board is using the *right* selective features, we must first find out what the *primary* ones are and what weights are given to them in practice. This requires some sort of measurement. Merely saying that certain factors are important in granting or denying parole oversimplifies the issue. Parole selection is not simply a yes-or-no decision; the question of *when* an inmate should be paroled is more complex than *whether* he should be. The trend toward abolition of minimum sentences imposes greater responsibility on a parole board, which must decide how much time, within the limits set by statute and the sentencing judge, the offender should serve before release.

Thus we have a starting point—the weights being given to the offense and to the offender's characteristics. Examining how these weights are applied in practice will provide a measure of unwritten or *implicit* policy and thus put the parole board in a good position to formulate *explicit* policy.

The National Advisory Commission on Criminal Justice Standards and Goals states:

> The major task of the parole board is articulation of criteria for making decisions and development of basic policies. This task is to be separated from the specific function of deciding individual parole grant and revocation cases, which may be performed either by the board in smaller states or by a hearing examiner.[1]

The issue of explicit general policy and its relation to discretion in parole selection has been considered by a number of authors.[2] A principal method suggested for controlling discretion is the stipulation that reasons for denial of parole be given in writing. While this is a start in the right direction, it cannot, by itself, resolve the matter of equity. True, the inmate may have a right to know the basis for his continued deprivation of liberty and he may be aided thereby in taking corrective action to increase the likelihood of rehabilitative gains and the probability of being granted parole at a later review. Similarly, the paroling authority may profit from the exercise by learning to state more explicitly what often are vague impressions. But these expected gains do not address the issue of fairness entirely. Providing reasons for parole denial identifies the criteria used but not the weights given to them.

For example, the Model Penal Code lists four primary reasons for denying a prisoner release on parole:

> a. There is substantial risk that he will not conform to the conditions of parole; or
> b. his release at that time would depreciate the seriousness of his crime or promote disrespect for law; or
> c. his release would have a substantially adverse effect on institutional discipline; or
> d. his continued correctional treatment, medical care, or vocational or other training in the institution will substantially enhance his capacity to lead a law-abiding life when released at a later date.[3]

If parole selection were truly an either-or (parole/no parole) decision—as it may be in jurisdictions with long minimum sentences—such reasons might suffice. However, when minimum sentences are short or are not given (following the present sentencing trend), parole selection is, in reality, more of a deferred sentencing decision—a decision on when to release—than a parole/no parole decision. Merely giving reasons for denial does not suffice because they relate only to the fact of the denial; they include no criteria on the length of the consequent "continuance" or "set off." Thus a parole board considering a bank robber may give him a continuance of three years for reasons (a) and (b) quoted above and in a similar case of another bank robber give a continuance of five years for the same reason. Without explicit guidelines that cover not only the criteria used but also the weights to be given them, a parole board will not be more likely to arrive at equitable decisions than it is when it gives no reasons at all, and observers will not have much more opportunity to challenge these decisions.

PRIMARY CRITERIA

One phase of the Parole Decision-making Project conducted by the NCCD Research Center was identification of weights given to various criteria in the parole decision. It became apparent early in the project that, as other research endeavors had shown, parole board members place little value on the mere presentation of the prediction device known as an "experience table."[4] A study of criteria used in making parole *decisions* (as distinguished from criteria used in predicting parole *outcome*), in which board members completed a set of subjective rating scales for a sample of actual decisions over a six-month period, showed that the primary concerns were severity of offense, parole prognosis, and institutional behavior and that a parole board's decision could be predicted fairly accurately by knowledge of its ratings on these three factors.[5]

From this knowledge, the development of an explicit indicant of parole selection policy was possible. For initial decisions a chart was constructed with one axis reflecting offense severity and the other reflecting parole prognosis (risk). The intersection of these axes gives the expected decision (in months to be served before the review hearing). In the examples presented in Figure 13.1, the expected decision in high severity/good prognosis cases (such as armed robbery, first offender) is 20 months to be served before review consideration; in low severity/poor prognosis cases, the expected decision is 14 months to be served before review consideration. At review considerations, cases with "adequate" or "very good" institutional adjustment (discipline and program progress ratings were highly correlated) were generally released; those with ratings of "below average" or "poor" were likely to be "set off" for another hearing.

As an aid in actual case decision making, this type of chart could be used in the following manner. After scoring the case on severity and prognosis, the parole board member or hearing examiner would check the table to see the expected decision. In practice, a range (e.g., 20 to 24 months) would be appropriate to allow for some variation within broad severity or risk categories. Should he wish to make a decision outside the expected range, he would be obligated to specify the factors which make that particular case unique (such as unusually good or poor institutional adjustment, credit for time spent

FIGURE 13.1   Time to Be Served Before Review (in Months)

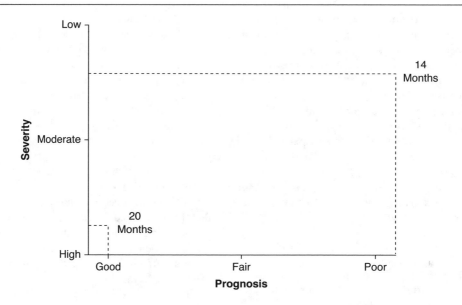

on a sentence of another jurisdiction, etc.). At the review hearing, the decision to parole or continue would be based primarily on institutional performance.

GUIDELINES: CONSTRUCTION AND USE

The United States Board of Parole showed considerable interest in implementing this model. Very likely, one reason was that the Board, under heavy criticism for several years, was attempting at that time to move ahead on its own proposal for change, which included regionalization, a plan that called for delegating the routine decision-making power (parole grants and revocations) to an expanded staff of hearing examiners, with the Board performing a policy-setting and appellate function. Obviously, decision guidelines of the type developed could enable the Board to exercise control more effectively over the decisions of the expanded and decentralized staff.

The result was that the Parole Decision-making Project staff was requested to formulate parole selection policy guidelines in as objective a format as possible. The staff replied that the Board itself might rank-order offense types by severity and then, for each risk classification (the determination of which could be aided by a

statistical predictive device), decide on an explicit policy. However, the Board expressed doubt about undertaking the task without having more familiarity with this type of device. The Project staff, therefore, was requested to provide two sets of policy guidelines—one set for adult offenders, the other for youth—based on the Project's coded material reflecting parole board policy during the preceding two years.[6] These guidelines were to be tested for six months, after which the Board would make any modifications deemed necessary. A plan to facilitate periodic consideration of guideline modifications was also requested.

The study cited above[7] yielded a set of guidelines based on subjective ratings. The new requirement was a table based on more objective measures. Thus, for the parole prognosis axis, an eleven-factor predictive (salient factor) score (see Appendix A) that have been worked out by the Project was substituted for the subjective ratings. These "experience table" scores were combined to form four classes of risk: very good (9–11), good (6–8), fair (4–5), and poor (0–3).[8]

For the severity scale, a different procedure was necessary. The median time served was calculated for each offense in each category of offense ratings coded by the Project.[9] Offense ratings with similar median times served were combined to produce six severity level classifications.[10]

The median time served for each severity/risk level was then tabulated (separately for youth and adult cases) for the large sample of final decisions (parole/mandatory release/expiration) coded by the Project. "Smoothing," based on agreement by two Project staff members after visual inspection, increased the consistency of these medians, although no attempt was made to force uniform or linear increments. Each median was then bracketed ($\pm x$ months) to provide a "discretion range"—the guideline table. Table 13.1 displays the original adult guidelines. The size of the appropriate range was determined after informal discussions with several board members and hearing examiners and, while arbitrary, is to some extent proportional to the size of the median. Since not all offenses were included in this listing, instructions were prepared which explained that an unlisted offenses' appropriate severity level could be determined by comparing that offense with others of similar severity that were listed. In addition, because not all offense ratings (e.g., vehicle theft) were specific enough to cover the scale of severity possible (e.g., theft of one vehicle for personal use up through large-scale theft for resale), the instructions indicated that the

offense ratings listed were to be used only as a guide and that the hearing panel's determination of the severity category should be supported by the description of the offense in the hearing summary. In other words, the severity rating is a subjective determination guided by objective indicants.

In October 1972 the United States Board of Parole launched a pilot project to test the feasibility of regionalization. Comprised of five institutions in the Northeast, making up about one-fifth of the Board's total workload, the project had a number of innovative features, including opportunity for the prisoner to be represented by an advocate, written reasons for parole denial, a two-stage administrative appeal process, and the use of decision guidelines.

For all initial hearings, the examiners were instructed to complete an evaluation form that included a severity rating scale and the salient factor score. Should they make a recommendation outside the guideline table, they were instructed to specify the case factors which compelled them to do so. The format of the hearing summary was designed so that the last section begins with the following standardized statement, the blanks to be filled in with the appropriate phrase or number:

TABLE 13.1   Average Total Time (Including Jail Time) Served Before Release
U.S. Board of Parole, Pilot Regionalization Project, Guidelines for Decision Making, Adult Cases

Offense Categories	Salient Factor Score (Probability of Favorable Parole Outcome)			
	9–11 (Very High)	6–8 (High)	4–5 (Fair)	0–3 (Low)
A—Low severity[a]	6–10 months	8–12 months	10–14 months	12–16 months
B—Low/moderate severity[b]	8–12 months	12–16 months	16–20 months	20–25 months
C—Moderate severity[c]	12–16 months	16–20 months	20–24 months	24–30 months
D—High severity[d]	16–20 months	20–26 months	26–32 months	32–38 months
E—Very high severity[e]	26–36 months	36–45 months	45–55 months	55–65 months
F—Highest severity[f]	Information not available because of limited number of cases			

NOTES: (1) If an offense can be classified in more than one category, the most serious applicable category is to be used. If an offense involved two or more separate offenses, the severity level may be increased. (2) If an offense is not listed above, the proper category may be obtained by comparing the offense with similar offenses listed. (3) If a continuance is to be recommended, subtract one month to allow for provision of release program.

a. Minor theft; walkaway (escape without use of force); immigration law; alcohol law.

b. Possess marijuana; possess heavy narcotics; less than $50; theft, unplanned; forgery or counterfeiting, less than $50; burglary, daytime.

c. Vehicle theft; forgery or counterfeiting, more than $500; sale of marijuana; planned theft; possess heavy narcotics, more than $50; escape; Mann Act, no force; Selective Service.

d. Sell heavy narcotics; burglary, weapon or nighttime; violence, "spur of the moment"; sexual act, force.

e. Armed robbery; criminal act, weapon; sexual act, force and injury; assault, serious bodily harm; Mann Act, force.

f. Willful homicide; kidnapping; armed robbery, weapon fired or serious injury.

The hearing panel considers this to be a [   ] offense severity case with a salient factor score of [   ] The subject has been in custody for a total of [   ] months.

A decision to [   ] is recommended. (Indicate reasons if the decision is outside the guidelines.)

For review hearings, completion of the evaluation form was required before any continuance was recommended for reasons other than institutional discipline or failure to complete specific institutional programs, so that the guidelines would not be exceeded by arbitrary continuances. If a parole grant was recommended, completion of the form was not necessary. At early review hearings (requested by institutional staff when, in their judgment, an inmate has shown exceptional institutional progress meriting earlier parole consideration) the guidelines are consulted also to see whether the exceptional progress justifies the advanced parole date recommended.

Statistical tabulations for the first four months (October 1972 through January 1973) show the numbers and percentages of panel recommendations within and outside the guidelines (Table 13.2). Of all initial decision recommendations (adult and youth) 6 per cent were within the decision guidelines. About one-third of panel recommendations outside the guidelines were for continuances of one, two, or three months under the guideline specification, partly because of a desire to allow more than the thirty-day release preparation period built into the guideline table. With continuing use of the guidelines, release at review consideration (given good institutional adjustment) will occur more frequently, uncertainty in release program planning will be lessened, and the need for lengthy post-decision release planning periods will be reduced.

During the course of this study, the project case summaries were examined to identify recurring explanations for decisions outside the guidelines, and a list of examples of such cases was prepared as a guideline supplement (see Appendix B). The list does not, in itself, justify a deviation from the guidelines in an individual case; it is merely a reminder that the deviation can be considered.

GUIDELINE MODIFICATION

Since usage of the guidelines may induce rigidity—just as the absence of guidelines produces disparity—the Board adopted two basic procedures for modifying and updating them.

First, the Board may modify any guideline category at any time. For example, after three months of guideline usage it decided to place three additional offenses on the guideline chart—Selective Service violation (determined by vote of the Board to be an offense of moderate severity), violation of the Mann Act with force (very high severity), and violation of the Mann Act without force for commercial purposes (moderate severity).[11]

Second, at six-month intervals the Board will be given feedback from the decision making of the previous six months and will examine each category to see whether the median time to be served has changed significantly. For example, the adult guidelines for the high severity/fair risk category show 26–32 months (see Appendix C), a median of 29 months ± 3. If after six months the median within this category is found to have statistically shifted—e.g., to 31 months—a new guideline of 28–34 months may be created.

TABLE 13.2   538 Initial Decision Recommendations, Pilot Project Guideline Usage, October 1972 to January 1973[a]

Site	Within[b] Decision Guideline	1–3 Months Longer	1–3 Months Shorter	4 or More Months Longer	4 or More Months Shorter
		Number and Percentage of Recommendations			
Adult institutions	266 (64.6%)	20 (4.9%)	59 (14.3%)	26 (6.3%)	41 (10.0%)
Youth institutions	73 (57.9%)	11 (8.7%)	10 (7.9%)	21 (16.7%)	11 (8.7%)
All institutions	339 (63.0%)	31 (5.8%)	69 (12.8%)	47 (8.7%)	52 (9.7%)

a. In the first four months of operation the panels failed to complete the evaluation form in only three cases out of 541 hearings.

b. Includes cases in which a decision within the guidelines was precluded by the minimum or maximum term.

At these policy meetings feedback will be provided the Board concerning the percentage of decisions falling outside each guideline category and the reasons given for these decisions. This will serve two purposes: The reasons for the deviations from the guidelines may be examined to certify their appropriateness, and the percentages of decisions within and outside the guidelines (and their distribution) for each category can be evaluated to determine whether the width for the category is appropriate. That is, too high a percentage of decisions outside the guideline range without adequate explanation may indicate either that a wider range is necessary or that the hearing panels are inappropriately exceeding their discretionary limits. On the other hand, a very high percentage of decisions within the guidelines may indicate excessive rigidity. The guidelines themselves cannot provide answers to these questions of policy.

IMPLICATIONS AND LIMITATIONS

By articulating the weights given to the major criteria under consideration, explicit decision guidelines permit assessment of the rationality and appropriateness of parole board policy. In individual cases they structure and control discretion—thus strengthening equity (fairness)—without eliminating it.

The decision guidelines method has implications not only for original parole selection decisions but also for decisions on parole violation and reparole. It appears equally applicable to judicial sentencing, in which similar problems of disparity arise.

The guidelines concept, the scales used, the procedures for applying them in individual cases, and the procedures to be used in their modification—all of these need to be refined; at present, they are admittedly crude. They appear, nevertheless, to be useful.

APPENDIX A: SALIENT FACTOR SCORE

_____ A. Commitment offense did not involve auto theft.

_____ B. Subject had one or more codefendants (whether brought to trial with subject or not).

_____ C. Subject has no prior (adult of juvenile) incarcerations.

_____ D. Subject has no other prior sentences (adult or juvenile)—i.e., probation, fine, suspended sentence.

_____ E. Subject has not served more than 18 consecutive months during any prior incarceration (adult or juvenile).

_____ F. Subject has completed the 12th grade or received G.E.D.

_____ G. Subject has never had probation or parole revoked (or been committed for a new offense while on probation or parole).

_____ H. Subject was 18 years old or older at first conviction (adult or juvenile).

_____ I. Subject was 18 years old or older at first commitment (adult or juvenile).

_____ J. Subject was employed, or a full-time student, for a total of at least six months during the last two years in the community.

_____ K. Subject plans to reside with his wife and/or children after release.

_____ Total number of correct statements = favorable factors = score

APPENDIX B: GUIDELINE USAGE—AUXILIARY EXAMPLES

The following are recurrent situations in which a decision outside the guidelines might be considered.

Decisions Longer Than Indicated by the Guidelines

1. The subject was committed for a probation violation which involved a new serious offense.

2. More time is necessary to complete a special institutional program (e.g., one-year drug abuse program).

3. The instant offense was actually a series of separate offenses (e.g., a series of bank robberies).

4. The salient factor score appears substantially inconsistent with clinical judgment (e.g., a high salient factor score for a person with a severe history of narcotic addiction).

5. A very high severity offense rating is normally indicated and there were additional aggravating circumstances (e.g., a bank

robbery in which a person was injured or a weapon was fired).

6. Extremely poor institutional conduct (e.g., serious or repeated disciplinary infractions).

Decisions Shorter Than Indicated by the Guidelines

1. Substantial medical problems.

2. Subject faces a substantial additional state-commitment sentence.

3. Subject has been in continuous custody on a separate charge for a substantial period of time.

4. The salient factor score appears substantially inconsistent with clinical judgment (e.g., a low salient factor score for a first offender).

5. Deportation-only cases.

6. Extremely good institutional program progress.

APPENDIX C: GUIDELINES FOR DECISION MAKING, ADULT CASES (REVISED APRIL 1973) AVERAGE TOTAL TIME (INCLUDING JAIL TIME) SERVED BEFORE RELEASE

	Salient Factor Score (Probability of Favorable Parole Outcome)			
Offense Categories	9–11 (Very High)	6–8 (High)	4–5 (Fair)	0–3 (Low)
A—Low severity[a]	6–10 months	8–12 months	10–14 months	12–16 months
B—Low/moderate severity[b]	8–12 months	12–16 months	16–20 months	20–25 months
C—Moderate severity[c]	12–16 months	16–20 months	20–24 months	24–30 months
D—High severity[d]	16–20 months	20–26 months	26–32 months	32–38 months
E—Very high severity[e]	26–36 months	36–45 months	45–55 months	55–65 months
F—greatest severity[f]	Information not available because of limited number of cases			

NOTES: (1) If an offense can be classified in more than one category, the most serious applicable category is to be used. If an offense involved two or more separate offenses, the severity level may be increased. (2) If an offense is not listed above, the proper category may be obtained by comparing the offense with similar offense listed. (3) If a continuance is to be recommended, subtract one month to allow for provision of release program.

a. Immigration law; walkaway (escape without use of force); minor theft (includes larceny and simple possession of stolen property less than $1,000).

b. Alcohol law; Selective Service; Mann Act (no force, commercial purposes); theft from mail; forgery/fraud (less than $1,000); possession of marijuana (less than $500); passing/possession of counterfeit currency (less than $1,000).

c. Simple theft of motor vehicle (not multiple theft or for resale); theft, forgery/fraud ($1,000–$20,000); possession of marijuana ($500 or over); possession of other "soft drugs" (less than $5,000); sale of marijuana (less than $5,000); sale of other "soft drugs" (less than $500); possession of "heavy narcotics" (by addict, less than $500); receiving stolen property with intent to resell (less than $20,000); embezzlement (less than $20,000); passing/possession of counterfeit currency ($1,000–$20,000); interstate transportation of stolen/forged securities (less than $20,000).

d. Theft, forgery/fraud (over $20,000); sale of marijuana ($5,000 or more); sale of other "soft drugs" ($500–$5,000); sale of "heavy narcotics" to support own habit; receiving stolen property ($20,000 or over); passing/possession of counterfeit currency (more than $20,000); counterfeiting; interstate transportation of stolen/forged securities ($20,000 or more); possession of "heavy narcotics" (by addict, $500 or more); sexual act (fear, no injury); burglary (bank or post office); robbery (no weapon or injury); organized vehicle theft.

e. Extortion; assault (serious injury); Mann Act (force); armed robbery; sexual act (force, injury); sale of "soft drugs" (other than marijuana—more than $5,000); possession of "heavy narcotics" (nonaddict); sale of "heavy narcotics" for profit.

f. Aggravated armed robbery or other felony—weapon fired or serious injury during offense; kidnapping; willful homicide.

APPENDIX D: GUIDELINES FOR DECISION MAKING, YOUTH CASES (REVISED APRIL 1973) AVERAGE TOTAL TIME (INCLUDING JAIL TIME) SERVED BEFORE RELEASE*

	Salient Factor Score (Probability of Favorable Parole Outcome)			
Offense Categories	9–11 (Very High)	6–8 (High)	4–5 (Fair)	0–3 (Low)
A—Low severity[a]	6–10 months	8–12 months	10–14 months	12–16 months
B—Low/moderate severity[b]	8–12 months	12–16 months	16–20 months	20–25 months
C—Moderate severity[c]	9–13 months	13–17 months	17–21 months	21–26 months
D—High severity[d]	12–16 months	16–20 months	20–24 months	24–28 months
E—Very high severity[e]	20–27 months	27–32 months	32–36 months	36–42 months
F—Greatest severity[f]	Information not available because of limited number of cases			

*Based on Supplemental Report No. 9 of the Parole Decision-making Project, conducted in collaboration with the United States Board of Parole, supported by a grant from the National Institute of Law Enforcement and Criminal Justice of the Law Enforcement Assistance Administration, and administered by the Research Center of the National Council on Crime and Delinquency.

NOTES: (1) If an offense can be classified in more than one category, the most serious applicable category is to be used. If an offense involved two or more separate offenses, the severity level may be increased. (2) If an offense is not listed above, the proper category may be obtained by comparing the offense with similar offenses listed. (3) If a continuance is to be recommended, subtract one month to allow for provision of release program.

a. Immigration law; walkaway (escape without use of force); minor theft (includes larceny and simple possession of stolen property less than $1,000).

b. Alcohol law; Selective Service; Mann Act (no force, commercial purposes); theft from mail; forgery/fraud (less than $1,000); possession of marijuana (less than $500); passing/possession of counterfeit currency (less than $1,000).

c. Simple theft of motor vehicle (not multiple theft or for resale); theft, forgery/fraud ($1,000–$20,000); possession of marijuana ($500 or over); possession of other "soft drugs" (less than $500); possession of "heavy narcotics" (by addict, less than $500); receiving stolen property with intent to resell (less than $20,000); embezzlement (less than $20,000); passing/possession of counterfeit currency ($1,000–$20,000); interstate transportation of stolen/forged securities (less than $20,000).

d. Theft, forgery/fraud (over $20,000); sale of marijuana ($5,000 or more); sale of other "soft drugs" ($500–$5,000); sale of "heavy narcotics" to support own habit; receiving stolen property ($20,000 or over); passing/possession of counterfeit currency (more than $20,000); counterfeiting interstate transportation of stolen/forged securities ($20,000 or more); possession of "heavy narcotics" (by addict, $500 or more); sexual act (fear, no injury); burglary (bank or post office); robbery (no weapon or injury); organized vehicle theft.

e. Extortion; assault (serious injury); Mann Act (force); armed robbery; sexual act (force, injury); sale of "soft drugs" (other than marijuana–more than $5,000); possession of "heavy narcotics" (nonaddict); sale of "heavy narcotics" for profit.

f. Aggravated armed robbery (or other felony)—weapon fired or serious injury during offense; kidnapping; willful homicide.

NOTES

1. National Advisory Commission on Criminal Justice Standards and Goals, *Report of the Task Force on Corrections: Summary Report on Corrections—Working Draft* (Austin, Texas: Office of the Governor, Criminal Justice Council, 1972), p. 39.

2. K. C. Davis, *Discretionary Justice* (Baton Rouge: Louisiana State University Press, 1969);

F. L. Bixby, "A New Role for Parole Boards," *Federal Probation*, June 1970, pp. 24–28; F. Remington et al., *Criminal Justice Administration* (Indianapolis: Bobbs-Merrill, 1969).

3. American Law Institute, *Model Penal Code* (May 4, 1962), § 305.9.

4. See P. Hoffman and H. Goldstein. *Do Experience Tables Matter?* Parole Decision-making Project, Report No. 4; and P. Hoffman et al., *The*

Operational Use of an Experience Table, Parole Decision-making Project, Report No. 7 (Davis, Calif.: NCCD Research Center, June 1973).

5.   P. Hoffman, *Paroling Policy Feedback,* Parole Decision-making Project, Report No. 8 (Davis, Calif.: NCCD Research Center, June 1973).

6.   For a description of sampling and coding procedures, see Susan M. Singer and D. M. Gottfredson, *Development of a Data Base for Parole Decision-making,* Parole Decision-making Project, Report No. 1 (Davis, Calif. NCCD Research Center, June 1973).

7.   See text *supra* at note 5.

8.   This was one of the Project's first predictive measures and was based on a relatively small sample. As soon as a more powerful device is formed, it can be readily substituted similarly, if a different combination of score categories is desired, the guidelines can be changed accordingly.

9.   For coding definitions and procedures see D. M. Gottfredson and Susan M. Singer. *Coding Manual,* Parole Decision-making Project, Report No. 2 (Davis, Calif: NCCD Research Center, June 1973).

10.   Some offense ratings had been excluded because of lack of specificity.

11.   The first set of guidelines used offense descriptions prepared in another context for use in a decision game. After the first six months, revised guidelines were prepared specifically for federal offenders; they are shown as Appendices C and D.

14

IMPEDIMENTS TO PENAL REFORM

NORVAL MORRIS

In this country, in contrast to Europe, criminology has not found a secure home in the law schools, nor have judges and lawyers manifested esteem for criminological and penological speculations. Happily, for reasons which pertain to the broad sweep of social and political change rather than to any process of intellectual conversion, the days of neglect are passing. The discipline of criminology, if discipline it be or can become, will hereafter play an increasing role in the life of the law schools of this country. For this reason, quite apart from proper reservations about any incumbent of the chair, the establishment of the Julius Kreeger Professorship of Law and Criminology is of importance to this law school, fixing these studies into the structure of our Faculty; of importance to the law schools of the United States as an act of leadership in legal education; and, I hope, of importance to the communities we seek to serve.

In an inaugural lecture one is permitted to make a testament about one's field, to offer a broad theoretical statement of an intellectual position. On the theme of penal reform my testament is easy to make and unchallengeable: We need more knowledge of the efficacy of our various penal sanctions in their deterrent and educative roles in the community at large and with the individual offender. None will challenge this; but its affirmation does not achieve much. It has truth but lacks momentum. The point has been made with wearisome repetitiveness.[1]

So I would like to pursue a narrower question. Why is it that so little headway is made? What are the impediments to the acquisition of these types of knowledge? It is probable that here, too, progress presupposes some degree of clarity in recognition of the obstacles to progress. I do not mean to dwell on the political and economic obstacles to penal reform. That these may on occasion be massive, no one can doubt. I have in mind rather the impediments of inadequate theory and the gaps in our knowledge that may well in the long run prove more intractable than the political exigencies and the chronic shortage of men, money, and materials with which a selfish community burdens its penal reformers.

It is to be noted that the handicaps of a defective theory and of exiguous information about our penal methods, to which I will point, have not precluded the development of an appreciably powerful and effective penal reform movement; there is no paradox here, since the mainspring of penal reform has been neither empirically validated knowledge nor a developed theory. Decency, empathy, the ability to feel at least to a degree the lash on another's back, the removal occasionally of our customary blinkers to human suffering, a respect for each individual springing from religious or humanitarian beliefs—these have been the motive forces of penal reform and not any validated knowledge concerning the better prevention of crime or recidivism. We have built an intellectual superstructure to our developing sense of identity with all fellow humans, criminals and delinquents not excepted, but it is an edifice of rationalizations. Perhaps this is an overstatement, perhaps a more precise analysis of this relationship between mind and heart in penal reform is that our uniform experience, critically analyzed, seems to be that we can indulge our sense of decency, of the reduction of suffering even by criminals, without any adverse effects on the incidence of criminality. The history of penal reform thus becomes the history of the diminution of gratuitous suffering.

Capital punishment moves from being the basic punishment for all felonies to an exceptionally inflicted indecency in which we place little trust and have little confidence. And the change is not the product of research studies that would satisfy the empiricists of this law school. The same is true of all the ornate and obscene forms of corporal punishment which constituted our heritage of penal sanctions for non-capital offenses. Likewise, that convicts ceased to be transported to the southeastern shores of this continent and to the pleasant sunny climes of Australia had little to do with any assessment of the effectiveness of the sanction of transportation in deterring men from criminal conduct. Yet again, many of the indignities and cruelties of that American invention, the prison, to be found in the original Auburn and Pennsylvania systems, have been eliminated or ameliorated, not because of developing knowledge about the more effective prevention of crime or of recidivism, but because they inflict needless suffering. The crime and recidivist situations at least did not deteriorate upon our casting aside the gallows, the lash, the lock-step, the broad arrow, and the rules of solitude and silence. And much indeed yet remains to be done along these lines. The diminution of gratuitous human suffering gratuitous in the sense that no social good whatsoever flows from it, that it in no wise diminishes the incidence or seriousness of crime and

delinquency, remains an important purpose of penal reform. One does not have to travel far from this place today to find thousands of convicted persons, adult and juvenile, subjected needlessly to such suffering and for grossly protracted periods. Moreover, most such suffering is more than useless; it is harmful to us. It tends to increase the social alienation of those we punish beyond our social needs, and it is highly probable that we pay a penalty in increased recidivism and increased severity of the crimes committed by those who do return from such punishment to crime. Studies of the inmate culture have confirmed the alienating effect of the prison, its creation of a community of the self-identified as aggrieved. The inmate culture has high efficiency in communicating criminal and anti-conventional values in a situation ideal for their transmission and consolidation. The prison engenders more than social alienation; it fosters and confirms maladjustment.

These, then, have been our main guidelines to penal reform: the humanitarian diminution of gratuitous suffering and the self-serving reduction of social alienation. It becomes clear, however, that these guidelines are gradually becoming insufficient. New directions must be charted. The Swedish adult correctional system provides an excellent case study in this impending need. In terms of the amelioration of penal conditions little remains to be done. There obtains in that country as little interference as reasonably possible with the convicted criminal's life, an energetic attempt is made to preserve his social ties by probation systems, and, if it should be necessary to incarcerate him, to do so briefly and in conditions of reasonable comfort with as little disruption of those social ties as possible. No large penal institutions; regular home leave; over a third of prisoners held in open conditions lacking bolts, bars, and walls; adequate work and vocational training; a sense of near equality in the relationships between prisoners and staff; these have become the hallmarks of the Swedish prison system. Along this path, in Sweden, they have gone about as far as they can go. Not quite; there are still a few remaining traditional lock-ups to be eradicated; there still remain a few needless indignities and hardships. Nevertheless, in the broad, the guidelines of empathy and minimizing alienation have served to their limit. Further guidance will not come from the heart; the head must be more directly engaged. And that means a program of research and training which is in Sweden hardly officially envisaged, let alone pursued. The same is true, though at a much earlier stage of development, in this country. Take, for example, the half-way house movement which is spreading so rapidly. It shortens prison sentences, it sometimes serves as an alternative to institutionalization, it provides a bridge between the institution and the community, it supports probation and parole arrangements for some offenders, and there is great enthusiasm for it. Yet, in my view there is no established information showing that it better protects the community or better reforms criminals than the sanctions it is supplanting. We are enthusiastic about it because it assists us to avoid harm; not because we know that it assists us to achieve positive good. It was for this same reason that we eliminated the lash.

What, then, are the limitations on this process of ameliorating the prisoner's lot and of reducing the punishment of the convicted criminal and young offender? Limitations there must be, else no punitive action whatsoever would be appropriate. We must recognize our present penal reform movement as an uneasy series of compromises between punitive aggression and rehabilitative empathy and build towards correctional systems, for adult and young offenders, rationally related to our social purposes. Penal reform must stretch beyond its traditional humanitarian purposes to achieve a larger social protection from crime and recidivism. There are obstacles to this effort; I propose to consider certain of them under the following four headings: deterrence; less eligibility; the limits of the rehabilitative ideal; and the ethics and strategy of research.

I. Deterrence

As Sir Arthur Goodhart recently wrote, if punishment "cannot deter, then we might as well scrap the whole of our criminal law."[2] Indeed, to my knowledge, every criminal law system in the world, except one,[3] has deterrence as its primary and essential postulate. It figures most prominently throughout our punishing and sentencing decisions—legislative, judicial, and administrative. We rely most heavily on deterrence; yet we know very little about it.

Ignorance of the consequences of penal sanctions on the community at large is a constant inhibitor of penal reform. Punishment sometimes deters, sometimes educates, sometimes has a habituative effect in conditioning human behavior; but when and how? Our ignorance is a serious obstacle, whatever our regulatory objectives. And of equal importance, we are hesitant to think only in terms of what the individual convicted offender needs to turn him away from crime because we fear that to do so would sacrifice the general deterrent, educative, and habituative effects of our penal sanctions. Thus, if penal reform is to become rational, it is essential that we begin to learn the extent to which our diverse sanctions serve prospective public purposes apart from their effects on the sentenced criminal; absent this knowledge, striking a just balance between social protection and individual reclamation is largely guesswork.

The deterrence argument is more frequently implicit than expressed; the debate more frequently polarized than the subject of a balanced discussion. When I listen to the dialogue between the punishers and the treaters, I hear the punishers making propositions based on the assumption that our penal sanctions deter others who are like-minded from committing crime. And I hear the treaters making propositions concerning the best treatment for a given offender or class of offenders which are based on the assumption that our penal sanctions do not at all alter. There is rarely any meeting of the minds on the issue central to the discourse. And it is not as if such knowledge is unobtainable; it has merely not been sought with anything like the energy and dedication that has been given to the expensively outfitted and numerous safaris that have searched for the source of criminality. The polar argument becomes a bore; a modest beginning on the search for more knowledge becomes a compelling need. We have endured a surfeit of unsubstantiated speculation, continuing quite literally since man first laboriously chipped out his penal codes on tablets of stone or scrawled them on chewed and pounded bark. It is time we did better. To do so it may be wise first to get our terms clear, then to assess what we now know, and then to suggest a strategy for our search.

European criminologists draw a distinction between special and general deterrence which is helpful to our purposes. By special deterrence they refer to the threat of further punishment of one who has already been convicted and punished for crime; it may be the same medicine that is threatened as a method of dissuading him from recidivism or it may be a threat of a larger or different dose. Special deterrence thus considers punishment in the microcosm of the group of convicted criminals. General deterrence looks to the macrocosm of society as a whole (including convicted criminals). It would seem hard to deny that for some types of crime and for some types of people, the individual superego is reinforced and to a certain extent conditioned by the existence of formal punishments imposed by society, and that we are influenced by the educative and stigmatizing functions of the criminal law. Further, it seems reasonable to aver that for some people and for some types of crime the existence of punishment prevents them as potential offenders from becoming actual offenders, by the very fear of the punishment that may be imposed upon them. These two broad effects can be regarded as processes of general deterrence. For purposes of research it may, of course, be necessary to separate these various strands that I have woven together in the concept of general deterrence.

The acquisition of knowledge concerning special deterrence may be achieved by substantially the same methods that will be suggested hereunder as means of dispelling our ignorance of the reformative effects of our treatment methods. In the meantime, this gap in our knowledge is less inhibitory of penal reform than our uncertainty about the general deterrent effects of criminal sanctions and of the possibly adverse consequences of too rapid a shift to predominantly reformative processes.

What, then, do we know of general deterrence? In September, 1965, at the Fifth International Congress of Criminology, held in Montreal, Professor Johannes Andenaes of Oslo University gave a paper, *Punishment and the Problem of General Prevention*[4] which better answers that question than anything else I know in the literature. My comments now are therefore confined to this reference to Professor Andenaes' paper and to an effort to underline its central theme which was that "the problem is not one of determining whether . . . [general deterrent] effects exist; it is one of determining the conditions under which they occur and the degree to which they occur."[5]

Perhaps the capital punishment controversy has produced the most reliable information we have on the general deterrent effects of a criminal sanction. It seems to me well established, as

well established as almost any other proposition in social sciences, that the existence or non-existence of capital punishment as a sanction alternative to protracted imprisonment for convicted murderers, makes no difference to the murder rate or the attempted murder rate. Suppose this is true; there is a temptation to extrapolate such a proposition to other crimes. This temptation should be resisted for it is quite easy to demonstrate contrary situations for other crimes where increased sanctions (maintaining stable reporting, detection, arrest, and conviction rates) lead to reduced incidence of the proscribed behavior. For example, by way of extreme contrast to murder, parking offenses can indeed be reduced by an increased severity of sanctions if one is determined about the matter. And, even with regard to capital punishment for murder, if the secret heart of an abolitionist must be bared, general deterrence still probably functions peripherally.

Let me conclude this theme by a possibly too whimsical allegory. Some people tell me that the world is flat; that if you punish one, that will deter the others. And it is plainly clear that for a variety of purposes they are correct, just as for many purposes—tennis, building a house—the world is clearly flat. But there is a certain roundness alleged by some dreamers. They claim that if you sail in one direction you get back to where you started. They suggest it is their long and tragic experience that those who would deter others from acting by threatening or even demonstrating that they will suffer, often experience the very action they seek to deter; that those who would reduce crime by terror often live deeply fearful of violent crime. Let us kill one in ten; that will stop their resistance! Hang the murderers; that will reduce the murder and attempted-murder rates! Bomb their cities; that will bring them to the conference table! And I conclude, on this topic, as I hope you do, that those who would pin their larger faith to deterrence are unwise; and that those who deny its operative relevance in many mundane and smaller areas of behavioral control are likewise unwise. What we need are some soundings in deterrence, some tracings of this shore, so that we shall begin to know where the flatness of the human personality is relevant and where the roundness; for what purpose this particular world is flat and for what purposes round. Given these insights, a massive impediment to penal reform would be cast aside.

II. LESS ELIGIBILITY

The principle of "less eligibility" is the reverse side of the coin of deterrence. Sidney and Beatrice Webb defined this principle, in relation to the 19th century Poor Laws in England, as follows: "The principle of less eligibility demanded that the conditions of existence afforded by the relief [of the pauper] should be less eligible to the applicant than those of the lowest grade of independent labourers."[6] When applied to penal sanctions, and certainly to prisons and reformatory institutions, it means that the conditions of the convicted criminal should be "less eligible" than those of any other section of the community. Jeremy Bentham, in his *Panopticon*, adopted this principle: "[T]he ordinary condition of a convict . . . ought not to be made more eligible than that of the poorest class of subjects in a state of innocence and liberty."[7]

The principle of less eligibility has, as you see, an attractive simplicity. If the conditions of the convicted criminal are to be better than those of any other group in the community, then that group, when they know of this fact, will hurry to join their more fortunate brethren—and the gates lie open via crime. Far from being deterred, they will be attracted. In 1939, Hermann Mannheim regarded this principle of less eligibility as "the most formidable obstacle in the way of penal reform."[8] In the years since Mannheim wrote, the principle seems to have declined in significance, certainly at the administrative level. The Federal Bureau of Prisons has for years in its institutions for young adults and older youths been providing vocational training programs which are only now gradually being emulated by the Job Corps and which have long been superior to the vocational training opportunities which would have been available to the inmates had they not been convicted of federal offences; and these training opportunities are offered in material and physical conditions manifestly superior to those in which otherwise all but a few would be living. The same is true in many prisons and reformatories—for example the forestry camps run by the Illinois Youth Commission. The conditions there are certainly not luxurious, but they are better physically than those in which many of the youths live in the depressed neighborhoods from which they come.

And if one goes further afield to test this, say to Polynesia, in the jail at Fiji a bell would ring loudly

at five in the afternoon to summon the prisoners working on the docks, it being well understood that those who were not within the walls by five fifteen would have to fend for themselves that night—and would be arrested the next morning. They rushed to jail at the summons of the bell; but few were thereby expressing an affection for jail life. And in the Nukulofa, on Tonga, in the Friendly Isles, the capital of the last kingdom in Oceania, where the unsylphlike Queen Salote has recently been succeeded by her son, King Tupou II, the main prison, an open institution, is known as "Government College."

The truth is that at all levels of cultural development we seem to accept that compulsory treatment, with the stigma of crime, and pursuant to a judicial sentence, is not likely to be positively attractive to other than those who by long institutionalization have been habituated to it.

Thus, though the principle of less eligibility remains a rationalization for the punitive emotions of men, it is not at present a serious bar to penal reform. There is, however, one other aspect of this principle of less eligibility that may merit a passing glance. Assume that to keep a prisoner costs the community about $2,500 a year. It may be cheaper, if our prediction instruments were at all reliable, to leave him at large and by weekly subsidy of $40 to reward his virtuous avoidance of crime; like a reverse income tax, a reverse crime prevention contribution. It may be cheaper, but it won't soon happen. We may doubt the deterrent efficacy of a sanction but we had better, for the time being, not make our punishments positively attractive. Nor do I fear that my successors in this chair will have serious difficulty in avoiding any problems of less eligibility as they discover and define the rules of sound penal practice in relation to our deterrent and reformative purposes.

III. THE LIMITS OF THE REHABILITATIVE IDEAL

A new but nevertheless serious impediment to penal reform is our growing skepticism about the wisdom of indulging in practice our desire better to treat convicted criminals by mobilizing for that purpose the developing skills of the relevant social sciences. We have come to fear that by so doing we will sacrifice many of the traditional and important values of justice under law. The rehabilitative ideal is seen to import unfettered discretion. Whereas the treaters seems convinced of the benevolence of their treatment methods, those being treated take a different view, and we, the observers, share their doubts. The jailer in a white coat and with a doctorate remains a jailer—but with larger powers over his fellows. It is clear that absent definition of the proper limits of the rehabilitative ideal, this lawyer-like skepticism of ours is a serious theoretical and practical impediment to penal reform.

The dangers of abuse of the rehabilitative ideal are real, but they must not tempt us to inaction; we must not let our skepticism of the reformer's simplistic enthusiasm lead us to a flat and unproductive opposition. We must not be entirely sicklied o'er with the pale cast of thought. Throughout all developed legal systems the rehabilitative ideal sweeps steadily over the jurisprudence of the criminal law and it is regrettable for lawyers to oppose it. We may be skeptical of any rounded Positivist theory, cautious of the School of Social Defence, and even doubt that Marc Ancel's recent graceful study[9] of the penal philosophy of that school accurately phrases correctional realities; but we can hardly oppose their aim or doubt their future significance.

I do not seek to rebut the thesis that the rehabilitative ideal can be abused and has frequently been abused; it seems to me proper to look with suspicion on those who seek power over the lives of others, including the criminal and the juvenile delinquent, on the ground that it will be exercised for their own good and hence for the larger social good. I offer, rather, some suggestions of principle by which we may have our cake and eat it—I hope to suggest principles by which the rehabilitative ideal may be accepted as a guide to social action while at the same time its threats to human rights, its 1984-ish potentialities, can be avoided.

Speaking in 1961 at this law school, on the occasion of the celebration of the enactment of the Illinois Criminal Code, I tried to sketch the dangers of abuse of human rights from assumptions of power for rehabilitative purposes and then offered the following two principles to avoid these dangers:

1. *Power over a criminal's life should not be taken in excess of that which would be taken were his reform not considered as one of our purposes.* The maximum of his punishment should never be greater than that which would be justified by the other aims of our criminal justice. Under the power ceiling of that sentence, we should utilize our reformative skills to assist him towards social readjustment; but we should never seek to justify an extension of power over him on the ground that we may thus more likely effect his reform. This principle should be applied to the exercise of legislative, judicial, and administrative power; it should be applied to substantive law as well as to procedural processes.

2. *Correctional practices must cease to rest on surmise and good intentions; they must be based on facts.* We are under a moral obligation to use our best intelligence to discover whether and to what extent our various penal sanctions do in fact reform.

I appreciate that I am advocating a natural law type of limitation to punishment, not easily capable of formulation in terms which exclude an imprecise individual and community sense of injustice; but that does not preclude its being a sound rule for avoiding the potentiality for injustice in the rehabilitative idea. The late C. S. Lewis was, it seems to me, clearly right when he argued:

> [T]he concept of Desert is the only connecting link between punishment and justice. It is only as deserved or undeserved that a sentence can be just or unjust. I do not here contend that the question "Is it deserved?" is the only one we can reasonably ask about a punishment. We may very properly ask whether it is likely to deter others and to reform the criminal. But neither of these last two questions is a question about justice. There is no sense in talking about a "just deterrent" or a "just cure." We demand of a deterrent not whether it is just but whether it will deter. . . . Thus when we cease to consider what the criminal deserves and consider only what will cure him or deter others, we have tacitly removed him from the sphere of justice altogether; instead of a person, a subject of rights, we now have a mere object, a patient, a "case."[10]

IV. Ethics and Strategy of Research

Earlier I noted gaps in our knowledge of deterrence and suggested means for filling them.

Knowledge of the deterrent efficacy of various punishments is, however, only half the basic necessary information, for if rational decisions are to be made concerning penal sanctions we need also to know the likely effect of the proposed punishment on the particular person to be punished. This likelihood can be judged at present only as a combined statistical and clinical prediction, and then only in terms of probability. Here too the gaps in our knowledge are chasms and we must consider how they can be filled.[11] It will be found that some serious obstacles of an ethical and strategic nature stand in the way of an easy acquisition of this knowledge.

Before considering them, it should be noted that these two areas of information relevant to any punishing decision (general deterrence and rehabilitative potential) interrelate differently at different stages of the punishing process, and interrelate differently for different types of crimes. Thus, the legislator when addressing himself to the definition of the available sanctions for a given type of criminal behavior will be thinking largely in terms of available knowledge concerning deterrence and to a lesser extent will need to take into account problems of individual treatment and rehabilitation. By contrast, the prison administrator or the probation administrator rarely has to give much consideration to problems of deterrence but stands in larger need of information about the likely therapeutic effects of his decisions on the individual offender. The judge imposing sentence faces a more complex balance between the deterrent and individual treatment processes of the criminal law. And for the judge, the relationship between these two processes, rehabilitative and deterrent, cannot be stated as an equation applicable to all crimes; it varies greatly from one type of crime to another. For example, many murderers could safely be released from the court without further punishment on the day that they are convicted of their murder. Deterrence will, however, be a primary and usually controlling consideration precluding such a decision. By contrast, a criminal frequently previously convicted of a relatively minor offense who has just been convicted for this offense again will raise problems in which his individual needs and the needs of society for protection from him will bulk very much larger than any questions of deterring others from the type of behavior of which he has been last convicted.

Though this interrelationship between the deterrent and treatment purposes of the criminal law is thus dynamic and diverse, in most sentencing situations a rational balancing can be achieved only if some information relevant to both aspects is available.

It has recently become fashionable to stress our lack of knowledge of the relative efficacy of our various treatment methods and I do not wish on this occasion to retrace that melancholy story. The central question eludes us: Which treatment methods are effective for which types of offenders and for how long should they be applied for optimum effect? Criminological research has been unwisely concentrated on the search for that will-o-the-wisp, the causes of crime, glossing over the likelihood that crime is not a unity capable of aetiological study. "What are the causes of disease?" is surely as hopelessly wide and methodologically inappropriate a question as is the question "what are the causes of crime?" At last, however, there is widespread verbal agreement (if not action) that we must critically test our developing armamentarium of prevention and treatment methods, and that to do so requires testing by means of controlled clinical trials. Follow-up studies, association analysis, predictive attributes analysis[12]—no matter how sophisticated other research techniques we apply, we cannot escape the need for direct evaluative research by means of clinical trials. And this leads me to the next impediment to penal reform—clinical trials themselves raise important ethical issues that demand consideration.

In medical and pharmacological research the clinical trial is well established and has proved of great value in the development of therapeutic methods. Where there is genuine doubt as to the choice between two or more treatments for a given condition, efficient experimentation requires that the competing methods be tested on matched groups of patients. Of course, the analogy between the doctor's "treatment" and the court's or penal administrator's "treatment" is imperfect. Both the subject of medical diagnosis and the criteria of successful treatment are better defined, and the patient consents to treatment while the criminal does not. Problems of abuse of human rights thus obtrude when it is sought to apply the clinical trial to correctional practice. Is it justifiable to impose a criminal sanction guided by the necessities of research and not the felt necessities of the case?

There is, however, a respectable and reasonable ethical argument against clinical trials of correctional treatment methods which must not be burked in our enthusiasm for the acquisition of knowledge. It runs like this: Terrestrially speaking, man is an end in himself; he must never be sacrificed to some self-appointed superman's belief that knowledge about man's behavior is of greater value than respect for his human rights. This is particularly true if the sacrifice is made without his uncoerced and fully informed choice. The explorer may, choosing thus freely, risk his life in the pursuit of knowledge. The citizen may, under certain controlled conditions, risk his life and physical well-being in furtherance of medical experiments. But when hint of coercion, or restraining or unduly influencing pressures appear, it is (choose your epithet) sinful, unethical, socially unwise, to permit such sacrifice of the individual to the supposed collective good.[13] The argument shifts, of course, in wartime; but then the threat to the collectivity is seen as the overwhelming value.

It is my view that the ethical argument against clinical trials is not convincing and that, given certain safeguards, it is entirely appropriate, indeed essential, for evaluative research projects of this type to be built into all new correctional developments. The two safeguards that I have in mind may not in perpetuity solve the problem, but they do at least provide sufficient protection of human rights for many decades of correctional research.

First, we do not have to apply such research techniques at the stage of judicial sentencing; they can well operate within the sentence that the judge has determined to be the just and appropriate sentence. Secondly, by applying a principle which might be called the principle of "less severity," abuse of human rights can be minimized.

Experiment at the judicial stage is not necessary since correctional sanctions already include wide diversities of treatment within the judicially imposed sentence. A defined term of imprisonment may in any one state involve a commitment to possibly extremely different types of institutions having substantially different reformative processes and with appreciably different degrees of social isolation. And given the operation of discretionary release procedures, including parole, most prison sentences permit widely differing periods of incarceration. Likewise, a sentence of probation can lead to a close personal supervision or to the most perfunctory experience of occasional reporting. The range of subtreatments within each correctional treatment is thus very wide; so wide that ample room for evaluative clinical research into these subtreatments exists without interference with judicial processes. Of course, as information relevant to sentencing emerges from such administratively created clinical trials, it will be fed into the judicial process and will then create new opportunities for further evaluative research. And knowledge will grow without experimentation at the judicial level.

"Less severity" is the other safeguard. By this I mean that the new treatment being studied should not be one that is regarded in the mind of the criminal subjected to it, or of the people imposing the new punishment, or of the community at large, as more severe than the traditional treatment against which it is being compared. To take a group of criminals who otherwise would be put on probation and to select some at random for institutional treatment would be unjust; conversely, to select at random a group who would otherwise be incarcerated and to treat them on probation or in a probation hostel would seem to be no abuse of human rights. Applying this principle it is possible to pursue many decades of valuable evaluative research.

In conclusion, let me say that it is my position that the ethical difficulties in empirical evaluation research are so slight as not to constitute a serious impediment to it. I confess that I feel happier when such projects test differences of practice within existing treatments, so that no burglar will bother to be furious, but I know that is no answer. My final reason for not being persuaded by the furious burglar, even in his precise situation, is this: the whole system of sanctions, from suspicion to arrest to trial to sentence, punishment, and release is now so full of irrational and unfair disparities that marginal arguments of the type the furious burglar produces are to me lost in the sea of injustice from which in the long run we can only be saved by these means. Yet I remain on his side to the extent that I abhor experimental design which is not anxiously perceptive of these ethical problems and does not do its utmost to minimize them.

Putting the ethical obstacles aside, I come to one last but serious strategic impediment to the immediate potentiality of empirical evaluative research to lighten our ignorance of treatment methods. It is peculiarly difficult to organize an effective evaluative program from outside the penal system itself. It may be that only from within the administration can effective and continuing research programs be mounted: and it is certain that it cannot be mounted from without unless there is enthusiastic and strong support for it from within. Thus, California is now producing more meaningful evaluative research than any other state or country in the world. One reason is that the Adult and Youth Authorities in that state have built their research programs deeply into their administrative structures. The same thing is in very small part true in the United Kingdom and to some degree in the federal systems and some of the more progressive states; but it is the rare exception and certainly not the rule.

Let me mention some of the difficulties of "outside research"; for example, research mounted by a university department with the permission of the relevant correctional authority. Let it be supposed that the senior administrators of that authority are wholly and fully persuaded of the need for such quality control of their product. Even so, what is in it for the front of the line staff who must be involved in the project? What effect does the project have on, for example, their mileage allowances? What can they gain from it for themselves? How can their quiet insidious lack of enthusiasm be reconciled with the supportive needs of an active research project? Only if research skills and supportive efforts are part of the career line to promotion is it likely that they will be fully supportive. Within the universities, where they are a part of the normal career promotion and status lines, it is well and easy to talk of the high challenge and value of the acquisition of this type of knowledge. It may appear quite otherwise when one is daily engaged in the treatment of criminals, particularly when the knowledge itself which is being sought is likely to be such as to cast a serious doubt on the social value of one's own efforts.

Politically, if the results of research evaluative of an existing practice are adverse to it, one's opponents and critics may use it unfairly to discredit not only those administering the correctional system but also the appointing authority who is politically responsible. Political battles may be fought while mounted on the charger of

research. Further, in the usual overcrowded, understaffed, exiguously budgeted correctional agency, the unanticipated extra work that is created by a research project for an already fully occupied staff leads not only to lack of enthusiasm for the research project, but may change the nature, methods, and objectives of the research.

These problems are multiplied when the responsible administrators are not totally persuaded of the value of such research but rather are convinced of the socially useful quality of their product as it stands. They need no quality controls of their product—they daily see that it is good. They have, in short, a vested interest in the preservation of current practices. I do not mean offensively to imply that those in charge of correctional agencies or institutions want, for any financial or personal reasons, to preserve inefficiencies in the system. If it were such a corrupt vested interest it would be a less serious obstacle to penal reform. The point is that their motives are of the best. They have total confidence in the quality of their agency or institution. They are ignorant of developments elsewhere and of existing theoretical speculations and research. They are suspicious of the outsider claiming research skills and critical capacities who yet obviously lacks comprehension of the day-to-day difficulties of correctional work. Many are fine people, devoted to minimizing human suffering, pursuing their work as a humanitarian dedication. Their salaries are not high nor is their status in the eyes of the community. Psychological mechanisms must come to their aid to convince them of the social value of what they are doing. Dr. Schweitzer would not have been easy to persuade that he was doing more harm than good in the Congo; and the analogy is close in the mind of the devoted and ambitious correctional officer and administrator.

Like the other impediments to penal reform to which I have pointed, this one is not an impossible obstacle. There is an increasing movement amongst the leading correctional administrators of the world gradually to incorporate some evaluative research programs into their new developments. The swell is slight, but it is perceptible. There will be setbacks, but the shape of future growth is clear. Likewise, the "outsider" in the university need not at all despair of gaining collaboration from those daily involved in correctional practice in his research enterprise, provided he realizes that it is necessary when designing his experiment to take into account the material and psychological needs not only of the subject of his experiment but also of those involved in their treatment. It is no good persuading correctional administrations to allow a research enterprise to be pursued within their organizations unless the collaboration includes the clearest understanding about the roles of those employed in that administration and incorporates advantages to them which will not adversely affect the experiment as an experiment but will provide an incentive for their interested collaboration.

V. CONCLUSIONS

1. To date, our guidelines to penal reform have been humanitarian and aimed at diminishing the prisoner's needless suffering and reducing his social isolation. This sentiment now provides an insufficient frame of reference for penal reform.

2. The fundamental postulate of the criminal law is that punishment deters, yet we have only random insights into the deterrent efficacy, if any, of our diverse sanctions. This knowledge, seriously pursued, would not long elude us.

3. The principle of "less eligibility" is no longer a practical impediment to penal reform.

4. There are no dangers in our espousing the rehabilitative ideal provided.
   a. power over a criminal's life is not taken in excess of that which would be taken were his reform not considered as one of our purposes, and
   b. all supposedly reformative processes are subjected to critical evaluation by empirical research methods.

5. Provided experiments are designed with an eye to avoiding abuse of human rights, and for the time avoid clinical testing at the judicial stage and adhere to the principle of "less severity," the clinical trial is as appropriate to penal form as it is to medical therapy.

6. Research directed towards penal reform is a responsibility of the penal administrator. The outsider, the scholar in a university, may be useful collaborator but only if the penal administrator is convinced of the necessity of such research and will organize his staff and their promotion lines to encompass research activities.

NOTES

1. Most emphatically I do not wish to be misunderstood as suggesting that we do not now have knowledge that could be applied to the better prevention and treatment of crime. There is a culture lag here too. The knowledge of the criminologist may be exiguous, but is ample indeed compared with that of those who are responsible for our legislation and practice in this field.

2. Goodhart, Book Review, 74 The Listener 1005 (1965).

3. Kriminalloven Og de Vestgrønlandske Samfund (Greenland Criminal Code 1962).

4. The paper is reprinted in Andenaes, The General Preventive Effects of Punishment, 114 U. PA. L. Rev. 949 (1966).

5. Andenaes, Punishment and the Problem of General Prevention 60 (September 1965). The quotation is from a summary by Professor Andenaes which was not reprinted in Andenaes, supra note 4.

6. Webb, English Poor Law Policy 11 (1963).

7. 4 Bentham, Works 122–23 (1893).

8. Mannheim, Dilemma of Penal Reform 59 (1939).

9. Angel, Social Defense—A Modern Approach to Criminal Problems (1965).

10. Lewis, the Humanitarian Theory of Punishment, 6 Res Judicatae 225 (1953).

11. It would be a disservice to exaggerate our lack of knowledge of the efficacy of certain penal sanctions. Cynicism is a cheap commodity and gives a spurious air of wisdom. We have, for example, reasonably securely established that there are large categories of criminal offenders, adult and juvenile, who can be treated better on probation than in institutions. By "better" here I mean that they have no higher recidivist rate (though their closer supervision would make it likely that a larger proportion of their offenses would be detected—that their "dark figure" of crime would be less than that of those sent to prison and observed after release), that it is cheaper to treat them on probation than in prison (quite apart from other welfare costs that are also minimized), and that when probation is given to this category of offenders there appears to be no consequential increase in the rate of crime for which the criminal sanctions alternatively used might be thought to have a deterrent effect. This type of knowledge is important, and has emerged from a multitude and variety of studies. It guides social planning to a degree, and there remains much to be done on the basis of the already acquired knowledge of this type and range. Yet it is not cynicism to mention its defects. It suffers from too gross a grouping of personality types and persons subject to social pressures, and omits any analysis of the dynamic relationships between personality and community

processes relevant to human behavior. It is highly probable that within the gross groups so tested there are some who need prison and not probation. And further, probation and prison are not unities, in themselves, but are rather diverse bundles of treatment and custody methods. The step from our present too broad analysis of competing treatment methods toward the gradual development of a treatment nosology demands much more refined and narrow controlled experimentation, and is an inevitable precursor of rational penal reform.

12. See Wilkins, Social Deviance, ch. 9 (1965).

13. See Do We Need New Rules for Experiments on People, Saturday Rev., Feb. 5, 1966, pp. 64–70.

PART IV

Breaking the Cycle of Violence

As noted in the first chapter, the National Council on Crime and Delinquency (NCCD) was an early advocate for specialized courts to deal with violence in families. From its inception, the council saw the link between child maltreatment and future delinquency. In 1993 the NCCD created the Children's Research Center (CRC) to focus its work on reforming the nation's child welfare system. Today that work takes us into 22 states and Australia.

Cathy Spatz Widom (1992)[1] coined the phrase "the cycle of violence" to describe the pattern of children who were victims or witnesses to violence in their homes that went on to be violent offenders themselves. Many longitudinal studies of chronic offenders have documented this tragic cycle (Kelley et al., 1997; Pasawerat, 1991; Thornberry, 1994).[2] In addition, pathbreaking research by NCCD Senior Researcher Madeline Wordes-Noya and her colleague Michelle Nuñez (2002)[3] found that recent violent victimization experienced by teenagers was the single most powerful factor predicting if these adolescents would commit a violent crime in the subsequent 12 months.

Children whose parents are incarcerated make up a particularly vulnerable population. Since the 1970s, the NCCD has highlighted the challenges faced by these children in a publication titled *Why Punish the Children?*[4] The NCCD was instrumental in improving the prison visiting policies for children in several state corrections systems and the federal Bureau of Prisons. The council collaborated with the Child Welfare League of America to establish a resource center for groups working with children whose parents were in prisons and jails. We helped a number of foundations in Pittsburgh, Pennsylvania, conduct a study of this issue, and currently the NCCD is helping several police departments develop better methods of responding when officers encounter a young child at a crime scene.

In this chapter, we present the core research that the NCCD used to help bring about major changes in child welfare in Michigan. Our approach involved developing and implementing a highly prescriptive Structured Decision Making (SDM™) system to cover most child welfare interventions. An evaluation of SDM in 13 Michigan counties showed improved outcomes for children and families, and fewer cases of subsequent maltreatment. The use of SDM also allowed Michigan to permit more children to safely remain with their families and avoid foster care placements. Another important article by Baird and Wagner shows the value of actuarial versus clinical decision making in a range of child welfare situations. The essay by Freitag and Wordes-Noya offers more detail on how SDM works and how to incorporate these tools in effective child welfare practice. The authors spell out the challenges to implementation and offer practical advice to judges and child welfare professionals on the advantages and limitations of the SDM approach.

The last article in Part IV is by NCCD board member Judge Carolyn Temin and NCCD President Barry Krisberg. Judge Temin served on the Court of Common Pleas in Philadelphia and was the President of the National Association of Women Judges. She is a strong advocate of better services and care for the children of the incarcerated. This essay summarizes the latest data and research on the topic. It includes an agenda for research, policy, and programming that would reduce harm to children whose parents are confined.

NOTES

1. Widom, C. S. (1992). *The cycle of violence.* Washington, DC: U.S. Department of Justice, Office of Justice Programs, National Institute of Justice.

2. Pasawerat, J. (1991). *Identifying Milwaukee youth in critical need of intervention: Lessons from the past, measure for the future.* Milwaukee: University of Wisconsin, Employment and Training Institute; Kelley, B. T., Thornberry, T. P., & Smith, C. A. (1997). *In the wake of childhood maltreatment.* Washington, DC: U.S. Department of Justice, Office of Justice Programs, Office of Juvenile Justice and Delinquency Prevention; Thornberry, T. P. (1994). *Violent families and youth violence: Fact sheet #21.* Washington, DC: U.S. Department of Justice, Office of Justice Programs, Office of Juvenile Justice and Delinquency Prevention.

3. Wordes-Noya, M., & Nuñez, M. (2002). *Our vulnerable teenagers: Their victimization, its consequences, and directions for prevention and intervention.* Oakland, CA: National Council on Crime and Delinquency.

4. Bloom, B., & Steinhart, D. (1993). *Why punish the children: A reappraisal of the children of incarcerated mothers in America.* San Francisco: National Council on Crime and Delinquency.

15

THE MICHIGAN STRUCTURED DECISION-MAKING SYSTEM

CHRISTOPHER BAIRD

DENNIS WAGNER

ROD CASKEY

DEBORAH NEUENFELDT

Child protective services (CPS) has one of the most difficult missions imaginable. When child abuse or neglect is suspected by the community, CPS workers must investigate the report, determine if maltreatment occurred, and then if abuse or neglect is confirmed, select a course of action that will ensure that the child(ren) is protected from future harm. The stakes are obviously very high, both in human and economic terms.

While there has been a threefold increase in reports of abuse and neglect nationwide since 1980, there is little data available to agencies to guide the selection of the most effective strategies for intervention. So little is known that CPS agencies even struggle with how effectiveness can be measured.

In the face of the rising number of reports of abuse and neglect, most child protection agencies have acknowledged that workers need help in assessing the degree of risk represented by each family entering the system. As a result,

many have adopted or developed systems of risk assessment. These systems vary greatly in terms of objectives, complexity, and content but all are designed to standardize the way risk to children is assessed with the overall goal of improving the effectiveness of the child protection system. Over five years ago, the State of Michigan, with assistance provided by the National Council on Crime and Delinquency's Children's Research Center, began the development of a comprehensive risk-based case management system. Drawing on knowledge gained in the development of similar approaches in both juvenile justice and child protection, the CRC worked with Michigan staff to establish the following principles to guide development.

- First, risk was defined as the probability of continued maltreatment. The assessment system was to be based on research conducted on Michigan cases. Its validity and reliability should be clearly documented.

- The assessment system should be simple to implement and drive all subsequent decisions regarding services to families and children.
- Finally, information generated by the assessment process should be aggregated to form the basis for policy development, budgeting, and resource allocation.

To develop risk assessment instruments for protective services in Michigan, an extensive data collection effort was undertaken. a stratified random sample of 1,896 cases was selected and relationships between family characteristics and case outcomes were examined. The results of this research were two simple risk assessment scales, one that classified cases based on the risk of continued abuse; the other according to the risk of subsequent neglect. Ratings from these scales were used to assign cases to one of four different service levels.

In 1994, a revalidation study was undertaken resulting in minor revisions to the instruments. This represents the first time a research-based risk assessment system has been subjected to a revalidation, underscoring Michigan's continued commitment to improving decision making in protective services. New substantiations reported ranged from 0% in the low-risk group to 29% for families classified as needing intensive services.

The importance of *validated* risk assessment instruments cannot be overstated. Such instruments provide CPS workers with a simple, straightforward method of determining the relative risk levels of families entering the system. This allows agencies to prioritize their efforts, focusing resources on cases with the highest proclivities for continued maltreatment.

It was recognized that improved assessments by themselves have limited impact on case practice unless there are clear expectations regarding service delivery and monitoring. Thus, service standards were developed to correspond directly to the level of risk of each family. These standards define the minimum frequency of contacts that workers should have with cases at each risk level. It is, in effect, an effort to differentiate services provided, giving priority to those families most likely to again abuse or neglect children.

The goal of the Michigan development effort was to provide structure to case decision making and to base services on the risk and need levels of families. To accomplish this, a comprehensive case management system called Structured Decision Making (SDM) was developed. In total, the system is comprised of the following components:

- Highly structured assessments of family risk and family needs.
- Service standards that clearly define different levels of case contacts, based on risk levels.[1]
- A workload accounting and budgeting system that translates service standards into resource requirements and helps deploy resources equitably throughout the organization.
- A system of case review and reassessment to expeditiously move cases through the system.
- A comprehensive information system to provide data for monitoring, planning, and evaluation.

Although the workload assignment and budgeting components of the system have not been fully implemented to date, the remaining elements were implemented in 13 Michigan counties beginning in 1992. The absence of workload budgeting and case assignment systems meant that the new service standards were difficult to meet, particularly for cases at the higher service levels as the mechanism for equating resources with needs was missing. Nevertheless, substantial changes were initiated in the counties that adopted SDM: Risk and need assessments were conducted on all families where neglect or abuse was substantiated and decisions regarding case services were made accordingly a new case planning protocol established clear expectations for service referrals and agency managers were provided detailed reports on case decisions, family and children needs, service provision, and the progress of cases served. These data provided the basis for monitoring actions taken bringing an unprecedented level of accountability to the agency. When patterns emerged that indicated actions were not in concert with good case practice, new policies were developed, directing workers toward more judicious use of resources, and helping to ensure that case decisions reflected the risk level of families served.

Michigan continues to improve and expand the system knowing that its ultimate impact may not be realized for several years. Most importantly, statewide implementation in CPS is planned and the SDM system will be extended to the foster care caseload. The goal is to move cases more expeditiously through out-of-home placements, shorten stays in temporary care, and enhance the potential for successful family reunification. Other important changes in policy regulating how cases are handled have emerged as information regarding actual practice and case outcomes have been produced.

The remaining sections of this report present results of a comprehensive evaluation of the Michigan Structured Decision-Making System. The same level of care taken in system design was applied to the evaluation. Controls implemented during the evaluation helped ensure that changes, both positive and negative, could be attributed to the new system.

While the primary focus of this report is to determine the impact of the new system on case outcomes, it is also important to assess how SDM actually changed the way cases are handled in Michigan. Unless the system produced differences in the management of CPS cases, there is little reason to expect that outcomes will change. Therefore, the first part of the study analyzed case decision making and service provision to determine the degree to which operations actually differed in the counties that implemented Michigan's SDM system.

EVALUATION DESIGN

A. Introduction

Two approaches to this evaluation were considered. The first, an interrupted time series design, was rejected because other changes that occurred at or about the time of the implementation of the new system meant that any pre/post program differences could be attributed to factors other than SDM. For example, a new perpetrator notification process was implemented during SDM implementation resulting in a rather dramatic decline in statewide substantiation rates. Such changes make an analysis across time periods difficult at best.

The second option was to establish a comparison group of substantiated cases that were subject to all of the policies and case procedures of the Michigan CPS system *except* those implemented with SDM. This design was chosen, and 11 comparison areas were selected based on economic, demographic, and protective service profiles similar to the counties that had been implemented in the new system. In the state's largest county (Wayne County, which includes the city of Detroit), SDM had been implemented in half of the CPS units; the other half operated under the old system. Hence, Wayne County served as its own "comparison group match." The remaining SDM counties were matched to others in the state based on the following criteria:

- Total Population of County
- Median Income of County
- Percent of Population Living in Poverty
- Percent Single Parent Households
- Number of Substantiated Abuse/Neglect Investigations Per Month
- Number of CPS Referrals Per Month
- Number of Full-Time CPS Employees

There were no significant differences between the two groups of counties prior to SDM implementation.

All cases from both the SDM and comparison counties that had abuse or neglect substantiated between September 1992 and October 1993 were tracked for 12 months. Independent case readers were trained in SDM assessment procedures and sent to the comparison counties to conduct risk and need assessments, and review files to collect data on service referrals and program participation. Results of the risk and need assessments were not shared with CPS workers in the comparison counties to avoid influencing case decisions or service provision. Outcome data (new referrals, investigations, and substantiations) were taken from Michigan's computerized information system. Data on SDM cases were collected from Michigan's SDM data base, augmented by file reviews conducted by the same case readers cited above.

B. Measuring Changes in Open/Close Decisions

The first step in the evaluation was to determine how the new system affected worker decisions to open or close cases and/or resulted in a different use of protective services, family preservation (Families First), and foster care. Changes at this level were minimal; there were no significant differences between the two groups in the percentage of cases that were closed, placed on protective services caseloads, placed in Families First, or transferred to foster care. There was, however, a general trend toward a greater degree of "triage" in the SDM counties, where about 3% more cases were closed without services and approximately 2% more cases were transferred to foster care.

Further analysis of this issue found some important and statistically significant differences between the two study groups. These differences included:

- SDM counties were significantly more likely to close low- and moderate-risk cases.

- Cases that were closed without services in SDM counties had significantly lower rates of re-referrals and new substantiations than closed cases in the comparison group, indicating that the "screening out" process was more effective in the SDM counties. In non-SDM counties, outcome data clearly indicate that many more cases where children were at risk of harm were closed without services.

It should also be noted that the SDM cases in this study entered the system before policies prohibiting closure of high and intensive cases were promulgated. Hence, studies of cases substantiated in 1994, for example, would, in all likelihood, find far greater differences in case closure statistics. The new policy appears to be well-grounded, given the relatively high rate of referrals for high-risk cases in both study groups. Indeed, the relatively high rate of re-referrals in both the SDM and comparison groups demonstrates that closing these cases puts children at risk.

In total, 51% of low and 38% of moderate-risk cases were closed following substantiation in the SDM counties compared to 35% of low-risk and 28% of moderate-risk cases in the comparison counties. On the other hand, comparison counties closed more high- and intensive-risk cases. Closing selected cases at lower risk is in concert with the goals of SDM. Such actions shift resources from cases where risk of continued abuse and neglect is low to families with higher-risk profiles. It appears that the process of completing risk and need assessments to help determine which cases can be closed significantly enhances the screening process. Cases closed in the SDM counties had much lower rates of re-referral and re-substantiations than cases that were closed following investigation in comparison counties.

At the other end of the service continuum, a higher proportion of cases sent to foster care in SDM counties were high or intensive risk. In fact, foster care was used for more cases in the SDM counties, but because the new case management system is not used, as yet, in foster care, no data on reunification and length of stay in out-of-home care were collected.

C. Changes in Services Provided to Families

The SDM system, as designed, is intended to: (1) focus more attention on higher-risk cases, and (2) focus case plans and services on needs identified during the assessment process.

As noted earlier, service standards requiring more contact with higher-risk families were implemented in the SDM counties. Time studies were then conducted to determine the degree of compliance with these standards, and the amount of time spent on cases at each service level. While service standards were not met in a high proportion of cases—due, in large part, to the fact that a workload-based budget was not in place—there were, at least, significant differences in time spent on low- or moderate-risk cases and high/intensive-risk cases.

When standards were met, the differences in time devoted to cases at each service level, of course, increased. At the low- and moderate-risk levels, cases in which standards were met had 3.3 and 4.2 hours per month of contact with families instead of 2 hours per month in all studied cases. At the high- and intensive-risk levels, cases in which standards were met had 6.6 and 7.7 hours per month of contact instead of 3 in all studied cases. The outcome portion of this evaluation demonstrates that increased services and case monitoring helps to protect children, lowering the rate of reported maltreatment over the next year. While no comparable time study data are available from non-SDM counties, prior studies conducted by NCCD/CRC have demonstrated that, unless clearly articulated standards are in place, there are generally only minimal differences in time devoted to cases at different risk levels.

A second and important measure of system impact is a comparison of program participation rates of families in each study group. Cases opened to protective services and the Families First program were identified and service referral and participation information was compared. For every major program category, service participation in the SDM counties occurred at significantly higher levels than in the comparison counties (see Figure 15.1). This was particularly true in areas outside of Wayne County. (In Wayne

FIGURE 15.1   Percent of High-Risk CPS Cases That Received Specific Services

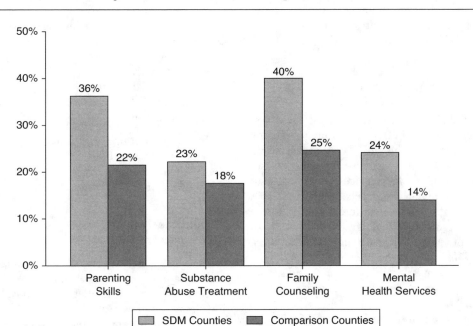

County, more cases are closed following substantiation and a much higher proportion of those remaining are transferred to foster care.)

The greatest increases in services provided are found in two critical areas: parenting skills and family counseling. In both of these service areas, SDM counties realized a 60% increase in the rate of referral.

Furthermore, an analysis of referral and outcome data *within* SDM counties illustrates that involvement in services *significantly* reduces the rate of subsequent maltreatment. Figure 15.6 compares outcome data from families with *serious* substance abuse problems who received treatment with those who did not. The rate of subsequent substantiated abuse or neglect declined markedly for the group receiving treatment. Similar results were found for families receiving other types of services. Almost half of the families with serious substance abuse problems received services. Those families had new substantiations at roughly one-third the rate of those families that did not receive services.

D. Process Evaluation Summary

The results of the process evaluation lead to the following conclusions:

- The SDM system resulted in better decisions as to which cases could be closed following substantiation. A higher proportion of cases were closed in SDM counties than in comparison counties, but a greater proportion of closures were low and moderate risk, and the rate of re-referral and re-substantiation of SDM closures was significantly lower than for cases closed in the comparison group.
- In SDM counties, more time was devoted to cases at higher risk levels. These differences are likely to increase if a workload-based budget is adopted and resources allocated accordingly.
- Cases in SDM counties, particularly those outside of Wayne County, received significantly more services than cases in comparison counties. The difference in services received was greatest for the highest-risk cases.
- Services provided to families with serious problems—particularly substance abuse treatment and parenting skills training—substantially reduced the incidence of subsequent maltreatment.
- Closing high-risk cases following substantiation leaves children unprotected.

The movement toward a policy prohibiting closing these cases—unless unusual circumstances warrant an exception—is supported by this evaluation.

MEASURING THE IMPACT OF SDM

Data cited above document that the SDM system resulted in better decisions regarding which cases could be closed without services, and substantial increases in services to cases that were opened for services, particularly to those at the higher risk levels. The next step in the evaluation was to determine if these changes resulted in a better overall system of child protection. *The principal issue is, in effect, did risk-based decision making, coupled with clear expectations regarding contacts and service provision, translate into lower rates of maltreatment in Michigan?*

The first step in the analysis was to determine if the samples from the SDM and comparison counties were indeed similar. The strategy of selecting comparison counties based on economic, demographic, and CPS profiles matching those of the SDM counties produced remarkably comparable samples. Risk profiles of each sample are presented in Table 15.1.

No significant differences in risk levels were found, either for the entire samples or when cases opened to protective services were compared. The SDM group did have a *slightly* higher risk profile, indicating that *marginally* higher rates of continued maltreatment could be expected, all other things being equal.

A 12-month follow-up period from the date of investigation was used for all cases in the study.[2] Five outcome variables were used to measure impact. These were:

- All new referrals on abuse and neglect complaints.
- Number of subsequent investigations conducted on each case.
- All new substantiations by type.
- All removals of children from homes of families in the samples.
- Any injuries reported as a result of maltreatment.

In combination, these outcome measures provide an excellent basis for determining both the frequency and severity of abuse and neglect during the follow-up period.

A. Outcome Comparisons: All Cases in Each Sample

Figure 15.2 presents overall results for all cases in each sample, regardless of actions taken. Rates of new referrals, substantiations, removals, and injuries reported were all lower in SDM counties. The most significant decreases were found in rates of substantiation; new substantiations in SDM counties occurred at less than half the rate found in comparison counties. While rates of subsequent removal and reports of injury were relatively low in both groups, these measures in SDM counties were also well below those observed in the comparison counties.

B. Outcome Comparisons: Cases Opened to Protective Services

Figure 15.3 compares overall results for cases opened to protective services (including those placed in Michigan's Family Preservation Program) from SDM and comparison counties. Again, the greatest difference was found in rates of new substantiations and again the SDM rate

TABLE 15.1   Risk Level Comparisons - SDM and Comparison Counties

	SDM Counties		Comparison Counties	
Risk Level	All Study Cases	CPS Cases Only*	All Study Cases	CPS Cases Only*
Low Risk	5.1%	3.9%	8.7%	8.2%
Moderate Risk	28.3%	26.6%	24.1%	23.3%
High Risk	66.6%	69.5%	67.3%	68.5%

*Includes those placed in the Families First program.

The Michigan Structured Descision-Making System   149

FIGURE 15.2   Outcomes for All Cases in Study 12-Month Follow-Up

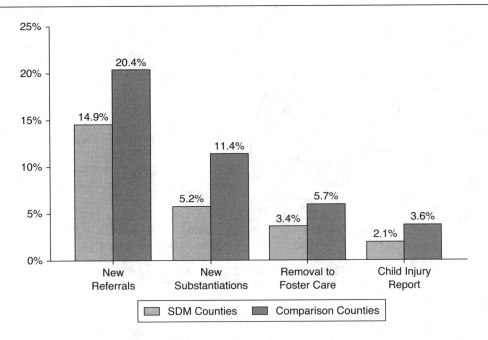

FIGURE 15.3   Outcomes for CPS Cases 12-Month Follow-Up

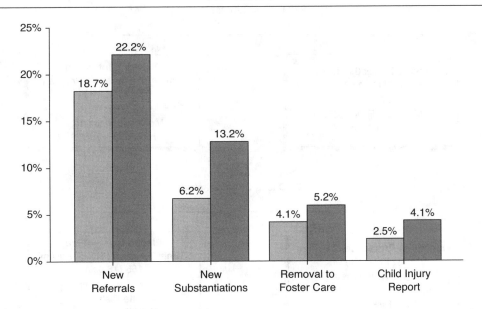

was less than 50% that reported in the comparison group. Rates of referrals, removals, and child injuries were also lower in the SDM group.

The final measure of impact analyzed, the average number of new investigations assigned was also significantly lower in SDM counties

(see Figure 15.4). This, in large part, explains why the SDM counties experienced a rate of substantiation less than half that experienced by comparison counties, while the rate of referral in SDM sites was only 16% below (in relative terms) that of the comparison counties. In

FIGURE 15.4   Average Number of New Investigations Assigned for CPS Cases

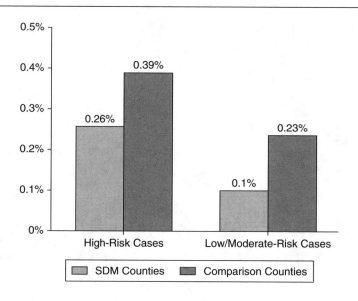

FIGURE 15.5   Action Taken Following Substantiation

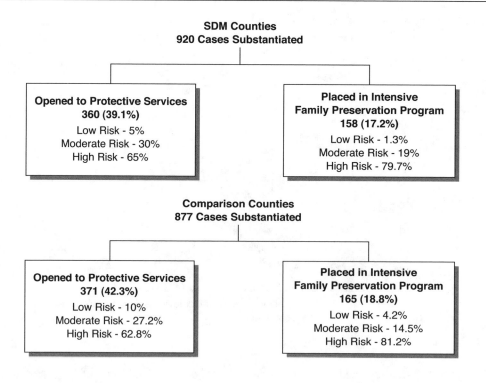

essence, *more cases in the comparison counties had multiple referrals, which, in turn, resulted in more substantiations.*

Because the SDM system was initially implemented only in child protection services, CPS cases, including those served by the Families First program, serve as the primary focus of the evaluation. Figure 15.5 presents a breakdown of these cases in both the SDM counties and the comparison group.

These figures indicate, as expected, a higher risk profile for families referred to Families First. However, they also illustrate part of the problem encountered in evaluating the impact of Family Preservation Programs throughout the nation. These programs have been established, in large part, as alternatives to foster care and theoretically target families where risk of placement is imminent. However, if many families referred to Family Preservation Programs do *not* have children at risk of placement, then the program's impact on foster care placement rates may be marginal at best.

Based on results from SDM counties, Michigan has established a policy reserving Family Preservation referrals for higher-risk families. Such a policy may well improve the impact of the program by ensuring the program serves the targeted population.

Figures 15.6 and 15.7 compare outcomes by risk level in SDM and comparison counties. (Because there were so few low-risk cases opened to protective services, the low- and moderate-risk groups are combined throughout this section to simplify presentations.)

FIGURE 15.6   Outcomes for High-Risk CPS Cases

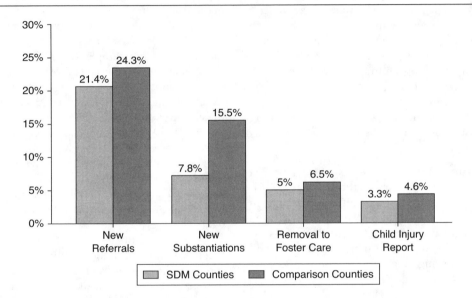

FIGURE 15.7   Outcomes for Low- and Moderate-Risk Cases

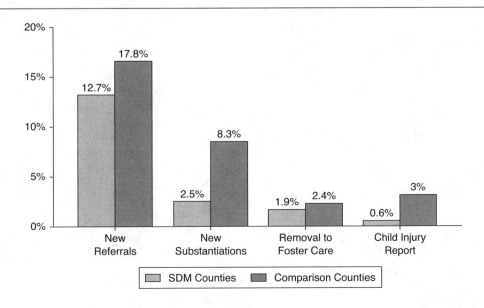

C. Summary of Impact Evaluation Findings

As the charts from the previous pages illustrate, all outcomes for CPS cases in SDM counties are substantially better than those found in comparison counties. Key findings include the following:

• The substantiation rate for high-risk cases in SDM counties was about half that recorded in comparison counties. Injury rates and foster care placement were lower in the SDM high-risk group. While referral rates were only marginally lower for high-risk SDM cases, the average number of new investigations assigned per case was significantly lower. The referral rate reflects all cases with one or more referrals; the mean number of investigations reflects the *number of referrals* per case that were investigated. Therefore, this measure is a more accurate reflection of both the frequency and severity of new referrals received on each sample case. As such, it helps to explain the larger difference found in substantiation rates between the two study samples.

• Outcomes for high-risk cases in SDM counties were similar to those obtained for moderate- and low-risk families in comparison counties. This is strong evidence that structured assessments using valid and reliable risk assessment tools, followed by increased services and case monitoring, does work to protect children while keeping families intact.

• The SDM system also produced significantly better outcomes for low- and moderate-risk families. Re-referrals and substantiations were markedly lower than rates observed in the comparison counties. Injury and foster care placement rates were also lower and the mean number of new investigations reported was less than half the average found in the comparison group.

D. Wayne County (Detroit) Findings

One of the key issues to be addressed in this evaluation was how well this system functioned in a major urban area: Wayne County. Child protective services in Wayne County operate quite differently than in other Michigan counties. Most notably, when abuse or neglect is substantiated in counties other than Wayne, the majority of cases are opened to protective services. A small percent are closed and another relatively small percentage are transferred to foster care. In Wayne County, only about one-third of all substantiated cases are opened to protective services, and the majority of these cases are placed with the Families First program. About one-third of all substantiated cases are transferred to foster care and the remaining 30–35% are closed. As a result, few cases (48) from the Wayne County sample were really affected by case management requirements of the new system.

Operations also vary among units in Wayne County, further complicating attempts to measure the effectiveness of SDM. Table 15.2 presents the risk levels of Wayne County cases opened to protective services from both study groups.

The comparison units in Wayne County made greater use of the Families First program and, conversely, made fewer foster care placements (31% of all substantiated cases versus 34.9%).

Overall, cases opened to protective services in the SDM units had slightly better outcomes than cases in the comparison units. However, the number of cases analyzed is not sufficient to permit a meaningful breakdown by risk levels.

While the analysis of Wayne County cases was limited by the low number of families receiving in-home services, separating these data did produce some valuable findings. These include:

• Overall, Wayne County cases are higher risk than in other counties. About 71% of Wayne

TABLE 15.2   Risk Levels of Cases Opened to Protective Services—Wayne County

Risk Level	SDM Group		Comparison Group	
	CPS	Families First	CPS	Families First
Low/Moderate	16	15	15	16
High/Intensive	32	50	37	85
TOTAL	46 (42.5%)	65 (57.5%)	62 (38.0%)	101 (62.0%)

FIGURE 15.8   Outcome Comparisons All Non-Wayne County CPS Cases

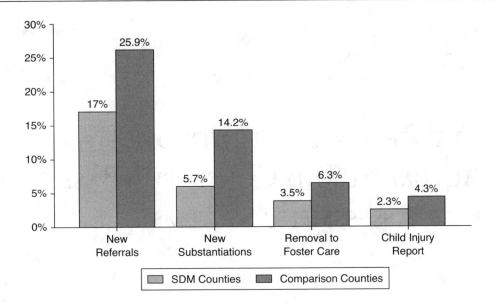

County cases (from the combined SDM and comparison groups) were high risk, compared to 64% of cases from other counties. However, this difference does not fully explain the greater use of foster care. CPS staff could, perhaps, adequately serve many of these cases through a combination of direct contacts and purchased services.

• Despite a much lower use of foster care and the Families First program, SDM counties (other than Wayne) had a lower rate of new substantiations, foster care placements, and child injuries than the Wayne County comparison group. Changes to the Wayne County service mix with enhanced use of CPS staff and purchased services may help to reduce the reliance on out-of-home placement.

When Wayne County cases are excluded from the analysis, differences between SDM and comparison counties are even more pronounced. Figure 15.8 compares outcomes for cases outside of Wayne County. The differences noted in substantiations, foster care placements, and child

injuries are extraordinary, given that some components of the case management system have yet to be implemented. The degree of structure and accountability offered by this system appears to substantially improve child protection in Michigan.

NOTES

1. Low-, moderate-, high-, or intensive-risk levels corresponded to one, two, three, or four (respectively) face-to-face monthly contacts with clients, plus the same number of collateral contacts on behalf of the client.

2. Eighteen months of follow-up data are available for the majority of cases. The conclusions listed in this report are fully supported by the 18-month data; however, since some cases did not have a full 18-month follow-up and because some data regarding events occurring near the end of the follow-up period may not have been captured in the agency's data system, a conservative approach was adopted to data presentation to ensure complete data on all cases studied.

16

THE RELATIVE VALIDITY OF ACTUARIAL AND CONSENSUS-BASED RISK ASSESSMENT SYSTEMS

CHRISTOPHER BAIRD

DENNIS WAGNER

I. CPS RISK ASSESSMENT SYSTEMS

The number of abuse and neglect allegations nationwide has risen dramatically over the last two decades. Most child welfare agencies have been hard pressed to respond effectively, as the new demands have outpaced available resources. The results have included lawsuits in more than 30 states, media exposés resulting from child deaths, increased concerns over worker and agency liability, and a continuous search for new strategies and resources to address the burgeoning problem.

The need for additional resources is obvious, but that is not the only issue. The increasing pressures have highlighted a problem that has long plagued human services agencies in general, and child welfare agencies in particular: the need for more efficient, consistent, and valid

decision making. Child protection workers are asked to make extremely difficult decisions, yet in many agencies, workers have widely different levels of training and experience. Consequently, decisions regarding case openings, child removal and reunification, and other service-related issues have long been criticized as inappropriate, inconsistent, or both. In fact, research has clearly demonstrated that decisions regarding the safety of children vary significantly from worker to worker, even among those considered to be child welfare experts (Rossi, Schuerman, and Budde, 1996). As pressure to make critical decisions affecting children and families rises, so does the potential for error. Inappropriate decisions can be costly, leading to an overuse of out-of-home placements, or tragic, resulting in the injury or death of a child.

Note: This article reports on the second phase of a three-year study funded by the National Center on Child Abuse and Neglect (grant #90-CA-1550), "Comparative Study of the Use and Effectiveness of Different Risk-Assessment Models in CPS Decision Making," to determine the relative reliability and validity of three approaches to risk assessment in child protective services.

To increase the consistency and validity of decision making, many agencies have turned to a variety of assessment systems. Most of these systems estimate the risk that a child will be abused or neglected in the future and thus fall under the general rubric of "risk assessment."

Risk assessment systems used in child protection services (CPS) are formalized methods that provide structure and criteria with the expectation that structure will increase the reliability and accuracy of CPS worker decision making, helping workers to more effectively provide services to families and better protect children. A variety of systems for estimating risk have been developed over the years. The American Public Welfare Association (APWA) conducted a survey in 1996 of 54 states, territories, and large county child welfare agencies to determine use and satisfaction with CPS risk assessment systems. Of the 44 jurisdictions that responded, 38 had some risk assessment or safety assessment in place. Of these states, 26 first implemented their risk assessment after 1987 (Tatara, 1996).

Some experts have expressed concern that the theoretical and empirical support for these systems is inadequate (Cicchinelli, 1991). Because different methods of risk assessment development have been employed over the last two decades, risk assessment procedures vary on a number of dimensions, and the task of comparing one to another is quite complex (Murphy-Berman, 1994). Generally, however, CPS risk assessment systems fall into two basic types (Johnson and L'Esperance, 1984).

Consensus-Based Systems

In these systems, workers assess specific client characteristics identified by the consensus judgment of experts and then exercise their own clinical judgment about the risk of future abuse or neglect.

Actuarial Systems

These systems are based on an empirical study of CPS cases and future abuse/neglect outcomes. The study identifies items/factors with a strong association with future abuse/neglect and constructs an actuarial instrument that workers score to identify low, medium, or high risk families.

This study, funded by the Office of Child Abuse and Neglect (OCAN), compared the reliability and validity of two consensus models and one actuarial model. Results of the reliability study were published earlier (Baird, Wagner, Healy, and Johnson, 1999). This article summarizes results of the validity study.

Consensus-Based Risk Assessment Models

Research in child abuse and neglect has served as a guide to the development of "expert" or consensus-based risk assessment systems. Although the volume of research on these systems is considered by some as "quite formidable" (Doueck, Levine, and Bronson, 1993), these systems have rarely undergone rigorous evaluations.

Historically, caseworkers have used the case study method, relying almost entirely upon clinical experience, interviewing skills, and intuition to estimate the risk of abuse or neglect to a child. In many states, such clinical assessments are structured by instruments or systems that identify specific case characteristics, often those selected after a review of the literature, for the worker to assess (Tatara, 1987). These instruments may be helpful to CPS workers in conducting a comprehensive case assessment, but they are typically not constructed from an empirical analysis of case outcomes in the jurisdiction where they are used (Wald and Woolverton, 1990). In other words, these instruments help organize the caseworker's clinical assessment of risk, but they are not based on research specific to the jurisdiction (Marks, McDonald, Bessey, and Palmer, 1989).

An early study illustrating a critical problem for clinical judgment was conducted by Margaret Blenkner in 1954. Three expert clinical social workers were asked to perform several clinical assessments of 47 clients using information recorded at intake in a private social service agency. After reading each file, making the assessments, and recording them on a data collection form, each clinician was asked to make a prognosis for future casework success (the cases were closed and outcomes had been established previously by other clinical judges).

In subsequent analysis, five of the assessment measures these clinicians had recorded demonstrated a strong relationship with case outcome and Blenkner added them together to create a summary score. Although the summary scores demonstrated a very high correlation with successful case outcome, the prognoses of the three clinical judges proved unrelated to outcomes and to one another. Meehl (1954) observed that, "Apparently these skilled case readers can rate relatively more specific but still fairly complex factors reliably enough so that an inefficient mathematical formula combining them can predict the criterion; whereas the same judges cannot combine the same data 'impressionistically' to yield results above chance" (p. 108).

Blenkner's work illustrated why many observers believe clinical judges perform poorly on predictive tasks: they differentially select and weight information about the subject (Wagner, 1992). Despite the fact that the variables in Blenkner's formula had been developed by clinicians and required clinical skill to observe, clinical judges performed poorly when asked to predict case outcomes.

Actuarial Systems

The evidence now available from actuarial studies of child abuse and neglect suggests a conclusion endorsed several years ago in many other fields, namely that actuarial risk assessments derived from simple, empirically validated instruments can efficiently estimate the risk of future maltreatment and, therefore, may substantially improve the clinical risk assessment performed by an individual caseworker (CRC, 1999). Actuarial assessment methods, which require extensive longitudinal research, have only recently been introduced in CPS. In their summary of this area of research, Marks and McDonald (1989) cite only two actuarial risk assessment studies in abuse and neglect: an Alameda County study conducted by Johnson and L'Esperance (1984) and an Alaska study conducted by the National Council on Crime and Delinquency (NCCD) (Baird, 1988). Since the 1989 Marks and McDonald publication, however, NCCD has conducted additional actuarial research in California, Colorado, Oklahoma, Michigan, Rhode Island, New Mexico, and Wisconsin. a large body of research evidence in experimental psychology and corrections (i.e., Meehl, 1954; Sawyer, 1966; Dawes, Faust, and Meehl, 1989) supports the view that actuarial instruments can estimate future behavior more accurately than an individual decision maker unaided by actuarial information can (even decision makers who have had extensive clinical training).

This study takes the next step by directly comparing the accuracy of risk designations derived using actuarial and consensus-based instruments.

II. Prior Risk Assessment Research

While there are many articles addressing issues of reliability and validity of risk assessment systems used in child welfare, there is a paucity of research directly comparing the relative validity of different systems. Camasso and Jagannathan (1995) compared the Washington and Illinois systems using a sample of CPS cases in New Jersey. This article is of particular interest because the same two systems were analyzed in this study (the California risk assessment system is a derivative of the Illinois model). The authors concluded that the performance of both instruments was poor. However, they also found that both systems did predict case recidivism, closings, and substantiation with probabilities greater than chance.

There have been several studies of individual systems conducted. For example, Sheets (1991) concluded that risk levels designated by the Child at Risk Field (CARF) had no relationship to subsequent maltreatment. Two studies have examined the predictive performance of the Washington instrument. English, Aubin, Fine, and Pecora (1993) used the Washington instrument to sort 2,209 CPS cases into either a "no or low risk" category or a "moderate or high risk" category. The rate of recidivism, defined as a report of maltreatment during a six-month follow-up, was 18% for the "no or low risk" group, but 26% for the "moderate or high risk group" (p < .001). Camasso and Jagannathan (1995) examined seven scales derived from items of the Washington instrument, and found that two of the seven scales significantly predicted case recidivism.

It appears that only one other direct comparison of actuarial and consensus-based models has occurred to date in child welfare. In New York, Falco (1997) compared a consensus-based risk assessment system developed for CPS with an actuarial device developed in a 1996 Children's Research Center (CRC)-facilitated research effort. The consensus-based instrument used in New York was unusually well constructed, having avoided some of the design problems discussed in the earlier review of model reliability (Baird et al., 1999). Falco found that risk designations provided by the consensus-based instrument did indeed have a significant relationship to subsequent maltreatment, but its classification power was largely dichotomous. In essence, it effectively identified two risk levels rather than the intended four-level designation. Still, the actuarial device proved significantly superior and is scheduled to replace the consensus-based model in New York.

Although "head to head" tests of actuarial and clinical-based models have been rare in child welfare, a substantial number of such tests have been conducted in other fields. Dawes (1993) has eloquently summarized the results of this research.

In the last 50 years or so, the question of whether a statistical or clinical approach is superior has been the subject of extensive empirical investigation; statistical vs. clinical methods of predicting important human outcomes have been compared with each other, in what might be described as a "contest." The results have been uniform. Even fairly simple statistical models outperform clinical judgment. The superiority of statistical prediction holds in diverse areas, ranging from diagnosing heart attacks and predicting who will survive them, to forecasting who will succeed in careers, stay out of jail on parole, or be dismissed from police forces.

Three years later, Grove and Meehl (1996) presented an exhaustive review of the literature citing 136 studies ranging from the 1928 Illinois Parole Board Study (Burgess, 1928) to the present, concluding that "a great preponderance of studies favor the actuarial approach." They did, however, find a few (eight) studies where clinical judgment outperformed actuarial models. For other reviews, both of which conclude that actuarial approaches are superior to clinical judgment, see Sawyer (1966) or Wiggins (1981).

III. Study Design

A. Selection of Risk Assessment Systems to Be Tested

Risk assessment models that typify both actuarial and consensus-based systems used in various jurisdictions nationwide were selected for this study.

Two of the more widely used versions of consensus-based systems are the Washington Risk Assessment Matrix, a risk assessment system developed by practitioners in the State of Washington, and the California Family Assessment Factor Analysis, a derivative of the Illinois Child Abuse and Neglect Tracking System (CANTS). Because it is the most widely used actuarial-based approach, the Michigan Structured Decision-Making (SDM) System's Family Risk Assessment of Abuse and Neglect was selected for this study. It is a research-based tool constructed during a study of 2,000 Michigan families (Baird, Wagner, and Neuenfeldt, 1992) and recently revalidated on a cohort of 1,000 families (Baird, Wagner, Caskey, and Neuenfeldt, 1995). This system is also used (or is being implemented) in Georgia, Indiana, Minnesota, and Cleveland, Ohio.

B. Site Selection

The site selection process sought to identify four distinct sites that would offer: (1) a broad geographical representation; (2) significant representation of ethnic and racial minorities, including African Americans and Latinos; and (3) a mixture of urban and rural sites. The need for a high volume of cases dictated that large urban centers be chosen as primary sites, and the need for geographical diversity demanded that cases from surrounding rural sites be systematically added to the study cohort when possible. Despite the objective of including cases from rural areas, the complexities encountered in the data collection phase limited this effort. It should be noted that the vast majority of cases in the study came from urban settings. In total, data on 1,400 families were gathered from four project sites: Alameda County, California; Dade County, Florida; Jackson County, Missouri; and Macomb, Muskegon, Ottawa, and Wayne Counties in Michigan.

At the time the study was conducted, the Alameda County site was using the consensus-based California Family Assessment Factor Analysis. The four counties in Michigan were all using the actuarial-based Michigan Family Risk Assessment of Abuse and Neglect. Neither Dade County (Miami, FL) nor Jackson County (Kansas City, MO) was using any of the three risk models included in this study. Before finalizing selection of these sites, files from each were obtained and reviewed. After careful review, file content in each site was judged to be representative of CPS files in general, and adequate for this study.

C. Data Collection/Inter-rater Reliability

In order to collect necessary data from each site, case reading teams of three people were selected and trained—one case reader for each risk assessment model at each site. Every attempt was made to recruit prospective readers who had child welfare experience and/or education. Once the teams had been identified, the case readers gathered for a three-day intensive training session. *One* member of each team was trained thoroughly by an expert to complete *one* risk assessment model. All training sessions included inter-rater reliability testing to ensure that case readers understood the system thoroughly. In addition to the extensive training in the risk assessment models, case readers were trained on cultural sensitivity and awareness. This interactive session, conducted by a nationally known expert in the field, assisted readers in recognizing and eliminating personal bias based on race or ethnicity from their work and motivated them to base their responses on facts provided in the case files.

An earlier phase of this study compared the reliability of the three risk assessment models (Baird et al., 1999). Eighty cases, 20 from each site, were used to assess reliability. In total, four different case readers assessed all 80 cases using each model. Two measures of reliability were used: simple percent agreement among readers and Cohen's Kappa. The latter is a measure of percent agreement adjusted for chance. Both the California and Washington models had serious reliability problems, a finding with obvious implications for the validity phase of the study.

D. Defining/Measuring CPS Outcomes

Although many CPS agencies have used risk assessment instruments for a decade or more, the validity of these instruments, until recently, has not been the subject of serious inquiry. There are a number of reasons many CPS risk instruments have not been validated. Foremost is that goals and objectives of many risk assessments were never clearly defined or, if defined, they were often so broad that validation was, at best, difficult. For example, seriousness of the

reported incident, probability of substantiation, immediate child safety, family and child needs, and probability of future maltreatment are sometimes addressed within a single "instrument" or system. In addition, risk to individual children within each household is often separately assessed, further complicating validation efforts. Risk assessment instruments have, in essence, been expected to inform a wide variety of CPS decisions (Baumann et al., 1997). Hence, it has been difficult to identify the criterion variables that could be used to evaluate the validity of instruments.

However, if risk assessment is, as Wald and Woolverton (1990) note, "a process for assessing the likelihood that a given person (usually a parent) will harm a child in the future," then subsequent harm becomes the criterion variable and validation is possible. The CPS field has gradually come to accept this definition of risk; similar definitions have been presented by others in recent years (Pecora, 1991; Ruscio, 1998). Subsequent harm is the principal criterion used in this study to measure the relative validity of the California, Michigan, and Washington risk assessment systems. The problems of defining "harm" as well as determining if harm has occurred, of course, remain. Harm comes in many forms and in different degrees and, because observation of families is necessarily limited, any maltreatment that occurs may go undetected. These problems have produced some skepticism about the reliability of outcome measures used in child welfare. Some researchers maintain that, because child maltreatment may be detected and reported at different rates based on social or economic status, using new reports of abuse/neglect as an outcome measure may not accurately represent what actually occurs. Further, critics of validation efforts feel that reports of abuse or neglect are often not accurate—that mere allegations cannot be accepted as an indication that harm actually occurred. These critics further argue that the CPS process of substantiation—because it is usually an "administrative process" not subject to legal standards of proof—may not be a sufficient basis on which to establish that maltreatment actually occurred (English, 1997). Even if sufficient, it still represents only those cases where maltreatment was detected.[1]

While there is little question that outcomes in any human service field are subject to the vagaries of reporting, inconsistencies in worker and agency responses to reports, and other problems, there is ample evidence that available outcome data are sufficient to develop risk assessment systems capable of identifying groups of cases with significantly different rates of success/failure (as defined by each field). While outcome data may not be totally accurate, there is no evidence to suggest that the patterns derived would change significantly if every event was detected, recorded accurately, and responded to in a consistent fashion by all decision makers. In other words, if subsequent maltreatment is "discovered" in 5% of low risk cases, the actual maltreatment rate may be somewhat higher (or lower), but it would still, in all probability, be substantially lower than the "real rate" of subsequent maltreatment found in the high risk population. It seems safe to assume that "error," in all probability, bears a proportional relationship to the reported rate for each risk group.

In research involving human subjects, a very controlled environment is required if all events (outcomes) are to be detected. Outside of a laboratory, such control is not possible. To insist that no research is legitimate because of the imperfections of data is to trap a field in its status quo. Severe criticism of both CPS policy and practice has been leveled by groups specifically appointed to review the child welfare system. For example, the National Commission on Children (1991) reported: "If the nation had deliberately designed a system that would frustrate the professionals who staff it, anger the public who finance it, and abandon the children who depend on it, it could not have done a better job than the present child welfare system." Clearly, the status quo is not an acceptable option.

E. Defining Validity

In addition to the question of what outcomes can and should be measured, CPS has struggled with the issue of *how* the validity of risk assessment instruments is best determined. Other fields—criminal justice, medicine, and meteorology, for example—have long struggled with the same issue and a body of literature has emerged which served as the foundation of this study. It is our belief that CPS research would benefit enormously by adopting the strategies and methods of inquiry developed in other fields.

Validity of decision systems has traditionally been measured by the degree to which "predictions" about case outcomes are realized. Ruscio (1998) defines validity in the following manner:

> The efficacy of your decision policy can be examined through the use of a simple fourfold classification table crossing the optimal outcome for each child (kept at home vs. placed into care) with the decision that is reached. There are two types of correct decisions, or "hits," that are possible: True positives are decisions that place children into care when appropriate, and true negatives are decisions that keep children at home when appropriate. There are also two types of incorrect decisions, or "misses," that are possible: False positives are decisions that unnecessarily place children into care, and false negatives are decisions that fail to place children into care when placement is necessary. Based on this classification table, the effectiveness of a decision policy may be evaluated in several ways. For instance, one could determine how many of the decisions to place a child into foster care were correct (true positives divided by the sum of true and false positives); how many children who optimally should have been kept in the home actually were (true negatives divided by the sum of true negatives and false positives); or how many placement decisions, overall, were correct (the sum of true positives and true negatives divided by the total number of cases).

While calculation of false positives, false negatives, and the overall percentage of correct predictions is useful in many settings, it may not be the best method for gauging the efficacy of a risk assessment system when the probability of success/ failure is substantially different than 50–50. When events are relatively rare, they are inherently difficult to predict. In such instances, simply assuming an event will not occur may produce more predictive accuracy than any attempt to determine where or when occurrence is likely. For example, if subsequent maltreatment (failure) is reported in only 15% of cases opened to protective services, then simply predicting no case opened to services will have subsequent maltreatment reported produces an 85% "hit rate." Obviously, such a prediction, while highly accurate, is of little value to a CPS agency. (In essence, the "sensitivity" of the prediction is .85, but the specificity—correct identification of those who do fail—is zero.) A valid and reliable risk assessment system may improve the "hit rate" marginally, but it is possible such a system

TABLE 16.1   Actual Versus Predicted Outcomes

		Predicted Outcomes	
		No Subsequent Maltreatment	Subsequent Maltreatment
Actual Outcomes	No Subsequent Maltreatment	71	14
	Subsequent Maltreatment	4	11

could result in a higher percentage of false positives and false negatives and still provide the agency with quality information about the relative probability of subsequent maltreatment. Consider the scenario where a CPS population ($N = 100$) has a subsequent maltreatment rate of 15%. A risk assessment identifies 25% of the population as "high risk," which, for this example, is equated with a prediction of subsequent maltreatment. Actual versus predicted outcomes are presented in Table 16.1.

In the above example, an overall "hit rate" of 82% is attained (3% lower than that attained when all cases are predicted to succeed) with a rate of false positives (subsequent maltreatment) of 56% and false negatives of 5.3%. Despite the high proportion of false positives, cases that were rated high risk experienced maltreatment at a 44% rate, while only 5.3% of those rated at lower risk levels had subsequent maltreatment reported. The ratio of "failures" in the high risk group to "failures" in the low risk group is more than 8:1. Such results help agencies identify which families are more likely to abuse or neglect their children. In addition, 11 of the 15 cases (73.3%) where subsequent maltreatment occurred were correctly identified (a relatively high rate of specificity).

Identifying 25% of this population as high risk (when only 15% again maltreat their children) may be due to cut points that were set artificially low or due to the fact there were no discernable differences among the 14 members of the high risk group that did not maltreat their children and the 11 cases where maltreatment was reported. Our experience with scale construction in child welfare, as well as adult and juvenile corrections, indicates the latter explanation is far more likely. When the rate of "failure" is low, there is a natural tendency toward false positives.

Other fields, such as juvenile justice, medicine, and adult corrections, have largely abandoned the idea that risk assessment is an exercise in prediction. Instead, terms such as "base expectancy rates" have replaced discussions of false positives and false negatives. In corrections, for example, high risk does not equal a prediction of failure—in fact, in most correctional systems, more high risk cases succeed than fail. Instead, high risk simply denotes inclusion in a group of offenders with significantly higher historical rates of recidivism than other groups.

The field of medicine offers similar examples. In cancer research, it is common practice to identify characteristics of malignancies and surrounding tissue and to classify patients as high, moderate, or low risk based on the observed rates of recurrence within a specified time period (Silverstein and Lagios, 1997). A designation of high risk of recurrence does not equate with a "prediction" that the cancer will recur. In fact, most medical professionals carefully avoid making such predictions. As treatment options expand and improve, recurrence-free survival rates have increased to the point where, if false positives and negatives were to be minimized, the best "prediction" for high risk cases would be "no recurrence." Still, knowing that cases with similar characteristics have experienced a recurrence rate of 10%, 25%, or 45% helps the doctor and patient select the most appropriate treatment plan.

Conceptually, the use of false positives and false negatives to evaluate risk assessment systems creates another dilemma. While outcomes are often dichotomous (an event will either occur or not occur), most risk assessment models assign cases to three or more different risk levels. One of the systems evaluated in this study (Washington) uses six levels of risk. If efficacy is based on predicting an outcome, it must be asked what prediction is being made for cases at intermediate risk levels: Is the designation "moderate risk" a prediction that subsequent maltreatment will or will not occur? We would submit that it is neither, but simply the recognition that these cases "recidivate" at higher rates than some and lower than others. Knowing this allows workers to establish appropriate service plans, just as similar information permits doctors and patients to decide on a particular course of action.

Therefore, in evaluating the relative efficacy of California, Michigan, and Washington risk assessment systems, it is imperative to be very clear about expectations. The terms prediction and classification are often used interchangeably, yet really connote different expectations. Prediction is more precise than classification. According to Webster's definition, prediction "declares in advance on the basis of observation, experience, or scientific reason." to predict accurately in any field is difficult; to accurately predict human behavior is especially complex as many factors contribute to determining how individuals will act. Classification, on the other hand, is simply "a systematic arrangement in groups or categories according to established criteria." While accurate prediction would greatly benefit child protective services and society, it has not proven feasible. We submit that goals of risk assessment are much more modest; it is simply meant to assign cases to different categories based on observed rates of behavior.

Risk scales, in general, explain little of the variance in outcomes—8% to 15% is common. This is true in nearly every field ranging from automobile insurance to criminal justice to child protective services. This fact leads some researchers to caution against the use of risk assessment, claiming these instruments are not valid because they fail to predict accurately who will succeed and who will fail. But if, as noted above, simple classification is the goal, explained variance in outcomes is of little consequence. What is important is the *degree* to which families in different risk groups perform differently. Furthermore, if prediction is not the goal, then the issue of false positives and false negatives is moot. Classification recognizes that a high risk designation is not a prediction of failure. It is, instead, a clear indication that such families may require more attention and more services, because cases in this designation tend to "fail" at higher rates than cases in other classifications.

Recently, new and potentially better methods of measuring the efficacy of risk assessment systems have emerged. One innovative measure, the Dispersion Index for Risk (DIFR) recognizes that "the primary utility of a risk classification model is in providing a continuum of risk estimates associated with a variety of conditions which can be used to guide a range of decision-making responses" (Silver and Banks, 1998). Hence, the authors conclude, "it is for this reason that traditional measures of 'predictive accuracy' which carry with them the assumption that dichotomous decisions will be made, have little utility for assessing the *potency* of a risk classification model."

The DIFR measures the potency of risk assessment systems by assessing how an entire cohort is partitioned into different groups and the extent to which group outcomes vary from the base rate for the entire cohort. In essence, it weights "base rate distance" by subgroup size to calibrate the "potency" of a classification system. This new method of measurement reflects the validity construct outlined on previous pages of this report. Because it considers proportionality and differences in outcome rates among *several* subgroups, it represents a significant advancement in measuring the efficacy of classification systems and produces a summary statistic for comparing the classification potency of different risk assessment systems.

IV. Comparing the Validity of Three Risk Assessment Models

A. Selection and Definition of the Criterion Variable(s)

The primary measure of validity used in this study was the ability of each system to classify cases into risk groups with significantly different rates of subsequent maltreatment reported. Outcome measures analyzed include:

- Subsequent investigations of abuse/neglect within 18 months of the investigation that brought each case into the study cohort;
- Substantiation resulting from these investigations over the 18-month follow-up period; and
- Placements in out-of-home care over the same 18-month follow-up period.

Initially, child injury was included as an outcome measure, but problems were encountered in collecting these data. In addition to a very low base rate (injuries were reported in a very small proportion of cases in the study), the manner in which child injuries were cited in case files varied substantially among agencies and among workers within the agencies participating in the study. After careful review, it was determined that the reliability of these data was insufficient for inclusion as an outcome measure.

In total, 1,400 families from four different states comprised the study sample. All were investigated in 1995 or 1996. However, all three risk assessments were not completed on all 1,400 families. For a variety of reasons, ranging from a lack of available data to the absence of a case reader on the day a case file was available, the number of cases for which each risk assessment was completed ranged from 1,335 to 1,396.

With different numbers of cases available for each risk instrument, two options were considered for comparing the validity of the three models. The first option was to use only cases where *all three* instruments were completed. The second option was to use all available cases for each system and to report results noting that a few cases in each analysis were not represented in the other samples. Preliminary analyses were conducted under both options. When only minute and statistically insignificant differences were found in the classification breakdown for each system under the two scenarios, it was decided that, to maximize sample size, results of all cases with a particular assessment completed would be used to compare results.

It was necessary, however, to exclude some cases from the analysis. In instances where a child was removed from the home *and* remained in placement at the close of the investigation, the family was not included in the validation study because placement may have greatly reduced or even completely eliminated any potential for future maltreatment (DePanfilis and Zuravin, 1998). In total, 188 families were removed from

analysis of the California system, 193 from the Washington analysis, and 194 from the analysis of the Michigan system.

One other serious problem was encountered with data collected during the follow-up period. In Alameda County, new investigation and substantiation data for 60 families in the sample could not be retrieved. In addition, new investigation and substantiation rates observed for the remaining Alameda County cases were much lower than those reported by other jurisdictions in this study as well as in five metropolitan California counties where similar case outcome data were available. This indicated that the missing Alameda County cases were unlikely to be a random subset of the total sample (Wagner, Freitag, & Johnson, 1998). While excluding Alameda cases from the validation study does not alter overall results (all patterns noted remain in place with Alameda data included), it was felt that both the large number of cases (60) with missing outcomes, and evidence that these cases were not missing on a random basis, supported the exclusion of Alameda County data when the three systems were directly compared.

When Alameda County cases and cases where a child remained in out-of-home placement at the end of the investigation were deleted from the primary analysis, the total samples remaining for each assessment system ranged from 876 (California), to 908 (Washington), to 929 (Michigan) families. The difference in sample size available for each instrument produced marginal differences in new investigation and substantiation rates recorded (never greater than 1%) for each outcome measure. Rates at which outcomes were reported for each cohort are shown in Table 16.2.

1. Sample Characteristics

All cases in the study were investigated in the fall of 1995 or early in 1996. For study cases,

TABLE 16.2   Outcome Rates for Samples Used to Analyze Each Risk Assessment Model

	California Model	Michigan Model	Washington Model
One or more new investigations recorded	33%	33%	34%
One or more new substantiations recorded	17%	17%	18%
One or more new placements recorded	4%	4%	4%

94.5% of the primary caretakers were the victim's birth parent and nearly 90% were female. The mean age of the primary caretakers was 32.9 years. In 47.9% of homes assessed there was a single caretaker. In 25.9% of all families, there was only one child present in the home at the time of the investigation. Nearly 32% had two children, 21.2% had three, and 21.1% had four or more. Although data on specific income levels was not collected, a large proportion of the sample was on some form of assistance; 44.4% received AFDC payments, and 35.3% were receiving food stamps at the time of the index investigation.

Selection of cases began on the project start-up date and continued with consecutive cases according to two rules: (1) all cases substantiated as a result of the index investigation were selected; and (2) every fourth case not substantiated at the conclusion of the index investigation was randomly selected. The lone exception to the second rule occurred in Michigan where risk instruments were completed only on substantiated cases. In the sample used for the primary analyses, the index investigation allegation was neglect in 57.4% of cases, for physical abuse in 45.3%, for sexual abuse in 10.5%, and for some other form of maltreatment in 2.5% of the cases. These percentages do not sum to 100% because more than one form of maltreatment was alleged in some cases. In response to the index investigation, CPS workers substantiated neglect in 40.7% of all investigations, physical abuse in 25.7%, sexual abuse in 7.9%, and other forms of maltreatment in 0.2% of all cases. It is important to note that substantiations for index investigations are not included in the outcome measures used for this study.

B. Results

Comparing the three instruments required that cut-off points or "thresholds" for risk levels be established for the Michigan instrument (the only instrument subject to scoring). In instances where other jurisdictions have adopted the Michigan instrument, cut-off scores used to designate high, moderate, and low risk levels have been dependent upon a number of factors including: (1) screen out procedures that affect the percentage of referrals investigated in each agency, (2) the level of resources available to provide service to cases at each risk level, and (3) risk assessment results from a representative sample of cases to determine how entire caseloads are likely to score in each jurisdiction.

Because these steps were not possible or even desirable for a prospective study, a conservative approach to setting cut-off points was selected. Once the entire sample was assessed, the mean scores for both the abuse and neglect instruments were computed. The moderate risk level was then established as the mean score plus or minus one standard deviation. Cut-off scores for each risk level were then rounded to whole numbers. To include more cases in both the high and low risk categories, the cut-off point for high risk was rounded down while the cut-off for low risk was rounded up. In essence, cases were simply triaged. Interestingly, this method produced percentages at each risk level almost identical to those found in Georgia, the largest state to date to adapt the Michigan system (Baird, Ereth, and Wagner, 1999).

To facilitate comparability, the six levels of risk in the Washington model were collapsed into three levels to match the number of risk classifications produced by the California and Michigan models. The no risk and low risk designations were combined as low risk; moderately low and moderate became moderate risk; moderately high and high risk designations were combined and designated as high risk families.

The three risk assessment systems analyzed in this study produced different classification results. While the proportion of cases rated low, moderate, and high risk was reasonably similar in the Michigan and Washington models, California ratings were, on the whole, much lower. The most notable difference among the systems is the proclivity of the California system to classify many more cases as low risk. Overall percentages of cases rated high, moderate, and low risk by each system are presented in Table 16.3.

Intercorrelations among the risk instruments were also calculated. All correlations are statistically significant ($p < .001$) and, surprisingly, the highest correlation (.524) was between the Washington and California models (surprising because these systems distribute cases very differently among the classification levels). The correlation between the California and Michigan models was .344; between Washington and Michigan .362.

1. Comparing Outcomes by Risk Level

Table 16.4 compares three outcome measures delineated by risk level for all three models.

TABLE 16.3   Percentage of Cases at Each Risk Level

	California Risk Assessment Model	Michigan Risk Assessment Model	Washington Risk Assessment Model
Low Risk	50.5%	14.9%	22.2%
Moderate Risk	34.7%	58.1%	52.3%
High Risk	14.8%	26.8%	25.4%

The overall results indicate that the Michigan model resulted in superior risk classifications. The new investigation rate increased from 16% to 32% to 46% as the Michigan risk level rose. These differences were all significant at the .001 level. The Washington risk model produced mixed results. The difference in new investigation rates between low and moderate risk (25% and 35%, respectively) was significant ($p < .001$) but the difference in the investigation rate between moderate and high risk cases (39% vs. 35%) was not significant ($p > .05$). Cases rated low risk by the California model also had a significantly lower re-investigation rate than families rated moderate risk (28% vs. 38%), but there was no difference in the investigation rate of moderate and high risk cases. The California model designates far fewer cases "high risk" than either the Michigan or Washington models. However, this "selectivity" aspect of the California model did not result in a more accurate designation of "high risk" on this or any other outcome measure.

When the rate of new substantiations was considered, differences among the three approaches to risk assessment were more pronounced. For the Michigan system, the new substantiation rate approximately doubled at each risk level, increasing from 7% for low risk families, to 15% for moderate risk families, and 28% for high risk families. These differences are all statistically significant ($p < .01$). However, differences in substantiation rates at each risk level were much narrower for both the California and Washington systems (15% to 18% and 16% to 21%, respectively). These differences were not statistically significant ($p > .05$) for either instrument.

Placement rates for high risk cases under both the Washington and Michigan systems were significantly higher than the rates recorded for either moderate or low risk cases ($p < .01$). While differences in placement between the moderate

TABLE 16.4   Outcomes Reported During 18-Month Follow-Up by Risk System

	Case Distribution	New Investigation Rate	New Substantiation Rate	New Placement Rate
	California Risk Assessment Model			
Low	50.5%	28%	15%	3%
Moderate	34.7%	38%	18%	1%
High	14.8%	38%	18%	6%
	Michigan Risk Assessment Model			
Low	14.9%	16%	7%	1%
Moderate	58.1%	32%	15%	3%
High	26.8%	46%	28%	7%
	Washington Risk Assessment Model			
Low	22.2%	25%	16%	2%
Moderate	52.3%	35%	16%	3%
High	25.4%	39%	21%	6%
Base Rates for Sample		33%	17%	4%

NOTE: This table excludes cases in out-of-home placement at the conclusion of the investigation and cases from Alameda County, CA.

and high risk classification in the California instrument were statistically significant, this result needs to be viewed with considerable caution. Cases rated at the moderate risk level by the California system actually had a lower placement rate than cases rated low risk. Hence, the differences in placement rates are not all in the expected and logical direction.

2. The Dispersion Index for Risk (DIFR)

In addition to simply comparing risk classifications for each system with actual outcomes as the primary measure of system validity, the Dispersion Index for Risk (DIFR), described earlier, is presented as a supplemental measure of validity. Although the DIFR is a new summary statistic for estimating the potency of classification systems, it was chosen because it best matches the concept of system validity employed in the study. The developers of this statistic argue that "traditional measures of predictive accuracy, such as sensitivity and specificity, are not the proper way to evaluate the potency of a risk classification model" (Silver and Banks, 1998, p. 3). They further state:

The primary utility of a risk classification model is in providing a continuum of risk estimates associated with a variety of conditions which can be used to guide a range of decision-making responses. This is true whether risk statements are issued in numerical or ranked-categorical terms (i.e., high, medium, and low risk). And it is for this reason that traditional measures of "*predictive* accuracy," which carry with them the assumption that dichotomous decisions will be made, have little utility for assessing the *potency* of a risk classification model.

DIFR is computed using the following formula:

$$DIFR = \sqrt{\sum_{i=1}^{k} \left(\ln\left(\frac{P}{1-P}\right) - \ln\left(\frac{p_i}{1-p_i}\right) \right)^2 * \frac{n_i}{N}}$$

In sum, the DIFR considers both the degree to which outcomes of each subgroup (classification level) differ from the mean for the study sample *and* the size of the group classified to each level. Its one drawback is that it is not monotonic. That is, it measures distance from the mean *without* considering whether it is in the expected or logical direction. Therefore, when outcome rates do not conform to the basic expectation, that "failure rates" will increase as risk levels increase, the test is inappropriate. Fortunately, this occurs in only one instance in this study. The rate of placement in the California system is lower for the moderate risk group (1%) than the low risk group (3%). Hence, a placement DIFR was not computed for the California system as the value derived would be misleading. All other DIFR values are provided below in Table 16.5.

As the above results indicate, the classification potency of the actuarial (Michigan) instrument far exceeds that of either of the consensus-based risk assessment models.

Based on experience assessing risk assessment systems with DIFR (albeit, somewhat limited to date), the developers of the measure provided the following conclusions:[2]

- The Michigan risk assessment system is a profoundly more potent classification device than either of the other two systems tested.
- Given the low base rate, the DIFR values indicate the Michigan system is a stronger classification device than many other systems they have tested to date.

It should be noted that the DIFR is an evolving statistical test. Early reviews from the research and statistics field have been positive, but adjustments could be forthcoming. Still, it is our view that the DIFR better represents the definition of classification than the more traditional measures of validity do and, therefore, provides a valuable test of a system's power to accurately classify cases. As such, it represents a significant contribution to the field of risk assessment research.

TABLE 16.5   Dispersion Index for Risk

	DIFR Value for Investigation Rates	DIFR Value for Substantiation Rates	DIFR Value for Placement Rates
California Risk Assessment Model	.228	.117	—
Michigan Risk Assessment Model	.464	.522	.666
Washington Risk Assessment Model	.235	.156	.454

3. Including Chronicity in the Outcome Measure

All outcome tables presented to this point reflect any *instance* of a new investigation, substantiation, or placement during the follow-up period, but do not take into account the *number of times* a family was investigated, substantiated, or had a child placed in out-of-home care. However, it is instructive to analyze the frequency of each event by risk level. Table 16.6 compares the *mean* number of investigations and substantiations for cases at each risk level. (The *mean* number of placements was very close to the *rate* recorded and, therefore, adds little to previous analyses and is not presented here.)

As Table 16.6 indicates, the Michigan actuarial system clearly outperformed the consensus-based systems when the number of new investigations and substantiations is considered. The mean number of investigations recorded for cases identified by the California and Washington systems as moderate risk actually exceeded the means for high risk cases, although the difference was not significant ($p > .05$). There was also no significant difference in substantiation rates reported for high and moderate risk cases for the California or Washington systems. There were, however, significant differences in both the mean number of investigations and substantiations at each Michigan risk level ($p < .05$). In fact, the mean number of substantiations more than doubled at each succeeding risk level.

Because chronicity as well as the severity of maltreatment is often an important factor in CPS decision making, the number of new investigations and substantiations constitutes an important measure of system validity. On this measure, the Washington system demonstrates

some ability to identify low risk cases, but there were no differences in outcomes between moderate and high risk families. There were no significant differences in the means at any risk level for the California system.

4. Case Comparisons

Clearly, the three risk assessment models performed differently in the aggregate. However, even when the overall proportions of cases falling into a particular risk level were similar, these proportions were comprised of different cases. For example, both the Michigan and Washington systems classified about one-fourth of the sample population as high risk, but that is where the similarity ends. Over half (54%) of the cases rated high risk by the Washington system were classified as low or moderate risk by the Michigan system. Conversely, 82% of families rated high risk by the Michigan system were placed at lower risk levels by the Washington system. Comparing outcomes from cases where the systems disagree helps to identify the social and economic costs of using different classification tools.

The 124 families rated high risk by the Washington system but rated low or moderate risk by the Michigan scales had investigation, substantiation, and placement rates nearly identical to the mean rates recorded for the study sample of the remaining 105 cases rated high risk by the Michigan system, nearly half had a subsequent investigation recorded, and their substantiation and placement rates were significantly above the base rate for the study sample ($p \leq .05$) (see Table 16.7). In essence, the Washington risk assessment system classified a

TABLE 16.6   Mean Number of New Investigations and Substantiations by Risk Level

	California Model		Michigan Model		Washington Model	
	Investigations	Substantiations	Investigations	Substantiations	Investigations	Substantiations
Low	.53	.22	.25	.09	.39	.18
Moderate	.66	.28	.54	.21	.67	.27
High	.59	.22	.87	.43	.64	.28
Base Rate	.58	.24	.59	.25	.60	.25

NOTE: Base rates for each system vary slightly because the number of cases for which each risk assessment was completed ranges from 929 for Michigan to 876 for California.

TABLE 16.7   Michigan/Washington Comparison Cases Rated High Risk by Washington Model N = 229

Michigan Risk Level	N	Investigation Rate	Substantiation Rate	Placement Rate
Low/Moderate	124	32%	16%	3%
High	105	49%	28%	10%

TABLE 16.8   Michigan/Washington Comparison Cases Rated High Risk by Michigan Model N = 144

Washington Risk Level	N	Investigation Rate	Substantiation Rate	Placement Rate
Low/Moderate	118	45%	28%	5%
High	26	49%	28%	10%

TABLE 16.9   Michigan/California Comparison Cases Rated High Risk by Michigan Model N = 238

California Risk Level	N	Investigation Rate	Substantiation Rate	Placement Rate
Low/Moderate	168	46%	29%	5%
High	70	47%	26%	10%

large group of families with outcome rates similar to the "average sample case" as high risk cases.

Table 16.8 demonstrates that the Washington system resulted in a low or moderate risk rating for the majority of cases rated high risk by the Michigan system. However, the rate of investigation and substantiation reported for these cases was nearly identical to the rates reported for families rated high risk by *both* systems. The placement rate was lower (5% vs. 10%), but the difference was not statistically significant ($p > .05$).

The implications of misclassification with the California system are more profound. Over 71% of *high risk* Michigan cases were rated *low* or *moderate risk* by the California system. However, these cases had investigation and substantiation rates well above the sample mean; rates that were nearly identical to cases rated high risk by *both* systems (see Table 16.9). Again, the difference noted between placement rates was not significant ($p \geq .05$).

Even when results of the two consensus-based systems were combined, classification potency added by the Michigan actuarial model is evident (see Table 16.10). There were 101 cases rated high risk by both the California and Washington systems. Of these, 45 were classified moderate risk by the Michigan system. These 45 families had a reinvestigation rate of 22% and only one (2%) of

these families was resubstantiated. Both rates are well under the mean rate of investigation and substantiation reported for the entire study sample. Of the remaining 56 cases rated high risk by the Michigan system, 46% were reinvestigated and 25% had abuse/neglect substantiated during the 18-month follow-up period. In essence, validity is not enhanced by adding results of the consensus system to those attained by the actuarial approach, but actuarial data can substantially increase validity when added to or used in place of consensus-based systems.

5. Site Comparisons

Comparisons of outcome rates are reported by site in Table 16.11. Caution should be exercised in interpreting these results as major fluctuations in rates can be attributed to a few cases. For example, the 64% rate of new investigations for Dade County cases rated moderate risk on the California system represents only 11 cases. In addition, because only substantiated cases are classified in Michigan, few cases in the Michigan sites were rated low risk by either the Michigan or Washington system.

Only investigation and substantiation rates are reported by site. The low base rate for placement, coupled with small numbers of cases at each risk level when data are reported by site,

TABLE 16.10   Michigan/California and Washington Comparison Cases Rated High Risk by Both the California and Washington Models, $N = 101$

Michigan Risk Level	N	Investigation Rate	Substantiation Rate
Low/Moderate	45	22%	2%
High	56	46%	25%

TABLE 16.11   Outcomes by Risk Levels at Each Study Site (Ns in parentheses)*

	California Model		Michigan Model		Washington Model	
Site	Investigation	Substantiation	Investigation	Substantiation	Investigation	Substantiation
			Dade County			
Low Risk	39% (160)	21%	24% (29)	14%	36% (102)	22%
Moderate Risk	64% (11)	36%	43% (129)	21%	49% (67)	21%
High Risk	36% (14)	29%	44% (71)	35%	44% (50)	36%
			Jackson County			
Low Risk	22% (232)	13%	15% (101)	6%	13% (89)	10%
Moderate Risk	40% (222)	20%	31% (272)	17%	34% (334)	18%
High Risk	53% (32)	31%	50% (116)	28%	51% (55)	27%
			Michigan Counties			
Low Risk	20% (50)	2%	0% (8)	0%	9% (11)	9%
Moderate Risk	27% (71)	11%	23% (141)	7%	24% (74)	5%
High Risk	33% (84)	12%	42% (62)	18%	32% (126)	13%

*Less long-term removal cases.

made placement rate comparisons rather meaningless. As noted earlier in the review of model reliability, the highest quality data came from Jackson County, Missouri, and the Michigan sites (Baird et al., 1999). Note that all three systems performed reasonably well in both jurisdictions. In essence, because California and Washington assessments were each completed by *one* recently trained case reader, the problems caused by a lack of inter-rater reliability may have been mitigated to a significant degree. The Washington system did particularly well at the Jackson County site, attaining the highest degree of discrimination for investigation rates. However, the Michigan system placed a higher percentage of cases into the high and low risk levels with only a marginal reduction in the level of discrimination attained. As a result, DIFR values were substantially higher for the Michigan system than for the Washington model in Jackson County. The reason for this is clear when one considers the Michigan system placed 110% more Jackson County cases in the high risk category (116 vs. 55) and 13.5% more cases at low risk than the Washington system (101 vs. 89), yet still attained very similar investigation and substantiation rates at each risk level. Overall, the Michigan system was the more effective classification instrument in each of the jurisdictions participating in this study.

6. Racial Breakdowns

When the entire cohort was considered, nearly equal percentages of African Americans and Whites were classified to each risk level by each of the risk assessment systems. However, when cases placed in foster care were removed—as they were for the validation study—differences were noted. All three systems classified fewer African American families than White families to the high risk level. The Washington system exhibited the greatest differences, classifying 8.3% more of the African American population to the low risk group.

The difference in the proportion of African Americans scoring low risk in the analysis sample (vs. the entire cohort) probably reflects the fact that more African American children were placed in foster care in most of these agencies (as well as in most other jurisdictions throughout the nation). Eliminating placement cases from the validity study removes more high risk African American families than high risk White families, leaving a greater percentage at lower risk levels.

When outcomes were computed by risk level, the Michigan risk model proved valid for both African Americans and Whites. Interestingly, both the California and Washington models classified African Americans fairly effectively, but there was little relationship between risk ratings and outcomes for Whites in either system. However, these results need to be viewed with caution because the sample, when divided by race and ethnicity, is too small to support conclusive findings.

7. Attempts to Improve Risk Assessment

With so many data elements available on sample cases, it was hoped that more effective classification instruments could be constructed. However, extensive testing, both within and among sites, produced only marginally better results than those already attained using the Michigan scales. In essence, despite the extensive amount of data available for this study, the current Michigan instruments produced results *comparable to those attained by any other combination of factors*. However, a larger sample from a *single* jurisdiction may well produce different results than those attained in this study. Research conducted in several states indicates that this is indeed the case (Wagner and Johnson, 1997; Wagner, Freitag, and Johnson, 1998), and therefore additional research in this area would be beneficial. Earlier research clearly indicates that site specific studies using large construction and validation samples can produce classification instruments somewhat superior to those "imported" from another CPS agency. Nevertheless, the Michigan scales do appear to be transferable to other jurisdictions. Site comparisons also indicate the Washington and California systems transfer well, but their ability to classify cases effectively in any jurisdiction is limited compared to Michigan's actuarial system.

V. Conclusions and Implications

A. Conclusions

Prior research comparing actuarial assessment systems with clinical decision making has clearly demonstrated the superiority of the actuarial approach (Meehl, 1954; Dawes et al., 1989; Grove and Meehl, 1996). Recent research has demonstrated that low reliability (or consistency) may well account for a substantial portion of lack of validity in clinical judgments (Rossi, Schuerman, and Budde, 1996). Consensus-based or expert risk assessment systems in child protection services attempt to overcome the problems inherent in clinical judgment by identifying what factors workers should assess and providing guidance in how each factor should be measured. The question is then "do these systems provide enough guidance to ensure consistency among workers *and* provide valid designations of risk?" Further, "do they match or surpass validity of actuarial assessment systems?"

This study may be the first national comparison of expert and actuarial systems conducted to date, although a similar study was conducted in one state, New York (Falco, 1997). Key findings are summarized below.

- The Michigan actuarial system demonstrated a significantly higher level of validity than the California or Washington consensus-based systems on all outcome measures. Differences between the actuarial and expert approaches were especially pronounced when chronicity (represented by the *number* of investigations and substantiations recorded during the follow-up period) was considered.

- When validity *within* each study site was analyzed, the Michigan system demonstrated the best overall performance. However, the Washington system demonstrated a strong relationship to outcomes in two sites and performed especially well in the Jackson County, Missouri site.

- Despite the fact that well over 100 variables were collected on each case in the study, only marginal improvements in the degree of discrimination attained by the Michigan system proved feasible. However, this could be due to limitations of the sample size within *each* jurisdiction and should therefore be the subject of continued research.

- Finally, the newly developed summary statistic, the Dispersion Index for Risk (DIFR) shows considerable promise as a method for measuring the potency of risk assessment systems. It appears to better reflect differences between risk models than do other more traditional measures of validity.

B. Implications

The implications of this study are clear: Actuarial-based systems are more accurate than consensus-based or expert systems and, therefore, have the potential to improve CPS decision making. The value of increased accuracy is perhaps best demonstrated by comparing cases classified to different risk levels by each system. Cases classified high risk by the Michigan system, but low or moderate risk by the Washington and California systems, had high rates of subsequent maltreatment. Conversely, families classified high risk by the Washington and California system but moderate or low risk by the Michigan scales had subsequent maltreatment rates at or below the average for the entire sample. Without question, the social and economic costs of misclassification could be substantial.

As computerization in child welfare agencies increases, both the quantity and quality of data available for research purposes *may* increase as well. Additional research using larger samples from a wider range of jurisdictions could further advance the knowledge base regarding the design and transferability of risk assessment instruments.

NOTES

1. The terms substantiation, confirmation, and indication are all used in child welfare. In most cases, to substantiate, confirm, or indicate that abuse or neglect occurred refers to a preponderance of evidence and is not necessarily reflective of legal standards of evidence needed to establish guilt beyond any reasonable doubt.

2. Steven Banks, co-developer of the Dispersion Index for Risk, graciously offered to review the study results and provided these conclusions in personal correspondence with the study authors.

REFERENCES

Baird, S. C., "Development of Risk Assessment Indices for the Alaska Department of Health and Social Services." in T. Tatara (Ed.) *Validation Research in CPS Risk Assessment: Three Recent Studies*, Occasional Monograph Series No. 2, Washington, D.C.: American Public Welfare Association, 1988.

Baird, S. C., Ereth, J., and Wagner, D., "Research-Based Risk Assessment: Adding Equity to CPS Decision Making." Children's Research Center, Madison, WI, June 1999.

Baird, S. C., Wagner, D., Healy, T., and Johnson, K., "Risk Assessment in Child Protective Services: Consensus and Actuarial Model Reliability." *Child Welfare*, Vol. LXXVIII, No. 6, pp. 723–748, November/December 1999.

Baird, S. C., Wagner, D., Caskey, R., and Neuenfeldt, D., "Michigan Department of Social Services Structured Decision Making System: an Evaluation of Its Impact on Child Protection Services," Children's Research Center, Madison, WI, March 1995.

Baird, S. C., Wagner, D., and Neuenfeldt, D., "Protecting Children: the Michigan Model," *Focus*, National Council on Crime and Delinquency, Madison, WI, March 1992.

Baumann, D. J., Esterline, J. A., Zuniga, G., Smith, S., Whiteside, D., Fluke, J., Goertz, B., and Cohen, M., "The Implementation of Risk Assessment," Chapter 8 in the WISDOM Project, Texas Department of Protective and Regulatory Services, Program Assessment Section, Austin, TX, 1997.

Blenkner, M., "Predictive Factors in the Initial Interview in Family Casework." *Social Science Review*, 28, 1954.

Burgess, E. W., "Factors determining the success or failure on parole." in A.A. Bruce (Ed.), *The workings of the indeterminate sentence law and the parole system in Illinois* (pp. 205–209), Illinois Committee on Indeterminate-Sentence Law and Parole, Springfield, IL, 1928.

Camasso, M. J., and Jagannathan, R., "Prediction accuracy of the Washington and Illinois risk assessment instruments: An application of receiver operating characteristic curve analysis," *Social Work Research*, Vol. 19, No. 3, pp. 174–183, September 1995.

Children's Research Center, *A New Approach to Child Protective Services; Structured Decision Making*, National Council on Crime and Delinquency, Children's Research Center, Madison, WI, 1999.

Cicchinelli, F. (ed.), *Proceedings from the Symposium on Risk Assessment in Child Protective Services*, National Center on Child Abuse and Neglect, Washington, D.C., 1991.

Dawes, R., "Finding Guidelines for Tough Decisions," *The Chronicle of Higher Education*, A40, June 1993.

Dawes, R. M., Faust, D., and Meehl, P. E., "Clinical Versus Actuarial Judgment." *Science*, 243, pp.1668–1674, 1989.

DePanfilis, D., and Zuravin, S. J., "Rates, Patterns, and Frequency of Child Maltreatment Recurrences Among Families Known to CPS." *Child Maltreatment*, Vol. 3, No. 1, pp. 27–42, February 1998.

Doueck, H., English, D., DePanfilis D., and Moote, G., "Decision Making in Child Protective Services: A Comparison of Selected Risk

Assessment Systems." *Child Welfare*, 72(5), pp. 441–452, 1993.

Doueck, J., Levine, M., and Bronson, D., "Risk Assessment in Child Protective Services: An Evaluation of the Child at Risk Field System," *Journal of Interpersonal Violence*, pp. 446–467, December 1993.

English, D. J., "Current Knowledge About CPS Decision Making," *Decision Making in Children's Protective Services*, pp. 56–74, National Resource Center on Child Maltreatment, 1997.

English, D. J., Aubin, S. W., Fine, D., and Pecora, P. J., "Improving the Accuracy and Cultural Sensitivity of Risk Assessment in Child Abuse and Neglect Cases," Office of Children's Administration Research, Olympia, WA, February 1993.

Falco, G., "Clinical vs. Actuarial Risk Assessment: Results from New York State." Office of Program Evaluation for the New York State Department of Social Services. July 1997.

Grove, W. M., and Meehl, P. E., "Comparative Efficiency of Informal (Subjective, Impressionistic) and Formal (Mechanical, Algorithmic) Prediction Procedures: The Clinical-Statistical Controversy," *Psychology, Public Policy, and Law*, Vol. 2, No. 2, pp. 293–323, 1996.

Johnson, W., and L'Esperance, J., "Predicting the Recurrence of Child Abuse." *Social Work Research and Abstracts*, 20 (2), pp. 21–26, 1984.

Marks, J., McDonald, T., Bessey, W., and Palmer, M., "Risk Factors Assessed by Instrument-based Models: A Review of the Literature." *Risk Assessment in Child Protective Services*, National Child Welfare Resource Center for Management and Administration, 1989.

Marks, J., and McDonald, T., "Predicting Recurrence of Child Maltreatment." *Risk Assessment in Child Protective Services*, National Child Welfare Resource Center for Management and Administration, 1989.

Meehl, P., "Clinical Versus Statistical Prediction: A Theoretical Analysis and a Review of the Evidence." Minneapolis, University of Minnesota Press, 1954.

Murphy-Berman, V., "A Conceptual Framework for Thinking About Risk Assessment and Case Management in Child Protective Services." *Child Abuse & Neglect*, Vol. 18, No. 2, pp. 193–201, 1994.

National Commission on Children, *Beyond Rhetoric: A New American Agenda for Children and Families*, 80, 1991.

Pecora, P. J., "Investigating allegations of child maltreatment: the strengths and limitations of current risk assessment systems." in M. Robin (Ed.), *Assessing child maltreatment reports: The problem of false allegations*, pp. 73–92, New York: Haworth Press, 1991.

Rossi, P., Schuerman, J., and Budde, S., "Understanding Child Maltreatment Decisions and Those Who Make Them." Chapin Hall Center for Children, University of Chicago, June 1996.

Ruscio, J., "Information Integration in Child Welfare Cases: An Introduction to Statistical Decision Making," *Child Maltreatment*, Vol. 3, No. 2, pp. 143–156, May 1998.

Sawyer, J., "Measurement and Prediction, Clinical, and Statistical." *Psychological Bulletin*, Vol. 66 No. 3, 178–200, 1966.

Sheets, D., *The Texas CARF evaluation.* Texas Department of Human Services, Austin, TX, 1991.

Silver, E., and Banks, S., "Calibrating the Potency of Violence Risk Classification Models: the Dispersion Index for Risk (DIFR)," Paper presented at the American Society of Criminology conference, 1998.

Silverstein, M. J., Lagios, M. D., "Use of Predictors of Recurrence to Plan Therapy for DCIS of the Breast," *Oncology*, Vol. II, No. 3, pp. 393–410, March 1997.

Tatara, T., "An Overview of Current Practices in CPS Risk Assessment and Family Systems Assessment in Public Child Welfare," *Summary of Highlights of the National Roundtable on CPS Risk Assessment and Family Systems Assessment*, American Public Welfare Association, Washington, D.C., 1987.

Tatara, T., "A Survey of States on CPS Risk Assessment Practice: Preliminary Findings," Presented at the Tenth National Roundtable on CPS Risk Assessment, American Public Welfare Association, Washington, D.C., 1996.

Wagner, D., "Development of Research-Based Risk Assessment Instruments in Oklahoma," National Council on Crime and Delinquency, February 1992.

Wagner, D., Freitag, R., and Johnson, K., "Preliminary California Risk Assessment: Risk Assessment Workgroup," Children's Research Center, Madison, WI, September 1998.

Wagner, D., and Johnson, K., "State of New Mexico Children, Youth, and Families Department: Preliminary Findings of the Child Protective Services Risk Assessment Study," Children's Research Center, Madison, WI, January 1997.

Wald, M. S., and Woolverton, M., "Risk Assessment: the Emperor's New Clothes?" *Child Welfare*, Vol. LXIX, No. 6, pp. 483–511, November-December 1990.

Wiggins, J. S., "Clinical and statistical prediction: Where are we and where do we go from here?" *Clinical Psychology Review*, 1, pp. 3–18, 1981.

17

IMPROVED DECISION MAKING IN CHILD MALTREATMENT CASES

RAELENE FREITAG

MADELINE WORDES-NOYA

Delinquency prevention efforts ideally encompass a broad array of interventions, from smaller class sizes in early school years to after-school recreation to gang crisis intervention and mediation to intensified motorized police patrols.[1] But even more fundamental to preventing delinquency is the reduction of child maltreatment.[2] An emerging body of research points persuasively to a strong link between the experience of abuse or neglect and subsequent delinquent behavior.

The National Council on Crime and Delinquency has conducted a number of actuarial research studies designed to develop tools to categorize juvenile parolees and probationers on the basis of their likelihood to repeat delinquent behavior. Repeatedly these actuarial studies identify prior history of abuse or neglect as a key indicator, for subsequent delinquency.[3] Other studies have found that maltreated children were significantly more likely to engage in behaviors considered high risk for delinquency, including teen pregnancy, drug use, lower grade-point averages, and assaultive

behaviors, and had more reported mental health problems than nonmaltreated children in matched control groups.[4] Court-referred juvenile offenders were found to include a striking proportion of youth who had previously been victims of substantiated abuse or neglect (66 percent of male offenders and 39 percent of female offenders).[5] In a longitudinal study comparing maltreated children with a matched control group, the maltreated children were more likely to be arrested for juvenile offenses (27 percent compared to 17 percent for the control group) and were arrested more often (an average of 3 arrests compared to 2.4 for the control group).[6]

Preventing child abuse and neglect ultimately involves its own array of interventions. This article does not address primary or secondary prevention efforts, though these are of no less importance. It describes one demonstrably effective and attainable tertiary prevention strategy. "Tertiary prevention efforts" are those directed toward families who have already come to the attention of a child protective service agency and are designed to reduce the likelihood

Source: From Freitag, R. and Wordes, M., "Improved Decision Making in Child Maltreatment Cases," in *Journal of the Center for Families, Children, & the Courts,* Volume 3, 2001. Reprinted with permission of the Judicial Council of California.

that children in those families will experience abuse or neglect in the future. Significant reduction in child abuse and neglect was achieved simply by improving the decision-making process in child protection agencies.

DECISIONS IN CHILD MALTREATMENT CASES

Decision making in child maltreatment cases is a daunting task with potentially grave consequences. Each case is unique, often involving complex and confusing facts, and the stakes—the safety and welfare of a child—are very high. Errors can result in children remaining in unsafe circumstances or in needless allocation of scarce resources and unwarranted interventions. Added to these concerns, child protective service (CPS) workers—the first line of decision-makers—are often overworked, overwhelmed by the gravity of the choices they must make, and, too often, new to the job and inexperienced.

The decisions child protective agencies make are complex and critical to reducing further maltreatment and potential delinquent behavior. Given the numbers and severity of cases that present to child agencies, the difficulty of making appropriate discretionary decisions, and limited staffing and services, agencies are looking to structured decision-making systems to help them respond appropriately to reports of abuse and neglect. This article describes principles and elements of the structured decision-making (SDM) system developed by the Children's Research Center of the National Council on Crime and Delinquency and reports results of studies on the use of this tool.

According to a 1993–94 survey, nearly 3 million children were identified as the victims of maltreatment.[7] Not all abused or neglected children are reported to official agencies; even so, CPS agencies across the country daily receive thousands of phone calls reporting possible abuse and neglect. Approximately 40 percent of these official reports are screened out in the initial call and not assigned for investigation.[8] About one-third of the investigated reports of child maltreatment are confirmed. Over 800,000 abused or neglected children had officially substantiated CPS cases in 1999.[9]

The system fails when the agency does not respond adequately and the abuse or neglect continues. The problem of ensuring adequate CPS response is national in scope: More than 30 states have experienced class-action lawsuits concerning the delivery of child protective services. The decision-making environment facing CPS agencies is increasingly complex because of a confluence of factors:

- While actual referrals to CPS agencies have declined slightly over the past several years, this modest reduction follows more than a decade of robust increase. Few agencies have been able to keep pace with referrals, so that existing workforce strength lags far behind the amount of time needed to conduct adequate investigations and provide adequate services.

- Scarcity of workers, especially in certain communities, results in both continued exacerbation of staff shortages and employment of staff with nontraditional academic preparation and experience.

- Because of rapid staff turnover, workers with minimal experience often conduct investigation and provide services.

Child protection assessment and service delivery require a vast array of skills and knowledge. Clear analysis and good judgment are required in deciding which cases to investigate and which cases to focus the agency's greatest attention on. But in this environment, even the most expert child welfare workers tend to reach different decisions about the safety of children when presented with the same case information.[10] Many agencies are seeking improved decision-making models as a fundamental step toward improving outcomes.

One promising decision-making tool for CPS workers is the structured decision-making (SDM) system. This article describes the principles and elements of the SDM model developed by the Children's Research Center of the National Council on Crime and Delinquency.

THE SDM MODEL

SDM is a strategy designed to reduce revictimization of children by improving the efficiency and effectiveness of CPS agencies. This improvement is accomplished by (1) increasing the consistency, objectivity, and validity of child welfare decisions and (2) focusing resources on families at the highest levels of risk for revictimization. SDM is currently in use in all or part of a number of states including Alaska, California, Georgia, Michigan, Minnesota, New Hampshire, New Mexico, Ohio, Rhode Island, and Wisconsin.

Underlying Principles of the SDM Model

The SDM model is based on four primary principles:

1. Decisions can be significantly improved when they are structured appropriately. Therefore, every worker in every case must consider a set of specific criteria using highly structured assessment procedures. Using common criteria across workers and across cases increases the consistency and accuracy of decisions.

2. Priorities assigned to cases and services delivered must correspond directly to the assessment process. Even best assessments are of little use unless the actions taken are related to the results of the assessment. Yet in many systems currently, families are served with "one-size-fits-all" approaches: Regulations often require the same level of contact with a family (i.e., one contact per month) regardless of the family assessed risk level, and case plans often require parenting classes and counseling regardless of the family's identified strength needs. Instead, SDM ensures that the agency's highest priority is given to the most serious/highest-risk cases. SDM further increases the likelihood that agency will address specifically identified service needs while reducing the often-automatic referrals to readily available, yet sometimes unnecessary, services.

3. Virtually everything that an agency does—from providing services in an individual case to allocating budgetary resources—should be a response to the assessment process. Data obtained from use of the SDM model provide a rich source of information on the range and extent of services needed in the community and shed light on the impact and effectiveness of agency policy and practice.

4. A single, rigidly defined model cannot meet the needs of agency. Organizational structures, agency mandates, governing statutes, and regulatory environments vary significantly from state to state. Rather than importing a decision system wholesale, each jurisdiction should tailor the system to its local needs and design a process that builds acceptance and local expertise into the model.

Principal Components of the SDM Model

The SDM model consists of a set of assessment tools along with related definitions, policies, and procedures. Each tool is designed specifically for use at a particular key decision point in the life of a CPS case. By focusing on individual decision points for each tool, rather than considering all case information as a whole, the SDM model enhances clarity and allows agencies to more effectively monitor compliance with established policies and procedures.

Although SDM is a highly structured system, it is not rigid. No set of factors can account for all unique case and family characteristics, and no set of definitions can encompass the vast array of case features. Therefore, most SDM tools incorporate an override provision that allows a worker to change the assessment-indicated decision when necessary. In this way, SDM does not replace worker judgment but forms a dynamic partnership between structure and judgment.

Initial Intake Assessment

At the time of referral, a worker must determine whether the report raises concerns that fall within the mandate of the CPS agency. Although statutes and regulations often define abuse and neglect, application of the definitions tends to be inconsistent. Reports of similar conduct to a CPS agency may result in an investigation at one time but not another. SDM's initial intake assessment tools include expanded and concrete examples to illustrate the kinds of situations the agency would investigate. The tools not only help screening workers improve consistency but also are useful for articulating agency policy to mandatory or voluntary reporters.

Response Priority Assessment

Once a workers has decided to assign a referral for investigation, he or she turns to a set of

FIGURE 17.1   Removal Rate by Response Time

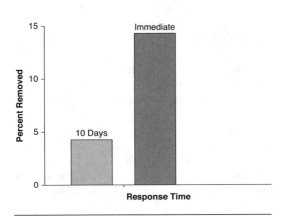

Source: Children's Research Ctr., Combined California Counties: Structured Decision Making Case Management Report. January-December 2000, at AI (Children's Research Ctr., Nat'l Council on Crime & Delinquency, 2001).

response priority tools that help determine how quickly to respond. Ideally, every call would receive an immediate response, but there are times when more calls come in than the available workers can process. A good triage process ensures that those calls deserving an urgent response will get one.

Response priority tools are typically built to address major categories of maltreatment (i.e., neglect, physical abuse, sexual abuse) and consist of decision trees that lay out a logical sequence of 3 to 10 critical questions. By answering these questions in order, a worker is guided to a response-time recommendation based on the characteristics of the report. Most jurisdictions sort referrals into two or three response times, such as immediate, 3-day, or 10-day. As with all SDM tools, the final step of the response priority assessment is to consider whether there are unique circumstances that warrant an override of the tool-derived decision.

Aggregate information from SDM jurisdictions suggests that the response priority instruments are effective. One way to examine effectiveness is by comparing the rates at which children are removed from their homes during the initial stage of the investigation. For investigations in which a nonimmediate response is recommended there should be very few instances in which conditions warrant removal of a child.

Conditions severe enough to result in removal would warrant an immediate response so that the child is not left in dangerous conditions before the investigation begins. Thus, the rate of removal is expected to be far higher in immediate-response investigations, reflecting that the allocation of resources is appropriate—that is, a worker is immediately dispatched when conditions warrant. Application of the response priority assessment in over 20,000 referrals in California counties using SDM resulted in removals of children in 14 percent of all immediate-response cases, compared to only 3 percent in nonimmediate-response cases (Figure 17.1).[11]

Safety Assessment

The next key decision point occurs as the worker completes his or her first face-to-face contact with the child and family. Whether using a systematic assessment tool or individual clinical judgment, every worker in every case effectively makes a safety decision at the moment he or she takes custody of a child or leaves without the child. The safety assessment is a determination of the imminent threat of harm to the child if he or she remains in the home.

In SDM, the safety assessment consists of three parts. In the first section, the worker answers a set of 10 to 12 questions to establish whether conditions in the home pose substantial immediate danger to a child. The importance of the assessment is twofold. First, it ensures that critical areas are not overlooked. Second, it ensures that consistent safety standards are applied. This consistency contributes to equity in removal decisions. If workers observe no safety issues, children are not removed.

If one or more safety factors are present, the worker proceeds to the second section of the assessment, identification of possible in-home interventions. The tool lists actions, services, or agreements that can be put in place to ensure child safety while the investigation proceeds. This step documents the agency's reasonable efforts to prevent removal and, more important, facilitates a dialogue between the worker, the parent, and, in some cases, the extended family or community that clearly articulates the agency's safety concerns and helps to create a safety plan. In situations where no safety plan would adequately ensure child safety in the home, removal is the only option. The third step in the assessment is to record the final decision.

Although safety assessments may be characterized as simple checklists, their value cannot be overstated. Simplicity is, in fact, key to successful implementation, because CPS investigators are required to make safety decisions within very limited time frames. By allowing an investigator to focus on a relatively small set of important factors, safety assessments help investigators avoid mistakes and improve consistency.

Risk Assessment

The heart of the SDM model is its actuarial risk-assessment tool. (See Scale 17.1 for an example.) Unlike almost all other CPS risk-assessment approaches in use, SDM risk assessment is based on actuarial research. This methodology has produced tools that demonstrate more reliability and validity than consensus-based tools.[12] Higher reliability and validity translate into decision making that is equitable for families and that optimizes an agency's resources.

When a highly reliable and valid risk assessment forms the backbone of a comprehensive decision-making system, an agency is well positioned to better protect children from revictimization.

In SDM, *risk* has a very specific definition: It is an estimate of the likelihood that a child who has come to the attention of a CPS agency will be victimized during the next 18 to 24 months. Recidivism rates for lower- and higher-risk families vary substantially. As shown in Figure 17.2, for example, in the California SDM model 93 percent of investigated low-risk families did not experience another substantiation within two years of the index investigation.[13] In contrast, among very high-risk families nearly half of those investigated once had at least one more substantiation within two years.[14]

The Actuarial Method

Prior to the appearance of actuarial risk assessments, consensus-based risk assessments were developed to bring some structure to the risk-assessment process. These consensus-based tools were typically developed by a group of child-protection experts, who used existing research, along with their experience, to determine what

factors to include in the tools. The SDM approach differs in its construction. The SDM process begins similarly, with experienced workers proposing characteristics that could be observed during an investigation and that they believe will distinguish families who will experience recurrent abuse from those who will not. Often, workgroups generate lists of 150 to 200 items. Here the similarity ends. Instead of using a consensus process to hone the list to a more manageable number of items, SDM uses actuarial research to measure all of the items in a large sample of actual cases. This measurement often consists of a retrospective review of case files for investigations that occurred 18 to 24 months prior to the study. For example, if the case reflects that at the time of the investigation it was known that the primary caregiver had been diagnosed with alcohol dependency, and the study includes an item for alcohol dependency, it would be coded as such for the primary caregiver. Each of hundreds of files is similarly coded for each of hundreds of characteristics. Only information known at the time of the investigation can be used to code the items.

The second step is to open the remainder of each case file, so that workers can determine whether the family experienced subsequent negative events. Multiple events indicative of negative outcomes are measured. These can include re-referrals, resubstantiations, subsequent injuries, subsequent severe injuries, and subsequent out-of-home placements. Multiple outcome measures are needed because no absolute measure of recurrence exists. Much maltreatment goes undetected, and single measures such as referrals and substantiations can reflect quite varied practices. Checking the risk tool for validity on the basis of multiple outcomes helps reduce any potential bias that could result if a tool were to be built on a single measure.

Next, analysis of the relationships between case characteristics and outcomes is conducted to identify a set of characteristics that have the strongest correlation. These items are used to construct the risk assessment. Our research has consistently found that the most valid tools include separate indexes for estimating future neglect and future abuse. The tools are quite brief: each index typically includes around 10 items. Moreover, many items include concrete and easily observable and verifiable characteristics

Scale 17.1

CALIFORNIA FAMILY RISK ASSESSMENT OF ABUSE/NEGLECT

Family Case Name: _____ Family Case #: _____

County Name: _____ County #:_____ Office: _____

Worker Name: _____ Worker #: _____CPS Referral Date: _____ Assessment Date: _____

Neglect _____ Score _____ Abues _____ Score _____

N1. Current investigation is for neglect
    a. No 0
    b. Yes .... 1 —

N2. Number of prior abuse/neglect investigations
    a. None 0
    b. One 1
    c. Two or more.................................. 2 —

N3. Number of children in the home
    a. Two or fewer.................................. 0
    b. Three or more .... 1 —

N4. Number of adults in home at time of investigation
    a. Two or more.................................. 0
    b. One/none .... I —

N5. Age of primary caregiver
    a. 30 or older 0
    b. 29 or younger .... 1 —

N6. Characteristics of primary caregiver (check & add for score)
    a. Not applicable 0
    b. Parenting skills are a major problem............................ 1
    c. Lacks self-esteem............................ 1
    d. Apathetic or feeling of hopelessness............................... 1 —

N7. Primary caregiver involved in harmful relationships
    a. No 0
    b. Yes, but not a victim of domestic violence 1
    c. Yes, as a victim of domestic violence........................... 2 —

N8. Primary caregiver has a current substance abuse problem
    a. No 0
    b. Alcohol *only*.................................... 1
    c. Other drug(s) (with or without alcohol)............................. 3 —

N9. Household is experiencing severe financial difficulty
    a. No 0
    b. Yes .... 1 —

A1. Current investigation is for physical, sexual or emotional abuse
    a. No 0
    b. Yes .... I —

A2. Prior abuse investigations
    a. None 0
    b. Physical/emotional abuse 1
    c. Sexual abuse............................... 2
    d. Both b and c .... 3 —

A3. Prior CPS service history
    a. No 0
    b. Yes .... 1 —

A4. Number of children in the home
    a. One 0
    b. Two or more .... 1 —

A5. Caregiver(s) abused as child(ren)
    a. No 0
    b. Yes .... 1 —

A6. Secondary caregiver has a current substance abuse problem
    a. No, or no secondary caregiver 0
    b. Yes (check all that apply)
        ____ Alcohol abuse problem
        ____ Drug abuse problem .... 1 —

A7. Primary or secondary caregiver employs excessive and/or inappropriate discipline
    a. No 0
    b. Yes .... 2 —

A8. Caregiver(s) has a history of domestic violence
    a. No 0
    b. Yes .... 1 —

A9. Caregiver(s) is an over-controlling parent
    a. No 0
    b. Yes .... 1 —

A10. Child in the home has special needs or history of delinquency
    a. No 0
    b. Yes (*check all that apply*)
        ____ Diagnosed special needs
        ____ History of delinquency .... 1 —

(Continued)

(Continued)

N10. Primary caregiver's motivation to improve
parenting skills
a. Motivated and realistic 0
b. Unmotivated 1
c Motivated but unrealistic .... 2 —

N11. Caregiver(s) response to investigation
and seriousness of complaint
a. Attitude consistent with
seriousness of allegation
and complied satisfactorily 0
b. Attitude not consistant with seriousness
of allegation (minimizes)................ 1
c Failed to comply satisfactorily 2
d. Both b and c .... 3 —

TOTAL NEGLECT RISK SCORE .... —

INITIAL RISK LEVEL
Assign the family's risk level based on the highest score
on either scale, using the following chart:

Neglect Scale	Abuse Scale	Risk Level
____ 0–4	____ 0–2	____ Low
____ 5–7	____ 3–5	____ Moderate
____ 8–12	____ 6–9	____ High
____ 13–20	____ 10–10	____ Very High

FINAL RISK LEVEL: ____ Low ____ Moderate
____ High ____ Very High

A11. Secondary caregiver motivated to
improve parenting skills
a. Yes, or no secondary
caregiver in home 0
b. No .... 2 —

A12. Primary caregiver's attitude is
consistent with the seriousness of
the allegation
a. Yes 0
b. No .... 1 —

TOTAL ABUSE RISK SCORE .... —

OVERRIDES
Policy: Override to Very High. Check appropriate
reason.
_____ 1. Sexual abuse cases where the perpetrator is likely to
have access to the child victim.
_____ 2. Cases with nonaccidental physical injury to
an infant.
_____ 3. Serious nonaccidental physical injury
requiring hospital or medical treatment.
_____ 4. Death (previous or current) of a sibling as a
result of abuse or neglect.
_____ 5. Positive tox screen (any drug, including
alcohol) of mother or child.
Discretionary: Override to increase one risk level
_____ 6. Reason: _____

_____   _____
Supervisor Review/Approval   Date

such as ages and number of children. This
enhances both the reliability and accountability
of the risk assessment. For example, items such
as "low self-esteem" are more subjective. Even
with clear definitions to guide whether to assess
a parent as having low self-esteem or not, it is
more difficult to have multiple workers reach
the same conclusion. In contrast, it is likely that
multiple workers would consistently agree on
the number or ages of children. It is also easier
for a supervisor to review case files and confirm
that the worker accurately completed the risk
assessment when items are concrete. To the
extent that these concrete items are capable of
accurately estimating risk, they are incorporated
into the risk-assessment tool.

Decisions Based on Risk

Because the risk tool accurately categorizes
substantial differences in outcomes for families
at various risk levels knowing the risk level of a
particular family helps target scarce agency
resources. Low-risk families have a low rate of
future substantiations, with or without agency
intervention, so there is little benefit in allocating
resources to them. In contrast, higher-risk
families are substantially more likely to maltreat
their children without agency intervention. More
important, there is reason to believe that CPS
intervention with higher-risk families is very
effective. In several southeastern Wisconsin counties using SDM, low- and moderate-risk families

Figure 17.2   Cases Resubstantiated Within Two Years, by Risk Level

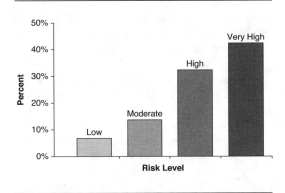

Source: Children's Research Ctr., California Preliminary Risk Assessment 6 (Children's Research Ctr., Nat'l Council on Crime & Deliquency 1998).

had about a 14 percent re-referral rate regardless of whether the CPS agency provided postinvestigation services. In contrast, high- and very high risk families who were provided CPS services after the investigation had re-referral rates that were only about half as high as families in the same risk classification who did not receive services.[15]

These data support the SDM principle that risk level should guide the decision whether to open a case for ongoing services after the initial investigation. Higher-risk cases should be opened and provided with CPS services, while lower-risk cases may be effectively served by community agencies or may need no service at all.

Differential contact standards are a second application of risk level to decision making. In SDM, the higher the risk level of an open case, the more time a worker is expected to be in contact with thes family. Differential contact standards set an expectation for worker contact and reflect the reality that certain cases consume far more worker time than others. Uniform standards that set the same expectation for worker time regardless of case characteristics simply do not reflect the need for variation. More important, without risk-based contact standards, worker time may accumulate among cases that are demanding but not necessarily high risk. In other words, workers can end up spending much time on activities that contribute little to the safety of children.

Limits of Risk Assessment

Although actuarial risk-assessment tools are highly effective, they have certain limitations. First, they are not predictive. That is, results of the risk assessment should not be considered a prediction of future behavior but only as a classification: They place a family in a group of families that share certain characteristics and have a known outcome rate. No tool can predict with certainty whether a family will maltreat a child in the future. A large percentage of even the highest-risk families will not maltreat their children again, and a small percentage of the lowest-risk families will do so. For this reason, risk level would be an inappropriate basis for the decision whether to remove a child from his or her parents. That decision is more effectively made by the safety assessment.

Second, the effectiveness of the method depends on the quality of the case files reviewed. It is possible that as knowledge of child abuse and neglect expands and case practice, including effective documentation, is strengthened, so too will actuarial tools capture increasingly robust items. There may be characteristics other than those typically appearing on current tools that are more highly correlated with outcomes but have been inconsistently documented in case files. Actuarial tools may miss these. Therefore, workers using tools have the right, and even the responsibility, to override a tool's risk estimate when they believe that a family presents unique considerations not captured by the tool. As mentioned above, this partnership between structure and judgment optimizes the value of the highly valid and reliable actuarial tools with the check-and-balance system of trusting the worker's knowledge and skill to identify exceptions.[16]

Finally, actuarial risk assessments are not designed to examine every aspect of a family that might be relevant to decisions about the most appropriate intervention for reducing the likelihood of future abuse or neglect. As a result, actuarial risk tools cannot form a basis for case planning. The family strength and need assessment is far better suited for this task.

Family Strength and Need Assessments

Families served by CPS agencies differ not only in their likelihood of experiencing recurrent problems, but also by their specific constellations

FIGURE 17.3   Sample Item From California Family Strength and Need Assessment

SN 1. Substance Abuse/Use
(Subsances: alcohol, illegal drugs,
inhalants, prescription/
over-the-counter drugs)

a.	Teaches and demonstrates healthy understanding of alcohol and drugs	+3
b.	Alcohol or prescribed drugs use	0
c.	Alcohol or drug abuse	−3
d.	Chronic alcohol/drug abuse	−5

for strengths and needs. Only by systematically assessing every family across a comprehensive set of domains does it become possible to identify the particular areas in which services are most needed.

SDM strength and need assessments typically consist of 10 to 12 critical domain areas, such as substance abuse/use, mental health, social support, and basis needs. The family is scored in each domain according to a scale ranging from "strength" to "severe need." (See Figure 17.3.) Each response within an item has a core based on how critical an issue is to reducing subsequent child abuse or neglect. Comparison of the scores on each item helps to identify the need areas to be addressed first. Case plans, then, typically focus on up to three main areas of need while incorporating identified strengths. When strength and need assessments are repeated over time, they help assess progress.

Reassessments

The risk assessment tools designed for the initial investigation typically do not work well at reassessment because they do not assess progress toward change. Reassessment tools better handle this function.

At regular intervals in the life of a case, reassessments help guide decisions about when to close the case, refocus case plans, and reset contact standards if the case remains open. Reassessments include some of the most significant risk factors considered in the initial risk tool and evaluate progress toward the case plan's goal. Using this tool helps reduce the potential for cases to remain open—continuing to consume agency resources—despite diminishing returns from the investment of CPS services.

Reassessments are particularly vital for children in out-of-home care. Based on local agency statutes and regulations, reunification must occur within specific time limits. Children returning to their parents must have lower risk levels at reassessment, and their parents must have demonstrated acceptable visitation. The final step toward reunification is an assessment of safety concerns. If any of these three conditions—risk level, visitation, or safety—falls below the acceptable level, the child will not be returned home. The decision model also incorporates the required time limits. Based on the time already in care and the age of the child, a decision tree guides the worker toward a recommendation either to continue to provide reunification services or to change the permanency-plan goal.

IMPLEMENTATION ISSUES

A decision model such as SDM requires several critical changes in work culture:

- A change from clinical judgment alone to a partnership between research, structure, and judgment

There is often initial resistance to SDM by a small segment of workers who prefer to continue to make decisions based on their own knowledge, experience, and values. Alternatively, some workers are prone to rely too mechanically on tools without exercising their responsibility to override results where appropriate. Skilled supervisors can help staff achieve the optimal balance between research, structure, and judgment.

- Refocusing resources toward higher-risk families, regardless of whether an investigation is substantiated or not

Practice in many jurisdictions has evolved in ways that make substantiated cases far more likely to be opened than unsubstantiated cases regardless of risk level. On the one hand, there is a reluctance to close lower-risk cases that are substantiated, even though an overwhelming percentage of low-risk families will not maltreat again. On the other hand, unsubstantiated or inconclusive higher-risk cases are rarely opened. Without evidence to support a court order, it is

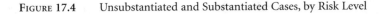

FIGURE 17.4   Unsubstantiated and Substantiated Cases, by Risk Level

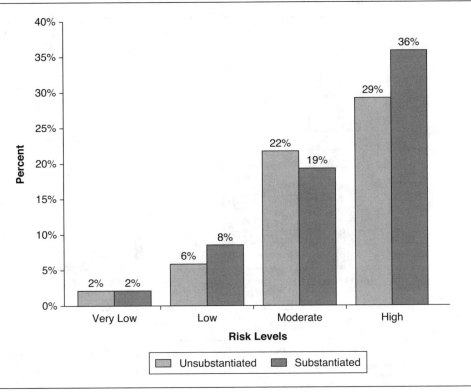

Source: D. Wagner & B. Meyer, Using Actuarial Risk Assessment to Identify Unsubstantiated Cases for Preventative Intervention in New Mexico 14 (1998) (paper presented at 12th National Roundtable on CPS Risk Assessment).

often suggested, there is little a CPS agency can do.

Children's Research Center research in New Mexico provides strong evidence that recurrence has little to do with current substantiation status. New maltreatment was about as likely in unsubstantiated cases as in substantiated ones when controlling for risk level. It is true for inconclusive or unsubstantiated cases, however, that families must be allowed to voluntarily accept or reject services. The SDM impetus to open all higher-risk cases, regardless of substantiation status, requires a commitment to work toward engaging a family in services based on a mutual concern for the child's safety and well-being. While this effort to engage families will sometimes fail, the New Mexico findings strongly suggest that when we fail to engage higher-risk families in treatment-oriented services today, those same families will probably consume investigation resources tomorrow. More critical, a child may be harmed while the system waits for evidence to substantiate. (See Figure 17.4.)

- Using data to inform decisions throughout the agency

While SDM has tremendous value for guiding decisions in individual cases, its value is enhanced when an agency uses aggregate data to make policy, program, and financial decisions. For example, the family strength and need assessment provides a thorough picture of the needs profiles of all families served by the agency. This information can serve as a basis for dialogue with community organizations about matching available services to actual needs.

EVALUATION OF SDM MODELS

Rarely has any new child welfare program or concept been as thoroughly examined as SDM. This examination is ongoing and is useful in both confirming that the model is working and pointing out areas requiring improvement. In addition to regularly gathered management

FIGURE 17.5   Cases with New Child Maltreatment outcomes in a 12-Month Follow-Up in SDM and non-SDM Counties

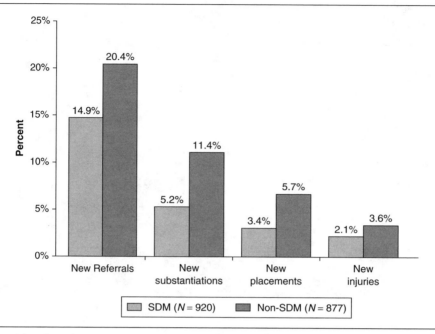

Source: S. C. Baird et al., Michigan Department of Social Services Structured Decision Making System: An Evaluation of Its Impact on Child Protective Services 17 (Children's Research Ctr., Nat'l Council on Crime & Deliquency 1995).

FIGURE 17.6   Cases Achieving Permanency Within 15 Months of Entering Foster Care in SDM and non-SDM Counties

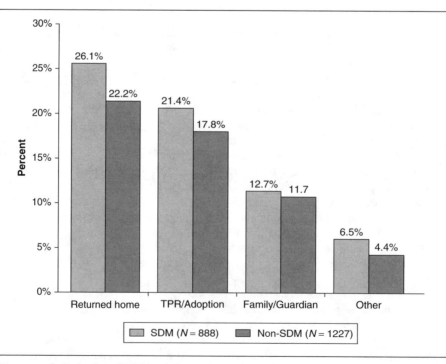

Source: D. Wagner et al., Evaluation of Michigan's Foster Care Structured Decision Making Case Management System 21 (Children's Research Ctr., Nat'l Council on Crime & Deliquency 2001).

data, several controlled research designs have examined the impact of SDM models. This section reports key findings from those studies.

Michigan began using SDM in 13 counties in 1992. An evaluation of SDM's effectiveness was conducted three years later.[17] Approximately 900 families investigated by the 13 SDM counties were compared to a similar number of families investigated by a matched set of 13 comparison counties. All families were followed for 12 months after the index investigation.

The study found that SDM jurisdictions apparently made more effective decisions about which families to serve postinvestigation. Even though SDM counties closed a higher percentage of cases immediately upon concluding the investigation, closed cases in SDM counties had fewer subsequent referrals, substantiations, injuries, and placements than did closed cases in non-SDM counties. SDM counties were also more effective at getting targeted services to families with specific identified needs. For example, among all families identified as needing family counseling in SDM counties, about 40 percent actually received family counseling. While this percentage is far below optimal, only 25 percent of families with an identified need for family counseling received it in non-SDM counties.

Finally, in terms of ultimate outcomes, families in SDM counties experienced significantly fewer new referrals, new substantiations, subsequent injuries, and foster placements compared to families in non-SDM counties. Figure 17.5 shows that for every outcome measured using official statistics, counties using SDM lowered the rates of child maltreatment.

The reunification assessment was evaluated in another study of SDM in Michigan.[18] Figure 17.6 shows that significantly more children were moved to permanency in SDM counties (67 percent) than in non-SDM counties (56 percent). Even more striking, increased permanency was achieved in all permanency-status categories.

CONCLUSION

SDM is not a panacea for the vast and complex issues facing CPS agencies. While SDM is an excellent teaching tool, it is not a substitute for comprehensive conceptual and theoretical education for workers. SDM may help newly hired workers learn critical decision-making skills

more quickly, but is should not replace efforts to reduce rapid turnover in the first place.

Moreover, while SDM can help in the allocation of existing CPS resources in ways that bring about the greatest reductions in subsequent victimization, existing resources may be insufficient to achieve optimal results. SDM can effectively categorize families on the basis of risk and identify critical needs to be addressed, but if services to meet those needs do not exist in the community, categorization alone will simply not be enough.

Implementing SDM is far from a "turnkey" operation. It is not enough for an agency to hand out a new set of assessment forms. SDM's full value depends on careful preimplementation planning, comprehensive training, and continued attention to the quality of implementation. It takes no small effort to make the paradigm shifts discussed in this article, especially when many CPS jurisdictions have a full plate of regulatory changes, automation issues, and a plethora of new policies, programs, and initiatives competing for attention.

It is encouraging, however, that even faced with the enormity of its task, a CPS agency can implement SDM with sufficient quality to achieve a measurable reduction in child victimization. The Michigan evaluation studies cited in this article suggest that, all else being equal, jurisdictions implementing SDM can achieve improved outcomes. SDM represents one practical and efficient way to improve the nation's CPS systems and, in turn, help reduce harm to children.

NOTES

1. Guide for Implementing the Comprehensive Strategy for Serious, Violent, and Chronic Juvenile Offenders (Office of Juvenile Justice & Delinquency Prevention 1995).

2. Richard Wiebush et al., Preventing Delinquency Through Improved Child Protection Services, Juv. Just. Bull. 1 (Office of Juvenile Justice & Delinquency Prevention, July 2001).

3. Nat'l Council on Crime & Delinquency, Assessing the Risk of Juvenile Offenders in Nebraska (1995); Nat'l Council on Crime & Delinquency, Development of an Empirically Based Risk Assessment Instrument for the Virginia Department of Juvenile Justice: Final Report (1999); Nat'l Council on Crime & Delinquency, Revalidation of the Michigan Juvenile Risk Assessment (1995); Nat'l Council on Crime & Delinquency, Rhode Island Juvenile Risk Assessment Findings (1995); Nat'l

Council on Crime & Delinquency, Wisconsin Juvenile Offender Classification Study: County Risk Assessment Revalidation Report (1997).

4. Barbara T. Kelley et al., in the Wake of Childhood Maltreatment, Juv. Just. Bull. 1 (Office of Juvenile Justice & Delinquency Prevention, Aug. 1997).

5. John Pawasarat, Identifying Milwaukee Youth in Critical Need of Intervention: Lessons from the Past, Measures for the Future 1 (Univ. of Wisconsin Employment & Training Inst. 1991).

6. Cathy S. Widom, the Cycle of Violence, Research in Brief 1 (U.S. Dep't of Justice, Oct. 1992); Cathy S. Widom, Victims of Childhood Sexual Abuse—Later Criminal Consequences, Research in Brief 1 (U.S. Dep't of Justice, Mar. 1995); Michael G. Maxfield & Cathy S. Widom, Childhood Victimization and Patterns of Offending Through the Life Cycle: Early Onset and Continuation (1995) (paper presented at the annual meeting of the American Society of Criminology).

7. Admin. on Children, Youth & Families, U.S. Dep't of Health & Human Servs., The Third National Incidence Study on Child Abuse and Neglect (1996), www.calib.com/nccanch/pubs/stainfo/nis3.cfm.

8. Admin. on Children, Youth & Families, U.S. Dep't of Health & Human Servs., Child Maltreatment 1997: Reports from the States to the National Child Abuse and Neglect Data System (1999), www.calib.com/nccanch/pubs/factsheets/canstats.cfm.

9. Id.

10. Peter H. Rossi et al., Understanding Child Maltreatment Decisions and Those Who Make Them (Chapin Hall Ctr. for Children, Univ. of Chicago 1996).

11. Children's Research Ctr., Combined California Counties: Structured Decision Making Case Management Report, January-December 2000, at A1 (Children's Research Ctr., Nat'l Council on Crime & Delinquency 2001).

12. S. Christopher Baird et al., Risk Assessment in Child Protective Services: Consensus and Actuarial Model Reliability, 78 Child Welfare 723 (1999); S. Christopher Baird & Dennis Wagner, the Relative Validity of Actuarial and Consensus-Based Risk Assessment Systems, 22 Child. & Youth Services Rev. 839 (2000); see George Falco, Clinical vs. Actuarial Risk Assessment: Results from New York State (Office of Program Evaluation, N.Y. Dep't of Soc. Servs., 1997).

13. The index investigation is the first investigation that occurred during the study period. For some families, this is the first-ever investigation, while others had prior CPS investigations as well.

14. Children's Research Ctr., California Preliminary Risk Assessment 5 (Children's Research Ctr., Nat'l Council on Crime & Delinquency 1998).

15. High risk: closed after investigation = 28%, re-referral rate vs. open for service = 15% re-referral rate. Very high risk: closed after investigation = 45%, re-referral rate vs. open for service = 24% re-referral rate. See Dennis Wagner & Pat Bell, the Use of Risk Assessment to Evaluate the Impact of Intensive Protective Service Intervention in a Practice Setting (Children's Research Ctr., Nat'l Council on Crime & Delinquency 1998).

16. In practice, SDM override rates generally range from 2 to 8 percent. Lower rates may suggest that tools were being used too mechanically, without attention to unique circumstances. Rates above 10 percent raise serious doubt about the tool's validity and utility or the effectiveness of training the appropriate use of the tool.

17. S. Christopher Baird et al., Michigan Department of Social Services Structured Decision Making System: an Evaluation of Its Impact on Child Protective Services (Children's Research Ctr., Nat'l Council on Crime & Delinquency 1995).

18. Dennis Wagner et al., Evaluation of Michigan's Foster Care Structured Decision Making Case Management System (Children's Research Ctr., Nat'l Council on Crime & Delinquency 2001).

18

THE PLIGHT OF CHILDREN
WHOSE PARENTS ARE IN PRISON

BARRY KRISBERG

CAROLYN ENGEL TEMIN

INCARCERATED PARENTS: A GROWING NATIONAL PROBLEM

Traditional discussions about sentencing policy pay scant attention to the effects of imprisonment on parents and their children. However, the enormous rise in the numbers of people behind bars, especially women, has brought this issue to prominence. In 1999, more than half of all state and federal prisoners reported having a child under the age of 18. Over 721,500 parents of an estimated 1,324,900 minor children are confined in prisons. Since 46 percent of these incarcerated parents reported that they resided with their children prior to entering prison, the Bureau of Justice Statistics estimates that 336,300 U.S. households with minor children are impacted by the imprisonment of a parent (Mumola, 2000). African American children are nine times more likely to have an incarcerated parent than white children. Latino children are three times more likely to have an imprisoned parent than white children. These numbers increased steadily during the 1990s—the number of minor children whose parents were locked up increased by over 500,000 during this period.

The alarming rise in the number of women inmates has exerted a profound impact on this issue. Children are far more likely to live with their mother rather than their father prior to parental incarceration (64 percent versus 44 percent, Mumola, ibid.). After parental incarceration, a child whose father is imprisoned usually lives with the mother, while the child of an incarcerated mother is much more likely to live with grandparents, other relatives, or to be placed with foster care agencies. The children of incarcerated women are more than five times more likely to enter the foster care system than children whose male parents were in prison. Thus, the decision to incarcerate a woman with minor children often creates immediate problems for the child welfare system (Bloom & Steinhart, 1993; Acoca & Raeder, 1999). There are several other important concerns unique to incarcerated mothers that we will discuss later in this paper.

The Bureau of Justice reports that the majority of children have never had a personal visit with their incarcerated parent after prison admission, although the vast majority of inmates say that they stay in touch with their children on a weekly basis via letters and telephone calls (Mumola, 2000). Sheer distance seems to be a major impediment to children visiting their imprisoned parents. Most parents are confined in facilities that are more than 100 miles from their last place of residence. Because there are fewer women's prisons, their children often must travel greater distances to visit with their mothers. The barriers to visits are especially difficult for federal prisoners whose place of incarceration is typically very remote from their place of last residence.

CHILDREN ADRIFT

Nearly a quarter century ago, the National Council on Crime and Delinquency (NCCD) and the Children's Defense Fund (CDF) chronicled the plight of children with incarcerated parents (McGowan & Blumenthal, 1978). Fifteen years later, the NCCD replicated this national study and found that the number of incarcerated women and men had grown tremendously, but there was little or no improvement in the response to their children (Bloom & Steinhart, 1993). Both studies used the title "Why Punish the Children?" The simple, but crucial point was that the children of offenders had committed no offenses, yet they were made to suffer from the "not so benign neglect" of governmental agencies. Both studies documented how neither courts, corrections departments, nor social welfare agencies took any meaningful actions to care for the children of incarcerated parents. These children were often adrift amid a range of official policies and procedures that seemed illogical, at best, and often anti-child at worst.

For example, children who visited their incarcerated parents had to participate in the mass visiting process of state prisons, with no provisions for their childhood needs. NCCD found that it was not unusual for infants and small children to be subjected to strip searches and body cavity intrusions. The children were often left to fend for themselves as the adult visitors discussed a range of complex legal and financial issues.

Social workers were rarely encouraged to facilitate prison visits between children and their parents. There were few provisions for transportation of children to remote prison locations. Those social welfare staff who did try to keep families connected were also subjected to humiliating treatment by corrections officials who claimed to be guarding against smuggling of illicit goods into the prisons. Children were often quickly moved into foster care settings with little planning for permanent living arrangements. A frequent social welfare response was to place the children with relatives (often grandparents)—this permitted the social welfare agency to provide minimal (or, in some cases, no) financial aid to the "kinship caretakers." Laws in some states prohibited foster care payments to the relatives of incarcerated parents (Bloom & Steinhart, 1993). Kinship care givers are often faced with immediate financial hardships, and they usually lack the legal advocacy resources to navigate through the complex web of welfare regulations. Further, there was little or no screening to determine the fitness of kinship care givers to take custody of a minor child.

Sometimes the children were told that their parent had died, later the story would change (McGowan & Blumenthal, 1978). Few, if any, counseling resources specifically designed to address the needs of those with incarcerated parents were available to the children themselves, or their care givers. Both NCCD studies found that the children of incarcerated parents did not thrive. Parents reported that the children experienced severe problems in school and showed signs of serious mental health and behavioral problems. There is growing research evidence that the children of incarcerated parents (especially those whose mothers are in prison) show much higher rates of subsequent criminal behavior and incarceration (Acoca, 2000; Acoca & Dedel, 1998; Gabel & Johnston, 1995; American Correctional Association, 1990). Thus, the problems of children whose parents are in prison, if not attended to, produce inter-generational patterns of crime and violence.

It is not difficult to imagine how the experience of having a parent locked away in a distant prison would create such adverse impacts on children. For example, the Center for Children of Incarcerated Parents studied the effects of incarceration on 56 children from South Central Los Angeles. The study noted that these children had been subject to a broad range of adverse experiences including extreme poverty, exposure to violence, pre-natal drug exposure, and violent deaths of family members. Added to these extreme stress factors was the forced removal of the parent from the household. The Center found that these children were even more vulnerable to the impact of separation from parents, leading to severe traumatic stress.

The traditional role of the parent in helping children deal with difficult life situations is greatly diminished in these families. Stable, nurturing home environments that are key to building resiliency among young children are often absent (Center for Children of Incarcerated Parents, 1992).

The overwhelming evidence from research on early childhood development demonstrates the critical importance of establishing a "strong and enduring attachment bond to at least one care giver during infancy" (*Yale Law Journal,* 1978:1411–1412). Many scholars have underscored the role of parental attachment in the formulation of healthy emotional and cognitive competencies (Bowlby, 1969; Ainsworth, 1973; Goldstein, Freud, & Solnit, 1973). Moreover, there is strong evidence that the removal of a child from a family may cause additional psychological damage (Wald, 1975). In particular, children who are shifted among multiple care givers often experience great difficulties in establishing close interpersonal relationships. Research has indicated that the first two years after a child's birth are particularly critical for forming parent-child attachments, although the long-term impact of early separation can be reduced if the child and parent are reunited within a brief time frame (*Yale Law Journal,* 1978). Little is known about whether the long-term negative consequences of lengthy early childhood separation from parents can be reversed later in life.

Decisions to sever parent-child ties must be grounded in a very careful analysis of potential harm to the child. Families awash in mental illness, drug abuse, violence, and other personal forms of dysfunction can be very hurtful to children. Child welfare professionals must make "life or death" decisions regarding the removal or maintenance of a child in an abusive or neglectful home environment. Social work professionals must also assess whether the provision of appropriate treatment services can greatly reduce the threats to the child while averting the problems created by separation (Wald, 1975). When the case involves incarcerated parents, careful assessment of "best interests of the child" is rare. Parental incarceration often is viewed, per se, as evidence of extreme neglect. The virtual absence of programs that could maintain infant and parent bonds during the criminal sentence makes such considerations moot (Morash et al., 1994). Since it is rare that criminal courts and family courts coordinate their planning, the question of what will become of the child is often an afterthought for the justice system.

SPECIAL BURDENS OF INCARCERATED MOTHERS

No analysis of the problems of children whose parents are incarcerated can ignore the special plight of women in prison. As noted earlier, women are most likely to be the prime and sole caretakers of their children, and they are more likely to be living in extreme poverty or homelessness prior to their imprisonment (Mumola, 2000). The incarceration of women has grown rapidly in recent years, particularly as states and the federal government have instituted tough new mandatory sentencing policies as part of the "War on Drugs" (Acoca & Raeder, 1999). Incarceration has displaced probation as the prime sentencing option for many women offenders. Sentencing guidelines have "bootstrapped" sentences for women to more closely resemble the statistical average for men (Acoca and Raeder, 1999). While these changes have been justified in terms of greater equity in the sentencing process, many believe that grave injustices are being perpetrated in the name of gender fairness (Amnesty International, 1999).

Research has consistently demonstrated that women are most likely to be imprisoned for non-violent crimes—almost 74 percent of women in state prisons were admitted for non-violent offenses, while the majority of men behind bars were convicted of violent crimes (Mumola, 2000). Women are more likely to be low level couriers in drug transactions, and to commit their offenses to satisfy their addictions (Acoca & Austin, 1996). Women are less likely to be disruptive inmates, and have lower rates of recidivism (Acoca & Raeder, 1999). Despite these findings, the reduced danger to public safety posed by women offenders it seems is not given any weight as jurisdictions move to more rigid sentencing schemes. Parenting considerations are almost never considered by judges as they set penalties within statutory guidelines systems. This is particularly ironic since an offender's value to his/her employer can be considered to ameliorate some sentencing guidelines, but their value as a sole care giver is not deemed relevant. Since men are more likely to be employed, and women more likely to be primary care givers, the superficial pursuit of "gender neutrality" produces greater gender discrimination (Raeder, 1993).

Women, unlike men, sometimes are pregnant and give birth while behind bars. Amnesty International (1999) and the United Nations Special Rapporteur on Violence Against Women (1999) have documented the virtual absence of prenatal care for incarcerated women. They have reported several incidences of women forced to give birth in prison cells or corridors, often while they are shackled. Moreover, it is customary that babies born to prison inmates are immediately separated from their mothers and placed in emergency foster care or with any relative willing to assume the burden.

This extreme cruelty toward women inmates fits a historical pattern in which women inmates have endured harsh conditions of confinement and been subject to sexual abuse by guards (Immarigeon and Chesney-Lind, 1992). Abusive experiences in prison are tragic continuations of physical and psychological abuse that many inmates have endured throughout their lives (Owen & Bloom, 1995; Acoca & Dedel, 1998).

Other social policies have exerted an adverse impact on inmate mothers. National and state reforms in welfare and adoption laws have made it easier to eliminate welfare benefits for women offenders, and have created nearly insurmountable barriers for inmate mothers who want to be eventually reunited with their children. For example, new federal laws had very negative impacts on inmate mothers. The Personal Responsibility and Work Reconciliation Act of 1996 made it far easier to drop families from the welfare rolls if the parents had criminal convictions for a drug offense. The Adoption and Safe Families Act of 1997 imposed tighter time frames for family courts and the provision of child welfare services to preserve families. Incarcerated women are now much more likely to lose their children to adoption, and less likely to qualify for family preservation services of any sort (Acoca & Raeder, 1999).

POLICY AND PROGRAM ALTERNATIVES

The problems of children whose parents are in prison must be addressed, not only for humanitarian reasons, but to attempt to interrupt the intergenerational cycle of crime and violence.

The nation can no longer tolerate having over 1.5 million minor children in limbo. The policy and program options are clear, and many sensible solutions have been advocated by many professional groups such as the National Association of Women Judges, the American Bar Association, the American Correctional Association, the Child Welfare League of America, and the National Council on Crime and Delinquency. It is now time for elected officials, courts, and public agencies to begin to implement the necessary reforms.

First and foremost, sentencing options must be expanded to be responsive to the needs of the children of incarcerated parents. This could mean changing sentencing provisions to allow for qualified, low-risk offenders to serve their sentences in non-institutional settings. Sentencing guidelines must be reexamined to determine if they are overly rigid, and if they create de facto discrimination against parents, especially the primary care givers. Whenever possible these reforms should create alternative sentencing options that permit children to continue to reside with their parents. Where current laws permit, judges should take the offender's care giver role into consideration as part of the pre-sentence investigation. Judges should consider a range of sentencing options that tend to preserve family attachments. These steps presuppose adequate funding of community corrections programs to give the courts appropriate sentencing alternatives that keep families together whenever this is feasible. Legislation enacted in California, and at the federal level, has attempted to dedicate funding for community-based correctional alternatives that keep children and their parents together, but funding for these programs has been woefully inadequate or virtually non-existent.

The child welfare system must accept increased responsibility for the grave challenges faced by children of incarcerated parents. Mechanisms must be established or strengthened to coordinate family reunification services with the courts and corrections agencies. Child welfare agencies should make reasonable efforts to keep siblings together, to place children with responsible relatives, and to facilitate visits between children and their incarcerated parents. Imprisonment, and the barriers faced by incarcerated parents in maintaining frequent contacts with their children, should not be the sole basis for recommendations to terminate parental rights. Policies denying full foster care benefits to legitimate kinship care givers should be eliminated. Government agencies should develop and fund community agencies which can provide a wide range of support services for incarcerated parents, and the children's care givers. These services should include legal advocacy, training and support for kinship care givers, and additional medical and mental health services for the children, as needed. Existing state and federal child welfare laws should be reviewed to eliminate any unnecessary obstacles or disadvantages created for the children of incarcerated parents.

Health care practices must be reformed to provide an appropriate level of care for pregnant inmates. Whenever possible, correctional officials should create non-institutional settings for pregnant inmates, and for an appropriate period after the child's birth. In-prison nurseries are a possible option but non-institutional placements are the preferred program option. Corrections agencies should contract with community agencies which have extensive experience working with low income families.

Pre-release programs for inmates should include training for inmate parents returning to their families, assisting them to regain custody of their children when appropriate, to help secure decent housing, and to find employment. Similar services for inmate parents should be included in parole planning.

CONCLUDING THOUGHTS

We are still punishing the children. Yet, in punishing the children of inmates, we are ultimately punishing ourselves. The ongoing pattern of societal neglect, and ofttimes hostility, comes back to haunt us in terms of creating more social problems such as violence, drug abuse, and mental illness. Ignoring the problem solves nothing. The number of innocent children who are impacted has grown geometrically, and they will be living in our communities for many years to come. In our collective zeal to condemn lawbreakers, we have inadvertently condemned their children. Basic humanitarian values and considerations of fairness demand that we change existing laws, policies, and practices.

Alleviating the plight of the children of incarcerated parents does not excuse the misdeeds of the parents, nor should it be viewed as ignoring the serious social and psychological problems faced by those inmate parents (many of whom were themselves the children of prison inmates) but, this growing social time bomb must be defused with sound and rational public policies. Greater public awareness of crises faced by these families is a good start. Frank reexaminations of criminal justice and child welfare policies that have worsened this problem should proceed immediately.

Judges can play a crucial leadership role in publicizing the inflexibility and dysfunctional aspects of existing sentencing codes. The judiciary can exercise their discretion to promote sentencing alternatives that attempt to preserve the bonds of parents and children. Advocacy and community-based social service agencies can play a key role in proposing meaningful alternative programs. Corrections and welfare officials need to provide greater training to their staff on the plight of these children and their parents. Budgets for remedial programs must be created and sustained.

It is sometimes fashionable in professional or political conversations to speak cynically about "writing off" this generation of incarcerated Americans. These spokespersons tell us to invest in the next generation—to provide better health care, more head start programs, more after school centers. The plight of the children of America's prisoners shows the obvious vacuousness of these views. Generations are connected. You cannot eliminate the parents without profoundly harming their children. Rescuing these children will require far more rational and enlightened legal policies toward their parents. In the end, saving the innocents is one sure way to save our communities and our own families from the cycle of violence that cannot be safely contained by prison walls.

REFERENCES

1978. "On Prisoners and Parenting: Preserving the Tie That Binds." *Yale Law Journal,* 87, (7): 1408–1429.

Acoca, Leslie. 2000. *Educate or Incarcerate: Girls in the Florida and Duval County Juvenile Justice Systems.* Oakland, California: National Council on Crime and Delinquency.

Acoca, Leslie and James Austin. 1996. *The Crisis—the Women Offender Sentencing Study and Alternative Sentencing Recommendations Project: Women in Prison.* Washington, DC: National Council on Crime & Delinquency.

Acoca, Leslie and Kelly Dedel. 1998. *No Place to Hide: Understanding and Meeting the Needs of Girls in the California Juvenile Justice System.* San Francisco, California: National Council on Crime and Delinquency.

Acoca, Leslie and Myrna S. Raeder. 1999. "Severing Family Ties: The Plight of Nonviolent Female Offenders and Their Children." *Stanford Law Policy Review,* 11, (1): 133–151.

Ainsworth, Peter B. 1973. "The Development of Infant-Mother Attachment." *Review of Child Development Research, I,* 3.

American Correctional Association Task Force on the Female Offender. 1990. *The Female Offender: What Does the Future Hold?* Laurel, Maryland: American Correctional Association.

Amnesty International. 1999. *Not Part of My Sentence: Violations of the Human Rights of Women in Custody.* New York, New York: Amnesty International.

Bloom, Barbara and David Steinhart. 1993. *Why Punish the Children? A Reappraisal of the Children of Incarcerated Mothers in America.* San Francisco, California: National Council on Crime and Delinquency.

Bowlby, J. 1969. *Attachment and Loss.* New York: Basic Books.

Center for Children of Incarcerated Parents. 1992. *Report No. 6: Children of Offenders.* Pasadena, California: Pacific Oaks College.

Gabel Katherine and Denise Johnston (Eds.). 1995. *Children of Incarcerated Parents.* New York: Lexington Books.

Goldstein, Joseph, Anna Freud, and Albert J. Solnit. 1973. *Beyond the Best Interests of the Child.* New York, New York: Free Press.

Immarigeon, Russ and Meda Chesney-Lind. 1992. *Women's Prisons: Overcrowded and Overused.* San Francisco, California: National Council on Crime and Delinquency.

McGowan, Brenda G. and Karen L. Blumenthal. 1978. *Why Punish the Children? A Study of Children of Women Prisoners.* Hackensack, New Jersey: National Council on Crime and Delinquency.

Morash, Merry, N. Haarr-Robin, and Lila Rucker. 1994. "A Comparison of Programming for Women and Men in U.S. Prisons in the 1980s." *Crime and Delinquency,* 40, (2), 197–221.

Mumola, Christopher J. 2000. "Incarcerated Parents and Their Children." *Bureau of Justice Statistics Special Report.* U.S. Department of Justice, Office of Justice Programs.

Owen, Barbara and Barbara Bloom. 1995. "Profiling Women Prisoners: Findings from National Surveys and a California Sample." *The Prison Journal,* 75: 165, 177.

Raeder, Myrna. 1993. "Gender Issues in the Federal Sentencing Guidelines and Mandatory Minimum Sentences." *Criminal Justice,* 8, (3): 20–25, 56–63.

Wald, Michael. 1975. "State Intervention on Behalf of 'Neglected' Children: A Search for Realistic Standards." *Stanford Law Review,* 27, (4).

PART V

THE LINK BETWEEN SOCIAL JUSTICE AND CRIMINAL JUSTICE

During the National Council on Crime and Delinquency's (NCCD's) 100 years of history, there have been profound changes in American society. Issues of racism, poverty, and sexism have formed tragic aspects of the nation's history. There was the Great Depression, which plunged many families into an economic nightmare. Legally sanctioned discrimination was the norm, hatred toward immigrants was epidemic, workers had few rights, women were second-class citizens, and there were many instances of racially motivated violence and urban riots. During the Second World War, over 100,000 Japanese Americans were labeled falsely as disloyal and held in internment camps. In the early years of NCCD's history, politically powerful groups in this country organized for a eugenics movement that called for the forced sterilization of individuals thought to be biologically inferior, including prisoners. This horrific idea saw its logical outcome in the death camps of Nazi Germany.

At the same time, there was a vibrant struggle for justice that confronted many of these deep problems. During the NCCD's first 100 years, the labor movement won critical victories for workers, and the New Deal ushered in the beginnings of a social safety net for senior citizens and children that was expanded during the War on Poverty. The civil rights movement produced impressive legal reforms that finally made the U.S. Constitution apply to all citizens. Advocates for full citizenship rights for women won impressive victories. The civil rights movement also inspired others to advance the struggle for justice for other classes of Americans who were facing discrimination due to age, disabilities, religious views, or sexual orientation. The struggle for justice led to a serious review of the rights of institutionalized persons and to persons suspected of criminal acts under the constitutional provisions of equal protection and due process of law.

While the struggle for justice is still a "work in progress," the volatile social environment exerts a profound impact on the criminal and juvenile justice systems. The NCCD always has and continues to ground its work in the inextricable link between social justice and the pursuit of a better justice system. Fairness in the application of laws and respect for all citizens is a core value of the NCCD. Earlier in our history, the NCCD challenged conventional notions that the legal system should criminalize private and consensual behavior by adults, including abortion, gambling, minor drug use, and prostitution. Presently, this focus is reflected in many NCCD programs that focus on race and justice and the treatment of women by the justice system. The work of the Children's Research Center (CRC) in child welfare reform places the very highest priority on increasing evenhanded responses to all families in crisis. The NCCD is deeply involved in ensuring that vulnerable groups, especially those with mental health issues, are

191

treated fairly and appropriately by law enforcement, the courts, and corrections.

The essays that follow offer a sampling of NCCD viewpoints on justice reforms that seek to overcome social barriers and conflicts while increasing democratic values and advancing freedom.

NCCD board member Patrick V. Murphy was a nationally respected expert on policing who took on the law enforcement establishment in his advocacy of community policing as a way to advance both public safety and social justice. His essay, "Organizing for Community Policing," set out a clear agenda on how to transform American law enforcement. America's most celebrated criminologist, and long-time NCCD board member, Marvin E. Wolfgang, delivered a memorable keynote address at an NCCD national conference that occurred within days of the assassination of Martin Luther King. With many cities experiencing riots, Wolfgang offered a calming perspective that urged the political leaders and justice system officials to exercise restraint and recommended that the nation work on expanding opportunities to all citizens.

Current NCCD board members Rose Matsui Ochi and Hubert G. Locke were early commentators on the problems of discrimination in sentencing and the policies and practices of police agencies. Their articles in Part V use empirical data to define the issues and offer very

practical remedies. NCCD board member Kim Taylor-Thompson illustrates how the link of social justice and criminal justice leads to new definitions for the roles of public defenders. Anthony Thompson extends the social justice and fairness principle to the vibrant movement to better respond to the challenges faced by prisoners returning home.

Finally, we have chosen to end this volume with Marvin E. Wolfgang's clarion call to abolish capital punishment "We Do Not Deserve to Kill." The NCCD spoke out against the death penalty in 1962. Over the next four decades, the board took a more cautious position on the topic, although Dr. Wolfgang used every opportunity to urge the NCCD board to adopt the strongest possible abolitionist stand. The NCCD called for a moratorium on executions in view of the evidence that many on death row were actually innocent. The council has participated in briefs before the U.S. Supreme Court to stop the execution of juveniles, and we have opposed putting to death persons with developmental disabilities. Both positions were accepted by the Supreme Court in recent years. In 2005, the NCCD once again called for ending capital punishment. There could be no more meaningful "birthday present" for this 100-year-old American institution than to see NCCD's advocacy to end the death penalty become the law once and for all.

19

RACIAL DISCRIMINATION IN CRIMINAL SENTENCING

ROSE MATSUI OCHI

The accepted symbol of justice in America—as completely impartial and unswayed by color of skin and economic status—and the reality of justice are very different. There is no getting around the evidence: Racial minorities receive disproportionately stiffer sentences for comparable crimes, in spite of our system of justice that provides more safeguards for accused persons than in any other country. We can and must do better. Justice in America should not depend upon whether a person is a member of a minority group and poor, or a member of the majority group and affluent.

The inequalities in our criminal justice system implicate the courts in racial discrimination and bring disrespect on an esteemed institution. This no doubt will come as a shock to those responsible for administering justice who have closed their eyes and continue to operate under the delusion that justice is color blind.

Even those of us who feel completely free of prejudice in our decisions need to recognize the role that our unconscious attitudes, values and biases play in our decision making. Each of us must own up to the fact that these attitudes exist and that we need to examine how they influence our judgments. Our concerns, however, should not be only with our immediate domains but with the problem of bias in its larger manifestation.

Judges' decisions do not alone account for racially disparate sentences—prosecutors, probation officers, and even defense attorneys all have input into the process. But judges' decisions represent the most important, final, and visible act in the criminal justice process. Judges, themselves, are also in the position of greatest power—they directly affect the liberty and property of thousands of people, and they can significantly influence what the other actors in the criminal justice process do.

This problem of a double standard of justice is very serious. We might well have less crime, if we can change those areas of our system in which bias occurs—and produce in the public's mind a single standard of justice for all.

The evidence that minorities receive harsher sentences than similarly situated whites comes from several studies. A 1982 report, *Inequality of Justice*, by the National Minority Advisory Council on Criminal Justice (NMACCJ) to the

Source: From "Racial Discrimination in Criminal Sentencing," by Rose Matsui Ochi, published in *Judges Journal,* 24(1), Winter 1985. © 1985 by the American Bar Association. Reprinted with permission.

Department of Justice concluded: "(G)laring disparities in the sentencing of poor and minority defendants, as compared to those convicted of crimes who are affluent and white, lack a principled basis. . . ."[1]

This conclusion was based on studies, consultations and testimony presented to NMACCJ in pubic hearings over a 24-month period. The NMACCJ report documented the pervasiveness of racial prejudice in the judicial system in setting bail, jury selection, plea bargaining, representation by counsel, hiring of court personnel and sentencing. The report also cites numerous prestigious fact-finding commissions and scholars who reached the same findings.

The President's Crime Commission, in a special 1967 report on the courts, found that racial prejudice permeates the system, whether racism operates purposefully by jury selection and sentencing, or unintentionally but inevitably through inequitable burdens on the poor and on those defendants with alien cultural customs.

> The law and court procedures are not understood by, and seem threatening to, many defendants. . . . [M]any defendants are not understood by and seem threatening to the courts and its officers. Even such simple matters as dress, speech, and manners may be misinterpreted. Most city prosecutors and judges have middleclass backgrounds and a high degree of education. When they are confronted with a poor, uneducated defendant, they may have difficulty judging how he fits into his own society or culture. They can easily mistake a certain manner of dress or speech, [as] alien or repugnant to them, but ordinary enough in the defendant's world as an index of moral worthlessness. They can mistake ignorance or fear of the law as indifference to it. They can mistake the defendant's resentment against social evils with which he lives as evidence of criminality. Or conversely, they may be led by neat dress, a polite and cheerful manner, and a show of humility to believe that a dangerous criminal is merely an oppressed and misunderstood man.[2]

The U.S. Commission on Civil Rights drew similar conclusions in its 1970 report which related:

> Our investigations reveal that Mexican-American citizens are subject to unduly harsh treatment by law enforcement offers, that they are often arrested on insufficient grounds, receive physical and verbal abuse and penalties which are disproportionately severe. We have found them to be deprived of proper use of bail and adequate representation by counsel. They are substantially underrepresented on grand and petit juries and excluded from full participation in law enforcement agencies. . . . [T]he ability to communicate between Spanish-speaking American citizens and English-speaking officials has complicated the problem of administering justice equally.[3]

Despite these decade-old reports, which recommended major reforms to decrease the number of miscarriages of justice perpetrated against minorities, the objective reality of injustice toward minority defendants in the courts continues today.

IS THIS DUE TO RACISM?

Observers have noted that minority criminal defendants still tend to receive more severe sentences than white defendants do. The question, "Is this due to racism?," has caused much debate among criminal justice researchers. Some of the researchers offer evidence of racial discrimination. Others claim that there is really no discrimination; and a few even suggest justifiable reasons for the differences that exist. Another claim is that the issue is poverty not race:

> Wealth discrimination [results] from poor defendants' inability to obtain a private attorney or pretrial release. As the effect of wealth discrimination on minority defendants is likely to be greater than on white defendants, since minorities are more likely to be poor, it amounts to indirect racial discrimination. Still others have suggested that this disparity is due to the effect of legal factors, such as the seriousness of the charge or prior criminal record. Since minorities are more likely to have a serious charge or prior criminal record, they are also likely to receive a more severe sentence.[4]

However, a review of the NMACCJ report reveals that there are numerous studies whose findings validate the theory that race is the predominant factor in sentencing bias.

In a study of sentencing practices of Texas courts, Henry Bullock points out that blacks are more likely than whites to bring into court a set of characteristics that tend to predispose judges and juries to assess longer sentences—no matter who happens to possess the attributes. These include type of offense, type of plea, number of previous felonies and place of residence. After stating the evidence for this assertion, Bullock goes on to make the following declaration: "However, control of these nonracial factors fails to reduce the gross association which we observe to exist between race and length of prison sentence. Instead, it increases the degree of this association, changes its direction, and strengthens its validity."[5]

Bullock's research also notes that blacks are likely to receive shorter sentences than whites for the crime of murder (an intraracial offense) but longer sentences than whites for the crime of burglary (an interracial offense). This observation is consistent with that of Judge Joseph Howard who notes that, in Maryland courts, 47 percent of all blacks convicted of raping blacks were returned to their community on probation,[6] but when the rapes involved white women, the death penalty was imposed in 55 cases. Of the offenders all but five were black. Furthermore, Bullock's survey shows that the average sentence meted out to white males is 5.7 years for raping a black woman and 4.7 years for raping a white woman. On the other hand, the average sentence given to a black male is 4.2 years for raping a black woman and 16.4 years for raping a white woman. Such data show a twofold inequity in the dispensation of justice.[7]

In another study, Morris Forsland found a difference in arrests between blacks and whites, as well as convictions and sentences. His study involved 4,319 offenses resulting in 3,724 arrests, out of which there were 2,719 convictions and 1,547 prison sentences. The data reveal that blacks were arrested 5.8 times more than whites and were sentenced to prison 9.8 times more than whites.[8] Forsland believes that the difference between blacks and whites in arrests and convictions is due to "decades of discrimination" and the concentration of blacks in the "lower social/economic strata of American society."[9]

There is as yet, however, no national compendium of systematically gathered data on sentencing or on the duration of time served by inmates of different racial groups.

At the NMACCJ hearings, in addition to the studies cited, numerous people testified about the arbitrary and harsher sentences minority defendants received. One person described "a Hispanic male who was sentenced to 1,800 years in prison for selling heroin valued at $10. Another pointed out situations in which American Indians were sentenced to two years' imprisonment for 'habitual drunkenness.' A third cited the case of six black chronic alcoholics who had served a collective total of 125 years in penal institutions for liquor-related offenses."[10]

Marvin Frankel in his book *Criminal Sentences* summarized the chaos of sentencing practices: "a defendant who comes up for sentencing has no way of knowing or reliably predicting whether he will walk out of a courtroom on probation or be locked up for a term of years that may consume the rest of his life, or something in-between."[11] He cites some examples:

- A former credit manager of a department store, convicted of a fraud and kickback scheme which netted him $16,800, was sentenced to 30 weekends in jail.
- An investment counselor who swindled more than $2 million from his clients was sentenced to one year and one day in prison.
- The compassionate judicial treatment of the Watergate defendants.
- A Dallas policeman convicted in 1973 of murdering a 12-year-old Mexican-American named Santos Rodriguez was sentenced to five years in prison.[12]

In another incident, two white men who were convicted of murdering Vincent Chin were each fined $3,700 and were placed on three years' probation. The simple facts were not in dispute. Chin, 27, a Chinese American, became involved in an argument in a bar with Ronald Ebens, an automobile factory foreman. Ebens mistook Chin for a Japanese and accused him and his "countrymen" of undermining the American economy with the sale of Japanese cars in the United States. They continued the dispute in the bar's parking lot and then down the street in front of a restaurant. It was there that Ebens, aided by a stepson, beat Chin to death with a baseball bat. After strong public protest, the Justice Department filed a civil rights action to determine whether Chin's civil rights were violated.

DEATH PENALTY IMPOSITION

At every stage of the criminal justice process, justice officials' discretion exacts its inequitable toll from the poor and nonwhite. An analysis of the imposition of the death penalty is a singularly instructive example.

The differential imposition of the death penalty on minority offenders, as the Supreme Court has noted, is the ultimate form of discrimination. It is both immoral and illegal. Even those who believe the death penalty is an appropriate social response must agree with this conclusion.

Research indicates that members of minority groups have been sentenced to death and executed in significantly higher proportions to whites convicted of similar crimes. Research on the use of capital punishment shows that some 54.6 percent of all persons executed since 1930 were black.[13] Given that the "white" category inaccurately includes Hispanics, the disparity is even greater than the figures illustrate.

In Pennsylvania, over a 40-year period (1914–1954), only 11 percent of all blacks sentenced to death had their sentences commuted. During the same period, some 20 percent of their white counterparts received commuted death sentences—all having been convicted of first degree murder. In 11 southern states, 13 percent of all blacks convicted of rape were sentenced to death as compared to 2 percent of all of their white counterparts.[14] Such illustrations might easily be multiplied. The clear facts are that the lives of minority group members have been less valued in the American justice system than the lives of white majority group members.

AFTER THE *FURMAN* DECISION

In 1972 the Supreme Court recognized the racial implications of the death penalty in *Furman v. Georgia*, 408 U.S. 238 (1972).[15] It declared the death penalty unconstitutional for, among other reasons, discriminating against the poor and members of minority groups. At the time of the *Furman* decision, a clear majority of the 600 persons on death row were minority persons, as had been those executed legally since 1930, when statistics began to be maintained. For example, 90 percent of all men executed for rape since 1930 have been black.

The racial implications have taken a seeming new turn since *Furman*. In response to *Furman*, over 30 states passed new capital sentencing laws with specific restrictions on when the death penalty could be imposed. In 1976, "the Supreme Court upheld these new laws, on theory that they contained enough safeguards to permit the courts to pick out the worst crimes and criminals in a fair and even-handed way. But the court had no real evidence that the new laws would work any more fairly than the old ones. All it said was that the new statutes looked good enough on paper."[16]

Today, 54 percent of those on death row are white, 41 percent black, and 5 percent other minorities. (Rape is no longer a capital offense.) The South still remains the area in which the death penalty is most often imposed. Seventy-six percent of those on death row are in the 11 southern states.[17]

But have the new statutes worked to eliminate bias? Sociologists William Bowers and Glenn Pierce undertook a detailed study of homicides in Florida over the five-year period between 1973 and 1977. They correlated the race of the victim with the race of the offender and developed the data given in Table 19.1.[18]

Their research shows that the 72 white men on Florida's death row at the beginning of 1978 had all killed other whites. Not one of the 111 whites who killed blacks received a death sentence. Although an almost identical number of murders of blacks and whites had occurred (2,432 offenders arrested for killing whites versus 2,431 offenders arrested for killing blacks), 92 percent of the men on death row—white or black—had killed whites.[19] The taking of a black

TABLE 19.1   Race and Sentencing in Florida Homicides 1973–1977

Victim/Offender Race	Estimated # of Offenders	Persons Sentenced to Death	Probability of the Death Penalty
Black kills white	286	48	.168
White kills white	2,146	72	.034
Black kills black	2,320	11	.005
White kills black	111	0	.000

life, even by another black, was one-tenth as likely to be punished by death as the taking of a white one. Yet, a black who took a white life was five times as likely to receive the death penalty as a white committing the same offense.[20]

Other studies, as well, are proving that bias continues. Dr. Ray Paternoster, a criminologist, conducted research on South Carolina's new capital punishment law passed in 1977. Proponents of the new law had argued that it "would eliminate arbitrariness and disparity" in the decision to execute in South Carolina, a state like others in the South with a history of racial disparity in the use of the death sentence. "The point was to see if the new statute purges the system of discrimination," Paternoster said.[21]

Paternoster analyzed 1500 South Carolina homicides occurring between June 1977 and December 1981 and found that the new law did not have its intended impact. While no differences were evident when focusing on the race of the defendant, the race of the victim was a crucial factor in the prosecutor's decision to seek the death sentence. Defendants with white victims were far more likely to be selected for execution, even when Paternoster took account of such factors as seriousness of the offense, prior record and other victim characteristics.

In cases without substantial aggravating circumstances, defendants with white victims were four times as likely to receive the death sentence. If the defendants were also black, the probability of selection was ten times as great.[22]

In 1982 John Eldon Smith, a white inmate on Georgia's death row, claimed in federal court that Georgia's new sentencing system, much like the one it had replaced, was in actual practice condemning to death only killers whose victims were white, while sparing almost all murderers whose victims were black. This claim was based on a study of Georgia homicide cases that showed that a white defendant convicted of killing a white victim stood an eight times greater chance of going to death row than did a black who had killed a black. (For a black defendant, the chances of a death sentence were 33 time greater if his victim were white than if his victim were black.) Since about 60 percent of all Georgia homicide victims are black, this claim that the death penalty was being reserved for the killers of whites raised a matter of no small importance. The U.S. Supreme Court, however,

turned down the appeal, arguing that the study had not established that these enormous disparities might not have been the result of some factor other than race. Smith was executed December 15, 1983.[23]

A recently completed study, however, seems to bear out all the claims that Smith was trying to make. Relying almost entirely on official Georgia state records, University of Iowa Law Professor David Baldus studied a thousand homicide arrests and trials occurring between 1973 and 1980. Baldus analyzed and reanalyzed factual variables in each case, in search of any explanation other than race that would account for the glaring disparities in Georgia's capital sentencing record. He could find none. And neither could a team of social scientists hired during the past year by the state of Georgia to try to refute Baldus' conclusions.[24]

Baldus even discovered that some of the legal guidelines by which the U.S. Supreme Court had set such store as a means of overcoming racial discrimination were themselves being applied discriminatorily. For example, Georgia juries are now invited to separate out the worst crimes for death sentences by determining whether the particular murder before them was or was not "outrageously vile, horrible or inhuman." While this guideline was supposed to provide a color-blind method of helping to ensure that only the worst crimes and criminals would end up on death row, Baldus' research has now revealed that Georgia juries are more likely to find a given murder to have been "outrageously vile, horrible or inhuman" when the victim is white, and likelier still when the defendant is black.[25]

What the study shows is that many of the 109 inmates now on Georgia's death row are not there because of the crime they committed but because of their own skin color or the skin color of their victim.[26]

This is the type of evidence that Georgia death row inmate Alpha Otis Stephens will present to the federal courts. On December 14, 1983, the Supreme Court stayed his execution date. "In issuing the stay for Stephens, a black prisoner who had been condemned to death by an all-white jury for the murder of a white man, the court indicated that it may be willing to look again at a perennial issue of capital punishment in the United States: the matter of race."[27]

In another death penalty case, *Spencer v. Zant*, the Eleventh U.S. Circuit Court of Appeals sitting en banc recently heard arguments that could affect death row inmates throughout the nation.

Lawyers for James Lee Spencer, a black defendant convicted of murdering a white victim, argued that Georgia's death penalty statute is applied more frequently when the victim is white than when the victim is black.

The case is important to death row inmates in other states because Georgia's statute had been singled out as a model by the U.S. Supreme Court, and because it is the first time a Stanford University study, which found disparate application of the death sentence in seven states, is being used in a death penalty appeal.[28]

The Stanford University study, like the Paternoster study, found that a victim's race is more important than the murderer's race in influencing who is sentenced to death. The data also showed a clear pattern of discrimination against suspects of either race whose victims are white. The researchers concluded that there was a "clear pattern of discrimination" in homicide cases.[29]

The Stanford University study is one of many studies being cited in the appeal. During oral argument, U.S. Circuit Court Judge Robert Vance said he had just read a Rand Corporation study showing that "there's a disparate impact everywhere." He said that that study showed a "wide and rampant disparity in crime rates and punishment."[30] These studies not only affect the Spencer case but Stephens as well.

THE RAND CORPORATION STUDY

When charges of racial bias in sentencing are made, typically those responsible for the administration of justice assign reasons other than racial discrimination as a cause of discrepancies.[31]

Joan Petersilia, who conducted a June 1983 Rand Corporation Study of the criminal justice system, commented that racial discrimination in criminal sentencing is seldom discussed in judicial circles. Yet such discrimination is widely perceived in minority communities and is also supported by statistics.[32] The study was conducted for the National Institute of Corrections to determine whether there was evidence of racial discrimination at any of the points between arrest and release from custody. The report is based on a comprehensive, two-year empirical examination of racial discrimination in the criminal justice systems of California, Michigan, and Texas.

Using research techniques to control other variables, their analysis revealed that there was sentencing bias based on ethnicity.[33] Blacks and Latinos were sentenced to prison more often, and received longer terms than whites convicted of similar crimes and with similar criminal records.[34]

In California, the average sentence is six and one-half months longer for Hispanics and almost a month and one-half longer for blacks.

In Michigan, sentences average more than seven months longer for blacks, while in Texas they average more than three and one-half months longer for blacks and two months longer for Hispanics.

The report indicated that not only do these minorities receive harsher sentences, but they are not paroled as early as whites, and thus serve proportionately more time in jail.[35] The extra time served accounted for an additional two to eight months.

When Petersilia was asked by a reporter for *Checklist*, "What accounts for differences in sentencing and time served?," she explained, "for one thing, in sentencing and in parole decisions, the probation officer's presentence investigation report plays a key role. Judges follow the probation officer's sentencing recommendation in 80 percent of cases, and the report also becomes the heart of the parole board's case summary file. This document usually presents a comprehensive portrait of the offender. It contains personal and socioeconomic information, as well as all available details on the offender's criminal habits and attitudes."

This information is assessed for "indicators" of rehabilitation or recidivism. To the extent that an offender's personal and socioeconomic characteristics reflect patterns associated with recidivism rather than rehabilitation, that offender's chances of a lesser sentence or an earlier parole are diminished. But as Petersilia points out, "Black and Hispanic offenders typically have more of the personal and socioeconomic characteristics associated with recidivism than white offenders have," i.e., lack of high school education, unemployment, family instability, past brushes with the law, gang affiliation, drug and alcohol use. The problem, as she sees it, is that such "indicators" of recidivism tend to reflect the black experience more often than the experience of whites, that is, more black offenders are likely to have histories of unemployment, family instability, etc., than white offenders. But, in fact, the survey data show that once an offender is involved in crime, his recidivism rate is the same, regardless of race. The study thus concludes that risk prediction using such indicators as unemployment and family instability may be suspect and perhaps ought not to be relied upon to indicate which offender will again commit crimes when he returns to society.[36]

Questioning deliberate discrimination as an explanation for sentencing and time disparities, Petersilia suggests that racial disparities "seem to have developed because the system adopted procedures without analyzing their possible effects on different racial groups. Thus, the kinds of information used by judges and parole officials in their decision making may be a systemic source of bias; the sentencing recommendations in the probation officer reports, . . . may, for example, contain personal and socioeconomic information that distinguishes between races better than it predicts which offender will again commit crimes when he returns to society."[37]

Therefore, racial disparities in sentencing can be a result of racial discrimination or of seemingly neutral procedures that impact differently on minorities. Consequently, minorities are subjected to more arbitrary and harsher treatment.

JUDICIAL ROLES AND SENTENCING

Petersilia believes that judges, like the rest of us, are more favorably disposed to the familiar, and fear or become frustrated with the unfamiliar. Most of us tend to sympathize with individuals who look and think as we do, and who share our same history, neighborhood and lifestyle.

Findings from other fields all show that cultural distance tends to determine attitude and tolerance, and the greater the distance, the greater the tendency for imagination and bias to influence judgments. Depending on our position in society and our experience, all of us relate differently to various crimes and defendants.[38]

Professor Thorsten Sellin argues that judges, like any other individuals, reflect their race and economic backgrounds. The convicted who stand before them are not merely offenders who must be dealt with according to law, but persons who represent a class in society toward whom

judges will have attitudes. It would be denying them the "ordinary attributes of humanity" if "we were to assume that they could render justice free from all preconceptions."[39] Former Supreme Court Justice William O. Douglas once remarked, "Ninety percent of any decision is emotion." Further, Douglas claimed, "the rational part of us supplies the reason for supporting our predilections."[40]

In another case study involving sentencing disparities, Dean Jaros and Robert Mendelsohn analyzed the judicial role and sentencing behavior in Detroit Traffic Court.[41] The authors began by outlining certain role expectations and norms that judges acquire through professional organizations. They then proceeded to describe the "disrespectful defendant behavior" in accordance with judicial expectations. This behavior is characterized as follows:

1. Failure to use an honorific title in addressing the judge;

2. Expression of disagreement with declarative statements of the judge;

3. Raising the voice;

4. Use of sarcasm;

5. Expression of disparagement of courts, law or police; and

6. Failure to express repentance.[42]

The researchers also examined whether defendants' dress had any effect on sentencing decisions. Among the findings is that jail sentences "decline monotonically" as the dress becomes more appropriate—appropriate being defined as ranging from everyday work clothes (garbage collectors, etc.) to coat and tie or hose and heels, as most appropriate. Their conclusion was that sentencing behavior can be explained by the "legal-professional role" of the judge. The observations about the influence of cultural distance at the sentencing level are certainly applicable to decisions made by police, prosecutors, and probation and prison officials as well.

The common tendency to mistake the behavioral patterns of a few for the character traits of an entire race may interfere with equitable sentencing. If a court visualizes the lifestyle of certain racial groups as settling their disputes with deadly weapons in city parks, it may subconsciously affect the judge's whole approach toward both the accused and the victims of that race. It may be assumed that their values and expectations are different from the court's and that some judges on the bench may even subconsciously believe that imprisonment does not hurt "them" as much, that for "these" people it is an expected and even normal experience, and that, in the final analysis, all "they" understand is harsh sentencing.

It is easy to clamor about eliminating the "scum" from our streets, for everyone believes in retribution against those who commit crimes, particularly heinous crimes. Yet how few are willing to decry the arbitrary and disproportionate sentences imposed against minorities.

WHAT JUDGES CAN DO

In a democratic society, the judiciary represents the spirit and reality of fairness and justice. Toward that end, judges can personally and collectively recognize that sentencing disparity based on race is a result of discrimination and bias. It is not enough that as individuals, we alone may be impartial. We have a duty beyond our limited domains to see that bias is eliminated. Judicial education programs should include courses designed to eliminate bias in sentencing. These programs should cover how unconscious biases may affect our ability to deal equitably with persons unlike us—whether of a different race, sex, economic status, or political orientation.

Additionally, each judicial council should institute a study of their state's sentencing practice. Alaska's Judicial Council concluded, after an exhaustive study, that the "race of the defendant seemed to be associated with strong variation in the length of the sentence" and that these associations were "statistically significant and of a large magnitude."[43]

The struggle to assure more equal justice is immensely difficult, but lack of resolve and courage to meet the challenge head-on is unacceptable if we are to remain true to the principle of our nation—to value justice for all.

For too long the system's response has been to "circle the wagons," and deal in denial and defenses. Particularly today, in a period of declining resources and hardening public sentiment, corrective action to lessen the disparities is politically difficult.

The easiest postures to espouse in society are those that tug at people's prejudices, biases, emotions and sometimes bigotry. The most difficult are those rooted in humaneness and justice. Such is the debate over racial disparities in sentencing.

NOTES

1. National Minority Council on Criminal Justice, The Inequality of Justice: A Report on Crime and the Administration of Justice in the Minority Communities, Washington D.C., 1982.

2. The President's Crime Commission, Task Force Report: The Courts (Washington D.C.: Government Printing Office 1972), p. 50.

3. U.S. Commission on Civil Rights: Report on Hearings in 1970 (Washington D.C.: Government Printing Office, 1970).

4. Cassia Spohn, et al., The Effect of Race on Sentencing: A Re-Examination of an Unsettled Question, Law & Soc'y. Rev., Vol. 16, Number 1, 71 (1981–82).

5. Henry Bullock, Significance of the Racial Factor in the Lengths of Prison Sentences, J. of Crim. Law, Criminology and Police Sci., Vol. 52 (1961).

6. Joseph Howard, Racial Discrimination in Sentencing, Am. Judicature, Vol. 59 (1961).

7. Id.

8. M.A. Forsland, A Comparison of Negro and White Crime Rates, 61 J. of Crim. Law, Criminology and Police Sci., 214, June 1970.

9. Id.

10. Id. p. 306.

11. Marvin L. Frankel, Criminal Justice (New York: Hill & Wang 1973).

12. Id. p. 280.

13. Sue Reid, Crime and Criminology (New York: Holt, Rinehart, and Winston, 1979, p. 578).

14. Id.

15. Furman v. Georgia, 408 U.S. 238 (1972).

16. David I. Bruck, Gray Areas in Color-Blind Justice, L.A. Times, January 8, 1984.

17. Id.

18. Id.

19. Id.

20. Id.

21. Criminal Justice Newsletter, Research, "Whither Academic Freedom," October 24, 1983.

22. Id.

23. Id.

24. Id.

25. Id.

26. Id.

27. David I. Bruck, L.A. Times, see endnote 16.

28. Bill Girdner, Criminal Law Notebook, Daily Journal, 1984.

29. Id.

30. Id.

31. Joan Petersilia, Racial Disparities in the Criminal Justice System, The Rand Corporation, June 1983.

32. Id.

33. Id.

34. Id.

35. Id.

36. Research Reports, Checklist, No. 315, p. 3, March 1984.

37. Racial Disparities in Sentencing, Crim. Just. Newsletter, Vol. 14–15 August 1, 1983.

38. Joan Petersilia, L.A. Times 1974.

39. Thorsten Sellin, Race Prejudice in the Administration of Justice, Am. J. of Soc., Vol. 41, September 1935, p. 212.

40. Id.

41. D. Jaros and R.J. Mendelsohn, The Judicial Role and Sentencing Behavior, Midwest J. Pol. Sci., Vol. 11 No. 4, November 1967, p. 471.

42. Id.

43. Irving Joyner, Legal Theories for Attacking Racial Disparity in Sentencing, Crim. Law Bull. Vol. 18, p. 101, 1982.

20

ORGANIZING FOR COMMUNITY POLICING

PATRICK V. MURPHY

The police are the public, and the public are the police. No matter how large the department, the principle must be honored or crime control is weakened.

Community policing means different things in different cities, but the anonymity of urban living works against friendly policing.

The task of organizing should begin with a clear understanding of the role of the police. Are all police officers qualified to assume the responsibilities associated with community policing?

A merican policing is a failure.[1] Its first responsibility is to prevent crime. Yet, the United States has the highest rates of crime and incarceration in the industrial world, although it is the wealthiest nation. Thousands of citizens who should be contributing to the economy are a drain on it, being supported by tax dollars in prison.

The police have misunderstood their role. They have attempted to accomplish their mission independently with minimal community involvement. It is a policy that reveals a fundamental misperception of the proper relationship between police and people in any democratic society. Ultimate responsibility for law observance and order rests with the community of citizens, not with the police. Every community must police itself. The function of the police is to assist parents, youth, neighbors, teachers, leaders and others to be a strong community whose eyes, ears and influence are essential in preventing crime.[2]

It is a cardinal principle of democratic societies that ultimate responsibility for peace, good order and law observance rests with the community of citizens of that society, not with an organized police force.

Although the very complexity of modern societies usually dictates that policing efforts be coordinated and directed by a force of paid professionals, their responsibility is derivative. Their role is to supplement and aid community efforts, not supplant them. And the powers permitted to these police must be carefully defined and limited.

A community which abandons its basic duty to police itself, to a professional police service, will soon find that the police can hope to provide no more than a bare modicum of public order and security, and this only through such repressive measures that the basic liberties of a free people are eroded, and the very democracy that the police seek to preserve is endangered. Only if the proper balance is maintained between the basic responsibility of the community and the derivative responsibility of the police can a safe and orderly society be preserved with the least burden on the individual rights and freedom.

It is unfortunate, therefore, that the history of the urban policing in America in the 20th century is a consistent record of efforts by the police service to assume a disproportionate share of the responsibility for maintaining social control, and the concurrent abandonment by American communities of their portion of this duty. The result has been an increasing lawlessness which even increasingly repressive measures have been unable to curb. The delicate balance between the traditional roles of the community and the police needs to be restored. Peacekeeping must again become a joint police-community effort to stand any reasonable chance for lasting success.

The police are a small part of the total effort involved in preventing/controlling crime and drug trafficking. When people have confidence in their neighborhood and their neighbors, they protect one another, are less fearful, and set behavioral standards, especially for youth. A community is a network of people exchanging information, assisting one another, observing, cooperating with police to identify violators, but also to help minor offenders to go straight.

Neighbors and relatives supplement parents in raising children. Problem families tend to produce problem offspring. Police/citizen teamwork is important in identifying such youngsters, obtaining special support for them, and removing them from their families—if necessary. Protecting children from physically abusive parents is a major part of crime prevention warranting police attention and community assistance. "It takes a village to raise a child."[3] The police play a critical role in making a city neighborhood function as an "urban village" for raising children, mutual protection, mutual assistance, and community empowerment.

Typically, there is only one patrol officer on duty for 5,000 people. The wise chief understands that his officers depend upon those who live and work in every neighborhood. He will appreciate the value of time spent obtaining citizen participation. Every officer hour can generate many hours of useful volunteer time. The job description for patrol officers should make clear that most of the work in reaching objectives is performed by community members rather than the officer directly. Although some tasks must be performed by an officer personally, he gets the job done principally through the volunteer efforts of those protected. The function is more that of manager than doer.

Although the national crime rate is high, the distribution of offenses varies widely by size of city and within large cities. The murder rate in one city is eight times the national average. Within another city, the murder rate in one precinct is 90 times that in another. Some parts of cities have crime rates as low as those in villages and small towns. Other parts have alarming rates. Poverty and other socioeconomic ills, which are the root causes of crime, are invariably found where crime is abundant. The middle class doesn't depend upon the police nearly as much as the poor do to protect them from criminals who live and operate in their neighborhoods. As Professor Egon Bittner has shown, policing is essentially a vocation of service to the poor.[4] Urban poverty presents especially challenging problems to officers. Large poor populations concentrated in inner cities over large areas unrelieved by any oases of middle class strength and weakened by the anonymity of urban life need police resources proportionate to their share of crime as well as creative approaches to their need for protection, partnerships with the police, and political empowerment to enable them to obtain social and economic justice.

Officers who protect the working poor need excellent training and inspired leadership to motivate and sustain them in their daily contact with so much human suffering and victimization. Their performance, for better or worse, will be strongly influenced by an attitude of compassion as contrasted with one of contempt. It is among the disadvantaged, more than the middle class or the affluent that the police must become part of the community. It is in the low-income neighborhoods with high crime rates, and more victims, that it is most important for the police and the people to be one.

Hundreds of departments are changing from police-oriented to community-oriented policing; from reactive to proactive relations with the people. It entails a transition from stronger policing to friendly policing.

In order to grasp the implications of this strong trend, it is necessary to understand the proper role of the police. The police themselves have misunderstood their role, attempted to do the job without sufficiently involving the community, and have failed to organize their departments to accomplish the mission. Many departments that have been in a "community policing" mode for several years continue to be organized in a manner that impedes success in preventing crime and fostering social control. Authority and responsibility are assigned inappropriately.

American policing is uniquely local. It has not been systematized. It is a fragmented, insular non-system. There are more than 15,000 agencies. They are extremely isolated from one another. The exchange of ideas, policies, and criminal intelligence are severely limited. Careers are confined to one department almost without exception. The profession has developed although there is a clear need for a fully professional entry standard for every officer given law enforcement authority.[5] States have failed to do enough to upgrade, coordinate and set standards for local policing within their borders. Fifteen thousand local departments cannot work successfully without a comprehensive national support structure of planning, coordination, intelligence, statistics, research, experimentation, demonstrations, technical assistance, training, education, personnel exchanges and standards. The federal government fails to provide anything resembling an adequate backup system. The entire police service suffers as a result. The American people are victimized by excessive crime, fear and drug trafficking.

Without the benefit of a body of knowledge or the resources that would be provided by an established profession, it is not surprising that individual departments are very different. Variations in policies, practices, values, goals and objectives are broad (see Behan's chapter). Yet, some common flaws in philosophy, organization and management can be identified. The problems are not found to the same extent among all kinds of departments. In fact, they are concentrated in large city departments where the highest crime rates, especially for violence, are found. Crime rates tend to be lowest in villages and sparsely populated areas. There are

about 1,000 single-officer departments. They have friendly policing. Life is naturally friendlier in small towns. As a result, people and police work closely. Crime is minimal.[6]

The single-officer department provides a model for larger agencies. The friendly teamwork that occurs so naturally in a village fulfills the principle enunciated by Sir Robert Peel in London in 1829 when the "New Police" were being formed: "the police are the public, and the public are the police." No matter how large a department, the principle must be honored or crime control will be weakened. Democracy is also weakened when police and people are separated rather than united. In working poor neighborhoods, where crime rates are highest and people most dependent on the police, the failure is compounded by not fulfilling their responsibility to be one with the public, the police actually deprive the people of their right to have a strong community for self-protection and political empowerment. In a city environment—so unlike that in a village—next door neighbors can be strangers rather than friends. If there are high levels of crime and fear, suspicion can alienate residents from one another. A sense of community can deteriorate to the point of collapse. Every police chief must understand that his department has a duty to assign officers to every neighborhood to become part of it. When the proper partnership is established between an officer(s) and a relatively small neighborhood population of 1,000 to 5,000 residents, a mutually supportive community develops.

In many cities, those who live and work in a neighborhood don't know the police officers responsible for protecting them. They are strangers. The people would be safer and officers more satisfied if they were friends. Frustration with officers because of crime and drugs, even anger because they are aloof, could change to appreciation and respect. Officers who are suspicious and cynical toward strangers could become empathetic, supportive partners to friends, even advocates for government services and programs to correct the social and economic injustices underlying the crime. The fundamental basis of policing is friendship—an officer and the people that the officer protects knowing one another, exchanging information, assisting and supporting one another, forming partnerships, engaging in teamwork. That is how crime is prevented and social control exercised *by the people* in a democracy. The police, at least theoretically, function with the consent of the people.

Of course, in a police state—a dictatorship—stranger policing is the standard. Government of the people, by the people, and for the people is not the operating principles. Regrettably, many departments inadvertently follow the police state model more closely than the democratic. Officers are overbearing rather than community partners.

Even in neighborhoods with the highest crime rates, more than 90 percent of the population is law abiding. Their participation with the police is indispensable in preventing crime and exercising social control. Friendly policing is needed in such areas even more than in low crime rate sectors. Crime rate invariably correlates with poverty, under/unemployment, and the other socioeconomic root causes of crime. A police strategy that fails to proactively build friendships with minority or poor populations is misdirected.

More than half of all police officers of all ranks are generalist patrol officers (GPOs). They wear uniforms, circulate in marked patrol cars within a beat area, and exchange information about crime, delinquency, suspicious activities and people. They interact with young people, parents, neighbors, teachers, clergy, social workers, employers, and probation/parole officers. They respond to crime scenes and emergencies.

At any time, only one GPO is on duty for approximately 5,000 residents. The people, not the police, have the largest role, by far, in preventing crime. The role of the GPO is to assist the people—coordinate, manage, and lead. Close, active, day-to-day teamwork between every small neighborhood community and a GPO responsible for its protection is essential. A friendly relationship between the protected and *their* protector is critical. The police depend upon the information obtained from the people. The people depend upon the police to inform them about crime patterns and criminals so they can better protect themselves. Information is the lifeblood of police work.

The organizational structure should support friendly policing. Unfortunately, in most urban departments it produces stranger policing. Many large city departments were deliberately organized historically for stranger policing, stranger supervision, and stranger management on the theory that friendships inevitably generated corruption.[7] It was a cruel myth that has had a serious negative impact even to the present.

Community policing means different things in different cities. In some it means a relatively small community relations unit of ten officers in a department of 500. In others, each precinct has a community relations officer in addition to a central unit. Members attend community meetings and attempt to resolve grievances concerning police policies or incidents—especially those involving minority residents.

In some cities, it means little more than block watches and citizen patrols. In others, citizens volunteer as receptionists, athletic coaches, or scout leaders. In some it means assigning some officers to foot patrol. Drug Abuse Resistance Education involving officers assigned full-time to schools teaching the dangers of drug use is the major component of "community-oriented policing" in some jurisdictions. School resource officers assigned full-time to high schools and junior high schools constitute the major component in others.

Where the concept has advanced further, it is seen more as a generalist function, less as a specialized function. The patrol division participates. However, it is common for community interaction to be a specialization within the generalist patrol function. Less than 10 percent of the patrol officers in a precinct are assigned to community liaison. More than 90 percent are basically call responders oriented to handling the work that occurs during their shift, but having no continuing responsibility for solving the problem of a neighborhood by means of a community/police partnership. The community policing idea is fully implemented when all patrol officers participate. They are the generalists. There are more of them, or certainly should be, than all of the others—supervisors, managers, and specialists. They interact more around the clock with victims, criminals, suspects, witnesses, rich, poor, powerful, powerless, homeless, mentally disturbed, injured, and all of the others across the spectrum. Although patrol officers regularly deal with a wide range of people and problems, their responsibility for prevention or follow-up varies. In some departments, the contacts and incidents are dealt with by a patrol officer as isolated events, rather than pieces of a larger picture requiring a conjunctive plan of action. Their function is seen as part of rapid response—handling, referring, and reporting incidents that occur during their on-duty shifts. They are not significantly involved in community policing.

When GPOs are fully immersed in community policing, the contacts and incidents are processed but not in isolation. They are seen as part of a larger picture. The people are informed about incidents in their area. They are mobilized to help in solving crimes, preventing violations, and working collectively for community betterment. A GPO with responsibility for liaison with a community focuses primarily on it as a collection of mutually protective and supportive families who together are more effective in partnership with a community-oriented officer than the police alone. Individual crimes and incidents are secondary considerations that should not distract from consistently strengthening the neighborhood as a community. It is the best way to reduce crime.

There is a tendency for large police departments to over-specialize. Generalist patrol officers are relieved of responsibility for certain kinds of crime or problems. It reduces the number of generalists. Each becomes responsible for the protection of more people. Specialization should be resisted. The more generalists, the smaller average population to which each will have to relate. Stronger partnerships and better community teamwork will result. Every chief is well advised to challenge the structure of his agency rather than assume it is adequate. A vigorous analysis asking the right tough questions may reveal waste, confusion, and low rates of cost-effectiveness compared with well organized departments. Police agencies are not objectively evaluated routinely. The public, news media, elected officials and police tend to accept existing organization, policies, personnel administration, and community relations as satisfactory even though a knowledgeable evaluator would find a low level of productivity. The mysteries of police work and administration are certainly beyond the grasp of the news media. They fail badly in informing the public about police budgets and effectiveness as they do concerning the crime and drug problems.

A conscientious chief introducing, or further developing, community policing will address the issues of organization, management, responsibility, authority, accountability, discretion, and community liaison.

A large city police department is a complex, decentralized bureaucracy. It functions 24 hours a day. Its officers operate with little direct supervision. They make difficult decisions, without consultation, concerning a broad range of human behaviors. It is essential that their responsibilities and authority be carefully defined if the mission of the agency is to be accomplished. They cannot operate like the single-officer village where the chief is often "available" at home rather than patrolling. Many officers may reside outside the city and commute long distances. They do not protect their own city. Community policing is most difficult to implement in a large department in a large city.

The anonymity of urban living works against friendly policing. Such a department must be organized with great care.

The function of the police is to assist every neighborhood community to exercise social control. Yet, the majority of the police, the motorized patrol officers, in many cities are principally call responders with little or no responsibility for effectively assisting people with the multi-faceted task of protecting their streets and homes. Without a responsibility for working closely with parents, students, teachers, neighbors, clergy, and the other members of a community, the officer is deprived of the opportunity to function as a friend and protector. He is under-challenged, under-fulfilled, and under-empowered to do the job an officer should do. Morale is weakened and the indispensable partnership of a small neighborhood community of about 1,000 people with an officer, who is primarily responsible for their protection, is unformed.

"The police are the public, and the public are the police." It is the most fundamental of all principles for policing a free society, formulated in 1829 in London when civilian police were created. The people and the police must work closely together exchanging information, planning, monitoring violators, intervening in troubled and violent families, and helping delinquents to go straight. A first consideration in organizing is to determine how to structure the liaison from the department to individual neighborhoods. Should call response and community policing be separated between two groups of officers, or should all officers be responsible for both?

Since the "split force" concept was tried in Wilmington, Delaware, in the 1970s, it has been replicated in many other cities. One group of officers is assigned exclusively to community policing. Another is assigned exclusively to answering calls and routine patrol. The fewer the liaison officers assigned, the larger the average number of people in each area. Specialized officers, not required to respond to calls, can devote full time to liaison activities. Of course, they would have larger citizen groups to work with than would all patrol officers if they were assigned to liaison as well as respond to calls. Dividing a city into as many sub-beats as there are GPOs would result in an average population of about 1,000. A neighborhood as small as 1,000 could develop with dedicated, creative leadership from its "own" officer into a cohesive urban village capable of generating many of the strengths of an isolated village including highly effective prevention of crime, disorder, and drug trafficking.

An advantage of a structure of small sub-beats, each with a single officer responsible for its protection, is that a more personal, intimate relationship is established between the officer and the people he is sworn to protect. A smaller number of people have their own officer to know and work with. The officer will identify more with his or her own people, learn more about them and the problems. Friendlier relationship will result in greater effectiveness. One officer in a community policing relationship with 1,000 people in a sub-beat is more logical than five officers assigned to a beat attempting to relate to 5,000 people. When five are responsible, often no one is responsible. When responsibility is undivided, it is unequivocally fixed.

Community policing involving all GPOs in a precinct has been experimented with intermittently in New York City since 1973. A demonstration is underway in two precincts.[8] The generalist, as contrasted with the specialist, approach has the advantage of involving all officers. It is an important consideration. Those who are not involved under the specialist model tend to remain aloof from the people. The loss of their participation is wasteful.

As policing motorized, it became possible for an officer to reach the scene of a crime or emergency more rapidly than one on foot could. Radios in patrol cars further reduced response time. New technology resulted in arrests that could not have been made previously and saved lives that would otherwise have been lost. Expectations then became unrealistic. Without the benefit of research to provide accurate information, it was assumed that rapidly responding to most calls would provide a result that more than justified the cost. The police world is not research oriented. Many policies and practices are based on myths or untested assumptions.

Eventually research was done in a number of cities. It revealed that only 10 to 15 percent of requests for dispatch to unwarranted situations—other than a crime in progress or life-threatening emergency—can be costly in several ways. Accidents to police cars can result in death or injuries to officers or citizens, or damage to vehicles. In fact, more officers are killed in car accidents than are killed by gunfire.

Time devoted to responding to calls that don't require a dispatch or an immediate dispatch is time that is not available for community policing, solving crimes, or monitoring known criminals.

Departments involved in the research and some others have developed criteria for differential police response (DPR). Alternatives to immediate dispatch include delayed dispatch, resolution by telephone by a specially trained advisor, or referrals.

All departments should use DPR. It is indispensable for a fully effective program of community-oriented policing.

Motorization generated another myth: The visibility of uniformed officers in marked police cars prevents crime. The Kansas City Preventive Patrol Experiment, designed and evaluated by the Police Foundation, found that preventive patrol had no significant impact on crime. The waste associated with so-called "preventive patrol" and unwarranted dispatches consumes enormous amounts of valuable patrol officer time which should be converted to highly productive community policing functions. The conversion from stranger to friendly policing definitely does not require additional personnel.

The challenges facing American policing are concentrated in the largest cities. Although there are more than 15,000 departments, the 200 largest cities have far more than their share of crime. Cities of over 100,000 have 25 percent of the population but 61 percent of murders.

The smaller the city, the friendlier life will be and the closer people and police. The smaller a department, the less bureaucratic and impersonal it will be. A friendlier type of policing will be practiced.

The larger a city, the more anonymous life will be. The larger a department, the more bureaucratic, impersonal and complex it will be. It may be decentralized into precincts or districts. Organizing patrol for 24 hours a day, 7 days a week coverage while fixing responsibility for an area, at the same time that adequate supervision is provided, is a difficult problem that deserves careful analysis and periodic reevaluation.

The task of organizing should begin with a clear understanding of the role of the police. Confusion has revolved around the question of whether all officers are qualified to assume the responsibilities associated with community policing—community organization, social work, family intervention, school liaison, making referrals, solving problems, and being a "street corner politician"[9]—participating in the governing of an urban village. Some believe it would be premature for GPOs to be assigned such duties before a four-year college degree is an entry requirement.

A four-year degree should be required—the sooner the better. The awesome powers and broad discretion possessed by every officer call for a baccalaureate as an entry standard. Community policing functions, however, do not involve more profound decision making for patrol officers beyond the duty they already have—different determinations, but not greater. Today's officers can be more effective as community partners than continuing what they are presently doing. In fact, the functions associated with community policing define the proper role of the police. Preventive patrolling monopolized by rapid response and cross-dispatching is an abandonment of the indispensable role.

A patrol division, or precinct, must be organized by time, by area, and for proper supervision. Each patrol officer must be allocated according to the hours he will be scheduled for duty, by assignment to a beat or other area, in order that the particular problems can be learned and the people known. Finally, a supervisor must be responsible for the officer's performance, training and evaluation.

The tendency has been to organize patrol primarily by time of day into watches. In a city, or precinct, of 100,000 population, a typical complement would consist of 100 GPOs, 15 sergeants, 4 lieutenants, and a captain divided into three or more watches. The focus of each lieutenant watch commander tends to be on events that occur when the watch is on duty. The lieutenant's responsibility should extend to days when he is off and a sergeant member of the watch is in charge.

The sergeants and patrol officers also tend to focus on that part of the day when their group is on duty. Less attention is paid to beat problems, many of which overlap watches. Ideally, when patrol is organized primarily by time of day, each sergeant will have a zone or sector for which he will have a responsibility for community liaison, knowing the problems and people, as well as being known.

Similarly, GPOs will be assigned to a beat on which they will concentrate between calls. The amount of time available for beat and sector work will depend upon how much remains after dispatches are serviced. That, in turn, depends upon the dispatching policy. Research has found that only 10 to 15 percent of calls for an officer warrant an immediate dispatch. They are for a crime in progress or life-threatening emergency. Departments which have adopted a policy of Differential Police Response (DPR) save large portions of valuable patrol officer time which can be devoted to community-oriented policing. It results in increased productivity, crime prevention, and neighborhood community teamwork.

Of course, GPOs and sergeants will share responsibility for their beats and sectors with their counterparts from other watches. To be most effective, information should be exchanged among members of different watches assigned to the same beat or sector on a daily basis. Efforts should be coordinated. Policies and initiatives should be consistent around the clock. It is especially important that relationships between officers and those who live or work in a beat be consistent. Community-police teamwork can be seriously undercut when different watch commanders, sergeants, or GPOs adopt different policies, within their discretion, or develop different attitudes toward a community leader, school principal, or block watch team. The citizens are frustrated and confused as to why the police department cannot have a coherent approach to the problems that generate crime and disorder in their neighborhoods.

When patrol is organized primarily by time of day, there are major problems to be overcome in developing strong, productive partnerships of police and citizens at the neighborhood beat level. A motorized beat tends to be in the range of 5,000 to 10,000 residents. It is at that level that the job must be accomplished. On any larger scale, too many relationships between too many officers and too many police create confusion. Too many large police departments in seeking efficiencies of scale have forgotten that the role of the police is to assist the members of a community to police themselves. Cross-dispatching cars across beats, especially when the policy is to respond rapidly to as many calls for service as possible, can result in GPOs being out of their beat for most of a shift. It is an example of false efficiency interfering with the construction of the essential foundation of effectiveness—community relations.

Relationships at the beat level are critical. They can be weakened when responsibility is shared as it usually is among those from different watches. Inconsistencies in policies and attitudes toward particular individuals or groups also reduce effectiveness. Are such impediments inevitable?

The conventional wisdom is that some such problems are unavoidable because patrol officers must be organized primarily by watches. Beat organization is secondary.

For community policing to yield its full potential, the conventional wisdom should be challenged. It is possible to organize patrol primarily by space and secondarily by time. A 100,000 population city, or precinct, can be divided into four zones, each headed by a lieutenant with 24-hour responsibility similar to that of a precinct captain or chief of patrol. At the next level, 10 to 20 beats can be established with populations ranging from 5,000 to 10,000. Each beat can be commanded by a sergeant who, in effect, is the "neighborhood chief of police." Between 5 and 10 patrol officers are assigned permanently to each beat. Finally, the beats are divided into sub-beats, each of which is the 24-hour responsibility of a single GPO. An officer will become the individual protector of about 1,000 people, no more than 2,000 depending upon the amount of crime measured according to a crime seriousness index.

Just as a chief of police, chief of patrol, or precinct captain has 24-hour responsibility, so would GPOs, sergeants and lieutenants. It provides for consistency in the liaison of the department with communities at the sub-beat, beat, and sector levels. It eliminates the divided responsibility among members of different watches. At the sub-beat level, the officer is able to know his or her people well since they are a relatively small number. The people will be able to relate on a friendly, personal basis to their *own* officer. A different, much stronger rapport will develop between protector and protected. The officer who had seen the work in an impersonal way, dealing with strangers who were little more than numbers, will now feel an attachment to the families and individuals who have become familiar friends.

Organizing patrol primarily by space requires that it be organized secondarily by time. Patrol officers, sergeants, and lieutenants must be scheduled to provide round-the-clock coverage. Each lieutenant-sector commander would receive a schedule in advance delineating the sector's responsibility for providing a watch commander, sector supervisors, and beat patrol officers for its share of shifts during a month. Patrol officers when "in-service" for dispatch would normally cover their own beats, except that during the low activity watch—approximately midnight to 8:00 a.m.—a car should cover two or more beats. Three 8-hour shifts beginning at midnight typically require strength ratios of 1:3. Calls for service and other workload factors generally follow that pattern. Also, very few opportunities for community interaction are available while a city sleeps. Community policing occurs principally on day and evening watches.

Beyond providing personnel for watch duty, sergeant-beat commanders should have flexibility in scheduling their officers to best meet the needs of the beat and the sub-beats. Approximately five officers are required to cover a position continuously, allowing for days off, court time, training, vacation and sick leave. However, on a midnight shift, one officer can cover two or three beats. The saving permits the use of extra officers for other necessary beat work—crime analysis, problem solving, criminal intelligence, coordination with probation/parole, preventing drugs in schools, etc. during day or evening hours. By placing all GPOs under the flexible control of beat sergeants, their time can be put to best use.

A majority of police are patrol officers. Where most crime is found, their valuable time is misused in "chasing calls" where they are not needed. The best use of their time is leveraging the eyes, ears, influence and networking of a small neighborhood community which can accomplish more than police in preventing crime. Patrol should be organized primarily by space, rather than time—sector, beat and sub-beat managers replacing watch commanders, watch sergeants, and call responders.

Community policing is the friendly kind. It is found in small towns. They enjoy low crime rates. To bring it to cities, departments must be organized to facilitate community partnerships at the sub-beat and beat levels. The people of every small neighborhood community and their officer must become one. The poor are the most dependent on the police for protection and mutual improvement. Every patrol officer, not just some, should be a community officer.

NOTES

1. Pierce, Neal R. *Baltimore Sun*, January 13, 1992.

2. Statement of Mission. Lincoln, Nebraska Police Department.

3. African proverb.

4. Bittner, Egon. *Local Government Police Management.* Washington, D.C.: International City Management Association, 1982, p. 8.

5. *President's Crime Commission Report.* Washington, D.C.: Government Printing Office, 1967.

6. *Uniform Crime Reports 1990.* Washington, D.C.: Federal Bureau of Investigation.

7. Wilson, O. W. *Police Administration.* New York: McGraw-Hill, 1950, p. 471.

8. Press Release, New York Police Department, December 13, 1990.

9. Muir, William Ker, Jr. *Police* (Street Corner Politicians). Chicago: University of Chicago Press, 1997.

21

VIOLENCE, U.S.A.

Riots and Crime

MARVIN E. WOLFGANG

Violence in America today is more than the society wishes to tolerate, but should be considered historically and cross-culturally. Labor and other riots in the nineteenth and twentieth centuries were probably more destructive than current disturbances. America is not a "sick" society but does have violence within an essentially nonviolent culture. The fear of being victimized from crimes of violence is real but greater than statistics on victimization indicate. To riot is a violation of the law and partially a reflection of inadequate response from government and other agencies to legitimate grievance and dissent. To resort to violence is a sign of despair and a failure to have alternative avenues of expression. A subculture of violence exists in many cities and is generated from the value system associated with the poor, the deprived, and the residents of segregation. Dispersal of the population from this subculture is the major solution for its elimination. The task of a democracy is to guarantee the right to dissent, to respond to protest, and to fortify freedom while maintaining social control.

The vanguard of the Renaissance of Western civilization was Florence, Italy. Scholars and tourists alike glowingly describe the rebirth of our classical heritage, the humanistic philosophy, new perspectives in art, the political structure and processes of the Florentine Commune, the new architecture and legal system. Yet, with this renascent spirit there was still mob violence, riots, and bloodshed in the streets.

When the dictatorial Duke of Athens was compelled by an angry mob to flee the city in 1343, some of his political assistants were grabbed on the street, tortured, and murdered. The apex of the mob fury was reached in the scene described as follows:

> Those who could not wound them while alive, wounded them after they were dead; and not satisfied with tearing them to pieces, they hewed their bodies with swords, tore them with their hands, and even with their teeth. And that every sense might be satiated with vengeance, having first heard their moans, seen their wounds, and touched their lacerated bodies, they wished even the stomach to be satisfied, that having glutted the extent sense, the one within might also have its share.[1]

Source: Keynote address, 15th National Institute on Crime and Delinquency, Dallas, June 16, 1968. Reprinted in *Crime & Delinquency* (National Council on Crime and Delinquency). 14:4-289–305. (Oct. 1968). Reprinted with permission.

The poor boy, only eighteen years of age, dressed with sorrowful significance in black, was thrust through the heavy portal of the palace by the Burgundian soldiers, and torn limb from limb in the sight of his father, on whom the same fate descended immediately afterwards. The limbs of these victims were paraded on sticks through the town, and some boasted that they had eaten the raw flesh.[2]

This mob action helped to sustain Machiavelli's insistence that "the rage of men is certainly always found greater, and their revenge more furious upon the recovery of liberty, than when it has only been defended."[3]

By 1378 a vicious circle of popular lawlessness and governmental retaliation had been formed. One chronicler described conditions this way:

The populace perpetually penetrated into the palace, and interfered with the Priors in the discharge of their functions, ordering any name which they did not like to be torn up; and as the ranks of the malcontents were increased by those whom the government had ejected as too democratic, it may be imagined how the restless suspicions of the people were utilized for personal ends. The town was honeycombed with conspiracy, the banished of all classes keeping up communications with their friends and adherents inside the walls. Torture was freely applied, and numerous people decapitated in consequence of "confessions" thus obtained. Every man went about with invisible eyes fixed upon him, and names of "suspects" were found written up at the corners of the streets.[4]

A century later, in 1478, at the time of the Pazzi conspiracy against the life of Lorenzo de' Medici, we read:

The streets of Florence were polluted with the dead bodies and mangled limbs of the slaughtered. The palace was recovered from its assailants, whose carcasses were thrown into the street, and dragged about for the amusement of the people. The name of the Medici echoed everywhere; and portions of the bodies of the slain were borne about the streets on lances by mobs, who incessantly raised the cry "Palle! Palle! Perish the traitors." As to the Pazzi, they became at once objects of universal detestation.[5]

My reason for referring to these scenes is patent: to draw upon examples of riot and violence from a beautiful city at the most glorious time in its history, to show the brutal side of man's behavior in the midst of another period's affluence, political enlightenment, and highly humanistic culture.

VIOLENCE THEN AND NOW, HERE AND THERE

We are faced today with the questions of whether American society is more violent than earlier and whether we are more violent than other societies.

I should preface these remarks with caution. Most of my own research experience is concerned with collecting and carefully examining empirical data, using appropriate statistical tools for computation, and analyzing computer printouts with supported interpretations. My penchant for speculation and leaping into sweeping generalizations about "national character," the American society, and our "culture style" is probably as great as the next fellow's. But I have been reared in the constraints of logic, the scientific method, and the language of critical analysis, and it is therefore with a sense of hypothesis-formation, tentative assumptions, and heuristic suggestion that I venture into the game of pontificating about the stance of our society with respect to violence.

Man is not innately criminal, violent, or aggressive. He responds to people, events, or other kinds of stimuli that precipitate violative, violent, or aggressive behavior. But he learns what is fearful or frustrating so that the things to which he reacts are interpreted by him as such, and the resolution of events which he defines as problems is also learned. Cats, dogs, monkeys do not shoot their adversaries because they cannot or have not learned to use guns. Only man has the capacity, to make and to use such artificial weapons designed to destroy himself and others.

I am enough of a behaviorist to believe that the normal human being is born amoral, with plasticity to his personality, capable of being molded not only by his genes but by the generations before him and beside him. I am sufficiently a collectivist to realize the power that groups have over me, from large-scale political and economic organizations to crowds, the amorphous public, neighborhoods, and professional peers. I am enough of an individualist to enjoy privacy, to want the right to be different, to believe that I have the capacity to use reason. I have been reared in values, learned from family and friends that oppose violence and crime. Like most others I refrain from crime not because of the negative fear of detection or punishment but because of the positive commitment to a moral system that views crime as socially dysfunctional and individually reprehensible. But I am also enough of a realist to know that these propositions contain inconsistencies and contradictions. At the extremes of social life and in the crises of history, the logic of love can change to hatred and sweet reason turn sour.

When colonies collected themselves in the eighteenth century to sever their maternal ties, we called the action revolution and good despite the violence it engendered. When some states in the nineteenth century sought to bifurcate the nation, we called the action civil war and bad and lamented the bloodshed. The Nazis gave justice to our bombs and enlisted the world's generation of youth to react violently to violence. Violence becomes viewed as a rapid collective problem solver, from the three and twenty stabs in Caesar, according to Suetonius, to riots in city streets. Riots, rebellion, and revolution—the words we use to describe the stages provide more than alliterative language of the process; the rapid transition from one action to the other now causes our restless and anxious point in history, and commands our attention for response.

When men perceive oppression as their lot and know of others not oppressed, when ordered avenues of change are blocked by kings or legislators or some vague variety of any social system, the oppressed will either resign themselves to fate or rise up to taste the fruit of freedom, and having tasted will want the feast.

Like whites, Negroes are men who have learned of their oppression. By forced migration they became slaves. The politics of war redefined their citizenry but little their status. Slaves became servants in the economics of change. The quiet process of elevation has been too slow for all but a trickle of black humanity to enjoy white privilege, and today color is a description not of the skin but of one's status in society. That status is a depressed, deprived, and now frustrating one.

There are those who argue that American society is "sick" with violence and worse today

than ever. The argument includes the following items, some of which are real, others exaggerated or false: crime rates are rising; there are more killings and rapes than ever before; students are going wild with violence on campuses across the country; assassinations are upon us from President Kennedy to Martin Luther King to Senator Kennedy, with Medgar Evers, Viola Liuzzo, Michael Schwerner, James Chaney, Andrew Goodman, and Malcolm X in between; race riots are changing our cities into battlefields.

The explanations for current violence often become each observer's special scapegoat theory: the frontier mores; machismo; our permissive society; poverty amidst affluence; rising expectations with angry disenchantment; violence on television and in comics; working mothers and broken homes; recent Supreme Court decisions; black power; the Vietnam war; mail-order guns.

I am not prepared with evidence to deny the validity of these assertions singly or in combination. What I suggest, however, is that there is evidence in rebuttal to the general interpretation of our society's being newly, excessively, distinctively violent. In contrast to an ideal of nonviolence, we obviously have violence. But it is in the comparative mode, over our own history and other nations that the assertion is made and the rebuttal is offered.

Recall some of our own history that suggests violence as severe as or worse than now. We might discount the Revolution and the War Between the States, the latter of which took approximately a half million lives. But we cannot neglect the Shay and Whiskey Rebellions over debts and taxes; the slaughter and subjugation of American Indians; the Know-Nothings who fought rising Irish political power, who had a 48-hour orgy of mob violence in St. Louis in 1854 in which a dozen persons were killed and fifty homes of Irish Catholics wrecked and looted, who killed twenty persons in a two-day riot in Louisville the next year and burned two churches and two parochial schools in Philadelphia; and the Irish antidraft riot in New York in 1863 that killed nearly 2,000 and injured 8,000 in four days.

There were the bloody railroad strikes in 1877 that killed 150; the Rocky Mountain mining wars that took the lives of 198, including a governor, at the turn of the century; the brutal Molly

Maguires, a secret band of Irish miners in Pennsylvania; the Wobblies, or Industrial Workers of the World; the industrial and railroad police who brutally beat laborers from Pennsylvania to California; the garment workers' strike in Chicago in 1910 that resulted in seven deaths, an unknown number seriously injured, and 874 arrests; the twenty lives lost in the Illinois Central Railroads strikes in 1911; the 1919 steel strike in which twenty persons perished; the national cotton textile labor dispute of 1934 that spread from Georgia and South Carolina to Alabama, even to Rhode Island and Connecticut, with twenty-one deaths and 10,000 soldiers on strike duty.[6]

By 1871, the invisible empire of the Ku Klux Klan had a membership of over half a million, and a Congressional investigation that year uncovered hangings, shootings, whippings, and mutilations in the thousands. In Louisiana alone, two thousand persons had been killed, wounded, or injured in a short few weeks before the election of 1868. The commanding general of federal forces in Texas reported: "Murders of Negroes are so common as to render it impossible to keep accurate accounts of them."[7]

That violence is not unique to the United States is an assertion that needs no more than a few illustrations. The aftermath of the French Revolution had a kind of terror and bloodshed never witnessed in this country; the 1845 student riots in France spread throughout Europe; assassinations occurred from Austrian Archduke Francis Ferdinand in 1914 to Prime Minister Vervoerd recently in South Africa. The Nazis need not even be mentioned. There is still fresh in history the tortures in French Algeria; the Stalinist terrors of a generation; the mob violence and riots off and on for another generation involving Pakistanis and Indians; the current Nigerian civil war; the student and union violence in France today; the *violencia* of Colombia for nearly twenty years that resulted in the assassination of Dr. Jorge Gaitan in 1948 and an estimated 200,000 deaths up to 1967; the confused "cultural revolution" in mainland China; and the horrendous, little-publicized massacre of 400,000 persons in recent years in Indonesia.

The homicide rate in the United States today is steadily around 4 or 5 per 100,000, with only slight variations from year to year. In 1933, it was over twice as high, or around 11. The murder rate for Colombia is 34; for Mexico, 30; Nicaragua, 29; Guatemala, 12; Ecuador, 6—even

with poorly collected statistics. Of course the United States stands high in comparison with England and most of northern Europe. Our homicide rate is four times as high as Canada's and Australia's. These two countries also had "frontier mores"; in fact, Australia was first colonized by convicts.

Today we have more police, more bookkeepers of crime statistics, more definitions of delinquency—like truancy, running away from home, being incorrigible—that include one-third of our delinquents, who are not defined as such in other countries. Most large cities have large Juvenile Aid Divisions or Bureaus with the opportunity to apprehend juveniles under the label of "nonarrest," "remedial," or "warned" who nonetheless are counted in the police delinquency statistics. In Philadelphia this category comprises two-thirds of those under eighteen years who are taken into custody. Recent studies of Boston and Buffalo, using police and court data that reach back to the eighteenth century, indicate that rates of serious crimes were higher in the nineteenth century than they are today.

Supreme Court decisions regarding appearance of suspects for hearings within forty-eight hours were also viewed as "tying the hands of the police" and blamed for crime waves that never existed. Technical means and institutional modes of adjusting to the requirement slowly quieted earlier opposition until the rule is now taken for granted. Violence on television is distasteful to many, but the link to violent behavior is deemed unproved. And although I would prefer all guns in private hands to be turned in to public authorities and believe that many lives would be saved by very restrictive gun legislation, I am also aware that there are probably twice as many guns around the country today as in the 1930s, and I note a steady decline in criminal homicides since then. The inverse correlation is not causative, but neither is a reverse interpretation.

Violence in our own past, in the past and present of other nations, does not diminish it in our current scene. But its present dimensions and our instant explanations should be viewed with these perspectives.

THE FEAR OF BEING VICTIMIZED

There appears to be a widespread fear in the United States, especially in central cities, of being assaulted, robbed, and raped on the streets. Most social analysts agree that the fear is present and real, although there is only meager evidence and much conjecture about the validity of facts to justify the fear. As the mass media present more information (news) more rapidly about a phenomenon (crime) to more consumers over wider areas, these consumers tend to assume that the frequency of the phenomenon is increasing. This kind of "instant" news may be partially responsible for the increased fear of being victimized.

Official rates of crimes of violence are among some offenses, moderately increasing. We do not know the extent to which the crime rate may be affected by improved methods of recording, higher proportions of civilian employees to tabulate and correctly calculate crime statistics in the city police departments, the increase in citizens' willingness to report crimes, and other such factors, but they may be contributing to some of the official rate increases.

Surveys conducted for the President's Commission on Law Enforcement and Administration of justice interestingly reveal that most people are not victimized sufficiently often for crime to make a major impact on their lives. Nonetheless, if the actual experience of victimization is not a major determinant of attitudes about crime, there is a sense in which vulnerability influences fear. The greater concern of Negroes is consistent with the risk of victimization suggested by police statistics. Negroes are far more likely to be victims of a serious offense against the person than are white persons. The greater anxiety of women than men, however, is not consistent with what is known of the victimization risks. When citizens in Washington, D.C. were asked what steps they took to protect themselves against crime, they commonly spoke of avoiding danger in the streets and indicated that they sometimes stayed home at night or used taxis, or that they avoided talking to strangers. Some spoke of measures to protect themselves and their property at home, such as keeping firearms or watchdogs or putting stronger locks on the doors and windows. The crimes which the public seems to fear most—crimes of violence are those which occur least frequently. People appear to be more tolerant of crimes against property. They fear most being attacked by strangers, although the probabilities of being assaulted by strangers, especially in the

streets, are very low. From abundant research we know that crimes of violence are commonly committed in the intimacy of the home; they are intra-ethnic and generally intra-group offenses. For example, only about 5 or 6 percent of all rapes in the United States involve strangers and victim-offender relationships that are at the same time interracial.

Urban Space and Victimization Probabilities

Although the rates of increase of crime in the city have not been alarming, especially when computed as age-specific rates that take into account the increase in the teenage and young adult population due to the high postwar birth rate, the probability of being victimized may have considerably increased over the past fifteen years.

Even if *rates* of violent crime have changed little over time, the *volume* of violent crime has increased simply because of the increase in population. From the perspective of the potential victim, what is critical is not the crime rate of offenders or even the rate at which persons become victims of crime but rather the probability of an individual's being victimized in a given dimension of space, like a city street corner, a given block, or the center of the city. While the crude rate of violent crime or even the rate of juvenile crime may have remained fairly steady, the population of the neighborhood and the number of youth of crime-prone age may indeed have increased over fifteen years. Yet, the spatial dimension of the neighborhood has not increased; a street intersection remains the same. The result is that the chances of a given citizen being assaulted at that intersection have increased.

It has also been observed that one of the historical methods of urban crime control has been to cluster the lower classes in densely populated and residentially restricted areas. This style of ghetto crime control, common from Greco-Roman times, medieval Paris, industrial London, and modern America, is declining as social policy mounts an increasing attack against poverty and ghetto living. As barriers of streets and prejudice break down, the lower socioeconomic classes are spreading throughout the city and slowly beginning to spill out of the city boundaries.

The long-range effects of this geographic dispersion should have widespread social benefits, but the immediate, transitory effect of a lower class dispersing and still harboring some of the deleterious markings of slum living and social values—often including those connected with the ready resort to violence—may be to increase the amount of crime in old sections of cities that previously were accustomed to low crime rates. Thus, the older residents of formerly low crime-rate areas begin to note that the old familiar streets are "not as safe as they used to be." And, their perception may indeed be correct.

If, however, a democratic society opts for increased opportunities for all citizens, including freedom of residential choice, the transition stage to which we referred must be faced and accelerated so that a change in lifestyle and value orientations toward property and the dignity of persons accompanies the change of residence.

CRIME AND RIOTS

Criminogenic Forces of the City

The forces that generate conditions conducive to crime and riots are stronger in an urban community than in rural areas. Urban living is more anonymous living. It releases the individual from community restraints more common in tradition-oriented societies. But more freedom from constraints and controls also provides greater freedom to deviate. And living in the more impersonalized, formally controlled urban society means that regulatory orders of conduct are often directed by distant bureaucrats. The police are strangers executing these prescriptions on, at worst, an alien subcommunity and, at best, anonymous set of subjects. Minor offenses in a small town or village are often handled without resort to official police action. As eufunctional as such action may seem to be, it nonetheless results in fewer recorded violations of the law compared to the city. Although perhaps causing some decision difficulties for the police in small towns, formal and objective law enforcement is not acceptable to the villagers.

Urban areas with mass populations, greater wealth, more commercial establishments, and more products of our technology also provide more frequent opportunities for theft. Victims are impersonalized, property is insured, consumer goods in more abundance are vividly displayed and are more portable.

Urban life is commonly characterized by population density, spatial mobility, ethnic and class heterogeneity, reduced family functions, and, as we have said, greater anonymity. All of these traits are expressed in comparison to nonurban life, or varying degrees of urbanism and urbanization. When, on a scale, these traits are found in high degree, and when they are combined with poverty, physical deterioration, low education, residence in industrial and commercial centers, unemployment or unskilled labor, economic dependency, marital instability or breaks, poor or absent male models for young boys, overcrowding, lack of legitimate opportunities to make a better life, the absence of positive anticriminal behavior patterns, higher frequency of organic diseases, and a cultural minority status of inferiority, it is generally assumed that social-psychological mechanisms leading to deviance are more likely to emerge. These include frustration, lack of motivation to obey external demands, internalized cultural strains of inconsistency between means available and ends desired, conflicting norms, anomie, and so forth. The link between these two conditions—physical features of subparts of a city and the social-psychological aspects—has not been fully researched to the point where the latter can be safely said to be invariable or highly probable consequences of the former. Thus, to move onto a third level—namely, a tradition of lawlessness, of delinquent or criminal behavior, as a further consequence of the physical and social-psychological conditions of much urban life—is an even more tenuous scientific position. Nonetheless, these are the assumptions under which the community of scholars and public administrators operate today. The assumptions are the most justified and logically adequate we can make unless or until successfully refuted.

It has often been suggested that high crime areas of a city (meaning both residence of offenders and place of crime occurrence) contain, in high numbers, new migrants, the residue of earlier residential groups that have mostly moved out, and competitive failure from better districts who were forced to move back to the cheaper rent areas. This "selective migration" thesis may have some validity, but it has also been noted that most of the criminals in the high crime areas had been reared in delinquency areas of other cities.

It is abundantly clear even to the most casual observer that Negroes in American society are the current carriers of a ghetto tradition. More than any other socially defined group, they are the recipients of urban deterioration and the social-psychological forces leading to legal deviance. And for this reason, concern with crime in the city is commonly a concern with Negro crime. Although there are good reasons for raising serious questions about criminal statistics that report race of the offender and the fact that Negro crime rates are in general three or four times higher than white rates, and although Negroes probably suffer more injustices than whites in the law enforcement process from arrest to imprisonment, it is no surprise that the most valid efforts to measure crime still find Negro crime rates high. When the untoward aspects of urban life are found among Italians, Germans, Poles, or almost any other group, their crime rates are similarly high. Relative deprivation and social disqualification are thus dramatically chained to despair and delinquency.

All of this is not meant to obscure the fact that poverty also exists in small towns and rural areas. But when multiplied by congested thousands and transmitted over generations, poverty becomes a culture. The expectations of social intercourse change and irritable, frustrated parents often become neglectful and aggressive. Their children inherit a *subculture of violence* where physically aggressive responses are either expected or required by all members sharing not only the tenement's plumbing but also its system of values. Ready access and resort to weapons in this milieu may be essential to protection against others who respond in similarly violent ways in certain situations. Carrying a knife or some other protective device becomes a common symbol of willingness to participate in violence, to expect violence, and to be ready for its retaliation.

A subculture of violence is not the product of cities alone. The Thugs of India, the *vendetta barbaricina* in Sardinia, the *mafioso* in Sicily have existed for a long time. But the contemporary American city has the accoutrements not only for the genesis but also for the highly accelerated development of this subculture, and it is from this subculture that most violent crimes come.

The Crime of Riot

Crimes do not cause riots, but riots cause and are themselves crimes. Studies of riots by the Brandeis University Lemberg Center for the Study of Violence and studies of the Watts and Detroit riots tell us that "high levels of discontent" about job opportunities, housing, school integration, police behavior, and the efforts of federal and local governments to encourage integration characterized the feelings of the Negro population in six riot cities. Inflammatory incidents, usually perceived as police brutality, are the common precipitating, triggering factors. Although rioters are usually from the "under-class," the Watts study indicated that Negro readiness to participate in violence is not confined to this group.

A Howard University study of the early days of Negro nonviolent sit-ins and demonstrations tells us that, during the period when these incidents occurred, the rate of delinquency went down, and it explains this reduction in part by the fact that adolescent boys who might otherwise have been engaged in malicious mischief, corner lounging, disorderly conduct, and other similar acts had their attention and energies diverted to the demonstrations. The participation of juvenile gangs in riot control in Chicago after the assassination of Martin Luther King has been recorded as somewhat successful.

But it is also recorded that a high proportion of persons arrested during riots have previous arrest and criminal records. Many of these persons were looters, and looters are the parasitical wave in the riot and its aftermath who take advantage of the anomic situation. In one sense, carrying off color television sets, guns, and even pianos is a collective symbolic gesture of stealing a piece of the rewards of privilege requested by but denied to the Negro poor.

While not having a firm political ideology any more than students who riot on campus, the "young militants" responsible for the firebombing and the sniping—the bitter and alienated activists—surely perceive the bureaucrats and the broader social order as distant impersonal targets for distaste and disruption. Having seen that it is possible to get attention and dethrone the complacency of the white establishment, and having gained hope that their lot can be improved, they regard their present deprivation as unendurable. In referring to the French Revolution, De Tocqueville said: "a people which has supported without complaint, as if they were not felt, the most oppressive laws, violently throws them off as soon as their weight is lightened. The social order destroyed by a revolution is always better than that which immediately preceded it. The end which was suffered patiently as inevitable seems unendurable as soon as the idea of escaping from it is conceived."[8]

To riot is a crime in any state penal code definition. To incite to riot, to loot, burglarize, set on fire, destroy property, rob, assault, shoot, carry deadly weapons—each of these is a crime. Surely, the unrecorded number of crimes and of unapprehended offenders is enormous. Deaths that occur from retaliation by the police are, in strictly legalistic terms in some states, felony murders because they occurred as a consequence of other felonious acts committed by the rioters.

In still another sense, not compatible with a legalistic proximate cause notion, the white society, as the Kerner Commission noted, is responsible for inciting to riot. While displaying before the Negro poor the democratic idealism of opportunity, it has inflicted on them the prejudice, the economic blockage of opportunities, the subjugation, and the alienation from power and participation in democracy that have produced among Negroes the power to respond, exploding now in attacks to express their feelings. The urban riots thus far are a mixed bag of some confusing revolutionary ideology among a few, gnomic acts expressive of social malaise among many, and almost adventuresome play among still others. Should there be another round of riot, it will be either moderate skirmishes in more muted tones, reflecting a skewness toward dissipation of the ghetto thrust, or more violent guerilla warfare that can result only in more stringent repressive force by the state. If riots this summer are few or more moderate, we might conclude that the massively diffused efforts for better police-community relations, coalitions of white business with the Negro community, and all our other strategies of solution that reject tokenism and gradualism are beginning to pay off.

I am inclined to link the causes of urban riots and those of urban crime. Where riots have begun, crime rates have been highest, especially crimes of violence. The social forces that have generated crime overlay the forces that erupt into riot. The players in both dramas are the same or similar. The parallelism is too strong to ignore or deny. Correct the conditions causing the one phenomenon and you change the other concomitantly.

CITIZEN RESPONSE

Dispersion of the Subculture of Violence[9]

I have spoken of the subculture of violence. Mostly with reference to high rates of crimes of violence, outside the domain of concern with riots. My personal theoretical proclivity is to disperse the subculture's members, thus eliminating that subcultural set of values attached to the use of violence. The form of this dispersal is subsidized relocation and redistribution of the population: to intervene socially means taking some kind of action designed to break into the information loop that links the subcultural representatives in a constant chain of reinforcement of the use of violence. Political, economic, and other forms of social action sometimes buttress the subculture by forcing it to seek strength and solace within itself as a defense against the larger culture and thereby more strongly establish the subcultural value system. Social inaction probably does the same in lesser degree, for inaction is not generally indifference and thereby does not produce zero response.

The residential propinquity of the actors in a subculture of violence has been noted. Breaking up this propinquity, dispersing the members who share intense commitment to the violence value, could also cause a break in the inter- and intra-generational communication of this value system. Dispersion can be done in many ways and does not necessarily imply massive population shifts, although urban renewal, slum clearance, and housing projects suggest feasible ways. Renewal programs that simply shift the location of the subculture from one part of the city to another do not destroy the subculture. For the subculture to be distributed so that it dissipates, the scattered units should be small. Housing projects and neighborhood areas should be microcosms of the social hierarchy and value system of the central dominant culture. It is in homogeneity that the subculture has strength and durability.

For all its apparent, but still questionable, virtues and victories, the detached-worker programs of handling juvenile and delinquent gangs must still be viewed as a kind of holding action, or containment policy, until a more or less "spontaneous remission" of gang members occurs through aging, marrying, or moving away. The occasionally reported solidifying of formerly diffused activities is an untoward turn of events in the detached-worker programs. The point is, however, that detached-worker action, like any program that moves into a subculture from the outside, even with the language and dress associated with it, is designed to introduce values from the dominant culture by subtly and slowly bending the subculture values to parallel the former. (Where deviant values are not delinquent, it is probably more propitious for the dominant culture to become more flexible and permit the deviancy to function freely.) But such purposeful action by the larger society has been only piecemeal, outnumbered and outmaneuvered by the subculture, which, to the invading team, itself becomes the dominant culture within this setting.

In a sense, then, the larger culture sets up its own outposts within a subculture and seeks by subversive action to undermine the subcultural values. The police in these neighborhoods are like enemy troops in alien territory; they are the most blatant large-culture bearers. The detached workers, while still not undercover agents, are the most subtle subversives. With neither form of control, however, has society been able to record much success; and certainly no, or at best few, claims can be made for destroying the subculture of violence by these means.

While operating within the subculture that uses nonlegal methods, the legal nonviolent methods of the invaders often appear to have little or no utility. In many cases, the larger culture invaders who seek to control the subculture of violence ultimately resort to violence themselves and hence use the very methods of the subculture to subdue it. This usage reinforces and provides new subcultural justification for violence.

Before one set of values can replace another, before the subculture of violence can be substituted by the establishment of nonviolence, the former must be disrupted, dispersed, disorganized. The resocialization, relearning process best takes place when the old socialization and old learning are forgotten or denied their validity. Once the subculture is disintegrated by dispersion of its members, aggressive attitudes are not supported by like companions, and violent behavior is not regularly on display to encourage initiation and repetition.

To be most immediately effective beyond this point, however, the normative system of the larger culture must be presented as a reasonably clear, if not codified statement. But neither national goals nor the middle-class value system in a democratic society constitutes a dogma. One virtue of a more doctrinal system is its clarification of principles. To remain fluid and flexible is another kind and perhaps a more enduring quality of strength. To reconvert, retrain, reform may require some exaggeration of the elements of the value system; i.e., a presentation of an ideal and idealized type. Most cultures can array a stronger consensus against violence, especially criminal homicide, than against anything else, and can be more explicit about it. Except for a somewhat schizoid attitude toward war, the larger culture values contain strong prescriptions for nonviolence. Thus, if the dominant middle-class ethic is clearly opposed to the use of violence in interpersonal relationships, the clarity of its opposition should be a useful element in its efforts to resocialize the dispersed members of a former subculture of violence.

The dominant culture value of nonviolence would be transmitted by new patterns of residential propinquity to families, schools, and peer groups that contain very few and muted expressions of violence in child rearing, marital life, playground activities, and other episodes in the dramas of personal interaction; the resocialization process would take place in the subtleties of daily social life, without the vast network of a previous subcultural communication system that reported events of violence as commonplace. Community service centers, less locked in the zones of poverty and deviance and more widely distributed throughout the city, could buttress the otherwise slow shift in attitudes and values.

Recreational facilities, child guidance clinics, boy and girl scout clubs, hobby clubs, Police Athletic League centers, Little League baseball, and neighborhood associations could function as demonstrably effective vehicles for conversion to nonviolent activities. There is no solid empirical evidence that the catalog of clubs and playgrounds in American cities has been effective in preventing delinquency or reducing violent crime. A common criticism is that they do not reach the delinquent or highly potential delinquent population. Even when they are located in congested neighborhoods with high crime rates, they are often viewed as unwanted invaders of the territory and are consequently unattended except by the bad area's "good boys."

When the families from the subculture of violence have been distributed and increasingly absorbed by the surrounding middle-class milieu, they will become conditioned to the behavior expectations around them. Instead of the old and consistent role models from generations before them and peers beside them, the territorially transplanted families could see, not inadequate images of middle-class conformity and lifestyle from mass media projections, but nearby neighbors with whom they could interact. The nearly compulsive adoption of middle-class roles by Negro families in integrated communities is well known. We are drawing attention here to the general social-psychological processes of norm learning, empathy, projection, identification, internalization, ego ideals, primary reference groups, and differential association theory.

There may be some concern that the middle-class value system too often requires overconformity, is "bourgeois" in a pejorative sense, produces neurotics, and is overly supplied with mediocrity and banality. One might well ask what are the alternatives to the middle-class ethic to which our policy decision-makers would have criminal deviants resocialized. The range of alternative forms of behavior and attitude within the broad spectrum of the middle class is wide enough to avoid the stultifying and stagnant homogenization feared by some observers.

Under the suggestions of dispersion and newly found attachments to the middle-class milieu, community treatment of delinquents and placement of offenders on probation or returned to the community on parole should facilitate the retraining process. Instead of returning to the old criminal subculture or subculture of violence, the offender would be placed in an environment predominantly nonviolent.

Response to Riot

Citizens respond to riots in ways that reflect their backgrounds and the status they occupy in society. With our cultural pluralism, ethnic heterogeneity, and class clusters, not to mention personality variations, it is dangerous to generalize. Young and poor Negro males living in ghettoes would be expected to have a response different from middle-aged, middle-class whites. In addressing myself to all men I hope to be saying something to at least some.

Crash programs of coalition groups are necessary all over the land. Bankers and bomb carriers must sit at the same table to explore grievances and devise ways for the former to provide money and the latter to provide people to do what reason and reality can suggest. Business leaders, community organization workers, fellowship commissions, local government, and other civic leaders must do more than talk to themselves about the problems and prospects of others. The colonialism of help is no longer an acceptable mode among those who are frustrated and historical victims of social injustice. Beneath and beyond the former riots there is an intense morality and a demand for clear commitments, coming from middle-class students as well as the Negro poor. Impatience, discontent, and dissatisfaction with the state of American society should be viewed as healthy reflections of a desire for change and for participation in directing the change. Those deprived or dethroned are seeking self-respect and the dignity of being listened to, of being taken seriously. The dialogue between haves and have-nots has begun, and if the former do not pay attention to and seek out the latter, violence that can end only in violent repression will be the outcome.

To say that the police need support is a truism, as it is to suggest that they should always approach all persons with courtesy. Pejorative remarks breed pejoratives, as does violence itself. When the police move to curtail a disorder and function with propriety, citizens in the area should be supportive of them. Those who enter a riot are forsaking all other alternatives of resolution. If a city government or university administration offers no procedural alternatives, it has itself contributed to its own victimization. If the white middle class turns its homes into armed fortresses, it is also contributing more to the climate of challenge and fear than to the dissolution of violence.

Citizens must continue to impress their representatives at all levels of government to enact effectives laws against the absurd sale of firearms. They should urge the formal and structured teaching of nonviolence as a virtue in the school's educational value system, and they should encourage their children to have enormous enthusiasm for any humane cause. War games and toys of violence can hardly be deemed a healthy environment, even as an outlet for hostility. The marketing of violence in toys or in media simply desensitizes generations to the display of and exposure to violence even if it teaches no techniques. Every citizen should become a part of one or more organizations seeking to talk to those who harbor hate and hostility. If social contacts do not always promote love, they should at least reduce fear and hatred and increase understanding.

LEST WE FORGET

The capacity for violence lies in all normal men. But aggression is learned behavior, not innate or instinctive and not unalterable. The stimuli that arouse anger or fear are learned from our environment. The "climate of a culture," the "mood of a generation," the "drift of sentiment" are phrases that represent a collectivity; they are also clichés formulated by the articulate, educated classes making pop sociology, pop psychology, and pop history. The grammar of violence and its physical manifestation in riots may in part be a reflection of the self-fulfilling rhetoric of the analysts. The quiet, tree-lined main street of America, the daily routines of breakfast, dish washing, parent-child play and learning are not dramatic incidents of a society, but they form the lifestyle of most of us. Garbage collection attracts no public interest until the garbage is uncollected.

The diffusion of many good acts, or even of bad ones, over time, space, and people rarely receives wide display and hence has muted drama. But compressed courage, congealed catastrophe, and focal violence on culture heroes receive immediate and wide display. Instant explanations abound and the depths of our collective despair are matched only by our confusion and inability to explain the complexities of causation.

Ten thousand acts of police service, of courtesy and assistance, are little more than IBM holes on computer cards that tally the troubles of the citizenry from domestic cats in trees or quarrels in the home to providing the fastest service to transport wounded and heart-attack victims to hospitals. But one observed act of brutality—or excessive force—wipes out the nine rows and eighty columns 10,000 IBM cards of service.

Fifty thousand automobile deaths a year are regularly recorded without fanfare; the catastrophe of one jet plane carrying 120 passengers is a more dramatic headline because the disaster is a single stroke. Ten thousand homicides a year are hard for the public to contemplate; even worse is the execution of six million Jews. The ingredients of one dramatic death make all the difference. Several major attempts were made on President Roosevelt's life, as on President Truman's. In one case, the bullet missed FDR by inches. The news was reported, but there was no flurry of pop psychiatric analysis of mass violence. Yet, this was the Depression, a time of labor violence, of hordes of unemployed, of poverty at its height, of the first major Harlem race riot when there were not "rising expectations" but declining ones. The press and radio gave no ready explanations for a "sick" society. Would three inches' difference in the flight of a bullet have produced editorials denouncing American society, indicting a hundred million people for generating a climate of violence?

In short, I am not persuaded that our society is morally decayed, that kids are worse today than they used to be, that there is anything particularly distinctive about the way we destroy one another, that the United States has any special gift for violence. The idiosyncrasies of disturbed minds and dreadful, dramatic tragedies do not make a pattern of culture.

That there is violence in America cannot be denied. Few would deny that our society would be better with less display of violence on television, no racial prejudice, no or fewer guns in private possession, the removal of ghettoes, education for nonviolence, and more efficacious treatment of criminal offenders.

But the case can be made with equal vigor and evidence that ours is a gentle society, that our culture has helped to elevate man to the dignity he deserves, that the rule of law has rarely enjoyed such a high stance in history, that a greater number of good things have come to a greater number of people, that the number of alternatives available to a people with more freedom of expression has never been greater.

In historical moments of calm and conformity we need to remind ourselves of our deficiencies, our faulty democracy, our fallacies of justice and decisions. In moments of tragedy and violence we need to remind ourselves and others of our continued determination to protect the harmony history has carved for us from chaos.

MIND OVER MUSCLE—THE RULE OF LAW

Violence is not power. It is a means of seeking power and may be defined as an act of despair committed when the door is closed to alternative resolutions of repression, depression, and conflict. It comes from the failure to have a more abundant repertoire of means to gain a goal. The existence of a society is dependent on the repression of violence within its borders.

Sporadic, limited acts of violence on the authority of a society are like pinpricks on the political corpus. Watts, Detroit, and Newark are like suicidal wrist slashes of a patient who wants the doctor to save him from total destruction. The convergence of family, friends, and physicians on the attempted suicide promotes the protection and attention the patient wanted. Law and order must always prevail if a society is to endure; hence, violent jabs against it can be tolerated only to a finite point before societal retaliation becomes imperative and itself often excessively repressive.

The lessons to be learned from current collective riot conduct seem clear: as Columbia University officials remarked recently, acts wherein muscles usurp the role of minds are alien to a university. I suggest the same dictum for the larger society. Where reason is ruined and collective violence is viable, the social system has failed to provide the kind of participatory democracy we basically extol.

In the abstract there can be no side of violence with virtue. The course of the dominant society built on law and intrinsically the inheritor of the value of nonviolence must be to maintain itself. The black militant who would burn cities in this land harbors no better way of life than the Ku Klux Klaner who would burn crosses or bomb Sunday schools. But the responsibility of that dominant society is to offer alternatives for expression, provide reasonable access to the thrones of power, permit grievances to be known, and execute the provisions of our Constitution with dispatch.

Our national goals and culture values are clearer than we realize because we take them much for granted and have failed to formulate them into the kind of belief system or ideology more tightly knitted in its own logic and represented, for example, by communism. Some of our political and social norms have stability, but the flexibility of others has probably prevented our establishing an ideological set of rubrics for our civilization. Yet, the values are there and should be announced with as much clarity and precision as we can muster. And in the light of those values we can judge the violence that defends injustice because we will better know our definitions of justice.

Change occurs in all societies, albeit the change in some may be slow or, even if rapid, unplanned. It is when those persons opposed to change become intransigent and those who wish consciously to promote change are willing to resort to violence that order becomes disorder. When protest moves to riot and riot to rebellion, dissent is transformed into disruption. The right to exercise dissent peaceably is our basic constitutional guarantee. When physical harm to persons and things occurs, another guarantee is called into focus and used to force assaulters to retreat. This kind of balance is a fundamental which the police and the courts are designed to protect and maintain.

Lincoln asked the question succinctly: "Must a government of necessity be too strong for the liberties of its own people, or too weak to maintain its own existence?" I trust that our nation is sufficiently sensitive to the liberties of all to listen and to act, and strong enough to maintain them under the rule of law.

NOTES

1. Niccolo Machiavelli, *History of Florence and of the Affairs of Italy* (London: M. Walter Dunne, 1901), Book II, p. 100.

2. Bella Duffy, *The Tuscan Republic* (New York: G. P. Putnam's Sons, 1893), p. 159.

3. Machiavelli, op. cit. supra note 1.

4. Duffy, op. cit. supra note 2, p. 194.

5. W. C. Stafford and Charles Ball, *Italy Illustrated* (London: The London Printing and Publishing Company), p. 278.

6. Most of this history of labor violence has been abstracted from Philip Taft, "Violence in American Labor Disputes," *Annals of the American Academy of Political and Social Science*, March 1966, pp. 127–40.

7. Arnold Forster, "Violence on the Fanatical Left and Right," *Annals of the American Academy of Political and Social Science*, March 1966, p. 143.

8. Alexis de Tocqueville, *L'Ancien Regime*, M. W. Patterson, translator (Oxford, England: Basic Blackwell, 1949), p. 186. Cited and brought to my attention by Judd Marmor, "Some Psychological Aspects of Contemporary Urban Violence," n.d. (mimeo.).

9. In this section I am drawing upon some notions similarly expressed in Marvin E. Wolfgang and Franco Ferracuti, *The Subculture of Violence* (London: Tavistock; New York: Barnes and Noble, 1967).

22

THE COLOR OF LAW
AND THE ISSUE OF COLOR

Race and the Abuse of Police Power

HUBERT G. LOCKE

Every public officer who under color of authority, without necessity, assaults or beats any person is guilty of a violation of [law].

—Judge Stanley Weisberg's instructions to the jury in
the state trial of the four officers accused of using
excessive force against Rodney G. King

This chapter addresses a feature of the issue of police use of excessive force in which the problems of discussion are as much definitional and political as they are empirical and analytical. The definitional and political problems are intertwined; a number of persons might prefer—perhaps insist—that the issue be stated as one of racism and police brutality, while others would bridle at these words. Both terms point to a volatile problem in American society today: race is a factor in the way some persons behave toward others, and, on occasion, police

officers do use more physical force than is lawfully necessary in interacting with citizens. It is the interconnection between these two realities—whether race is a factor in circumstances in which police use excessive force—which has long been subject to fierce debate, one that has been raised to unprecedented visibility, if not volatility, by the events surrounding the videotaped assault on Rodney G. King by Los Angeles police officers on March 3, 1991.

To defuse the discussion of an issue raised to intense national prominence by the King assault,

Source: From Locke, H. G., "The color of law and the issue of color: race and abuse of police power," in W. A. Geller & Hans Toch (eds.) *Police Violence,* copyright © 1996 by Yale University Press. Reprinted with permission.

state trial of the accused police officers, verdict, violent aftermath, and subsequent federal trial of the accused officers, this chapter has a less politicized title. The acknowledged risk of losing the attention of those who believe that the problem of police excessive force toward persons of color persists, in part, because of an inability of analysts to "tell it like it is" is assumed precisely because of the persistence and volatility of the problem. Its control and, it is to be hoped, eventual eradication depend in large measure on the degree to which the issue can be stripped of its emotional content and consequences and instead viewed as a problem of gross lawlessness by those sworn to uphold the law.

Viewing the problem from the perspective of law—what is licit or illicit behavior—provides a relatively precise definition of what is at issue. In some quarters, any unwarranted or unwelcome police conduct may constitute brutality—including the use of a racial slur or profane or abusive language. As crude and inappropriate as such language may be, it does not aid the examination of the issue to lump it together with excessive physical force under the rubric "brutality." Any definition or category that designates too much ultimately describes nothing usefully. Moreover, and by extension, a legal perspective on excessive force offers a reasonably clear and concrete set of examples of the events and circumstances in which specific and, on occasion, documented behavior is at issue.

Ironically, while some might wish to broaden its application, it is the narrow, legal definition of police use of excessive force—acting "under color of authority, without lawful necessity"— that most persons of color would agree is at the core of their complaints about police misconduct.[1] One of the reasons that the Rodney King beating engendered so widespread and uniform a reaction from nonwhite Americans is the perception that police officers frequently act toward "minorities" in ways that are demeaning, if not physically abusive, because they enjoy the protective color and authority of their office.

Violence is an experience far too common in the cultures of poverty. What may appear to be officially sanctioned violence—excessive force "under color of authority"—therefore becomes especially odious to a person of color, who through diligence may escape other circumstances of violence only to be subject to violence at the hands of the police. What a single incident in Los Angeles in March 1991 made an issue of intense public attention has long been a problem that aroused passion in urban ghettos across the United States.

THE LEGACY OF THE 1960s

In December 1964, just after the first in what would be a four-year wave of summer civil disorders, the Practicing Law Institute (New York), with the assistance of the Rockefeller Fund, convened a three-day forum on "the Community and Racial Crises." The meetings were attended by municipal, state and federal officials, police chiefs, prosecutors, law professors, and representatives of civil rights and community relations agencies. Both the agenda and the discussions were reflective of the national mood of the time and, among the agency representatives present, of the relative levels of awareness and sensitivity to issues of race in their various fields. One of the topics of discussion, "Racial Tensions and the Police," touched off a fierce exchange between representatives of the police and civil rights agencies on the issue of police brutality (Stahl et al. 1966).

Two articles from *The Police Chief* among the background materials presented to conferees encapsulate attitudes toward police brutality by police administrators in the 1960s. The thrust of the first article, by the International Association of Chiefs of Police's executive director, was evident in its opening sentence: "I know of no period in recent history when the police have been the subject of so many unjustified charges of brutality, harassment and ineptness." With references to an editorial in the same journal, the author went on to decry "baseless charges of police brutality" made to cover "excesses and illegal conduct on the part of some demonstrators involved in the current racial tensions," as well as the excesses of "hoodlums" who "falsely [fly] the banner of civil rights" (Stahl et al. 1966: 120).

The same theme was echoed by the second IACP official, who described police brutality as "a commonplace and almost automatic accusation attached to any physical action taken by an official to control disorder" and as "a battle-cry . . . used by supposedly responsible Negro leaders to whip up support among their followers" (ibid.: 126). Police positions on the issue at the time tended to be reinforced by elements of the media; a *U.S. News and World Report* article listed Supreme Court rulings, civil rights pressures, and cries of police brutality "as signs of an impending breakdown in law and order throughout the nation" (Locke 1967: 625).

In less strident tones, the community side of the controversy was stated by an official of the NAACP:

> Concerning the basic facts, there can hardly be any dispute. Police brutality does occur, and the only question is how much of it there is, and where . . . . Unnecessary force is sometimes used in making arrests, although the determination of what is and is not "unnecessary force" is often extremely difficult.
>
> Neither can it be denied that, at present, large numbers (majorities in some instances) of Negroes have come to regard policemen as oppressors rather than protectors. . . . Finally, it is clear that no police force, operating under conditions short of a police state, can hope to function effectively for very long in a situation of crisis deriving from resentment or resistance on the part of massive proportions of the community in which it works.[2] (Stahl et al. 1966: 169)

During the 1960s the issue of police use of excessive force polarized police officials and large segments of the nation's Black populace and civil rights community (on the role of the civil rights community in forcing reform on American policing, see Williams and Murphy 1990). Three decades later, the assertions by the NAACP representative remain at the core of current discussions regarding the police and their behavior in communities of color across the nation: How widespread are incidents of the use of excessive force, where and under what circumstances do they occur, and does the excessive force problem cause the police to be viewed in nonwhite communities as oppressors rather than as protectors?

THE LITERATURE

What may be one of the earliest research inquiries concerning the police and "minority community relations" was also a subject of discussion at the 1964 conference. A collaborative study by the IACP and the U.S. Conference of Mayors had been designed to "gather information on police policies, practices and problems with respect to community relations and racial demonstrations in U.S. cities of over 30,000 population." The study serves as a benchmark on the police and their relationships with communities of color on the eve of what would become an era of immense change in American policing (Stahl et al. 1966: 143–58).

Much of the survey, which covered 165 cities, was calculated to discover the extent to which the cities were prepared for handling large-scale racial demonstrations; several questions, however, elicited findings on more basic race-related concerns. For example:

- One-half ($N = 83$) of the cities reported difficulties in recruiting Black officers because "applicants fail exams and standards."[3]

- Six departments, in their personnel assignments, restricted the arrest powers of nonwhite officers; thirty-four assigned nonwhite officers to predominantly nonwhite sectors of the city (see also Williams and Murphy 1990: 8); forty departments paired white and nonwhite officers only on special details.[4]

- Forty-eight departments reported they were under charges of brutality; forty-six were charged with "differential treatment" (of white and nonwhite citizens). Only two departments processed citizen complaints through a police review board.

The IACP-U.S. Conference of Mayors' early 1960s survey appeared just as academic interest in American policing was taking off. By 1970, the first of a torrent of research on police behavior began to appear in scholarly and professional journals (Sherman 1980a: 69). A quarter-century later, that research has produced an avalanche of publications. On the critical issue of the police use of excessive force, however, the research tells us far less than we would like to know about a problem that has been at the center of a long-standing debate between police and communities of color.

The questions that concern persons of color and researchers alike are fairly easy to specify. Are white police officers inclined to be racially and ethnically prejudiced? Do they discriminate against nonwhite citizens? Are incidents of excessive force the consequence of a few "rotten apples" in the ranks of policing, or does the police system encourage and support such behavior? To what extent is the disproportionately high number of Black (and, increasingly, Latino) victims of excessive force due to internal police practices (e.g., police are more inclined to use excessive force against nonwhite citizens) or to external circumstances (e.g., a greater involvement by persons of color in criminal activity)? Are "minority" police officers disproportionately represented among those who use excessive force? Is there an organizational or occupational climate (i.e., a police culture) or a tank-and-file climate (a police subculture) that actively encourages or tacitly condones the use of excessive force?

Problems of Inquiry

The search for answers to these questions has encountered innumerable problems that aggrieved citizens would consider insignificant, if not trivial, but which are of fundamental importance to scholars and legal system officials. One has to do with collecting the facts. As late as 1978, the Federal Bureau of Investigation would not release data on the police use of force (Takagi 1978); much has changed in this regard at both the federal and local levels, although there is still a need for more standardization and goal-oriented compilation and reporting of data (Geller and Scott 1992).[5] In 1992, there was a pitched dispute between the chair of the House Government Operations Committee and the U.S. Department of Justice over the release of a review of 15,000 complaints against police (some, but not all, concerning excessive force) received by the Department's Civil Rights Division, its Federal Bureau of Investigation, and United States Attorneys over the previous six years (*Seattle Times,* March 4, 1992: A9; DeParle 1992).

A similar controversy surrounded a Chicago Police Department internal study of fifty persons allegedly abused by police; its release had to be ordered by a federal judge (*Chicago Sun-Times,* February 8, 1992: 4). By contrast, however, Chicago's and many other big-city police departments have for several years been releasing data on shootings in which police were involved, albeit shootings the vast majority of which are considered justifiable by police administrators (Geller and Scott 1992).

Next to the importance of adequate data are the methods of analysis. Griswold reviewed most of the research literature up to 1978 to see whether the police discriminate against "minority group members." For nearly every finding presented, criticism of the measures used or the failure to control for other possible influences, or counterevidence could be offered that pointed to other possible explanations. Griswold (1978: 65) states: "What conclusions, if any, can be made about differential treatment of Blacks by the police? The conflicting evidence paints a rather fuzzy picture, with no clear evidence which can be presented to resolve the issue."

Two years later, Sherman (1980a: 69) noted that the preponderance of police research tended to examine two-factor assumptions about the causes or associational features of police behavior. "The present state of the field," he wrote, "is best characterized as a series of bivariate assertions about the impact of certain variables on police behavior about which a moderate amount of empirical evidence has accumulated." A decade later, the evidence is much more extensive; the findings, however, continue to show what Sherman termed "weak relationships between a wide range of the hypothesized causes and police behavior" (see also Sherman 1980b). In lay terms, this simply means that researchers do not know or cannot assert much, with empirical reliability, about whether there are racial reasons for police behavior because other possible explanations cannot be ruled out.[6]

After data have been collected and analyzed, there is the problem of the generalizability of findings. Most studies, for reasons of accessibility, manageability, and funding, are of local police agencies or samples of police documents, officer attitudes, court cases, or other data sources in one or several police jurisdictions. Occasionally, as with the studies by Fyfe on the police use of deadly force, the insights or conclusions gathered from a single department or several-department study are sufficient to prompt significant policy initiatives (Fyfe 1982). Often, however, the findings from a single department have—or are treated as having—significance only for the department. The cumulative evidence from single-department inquiries may confound rather than clarify an issue, reducing the likelihood that any general conclusions can be drawn.

I do not mean to imply, however, that it is impossible for generalizable, single-agency studies to be devised to answer questions about whether race is a contributing factor in police use of improper force. If the evidence from a series of such studies seems impossible and inconsistent—as it often does—then perhaps researchers are asking the wrong questions. Perhaps one of the questions to ask would be under what *conditions* race is a factor in abuses of force. It may be that the effect of race is contingent on the social context, as some studies of sentencing have revealed, or it may be, as Fyfe has found in the context of police use of *deadly* force, that the effect of race is contingent on organizational context (e.g., the values expressed by the police chief). Much remains to be learned, given the primitive nature of the research data to date.

Finally, there is the awkward, seldom discussed, but not infrequent problem of research bias. Research is generally viewed as important for, among other reasons, its capacity to set aside political or other assumptions in order to examine an issue dispassionately and without preconceived notions.[7] Since the monumental study of Gunnar Myrdal on race in America (1962), we have known this general proposition is considerably weaker when questions of race are at stake (pp. 1035–64). Scholars are seldom comfortable with the reminder that their work might be affected by other than scientific dictates; the comparative inattention to the issue of police use of excessive force against persons of color, for example, when placed against the unending examination of correlates between race and crime, suggests that research and the setting of research priorities may not be value-free.

This is not a sweeping indictment of the entire research community. To be sure, virtually every study of police behavior, in general, and of the use of force in particular, has attempted to address the effects of race, and many of these studies have been motivated by the issue of differential treatment by race. Some of the scholarly inattention to the use of nonlethal force and the effects of race may be due to the paucity of existing data and the difficulty of primary data collection. Still, as the will to learn about a problem rises, the funds to enable the learning may increase (depending largely, of course, on the power of those who wish the learning to occur).

What Do We Know?

The evidence is indisputable that, compared to general population distributions, persons of color are disproportionately represented among those subjected to police use of force where the discharge of a firearm is involved (Binder and Scharf 1982; Mendez 1983; Trujillo 1981; Geller and Karales 1981b; Fyfe 1981a, 1981b; Geller and Scott 1992). Beyond this finding, researchers can assert little empirically about the police use of appropriate and excessive force that is not in dispute.

For reasons related to the protocols of research, many inquiries regarding excessive force have focused on police shootings, because shooting incidents tend to be unambiguous as to whether force is involved (although whether the force is excessive remains an open question), and since the early 1980s the data (police shooting review reports, autopsy and coroners' inquest reports, newspaper accounts, etc.) have been relatively abundant and accessible. A large number of police shooting studies (summarized in Geller and Scott 1992) find that nonwhites constitute a disproportionately high number—compared to their percentages in the general populace—of victims of such incidents.

If we pursue the matter further, however, we find many individual, situational, organizational, or legal circumstances that have a potential impact on this general finding. Friedrich, in the same year in which Sherman summarized the state-of-research knowledge regarding four aspects of police behavior (service, detection, arrest, and violence—Sherman 1980a), offered a summary analysis of research on police use of force. Friedrich reviewed the three primary explanations advanced for variations in the use-of-force phenomenon: individual characteristics of police officers, situational characteristics of encounters between police and citizens, and the organizational culture of police work. He concluded, a decade after extensive research inquiries had been undertaken on the topic, that "many factors commonly thought to affect the use of force have little effect" (1980).

As noted above, what every study of police use of fatal force has found is that persons of color (principally Black males) are a disproportionately high percentage of the persons shot by police compared to their representation in the general population (Goldkamp 1970; Kobler 1975; Peirson 1978; Takagi 1978; Fyfe 1978, 1981a, 1981b, 1982; Geller and Karales 1981b; Binder and Scharf 1982; Binder and Fridell 1984; Horvath 1987; Sulton and Cooper n.d.; Geller and Scott 1992). Where the studies diverge are the reasons for such disproportionality. Fyfe found uses of force to depend in part on real and immediate police hazard in specific incidents in one police jurisdiction (1981c) and in part on internal police practices in another (1982). Takagi (1978) questioned both the assumption-of-danger thesis as well as the culture-of-violence explanation, pointing to a number of compounding problems in the data which make for poor inquiries on the issue. Geller and Karales (1981b) found that Blacks and whites were equally likely to be shot by police, given their exposure to forcible felony arrests. In a related Chicago study, Geller (1981) found most variances in shooting participation by officers of different races to be explainable by the residency and deployment patterns of the officers involved. Binder and Scharf (1982) attribute the disproportionality of Blacks who are shot by police to community characteristics (e.g., the high rates of violence in inner cities); Goldkamp (1970) tentatively advanced a corresponding explanation based on arrest rates for violent crime.

Mendez (1983), after analyzing deadly force rates and population in relation to violent crime arrests, property crime arrests, reported crime, and the length of public service, found only two offense rates related to the use of deadly force: robbery and larceny (the first, positively related; the second, negatively related). Binder and Fridell (1984), in a review of police shooting studies, found any conclusion about a pattern of racial discrimination in police shootings to be confounded by variables that support alternative explanations. Horvath (1987), reanalyzing the data used by Fyfe (1980a), disputed Fyfe's conclusion that there might be a geographic relationship between the rates of police shootings and the incidence of criminal homicides; Horvath found the relationship "spurious" and suggested the correlation is probably due to a third, unknown factor. Significantly, none of these studies, with the exception of Takagi (1978) and Fyfe's 1982 study of Memphis, suggest a racial motivation behind the high number of deaths of persons of color at the hands of the police or find any evidence to support the allegation that racial bias operates *systematically* as a factor in police shooting (see generally, Geller and Scott 1992). Worden departs from most prior findings by suggesting that race may play a contributing role in police use and misuse of *nonlethal* force (see also Black 1980).[8]

The notoriety surrounding the Los Angeles Police Department, highlighted by the Rodney King affair, prompts special attention to a study of firearms discharges by Los Angeles police officers (Meyer 1980). Based on information supplied by the department, the study found that of 584 suspects shot at during a five-year period (1974–78), in cases where the race of the suspect was known, 321 (55 percent) were Black, 126 (22 percent) were Hispanic, 131 (22 percent) were white, and 6 (1 percent) were of other nonwhite origin. The race of 21 suspects was unascertainable (they were excluded from the total in calculating percentages). In 1979, 46 (45 percent) of the 102 suspects shot at were Black, 32 (31 percent) were Hispanic, and 23 (23 percent) were white.

Meyer's Los Angeles study also found that a higher proportion of shootings at Black suspects were reported as caused by suspects disobeying the order of officers to halt and by suspects appearing to reach for weapons. A greater proportion of Black (28 percent) than Hispanic (22 percent) or white (20 percent) persons shot at by police were ultimately determined to have been unarmed, although a somewhat greater percentage of Black (54 percent) than Hispanic (48 percent) or white (49 percent) victims were carrying guns. There was no significant difference in the number of shots fired at suspects by race when other circumstances surrounding the shootings were controlled statistically.

Looking at the Los Angeles Police Department about a decade later than Meyer, the Christopher Commission (Independent Commission on the LAPD 1991) implied a pervasive relationship between officer prejudice and mistreatment by the department of minority citizens. Polling of officers in the LAPD even disclosed some belief among the rank and file that prejudice contributed to such abuses of force. The Christopher Commission stated:

> If combined with racial and ethnic bias, the Department's active style of policing creates a potentially grave problem. Because of the concentration of . . . crime in Los Angeles' minority communities, the Department's aggressive style—its self-described 'war on crime'—in some cases seems to become an attack on those communities at large. The communities, and all within them, become painted with the brush of latent criminality (p. 74).

Perhaps the most important policy contribution of two decades of research on the issue comes from a line of studies on the control of police use of deadly force. Fyfe (1978a, 1980a, 1981b, 1981c) discovered a significant impact on the nature and frequency of police-citizen violence in New York City from stringent departmental guidelines and shooting review procedures. This finding was reinforced by Fyfe's study in Memphis (1982), where he found that police officers frequently engaged in "elective" shootings (i.e., where the officer's life or that of a citizen other than the person confronted is not in danger). Geller and Karales (1981b), Geller and Scott (1992), Binder and Fridell (1984), and Wilson (1980) have all commented on restrictive shooting policies as control strategies for reducing police shooting incidents (particularly when such policies are coupled with other training and officer safety initiatives).

Perceptions

Although the role of race in police use of excessive force may remain empirically uncertain to researchers, it is far from problematic for countless citizens of color in America. Murty et al. (1990) found that most citizens are satisfied most of the time with the police, except for Black Americans (see also chapter 5). Lasley (1994) found that the attitudes of poor Hispanics and poor whites were more favorable toward Los Angeles police than were the attitudes of poor African Americans. Lasley (1994: 249) also reports that "numerous studies . . . have found attitudes toward police to be most favorable among Caucasians and lowest among African Americans, even while controlling for community context and demographic differences (Bayley and Mendelsohn 1969; Hahn 1971; Benson 1981)." Wagner (1980), reporting on a city in which Black residents were 41 percent of the populace, found that they filed twice as many complaints against the police as white residents (compare the findings of the Police Foundation's NIJ-funded study of excessive force—Pate and Fridell 1993). Davis (1990) found the urban poor and minorities to have the least favorable attitudes toward the police in New York City; Murty et al. (1990) found the same to be the case in Atlanta; and Lasley (1994) reached a similar conclusion in a study of inner-city Los Angeles residents. The findings transcend social status, as Boggs and Galliher (1975) found persons of higher socioeconomic status among Black citizens to hold more negative attitudes toward the police than whites of similar status.

The recency of several of the articles mentioned suggests that these perceptions persist even though policing has made significant progress in overcoming the conventions of law enforcement of the 1960s. In many communities a new generation of police leaders presides over a new generation of officers who come to police service with higher educational backgrounds and far better professional training than that of three decades ago. The ranks of policing are relatively more diverse today, with respect to both race/ethnicity and gender (see Williams and Murphy 1990: 12). The fact, however, that resentment in communities of color is not directed only toward white police officers and that studies show that nonwhite as well as white officers are likely to be high-rate users (but not necessarily abusers) of force (Fyfe 1978; Geller and Karales 1982; Geller and Scott 1992) suggest the problem is more complex than white/nonwhite equations. One study (Brandl et al. 1994) suggests that citizens' *attitudes* toward the police shape their perceptions and evaluations of their *contacts* with the police as much as, or more than, their *contacts* with the police affect their *attitudes* toward the police. The implication seems to be that changing citizens' attitudes may require more than changing the nature of their direct experiences.

Issues

If the bulk of the social science evidence remains unclear as to the salience of race in excessive force situations, the issues surrounding color and the police abuse of power are far less so. To some extent, the sifting of the evidence has contributed to a sharpening of the issues which, in turn, have become specific foci of attention for analysts, activists, and police administrations alike.

It had been commonplace in law enforcement for decades to blame the failures of police work—from corruption scandals to brutality charges—on a few "bad cops." By focusing too much on rotten apples, one can miss the possibility that the barrel is rotten and is spoiling the contents. These are perspectives on *causation*—officer predisposition versus socialization to a brutal work group. No matter which is the case, it is important to know whether officers accused of using excessive force are likely to be multiple offenders. Conventional wisdom and healthy suspicion combine, in this instance, to underscore a belief that the disproportionately high number of citizens of color involved in excessive force incidents are victims of a relatively small proportion of officers, who commit these offenses several times.

An early clue to the repeat-offender phenomenon came from a source that, while it would not rank high on the scale of academic research, proved to be an important source of data. In February 1983, an investigative report on WMAQ-TV in Chicago was announced as the exposure of "a police system which fails to deal with the cops who are beating justice." The five-part telecast was based on a review of all lawsuits brought in federal court over a five-year period (1978–82) in which police brutality was alleged (see chapter 13 for additional discussion of such litigation). In all, 435 Chicago police officers were identified in the suits, 107 of whom subsequently were found to have been charged in two or more official complaints during the previous ten years, either in court or at the police department. Further investigation found that 13 of 68 officers in a single police district had been the subject of complaints three or more times over a two-year period.

The investigative report was not research in any academic sense, nor did it claim to be. Ironically, it did not set out to deal with police brutality nor, after shifting to the excessive force issue, with repeat offenders. Both were accidental discoveries that led to a report which set the agenda for Chicago mayoral politics during the winter of 1983 (Leff et al. 1986) and made a contribution to knowledge about excessive force complaints.

Academic research provides some evidence to support the Chicago discovery about repeat offenders. In a study of police shootings in Philadelphia between 1970 and 1978, Waegel (1984a) discovered that 0.2 percent of the sworn force (13 of 8,000 officers) accounted for 10 percent of all shooting incidents. Sixty-seven officers in Philadelphia—0.8 percent of the force—were involved in more than one shooting incident and accounted for 34 percent of all shootings.

A more recent study of the Los Angeles Police Department finds the same basic pattern. From 1986 through 1990, allegations of excessive force

or improper tactics were filed against approximately 1,800 officers, more than 1,400 of whom had only one or two complaints. But 183 officers had 4 or more allegations, 44 had 6 or more, 16 had 8 or more, and one officer had 16 complaints. The 10 percent of officers with the highest number of excessive force or improper tactics allegations accounted for 27.5 percent of all such complaints (Independent Commission on the LAPD 1991).

The data involve only two urban police forces. Moreover, they do not control for the areas in which the officers were assigned, the race of the involved officers or civilians, the level of violence or the rates of arrest in the assigned areas, whether the officers were on or off duty when the alleged abuses of force occurred, whether the persons against whom force was used were found to be armed or unarmed, or any of a number of other variables (see also Renner and Gierach 1975).

The raw complaint data, however, even without measuring possible influences, are sufficiently striking that police administrators and others in a position to influence law enforcement policy are not apt to await regression analyses to screen out relevant from irrelevant factors, important as they are. Assuming a sizable organization, a department is at its peril if less than 1 percent of its officers are involved in over one-third of its shooting or other use-of-force incidents. In all but very small organizations, for so minuscule a portion of personnel to account for a potentially sizable performance problem would be a red flag alerting administrators to the need for immediate analysis and possible personnel action. Absent clear evidence that an officer's assignment to unusually dangerous tasks has occasioned his or her string of violent encounters, police managers would do well to err on the side of caution and, at least for an evaluative period, change the officer's assignment. And, in the interest of the officer's career longevity and the department's preservation of good public relations, empathetic police commanders might well want to reassign the officer in question even if they conclude that it was the *assignment* rather than a *predisposition* to violent tactics that accounted for the pattern of violent encounters. To simply ignore the reasons for a growing string of shootings or other serious uses of force by a small number of officers (even if each episode has been determined to be within departmental policy) would pose important questions about how concerned a police commander is about officers who use (or possibly abuse) force frequently.

The issue of how seriously the excessive force problem is taken by police also is illumined by the research literature reviewed by Lester. In a survey of police officer attitudes in a small Southern city, Barker (1978) examined the extent to which officers tolerated "deviant" behavior, i.e., behavior contrary to accepted standards among other officers in the department. "Deviant" behavior in the survey was measured by attitudes toward police perjury, drinking, sleeping or having sex on duty, and police brutality.

The study found that, first, the more officers perceived a given "deviant" behavior to occur, the more tolerant they were of it, and, second, the less deviant the officers considered a given behavior, the more common they perceived its occurrence to be. Third, and most striking, police brutality was perceived to be one of the least deviant behaviors, equal in seriousness to sleeping on duty and, simultaneously, one of the most prevalent behaviors; 40 percent of the force were perceived to have committed acts of brutality at some point in their careers. As brutality was considered a less serious form of deviance, officers indicated they would report a fellow officer for brutality less often than for any other of the stated "deviances."

A corresponding study of officers in a medium-sized department (Lester and Ten Brink 1985) found that officers most likely to report fellow officers for acts of excessive force were also most likely to report them for other offenses, like drinking on duty or accepting a bribe. Taken together, the two studies suggest that brutality or the excessive use of force is part of a range of deviant behaviors that are not considered by some officers to be any more serious than other offenses—perhaps, among some, less serious—and that those officers who have the professional integrity to report excessive force offenses would be just as likely to report other violations of professional norms. A federally funded study under way in Ohio and Illinois should provide additional findings of interest concerning the prevalence of police abuse of force and officers' willingness to report their colleagues' misconduct to supervisors.

Perhaps more important, Carter (1976) learned that 62 percent of his officer respondents

(in a single police agency) believed officers were entitled to use excessive force in retaliation for assaults against officers. If people of color are disproportionately engaged in what police see as resisting arrest, an officer's propensity to respond with avowedly excessive force could well produce patterns of abuse with racial dimensions. Sykes and Clark (1975) offered a theoretical framework, which they termed a theory of "deference exchange," for thinking about such problems. They argue that police expect acknowledgment by the citizen that police-citizen interactions are governed by an asymmetrical status norm—the police are the boss. If people disproportionately reject this norm, then police encounters with people of color are correspondingly more likely to give rise to behaviors by citizens that officers interpret as disrespect.[9]

Given the extent to which the excessive force issue involves persons of color, the relative seriousness that officers attach to the excessive use of force is of considerable importance. If some police officers are inclined to consider the excessive use of force as less serious than drinking, or no more serious than sleeping on duty, some officers of the law and many citizens of color are assessing police behavior by fundamentally different norms. The state court acquittal of the officers who assaulted Rodney King and its bloody aftermath suggest just how dangerous such differences can be. The beating and the verdict essentially reflected the norms of those who do not attach great seriousness to excessive force. The subsequent disorder in Los Angeles depicted just how much those norms of four police officers and eight of twelve state court jurors were at odds with people of color in the nation's second largest city.

Some encouragement may be derived from the Lester and Ten Brink study (1985), which suggests that there is a cadre of police officers who do attach significance to the excessive use of force and who are willing to report offenders. It is about such officers that we wish to know much more than we do: their representation among police officers, their values and other possible motivations, their backgrounds, their view of their work and of the communities they serve, especially if they serve in communities of color.

"Police culture" has long been a topic of interest and inquiry among researchers and observers of the law enforcement scene. The best literature on the police culture has been the writing of police officers themselves, sometimes as reflections on their own careers (Niederhoffer 1967; Niederhoffer and Blumberg 1970) or as the observations of "insiders" (Rubenstein 1973), and occasionally as popular fiction (e.g., Joseph Wambaugh's work). The writings of police tell of an occupational world characterized by immense solidarity among those who enter its ranks, one which comes to divide society between "us" and "them," and one whose protocols dictate a strict code of silence if misconduct on the part of another officer is at issue. With respect to excessive force and persons of color, officer attitudes, values, and behavior may be shaped as much by peer group pressure or the unwritten codes of conduct as by the administrative directives or the professional norms of policing.

The finding in many studies (Fyfe 1978; Geller and Karales 1982; Geller 1981; and others) that nonwhite officers in some locales use force in more incidents than might be expected given their representation on police forces is, on occasion, reported as if it were evidence in support of the proposition that the police are not racially discriminatory, i.e., if nonwhite officers use force (albeit not necessarily *excessive* force) frequently, the problem of police misuse of force cannot be one of racial attitudes or bias. An alternative conclusion might be that the overaggressive peer culture of policing in some agencies is so strong that it pressures Black officers, who might know better, into abusing minority-race citizens.

In point of fact, most of the studies showing disproportionate use of *deadly* force by minority-race officers do not attribute these patterns to punitive or other inappropriate motives. Instead, the studies suggest that residential and deployment patterns in many jurisdictions place officers of color in exceptionally dangerous places—where they are, more than fellow white officers, likely to have to use deadly force *legitimately*, both on and off duty. But the careful presentation of such findings by most researchers cannot prevent others from consciously or unconsciously twisting the conclusions to meet a preconceived text exonerating white officers of abuses solely because their nonwhite colleagues use violence just as or more often. If empirical evidence were to suggest disproportionate use of *excessive* force by officers of color, then it might indeed be valuable to research whether organizational climate and peer pressure—the culture

and subculture of policing—are so influential as to override even racial background in shaping officer behavior.

Several studies also found that the demeanor of the citizen may have much to do with the behavior of the police officer. In common parlance, this problem is known as "flunking the attitude test" or "contempt of cop"; in the research literature, it first appeared as an almost incidental discovery or was reported inadvertently as a rationale for police conduct (Ferdinand and Luchterhand 1970). Piliavin and Briar (1964) were the first to note that demeanor was an important factor in police contacts with juveniles; Friedrich (1980) found demeanor to be one of two significant factors in the police use of force.

The demeanor of offenders is itself a complex issue, quite apart from questions of race. In innumerable instances an officer must deal with someone who is inebriated, under the influence of drugs, or, especially following the era of deinstitutionalization of mental health patients, mentally ill. Force use in these circumstances, if it is reasonably applied, is likely to be less problematic or, at the least, to be viewed with greater sympathy in doubtful situations.

Problems arise more often when force is used in circumstances where initial police conduct (e.g., the reason for a pedestrian or vehicle stop) is doubtful and where the resulting legal uncertainty of the situation triggers a verbal and then physical confrontation. When such problems repeatedly or disproportionately occur in encounters between police officers and persons of color, a serious problem in police-citizen relations as well as in police administrative responsibility occurs. This is best described by an assistant chief of the Los Angeles Police Department:

> We expect people to go out and aggressively identify people, and then investigate them, and that puts these police officers in the middle between what we evaluate them on and what they are able to do legally. And so it results in police officers bluffing their way into situations and, when they stop people on the street, frequently the guy knows, you don't have any reason, and he knows that very well. And he knows they're bluffing and that gets us in, time after time, into these conflict situations that end up, frequently, with use of force, frequently with manufacturing or at least puffing of the probable cause (Independent Commission on the LAPD 1991; see also Muir 1977).

Two other interesting clues are to be found in the research literature. Friedrich (1980) was among the first to note the visibility of a police-citizen encounter to other officers and to the public as a significant factor in the police use of force. Wagner (1980) found the officers in two-person patrols were more likely to be targets of excessive force complaints than one-person patrols, supporting observations in an earlier monograph by the Police Foundation (Milton et al. 1977; see also Heaphy 1978). Finally, in the few studies to assert that the police may discriminate for racial reasons (e.g., Powell 1981, 1990), the bias was found to be prevalent primarily in "nonfelony mid-level types of offenses" (such as domestic disturbances, speeding, driving while intoxicated), perhaps because officers have the greatest discretion in such cases (see also Fyfe 1982; Tonry 1995).

The methodology of such studies typically limits their generalizability, as is often true also with studies of single jurisdiction.[10] Accordingly, it is prudent to consider these studies primarily as offering clues and informed speculations about the circumstances that surround certain police behavior. These clues are sufficient, however, to permit a hypothetical typology or profile of the circumstances under which the use of excessive force is most likely to occur.

> Police use of excessive force is likely to occur in a proactive encounter (initiated by the officer and a citizen) when more than one officer is present. The officers will be from a department in which abuse of physical force is considered a minor to mid-level offense. Perhaps most important, the suspect will not act with complete deference toward the officer and probably will be disrespectful.

This hypothesized typology also describes with accuracy the Rodney King incident. The episode began with a police chase of King's vehicle by two California Highway Patrol officers; when King's vehicle was finally halted, ten minutes after pursuit began, twenty-two police officers were at the scene. All but two were officers of the Los Angeles Police Department. Testimony to the Christopher Commission by a retired thirty-eight-year veteran of the LAPD who served as assistant chief indicates the extent to which excessive force was, at the time (1991), considered a relatively minor problem:

> I don't see anyone bringing these people up and saying, "Look, you are not . . . measuring up . . ." I don't see that occurring.
>
> The sergeants . . . are not held accountable so why should they be that much concerned . . . ?
> I have a feeling that they don't think that much is going to happen . . . if they try to take action and perhaps [they think they won't] even be supported by the lieutenant or the captain . . . when they do take action against some individual. (Report of the Independent Commission 1991: 32)

A second assistant chief of the department testified: "and, so that's an area that I believe we have failed miserably in, is holding people accountable for the action of these people" (ibid.: 33).

Finally, there are the computer and radio messages transmitted between officers immediately following the beating of King. The comments of the officers ("he pissed us off, so I guess he needs an ambulance now"; "we had to chase him. . . . I think that kind of irritated us a little") reflect their perception that King had not acted toward them with the proper deference.

FUTURE DIRECTIONS FOR RESEARCH

While police chiefs and commanders continue to grapple with the volatile problem of excessive force and with particularly explosive racial and ethnic features, scholars and researchers will continue to probe the multiple aspects of this phenomenon. What new lines of inquiry might be explored that could produce insights helpful to police administrators and policymakers?

In addition to those suggested earlier (e.g., learning more about officers who will stand up against peer pressure and criticize colleague's abuses of force), the most promising pursuits may be avenues of professionalism and community policing. While community policing in some respects is a catch phrase for a host of new (and often untested) police strategies and tactics (Goldstein 1993; Mastrofski 1993; compare Sparrow et al. 1993), it has the primary virtue of focusing attention on the relationship between those who deliver police services and the public. Professionalism, on the other hand, is a matter of continuing interest in policing. Taken together, community policing and professionalism constitute major elements in a research agenda that, politically, police officers can view positively rather than as adverse to their interests (Kelling and Kliesmet also advance this point). Substantively, such a research agenda would be based on the premise that police professionalism is measured, in part, by the way in which police services are delivered to various communities. The interests of both the police and the public may be served by research efforts that examine the quality of policing through the eyes of different segments of the service populations.[11]

Inquiries on the police and "minority" problems in the past seldom have been undertaken by asking what the interests and priorities of minorities might be. For example, it will be instructive to learn how communities of color assess "effective" policing. What priorities would citizens of color set for the police in their communities? By what criteria would such citizens measure police performance? How do citizens of color assess police professional conduct? How significant is the race or ethnicity of a police officer in measures of police effectiveness by citizens of color?

Quite possibly, one would find little divergence between the views of citizens of color (or within communities of color[12]) and the views of professional-minded police officers on these questions. It is also possible that some unexpected, helpful insights might emerge concerning differences between police and public opinions.

When the community policing and problem-oriented policing notions were first advanced, some scholars were surprised to discover the priority the residents placed on the removal of abandoned cars in their neighborhoods—symbols of community decay and public neglect that did not rank high on the priorities of the police; in all likelihood, few researchers would have attached much importance to them (see, generally, Goldstein 1990; Wilson and Kelling 1982). Similar discoveries might come from research inquiries that begin with identifying the concerns of people of color about policing (see Williams and Murphy 1990).

CONCLUSION

Research often proves frustrating or disappointing to those who do not engage in it (and not infrequently to those who do). What may appear as obvious or self-evident can, on careful analysis, turn out to be neither. Social science research

is important to the extent that it forces those who are not content with unproven answers or unprovable propositions to continue probing the hard question that confront societies.

In the wake of the state court trial of the LAPD officers who beat Rodney King and the subsequent riot, reporting on almost three decades of research most (but not all) of which fails to document a systematic relationship between race and the police use of excessive force risks being dismissed, if not scorned, in some quarters as of the same piece as the acquittal of King's assailants. To reject this body of research findings—or the present summary of it—because it seems to fly in the face of common knowledge would be a serious error, for at least two reasons.

In the absence of being able to confirm that racist acts—behaviors that are racially motivated—are pervasive in policing, we nevertheless have to deal with racially linked outcomes in law enforcement. The disproportionately high number of complaints filed by citizens of color which allege police misconduct (documented by Pate and Fridell 1993), the disproportionately high number of persons of color who are shot at, injured, or killed by police, the significant number of civil damage suits involving excessive force claims in which plaintiffs of color receive significant monetary awards all point to a police-minority community problem of considerable proportions. The problem of disproportionate harm to persons of color at the hands of police is much greater in some communities than in others; police and community leaders have worked at its resolution more urgently in some cities than in others.

In the final analysis, it may be more important to know that police abuse of force can be curbed or controlled (without impeding good, necessary police work) than it would be to establish whether it is race-neutral or race-biased (Tonry 1995). In terms of the concerns of communities of color, this is probably the most significant finding of the research literature on police use of force. Stringent guidelines on the use of force, accompanied by administrative directives that make clear to the rank-and-file that the guidelines will be enforced and followed by a review mechanism that assesses use-of-force situations and apportions the appropriate remedial or punitive action, succeeded in sharply curtailing police shootings (justified or otherwise) in many locales. As others in this volume have observed, it is important to realize that these positive results were obtained with the relatively visible police decisions to use deadly force; as yet we have little or no social science evidence that similar results can be obtained with nonlethal force.

Perhaps we will discover if such control mechanisms are effective against nonlethal abuses of force only when more police leaders take bold initiatives to shift police culture specifically on use-of-force issues and, more generally, on matters of police protection of the diverse communities they are sworn to serve. The at best dubious testimony of Los Angeles police detective Mark Fuhrman during the trial of *People of the State of California v. Orenthal James Simpson,* while not an abuse-of-force issue in physical terms, reflects an equally critical dimension of the problem of race and abuse of power in policing. Like periodic revelations of corruption in police ranks, Fuhrman's statements are powerful indicators that, in spite of the gains in policing over the past three decades, race remains the litmus test of progress or its lack in efforts to professionalize modern law enforcement. If techniques can be found to reduce police abuse of force against persons of *all* backgrounds, significant headway might be made in reducing a major problem in local policing, municipal governance, and American race relations.

NOTES

I am grateful to my graduate research assistants, Catherine Cornwall and Steven Klusman, for their stellar contributions to this essay. The typology of excessive force situations in the "Issues" section of this chapter is the work of Steven Klusman.

1. Obviously, there is no unanimity of opinion among communities of color on any topic, although there may be more agreement concerning issues of police service quality than on many other topics (Murty et al. 1990; Boggs and Galliher 1975). But Lasley (1994: 250–51) found differences between poor Black and poor Hispanic residents of South Central Los Angeles in attitudes toward Los Angeles police officers. Before the Rodney King beating, Hispanics' attitudes were not as favorable as those of whites but not as negative as those of Blacks; and during the four months following the beating, African Americans' negative attitudes toward the LAPD "were much more profound and 'longer-term'" than were the critical perceptions held by whites and Hispanics.

2. Historically, there can be little doubt that for generations after the involuntary arrival of Black people in this country, the formal, officially approved role of police, both in the South and often in the Northern "free" states, was that of oppressor of these people of color—keeping slaves in their place and capturing and returning runaways to their owners and, later, enforcing Jim Crow segregation laws (Williams and Murphy 1990: 3–5; Richardson 1970: 19). Important for the purpose of this chapter, the early role of many Southern police in the "slave patrols" formally included corporal punishment on offenders (runaway or disobedient slaves) without prior judicial process (Williams and Murphy 1990: 4; Wood 1984: 123–24; Foner 1975: 206). White corporal punishment of Blacks—by today's standards grossly excessive force—may have been a formal police function in the slave states, history has recorded the attitudinal climate that prevailed toward Blacks in many Northern communities. When Alexis de Tocqueville studied American prisons during his travels in 1830, he not only discovered many Northern police capturing and holding runaway slaves, as applicable laws required them to do, but also "was surprised to discover that there was more overt hostility and hatred toward Blacks in the North, where slavery did not exist, than in the South, where it did" (Williams and Murphy 1990: 4).

3. Williams and Murphy (1990: 2, 9–10) observe that "several of the hiring and promotional standards, although influential as antibodies to the rampant nepotism and political favoritism that had characterized policing [for generations], proved to be detrimental to Blacks—just at a time when, to a limited extent, because of their increasing political power, they were beginning to acquire the credential that would have allowed them to qualify by the old standards." By contrast, the first Blacks appointed to Northern police forces in the two or three decades after the Civil War were substantially *overqualified* compared to their white cohorts (Williams and Murphy 1990: 8; Lane 1986: 64–65).

4. Such practices had a long and sordid history. When Blacks were first appointed to some Southern police departments after the Civil War, whites often protested—and occasionally rioted over—the efforts of Black officers to use their lawful authority over whites (Williams and Murphy 1990: 8; Wharton 1965: 167). Williams and Murphy (1990: 8) report that a 1961 study "found that 31 percent of the departments surveyed restricted the right of Blacks to make felony arrests; the power of Black officers to make misdemeanor arrests was even more limited." This study was reported initially by the President's Commission on Law Enforcement and Administration of Justice (1967: 170). When a number of the current leading Black police chiefs in

America began their careers as rookie officers in the 1960s, they were restricted to working in Black communities and could routinely neither partner with white colleagues nor arrest white lawbreakers. Some of their supervisors and fellow officers called them "niggers," and some departments would take a squad car out of service before allowing an officer of color to drive it. The outlaw subculture of some police departments was also a whites-only enterprise, excluding Black officers from any—or at least from their proportionate—share of payoffs. Black officers on patrol not infrequently were reported as "suspicious men" in citizens' calls to police emergency numbers. One former police chief who exemplifies this poignant career odyssey is attorney Gerald Cooper, who headed the Evanston (Illinois) Police Department and formerly served with the Chicago Police Department. He candidly discussed these "bad old days" with his officers at an organizational retreat (Cooper 1994).

5. While the FBI is now more willing to release data, the data available for release remain superficial and incomplete concerning use of *deadly* force (Geller and Scott 1992) and so sporadic and ambiguous concerning police use of *nonlethal* force as to be worthless.

6. Tonry (1995) reports in detail on a line of research that examined racism as a possible explanation of *arrest* decisions and found very little evidence of its *systematic* influence with the important exception of arrests for less serious offenses (a category in which Powell [1981, 1990] suggests that police are more likely to abuse force for racial reasons), the studies generally reveal that police arrest persons of color in proportion to their participation in committing crimes. Crime participation rates are identified through victimization surveys—Census Bureau surveys in which victims report the nature of their victimization and, among other characteristics, the race/ethnicity of their alleged offender.

7. Compare Cordner (1985), on the limited power of research findings to shift organizational priorities except in directions the organization was leaning anyway.

8. Friedrich (1980), studying police use of *nonlethal* force, found that only the behavior of the offender and the visibility of the encounter to police peers and the public were significant influences on police use of force; race was not.

9. Theoretical frameworks are useful to the extent they serve as possible explanations—not necessarily justifications—for certain activities or behavior. Disrespectful citizens have long been triggers to police violence, and disrespectful officers have lit many a fuse on a hot-tempered citizen. Today, "dissing" seems also to be an increasing cause of interpersonal violence for urban street gangs.

10. As noted above, the methodology of single-city studies can be improved to strengthen their generalizability, such as by making the central research questions, ones like: under *what organizational and social conditions* is race a factor in use- and abuse-of-force episodes?

11. Crawford (1973), in an officer and public opinion survey, discovered that officer prejudice stands as an impediment to police-community rapport of the sort required to make community policing work. Crawford found that "prejudiced" officers overestimate the resentment that the public actually feels toward the police.

12. But compare Waddington and Braddock (1991: 32).

For a complete list of references please see original article.

23

NAVIGATING THE HIDDEN OBSTACLES TO EX-OFFENDER REENTRY

ANTHONY C. THOMPSON

The distance between a prison and an ex-offender's home community generally can be traversed by bus. But this conventional form of transportation masks the real distance the ex-offender must travel from incarceration to a successful reintegration into her community. Indeed, in many ways, the space that she must cross is more akin to what one imagines takes place in time travel. The ex-offender, of course, remains the one constant throughout the trip across time. She possesses the personal strengths and weaknesses that she has always had. But because time has effectively stood still for her, she has no real frame of reference for the changes she will encounter. Armed with little more than her own instincts and innate abilities, she is thrust instantaneously into a world that is at once foreign and intimidating in its differences and complexities. Her home community barely resembles that which she left behind. Yet, more than physical changes await her. The community that she enters has undergone significant economic, technological, and social changes that perhaps its insider

now takes for granted, but that will be all too apparent to our time traveler—the outsider. The insider will be familiar with the norms of conduct, the formal and informal structures that exist in this environment, and the relationships that govern how residents interact and thrive. The outsider will not know the rules. And yet, we will expect the ex-offender—the quintessential stranger in a strange land—to enter this dramatically different environment and simply fit in without information, without significant support, and without meaningful preparation. If she does not manage to succeed on her own, she must then face the ultimate consequence—a return to her own time, a return to prison.

The problem posed by inmates being released from prison and struggling to make successful transitions is not science fiction. Nor is it new. What is new, though, is the scale of the current problem. The United States has commenced the largest multi-year discharge of prisoners from state and federal custody in history. This release is a direct consequence of the explosion in incarceration that this country endorsed and

---

Source: From Thompson, A. C., "Navigating the hidden obstacles to ex-offender reentry," in *Boston College Law Review*, copyright © 2004. Reprinted with permission.

experienced over the last two decades. In the twenty-five-year period between 1972 and 1997, the number of state and federal prisoners soared from 196,000 to a record 1,159,000.[1] In the year 2000 alone, corrections officials discharged approximately 600,000 individuals, with most returning to core communities from which they came.[2] The repercussions of this massive release effort are only now beginning to be felt. Staggering numbers of ex-offenders have been returning to the communities from which they originally came, having completed their sentences.[3] Research suggests that a large share of reentering offenders come from a relatively small number of neighborhoods.[4] Typically, these communities are located within central cities in a core group of states already straining under the load of their existing social and economic problems.[5] Without in-depth planning, these neighborhoods will remain ill prepared to take on the additional demands of the burgeoning reentering ex-offender population.

Prison officials, criminal justice experts, elected officials, and other interested community activists are rapidly coming to this realization. To head off the huge upheavals that this record number of releases could spark, many actors in the criminal justice system are beginning to engage in some form of planning to prepare both returning individuals and their communities for this change.[6] Unfortunately, the efforts are belated. Worse still, they may be inadequate to the task. One of the principal complications for which communities must prepare is that significant numbers of ex-offenders will rejoin their communities without the safety net of minimal supervision or support mechanisms to aid in this reintegration. Of the more than 600,000 prisoners returning home annually, about 130,000 individuals will be released simply without any form of oversight after having completed their sentences fully.[7] These individuals will not be on parole; they will not be subject to any release conditions; they will have no duty to report to—or work with—a parole officer.[8] Instead, record numbers of ex-offenders will be left on their own to navigate their release and reintegration into the very communities in which they first found themselves enmeshed in the criminal justice system.

Of course, the lack of supervision is not an entirely new phenomenon. Even when the criminal justice system expected the vast majority of ex-offenders to report to parole officers, the interaction too often degenerated into little

more than a superficial reporting relationship. Individuals on parole would be required to meet with their parole officers according to a set schedule and to report their activities.[9] Failure to appear for a parole meeting or to comply with parole conditions could lead to sanctions or revocation of parole.[10] But the sort of guidance or help that one might imagine a parole officer could supply too often was rendered impossible due to case overload and a lack of both will and resources to engage in any meaningful intervention in the lives of individuals released on parole.[11] Thus, even under a traditional model, society has relied on ex-offenders largely to manage their own reintegration.[12]

This reliance has been greatly misplaced. It ignores the reality that an overwhelming number of ex-offenders entered prison with disabilities that continue to plague them upon reentry into their communities. A prison record, in addition to minimal education and a lack of job skills, limits ex-offenders' employability in many cases.[13] In addition, society has created a vast network of collateral consequences that severely inhibit an ex-offender's ability to reconnect to the social and economic structures that would lead to full participation in society.[14] These structural disabilities often include bars to obtaining government benefits, voting disenfranchisement, disqualification from educational grants, exclusion from certain business and professional licenses, and exclusion from public housing.[15] Without structural support or intervention, these individuals face a wide range of obstacles making it virtually impossible for them to pursue legitimate means of survival.

Economic obstacles are complicated by the profound physical and mental health problems that often haunt ex-offenders. To the extent that mental health problems have manifested prior to incarceration, they more often than not remain untreated in prison.[16] Eighty percent of the state prison population reports a history of drug or alcohol use.[17] These individuals often face serious, sometimes life-threatening, health problems. Mental disorders are also prevalent among the inmate population. Rates of mental illness are, by some estimates, as high as four times the rate in the general population.[18] Providing more accessible treatment for mental and physical illnesses could help stabilize these conditions and enable individuals to maintain housing and employment. Instead, little help is available.[19] Equally troubling is the pressure placed on limited public health resources in low-income communities due to the lack of foresight regarding the escalating numbers of reentering individuals with health problems.

This laissez-faire attitude about reentry has had a predictable effect on crime. The ex-offender population has tended to recidivate due in part to an unavailability of economic and social supports. The majority of ex-offenders released from prison reoffend.[20] The largest study of recidivism conducted by the Bureau of Justice Statistics showed that eleven states accounted for 57% of all state prison releases in 1983.[21] Of those prisoners released in 1983, 63% were rearrested at least once for a felony or serious misdemeanor.[22] Concern about stopping the cycle of crime would seem to mandate that we as a society address issues of reentry and devise plans for the successful reintegration of ex-offenders into society. Large numbers of community groups, youth workers, law enforcement representatives, and faith institutions have begun to take this problem seriously. Their motives may vary, but each of these groups has realized the benefits of planning for returning prisoners due, in part, to the impact on both services and safety.[23] Jerry Brown, Mayor of Oakland, California, for example, attributes the city's gradual increase in homicide and general crime rates, in part, to "parolees hitting the streets."[24] As a result, the city has openly acknowledged the need to initiate programs with inmates in the state prison system prior to their release back into the neighborhoods from which they came.[25]

The federal government has taken some initial steps to tackle this problem as well. In 2000, then Attorney General Janet Reno called prisoner reentry "one of the most pressing problems we face as a nation."[26] In the 2000–2001 federal budget, then President Bill Clinton included $60 million for "Project Reentry," a federal program designed to encourage parental responsibility among offenders, job training for parolees, and the establishment of reentry courts.[27] Under the federal design, reentry courts would operate as a substitute for parole supervision, conferring on judges the responsibility to monitor the progress and problems of released ex-offenders.[28]

Although these efforts represent an important component in any effort to address the problem of reentry, little attention has been paid to the role that the legal community should play. Legal institutions have begun to weigh in on the issue of collateral consequences and reentry. Recently, the American Bar Association has promulgated a resolution calling for the reevaluation and, where appropriate, the abolition of collateral sanctions that states automatically impose on individuals convicted of certain offenses.[29] But more remains to be done. Effectively tackling the problems posed by reentry may require a shift in the ways that lawyers currently conceive of—and provide—representation to this population. The shift proposed in this article actually may require that lawyers revive and reinvigorate a paradigm of the past: the lawyer as general practitioner. The funding streams of governmental poverty practice coupled with the efficiencies of modern-day compartmentalization and specialization have caused perhaps unintentional schisms in the public interest sector. In much the same way that lawyers in private practice have come to specialize, public interest lawyers have developed areas of expertise that both deepen their knowledge of the matters that fall within their practices and narrow the range of matters that they will tackle.[30] The political and economic forces that drove lawyers to specialization may have caused them to lose sight of what fell out of the picture as they moved away from the traditional model of general practice.

Given the need to reorient the thinking of lawyers and their sense of their mission, law schools may have an important role to play. In particular, law clinics may provide the precise vehicle to try this new role on for size. Law school clinics ideally operate as laboratories for exposing young lawyers about to enter the profession to the realities and potential of practice. In the reentry context, law clinics might serve as a location for developing new advocacy strategies that cut across disciplines and practice lines. On a more practical level, law students may also begin to provide ex-offenders a resource of support and services in the process of reintegration.

Recognizing that any proposals for change must take account of the current situation and the factors that led to it, this article attempts to explore the root causes of the reentry problem the nation now faces and the new challenges that reentry poses for both individual ex-offenders and for their communities. Part I of this article examines the typical challenges that ex-offenders encounter upon their return to communities.[31] A careful understanding of the extent and range of problems that they face is a necessary prerequisite to the development of any meaningful strategies or policy initiatives to ease the transition of this population. Part II looks at the role of lawyers in helping to manage reentry and offers modest proposals for involving law students in the challenge of reintegration of these ex-offenders into society.[32]

I. THE CHALLENGES OF REENTRY FOR EX-OFFENDERS AND THEIR COMMUNITIES

Much of what ex-offenders encounter upon release to their communities can be anticipated and addressed. The problem is that for too long the standard approach has been to allow ex-offenders to fend for themselves with little or no support or guidance. A critical first step in unraveling the tangle of issues that ex-offenders face is open acknowledgment that there are common difficulties. Mapping a path for ex-offenders to follow given those difficulties would seem a logical second step. Issues of gender and geography also bear consideration in developing any strategy to address the morass of reentry problems facing the returning offender.

As a first step toward coordination, one might begin by examining the various points of contact for the offender on the continuum from prison to home. Such an examination would likely suggest a role for corrections officials prior to the offender's release. Meaningful coordination of programs for the offender means assessing the offender's needs while in prison and providing information about programs that he or she might tap upon release. At a minimum, for example, corrections officials might ensure that upon release an offender will receive adequate state-issued identifications. Healthcare services, drug treatment placements and employment services should all be connected from facilities to communities, so the ex-offender has a map of sorts to follow that might prevent interruption of services and might provide a transitional support as he or she begins reintegration.

Still, the most pressing problems that the ex-offender encounters are the obstacles that interfere with the ability to make a smooth transition to being a productive member of the community. Collaborative efforts will need to take into consideration that the communities receiving the largest number of ex-offenders are also the communities most often at risk.[33] Overwhelmingly,

commentators and statistics demonstrate that the primary recipients of prison sentences during the height of the war on drugs and the war on crime have been African Americans.[34] This high rate of incarceration has placed added stresses on low-income communities of color. The loss of young men who are potential wage earners and supports for families has a detrimental effect on the social organization of poor communities while the offender is in prison. After the offender is released, the problems of lack of employment and lack of meaningful connection with the community can persist.[35]

So the question remains that if conditions continue to worsen, what can and should communities do to provide resources for returning ex-offenders? At a minimum, a coordinated effort to develop public education programs geared to individuals and communities about the impact of reentry and the need to provide services would seem appropriate. These programs should identify common issues facing all ex-offenders in the particular community. For those groups of ex-offenders that may experience unique difficulties—women with children, or those ex-offenders with particular mental or physical health problems—communities should enlist broad support and input into methods to serve this population.

A. Barriers to Reentry

One of the principal but largely hidden barriers to successful reentry is the complex network of legal and administrative regulations barring access to many services.[36] Where specific legal barriers are not in place, powerful incentives drive local authorities to exercise their discretion in a manner that limits access to services for ex-offenders in the interest of the larger community.[37]

1. Housing

For example, the federal government rewards public housing agencies points in the Public Housing Assessment System for documenting that they have adopted policies and procedures to evict individuals who engage in activity considered detrimental to the public housing community.[38] On its face, such a system makes sense. It is designed to ensure safety of public housing tenants by empowering officials to remove a current threat.[39] Public housing officials, however, have interpreted this mandate to cover individuals who may pose no current danger, but who happen to have criminal histories.[40]

Housing has always presented a problem for individuals returning to their communities following a period of incarceration. Private property owners often inquire into the individual's background and tend to deny housing to anyone with a criminal record.[41] But, in the past, when private housing options seemed foreclosed, public housing remained an option. Ex-offenders were placed on a list like other public housing applicants and were considered based on a number of factors including their age, marital status, and parental status.[42] In 1988, however, Congress removed that safety net through an amendment to the public housing statute adopting a one-strike eviction policy from federal public housing.[43] The intent of the amendment was to prohibit admission to applicants and to evict or terminate leases of residents who engaged in certain types of criminal activity.[44] More than just adversely affecting the individual, the one-strike provision has had a profound impact on families. It has fractured family structures and increased pressure on already at-risk communities by limiting housing options for those who have convictions or are returning from incarceration.[45] Families who reside in public housing often have had to sign agreements that ex-offender family members not only could not live with them but also would not visit the public housing unit.[46]

2. Employment

Although it is tempting to think in isolation about each of the problems reentering ex-offenders face, they tend to be linked. For example, the difficulty in finding housing also affects the ability of ex-offenders to secure and maintain employment.[47] The relationship between stable housing and seeking and maintaining employment has been described as interconnected.[48] Ex-offenders applying for work need to have an address and telephone number where they can be reached. Once employment is obtained, the newly employed need the stability that comes from some level of permanence to be able to handle the day-to-day stresses associated with work.

If families cannot or do not provide housing options for those returning from incarceration,

then options are few. The temporary housing stock in most central cities—the primary communities in which large numbers of offenders are located—consists primarily of homeless shelters. Homeless shelters are more often than not unsafe.[49] Moreover, these facilities tend to be crowded and lack any sense of privacy, making it difficult for occupants to regard the shelter as anything other than temporary lodging.[50] This situation adds to the feeling of instability in the lives of ex-offenders when stability is precisely what they need.[51]

In addition to limitations on access to public housing, felony convictions lead to a number of employment barriers. Throughout the 1980s, a number of states restricted the employment opportunities for ex-offenders to show their tough-on-crime stance.[52] Rather than focusing on employment that might be related to an offense, these prohibitions generally assume the form of blanket restrictions based on the individual's status as an ex-offender as opposed to some specific relationship to conduct.[53] A number of states permanently bar ex-offenders from public employment.[54] California, for example, prohibits parolees from working in real estate, nursing, or physical therapy.[55]

On one hand, some might argue that the nature of certain offenses might warrant exclusion from specific occupations, such as barring a convicted sex offender from working with children. The logic of this sort of exclusion lies in its direct relationship to the nature of the offense of which the ex-offender was convicted. On the other hand, some still might argue against these specific exclusions because the exclusions fail to acknowledge the effect of therapy and the potential for changes in the offender's conduct and character. Regardless of how one might resolve this debate, it is hard to construct a justification for blanket restrictions that makes sense. Applicants for employment should be reviewed individually rather than having to face the additional punishment of being barred from a position regardless of the offense. By precluding every ex-offender from specific occupations, states may be preventing too broad an array of potential workers from becoming productive members of the community.[56]

Complicating the bars to employment are occupational licensing restrictions that apply to ex-felons nationwide.[57] Professional licensing is the primary method for maintaining some measure of regulatory control over professional qualifications and over the quality of service provided by individuals within that business. Ex-offenders are routinely excluded from many employment opportunities that require professional licenses.[58] Many federal, state, and municipal laws exclude ex-felons from "regulated occupations" by requiring that the applicant show "good moral character" or by barring entry into the profession by anyone who has been convicted of a crime.[59]

Good moral character statutes pose a significant barrier to the ex-felon obtaining an occupational license.[60] These statutes rarely define "good moral character" with any specificity making statutory interpretations of this term ambiguous at best.[61] Without a reasonably clear legislative or judicial understanding of what "good moral character" means, licensing boards and agencies have tremendous latitude in defining the term.[62] Therefore, someone with a criminal conviction applying for a license that contains the good moral character requirement is barred, for all intents and purposes, from obtaining a license.[63] Further, without adequate guidelines, different licensing agencies can apply varying interpretations of good moral character, which can lead to inconsistent application of the same licensing statutes.

The provision that any criminal conviction will bar an individual from obtaining a license can be similarly overbroad.[64] Licensing requirements apply to a wide spectrum of professions—from lawyer to bartender, nurse to barber, and plumber to beautician.[65] Professional disqualifications do not depend on the existence of a nexus between the prior offense and the employment.[66] Therefore, an individual might face exclusion from the plumbing profession, for example, because of an assault conviction that occurred in a unique situation wholly divorced from an employment context. Still, professional disqualifications have been hailed as necessary "to foster high professional standards."[67] As these restrictions indicate, felony convictions "impose . . . a status upon a person which not only makes him vulnerable to future sanctions . . . but which also seriously affects his reputation and economic opportunities."[68] The end result of these wide-ranging restrictions on ex-offenders' ability to obtain employment is to further restrict their ability to reintegrate into society.

One unforeseen complication has been that prisons have continued to provide vocational training to inmates in certain occupations from which they will be barred upon release. Consider the case of Marc LaCloche.[69] Mr. LaCloche served a term in the Clinton Correctional Facility in New York after being convicted of first-degree robbery.[70] He spent 1200 hours in prison learning a barber's trade so that upon release he would have a means of building a new life.[71] Shortly before LaCloche was due to be paroled, he applied for a license as a barber's apprentice, but the state refused his application on the ground that the "applicant's criminal history indicates lack of good moral character."[72] At least one judge in New York appreciated the irony of this situation, noting, "if the state offers this vocational-training program to persons who are incarcerated, it must offer them a reasonable opportunity to use the skills learned thereby after they are released from prison."[73] Yet the disconnect continues.

3. Voting

Perhaps the most public bar to reentry is the inability for ex-offenders to participate in the electoral process. Felon disenfranchisement arguably has altered the outcome of elections.[74] States address the participation of ex-felons in the voting franchise in a variety of ways. A number of states disenfranchise felons permanently but allow some limited opportunities for formal restoration of rights.[75] Others either permanently disenfranchise after a second felony conviction or allow ex-felons to vote only after they finish probation or parole.[76] The loss of voting power has ramifications not only for the individual ex-offender, but also for the communities to which ex-offenders return, which will then include growing numbers of residents without a recognized political voice.

B. Reentry Is Complicated by Gender

To the extent that policymakers consider the plight of the returning ex-offender, they treat reentry problems generically more often than not. That tendency has almost hidden from view the unique but quite compelling difficulties that female ex-offenders face upon release.[77] Women who are incarcerated have unique health needs and often experience different mental health issues that may have contributed to or arisen out of their confinement.[78] Yet, perhaps the most significant factor that distinguishes women from their male counterparts relates to their real and perceived responsibility for their children.[79] It is the impact of the parental role that often weighs most heavily on the woman ex-offender and guides her choices upon release—a factor too often ignored in examinations of the problems posed upon reentry.

The majority of mothers currently incarcerated had been the sole caretakers for their children prior to incarceration.[80] Generally, when a father goes to prison, the mother keeps the family intact.[81] When a mother enters prison, however, the father too often does not remain involved in the caretaking of the children.[82] Therefore, families are more likely to be broken as a result of mothers being incarcerated than fathers.[83] Although some children live with a relative during their mother's incarceration, many enter the foster care system because no family member is available to care for them.[84] Thus, an overriding concern for many women upon release is regaining custody of their children.

The lack of planning for reentry for the female population has a disproportionate impact on children and families. Approximately 2.1% of all children under the age of eighteen have a parent in state or federal prison.[85] This means that 1.5 million children in the United States are affected by the lack of any coherent reentry policy.[86] In addition, between 1985 and 1997 the number of women in jails and prisons nearly tripled.[87] Upon release, this growing number of women faces the burden of trying to find housing and employment often at the same time that they are fighting to be reunited with their children.[88]

Additionally, the fight for custody can be overwhelming. Federal welfare and adoption legislation create significant obstacles for women ex-offenders.[89] Welfare laws reduce their access to benefits that might provide transitional support as they seek employment.[90] Adoption laws add pressure to returning mothers by reducing the amount of time that parents have to reunite with their children before permanently losing custody.[91] At the same time, increased rates of incarceration of men and women of color have meant an increase in fragmented families in those communities.[92]

Although measuring emotional harm is difficult, some judgments about the ways in which high imprisonment affects families, the life chances of children, and the economic circumstances of at-risk communities are possible.[93]

A brief examination of the problems that women encounter on reentry may lead to a decision to have gender-specific approaches to reentry. For example, in communities of color, women offenders tend to be stigmatized by their community.[94] Although men who commit crimes are not necessarily seen as good members of the community, they are rarely ostracized.[95] Women who engage in crime are often seen as defying gender roles, which is perceived by communities as deviance of a higher order.[96] In addition, women's transition back into their communities becomes more difficult because they often have trouble maintaining connections during their period of incarceration. The few women's prisons that exist tend to be located far from the women's homes.[97] This distance means fewer visits and limited contact with family members.[98] This distance has consequences such as loss of physical or legal custody of children.[99] Once released, women face multiple tasks simultaneously—getting children back, getting a job, getting housing, getting treatment—which only exacerbates the already difficult process of reentry.

C. Challenges to Communities with Reentering Residents

As a general rule, communities are quite adept at considering and anticipating the potential safety issues posed by the release of offenders. Still, they tend to ignore the drain on political influence and financial support when large numbers of ex-offenders return.

A principal financial impact has occurred as a result of the mechanics of the most recent national census. At the end of the millennium, the Census Bureau engaged in a comprehensive effort to count every living body in the country.[100] The Bureau counted bodies where they were located, which had an often-devastating impact on low-income communities, because prisons are often located somewhere else.[101] The twin circumstances of high incarceration rates of individuals from low-income urban communities and the Census Bureau's decision to count prisoners as residents of the communities in which prisons were located meant that low-income communities lost numbers for purposes of the Census.[102] Financial resources in the form of state and federal aid are tied, in part, to census figures. States such as Arizona, Illinois, and Wyoming use census figures to distribute state tax revenue and other funds.[103] One hundred and eighty-five billion dollars a year in federal aid are distributed on the basis of census figures.[104] Federal programs based at least partially on census data include job training programs, school funding, national school lunch programs, Medicaid, and community development programs.[105] The loss of population numbers can diminish the financial health of communities that rely on such programs. Indeed, as urban communities lost out, some rural communities stood to gain. Towns located close to prisons were able to include prisoners' low incomes in their per capita income figures.[106] Thus, the towns appeared poorer and became eligible for more poverty-related grants.[107]

What rural communities stood to gain from the inclusion of prison populations in their census figures, poorer urban communities lost. Funding follows prisoners who are transferred out of their home communities. In the 1990s, for example, Lorton prison, filled with District of Columbia residents, was placed in Virginia at a cost to the city of $60 million.[108] Such transfers of people and funds reduce the money available for resources that have been proven to reduce crime, such as schools and poverty programs.[109]

The census count simultaneously reduced the political power of low-income urban communities.[110] Even though inmates are prohibited from voting in forty-eight states, including New York, they are counted for the purpose of legislative apportionment and redistricting.[111] The fact that they are recorded by the census as residing in their prisons results in a decrease in the number of politicians representing urban interests.[112] In New York, for example, where 65.5% of state prisoners are from New York City, the census count costs the city 43,740 residents.[113] The loss of political power is particularly severe for minority communities in New York, because 80% of New York's prisoners are black or Latino, but New York's prisons are predominantly in white rural areas.[114] All prisons built in New York since 1982 have been built upstate, and although only 24% of New York prisoners are from the upstate region, over 91% of its prisoners are incarcerated there.[115]

In a number of states, the decrease in political power in mostly inner-city neighborhoods of color is matched by an increase of political power in the predominantly white rural areas in which prisons are located.[116] The votes of rural residents are said to be weighted more heavily than those of urban residents, because, with so many of their constituents incarcerated, rural politicians are able to devote more of their attention to their "real constituents."[117] With a considerable proportion of those included within their constituencies unable to react by means of the vote, politicians become better able to maintain the supply of local prison-related jobs through policies involving lengthy sentences and prison expansion.[118] In New York, for example, the leading defenders of the Rockefeller Drug Laws, which impose long mandatory drug sentences, and which precipitated the prison boom, are state senators who represent upstate areas.[119] The combination of the weakening of the political representation available to the urban communities most affected by these policies with the strengthening of those who stand to gain from them results in a cycle of prison expansion that appears to lack a democratic check.[120]

D. Government's Limited Response

The federal government only in recent years has recognized the enormity of the reentry crisis. In the late 1990s, Jeremy Travis, then Director of the National Institute of Justice (the "NIJ"), began to trumpet the call for increased attention to the problem.[121] Members of the Justice Department and the NIJ initiated a national discussion of an idea: the development of reentry courts to provide at least one response to the challenges posed by reentry.[122] First proposed by Travis and Attorney General Reno in 1999, reentry courts were expected to provide a central location for the coordination of services, support, and supervision for the returning offender.[123] The government provided considerable funds for the development of these prototype courts to give the states and local jurisdictions the incentive to undertake such projects.[124]

In theory, these courts would provide just the sort of organization that was missing upon reentry. Building on the success of drug courts in the 1990s, the reentry courts were to become the latest incarnation of problem-solving courts. This time the mission would be to "institutionalize redempt[ion]" while at the same time to provide treatment and other services to the returning ex-offender.[125] Typically, these courts include four core components: a reentry transition plan, a range of supportive services, regular appearances for oversight of the plan, and accountability to victims or communities.[126] The reentry transition plan was designed to be a specialized program for ex-prisoners that focused on each individual's specific employment, treatment, housing, family, and supervision issues.[127] Like their predecessor, the drug courts, reentry courts mandate regular meetings where the judge monitors the progress of an individual's transition.[128] In this way, judges have assumed the traditional role of parole officers as the primary overseers in an ex-offender's reentry.[129]

In practice, the experiment with reentry courts does respond to the one critical concern with regard to coordination: the courts can serve as a single entity that focuses on an individual's reentry. But reentry courts simultaneously raise a host of questions. Should judges engage in hands-on methods in this type of setting? Similar questions have been raised about the role of judges in drug courts.[130] The safeguard that judicial detachment is designed to provide, namely "reduc[ing] the likelihood of decision making based on favor or bias," is absent from a "hands-on" court.[131] Questions arise about the amount of judicial discretion available in reentry courts and other types of "problem-solving courts."[132] The judge who offers support to the person appearing before her will later be the one who decides whether and how to punish that person.[133] Will that judge "become personally invested in the success" of the efforts of that person, and perhaps react to failure "personally" and "inappropriately"?[134]

Thus, the federal government's response to reentry seems to raise more questions than answers. Do reentry courts require judges not only to stray too far beyond their traditional function, but also beyond their realm of expertise?[135] Judges have only limited training in the areas of responsibility required by these courts and, consequently, may not perform this role well.[136] And finally, are judges in a better position to oversee reentry than parole agents? By limiting the caseload of parole agents and providing them with the same range of service referrals, perhaps the system could achieve the same goals without the establishment of an entirely new court system.

II. THE ROLE OF LAWYERS IN MANAGING REENTRY

At a minimum, comprehensive reentry programming would require identifying an individual or entity with ultimate responsibility for assisting ex-offenders with the management of their reintegration into society. Some communities have begun to take steps to provide programs to support returning prisoners and their families.[137] Some local defender offices have begun to focus staff and other resources on developing reentry programs.[138] Meanwhile, some civil legal services providers have chosen to address problems facing ex-offenders to the extent that their problems fall within the office's areas of expertise.[139] Through probation services and other agencies, local governments also are attempting to coordinate services, but for the most part, these services happen on an ad hoc basis and remain largely uncoordinated.[140]

One group that could potentially intervene to coordinate services to this ever-increasing client population is lawyers. Lawyers are beginning sporadically to think about the challenge of representing ex-prisoners. As defense lawyers begin to embrace the concept of "whole-client" representation, they are recognizing that a client's social circumstances may have bearing on the client's involvement with the legal system.[141] Perhaps this broader conception of representation might lead them to recognize that those circumstances may continue to be at issue even once a client has completed a sentence. Civil legal services lawyers also are encountering a growing demand by ex-offenders for their assistance.[142] Rather than categorically rejecting such clients as having matters that flow from a criminal involvement, these lawyers may need to broaden their mandate to help fill the gap in service to these clients.

Right now, the types of issues confronting ex-offenders cross substantive legal categories. Matters related to housing and employment fall in the civil arena. Legal issues regarding the custody and care of children are also deemed civil. Ex-offenders may continue to interact with the criminal justice system if their release contains specific conditions that must be met to avoid revocation of release status. Although a single client may encounter all of these issues simultaneously, the traditional legal offices that handle such matters are often separate entities that will only address those issues that fall within their range of expertise. This leads the ex-offender from one office to another in search of assistance with reentry.

One possible way to reduce the chaos in legal representation that an ex-offender must negotiate would be to have one legal entity serve as the entry point for the offender. That office could then help map a strategy for the offender that might involve working with separate legal and social entities. The offender would thus have a point person from whom he or she could obtain some guidance in the process.

A. Adapting Traditional Advocacy Approaches to Facilitate Reentry

Practice areas have developed largely in response to the types of issues that both the civil and criminal justice systems yield. With ever-increasing complexity of legal cases, civil and criminal defense lawyers have come to appreciate the need to organize around specialty areas. This design strategy has permitted lawyers to focus their attention on specific substantive areas, learning the law that develops, and shaping practices to benefit their clients. For example, public defender offices generally organize into various divisions that focus on separate aspects of their clients' legal matters.[143] The office assigns lawyers to misdemeanor units or appellate divisions, enabling those lawyers to develop a level of expertise in that arena. To the extent that a defender office has broadened its mission to include a client's extra-legal needs, the office typically accomplishes this mission by assigning social workers to a support division.[144] In all offices, the volume of cases that they must handle makes compartmentalizing the defense function all the more necessary.

Similar practice pressures occur in the civil legal services arena. Civil cases have taken on a level of complexity that demands specialized skill sets of practitioners. As importantly, the restrictions that the federal government has placed on funding for legal services lawyers has dictated, and often limited, the services that legal service providers can offer.[145] Indeed, out of fear

that funding might be jeopardized, civil legal service practitioners have begun to exercise extreme caution in accepting cases or engaging in any activities that might appear to cross a regulated line.[146]

Still, when the client's problems cross the civil and criminal divide during the pendency of a legal matter, standard practice involves a general referral to another legal entity. Far from uniform, this referral process takes a variety of forms. Lawyers will rely on sometimes outdated lists or telephone numbers in their effort to direct the client to help. Clients then must juggle appointments, names, and addresses of various providers to get that help. But what might occur if lawyers developed more robust systems of referral or engaged in partnerships across substantive legal divides?

1. Creating More Robust Referral Processes

If legal organizations find it necessary for whatever reason to maintain substantive divisions, they still can provide their clients with improved assistance by taking the referral process more seriously. Even a moment's consideration of what would be required to facilitate a client's access to and use of referral services would reveal some steps that any organization could take to make this process operate more effectively. Developing and maintaining a strong referral process means identifying the range of services that clients need. In addition, identifying particularly strong and very weak organizations is very important and should involve at the very least a canvassing of staff (legal and support) and tracking and documenting clients' impressions of the services providers when possible.

More ambitious efforts might entail assigning an intern under the supervision of a lawyer or social worker to go to the most frequently used offices. That intern could then obtain information directly from the provider. This more ambitious effort could help the office begin to think more methodically about community relations. In doing so, legal organizations could reach out to churches and community organizations and offer know-your-rights workshops in the community. Ultimately, through formal and informal connections, defenders would become more aware of the providers in their clients' communities. The primary goal of this effort would be to create a viable system of referrals that both staff and clients could access to find help in addressing reentry concerns.

Even more ambitious plans might involve implementing a strategy where public defenders and civil legal service providers would engage in partnerships to weave a network of services for returning ex-offenders. For both defender offices and civil legal services providers, this would necessitate redefining their notions of what constitutes a case. Rather than limiting representation to clients who have pending cases or cases that fall within a specific substantive area, these offices would need to stretch their concept of representation. The new definition would include addressing a client's needs even once the initial legal matter had resolved. What follows is a proposal for embarking on such a new approach.

2. Identifying One Entry Point for Reentry Services

A critical failing of most efforts to address reentry is the lack of a single entity or point of contact for the coordination of services that ex-offenders would feel comfortable using. In theory, the parole officer concept in part was designed to serve this purpose: The parole agent represented a single point of entry for the ex-offender.[147] Despite its goals, however, the interaction between parole officer and ex-offender devolved into a monitoring/policing function. This article proposes a return to the theoretical underpinnings that led to the development of the parole agent, but vesting the coordination authority in a different entity: the public defender office. By providing a single stop for referral, support, and guidance, the defender would breathe life into the coordinating function that parole officers were once expected to fulfill. Defenders in this context would help to assess ex-offenders' needs, link them to services, and provide them with information about barriers, so that the ex-offenders would not have to learn these for themselves in a frustrating dance of trial and error.

Obviously, a number of legal, civic, or community-based organizations could fill this role. but the public defender office seems most logically suited to assume this function. Although defender offices are more often than not struggling to stretch resources to handle a growing caseload, these offices tend to have the institutional resources and structures that might allow them to coordinate a reentry effort.[148] They tend to employ staff and support personnel who could offer some stability to such an initiative. They may already have a relationship with the offenders, because it is likely that someone in the office represented them and may have continued to work with them during their incarceration.[149] That is not meant to suggest that undertaking such a role would be easy. Defenders would be electing to undertake a role that extends beyond their central mandate as contemplated by law and by funding authorities.[150] They would also need to stretch their concept of representation to cover a new substantive area. Still, the defender office seems at least a logical place to begin such coordination.

Some defender offices have already taken steps to work across substantive boundaries on behalf of their clients.[151] Neighborhood or community defenders represent all of their clients' legal needs based upon a geographical "catchment area."[152] These innovative offices can provide a wide range of services.[153] The structure of these offices often includes community members on their boards of directors, which also assists in recognizing the needs of clients.[154] These offices, although small in number nationally, represent a new and different way to provide comprehensive services (civil and criminal) for those experiencing difficulty with reentry.[155]

This approach to providing indigent legal services raises some questions of design. In thinking about providing direct representation to criminal defendants, the design of neighborhood or community defenders offices attempts to address clients' problems in a context broader than that of formal pending criminal charges. Employing teams rather than a single lawyer, the project represents clients in any forum in cases related to their difficulties with the criminal justice system. The design and structure of these offices provide some departure from the traditional means by which defenders normally deliver services. These offices do, however, provide an example of innovative or nontraditional ways to think about providing reentry services.

In many ways, what this article proposes may seem consistent with a view of lawyering that prevailed in the past: the general practitioner. Under that model, the lawyer attempted to help the client with the full range of issues that the client might bring to the lawyer. In reconceiving that concept and applying it to this context, some important distinctions bear mention. First, the defender office would not lose sight of its principal function—to provide zealous representation to indigent clients charged with crimes and facing the loss of their liberty or their lives. This would simply be a service that would be added to the complement of services that defender offices already provide. Second, the defender office would not have to become everything to every client. Instead, by conceiving of this role as a facilitative one, the defender simply could perform the function of referring the ex-offender to those with more specialized training in certain relevant practice areas. So, what is contemplated under this model is that the defender would work with civil legal services lawyers to address the clients' needs. The defender similarly would look to tap a larger social network of services that might meet the clients' treatment needs. Essentially, the defender office would play a coordinating role, guiding clients to the assistance they might require.

Of course, an inherent concern arising out of the general practitioner role is that the lawyer would give less-than-adequate advice to the client who might need a level of expertise. This would make the development of collaborative networks all the more important for both the defender and the ex-offender. One way to think of the role might be to borrow from the concept of in-house counsel in a corporation. In-house counsel must learn the nature of the business and understand and anticipate legal issues facing the business.[156] Yet, in handling many of the legal matters that develop, in-house counsel will enlist the services of outside counsel to assume primary responsibility for the matter.[157] In much the same way, the defender would perform such a coordinating role rather than a principal representational role. Understanding the client's needs, the defender would try to help the ex-offender identify the resource that might best address those needs. Thus, if defender offices were indeed willing to assume such a role, they might offer ex-offenders the single point of entry they now lack.

B. Preparing Lawyers for a Role in Reentry

Although lawyers could play a pivotal role in guiding ex-offenders through the maze of reentry, lawyers typically are not prepared to assume this responsibility. As indicated above, conventional legal practice has carved out separate substantive practice areas, leaving reentry in a limbo space that is neither purely civil nor purely criminal. Yet, practitioners do not bear entire responsibility for neglecting reentry as an area of focus. Law schools have done little to prepare new lawyers to deal with the myriad of legal, social, and administrative problems offenders reentering communities face.[158] Law schools have tended to perpetuate the notion that their mission is to prepare students to engage in conventional notions of legal advocacy.[159] So the following question remains: Is there some vehicle to expand the thinking and approaches of law students, young lawyers, and law faculties such that they recognize the pressing need to assist ex-offenders?

Law school clinics may offer an answer. By design, they differ from conventional methods of law teaching in that clinic students are called upon to represent clients and, at the same time, to develop a critical view of the legal system.[160] Clinical legal education has maintained a primary objective of teaching students the importance of advocacy in helping individuals solve problems, defend rights, and achieve their goals.[161] Those involved in clinical teaching, however, recognize that students must do more than merely glimpse the world through the representation of clients. Clinical teachers try to "sensitize students to what they are seeing, to guide them to a deeper understanding of their clients' lives and their relationship to the social, economic, and political forces that affect their lives, and to help students develop a critical consciousness imbued with a concern for social justice."[162] Given the complexities of reentry, the law school clinic provides an excellent vehicle to think more creatively about representing those trying to reintegrate into society.

In the same way that some legal scholars have advocated for a more activist role for community lawyers through clinical teaching, law schools can encourage law students to take a broader view of the needs and problems of returning ex-offenders.[163] Encouraging law students to work on behalf of ex-offenders trying to reintegrate requires the students to consider problems that may lie outside of conventional legal representation. For the first time, many students may need to consider lobbying housing administrators informally to rethink automatic exclusions from public housing, where the law clearly provides for such exclusions.[164] Law students may need to contact employers to advocate for the hiring of ex-offenders, where the same employers may have shown reluctance to do so in the past.[165] In some instances, supervised law students might be called upon to meet with legislators about lifting categorical employment bans of whole classes of jobs unavailable to those with felony convictions.

Law school clinics produce wonderful opportunities to infuse the thinking of law students with the notion of collaborative lawyering.[166] In the area of reentry, the partnering of law students, young lawyers with nonprofit organizations, and legal service providers can begin the process of forming partnerships to address the needs of the ex-offender population. Once law students begin to learn the dynamics of collaboration and, perhaps, experience its benefits, they may enter practice recognizing that collaboration may be an additional weapon in their arsenal when attacking complex problems.

1. Teaching Reentry

In the fall of 2002, New York University School of Law launched the first-ever Offender Reentry Clinic. The clinic aimed to provide direct representation for ex-offenders as well as to expose students in the clinic to a wide range of policy and administrative issues in reentry. The clinic partnered with the Legal Action Center, an East-Coast nonprofit organization with a long history of advocacy in areas of public health and criminal justice.[167]

The objectives of the clinic were twofold. First, the course sought to familiarize students with the range of legal, administrative, and social restrictions imposed on individuals with criminal records as well as on their families and communities. Second, the course was designed to examine the role that lawyers might play in helping ex-offenders navigate the obstacles that they face. Given these objectives, the course used a number of pedagogical tools to expose the students to the substantive law and the practical challenges of engaging in this work. So, for example, the students covered a range of substantive legal issues, including felon disenfranchisement and laws governing occupational bars and licensing restrictions. Because students

would also be representing actual clients, the course also offered training in litigation to help the students develop theories and hone formal advocacy skills.

Still, the clinic had broader objectives. The challenges facing individual ex-offenders and their communities seem to require twin approaches: working with individual clients to help them effect a smooth transition, and working to change the political, legal, and social environment in which reentry decisions are made. This latter focus meant that the clinic needed to examine the factors that might influence the delicate balance between promoting public safety and stigmatizing people who have paid their debt to society. Such an examination led to classes focused on the ways that legislation and the media shape the reentry issue. To help students develop practical approaches that they might use in legislative, media, and community advocacy, a wide range of guest speakers offered their experiences and expertise to the class. Thus, the class helped expose students to issues in reentry on a micro and macro level.

In an attempt to break down the traditional civil/criminal divide that exists in most poverty law practices, the clinic engaged in a range of simulations that contained both criminal law and civil law problems. The students used current issues and worked to develop a media advocacy plan that included writing opinion editorials that might begin to shape public opinion about issues in reentry. They had the opportunity to hear from a journalist whose area of expertise was ex-offender reentry.[168] They questioned her about pitching stories to editorial boards and educating reporters about criminal justice issues. The students also had a unique opportunity to brief and argue a Florida felon disenfranchisement case before counsel for the ex-offenders. Counsel would argue the same case before the U.S. Court of Appeals for the Eleventh Circuit two months after the students' simulation.[169] This gave the students a more traditional appellate argument experience. Finally, the students designed programs to deliver needed services to ex-offenders and had the opportunity to argue for funding before program managers for two national foundations. This gave the students a different experience in preparation for the varied types of services with which they would need to familiarize themselves before going into this type of practice. In addition to the more nontraditional preparation, the students also had extensive simulations in trial practice including openings, closings, and direct and cross-examination. These simulations also included individual critiques.

One of the unexpected experiences came through the clinic's interaction with a group of young lawyers working in local legal aid and public defender offices. These lawyers were working primarily as "fellows" in the offices on special projects regarding reentry. As these recent graduates began their fellowships, they soon discovered that they had little, if any, guidance on how to address the issue of reentry. The reentry effort in these offices, for the most part, was left entirely to these fellows to develop and implement. This experience underscored the need for defender and civil legal aid offices to accept this responsibility and the need for them to devote resources to training and preparation. Hearing about the new attorneys' experiences helped elucidate for the students the need to bring into practice a different mindset and a different skill set in preparing for the representation of ex-offenders.

2. A Case Study in Reentry

One of the matters that the clinic handled exemplified the range of skills and knowledge that reentry involves. The case involved John, a young man who had long since paid his debt to society and reintegrated into his community, only to be haunted by a mistake he had made in the past.[170] The clinic chose this case, in part, because of the substantive issues it posed, but also elected to represent him because, given his track record in the community, his circumstances presented a compelling, though not unusual, case for relief. The client, who had been employed by the New York City Department of Education in an after-school program, received a notice of termination because a decade earlier he had been convicted of a drug offense. The program in which our client worked operated in the New York City schools and provided a range of services for at-risk youth and for adults interested in completing their education. With virtually no notice and no explanation, the Human Relations Department of the Department of Education issued letters to all employees informing them of their obligation to be fingerprinted so that the Department of Education

could determine whether they had a criminal background. The Department further explained that individuals with criminal records would be barred from school property, effectively terminating their employment. The only recourse that the Department offered employees who received such a bar was an administrative hearing before a Department of Education administrative law judge. Administrators in the after-school program in which the clinic's client worked contacted the Legal Action Center, which, in turn, asked the clinic for assistance. Together, the clinic and the Legal Action Center worked to develop a policy strategy to propose to the city. In addition, the clinic agreed to represent some of the individuals who faced termination. This particular client came to the clinic after a referral by the Legal Action Center.

John's story was not unlike that of other young men of color. He had been involved with the criminal justice system since the age of seventeen, when he was convicted of a drug offense. He certainly was old enough to know better than to engage in unlawful behavior, but still young enough to make the sort of immature choices that typically occur in adolescence. From there, however, John's activities were far from average. As a result of his drug conviction, he attended a special boot-camp program in lieu of a standard prison commitment. As the name implies, the boot-camp program sought to mimic a military environment. He rose before dawn, engaged in a range of physical activities, and participated in mandatory programming. In the midst of this structure—and perhaps because of it—he managed to obtain his high school equivalency diploma. When John successfully completed the boot camp, state authorities released him to intensive parole supervision. His parole agent soon after reduced the level of supervision because John's conduct and attitude convinced the agent that John needed only minimal intervention and monitoring.

John had learned from his mistake. Because of his performance on parole, the parole officer granted early termination. John then obtained the job in the after-school program. After working successfully as a summer counselor, his supervisor asked him to stay on during the school year. Within a year on the job, he sought out and completed a number of training programs. Within three years, he had received specialized training for a wide range of counseling and after-school literacy programs. He completed all of the training seminars and some college courses while employed by the program. He ascended the ranks and eventually began to supervise other program counselors. At the time that he was given the Department of Education notice, he had been working as an administrator in the program for seven years. Despite the demands of his leadership position, he still made time to counsel youth. His supervisors were very pleased with his work, describing him as one of the program's most valuable assets. Upon learning of his situation, John's employers were supportive and made clear that they did not want him to be barred from the workplace.

John initially tried to handle the administrative proceeding on his own. Like most other ex-offenders, he simply was unsure of where to turn. So he took the course that was most familiar: He relied on his own instincts to guide him through this foreign system. This proved problematic. When John attended the hearing before the administrative law judge on his own without counsel, the judge ruled against him. When he was notified by mail that he effectively was being terminated and that he would be entitled to an appeal hearing, he knew he needed help. When the clinic decided to undertake representation, its participants immediately contacted the office of the administrative law judge indicating an intent to undertake representation of John. The court informed the clinic that there would be some restrictions on its representation. Among these restrictions was the limitation on who could "speak" at the hearing. The students had entered the world of departmental administrative hearings.

The students used the tools familiar to lawyers. They relied on New York state law in the brief that they filed to show that the judge had not engaged in the proper assessment of the conviction and John's conduct.[171] New York law required that the hearing officer weigh the conviction and subsequent behavior in determining the proper result. This weighing did not take place in the first hearing. While one part of the team prepared the legal documents, the other members of the team worked with the client to obtain a certificate of rehabilitation from the New York Department of Corrections, which indicated that John had done all that was required of him by the state. Nothing more could have been presented on John's behalf, but the administrative law judge was not inclined to

reverse himself. Indeed, the administrative law judge's findings simply stated that the severity of the crime justified our client's immediate termination. Even with representation, the appeal hearing turned out to be little more than a rehashing of the previous hearing at which John had been unrepresented.

So, the students recognized that they needed to broaden their strategy beyond conventional legal moves. They adopted a three-prong approach to gain relief for their client and to help change the policy that led to John's predicament. First, students engaged in some outreach work. The objective of this work was to collaborate with the program administrators and community activists who opposed the blanket termination policy.

The second aspect of the work involved political action. Essentially, the clinic worked with a larger coalition to help develop a political strategy designed to persuade city officials to cease blanket terminations of ex-offenders. The coalition sought to identify government officials to lobby for changes in this policy. The clinic also assisted in the development of talking points that activists could use to educate officials about the problems blanket terminations posed and the benefits of a policy that would involve individual review of the cases and facts.

The third strategy—pursuing a civil action in state court—was the principal means of obtaining individual relief for John. In working with John, the students advised him that they believed that the arguments that they had raised in the brief submitted to the administrative law judge would have perhaps greater persuasive power in a civil action reviewing the administrative actions. With John's agreement, the students filed suit in New York State District Court. The Assistant Corporation Counsel assigned to the case requested and received an extension of time within which to reply to the students' complaint.[172] During the period of the extension, the students engaged in a series of negotiations with the lawyer, urging that the city consider settlement. Ultimately, the city agreed to the students' terms. They agreed to reinstate John to his former position with full salary and benefits.

3. Lessons Learned in Rethinking Reentry

The problems posed by reentry are complex and necessarily demand multidimensional strategies. The New York University School of Law clinic found value in a combination of individual strategies on both the administrative level and the more formal legal level. The participants recognized, however, that the larger problem cannot be solved one case at a time. There are simply too many ex-offenders and too few resources for the participants to guide them to relief. Therefore, collaborative efforts to change the social and political context become critical.

One key component in the clinic's success was that students did not approach the effort with pre-established notions about the boundaries of their representation. They had not yet been sucked into the compartmentalization that defines and simultaneously limits practice strategies. Instead, the students were constantly brainstorming ways to influence both the outcome of the instant case as well as the overall policies that burden ex-offenders because of their status. Before each activity, interview, investigation, filing, and appearance, the students met and prepared for the various potential outcomes. This team meeting illustrated to the students that working collaboratively with the rest of the team provides a broader source of information and options than working solo on a case by case approach. The post-session meetings after each activity provided necessary feedback and reflection in the students' learning process and also helped foreshadow planning for the next stage of the litigation.

This approach varied dramatically from the conventional approach to individual representation in a legal aid or public defender setting. It also served to reinforce to the students that they are part of a dynamic process that is not limited in scope to a set group of actors or institutions. Rather, their representation of ex-offenders in the reentry context is limited only by their creativity and their contacts in the communities in which they work. In addition, by mixing traditional litigation strategies with media advocacy, legislative advocacy, and foundation advocacy, students immediately recognized that lawyering and lawyering skills are not mastered in one context alone. Rather, lawyers must maintain the ability to be flexible to changing moments in the representation and to be sensitive to a wide range of solution possibilities at those critical junctures. Overall, these lessons were a central part of the clinic and the larger effort to think creatively about the difficult problem of ex-offender reentry.

Of course, the task of addressing reentry cannot be left to law students or law fellows. They may be able to offer some help in filling the representational gap, but the magnitude of the reentry crisis demands the contribution of more than just the least experienced lawyers in the system.[173] Lawyers across disciplines and specialties will need to work with government officials, community activists, and ex-offenders in devising comprehensive strategies to resolve this crisis.

CONCLUSION

Instead of expecting individual ex-offenders to navigate their transitions back into their communities without help, the legal community needs to give them the tools that might better guarantee success. At a minimum, ex-offenders will need a point of entry where they can seek assistance ranging from information about what they can expect to more specific representational assistance particularly in the areas of employment, housing, and family law. Through coordinating the types of interventions that ex-offenders tend to need, these individuals might be less likely to fall through the cracks. As important, this type of coordination will necessitate a fundamental shift in how lawyers engaged in civil and criminal public interest practices conceive of their roles.

A similar recognition of the enormity of the reentry problem will need to take place at the local community level as well as within local and state governments. Until officials begin to see the economic and social impact of shortsighted policy making in this area, affected communities will continue to suffer economic and political losses. Legal educators should begin to think critically and creatively about what preparation and training lawyers for ex-offenders need. As the number of ex-offenders being released continues to increase, lawyers and communities hopefully will learn to collaborate on devising approaches to providing quality services.

NOTES

I am grateful to Professor Randy Hertz and especially Professor Kim Taylor-Thompson. I also would like to thank Anna Roberts and Liyah Brown for their research assistance and Dulcie Ingleton for her administrative support. I gratefully acknowledge financial support from the Filomen D'Agostino and Max Greenberg Research Fund at the New York University School of Law.

1. Marc Mauer, the Sentencing Project, Race to Incarcerate 114 (1999).

2. James P. Lynch & William J. Sabol, Prisoner Reentry in Perspective, CRIME POL'Y REP. (Urban Inst. Justice Policy Ctr., Washington, D.C.), Sept. 2001, at 4, 15, http://www.urban.org/UploadedPDF/410213_reentry.pdf.

3. See Jeremy Travis et al., Urban Inst. Justice Policy Ctr., from Prison to Home: the Dimensions and Consequences of Prisoner Reentry 1 (2001). http://www.urban.org/UploadedPDF/from_prison_to_home.pdf.

4. Lynch & Sabol, supra note 2, at 16.

5. Id.

6. See Travis et al., supra note 3, at 43.

7. See Lynch & Sabol, supra note 2, at 13.

8. Travis et al., supra note 3, at 15–16.

9. Id. at 21–22; see Joan Petersilia & Susan Turner, Intensive Probation and Parole, 17 CRIME & JUST. 281, 282 (1993) (discussing the elements of a generic intensive supervision program to include "some combination of multiple weekly contacts with a supervising officer, unscheduled drug testing, strict enforcement of probation or parole conditions, and requirements to attend treatment, to work, and to perform community service").

10. Travis et al., supra note 3, at 22; see Petersilia & Turner, supra note 9, at 282 (describing "intermediate sanctions").

11. See Travis et al., supra note 3, at 21.

12. See Jeremy Travis, but They All Come Back: Rethinking Prisoner Reentry, SENTENCING & CORRECTIONS (U.S. Dep't of Justice, Washington, D.C.), May 2000, at http://www.ncjrs.org/txtfilesl/nij/181413.txt (comparing parole supervision to more collaborative programs such as drug treatment and pretrial services).

13. See Travis et al., supra note 3, at 31–32; Lynch & Sabol, supra note 2, at 18.

14. See Gabriel J. Chin & Richard W. Holmes, Jr., Effective Assistance of Counsel and the Consequences of Guilty Pleas, 87 CORNELL L. REV. 697, 699–700 (2002).

15. Velmer S. Burton, Jr. et al., the Collateral Consequences of a Felony Conviction: a National Study of State Statutes, FED. PROBATION, Sept. 1987, at 52, 52 (identifying legally mandated collateral consequences of the loss of voting rights, the holding of public office and offices of private trust, service as a juror, employment opportunities, professional licenses, and domestic rights); Chin & Holmes, supra note 14, at 705–06; see 20 U.S.C.

§ 1091(r) (2000) (suspending eligibility for federal loans and grants for drug convictions); Anti-Drug Abuse Act of 1988 § 5101, 42 U.S.C. § 1437d(1) (2000) (permitting eviction from public housing for "criminal activity" by tenants or their guests); Developments in the Law—One Person. No Vote: the Laws of Felon Disenfranchisement, 115 HARV. L. REV. 1939, 1939–40 (2002) [hereinafter One Person. No Vote].

16. Mark J. Heyrman, Mental Illness in Prisons and Jails, 7 U. CHI. L. SCH. ROUNDTABLE 113, 118 (2000).

17. Travis et al., supra note 3, at 25.

18. Id. at 29; see Heyrman, supra note 16, at 118; James R.P. Ogloff et al., Mental Health Services in Jails and Prisons: Legal, Clinical, and Policy Issues, 18 L. & PSYCHOL. REV. 109, 112–15 (1994) (describing a study involving 3684 offenders incarcerated in New York prisons, which found that eight percent were suffering from severe psychiatric or functional disabilities of the severity ordinarily found among patients in a psychiatric hospital); T. Howard Stone, Therapeutic Implications of Incarceration for Persons with Severe Mental Disorders: Searching for Rational Health Policy, 24 AM. J. CRIM. L. 283, 287–90 (1997).

19. Heyrman, supra note 16, at 118.

20. See Travis et al., supra note 3, at 1.

21. Allen J. Beck & Bernard E. Shipley, Office of Justice Programs, U.S. Dep't of Justice, Bureau of Justice Special Report: Recidivism of Prisoners Released in 1983, at 1 (1989), http://www.ojp.usdoj.gov/bjs/pub/pdf/rpr83.pdf. The eleven states are California, Florida, Illinois, Michigan, Minnesota, New Jersey, New York, North Carolina, Ohio, Oregon, and Texas. Id.

22. Id.

23. Travis et al., supra note 3, at 43.

24. Evelyn Nieves, Homicides Rise Again, Threatening Oakland's Renaissance, N.Y. TIMES, Aug. 11, 2002, at A18.

25. Id.

26. See Attorney General Janet Reno, Remarks at John Jay College of Criminal Justice on the Reentry Court Initiative (Feb. 10, 2000), http://www.usdoj.gov/archive/ag/speeches/2000/doc2.htm.

27. Id.

28. See Travis, supra note 12.

29. See Standards Relating to Collateral Sanctions & Disqualification of Convicted Pers. § 19–1.2 (2003), http:// www.abanet.org/crimjust/standards/collateralblk.html#1.2.

30. See Robert L. Rabin, Lawyers for Social Change: Perspectives on Public Interest Law, 28 STAN. L. REV. 207, 232 (1976) (emphasizing the degree of specialization in public interest law firms).

31. See infra notes 33–136 and accompanying text.

32. See infra notes 137–163 and accompanying text.

33. Lynch & Sabol, supra note 2, at 15–16.

34. Jerome G. Miller, Search and Destroy: African-American Males in the Criminal Justice System 80–82 (1996); Alfred Blumstein, Incarceration Trends, 7 U. CHI. L. SCH. ROUND-TABLE 95, 103 (2000) (Stating that the incarceration rate of African Americans is 8.2 times that of whites); Punishment and Prejudice: Racial Disparities in the War on Drugs, HUM. RTS. WATCH, May 1, 2000, http://www.hrw.org/Reports/2000/Usa/Rcedrg00.htm#P54_1086.

35. John Hagan & Ronit Dinovitzer, Collateral Consequences of Imprisonment for Children, Communities, and Prisoners, in 26 PRISONS: CRIME AND JUSTICE 121, 121–22 (Michael Tonry & Joan Petersilia, Eds., 1999).

36. See Margaret Colgate Love, Starting Over With a Clean Slate: In Praise of a Forgotten Section of the Model Penal Code, 30 FORDHAM URB. L. J. 1705, 1716–19 (2003).

37. 42 U.S.C. § 1437d(Q) (2000) (Permitting Public Housing Agencies to Access Criminal Records); 24 C.F.R. § 5.903 (2003).

38. 24 C.F.R. § 966.4(1)(5)(vii).

39. Id.

40. See Id. § 902.43(a)(5); Michael Barbosa, Lawyering at the Margins, 11 AM. U. J. GENDER SOC. POL'Y & L. 135, 139 (2003).

41. Heidi Lee Cain, Comment, Housing Our Criminals: Finding Housing for the Ex-Offender in the Twenty-First Century, 33 GOLDEN GATE U. L. REV. 131, 149–50 (2003).

42. Id.

43. Anti-Drug Abuse Act of 1988, Pub. L. No. 100–690, § 5101, 102 Stat. 4181, 4300 (Codified at 42 U.S.C. § 1437d(1) (2000)).

44. Id.

45. See Fox Butterfield, Invisible Penalties Stalking Ex-Convicts, Sanctions Target Jobs, Housing, Welfare, Voting, PITTSBURGH POST-GAZETTE, Dec. 29, 2002, at A9.

46. See Id.

47. See Id.

48. See Brian Maney & Sheila Crowley, Scarcity and Success: Perspectives on Assisted Housing, 9 J. AFFORDABLE HOUSING & COMMUNITY DEV. L. 319, 328 (2000).

49. Christina Victoria Tusan, Homeless Families from 1980–1996: Casualties of Declining Support for the War on Poverty, 70 S. CAL. L. REV. 1141, 1190–93 (1997); Suzanne Daley, Robert Hayes: Anatomy of a Crusader, N.Y. TIMES, Oct. 2, 1987, at B1 (Describing View of Homeless That Shelters Are Dangerous Places).

50. See Tusan, supra note 154, at 1190–92; K. Scott Mathews, Note, Rights of the Homeless in the

1990s: What Role Will the Courts Play?, 60 UMKC L. REV. 343, 344 (1991); See also Daley, supra note 154, at B1.

51. See Paul Ades, the Constitutionality of "Antihomeless" Laws: Ordinances Prohibiting Sleeping in Outdoor Public Areas As a Violation of the Right to Travel, 77 CAL. L. REV. 595, 620 N.183 (1989) ("[E]ven if shelter beds are accessible, it can be argued that homeless people are offered no real choice if, as is likely, the shelter is dangerous, drug-infested, crime-ridden, or especially unsanitary. . . . Giving one the option of sleeping in a space where one's health and possessions are seriously endangered provides no more choice than does the option of arrest and prosecution.").

52. Nora V. Demleitner, Collateral Damage: No Re-Entry for Drug Offenders, 47 VILL. L. REV. 1027, 1038 (2002).

53. Id. at 1038–39.

54. Id. at 1038.

55. Id.

56. See Id.

57. Bruce E. May, the Character Component of Occupational Licensing Laws: A Continuing Barrier to the Ex-Felon's Employment Opportunities, 71 N.D. L. REV. 187, 193 (1995).

58. See Id. at 193–94.

59. See Id.

60. Id. at 197.

61. Id.; See Bayside Enters., Inc. v. Carson, 450 F. Supp. 696, 707 (M.D. Fla. 1978) (Stating that the character requirement is "So imprecise as to be virtually unreviewable"); Deborah L. Rhode, Moral Character as a Professional Credential, 94 YALE L. J. 491. 571 (1985).

62. See May, supra note 162, at 197.

63. See Id.

64. See Id. at 195–96.

65. See Id. at 193–94 & N.52 (Listing licensed occupations that exclude former offenders).

66. Id. at 206–07.

67. Note, Civil Disabilities of Felons, 53 VA. L. REV. 403, 406 (1967).

68. Parker v. Ellis, 362 U.S. 574, 593–94 (1960) (Warren, C.J., Dissenting).

69. Dareh Gregorian & Pia Akerman, Ex-Con Barber in Hair Tangle, N.Y. POST, Feb. 21, 2003, at 3.

70. Id.

71. Id.

72. Id.

73. Id.

74. See One Person, No Vote, supra note 15, at 1941.

75. See Jamie Fellner & Marc Mauer, Human Rights Watch & the Sentencing Project, Losing the Vote: The Impact of Felony Disenfranchisement Laws in the United States 4 (1998); The Sentencing Project, Legislative Changes on Felony

Disenfranchisement 1996–2003, at 3 (2003),
http://www.sentencingproject.org/Pdfs/Legchanges
report.Pdf (Providing updates from several states).

76. Fellner & Mauer, supra note 180, at 4; See
Patricia Allard & Marc Mauer, Regaining the Vote:
An Assessment of Activity Relating to Felon
Disenfranchisement Laws 3–4 (2000),
http://www.sentencingproject.org/Pdfs/9085.Pdf
(For an overview of current laws and initiatives
relating to felon disenfranchisement).

77. See Leslie Acoca & Myrna S. Raeder,
Severing Family Ties: The Plight of Nonviolent
Female Offenders and Their Children, 11 STAN. L. &
POL'Y REV. 133, 140 (1999).

78. Ellen M. Barry, Bad Medicine: Health Care
Inadequacies in Women's Prisons, CRIM. JUST.,
Spring 2001, at 39, 39–42.

79. See Acoca & Raeder, supra note 182, at
135–36.

80. Id.; Myrna S. Raeder, Gender and
Sentencing: Single Moms, Battered Women, and
Other Sex-Based Anomalies in the Gender-Free
World of the Federal Sentencing Guidelines, 20
PEPP. L. REV. 905, 949 (1993).

81. See Raeder, supra note 185, at 952
(Revealing that ninety percent of male inmates
reported that their children's mother was caring for
their children).

82. See Acoca & Raeder, supra note 182, at
135–36 (Reporting that only twenty-six percent of
female inmates indicated their children's father was
caring for their children).

83. See Marilyn C. Moses, Nat'l Inst. of Justice,
U.S. Dep't of Justice, Keeping Incarcerated Mothers
and Their Daughters Together 4 (1995),
http://www.ncjrs.org/Pdffiles/Girlsct.pdf.

84. See Id.

85. Amy E. Hirsch, Introduction to Every Door
Closed: Barriers Facing Parents with Criminal
Records 7, 7 (Ctr. for Law & Soc. Policy & Cmty.
Legal Servs., Inc. Ed., 2002).

86. Id.

87. See Acoca & Raeder, supra note 182, at 134.

88. See Stephanie R. Bush-Baskette, The War on
Drugs as a War Against Black Women, in Crime
Control and Women: Feminist Implications of
Criminal Justice Policy 113, 113–15 (Susan L. Miller
Ed., 1998) (Crediting the increase in black women's
incarceration rates to the war on drugs and
indicating that black women are a greater percentage
of the female prison population than black men are
of the male prison population).

89. Acoca & Raeder, supra note 182, at 140–41.

90. 42 U.S.C. § 608(a)(9) (2000); Personal
Responsibility and Work Opportunity Reconciliation
Act of 1996 § 115, Id. § 862a; Acoca & Raeder, supra
note 182, at 140–41; Recent Legislation, Welfare
Reform—Punishment of Drug Offenders—Congress

Denies Cash Assistance and Food Stamps to Drug
Felons, 110 HARV. L. REV. 983, 985 (1997).

91. Adoption and Safe Families Act of 1997,
Pub. L. No. 105–89, 111 Stat. 2115 (Codified in
scattered sections of 42 U.S.C.).

92. Tracey L. Meares, Social Organization and
Drug Law Enforcement, 35 AM. CRIM. L. REV. 191,
206 (1998).

93. The family disorganization that results from
the imprisonment of an adult member not only
increases the likelihood that juveniles will become
enmeshed in the justice system but also decreases the
likelihood that they will be able to disentangle from
it. For example, one study reporting that
institutionalization had an adverse effect on the
likelihood that juvenile offenders would commit future
parole violations also found that the most potent
predictor of parole outcomes was the level of "family
problems" they confronted once released. Michael
Fendrich, Institutionalization and Parole Behavior:
Assessing the Influence of Individual and Family
Characteristics, 19 J. COMMUNITY PSYCHOL. 109,
119 (1991); See Meares, supra note 92, at 206.

94. See Regina Austin, "The Black Community,"
Its Lawbreakers, and a Politics of Identification, 65
S. CAL. L. REV. 1769, 1791–92 (1992).

95. Id.

96. Id.

97. Report of the Special Committee on Gender
to the D.C. Circuit Task Force on Gender, Race, and
Ethnic Bias (1995), Excerpted in 84 GEO. L.J. 1657.
1796 (1996).

98. Id.

99. Raeder, supra note 185, at 951–54. For
approximately twenty-eight percent of women state
prisoners nationally, imprisonment means permanent
loss of legal custody of their children. Id. at 954.

100. Peter Wagner, Prison Policy Initiative,
Importing Constituents: Prisoners and Political
Clout in New York 1, 4 (2002), http://www
.prisonpolicy.org/Importing/Importing.shtml; Fred
Alvarez, Census Bureau Counts on Huge
Campaign to Get Numbers Right, L.A. TIMES.
Nov. 28, 1999, at B1.

101. Wagner, supra note 100, at 4.

102. Id. at 4–6.

103. Peter Wagner, Prison Policy Initiative.
Detaining for Dollars: Federal Aid Follows Inner-
City Prisoners to Rural Town Coffers 1 (2002)
(On file with author).

104. Id.

105. See Id.

106. Id.

107. Id.

108. Wagner, supra note 103, at 1.

109. See Id.

110. See Prison Policy Initiative, Diluting
Democracy: Census Quirk Fuels Prison Expansion 1

(2003), at http://www.prisonpolicy.org/Articles/ Dilutingdemocracy.pdf.

111. Id.; Wagner, supra note 100, at 4.

112. Peter Wagner, Locked Up, Then Counted Out: Prisoners and the Census, FORTUNE NEWS, Winter 2002–2003, at 22, 22, http://www.fortune society.org/Deathpenalty.pdf.

113. Id.

114. Press Release, Prison Policy Initiative, Study Says Prison Populations Skew New York Districts; City Loses, Rural Legislators Gain, From New Districts (Apr. 22, 2002), at http://www.prison policy.org/Importing/Pr.shtml. New York is a majority white state (54%), but the overwhelming majority of prison growth (87.6%) since 1970 has been of minorities. Wagner, supra note 100, at 12. During that period of growth, the New York prison population became 5.6 times larger. Id. Of the two million Americans now behind bars in local, state, and federal facilities across the nation, nearly half are Black and 16% are Hispanic. Jonathan Tilove, Minority Prison Inmates Skew Local Populations as States Redistrict. NEWHOUSE NEWS SERVICE, Mar. 12, 2002, at A1, http://www.newhousenews. com/ Archive/Storyla031202.html.

115. Peter Wagner, Census Quirk Sustains New York's Love Affair With Prisons, ALB. CENTER L. & JUST. NEWSL., Aug. 2002, http://www.prison policy.org/Articles/Clj0802.shtml; Wagner, supra note 112, at 22.

116. Tilove, supra note 114, at A1.

117. See Prison Policy Initiative, supra note 110, at 1.

118. See Id.

119. Id.

120. See Id. ("On a political level, it is the urban minority communities ravaged by the war on drugs that have the greatest desire to see drug law reform."). Jonathan Tilove describes a case study conducted by Peter Wagner in New York:

Almost half the state's prisons are in the state senate districts of four upstate Republicans who, if they could not count inmates, would have to stretch their district lines to encompass more people, setting in motion a ripple effect that eventually would reduce the Republican electorate in competitive districts closer to New York City.

And if those same prison inmates were instead counted in the communities whence they came, the population of urban districts would swell, setting in motion reciprocal ripples that would increase the Democratic electorate in those same competitive districts. Wagner estimates the net effect of changing how prisoners are counted could gain urban democrats two seats in both the New York House and Senate.

Tilove, supra note 114, at A1.

121. See Travis, supra note 12.

122. Id.

123. Reentry Courts.

124. See U.S. Dep't of Justice, Reentry Courts: Managing the Transition From Prison to Community: A Call for Concept Papers 12–19 (1999) (Developed by NIJ Director Jeremy Travis).

125. William Schma, Kalamazoo County Circuit Court, 29 FORDHAM URB. L. J. 2016, 2019 (2002).

126. Reentry Courts.

127. See Id.

128. Id.

129. See Id. For a description of the judge-centered model. By contrast, "[U]sually a court's responsibility ends when a defendant is found or pleads guilty and is sentenced by the judge. . . . [T]he trial judge's responsibility ends when the trial ends." U.S. Dep't of Justice, supra note 124, at 5.

130. See Morris Hoffman, Commentary: the Drug Court Scandal, 78 N.C. L. REV. 1437, 1533 (2000).

131. Anthony C. Thompson, Courting Disorder: Some Thoughts on Community Courts, 10 WASH. U. J. L. & POL'Y 63, 78 (2002).

132. See John S. Goldkamp, The Drug Court Response: Issues and Implications for Justice Change, 63 ALB. L. REV. 923, 953 (2000) (Raising the question: "What guides the drug court's use of incarceration during the informal, nonadversarial proceedings, which emphasize judicial discretion, and even, some might say, raise it to new heights?").

133. See Id. at 950 N.146 ("The judge in drug court can be encouraging and supportive, even engaging the defendant in direct conversation. . . . However, if the defendant is not participating effectively in treatment, . . . the judge may order confinement.").

134. Thompson, supra note 131, at 79.

135. See Goldkamp, supra note 132, at 927 (Describing a "hands-off critique" of drug courts and other types of "problem-solving courts" that view "intervention into the problems of the individuals involved in criminal cases as inappropriate and compromising to the 'neutral' judicial adjudication function").

136. See Thompson, supra note 131, at 79 (Noting that drug court judges "typically do not have the sort of professional or specialized training that one would expect from someone vested with the responsibility to choose and design treatment programs"); Id. at 93 (Raising the question: "Are we expecting too much of judges if we charge them with resolving complex social problems through the criminal justice system?").

137. See Travis et al., supra note 3, at 43; Reentry Courts.

138. See The Bronx Defenders, the Civil Action Project, at http://www.bronx-defenders.org/ Comm/Index.cfm?Code=006 (2003).

139. The Legal Aid Society of New York has run two programs, one out of its Brooklyn office,

administered by Ann Cammett, and the other, entitled "Second Chance," out of its Harlem office, administered by Mike Barbosa. The Second Chance program is now defunct, but represents the type of program that can be focused on services for ex-offenders.

140. See Petersilia.

141. See Cynthia Works & Cait Clarke, Preparing for the Tidal Wave of Prisoner Reentry: Equipping Civil Legal Aid and Defense Lawyers to Represent the Whole Client, CORNERSTONE (Nat'l Legal Aid & Defender Ass'n, Washington, D.C.). Fall 2002, at 3, 3. http://www.nlada.org/DMS/Documents/1044986725. 85/Fall%202002%CCC20Cornerstone%20final.pdf.

142. Anthony Thompson, Address to the National Legal Aid and Defender Association ("NLADA") Annual Conference (Nov. 14, 2002), http://www.nlada.org/DMS/Documents/1038340494. 03/Anthony%20Thompson%20Re-Entry20% Speech.doc.

143. See, e.g., The Pub. Defender Serv. for the Dist. of Columbia, About us, at http://www.pdsdc.org/Aboutus/Index.asp (Last visited Apr. 6, 2004).

144. The Bronx Defenders, Who we are, at http://www.bronxdefenders.org/Whow/Index.cfm (2003).

145. Deborah Rhode, Access to Justice, 69 FORDHAM L. REV. 1785, 1786 (2001); See Raymond H. Brescia et al., Who's in Charge, Anyway? A Proposal for Community-Based Legal Services, 25 FORDHAM URB. L.J. 831, 840 (1998) (Describing funding cuts to legal services programs that limited their ability to assist the community).

146. This author was the keynote speaker at the 2002 NLADA Annual Convention. The topic was The Need for More Focus and Collaboration on Offender Reentry. Concerned that attending such a speech might violate some federal mandates, civil legal service providers would only attend after an opinion was sought and circulated approving attendance at the keynote luncheon.

147. Vincent D. Basile, A Model for Developing a Reentry Program, FED. PROBATION, Dec. 2002, at 55, 58.

148. See The Bronx Defenders, Resources and Opportunities, at http://www.bronxdefenders.org/Reso/Index.cfm (2003); The Pub. Defender Serv. for the Dist. of Columbia, The Community Defender Program, at http://www.pdsdc.org/Communitydefender/Index .asp (Last visited Apr. 6, 2004).

149. The Public Defender Service for the District of Columbia, for example, has a division that works with inmates on civil matters while in prison. See The Pub. Defender Serv. for the Dist. of Columbia. The Civil Division, at http://www.pdsdc.org/Civil/ Index.asp (Last visited Apr. 6, 2004).

150. Gidcon V. Wainwright, Argersinger V. Hamlin, and Progeny Contemplate Representation Flowing From a Criminal Charge. See Argersinger, 407 U.S. 25, 25 (1972); Gidcon, 372 U.S. 335, 335 (1963).

151. See Susan Finlay, Center for Problem Solving Courts, 29 FORDHAM URB. L. J. 1982, 1997 (2002).

152. See Id. for a description of the neighborhood defender model. Judge Susan Finlay, Director of Education of the Center for Problem Solving Courts, Commented:

This [client] has multidimensional legal problems. They have a housing case and they have a criminal case. Wouldn't it be interesting if we actually provided some form of civil representation for them? And then that model is expanded even more by the Vera Institute of Justice in what is called the Neighborhood Defender Model. There is one up in Harlem which explores the idea that people who come to the defender service are of a certain character within a certain area. In other words, they are going to have a certain set of demographic characteristics which are going to cause them to have a whole host of problems that lead them to the criminal justice system; in other words that sense that we all had in law school that a person's legal issue is a very narrow set of problems the person has, and if we just solve that person's case, it is not really going to solve that crisis that they are in at that moment.

Id.; See also Terry Brooks & Shubhangi Deoras, New Frontiers in Public Defense, CRIM. JUST., Spring 2002, at 51, 51.

153. See Cait Clarke, Problem-Solving Defenders in the Community: Expanding the Conceptual and Institutional Boundaries of Providing Counsel to the Poor, 14 GEO. J. LEGAL ETHICS 401, 401–05 (2001).

154. See Kim Taylor-Thompson, Institutional Actor v. Individual Player: Alternating Visions of the Public Defender, 84 GEO. L. J. 2419, 2469–70 (1996).

155. Id.

156. See Jeffrey R. Parsons, Litigation Management: In-House and Outside Counsel— Who's in Charge? 219, 221–33 (Practising Law Inst., Corporate Law and Practice Course Handbook Series, PLI Order No. B4–6918, 1990), WL 684 PLI/Corp 219.

157. Maryellen B. Cattani, Managing Outside Counsel 75, 79 (Practising Law Inst., Corporate Law and Practice Course Handbook Series, PLI Order No. B4–6986, 1991), WL 760 PLI/Corp. 75.

158. Prior to the New York University Law School Offender Reentry Clinic, No Law School in the United States Offered a Clinical Course on Issues Ex-Offenders Face.

159. Stephen Wizner, The Law School Clinic: Legal Education in the Interests of Justice, 70 FORD-HAM L. REV. 1929, 1930 (2002).

160. Id.

161. Stephen Wizner, Beyond Skills Training, 7 CLINICAL L. REV. 327, 328 (2001).

162. Id. at 338–39.

163. See Andrea M. Seielstad, Community Building as a Means of Teaching Creative, Cooperative, and Complex Problem Solving in Clinical Legal Education, 8 CLINICAL L. REV. 445, 447 (2002) (Describing a model for a clinical program that combines independent representation of clients with community lawyering).

164. Dep't of Hous. & Urban Dev. v. Rucker, 535 U.S. 125, 136 (2002) (Holding that 42 U.S.C. § 1437(D)(1)(6), permitting eviction from public housing for drug-related activity, is constitutional).

165. See Shelley Albright & Furjen Denq, Employer Attitudes Toward Hiring Ex-Offenders, 76 PRISON J. 118, 127–35 (1996) (Describing results of a study of the factors that affect employers' decisions to hire ex-offenders).

166. The major theorist of collaborative lawyering is Gerald Lopez. See, e.g., Gerald P. Lopez, Lay Lawyering, 32 UCLA L. REV. 1, 2–3 (1984); Gerald P. Lopez. The Work We Know So Little About, 42 STAN. L. REV. 1, 10 (1989).

167. For more information about the Legal Action Center's areas of advocacy, see Legal Action Center, LAC Programs, at http://www.lac.org/Programs/Programs_Top.html (Last visited Mar. 18, 2004).

168. The journalist was Jennifer Gonnerman of the *Village Voice*, whose recent book chronicles the reentry of an ex-offender. See Jennifer Gonnerman, Life on the Outside: The Prison Odyssey of Elaine Bartlett (2004).

169. The case was Johnson v. Governor of Florida, 353 F.3d 1287 (11th Cir. 2003).

170. His name has been changed for purposes of confidentiality.

171. See N.Y. CORRECT. LAW §§ 750–755 (Consol. 2003).

172. The Corporation Counsel, a Division of the New York City Law Department, represents the city and its agencies in a variety of legal matters ranging from personal injury to constitutional challenges. N. Y. City Law Dep't, Message from the Corporation Counsel, at http://www.nyc.Gov/Html/Law/Html/Ccmsg.html (Last visited Mar. 18, 2004).

173. At a similar juncture in our legal history, the U.S. Supreme Court in 1972, in Argersinger, extended the right to counsel to misdemeanor cases, recognizing that this mandate would place demands on an already overtaxed legal system. See 407 U.S. at 34 & N.4, 37. At that time, the court offered no real guidance regarding how to implement its ruling. See Id. at 38. Indeed, Justice William Brennan suggested that states enlist law students in supervised clinics to provide representation. Id. at 40 (Brennan, J., Concurring). In hindsight, it is clear that such a proposal could not possibly meet the demand of the system.

24

TAKING IT TO THE STREETS

KIM TAYLOR-THOMPSON

Few contemporary challenges command our attention as compellingly as the need to improve the ways that the nation understands, discusses, and makes choices about criminal justice. The criminal justice system reflects, and is driven by, often unstated assumptions about who commits crimes, who poses a danger, and who deserves fair treatment. These assumptions, in turn, animate choices about the allocation of resources, the deployment of law enforcement personnel, and the evaluation and implementation of policies. Perhaps most unsettling is that vigilant scrutiny of these policies and practices reveals an utterly common if nonetheless flawed pattern: top-down decision making in which the most powerful—the wealthy, the privileged, and the politically well-connected—define justice priorities and initiatives to the exclusion of the vast majority in our society.

Lawmakers offer perhaps the most visible manifestation of this problem. Confronted with episodic increases in crime and violence, federal, state, and local officials succumb to the magnetic pull of familiar strategies. They wage battles against crime, fight wars on drugs, or mount "quality-of-life" campaigns in others' neighborhoods—low-income communities and communities of color—all the while presupposing the virtues of their own proposals. These legislators and political leaders routinely make sweeping claims about the latest campaign to reduce crime without having tested their operative assumptions, much less having invited informed and open debate. And the very communities in whose name and on whose streets these battles are fiercely fought rarely are permitted to play a role in evaluating such strategies or in determining whether they should be implemented at all. What results is a politically constructed vision of "justice for all" imposed by the few.

Still, politicians do not bear the entire blame. Other key players in the criminal justice system have been complicit. All too frequently, criminal justice actors have ignored the poor, the disenfranchised, the political outsiders—the precise individuals and communities whom these actors claim to serve. These appointed and elected public representatives have formulated plans and policies that they deem appropriate in the absence of any meaningful exchanges about whether they have adequately perceived, understood, or framed the problem to be addressed. But once-complacent communities have awakened of late. More particularly, they have begun to balk at their

Source: From Taylor-Thompson, K., "Taking it to the streets," in *New York University Review of Law and Social Change,* copyright © 2004. Reprinted with permission.

virtual exclusion from criminal justice decision making that directly affects them. These citizens have chosen on their own to explore avenues to insert and amplify their voices in decisions about justice.[1] No matter what form this community activism has assumed—police oversight boards, neighborhood watch programs, court observation teams—the initial efforts of these individuals and communities to monitor the behavior of criminal justice actors and institutions have only deepened their resolve to become more actively engaged.

And they expect to have their voices heard. Largely in response to this vocal and dissatisfied public, many criminal justice institutions have begun experimenting with varying levels of commitment and success, these institutions have adopted a wide range of strategies and practices designed to increase their responsiveness to community needs. Law enforcement offices have shifted from a singular reliance on reactive policing strategies to activities that add and incorporate community policing components.[2] Courts have targeted recurring criminal justice issues through problem-solving courts.[3] Corrections and parole authorities, in conjunction with community partners, have launched reentry programs for offenders to ease their transition back into society.[4] And prosecutors have begun experimenting with community prosecution models to align their offices' policies and priorities with community concerns and interests.[5] But notably, public defenders and other indigent defense service providers as a whole lag behind other criminal justice players in embracing a community orientation.[6]

What accounts for defenders' delay? Few indigent defense service providers have taken the time to consider squarely just how well-grounded they are—or should be—in the communities whose residents they serve. Fewer still have recognized the importance of becoming better informed about, and more involved in, community worries and aims. But paying attention to communities and their concerns could add an important dimension to the defender's role that is currently missing. Certainly, defenders have long recognized that in defining justice, too few voices are invited to the table.[7] Reforming our system of justice and making it more accessible to historically excluded voices would seem a goal that defenders would readily embrace. A community orientation could ultimately enable defenders to perceive common needs among clients and residents of communities as defenders examine the system as a whole. In the end, being alert to patterns of injustice may push defenders to perform more effectively on behalf of all of their clients—current and prospective.[8]

But even at the theoretical level, constructing a model of collaboration between defenders and communities is complicated at best.[9] Determining the nature of the interaction between defenders and residents of communities, particularly when the interests of individual clients may stand at odds with those of the community, is far from easy. And on a more fundamental level, as more voices enter the conversation about crime and the strategies to combat it, the process by which we administer justice could actually change. Currently, individual defenders can focus exclusively on the interests of a single client; the client's objectives and concerns guide the defender's strategic choices.[10] This well-defended, but perhaps not fully appreciated luxury of singular attention has historically reduced some of the complexity inherent in the defender's role.

If a defender office introduces a model of practice that invites community input and collaboration, that choice could subject even the individual defender's choices to scrutiny: community residents, for example, could perceive not just an opportunity but a right to express a view about defenders' policy choices. This, in turn, could force defenders at least to acknowledge, if not address, concerns that extend beyond those of the individual client.[11] This is not meant to suggest that defenders never consider issues external to the relationship with their client. Ethical considerations can impose competing duties on the lawyer, but this is typically confined to the exceptional circumstance.[12] Changing the nature of a defender office's relationship with its community could alter the frequency with which defenders consider viewpoints that fall outside of the lawyer-client relationship. In the end, envisioning and exploring the dimensions of collaboration would likely present a considerable challenge.

And it is that precise challenge that a growing number of defender offices have chosen to embrace.[13] They perceive mutual advantage in moving beyond reactive roles and forging partnerships that are at once community oriented and problem solving. Initially, the impulse to work more closely with the communities from which the defender offices' clients come seemed confined to smaller offices that chose explicitly to organize around and serve the neighborhoods in which they were located.[14] Defenders launched these offices as a tacit rejection of the conventional vision of the defender, which, at least in practice, seemed to embrace a role isolated from subordinated communities. But the choice to work in collaboration with communities has become somewhat less idiosyncratic. Of particular interest is that a number of traditional offices have begun to embrace more of a community orientation.[15] Perhaps the choice to reach beyond the defender office's walls can be traced to the power of necessity: operating without allies in the highly politicized environment of criminal justice is tricky at best,[16] or perhaps the choice to engage community problems flows from a willingness to assume less reactive forms of action.[17] Whatever the reason, defender offices of all sizes and in a wide variety of jurisdictions are choosing to embark on barely charted paths, entering into partnerships with neighborhood groups and developing justice initiatives that aim to advance the twin goals of fairness and safety.

In light of this apparent trend, the multiple and elusive dimensions of community-oriented defense bear examining. The first part of this article takes an empirical look at one traditional defender office's experience with adopting a community-based project aimed at addressing racial disparities in the criminal justice system. The second part examines the institutional, organizational, and office design questions that are necessarily implicated in choosing to carve out a community-oriented role for defenders.

I. COMMUNITY-ORIENTED PUBLIC DEFENSE IN PRACTICE: A CASE STUDY

A. Seattle Defender Association's Racial Disparity Project

In 1999, the Seattle Defender Association applied for and received a $146,000 grant from the U.S. Department of Justice to establish a Racial Disparity Project (RDP). With this seed money, the RDP set as its admittedly bold ambition the reduction of racial disparity and racial bias in the criminal justice system. To meet this objective, the RDP identified three strategies: client representation, training of defenders and other justice system professionals about ways to raise and address these issues, and public education. The project grew out of the Defender Association's view that defenders could play a role in shaping policy and in advocating for

their clients in a broader political context by working closely with communities.

The work of the RDP differs from conventional public defender work in fundamental ways. The RDP has chosen to initiate activities around the issue of race in the criminal justice system rather than simply reacting to problems as they occur. This means specifically selecting cases that have racial implications, using those cases as opportunities to educate judges, the public and the office about the role of race in the system. RDP lawyers have not abandoned their commitment to individual representation. On the contrary, the RDP team's focus on issues of race has heightened their awareness of the racial dynamics involved in, for example, a police officer's decision to stop or detain an individual, and has influenced the team's advocacy on behalf of individual clients. But perhaps the most visible difference in approach has been the RDP team's concerted and organized effort to form and maintain alliances on criminal justice issues. Whether the team is developing partnerships with community groups representing the same constituency as the Defender Association or working to maintain open lines of communication with other players in the criminal justice system, the RDP team embraces collaborative work to address racial disparity.

1. The Office's Activist Origins

The Defender Association's broader political orientation has deep roots in its past. The Defender Association began in 1969 as a small non-profit corporation founded by the federal Model Cities Program.[18] Seattle had experienced much of the same unrest that erupted throughout the country in the late 1960s. In the midst of this upheaval, the Model Cities program held weekly meetings for Seattle citizens focused on education, health and public safety. Many of those citizens interested in public safety sought to develop a plan for an independent public defender office patterned after the San Diego Federal Defender office. They then established that the office's principal mandate was to represent indigent clients. But they also insisted that the office commit itself to the practice of law reform by working both to remove procedural roadblocks to justice and to change practices that led to unfairness in the system.[19] A coalition that included the Mayor, the County Executive, the County Bar Association and the Urban League made appointments to the Defender Association's Board of Directors in the spring of 1969.

One of the office's first legal acts marked its initial foray into the political arena. Early in 1970, a protest at the federal courthouse in Seattle ended with seventy-five arrests by the police. Not only did the defender office receive more than enough clients, it used this opportunity to forge a coalition with other community activists. The Defender Association, along with representatives of the Lawyers Committee for Civil Rights under Law, the American Civil Liberties Union, and the Medical Committee for Human Rights, held a press conference in which these organizations criticized the conduct of the police, highlighting the instances of abuse. This mix of politics and law characterized the Defender Association's practice over the next few years as defenders set up offices on college campuses to gather information about and document instances of police abuse during political demonstrations. In this period, the office hired a full complement of staff and successfully represented individuals charged in the political and social unrest that continued to occur in the Seattle area in that decade.

The Defender Association's innovative practice throughout its thirty-four year history has earned the office a reputation for setting the standard for criminal defense.[20] It established a pre-sentencing counseling unit staffed primarily by ex-offenders in 1972 that ultimately evolved into a professional social work and dispositional planning unit. The office pioneered a "holistic" approach to juvenile advocacy that treats the client as a whole person rather than as the personification of her charge. To that end, it collaborated with Columbia Legal Services and the Washington Defender Association to form TeamChild, an independent office that seeks to assist juveniles charged in Juvenile Court with their education and other non-criminal needs.[21]

Individualized criminal defense necessarily took precedence over other political issues in the 1980s and early 1990s. Seattle defenders and their clients encountered a virtual revolution in criminal law. Clients faced charges growing out of new statutes; they could expect to receive longer penalties due to the onslaught of mandatory sentencing schemes such as three-strikes laws and "sexually violent predator" laws;[22] and their adolescent clients faced increasing incidences of prosecution in adult court.[23] Coinciding with these fundamental changes in the practice of criminal law—or perhaps in response to the media attention to crime that may have led to these initiatives—the public became more fearful of crime and less receptive to appeals for leniency. Jurors and judges mirrored this retributive response. Thus, gaining acquittals or otherwise favorable results for clients posed greater challenges during this period than in the office's previous history.

Still, the Defender Association embraced a broader mission. In representing individual clients, defenders recognized more than ever the importance of seeing their clients as whole human beings and conveying a complete picture to decision makers in the courtroom who might otherwise attempt to objectify them.[24] This meant working with social work staff, families, and individuals in their clients' neighborhoods to compile information that might help a fact finder empathize with their clients through a fuller understanding of their clients' circumstances and motivations. Even the office's external advocacy agenda focused on improving the quality of representation that could be provided to the individual accused. The Defender Association worked with courts, other defenders and legislators to advance the idea of workload standards for defenders both in Seattle and nationally.[25] Their advocacy helped to produce the Seattle and King County Bar Association standards, which included individual lawyer annual caseload ceilings.[26] The Defender Association also worked to ensure the adoption of caseload standards in its contract with the City of Seattle[27] and the provision of comprehensive and consistent training to all lawyers charged with the defense of the accused.

The representation of an ever growing number of clients offered defenders a unique perspective. They were positioned to identify issues that recurred over time. One issue that stared defenders in the face was the racial disparity involved in the decisions to arrest and prosecute. Staggering numbers of people of color faced charges in the criminal justice system. Like most defenders, the Seattle lawyers raised matters of race in the context of individual cases where appropriate. But the sheer volume of individuals needing representation overwhelmed the office, often leaving insufficient time to focus on attacking this problem in any systematic or sustained manner.

2. Framing the Problem

Still, the Defender Association's concern over the racial dynamics in the criminal justice system continued to mount. More often than not, clients facing criminal charges were people of color. But the individualized strategy, in which defenders raised race in the context of a given case, only allowed defenders to react to, rather than prevent, race-based stops and arrests of their clients. Even on those occasions when defenders managed to persuade a court to suppress evidence or to convince a prosecutor to dismiss charges in an individual case, these successes predictably failed to stem the tide of cases flowing into the system. The Defender Association recognized a need to do more and chose to act. In 1999, when the office sought and received a grant from the U.S. Department of Justice to develop a project aimed at uncovering and addressing racial disparity in the criminal justice system, it gained the resources to develop a systematic attack.

The problem was that the defenders were unsure where to begin. Framing the problem and constructing a strategy offered entirely new challenges. In an individual case, the strategies that defenders would adopt were well known. But the boundaries of the systemic problem that they were planning to address seemed less clear and the depth and breadth of this problem seemed almost limitless. The defenders conceded that while they possessed some experience with issues of race in the context of the criminal justice system, they could not on their own establish priorities that would ensure their efforts had an impact on the intended constituency.

So they sought help. As a first step, they chose to consult with community organizations in Seattle. This choice in itself marked a radical departure from strategies that defenders typically employ. Instead of relying on their own judgment about the issues of greatest concern to the communities that they represented, they chose to inquire. The defenders did not reflexively assume that the community would express opposition to issues that the defender might choose to pursue. Rather, community residents were seen as critical partners in this venture because they had expertise that the defenders lacked. Because these community residents experienced the impact of criminal justice policies, they could offer insights about priorities. Of course, not only might communities' evaluation of issues differ from those of defenders, but defenders were not confident that criminal justice issues would rise to the top of communities' own list of priorities. Concerns

about the operation of the criminal justice system may have been less pressing than, for example, economic issues confronting the residents of Seattle's low-income neighborhoods.[28] Interestingly, the Defender Association discovered that residents in certain low-income communities perceived real links between economic issues and criminal justice concerns.

The Central Area Motivation Program (CAMP) offered the defenders their starting place. CAMP, a Seattle social service organization, had conducted a survey of its constituents regarding major barriers to success in obtaining and retaining jobs. The first two issues mentioned were expected: a lack of housing and day care for children. But the survey identified a third impediment that incorporated a criminal justice issue: lack of driver's license privileges.[29] Washington State law mandates the suspension of a person's license if she fails to pay the fines assessed for traffic violations.[30] Anyone who subsequently drives can be charged with a misdemeanor offense: Driving While License Suspended (DWLS) in the third degree.

The issues of racial and economic disparity were stark. The defenders discovered that enforcement of this particular law had a disparate impact on low-income communities of color. Although African Americans represented approximately 9% of the city's drivers, African American drivers received 16.8% of traffic citations in 1999.[31] Twenty percent of those cases involved driving with a suspended license.[32] The disproportionately high numbers of people of color who were stopped for traffic violations raised the specter of racial profiling.[33] Economic survival coupled with the geographic location of employment opportunities seemed to be creating a vicious circle. Once ticketed for traffic violations, many individuals could not afford to pay the substantial fees. The only hope these individuals had of acquiring sufficient funds to pay fines was to continue to go to work. The heart of the problem was that they needed to use their cars to get to and from work. So, these individuals typically drove cars even though their licenses had been suspended. Because drivers of color were more likely stopped by the police, they were also more likely to be found driving with a suspended license.

Yet another racial impact became apparent. In Seattle, the handling of DWLS cases was different depending on which police agency performed the arrest. An arrest by the city police would be channeled through Seattle Municipal Court. The county sheriff's office processed its arrest through King County District Court. The principal difference between the ways that the city and county addressed the DWLS offense involved impoundment of vehicles. In 1998, the Seattle City Council had adopted a rule that the King County Council had rejected. That rule authorized city police officials to impound a vehicle driven by a person charged with DWLS for a period from fifteen to ninety days.[34] The owner of the car, even if she had not been driving, could not redeem the car until the conclusion of the impoundment period. At that time, the city assessed an administrative fee, the cost of removal, towing, and storage in addition to the fines for the underlying traffic offenses. The owner could only recover the car once those costs were paid and upon proof that the owner had a valid driver's license.[35] African Americans drove 39.5% of the vehicles impounded under Operation Impound in 1999.[36] Statistics revealed that black drivers were six times as likely as white drivers to have their cars impounded.[37]

The Defender Association had found its starting point. The director of the office assembled a team of three defenders who would constitute the Racial Disparity Project (RDP). Leo Hamaji, the Defender Training Coordinator with seventeen years of public defense experience, would devote 20% of his time to the RDP. Lisa Daugaard, who had spent three years working in the Defender Association, brought community experience to the equation. Before joining the Defender Association, she had served as the director of the Urban Justice Center in New York and the legal director for the Coalition for the Homeless. The third lawyer on the team was Song Richardson, who had previously worked with the NAACP Legal Defense Fund and the New York Legal Aid Society. Both Daugaard and Richardson spent 40% of their time on the project. Finally, Director Robert Boruchowitz, with twenty-six years of defender experience, served as the team leader. Together, the team's time commitment to the project amounted to that of one full-time employee.

This division of labor served two critical purposes. First, although Boruchowitz had proposed in his grant application—and had received funds for—only one full-time employee, he soon began to reconsider that choice. The person assigned to the project would need to draw on specialized skills to perform the wide-ranging and varied tasks that he envisioned for the RDP. This led Boruchowitz to conclude that utilizing several individuals might prove more effective than expecting a single individual to have such a broad array of skills.

The second purpose is perhaps more apparent. Allowing three defenders to collaborate reduced the burden on any single lawyer to develop the RDP. The team approach ensured against isolation and encouraged a cross-pollination of ideas among the team members. Using teams was not new to the Defender Association. It had developed this approach to handle serious cases such as when individuals faced the possibility of the death penalty or a conviction under "three-strikes" laws. The decision to employ the team model reflected the view that racial disparity was no less serious and no less complex. And this approach reinforced what these team members already knew: the importance of building on each other's expertise and taking care not to assume that they knew everything or had anything approaching all of the answers. They embraced and modeled the value of collaboration.

3. Differently Configured Vision of Practice

The team initially used familiar strategies and approaches. The RDP team chose to represent individuals in DWLS proceedings in court. But the implementation of these choices soon illuminated a broader vision of practice. Despite the often devastating impact of DWLS charges, individuals who faced the impoundment of their cars had no right to counsel. Still, the RDP team observed that on those rare occasions when an individual could afford representation, she could successfully challenge and, in the end, reduce the fines to be paid. So the RDP team began by providing free counsel to a select number of clients who had chosen to appeal the impoundments of their vehicles. The team met with remarkable success in the impoundment cases they handled, often persuasively raising issues of race and racial profiling with respect to the initial stops of their clients.[38] But this form of assistance, while important, particularly to the clients who otherwise would not have had representation, seemed inadequate to the task. The already stretched resources of the Defender Association only permitted RDP to handle a small number of cases on behalf of people whose cars had been impounded.[39]

The key effect of the impoundment law continued to loom: thousands of people were suffering under its disproportionate impact. To address this concern, the RDP team implemented two strategies. The first related to their decision about which cases to take on. Rather than taking the first case to come forward,[40] RDP consciously chose to link their representation with the team's broader goals. In selecting clients, they picked cases in which the client would likely choose to become actively involved in fighting the issue and working to organize other residents of the community who had been caught in the DWLS net. Particularly when they won—but interestingly, even when they did not—these clients worked to help others appreciate the significance of this issue.

The second mechanism that RDP employed to reach larger numbers of affected individuals involved self-help training. The court had the authority to allow relicensing by establishing a payment plan for unpaid tickets, but only implemented such plans when lawyers advocated for them. So the Defender Association, in collaboration with CAMP, offered clinics designed to inform individuals about the processes available to regain their licenses. Hundreds of interested residents attended the clinics. Lisa Daugaard wrote a twelve-page relicensing manual for CAMP that outlined the process and prepared individuals for the common types of arguments they could make and expect to hear. CAMP and the Defender Association originally planned to distribute these self-help kits as guides through the court process.

This choice of tactics in itself proved innovative. The Defender Association lawyers recognized that they could tap the advocacy talents of community residents. The team appreciated that lawyering at its core involves persuasion and that the individuals who were now facing an unfamiliar forum certainly had learned to use persuasive power in their daily interactions.[41] This did not mean that these individuals could immediately navigate their way through a court hearing. They needed the tools of information and rules of the game that the lawyers possessed and could provide. But once armed with that information, these individuals could fight battles on their own behalf.

But these plans were soon interrupted. Once the Seattle Municipal Court learned of the plan,

the judges both worried about the potential increase in their caseloads and suspected that the development of the clinics was a tool to put pressure on the court. So the court summoned Defender Association representatives to meet with judges and the City Attorney to discuss the clinics. This led to an unprecedented negotiation. The Defender Association eased the court's fears about its motivations and was able to proceed with a relicensing program at CAMP with the court's blessing. The Defender Association helped to secure $300,000 from the City Council to fund what became known as the Revenue Recovery Program in the municipal court. The funds covered the cost of helping people chart their way through this process and enabled them to take advantage of time payment arrangements. The City Council budget also paid for a relicensing coordinator. On the third Tuesday of each month, CAMP held relicensing meetings conducted by the relicensing coordinator. Anyone who proceeded through CAMP's relicensing program would have her case taken out of the collections process and would thereby reduce the amount of fees that she would need to pay.

Building on this success, RDP aimed to cross traditional adversarial lines. It proposed a partnership with the King County Prosecutor's office to develop alternatives to both prosecution and punishment for DWLS offenses. What emerged from this collaboration was the King County Re-licensing Project, a more comprehensive diversion program. The program permits anyone with a DWLS charge to participate, except those who have prior convictions for driving while intoxicated or other serious driving offenses. The prosecutor's office agrees to dismiss an individual's DWLS charge if the accused sets up and maintains a payment schedule for paying the underlying fine. At the individual's first appearance in court, the judge explains the terms of the program. If an individual chooses to participate, she must waive her right to a speedy trial for one year and agree to meet a schedule that requires a monthly payment of a minimum of 10% of the total amount owed. In return, the court withdraws the fines from the collections process and has the authority either to reduce the fines or to convert some of the fines to community service. Once the person begins making payments, the court lifts the suspension on her license. Upon completion of the payment schedule, the court dismisses the charge. If successful, this program will divert thousands of people from prosecution and possible jail sentences.

But more remained to be accomplished. Although these strategies reached greater numbers of affected individuals, the RDP team often conceived of the problem in somewhat conventional terms. The team was acquiescing in the state's framing of the issue as a legal problem that required a resolution in court. But realizing this, RDP lawyers had already begun to imagine the problem from other angles. The alternative approaches to this issue at the city council level revealed a political problem. The far-reaching impact on community residents presented a social and economic problem. And when framed in this way, the racial disparity problem posed by DWLS seemed to call for different allies, different strategies, and different tools.

B. Implementing Community-Oriented Defense Strategies

The Defender Association had always recognized the importance of legislative advocacy. In 1998, when the Seattle City Council had adopted the impoundment ordinance, the Defender Association had not yet implemented its Racial Disparity Project. Still, the Defender Association's director saw tremendous problems with the proposed ordinance. He sent a letter to the council detailing his concerns, including the potential racial and economic impact of such a rule. Though the Council did not vote the ordinance down, it did make an important concession: it directed Seattle police to maintain data on the race of drivers whose cars were seized and impounded and to issue a quarterly report with those figures.[42] This constituted a success.

But in 2000, RDP had more ambitious plans. They participated in a campaign to repeal the ordinance. Building on relationships they had developed through the course of representation and work with CAMP, the defenders set out to create a political environment in which policy makers were more aware of the devastating impact of the ordinance and more inclined to be open to arguments for repeal. RDP knew that they needed to help orchestrate a media campaign. They needed to highlight the common, but perhaps unintended, consequences of impoundment. Having been exposed to individuals

affected by the impoundment law, RDP set about identifying those individuals who might exemplify the real problems caused by this law. Their consistency and hard work on this issue helped residents trust that RDP would be a good political partner in this strategy.

1. Working Collaboratively With Individuals and the Community

Putting a public face on the problem was essential. The face that they found would not have been available to them but for the trust they had engendered. An African American grandmother, who in her seventy-four years had never received a traffic infraction nor had any involvement with the justice system, had her car impounded. She had allowed her granddaughter to use her car one day. The grandmother had no way of knowing that her granddaughter's license had been suspended; nor would it have occurred to her to cross-examine her granddaughter about this possibility before letting her borrow the car. Shortly after the granddaughter had borrowed the car, she was stopped by the police for a traffic violation. A routine check revealed that she was driving with a suspended license. Despite her protests that the car was not hers, the police officers seized and impounded the car, which they could lawfully do under the terms of the ordinance. RDP successfully fought the impoundment of the car and arranged for the return of the car.

An elderly activist was born; this grandmother's case graphically demonstrated that the ordinances' reach extended too far. Although she objected at first to the idea of appearing on television with her old car, she ultimately decided that the larger issue should win out over her personal concerns. She made it clear that this ordinance harmed individuals who were otherwise law-abiding citizens. Her story, along with others detailing similar effects, began to gain greater coverage by the local media. Indeed, RDP met with editors of the local newspapers and managed to place opinion pieces by RDP[43] and one City Council member[44] in the major local newspapers. These newspapers also covered the DWLS issue as news stories.[45] The press coverage permitted RDP to reach an even broader audience within the Seattle community.

The City Council entertained a vote to repeal the impoundment ordinance in June 2000.[46] RDP had organized community residents to testify at the hearings and to meet with individual council members. Rather than viewing themselves as directors of this effort and taking a leadership role, the RDP team played a facilitative role. They assisted and coordinated the legislative effort so that affected residents could speak for themselves and could stand in the forefront. RDP advised residents on strategies and encouraged their efforts to mobilize untapped groups within communities. Despite their efforts, the City Council voted against repeal of the ordinance, but only by a five-to-four margin. This vote revealed a remarkable shift from the initial vote for the ordinance two years earlier when it had passed by an eight-to-one margin.

RDP and community residents did not see this as a loss. Instead, it spurred them on to further efforts. Shortly after the vote, Lisa Daugaard testified before the council's public safety committee in support of a proposal that the city provide public defender representation to drivers who elect to appeal their impoundments to the municipal court.

RDP did not limit its political campaign to the impoundment issue. The team recognized that racial profiling exacerbated many of the racial problems inherent in the criminal justice system. Anecdotal evidence suggested that the practice was rampant in Seattle. But like most activists engaged in attacking the practice of racial profiling, the RDP team understood that anecdotes would not suffice. They needed to gain a clearer understanding of the numbers involved. So, together with CAMP, they mounted a media[47] and legislative campaign directed at city and state officials to mandate data collection on the race of all drivers stopped by law enforcement officers. They engaged in discussions with the Seattle police department and testified before the legislature in favor of data collection. Beginning in March 2000, they began to see results. The Washington State Legislature became one of the first legislative bodies to enact a law requiring the state patrol to record and report on the race of all drivers stopped by its officers.[48] Then, five months later, the newly elected police chief for Seattle announced that the police department would voluntarily collect racial data in the course of all traffic stops to determine whether Seattle was engaging in racial profiling.[49]

The alliances that RDP formed have led to other collaborative efforts. For example, RDP played an instrumental role in the development of a grassroots committee, Drive to Survive, in response to the impoundment law. Drive to Survive grew out of community-organizing meetings held by RDP, CAMP, the Northwest Labor and Employment Office, and a member of the County Council. The program is run by a Seattle resident, not by RDP. It lobbies local legislators on issues related to impoundment, engages in public outreach, and works to mobilize community residents in opposition to the impoundment law.

Efforts to make known the racial impact of the impoundment law raised the Defender Association's visibility. As a result, local community organizations began to refer cases involving racial issues to the RDP team. One program's referral resulted in a new but related direction for the RDP team. Youth at Risk sent the case of an Asian adolescent who had been rousted by the gang unit of the Seattle Police Department and subsequently charged with obstruction of justice. RDP ultimately won a dismissal of the case, but that did not end their involvement. Leo Hamaji, the senior staff lawyer on RDP, developed a relationship with a group of about ten Asian teenagers to discuss their experiences with local police authorities. Largely as a result of these ongoing discussions and at the urging of RDP, the ten teenagers testified about the activities of the gang unit. Since that testimony, the gang unit has been less active.

The community work of RDP has enhancement in its representation of individual clients. For example, Song Richardson defended an African American man pulled over by a sheriff's deputy for a traffic violation and then ultimately charged with possession of crack when a small quantity was discovered in his car. Richardson filed a discovery motion requesting access to the deputy's disciplinary records and the training materials of the sheriff's department. Similar motions had been filed and denied in other cases brought by the Defender Association. What differed in this instance was Richardson's ability to support the request with several affidavits from community residents. This time the court granted the discovery motion. The sheriff's department's training documents revealed that the deputy had not only been taught to use pretextual stops, but that his supervisors praised him for making stops of "dirtbag types."[50] Because of the relationships that the RDP team had developed with the community, they were in a better position to advance the interests of their individual clients.

2. Impact on Community's Perceptions of Defenders

RDP has worked hard to develop and maintain relations with communities of color in Seattle. Rather than accepting that the community and the defender office should operate on separate tracks, RDP actively sought to discover common ground that might permit collaboration on issues of mutual interest. The team did not perceive its role as making a decision and then seeking allies. It chose instead to listen to community concerns and to determine if the team could respond to, or provide assistance on those issues in a meaningful way. In looking at the partnerships that began in 1998 and continue today, it becomes clear that RDP has engendered a level of trust within the communities it serves. Building on that trust, the communities and RDP have successfully mounted campaigns to reform laws and rules that could reap substantial benefits for low-income communities. On the level of the individual case, this community interaction has helped to improve the quality of the Defender Association's representation.

Representatives of the community groups with whom RDP has forged relationships express the highest praise for the work of the team. During the course of its evaluation of the RDP program, a team of evaluators met with members of CAMP and Drive to Survive.[51] A founding member of Drive to Survive admitted that she had always viewed lawyers with some degree of skepticism: as she saw it, lawyers always put themselves in the spotlight and wavered in their commitment to communities. RDP changed her view of lawyers. She reported that she can tell residents of her community that while every public defender office is not the same, "we have a jewel, because they really want to do what is right by the community. . . . [W]e can trust this public defender office."[52]

The Executive Director of CAMP echoed these views. Before RDP's inception, CAMP's contact with the Defender Association had been limited. But since the RDP team had begun to work with the community to identify and alleviate the problems associated with racial disparity, their relationship had flourished. The Executive Director of CAMP noted his appreciation of the way that RDP operates as a team. He observed that they work together to develop strategies and approaches, and that this method of doing business carries over into their working relationship with community residents. RDP demonstrated its respect for the talents of residents by soliciting and listening to their ideas and by playing a facilitative role enabling residents to gain access to decision makers. He remarked that they possessed a genuine grassroots orientation and that he had not seen this level of activism in a long time.[53]

As with the residential community in Seattle, RDP has begun to alter its working relationships with actors in the criminal justice community. Instead of being left out of the dialogue, the defenders have come to be seen as important players with the ability to mobilize residents in support of their positions. The King County Prosecutor considers his office's working relationship with RDP beneficial to all parties involved. The prosecutor's office viewed its work on the development of the relicensing diversion program as advantageous because it met an efficiency objective: In a world in which criminal justice resources remain static or dwindle, innovative cost-savings approaches become all the more important. The initial collaboration led the County Prosecutor to work with the Defender Association on the development of drug courts and domestic violence courts that would satisfy defense concerns. Of course, the non-adversarial relationship on policy matters did not mean that in individual cases either side would see their roles differently. But outside of the traditional setting, they perceived tremendous promise in their working relationships.

Thus, by developing partnerships with community groups and moving beyond familiar but limiting traditional roles with prosecutors, the Defender Association has begun to change the public's perception of the scope of the defender's role and the potential for discovering common ground and common objectives.

3. Political Considerations and Side Effects

As the Defender Association embarked on this path, it needed to pay particular attention to the political implications of its choice to become more active and more visible. Interestingly, its first project involved a low-level crime about which the defenders could reasonably anticipate little if any political or public outcry.[54] Concentrating on an offense that does not tap fears about threats to safety made sense from a public relations standpoint. The community residents had identified it as an issue about which they cared, and this helped stave off any criticism that the defenders were imposing their views. From a legal perspective, neither the courts nor the prosecutors' offices had reason to resist reform efforts. DWLS cases clogged the system: they accounted for thousands of filings annually and constituted about 35% to 40% of all criminal case filings in King County District Court. The court and prosecutors eagerly accepted any proposal that might ease that docket. Thus, the choice itself made sense given the constituencies involved.

The work of the RDP team also generated good will. The residents of various low-income communities in Seattle witnessed time and again the team's dedication to this issue and the team's commitment to collaboration. Their successes encouraged groups within these communities to believe in their own ability to work for and achieve positive changes in the criminal justice system.

The resulting good will has had practical benefits for the defender office. Regardless of their success, defender offices must still justify their time and expenses to funding authorities. The funding for the Racial Disparity Project had come from a federal grant, but the office could have faced problems from its principal funding authorities if they perceived that defenders were engaging in work that took them away from their principal mission. Because the defenders were now moving beyond expectations, it was not hard to imagine that they might continue along this path. Interestingly, community residents made a point of attending the defender office's budget hearings and specifically testified on its behalf. These constituents had come to' recognize that the defender office has an important role to play in ensuring fairness in the justice system, and they made clear that they expected funding to continue.

II. Organizational Concerns

A. Internal Dynamics

The task of selling a new vision internally and externally is no small matter. Demonstrating that community-oriented defense strategies supplement rather than supplant the individualized vision of practice is important in helping the variety of audiences with which the defender office interacts appreciate the importance of community-oriented advocacy. As importantly, thinking about the design of public defender offices will help defenders explore how they might better respond to the demands of clients and their communities.

Current organizational design of public defender offices may reflect more of a reaction than a choice. From their inception, defender offices have faced the prospect of needing to respond to the demands of the criminal justice system. Consequently, the organizational structures adopted by defender offices were intended to assist them in handling the legal proceedings for large numbers of indigent clients. Such divisions typically took the form of specialized units that handled particular types of proceedings—trial divisions, appellate bureaus, juvenile branches. These divisions reflected the office's desire to provide focused attention to the diverse matters facing a client. But perhaps as an unexpected consequence, the organizational structure over time has defined and shaped the way that individual defenders conceive their role.

Today, the demands on the defender office have only increased. The growing number of cases, coupled with greater complexity presented in those cases, has meant that defenders have had to adapt themselves and their organizations to the ever changing needs of both clients and the criminal justice system. This has typically occurred within the organizational boundaries that have existed for the past forty years. But imagine what might look different if public defenders chose to design their organizations more affirmatively. What if they thought about their workplace without entirely acquiescing in what others in the criminal justice system define as the role and practice of a defender?

Adopting such an outlook might lead defenders to ask new sorts of questions and consult new sorts of people. For example, curiosity about clients and their communities can sometimes stem from the simple desire to connect. But what might begin as an interest in connecting could then evolve into something considerably more profound. Defenders might encounter other problem solvers—lay and professional—whose vision of their own "practices" (as parents, community activists, social workers, shopkeepers, ministers, etc.) could inspire defenders to see their own roles in a new light. For the first time, defenders might come to understand new ideas about possible strategies, possible collaborations, and possible ways of measuring the impact of their own efforts. Such inspiration could, in turn, raise questions about how the office is organized and how it might be better designed to serve a newly conceived idea of public defender work.

At its roots, community-oriented defense must stem from a belief that the community from which defenders' clients come is at once a valuable resource and an ally in the effort to improve the justice system. Too often, low-income communities and communities of color defined by their deficiencies. They seem to lack stability, good schools, safe streets. Changing the lens through which defenders see communities might allow them to perceive these communities in less pathological terms than do others outside those communities. Most defenders have come to recognize their own clients as individuals with a range of talent and knowledge who can be important partners in the defense of a case. Indeed, defenders tend to accept the premise that assets and allies can come in unexpected packages; extending this view to communities would be indispensable. But convincing defenders to move beyond their own preconceptions of the larger community may nonetheless prove difficult.

A critical first step in convincing defenders of the need to change their orientation may be to begin by focusing on ways that community ties can improve outcomes for their clients. Contacts with residents in a client's neighborhood can increase the likelihood of mounting a viable defense. Knowing people in a given neighborhood can facilitate investigation of a case, and can help the defender develop facts and identify witnesses who might provide jurors with a different or more complete understanding of what transpired in a given case. Forging relationships with service providers or employers can assist in securing favorable dispositions for clients and maintaining support networks to prevent recidivism. If defender clients are homeless, allies might include local housing authorities. If clients face mental health issues, psychologists, psychiatrists, and other mental health experts might provide community-based services. Not only might these allies share concerns about the populations

with whom the defenders work, but they may share defenders' disdain for the criminal justice system's heavy reliance on retributive measures rather than rehabilitative methods that may be cost effective and increase community safety.

1. Building on Community Ties Within the Defender Office

Some defenders already have developed their own community connections.[55] These contacts may arise from relationships cultivated outside of the workplace that may have little or no relationship to public defense. Like most people, individual defenders may have religious affiliations, may engage in volunteer work, or may participate in a child's school or sports activities. As an initial step toward developing relations with communities, the defender office may want to take stock of those connections. Once the defender office has catalogued already existing ties, it can begin to identify issues of concern that it shares with those entities. For example, if the office intends to take a public stand opposing proposed death penalty legislation, it will have access to a list of religious leaders in the area who may be willing to join the effort. If the police department engages in a campaign to arrest homeless individuals as part of a "quality-of-life" initiative, the office might seek support from individuals who work at the shelter where a defender volunteers once a month.

As defenders draw on their own connections, they should begin to consider what they bring to these community relationships. The defenders' legal expertise seems an obvious asset that they can contribute. For example, defenders can offer "know-your-rights" courses that attempt to deconstruct complex legal issues for the average citizen and provide an important service to citizens who might not otherwise have ready access to such information. Some defenders might elect to extend their efforts further. The Miami Dade County Public Defender undertook an anti-violence initiative that makes defenders available to schools and community organizations to discuss ways to resolve disputes short of violence and to avoid involvement in the criminal justice system. Defenders can be seen as contributing a service to the communities with which they engage and in which they operate.

Perhaps the community defender's greatest contribution would be to make oneself available to listen to community concerns. More often than not, community voices are ignored in policy debates, even when those policies will directly affect that community. Defenders have an opportunity to step into the breach and to make an effort to improve communication with communities that have specific concerns about the criminal justice system, the defender office, or larger issues of policy. Overcoming the almost natural skepticism that communities may harbor can be daunting. Defenders will need to earn the trust and respect of communities, but listening and being willing to address the community's concerns will likely move the defender office toward more meaningful relations with community residents.

The defender office's community involvement does not only extend to the work of lawyers. It should also include other members of the office's staff. In many ways, the non-legal staff members of the defender office are the face of the practice. Too often, though, the critical role they play is either ignored or taken for granted.[56] Receptionists and assistants field calls from clients and families. Investigators locate and interview a wide array of witnesses. In a growing number of offices, social workers or sentencing advocates work closely with clients and their families, evaluating clients and directing them to particularized services. As a practical matter, involving all staff makes community-oriented advocacy much more likely to succeed. Rather than expecting a limited number of individuals within the organization to shoulder outreach responsibilities, the defender office can spread the task around. This increases the likelihood that community outreach will occur and will be consistent by tapping into passions that staff members already have, the defender office increases the odds that its staff will remain motivated and involved in a community effort.

2. Incorporating the Team Approach

Asking defenders who are already overworked to incorporate community work into their practice may seem too demanding. Providing comprehensive representation to an individual client can overwhelm the most committed lawyers. Given the prevalence of three-strikes legislation, many of the cases that defenders handle involve potential life sentences. These draconian sentencing consequences make preparation for mounting a defense all the more critical. The task of developing such a defense becomes even more complicated if the accused is detained pending trial because she is effectively unable to assist the defender in her defense. She cannot help to locate witnesses as she might if released. Add to that complexity the likelihood that the bulk of clients whom the defender represents will have mental health problems, and the task of defending the case alone is crushing.

To address these realities, some defender offices have chosen to incorporate a team approach to representation. At first, only smaller experimental offices utilized this approach. The choice to design an office that challenged conventional views of representation led some community-based offices like the Neighborhood Defender Service (NDS) of Harlem to adopt team representation in individual cases.[57] The team concept evolved out of a desire to provide comprehensive services to an individual client. NDS, for example, utilized teams that consisted of lawyers, investigators, and community workers to work with each client from a variety of angles. The team shared files and strategies in an effort to address all of the client's needs. But as importantly, sharing of responsibilities enabled the team to produce high-quality work without overwhelming any single member of the team.

As this model enjoys more widespread use in traditional defender offices for the representation of clients, new possibilities arise for those offices hoping to develop a community orientation. Not every defender will possess or develop the skills to engage effectively with the community. Many of the traits that help to increase a lawyer's success in a trial setting—identifying and targeting flaws in an opponent's arguments, using confrontational tactics to expose those weaknesses—tend to be diametrically opposed to the characteristics that enhance community interaction. Dedicating training resources to the development of these skills would be an important component in a defender office's strategy to transform the office's orientation. But even following such training, some staff may be better suited to engage in this work than others. The team model would enable the defender office to recognize those unique strengths in its staff and to utilize their skills most effectively. Placing individuals with complementary skills on teams together could enable the office to provide comprehensive individual attention to its clients and engage in strategies that move the office into its community.

The Racial Disparity Project in Seattle offered one possible example of the benefits of a team approach by assigning three staff lawyers to the project at roughly one third of their time, the defender office capitalized on the thinking of three of its lawyers in addressing community issues, but for budget purposes assigned only one position to the community aspect of the work. Since RDP's inception, the defender office has continued to explore ways to extend this model throughout the office. One possibility that the office is considering involves arranging to have racial disparity units in each of the office's divisions. The unit would involve three lawyers from each division who would address racial issues unique to their division. The community involvement would be limited to members of that team, but lawyers would rotate through that team to expose them to this work.

Rotation of defenders through the team does raise questions about whose interests such a system might serve. The need to maintain some measure of consistency with community partners with whom the team has developed relations would seem to militate against short rotations. Given this concern, the team might choose to keep certain members constant and to allow only one position to rotate. But the overall ambition of the rotation system would be twofold. First, it would enable a broader array of lawyers—with presumably an equally broad array of talents—to engage in these activities and to bring their ideas to bear on common problems. Second, by creating an ever expanding cadre of community-sensitive defenders, the office would increase the number of lawyers whom community residents might contact even if those lawyers did not happen to be assigned to the team at that moment.

B. Questions of Accountability

Any expansion of the defender's work should raise questions about the impact on the office's core function: providing legal representation to individuals who are accused of a crime. In any effort to focus on broader issues, there is a real danger of losing sight of the defender's paramount task. Providing high-quality representation to the client, understanding her goals and working with her to resolve the case favorably remain critical defense functions. But if community work adds an important dimension to that practice, defender offices will need to remain alert to methods for holding themselves accountable to the clients whom they seek to serve.

This is no small task. Defenders, like most professionals, rarely engage in the sort of self-conscious evaluation of objectives and outcomes that might be necessary to determine whether they are indeed achieving the goals they have set. But if they hope to provide a certain level of representation and guard against dilution of that mission, then defender offices will need to think hard about who should hold them accountable and the measures for doing so.

1. Continual Reexamination of Office Focus

To facilitate a community orientation and to ensure its success, the defender office will need to engage in a regular process of reflection on the actions it has taken. Defenders could hold regular meetings with staff to discuss and assess outreach efforts. Such an assessment might mean holding meetings with current and former clients to determine whether these community efforts have impeded or enhanced the office's work on individual cases. Facilitating regular conversations between the office and the community organizations with whom the office interacts is essential. Regular dialogue—perhaps at monthly lunch meetings—might enable the defender office to monitor its progress and to address concerns raised by community partners.

The central purpose of such meetings would be to provide feedback and data that might help the defender office understand the impact of this orientation. If, in the course of such discussions, it becomes apparent that defenders are surrendering zealous advocacy by becoming more involved in the community, then the defender office would need to adjust its activities to remain true to its principal mission. A key component in engaging in this expanded range of activities would be to remain mindful that community involvement may have limits. The defender's office would quickly lose internal support if it were to take positions on policy that seemed inconsistent with the needs of its clients. It might also lose necessary external support if it raises expectations that it would engage in certain community activities and then only performed those activities haphazardly. Monitoring the office's work and readjusting its focus would help to guard against slippage.

2. Changing External
Perceptions of the Defender's Job

Central to any effort to engage in activities that fall outside the defender's recognized mandate is engaging in concerted public education about the nature of the defense function. Unless defenders take it upon themselves carefully to articulate this expanded view of their role, they will encounter resistance that may well impede any effort they may make to change their orientation and to provide more comprehensive service. Mounting a campaign to utilize every available opportunity to educate the public about the role of public defense in securing justice and maintaining fairness for individuals and communities will assist the defender office steering its activities in a somewhat different direction.

Defenders will need to overcome a general reluctance to articulate that which they do. Too often, defenders have chosen to say as little as possible about their role for fear of retribution in the form of budget cuts or unfavorable publicity. But in any effort to move an institution, the groundwork must first be laid to prepare others for the change. This education can mean the difference between resistance and success.

CONCLUSION

Choosing to carve out a community-oriented role for defenders is fraught with challenge and risk. Reorienting any institution, let alone one that has operated in a particular way for more than forty years, can seem too overwhelming a challenge to tackle. But despite the risks, a growing number of defender offices are embracing this task and making strides toward changing the public defense landscape. More remains to be done in examining their efforts and evaluating their success. At a minimum, defenders seem to recognize that in conjunction with their clients and their clients' communities, they may have tapped a new-found power: the power to define justice priorities, to evaluate criminal justice policies, and to create a system that includes the voices of those individuals and communities

that have historically been excluded from decision making. In this partnership, defenders may find a new role for themselves and their offices that complements and expands their traditional function as they work to construct a more inclusive vision of justice for all.

NOTES

I am enormously grateful for the comments and suggestions of Robert Boruchowitz, Lisa Daugaard, Leo Hamaji, Randy Hertz, Kirsten Levingston, Jerry López, Song Richardson, Anika Singh, and especially Anthony Thompson. I gratefully acknowledge the financial support of the Filoman D'Agostino and Max E. Greenberg Research Fund at the New York University School of Law.

1. See, e.g., Susan F. Bennett, *Community Organizations and Crime*, in Community Justice: An Emerging Field 31 (David R. Karp ed., 1998).

2. See Jerome H. Skolnick, *Justice Without Trial: Law Enforcement*, in Democratic Society 295 (1994); cf. Dan M. Kahan, *Reciprocity, Collective Action, and Community Policing*, 90 Cal. L. Rev. 1513 (2002); Tracey L. Meares, *Praying for Community Policing*, 90 Cal. L. Rev. 1593 (2002); Lawrence Rosenthal, *Policing and Equal Protection*, 21 Yale L. & Pol'y Rev. 53 (2003) (critiquing the use of problem-oriented order-maintenance strategies).

3. See, e.g., Todd R. Clear & David R. Karp, *The Community Justice Movement*, in Community Justice: An Emerging Field 9 (David R. Karp ed., 1998); John Feinblatt, Greg Berman & Michele Sviridoff, *Neighborhood Justice at the Midtown Community Court*, in Crime and Place: Plenary Papers of the 1997 Conference on Criminal Justice Research and Evaluation, 1998 Nat'l Inst. of Just. 81; Judith S. Kaye, *Changing Courts in Changing Times: The Need for a Fresh Look at How Courts Are Run*, 48 Hastings L. J. 851 (1997); Anthony C. Thompson, *Courting Disorder: Some Thoughts on Community Courts*, 10 Wash. U.J.L. & Pol'y 63 (2002).

4. See James P. Lynch & William J. Sabol, *Prisoner Reentry in Perspective*, 3 Urb. Inst. Just. Pol'y Center Crime Pol'y Rep. 2 (2001), at http://www. urban.org/pdfs/410213_reentry.pdf; Jeremy Travis, Amy L. Solomon & Michelle Waul, *From Prison to Home: The Dimensions and Consequences of Prisoner Reentry*, Urb. Inst. Just. Pol'y Center (2001), at http:// www.urban.org/UploadedPDF/from_prison_ to_home.pdf.

5. See Barbara Boland, *Community Prosecution: Portland's Experience*, in Community Justice: An

Emerging Field 253 (David R. Karp ed., 1998); Anthony V. Alfieri, *Prosecuting Violence/Reconstructing Community,* 52 Stan. L. Rev. 809 (2000); Anthony C. Thompson, *It Takes a Community to Prosecute,* 77 Notre Dame L. Rev. 321 (2002).

6.   *See* Kim Taylor-Thompson, *Effective Assistance: Reconceiving the Role of the Chief Public Defender,* 2 J. Inst. for Study Legal Ethics 199 (1999) [hereinafter Taylor-Thompson, *Effective Assistance*] (discussing need for chief defenders to break out of traditionally isolated roles and to begin conceiving of themselves and their offices as key players in the criminal justice system).

7.   *See, e.g.,* Kenneth B. Nunn, *The Trial as Text: Allegory, Myth and Symbol in the Adversarial Criminal Process—A Critique of the Role of the Public Defender and a Proposal for Reform,* 32 Am. Crim. L. Rev. 743, 761–68 (1995) (discussing the ways in which alternative viewpoints are marginalized and de-legitimated in the social "consensus" on crime).

8.   *See, e.g.,* Taylor-Thompson, *Effective Assistance, supra* note 6, at 200.

9.   The merits and challenges inherent in collaborations between lawyers and communities have been extensively debated in the context of civil legal services. *See, e.g.,* Gerald P. López, *Rebellious Lawyering: One Chicano's Vision of Progressive Law Practice* 23 (1992); Joel F. Handler, *Postmodernism, Protest, and the New Social Movements,* 26 Law & Soc'y Rev. 697 (1992); Ascanio Piomelli, *Appreciating Collaborative Lawyering,* 6 Clinical L. Rev. 427 (2000); *cf.* William H. Simon, *The Dark Secret of Progressive Lawyering: A Comment on Poverty Law Scholarship in the Post-Modern, Post-Reagan, Era,* 48 U. Miami L. Rev. 1099 (1994); Lucie E. White, *Collaborative Lawyering in the Field? On Mapping the Paths from Rhetoric to Practice,* 1 Clinical L. Rev. 157 (1994).

10.   *See* Kim Taylor-Thompson, *Individual Actor v. Institutional Player: Alternating Visions of the Public Defender,* 84 Geo. L.J. 2419, 2425–29 (1996) [hereinafter Taylor-Thompson, *Alternating Visions*].

11.   Largely in response to the ways that the criminal justice system treated—and ignored—victims of crimes, victims' rights advocates, over the past two decades, have sought to empower victims of crime to push for changes in the ways that prosecutors' offices work with them and make decisions that affect victims' interests. *See generally* Walker A. Matthews, III, *Proposed Victims' Rights Amendment: Ethical Considerations for the Prudent Prosecutor,* 11 Geo. J. Legal Ethics 735 (1998).

12.   Model Rule 1.6(b)(1) pierces the veil of attorney-client privilege and permits the lawyer to reveal information relating to the representation of the client if she reasonably believes such disclosure to be necessary to prevent reasonably certain death or substantial bodily harm. Model Rules of Prof'l Conduct R. 1.6(b)(1) (2002).

13.   I served as Academic Director of the Criminal Justice Program of the Brennan Center for Justice from 2000 to 2002. Our principal project during that time was the development of the Community Justice Institute, which provides technical assistance to defenders and community activists seeking to collaborate on criminal justice issues. The Community Justice Institute surveyed defenders across the country in 2001; some 127 defenders responded. Over one-half of the respondents indicated that they were currently collaborating with community residents, groups, or activists in their jurisdiction. *See* Brennan Center for Justice, Community-Oriented Defense Fact Sheet, at http://www.brennancenter.org/programs/cj/factsheet_cji.html (Feb. 2002).

14.   One of the earliest examples of a program designed as a neighborhood-oriented office was the Roxbury Defenders in an inner-city community in Boston. *See* Harold R. Washington & Geraldine S. Hines, *"Call My Lawyer": Styling a Community Based Defender Program,* 8 Black L. J. 186 (1983). Building on this example, other community-based defender offices were launched in the 1990s. In 1990, the Vera Institute of Justice began a pilot community defender office, the Neighborhood Defender Service of Harlem, designed to provide better public representation to indigent criminal defendants through what it described as a complete redefinition and restructuring of the system of representation. Vera Institute for Justice, Program Plan for the Neighborhood Defender Service 1–7 (May 2, 1990) (draft, on file with author). Five years later, a former staff attorney with the Neighborhood Defender Service took the concept to the Bronx where she began a community defender office called the Bronx Defenders. For more information about this office, *see* http://www.bronxdefenders.org.

15.   Representatives of the Seattle King County Defender Association, the Public Defender Service of the District of Columbia, the Dade County Defender, the Los Angeles Public Defender, and the Legal Aid Society of New York mentioned in discussions with me in my capacity as Academic Director of the Brennan Center that they had embarked on extended community projects.

The Knox County Public Defender in Knoxville, Tennessee recently revamped its method of service delivery and created the Knox County Public Defenders' Community Law Office. This office seeks to achieve five primary goals:

1. to prevent crime

2. to reduce recidivism

3. to empower clients to live a fuller, more meaningful, independent life

4. to increase community involvement in the criminal justice system

5. to demonstrate an innovative, effective service model

Office of the District Public Defender, Community Law Office Concept Paper 1, available at http://www.pdknox.org/Downloadable/CLOconcept.pdf (last visited Sept. 19, 2003).

16. Taylor-Thompson, *Effective Assistance, supra* note 6, at 204.

17. *See* Taylor-Thompson, *Alternating Visions, supra* note 10, at 2448.

18. The Defender Association, Thirtieth Anniversary Report 1969–1999 1 (1999) (on file with author) [hereinafter Anniversary Report].

19. *Id.* at 2.

20. *See* Charles E. Silberman, *Criminal Violence,* Criminal Justice 306 (1978) (recognizing the office's use of investigators, social workers and senior supervisors as providing comprehensive and professional service to clients).

21. TeamChild was founded on the premise that many children "can be diverted from delinquency or other trouble if their basic needs are met." TeamChild web site, at http://www.teamchild.org (last visited Sept. 19, 2003).

22. Wash. Rev. Code Ann. § 71.09.010–.09.350. (West 2002); *see also* Seling v. Young, 531 U.S. 250, 260 (2001) (upholding Washington's sexual predator laws).

23. Anniversary Report, *supra* note 18, at 9.

24. *See e.g.,* Ogletree, *Beyond Justifications*; Kim Taylor-Thompson, *Empty Votes in Jury Deliberations,* 113 Harv. L. Rev. 1261, 1287 (2000).

25. In 1983, the Defender Association helped to found the Washington Defender Association (WDA), a membership and support group for defenders across the state of Washington. The Defender Association director has served as its president since its founding. The WDA developed a set of standards which were endorsed by the Washington State Bar Association Board of Governors in 1985. That same year, the American Bar Association House of Delegates endorsed a set of defender caseload standards based largely on recommendations by the Defender Association. *See Report to the House of Delegates,* 1985 a.B.a. Sec. Crim. Just. Rep. 1, at http://www.sado.org/misc/nladap2.html.

26. *See* http://www.defensenet.org; *see also* Anniversary Report, *supra* note 18, at 4.

27. Interview with Bob Boruchowitz, the Defender Association (Sept. 4, 2003).

28. *See, e.g.,* Randall Kennedy, *Race, Crime, and the Law* 75, 305 (1997) (discussing the fact that because most residents in low-income communities of color are law-abiding and highly vulnerable to serious crime, treatment of individuals in the criminal justice system, while important, might not be of paramount concern to residents, and that residents may support measures considered "tough on crime").

29. John Powell, Seattle Defender Association's Racial Disparity Project (RDP) 2 (1993) (unpublished report prepared for the Institute on Race and Poverty at the University of Minnesota, on file with author) [hereinafter Evaluation Report].

30. Wash. Rev. Code Ann. § 46.20.289 (West 2002 & Supp. 2003).

31. *Seattle Police Say Blacks Ticketed Disproportionately,* Oregonian (Portland), July 21, 2000, at C6.

32. *Id.*

33. For a general discussion of how race plays a role in police officers' decisions to arrest, stop, or frisk, *see* David Cole, *No Equal Justice: Race and Class in the American Criminal Justice System* 16–62 (1999) (discussing police practices focusing on "poor black and Hispanic people living in the inner city"); Angela J. Davis, *Race, Cops, and Traffic Stops,* 51 U. Miami L. Rev. 425, 425 (1997) (describing "Driving While Black" as a social phenomenon); David A. Harris, *Factors for Reasonable Suspicion: When Black and Poor Means Stopped and Frisked,* 69 IND. L.J. 659, 677–81 (1994) (asserting that police target minority neighborhoods for police stops and searches); Anthony C. Thompson, *Stopping the Usual Suspects: Race and the Fourth Amendment,* 74 N.Y.U. L. Rev. 956 (1999) (discussing the constitutional and policy implications of race-based stops by police).

34. Seattle, Wash., Mun. Code §11.30.105 (2002), http://clerk.ci.seattle.wa.us.

35. *Id.* § 11.30.120.

36. Evaluation Report, *supra* note 96, at 3; *see also* Lisa Daugaard, *Impound Policy Goes After the Poor,* Seattle Post-Intelligencer, Aug. 17, 1999, at A9, available at 1999 WL 6599130.

37. Evaluation Report, *supra* note 29, at 3.

38. See Heath Foster, *Impoundment a Threat to Many; Simple Necessities Can Depend on a Furtive Drive to the Store,* Seattle Post-Intelligencer, Aug. 27, 2001, at A1, available at 2001 WL 3565417 (noting that in the nineteen cases of impoundment appeals handled by public defenders in 1999 and 2000, eighteen were overturned); *see also* Jim Brunner, *Impound Law Dealt Setback by Judge,* Seattle Times, May 16, 2001, at B1.

39. Largely due to the RDP's recognition that counsel mattered in these hearings, the Defender Association Director Boruchowitz has worked with the University of Washington Law School to establish an impoundment clinic where law students can provide representation to individuals whose cars have been impounded. *See* Bobbi Nodell, *Steering Help in Right Direction: UW Law Students Assist*

People Whose Cars Have Been Impounded, Seattle Times, Sept. 30, 2002, at B1.

40.   Taylor-Thompson, *Alternating Visions, supra* note 10, at 2441 (discussing the tendency among defender offices to follow a first-come first-served approach rather than engaging in case selection).

41.   *See* López, *supra* note 9, at 39 ("When problem-solving requires persuading others to act in a compelling way, we can call it lawyering. . . ."); Gerald P. López, *Lay Lawyering,* 32 UCLA L. Rev. 1 (1984) (describing lawyering as problem solving that involves persuasion).

42.   Seattle City Council Resolution 30467 (2002) (adopted as amended), available at www .cityofseattle.net/leg/clerk/sv2002.htm.

43.   *See* Robert C. Boruchowitz & Fred Bonner, *Better Court Practices, Not Impoundment, Have Reduced DWLS,* Seattle Post-Intelligence, Feb. 7, 2001, at B5, available at 2001 WL 3552916; Nick Licata & Lisa Daugaard, *Ruling on Impounds Restores Rights,* Seattle Post-Intelligencer, May 29, 2001, at B5, available at 2001 WL 3560135.

44.   *See* Larry Gossett & Robert C. Boruchowitz, *Reasons to Change City's Impound Law,* Seattle Post-Intelligencer, May 2, 2000, at A13, available at 2000 WL 5294252.

45.   *See, e.g.,* Kerry Murakami, *Judge Puts Brake on Sidran's Use of Car-Impoundment Law,* Seattle Post-Intelligencer, May 16, 2001, at B1, available at 2001 WL 3559305; Mike Roarke, *Some Say Law Impounds Rights; Crackdown on Bad Drivers May Hurt Innocents, Critics Say,* Spokesman-Review (Spokane, Wash.), July 5, 2000, at A1 (describing unfair reach of impoundment law), available at 2000 WL 22731123.

46.   *See* Jim Brunner, *Cries of 'Shame' as Law Is Retained; Impound-Ordinance Foes Berate Council,* Seattle Times, June 27, 2000, at B1 (covering City Council rejection of proposal to repeal impoundment ordinance).

47.   *See, e.g., We Should Prevent Racial Profiling,* Seattle Post-Intelligencer, May 13, 1999, at A12, available at 1999 WL 6590624.

48.   *See* Wash Rev. Code Ann. §43.43.480 (West 1998 & Supp. 2003).

49.   *See, e.g.,* Kimberly A.C. Wilson, *Police to Track Race Factor: Officers Will Help Learn If Profiling Occurs During Traffic, Pedestrian Stops in Seattle,* Seattle Post-Intelligencer, Aug. 22, 2000, at A1, available at 2000 WL 5301952.

50.   *See* Evaluation Report, *supra* note 29, at 9.

51.   In compliance with the initial grant to implement the Racial Disparity Project, the Defender Association engaged the services of the Institute on Race and Poverty at the University of Minnesota to develop a team to evaluate the program. This resulted in the Evaluation Report, *supra* note 29.

52.   Evaluation Report, *supra* note 29, at 6.

53.   *Id.* at 7.

54.   *See* Taylor-Thompson, *Effective Assistance, supra* note 6, at 215 (suggesting that defenders choose community projects that might garner widespread support while still reflecting the defender office's values).

55.   *See, e.g.,* Brennan Center for Justice, Community-Oriented Defense Fact Sheet, *supra* note 13.

56.   López, *supra* note 9, at 87–101.

57.   *See* Vera Institute of Justice Program Plan for the Neighborhood Defender Service, *supra* note 14, at 5–6 (stating that Neighborhood Defender Services will designate defense teams, consisting of attorneys, community workers and administrative assistants, rather than individual lawyers to represent clients).

25

WE DO NOT DESERVE TO KILL

MARVIN E. WOLFGANG

PUNISHMENT THAT IS DESERVED

The major purposes of punishment historically have been retribution, expiation, deterrence, reformation, and social defense. Throughout history, an eye for an eye, the payment of one's debt to society by expiation, general deterrence of crime by exemplary punishment and specific or special deterrence of an individual offender, reformation of the individual so that he or she will not commit further crime, and protection of society against criminality by detaining or imprisoning offenders have been the principal rationales for the disposition of criminal offenders.

These rationales have not moved through history like a Roman army phalanx but have moved instead, as the historian Crane Brinton has said, "Like a train-wreck in time, a telescoping of historical thought." Periods in history gave dominant position to each of these penal purposes. The Hammurabi Code was a brilliant civilization advance in 1700 B.C., with its emphasis on retribution, the call for talion, partly because it represented an attempt to keep cruelty within bounds.

But Hammurabi's code, we should remember, was not always the strict proportionality often attributed to it, that is, approximating the punishment to the crime. Professor James B. Pritchard (1955) from the University of Pennsylvania reminds us that if a noble destroyed the eye of another noble, his eye shall be destroyed; if he has broken the bone of another noble, "they shall break his bone"; and if he has knocked out the teeth of a noble "of his own rank, they shall knock out his tooth." But if the victim is not a noble, the punishment is a fine, as was the case of a commoner striking the cheek of a commoner. If a noble struck the cheek of a noble of higher rank, he received 60 lashes with an oxtail whip. Striking a noble of equal rank resulted in a fine. But if a slave struck a noble, off came his ear; if a son struck his father, they cut off his hand (Pritchard 1955, pp. 163–80).

The Law of Moses is usually claimed to be retributive, based on the principle of an eye for an eye, but as Princeton's Professor Walter Kaufman (1973) points out, careful reading of Exodus, Leviticus, Numbers, and Deuteronomy may show that the phrase appears three times,

Author's Note: This article was part of the 1996 Death Penalty Symposium and is reprinted with the permission of the Thomas M. Cooley Law Review. Parts 2 and 3 are adapted with permission from Marvin E. Wolfgang, "The Death Penalty: Social Philosophy and Social Science Research," *Crim. L. Bull.* 14 (18): 18–25.

Source: From Wolfgang, M. E., "We do not deserve to kill," in *Cooley Law Review,* pp. 375-386. Reprinted with permission.

but that the utilitarian notion of deterrence is also present, as in Deuteronomy: "The rest shall hear and fear, and shall never again commit any such evil in your midst" (Deuteronomy 19:20).

Moreover, it has been asserted that even with the rationale of retribution, with an effort to produce a kind of equilibrium or homeostasis, the meaning of an eye *under* an eye refers to the letters of the Hebrew alphabet, and the letters preceding the "eye," *ayian tachat ayian,* spell money, which is interpreted as monetary compensation or restitution to the victim by the offender.[1] The Talmud makes a clear effort to avoid the literal translation. Now this interpretation is, from my viewpoint, extremely important because it raises the issue of retributive equivalences. The claim is, therefore, that corresponding and proportional sanctions—that is, the punishment proportionate to the crime—even with precision are possible without requiring exactly the same pain. Similarity, not sameness, becomes the consequence of equivalences. This principle becomes more important with respect to the death penalty.

Although Socrates, through Plato and Aristotle, are more future oriented than past oriented relative to punishment, Plato, in particular, also refers to retribution as just deserts. Deterrence is future minded, meant to cause others or the same offender from committing crimes in the future. To punish an offender for what he or she has done and now what he or she might do in the future is, of course, past oriented. To punish one based on what he or she deserves to receive is retributive. Plato (427–347 B.C.) said, "Let the penalty be according to his deserts" (Hutchins 1952, Book IX, pp. 743, 744).

Plato sounds quite modern:

> When a man does another any injury by theft or violence, for the greater injury let him pay greater damages to the injured man and less for the smaller injury; but in all cases, whatever the injury may have been, as much as will compensate the loss. And besides the compensation of the wrong, let a man pay a further penalty for the chastisement of his offence: he who has done the wrong instigated by the folly of another, through the lightheartedness of youth or the like, shall pay a lighter penalty; but the one who has injured another through his own folly, when overcome by pleasure or pain, in cowardly fear, or lust, or envy, or implacable anger, shall endure a heavier punishment. . . . the

law, like a good archer, should aim at the *right measure* of *punishment,* and in all cases at the *deserved punishment.* (Hutchins 1952, Book IX, pp. 743, 744, emphasis added)

I should like to put the death penalty into this analysis.

Neither the absolute determinist nor the partial determinist should favor the death penalty for any reason. On examining Pythagorean, Epicurean, Stoic, Aristotelian, and Platonic views of determinism, one can see that only Plato fails the test of consistency. In Aristotelian terms, even a just man can act unjustly or be treated unjustly.[2] But Aristotle seems to skirt the issue of the penalty of death. He is a partial determinist when he speaks of voluntarism and involuntarism relative to passion connected to a man's sleeping with his neighbor's wife or striking the neighbor or his father.

> For a man might even lie with a woman knowing who she was, but the origin of his act might be not deliberate choice but passion. He acts unjustly, then, but is not unjust; e.g., a man is not a thief, yet he stole, nor an adulterer, yet he committed adultery; and similarly in all other cases. (Hutchins 1952, p. 339)

The inference to be drawn is that even when committing a crime—an unjust act—the person may nonetheless be just, and therefore punishment should be tempered.

Plato, I admit, is different. He is at once retributive in calling for punishment that is deserved and nods noticeably toward reformation. Hear him in Book IX of *Laws*:

> Such are the preludes which we sing to all who have thoughts of unholy and treasonable actions, and to him who hearkens to them the law has nothing to say. But to him who is disobedient when the prelude is over, cry with a loud voice—He who is taken in the act of robbing temples, if he be a slave or a stranger, shall have his evil deed engraven on his face and hands, and shall be beaten with as many stripes as may seem good to the judges, and be cast naked beyond the borders of the land. And if he suffers this punishment he will probably return to his right mind and be improved; for no penalty which the law inflicts is designed for evil, but always makes him who suffers either better or not so much worse as he would have been. (Hutchins 1952, p. 743)

However, he favors the death penalty for the "greatest of crimes," as the following passage from Book IX of *Laws* shows:

> But if any citizen be found guilty of any great or unmentionable wrong, either in relation to the gods, or his parents, or the state, let the judge deem him to be incurable, remembering that after receiving such an excellent education and training from youth upward, he has not abstained from the greatest of crimes. His punishment shall be death, which to him will be the least of evils; and his example will benefit others, if he perish ingloriously, and be cast beyond the borders of the land. (Hutchins 1952, p. 743)

Hence, Plato claims cognitive, rational free will in committing an "unmentionable wrong." However, in the dialogues between Cleinias and an Athenian Stranger, beginning in Book IX of *Laws*, Plato recognizes, in the words of the Athenian Stranger, ignorance as a cause of crime.

> A man may truly say that ignorance is a third cause of crimes. Ignorance, however, may be conveniently divided by the legislator into two sorts: there is simple ignorance, which is the source of lighter offenses, and double ignorance, which is accompanied by a conceit of wisdom; and he who is under the influence of the latter fancies that he knows all about matters of which he knows nothing. This second kind of ignorance, when possessed of power and strength, will be held by the legislator to be the source of great and monstrous crimes, but when attended with weakness, will only result in the errors of children and old men; and these he will treat as errors, and will make laws accordingly for those who commit them, which will be the mildest and most merciful of all laws. (Hutchins 1952, p. 748)

Plato's sense of retributive justice is very clear in a fuller passage from Book IX of *Laws* (Athenian Stranger speaking):

> But if any one seems to deserve a greater penalty, let him undergo a long and public imprisonment and be dishonoured, unless some of his friends are willing to be surety for him, and liberate him by assisting him to pay the fine. No criminal shall go unpunished, not even for a single offence, nor if he have fled the country; but let the penalty be according to his deserts—death, or bonds, or blows, or degrading places of sitting or standing, or removal to some temple on the borders of the

land; or let him pay fines, as we said before. (Hutchins 1952, p. 744)

DEATH AND RETRIBUTION

There is no rationale of punishment or disposition of a convicted offender that requires the death penalty. No logic of any rationale leads ineluctably to the death penalty. What are these rationales? Retribution, expiation, the utilitarian notion of deterrence, rehabilitation, social protection, or defense. We know they are not mutually exclusive except in abstract analysis, perhaps not even in that.

Several of these I should like to dispense with quickly because either the argument of the rationale clearly does not lead to the death penalty, or the evidence required to support the argument for the death penalty is weak, inadequate, or inconclusive. Death is not expiatory for the offender, for expiation implies that the offender has atoned for his guilt and is now cleansed in this life so he is free to accept the grace of God or a God—surrogate in the name of the state. Rehabilitation also requires life to continue so the former offending person can be restored to a life of social conformity. Deterrence is an unproven case. The Committee on Deterrent and Incapacitative Effects, of the National Research Council, National Academy of Science, concluded, after extensive research on crime in general and the death penalty in particular, that "in summary, the flaws . . . lead the Panel to conclude that the results of the analyses on capital punishment provide no useful evidence on the deterrent effect of capital punishment" (Blumstein et al., 1978, p. 62). What is left? Social protection and retribution. But social protection is so closely linked to deterrence and the utilitarian position that we need not pursue it further. Moreover, the social protection argument can lead to the undesirable consequences of executing potentially "dangerous" violent offenders and those who, as in the case of the Soviet penal code of the late 1920s and early 1930s, are "socially dangerous" to the state, even though they may not have committed any other specifically designated capital crime.

Retribution would appear to contain the most reasonable logic leading to the death penalty. Part of the reasoning in retribution theory includes Hobbes's notion of establishing an equilibrium, of restoring the state of being to what it had been before the offensive behavior had been committed. Strict homeostasis cannot be achieved with the death penalty for, as we all know, the victim of a killing cannot be restored. Nor is the abstract sense of equilibrium satisfied by execution, that is, the lex talionis, eye for an eye, tooth for a tooth (see Pritchard 1955). For retribution requires pain equal to that inflicted on the victim, plus an additional pain for committing the crime, crossing the threshold from law-abiding to law-violative behavior (see Hutchins 1952, Book IX, p. 782).

The state's killing of a convicted offender, especially under the medically protective circumstances now used, is not likely to cause him as much pain as he inflicted on his victim. Even if the pain to each were the same, the second requirement of retribution is not met—namely, the pain to be inflicted for the crime per se. What then would meet the requirement? A torturous execution? Perhaps, but that solution conflicts with other attitudes in our society, particularly those concerned with physical assaults by or in the name of the state. Apparently, Western society considers corporal punishment an anathema of civilization. We permit the police to shoot at fleeing felons under certain circumstances, but even this act is discouraged unless life is endangered.[3] Physical force may be used to arrest a suspect. But once a suspect is arrested, we mount glorious attacks against any physical abuse of arrestees, detainees, and defendants. We decry inadequate diets and urge good medical care for prisoners. The philosophy of our health delivery system is such that we must present our sacrifice to the rationalization for death in good physical condition. The state has made efforts to reduce the suffering of death in most exquisite ways.

Thus, there is a strong cultural opposition to corporal punishment. Western society today would not tolerate, I am sure, cutting off limbs, gouging out eyes, or splitting the tongue. Even for murder, there would be opposition to "partial execution" (i.e., cutting off legs, cutting of the penis, etc.). If we cringe at the thought of eliminating part of the corporal substance, is it logical to eliminate the total corpus?

A principal part of the rationale of retribution is proportional sentencing. Beccaria, Bentham, and other rationalists recognized the principle. The "just deserts" or "commensurate deserts" model amply anticipates it. Beccaria's scales of seriousness of crime and severity of sanction were meant to be proportional. Equal punishment for equal crime does not mean that the punishment should be exactly like the crime but that the ratios of sanction severity should have a corresponding set of ratios of crime seriousness.

Moreover, punishment can or should be expressed in equivalences rather than in the same physical form of the crime. For example, we do not prescribe state-inflicted injuries for offenders who have injured but not killed their victims. It is not banal to argue this point because it is critical to the logic of capital punishment. If the victim has been assaulted and then treated by a physician and discharged or is hospitalized, the state does not exact the same penalty for the offender. We do not in the name of the state stab, shoot, throw acid, maim, or mug persons convicted of such aggravated assaults. Where, then, is the rational logic for retention of the death penalty for inflicting death?

Instead, equivalences in pain are sought in kind, not in physical exactitude. The common commodity of pain in our democratic society is deprivation of liberty over time, measured in days, months, and years. Other forms of deprivation are subsumed under this deprivation. It is but a reasonable extension of the equivalences between deprivation of liberty for crimes less than murder and the same deprivation for longer periods of time for the crime of homicide.

In the Beccarian mode, more can be said about the "pains of imprisonment." Death eliminates all. It does away with guilt, frustration, aspiration, achievement disparities, desires for unattained and unattainable things, anxieties, and fears. By execution, the state deprives itself of the functioning of these self-inflicted punishments and of those punishments derived from the deprivation of liberty. Death ends all pain, and the offender is punished no more.

By "slavery," Beccaria means the restraints that accompany imprisonment when he says,

> Were one to say that slavery for life is as sinful as death and therefore equally cruel, I would reply that, adding all the unhappy moments of slavery together, the former would be even worse, but these moments are spread over a lifetime, while the death penalty expends its total influence in a single moment. . . . Therefore the intensity of the punishment of penal slavery, as substitute for the

death penalty, possesses that which suffices to deter any determined soul. I say that it has more. Many look on death with a firm and calm regard—some from fanaticism, some from vanity which always accompanies men beyond the tomb, some in a last desperate attempt either to live no longer or to escape misery—but neither fanaticism nor vanity dwells among fetters and chains, under the rod, under the yoke or in an iron cage, when the evildoer begins his sufferings instead of terminating them.[4]

The historical consequence of implementing a penalty "worse than death" has recently been described by Sellin, who said that Beccaria's "advocacy of penal slavery encouraged [in Austria, Hungary and elsewhere] the invention of horrid forms of imprisonment believed to be more deterrent than death" (Sellin 1977, p. 8). But the point I wish to emphasize is the psychological one made by Beccaria about pain that ends quickly with execution but lingers on with imprisonment. The issue is empirical, and the evidence today is little more than the 18th century could offer.

Beccaria also speaks of a punishment more deterrent than death that he thought he found in penal slavery, which in its very duration would be a constant reminder of the consequences of crime: "In the case of an execution a crime can furnish only one example to the nation, but in the case of lifelong penal slavery a single crime can provide numerous and lasting warnings" (Sellin 1977, p. 4). In short, the speed and for us now the secrecy of death and the socially intended meaning of execution are of little moment in the minds of the survivors. We can identify only momentarily with death. But the lingering reminder of deprived liberty is more of a sustained constant. It is easier to identify with a living example than with a dead and past example of suffering.

There is one other comment I should like to make at this point about deterrence without reference to the social science literature on the topic. Relative to the death penalty, there seems to be a greater willingness by the U.S. Supreme Court to listen to and be affected by arguments about deterrence than by arguments about racial, social class, or sex discrimination. Deterrence may be related to protection of society and legally is a state interest issue, but it is not rooted to any article or amendment in the Constitution. Discrimination is tied to due process in the 5th and 14th Amendments, to impartial juries in the 6th Amendment, and to equal protection also in the 14th Amendment. Further claims of cruelty are linked with the 8th Amendment, as it is claimed that the death penalty is inflicted disproportionately on the poor and on Blacks. But, to repeat, deterrence has no immediately recognizable legal isomorphism in the Constitution. It is related to legislative intent but not to specific constitutional issues to be decided by judicial review.[5]

Failure Systems: A Socratic Dialogue

I should like now to introduce the notion of system failures as a sociophilosophical argument against the death penalty. The first is social system failure; the second is criminal justice system failure.

To some extent, this position is similar to Gabriel Tarde's reference that society has the criminals it deserves. The point is that the social system that has crime has failed to educate, to form, to socialize its citizens to conform to the pre- and proscriptions. Such failure may be nearly inevitable, may vary by degree, but nonetheless exists. Individuals may share some portion of failure, some responsibility for the crime, but a social system that is not totally just—in the sense expressed from Plato to Rawls, or in Marx and Engels—has also failed. Such failure denudes the state's right to take away the lives of its failures. The philosophy does not apply to crimes less serious than murder.

"But why not?" Socrates' pupil, Adeimantus, might ask.[6]

"Because," Socrates would say, "We still imply with punishment, even with retribution, a restoration to an earlier state and, simultaneously, or hoped for, reformation. Death precludes both the restorative and the rehabilitative functions of punishment. By execution the state has dramatically and clearly proclaimed its failure and shut off any chance of rectifying it. Moreover, execution is an unjust finality to the failure the state itself has caused."

The criminal justice system also fails, and this failure should prevent the punishment of death.

"But what about the premeditated murderer, or the hired killer?" questions Adeimantus. "Surely he knows what he is doing, and although society may have failed to educate him in the virtues, he does not respond properly to the fear of punishment and when he is caught should be used as an example to others. Execution will function in an exemplary way and serves the interest of education."

"Not so," says Socrates. "It is an unjust punishment because it is an unequal punishment. The premeditated murder is planned not out of fear of being arrested, but on the perceived or real probability of not being caught, convicted, and punished. The criminal justice system is not totally efficient. It fails to arrest, convict, and punish most criminal offenders and many murderers. The failure, the inefficiency of the criminal justice system to capture and convict *all* murderers, promotes the cognitive stance of the offender's willingness to risk the probabilities."

Adeimantus rises to the reasoning and responds with enthusiastic cogency: "Should not this selective efficiency then be used to justify the execution of the few who are caught?"

"But again I remind you of equal protection and due process," says his mentor. "For if the criminal justice system were totally efficient, all murderers would be caught and the certainty of punishment principle could be invoked to deter without having to resort to greater severity of punishment. If we review this drama as a probability game instead of a battle of right against wrong, of the mammoth power of the state, with law enforcement and the prosecutorial armamentaria, against the individual, the state should be expected to win, to capture its attackers. The capacity to capture only some offenders produces reduced risk in the game of the individual against the state. Hence, the more the system fails (low 'clearance' rates, low conviction rates), the more the burden of the death penalty falls on the few who are captured. Execution of the few is thus an inequity on all, the total universe, because of the failure of pursuit by the state."

"Again, this logic does not apply to less severe sanctions for less serious offenses because the punished offender, not executed, can be restored and permitted to play the game again."

PROPORTIONALITY AND DEPRIVATION OF LIBERTY

In 1764, Beccaria, in his classic book *Dei delitti e delle pene,* wrote that there should be a scale of the seriousness of crime with a corresponding scale of the severity of sanctions (Beccaria 1963). In the Age of Reason in the 18th century, with an emphasis on the rationality of man, deterrence was the principal purpose of punishment. And Beccaria wrote poignantly about this rationale. One of his major statements—which surely has contemporary value—was that it is not the severity but the certainty of punishment that deters.

Despite Beccaria's focus on deterrence as the main purpose of punishment, the principle of proportionality between the gravity of the crime and the severity of the sanction, was an integral part of his philosophy and can be applied to the just deserts model. The principle of proportionality, equivalences, and punishment based on what is deserved all are now linked in a way that permits construction of a logical sequencing of scaling of sanctions. We need not agree with Professor Kaufman's (1973) assertion that there is no proportional punishment for raping a child or for treason or genocide, although admittedly these present difficult solutions.

Thomas Jefferson knew of Beccaria's essay and in his first inaugural address proposed what he called "Equal and exact justice to all men" (cited in Kaufman 1973, p. 223). In 1779, he drafted "a Bill for Proportioning Crimes and Punishments" (Padover 1943). For example, "Whosoever shall be guilty of rape, polygamy, or sodomy with man or woman, shall be punished, if a man, by castration, if a woman, by cutting through the cartilage of her nose a hole of one half inch in diameter at the least" (Padover 1943, pp. 95–96). He also wrote,

> Whosoever on purpose, and of malice forethought, shall maim another, or shall disfigure him, by cutting out or disabling the tongue, slitting or cutting of a nose, lip, or ear, branding, or otherwise, shall be maimed, or disfigured in *like sort:* or if that cannot be, for want of the same part, then *as nearly as may be,* in some other part of at least equal value and estimation, in the opinion of the jury, and moreover, shall forfeit one half of his lands and goods to the sufferer. (Padover 1943, p. 96)

Although some of what Jefferson says here may sound bizarre, he nonetheless nods in the direction of equivalences and proportionality.

I have tried to show elsewhere that sanctioning equivalences took an important step forward when, in 14th-century Florence, imprisonment became a form of punishment per se and essentially was meant to replace corporal punishments (Wolfgang 1960). Previously, prisons were used to detain defendants awaiting trial or awaiting flogging, branding, mutilation, exile, and banishment, but not as a punishment. In 1300, Florence opened its new prison, Le Stinche, and under the Ordinances of Justice of 1298 for the first time sentenced convicted offenders to the cells for definite, flat periods of time—without corporal punishment: 2 years for simple theft, 4 years for robbery, 4 years for sodomy (as I have found in the archives of the Uffizi for Benvenuto Cellini, although he never served the term), and so forth (Wolfgang 1960, p. 150).

I have no time to develop this thesis here a la Jacob Burkhardt, or Georg Simmel with his theory of money, or Arnold Hauser on Renaissance art, but the thesis claims that moving from the other worldliness and timelessness of the Middle Ages to the this-worldly orientation, to an economy based on mercantile capitalism, to building the Pitti Palace during the lifetime of the Patriarch of the Pitti family, to the chiming of clocks in the city piazzas, to new concise perspective in art, to Petrarch's climbing of Mt. Vesuvius just for the view, all converged to make equivalences of man's labor, his time and his money. Moreover, there was an effort to promote new political freedom. When time, labor, and money can be equated, when liberty becomes a precious commodity, then deprivation of liberty for given and specific amounts of time can become a disutility and a proper and just punishment.

In 1790, the Walnut Street Jail in Philadelphia opened a wing that was designated as the state prison. On October 29, 1829, the famous Eastern State Penitentiary was opened for prisoners and the term *penitentiary* came into use, a place for prisoners to do penance. Here was born the so-called Pennsylvania System of punishment that, like its Florentine counterpart, used imprisonment for specific periods of time as punishment sufficient unto itself. No more whippings, no more brandings, ducking stools, or corporal tortures. Specific periods of time in prison became equivalences for the gravity of crime.

Conclusion

I have mentioned proportionality, equivalence, retribution, capital punishment, and deprivation of liberty because I have tried to show their linkages and that death is not a punishment required by any logically consistent philosophy.

I have drawn on ancient Greek scholars for ideas concerning punishment, including the death penalty, because early on they thoroughly explored these issues, long before society became involved in the complexities of the costs of capital punishment versus life imprisonment, before racial discrimination was an issue, before Bedau and Radelet (1987) gave us studies of innocents executed or sentenced to death, and before Sellin's studies of the lack of deterrence appeared before the Royal Commission on Capital Punishment (Her Majesty's Stationery Office 1953).

As we all know, the United States is alone among Western industrialized countries that retain the death penalty. And South Africa last year became the 42nd nation since World War II to abolish capital punishment and declare it unconstitutional. If we can pull the thinking of ancient scholars of more than 2,000 years ago into our century of the unjust administration of justice of laws that still permit our government to kill people with premeditation, we might be more humble, more respectful of the dignity of human life, however horrible the acts of the offender.

As Sister Helen Prejean (1993) has observed, "You could say, 'They deserve to die,' but the key moral question is, 'Do we deserve to kill them?'"

The philosophy of logic, ethics, and morality is surely the bulwark of opposition to the death penalty. But so are our emotions. Some time ago, the governor of Pennsylvania asked me to be a state witness to an execution. I hesitated at first. I had seen men next to me die in combat during the war. I was not a stranger to seeing death before me. I accepted the offer because I wondered if my cool, intellectual, and philosophical opposition to the death penalty was shared by my emotions.

I shall not describe the horribleness of an electrical execution. There are descriptions better than I could write. I wish only to report that death in wartime combat, as ugly as it is, has no parallel to the state's premeditated, highly organized, calculated death of a human being, however heinous his crimes. I was moved to a new emotional height of opposition to capital punishment upon witnessing a clearly violent, ugly, truly premeditated state killing.

The state of Michigan must be applauded for having abolished the death penalty a century and a half ago, the first political jurisdiction in the English-speaking world to do so (see Bedau and Radelet 1987) and for maintaining abolition despite political rhetoric for the penalty. Michigan was there even before Western Europe (Bedau and Radelet 1987). I salute you, Michigan, for your original stance and for your proper perseverance against the death penalty.

NOTES

1. I am grateful to Edna Erez for bringing this use of the Hebrew alphabet and the interpretation by the Gaon Mevilna (the genius of Vilma) to my attention.

2. See Aristotle, *Nichomachean Ethics*, in Hutchins (1952).

3. See, for example, *Tennessee v. Garner* (1985) (holding that deadly force may not be used to prevent the escape of a criminal suspect unless a significant threat of harm exists).

4. This translation appears in Sellin (1977). A similar phrasing in English appears in Cesare Beccaria (1963), *Dei delitti e delle pene,* which was originally published in 1764.

5. The assertion that I have made here is buttressed by my dialogue with Louis H. Pollack, Dean of the Law School, University of Pennsylvania, and one of the leading constitutional lawyers in the United States.

6. I have used Adeimantus here in the hypothetical dialogue with Socrates because Adeimantus was one of the delightful questioners in Plato's Republic.

REFERENCES

Beccaria, Cesare. (1963). *On Crimes and Punishments.* Trans. Henry Paolucci. NY: Botts-Merrill. (Original publication, *Dei delitti e delle pene,* in 1764.)

Bedau, Hugo Adam and Michael L. Radelet. (1987). "Miscarriages of Justice in Potentially Capital Cases." *Stanford Law Review* 40 (21).

Blumstein, Alfred, et al. (1978). *Estimating the Effects of Criminal Sanctions on Crime Rates.* Washington, DC: Panel on Research on Deterrent and Incapacitation Effects, National Academy of Science, Deterrence and Incapacitation.

Her Majesty's Stationery Office. (1953). *Royal Commission on Capital Punishment, 1949–1953 Report.* London: Her Majesty's Stationery Office.

Hutchins, Robert Maynard. (1952.9). *Great Books of the Western World.* Trans. Benjamin Jowett. Chicago: Encyclopedia Britannica.

Kaufman, Walter. (1973). *Without Guilt and Justice.* New York: Dell.

Padover, Saul K., ed. (1943). *The Complete Jefferson.*

Prejean, H. (1993). *Dead Man Walking: An Eyewitness Account of the Death Penalty in the United States.*

Pritchard, James B. (1955). *Ancient Near Eastern Texts Relating to the Old Testament* (2nd ed.). Princeton, NJ: Princeton University Press.

Sellin, Thorsten. (1977). "Beccaria's Substitute for the Death Penalty." In *Criminology in Perspective,* edited by Simha F. Landau and Leslie Sebba.

Tennessee v. Garner. (1985). 471 U.S. 1.

Wolfgang, Marvin E. (1960). "A Florentine Prison: Le Carceri delle Stinche." *Studies in the Renaissance,* 148–66. New York: Renaissance Society of America.

PART VI

CONCLUSION

Continuing the Struggle for Justice

CHRISTOPHER BAIRD

When I was asked to write the concluding chapter for the NCCD Centennial Publication, there seemed little I could add to what was already eloquently covered by scholars and correctional experts like Norval Morris, Marvin E. Wolfgang, Allen Breed, and Barry Krisberg. Then I happened on the wonderfully optimistic writing of one of NCCD's founding fathers, Charles L. Chute. Unfortunately, most of what Chute wrote about in the 1920s is still relevant today. Obviously, the reforms he envisioned 80 years ago are not yet in place.

Chute was convinced that increased knowledge of crime and psychology would inevitably lead to a major reform of the nation's correctional system. But knowledge, like beauty, it seems, is in the eye of the beholder. This essay explores reasons why Chute's vision has been largely derailed and what is needed to see it fulfilled.

When Charles L. Chute, an early director of the National Probation Association, optimistically stated that advancements in knowledge (application of the scientific approach to social concerns) would change the way we treat offenders, he could not have foreseen events as they would unfold 60 to 80 years later. "We are so far today from the rational program of crime treatment," he wrote in 1923, "that it will take time to attain it, but progress should be more rapid than at any previous time in history because of the growing scientific spirit and approach to the problem." This 83-year-old sentiment is jarringly similar to what we might hear today at any current evidence-based practice seminar. Since history so often repeats itself, the challenge is to ensure that we do not hear the same lament 80 years hence.

Advances in knowledge and technology over the last 20 years may be beyond anything Chute could have imagined. If this is true, the way this nation now treats its offenders, both adult and juvenile, would undoubtedly have left him bewildered. A chasm separates knowledge (and, for that matter, simple common sense) from practice. Closing this gap presents one of the greatest challenges facing progressives in the 21st century.

Chute's optimistic view that society's understanding of abhorrent behavior would rapidly expand and that this knowledge would be used to reform the treatment of offenders was obviously wrong. His "prophecy" seemed somewhat on track in the late 1900s when the Law Enforcement Assistance Administration (LEAA) provided funding for new approaches to probation and parole, and the Office of Juvenile Justice and Delinquency Prevention (OJJDP) created standards for the care of juvenile offenders. But it all collapsed rather quickly, replaced by tough political rhetoric, draconian sentencing policies, and a near total retreat from the rehabilitation ideal. Allen Breed identifies the moment of death of rehabilitation at the point when Attorney General Edwin Meese stated, "the money has been wasted on so-called crime prevention and treatment programs, which are lining the pockets of social workers" (Breed, 1987, reproduced in Chapter 11 of this volume).

In the 1980s, three forces combined to create a "perfect storm" that focused attention on the national punishment of offenders as a crime prevention strategy. First, voters had become accustomed to the instant analysis so often presented by television news. The public, it seems, is looking for quick and easy answers to society's problems. Second, the creation of ideological "think tanks" with vast resources and a set agenda produced a plethora of studies that dominated political discussion throughout the 1980s. And third, the focus placed on public opinion polls and short-term solutions to virtually everything has produced an unprecedented level of timidity in politicians. No politician wants to appear to be soft on crime, even when sentencing policies and correctional practices are obviously counterproductive to long-term solutions.

The punishment "storm" was fueled by societal changes as well. Crime rates began to decline as baby boomers aged out of their crime-prone years. This provided powerful ammunition for those supporting increased incarceration. Reductions in crime rates became "proof" that "get-tough" policies were making the United States a safer place to live. It was a wonderfully simple message. Governors and state legislatures were quick to adopt positions that quelled public fears and were so easy to articulate.

The professional research community should have seen the storm brewing, but many did not. When it did respond, the response was too late and the message too complex to gain the attention of the broadcast industry. This failure is somewhat understandable. Good research cannot be conveyed in sound bites. Further, most correctional researchers had grown up in a time when news was dispensed in 30-minute segments by journalists with exceptional credentials. In those days, news professionals guarded the separation of news and entertainment with the same commitment our forefathers afforded the separation of church and state. News reporting was serious business. Sources were scrutinized and editorializing was clearly labeled as such.

In just a few decades, this changed dramatically. Information and the technology that produces and distributes information have become a major economic force. As profits in this industry soared, the lines between news, ideology, and entertainment have blurred, giving rise to a new political reality that Bill Moyers has dubbed "the politics of delusion."[1] "Facts" too often carry the baggage of doctrine or ideology.

No one should suggest that the way information is provided by the media is responsible for the lack of progress in criminal justice. Still, it is hard to imagine that it has not played a significant role in shaping the political response to almost everything in the United States. Several years ago, the Public Broadcasting System posed the question, "Can democracy survive television?" A panel of experts opined that it would, but barely. Television allows all issues to be reduced to sound bites, sometimes completely devoid of substance and nearly always designed to convince rather than inform. Over time, this has helped to create a public with a short attention span, demanding quick and simple solutions to complex problems. Public relations specialists invoking the old premise, "a picture is worth a thousand words," realize that visuals have enormous emotional power and can trump even the most rational discourse. Hence, when a president dons a jumpsuit, lands on an aircraft carrier, and declares "mission accomplished," his popularity soars.

The problems with current media coverage of complex social issues go well beyond what can be presented here. A more lengthy review is required, and that is best left to those who regularly study how information is conveyed by our nation's media outlets. It is enough to say that the task of converting knowledge to practice has become more difficult than Charles L. Chute ever envisioned.

Science has always struggled to overcome doctrine, ideology, and bias, but in today's information age, the struggle not only continues, it has also intensified. Political leaders have always recognized that information, or more accurately, the control of information, is a powerful political tool. The information age, however, requires that the message be backed by some semblance of evidence, giving rise to the second element crucial to the vast expansion of what is often called "the correctional industrial complex."

To justify spending more on a state's correctional system than its universities, social conservatives have created and funded "think tanks" to produce the evidence required. The tactics of these organizations are simple but effective, and they soon came to dominate the nation's discussion of crime and justice issues. Their approach incorporates the following principles:

- Create a name for the organization that connotes the ideal of academic, unbiased research.
- Be first with the message and disseminate it widely in the popular news media.
- Promote the message using dramatic language easily converted to political sound bites.
- Label all reports as research or policy analysis.

Crime was a major political issue in the 1980s and early 1990s and became the topic of choice of the conservative think tanks. The work of John DiIulio, Jr., the Legislative Exchange Council, Morgan Reynolds (who, ironically, now promotes the idea that the attacks of 9/11 were an "inside job" and that the twin towers were never really hit by aircraft), Eugene Methvin, and others quickly gained the attention of the popular news media. Their shrill warnings of pending crime epidemics and their slanted and often simplistic analyses promoting the increased use of incarceration struck a chord with politicians eager to please their constituents. At the peak of the hyperbole, the public was introduced to the concept of teenage "super predators" and the claim that each additional incarceration prevented 187 new offenses. By the time reasoned responses from Zimring, Austin, Mauer, and others from the research community thoroughly demolished these ideas, it hardly mattered. The fear of crime and the supposed effectiveness of prison sanctions were firmly entrenched in the collective psyche of politicians.

The social and economic costs of the imprisonment binge have been enormous. The United States has the highest rate of incarceration in the world, more than six times that of Western Europe. Our prisons are severely overcrowded, conspicuously devoid of meaningful treatment programs, and huge numbers of offenders are being returned to their communities with very little resources or assistance. Probation and parole caseloads have ballooned, and revocation rates in some jurisdictions are at unprecedented levels. The use of "super maximum" institutions to house disruptive prisoners, many of whom are mentally ill, is common practice. The recent sentencing of 9/11 conspirator, Zacarias Moussaoui, stands as testament to the current state of penology. Placement in a small, concrete, soundproof cell for 23 hours a day with 1 hour of isolated "recreation" in a small space adjacent to the cell was deemed a fate worse than death. If Moussaoui is not already mentally ill, such conditions of confinement practically guarantee he will be in the near future. Although Moussaoui's fate may garner little sympathy, it might at least increase awareness that many other prisoners are housed in identical or similar conditions. Indeed, a recent lawsuit found that some wards of California's Department of Juvenile Justice were kept in cells 23 hours a day and allowed 1 hour of isolated "recreation."

The deficiencies of our current system of justice do not need greater elaboration here. They are extensively covered in other essays in this compendium. The purpose of this essay is to examine why there has been so little progress and what can be done to resurrect Charles L. Chute's vision of humane, evidence-based treatment of offenders.

Social conservatives have clearly gained control of the national agenda in the justice arena. While progressives may decry the methods used to gain control, it is also necessary to accept that we have failed and must heed the lessons that failure offers. There is reason to believe, however, that a shift in the political climate is possible.[2] Based on the collective wisdom of the essays presented in this document as well as other recent social commentary, there seem to be three primary ingredients needed to change the direction of correctional practice in the United States: (a) leadership, (b) a clear, vigorous strategy and an organization with an abiding interest in the issue, and (c) the means to provide the infrastructure needed to sustain the effort as long as it is needed.

LEADERSHIP

In his speech, *The State of Corrections Today: A Triumph of Pluralistic Ignorance,* Allen Breed not only asked where our corrections leaders have gone, but also offered a blunt assessment of differences in what we say and what we do.

> Leaders in corrections articulated the most noble objectives while presiding over squalor, fear, and degradation. We have supported the principles of fairness, justice, and humane treatment for those who are wards of the state, yet our daily practices have often been, and often are, at odds with the ideals given voice in oration. (Breed, 1987, p. 265; see Chapter 11, this volume)

To reclaim Chute's vision of what corrections could be in this country, this must change. Those in charge of the nation's prisons should be the most eloquent and powerful voices for reform. They best understand the dire consequences of overcrowding, lack of adequate programming, and inordinately long sentences that drain hope from those incarcerated. Strong, individual voices have been raised, but it is well beyond the point where individual efforts can "right the ship." A strong, collective voice that cannot be ignored is required, and it is this group that needs to step forward.

The right combination of experience, expertise, and evidence, coupled with a sense of urgency and the means to focus public attention on justice issues, may well be the vehicle that could produce change. A commission, formed not by government but by a group of concerned corrections professionals, could develop a blueprint for change and membership. Such a commission could be assisted by a consortium of research groups working together to assemble the evidence needed to support their positions.

To increase credibility and fend off attacks from social conservatives, the commission should recruit a major spokesperson for the group who is a well-known conservative with a clear understanding of just how dysfunctional our current correctional system has become. They do exist. Former Supreme Court Chief Justice Warren Burger, for example, spoke eloquently about the need to reform the nation's prisons.

A CLEAR STRATEGY TO EFFECT REFORM

The goal of such a commission cannot be the production of another policy paper that few will read. Nor can it be to simply educate the public. It must be to *motivate* the public to *demand* reform of the nation's correctional systems. It is to make the public care about the issue, to understand how it affects them directly, and to see the damage it does to society. Quite obviously, this will require an ongoing effort to keep these issues in front of the American people. In essence, an extensive, well-funded media campaign, promoted with the same ferocity exhibited by conservative think tanks, is needed. The message must be simple, dramatic, and targeted to specific audiences using methods perfected by the prison-building advocates of the 1980s and 1990s. An effort of this magnitude cannot be sustained without adequate funding, the third basic ingredient needed to win the war of words and ideas.

FUNDING A REFORM EFFORT

Progressives will never be able to match the funds available to conservative think tanks, whose lists of sponsors often include dozens of Fortune 500 companies. Funding for such an effort can only come from the foundation world, and it is time for foundations to lead on this issue. Our prisons and jails are vastly overcrowded and without a major political awakening, continued construction seems inevitable. States keep adding to a broken system, consuming resources that would be better spent on schools, communities, and public health. The right coalition of correctional administrators, research organizations, armed with a cohesive, sophisticated strategy and solid evidence to support that strategy, might well instill the level of confidence needed to attract foundation support. Certainly, there must be a foundation willing to fund the development of the commission and the framing of the campaign.

Could such a campaign assure that science and knowledge will assume the role in the treatment of offenders that Charles L. Chute envisioned so long ago? History indicates that the chances of success are not good. But pessimism is also the enemy. Too frequently, new ideas are abandoned because conventional wisdom says that they just won't work, because "the current political climate is not amenable to change." Progress has been excruciatingly slow, but because our treatment of others defines who we are, the struggle to reform corrections must continue.

NOTES

1.   Many conservatives have expressed similar views. For example, see Kevin Phillips, American Theocracy, 2006.

2.   Despite media manipulation and political pandering, the US public now seems to recognize the folly of punishment as the sole purpose of imprisonment. According to a recent poll by Zogby International titled "Attitudes of US Voters toward Prisoner Rehabilitation and Reentry Policies," US voters are 8 to 1 in favor of rehabilitation and reentry services such as substance abuse treatment, employment development, and mental and medical health care for nonviolent prisoners returning home. As Allen Breed pointed out in his essay in this volume, public opinion has favored rehabilitation in the past and been ignored.

INDEX

ABOUT THE EDITORS

Barry Krisberg has been the President of the National Council on Crime and Delinquency (NCCD) for 15 years. He is currently a Visiting Lecturer in Legal Studies at UC Berkeley. He is known nationally for his research and expertise on juvenile justice issues and is called on as a resource for professionals and the media. Prior to joining NCCD, he held several education posts. He held an adjunct Professorship in the Department of Psychiatry at the University of Hawai'i and was also an adjunct professor with the Hubert Humphrey Institute of Public Affairs School at the University of Minnesota. He received both his master's degree in criminology and his doctorate in sociology from the University of Pennsylvania.

Susan Marchionna has been with the NCCD for 5 years, first as Executive Assistant and currently as Director of Communication. Prior to joining NCCD, she worked independently as an editor, technical writer, and custom dressmaker. She has a bachelor's degree from the University of California, Santa Cruz.

Christopher Baird is the Executive Vice President of the NCCD/Children's Research Center and has directed the Midwest Office in Madison, Wisconsin, since 1985. He has designed risk assessment, classification, and case management systems for child welfare, adult probation and parole, and juvenile justice systems. He has also authored numerous journal articles and other publications on research, program development, and management issues in child welfare, juvenile justice, and corrections.